The Springer series "Management for Professionals" comprises high-level business and management books for executives, MBA students, and practice-oriented business researchers. The topics cover all themes relevant to businesses and the business ecosystem. The authors are experienced business professionals and renowned professors who combine scientific backgrounds, best practices, and entrepreneurial vision to provide powerful insights into achieving business excellence.

The Series is SCOPUS-indexed.

AF905320

Management for Professionals

B. Rajesh Kumar

Rising Stars

Integrative Case Studies on the 100 Fastest-Growing Companies

Springer

B. Rajesh Kumar
Institute of Management Technology
Dubai, United Arab Emirates

ISSN 2192-8096 ISSN 2192-810X (electronic)
Management for Professionals
ISBN 978-3-031-50031-2 ISBN 978-3-031-50032-9 (eBook)
https://doi.org/10.1007/978-3-031-50032-9

© The Editor(s) (if applicable) and The Author(s), under exclusive license to Springer Nature Switzerland AG 2024
This work is subject to copyright. All rights are solely and exclusively licensed by the Publisher, whether the whole or part of the material is concerned, specifically the rights of translation, reprinting, reuse of illustrations, recitation, broadcasting, reproduction on microfilms or in any other physical way, and transmission or information storage and retrieval, electronic adaptation, computer software, or by similar or dissimilar methodology now known or hereafter developed.
The use of general descriptive names, registered names, trademarks, service marks, etc. in this publication does not imply, even in the absence of a specific statement, that such names are exempt from the relevant protective laws and regulations and therefore free for general use.
The publisher, the authors, and the editors are safe to assume that the advice and information in this book are believed to be true and accurate at the date of publication. Neither the publisher nor the authors or the editors give a warranty, expressed or implied, with respect to the material contained herein or for any errors or omissions that may have been made. The publisher remains neutral with regard to jurisdictional claims in published maps and institutional affiliations.

This Springer imprint is published by the registered company Springer Nature Switzerland AG
The registered company address is: Gewerbestrasse 11, 6330 Cham, Switzerland

Paper in this product is recyclable.

To my children.
Lakshmi and Appu

Preface

This integrative casebook focuses on analyzing the growth strategies of 100 fastest-growing companies based on the list of Fortune Survey 2021. Each case study focuses on the market overview, business segments, growth strategy, risk factor analysis along with sustainability initiatives of each company. In the final part of each case study, the financial performance, in terms of both market and operating performance of the company, is analyzed for a maximum period of 4 or 5 years. The growth trend analysis focuses on stock returns, excess market returns, growth rates of important financial parameters such as assets, revenues, net income, market capitalization, and enterprise value. As part of their growth strategy, 57% of the companies have adopted mergers and acquisitions as a strategic pursuit for growth. These companies have carried out multiple M&A transactions in different time periods. Approximately half of the companies have active sustainability initiatives with a focus on ESG (Environmental, Social, and Governance) principles. The healthcare service sector firm, Cigna, is the oldest firm with a history spanning 225 years of establishment. MYR Group, an electrical infrastructure contracting firm, has a rich history, having been established 130 years ago. Companies such as Medpace Holdings and Charles River Lab are established life science-based contract research organizations. Large market capitalization-based companies such as Alphabet, Meta Platform, Amazon, Adobe, Dupont, AMD, Netflix are among the fastest-growing companies in the world. Among the fastest-growing companies, there are companies belonging to industry sectors such as home care services, health and well-being, floral industry, education industry, recreational power boats, home building, and global health care services. Approximately 32 of the fastest-growing companies are in the financial services sector, 21 are in technology and related fields, 11 operate within the healthcare industry, 3 are in the apparel sector, and there are five in the real estate and construction industry.

The average five-year stock holding period returns for these fastest-growing companies were 725%. The average cumulative total monthly returns for the stocks of these companies were 117% during the recent five-year period. The average book value of equity as percent of market value of equity for the companies was 44% during the recent five-year period. The 5-year average growth rate of assets and revenues for the companies was approximately 28%. The average growth rate of net income for the companies was 79% during the recent five-year period. In terms of performance measures, the average profitability ratios of net margin, ROE, and ROA for these firms were 13%, 21%, and 9%, respectively, during the period 2018–2022. Financial services firm Freedom Holding Corporation had 5-year holding period return of 18,972% followed by technology firm Trade Desk with 5-year holding period return of 3211.9% and fintech firm Atlanticus Corporation with 5-year holding period returns of 2400%. The E-Commerce firm Etsy had holding period return of 1743%. Financial Specialty service-based firm Riley Financial had 5-year holding period return of 1332%. Technology firms such as ACM Research, Advanced Micro Devices, and Cybersecurity-based technology firm Fortinet had 5-year holding period return of approximately 1309%, 1189%, and 1093%, respectively. In terms of excess market value created, the five-year average book value of equity as percent of market value of equity for health care services firm, The Joint Corp, technology companies such as Paylocity, AppFolio, E-commerce firm Etsy were 3%, 4.50%, 4.90%, and 5%, respectively. The five-year average book value of equity as percent of market value of equity for technology firms such as Trade Desk and Fortinet was approximately 5%. For 20 fastest-growing companies, the average book value of equity was only approximately 10% of the market value of equity during the 5-year analysis period reflecting the excess value created by these companies in stock market. Firms such as Atlanticus Corporation, Trade Desk, ACM Research, and STAAR Surgical had 5-year total cumulative monthly returns of 378%, 340%, and 333.50%, respectively.

In terms of operating performance, financial services firm Freedom Holding Corporation had the highest average asset growth of 140% during the recent five-year period. Firms such as ACM Research, PennyMac Financial Services, Etsy, Kornit Digital, The Joint Corporation (Healthcare service) had average asset growth rate of 125%, 69%, 62%, and 57%, respectively, during the recent 5-year period. Approximately 40 companies had average revenue growth rate of 25% and above during the recent 5-year period. The 5-year average growth rate of revenues for Freedom Holding Corporation was 104%. Healthcare services firm Quidel Corporation and Riley Financial Inc. had five-year average revenue growth rate of 72% and 62%, respectively. The 5-year average growth rate of revenues for firms like PennyMac Financial Services, Salesforce, and Cigna was 58%.

In terms of average net income growth rate, 14 companies had average growth rate of over 100% during the past 5 years. Healthcare services firm, The Joint Corp topped the list with average net income growth rate of 787% followed by financial services firm Merchants Bancorp and technology sector firm AppFolio with average net income growth rate of 379% and 335%, respectively, during the period 2018–2022. Firms like Quidel Corporation (Healthcare), Riley Financial Inc. (Financial specialty services), and Advanced Micro Devices (Technology) had average net income growth rate of 335%, 332%, and 227% during the past five-year period. The top five firms with the highest average return on assets were consumer services firm Medifast (38.25%), Riley Financial (38.17%), Meta Platform (30.59%), Quidel Corp (27%), and Brooks Automation (26.77%). The five top firms in terms of 5-year average return on equity were Atlanticus Corporation (143.96%); Tech firm KLA (74.76%); Medifast (64.18%); Joint Corporation (61%); and Gardening firm Scotts Miracle (53.79%). Brooks Automation had the highest average net profit margin of 114.31% during the past 5 years.

Dubai, United Arab Emirates B. Rajesh Kumar

Acknowledgments

I would like to thank the editorial and production staff at Springer who guided this book through the publishing process. I wish to acknowledge the valuable guidance and support of Rocio Torregrosa, Editor at Springer. I thank Sneha Arunagiri, Project Coordinator and her team for all the support. I acknowledge the contents of various company websites, annual reports, and other sources of information, including the 2021 Fortune list of 100 fastest-growing companies, to which I referred for the preparation of this book.

Contents

Case 1 Atlanticus Corporation

Introduction

Atlanticus is a financial technology company established in Georgia, USA, by David G Hanna in 1996 and is headquartered in Atlanta. The company leverage data, analytics, and innovative technology to provide financial solutions to millions of people in America. Over the 25-year period, Atlanticus have serviced 18 million consumers and provided $26 billion loans. The company's predictive platform is built on years of investment in data, people, and technology. The products offered by Atlanticus include retail credit and general-purpose credit cards which are marketed through the omnichannel platform consisting of retail point of sale, direct mail solicitation, Internet-based marketing, and partnerships with third parties. Atlanticus through its CAR subsidiary provides multiple financing and service programs to automotive dealers and automotive non-prime financial organizations.

The company aims to satisfy the financial credit needs of millions of Americans who are not catered by large financial institutions. The company focusses on the strategy of facilitating appropriately priced consumer credit and financial services with value-added features and benefits to service millions of consumers in the United States. The company provides products and services to lenders in the United States. The firm invests in the receivables which are originated by lenders who utilize the technology platform and related services of the company. The company also purchases receivable portfolios from third parties. Atlanticus facilitates banks to offer flexible options to consumers for everyday purchases through the Fortiva® and Aspire® branded general-purpose credit cards. Fortiva Retail Credit is the premier second-look consumer credit program of the company. The company provides access to flexible patient payment options in the healthcare sector through the CURAE healthcare financing product. Dealer solutions of CAR financial services provide financing and servicing solutions to dealers in the buy here/pay market.

According to company news report, ever since the pandemic began, the company has funded over $1 billion of purchases for financially underserved consumers and provided support to thousands of merchant partners across the United States. The

© The Author(s), under exclusive license to Springer Nature Switzerland AG 2024

B. R. Kumar, *Rising Stars*, Management for Professionals,
https://doi.org/10.1007/978-3-031-50032-9_1

company has become the leading provider of second-look buy-now-pay later solutions in the market with the point-of-sale assets estimated at over 35% annually over the 3-year period, 2019–2021. The general-purpose credit assets have increased by approximately 100% during the above period. The servicing costs per account have been reduced by 35% over the past 3 years. The company serves over 1.6 million customers.

By the end of 2021, the company employed 331 employees in the United States.

Business Divisions

Credit Service Segment

This segment has serviced over $27 billion in consumer loans over the 25-year period. The segment supports lenders in offering inclusive financial services by offering products like private label credit and general-purpose credit cards which are originated by lenders through multiple channels such as retail and healthcare, digital marketing, and partnership with third parties. The company specializes in supporting the "second-look" credit service by extending the services of bank partners to consumers who do not have the accessibility for the financing options with larger financial institutions. The flexible technology solutions offered by Atlanticus facilitate the bank's partners to integrate the quick decision-making process with the infrastructure of participating retailers and service providers. The bank lenders can take instant credit decisions using the company's technology and proprietary predictive analytics thereby offering credit to consumers who are often rejected by lenders due to the focus only on higher FICO scores. The artificial intelligence– and machine learning–based underwriting process of Atlanticus facilitates banking partners to make effective decisions regarding credit service. The segment also provides loan servicing such as risk management and customer service outsourcing for third parties.

Auto Finance Segment

Auto finance segment basically purchases and/or service loans secured by automobiles and also facilitates floor plan financing for a pre-qualified network of independent automotive dealers and automotive finance companies involved in used car business. The services provided also include installment lending products. This segment generates revenues on purchased loans through interest earned on the face value of the installment agreements. Additional revenues are obtained with the accretion of discounts on loans purchased. The division has served more than 600 dealers in 34 states of the United States.

Strategic Perspective of Growth

Atlanticus manages investments in receivables using well-developed proprietary risk evaluation systems over a period of 25 years. The management of investments are done using credit scoring, credit file data, and other noncredit bureau attributes. The lending partners are assisted by the company with respect to the management of transaction authorizations, account renewals, credit line modifications, and collection programs. The adaptive control system of the company enables to develop and test multiple strategies for account management processes. In addition to standard credit behavior scores used in industry, the company uses proprietary risk scores in the control system to segment, evaluate, and manage the receivables.

With respect to private label credit and general-purpose credit finance activities, the company assists the lending partners to manage credit lines. Strategies are employed to reduce open credit lines for risky customers showing signs of increased credit or bankruptcy risks. Account management strategies are adjusted based on the analysis of data related to account performance through the proprietary database. The firm also uses industry standard fraud detection software to manage the portfolio.

The auto segment adopts the strategy of implementation of dealer-specific loss reserve accounts to manage credit quality and loss mitigation at the portfolio level. The segment basically focusses on cross-collateralization of the reserve accounts held by a single dealer. The strategy involves monitoring the performance of the dealer-based portfolio by adjusting pricings and the reserve account. The size and scope of future account purchases from the dealers are also analyzed. The dealers are provided with specific purchase guidelines for each product offering and the firm assists them with respect to monitoring of transactions during the loan acquisition process.

The collection strategy of the company has evolved with the utilization of digital and mobile processes. The company also oversees and manages third-party collectors. Collectors are often given flexibility to vary the general payment application priority in terms of payment of principal, finance charges, and fees. Collectors employ programs under which the contractual interest associated with a receivable are adjusted in terms of reduction or elimination or waiver of a certain amount of accrued fees under the condition that a minimum amount of payment has been made. These programs include the voluntary consumer credit counseling service.

Risk Analysis

COVID-19 has significantly impacted the consumer spending behavior related to financial services. US government stimulus programs have resulted in decreased consumer need for credit products and led to an increase in customer payments. Labor shortages and supply chain disruptions would lead to delay in consumer spending and affect the receivable growth of Atlanticus company. The company faces stiff competition from both financial service and financial technology companies. The private label credit and general-purpose credit card finance segments of lending partners face competition from national, regional, and local bankcard and consumer credit issuers. In the auto finance segment, the firm faces competition from national and regional companies.

The cash flows of the company are dependent on the payments received from the investments in receivables. The collection efficiency of the investments in receivables is dependent on many factors such as consumer profile, pricing of products, economic conditions, the rate at which consumers repay their accounts, and the consumer borrowing rate. The portfolio of receivables of the firm is not diversified and basically derived from consumers whose credit worthiness is estimated as less than the prime. The company invests in receivables either which are originated by lenders who utilize the services of the company or invest in or purchased pools of receivables from other issuers. The focus on such receivables may have an adverse impact on the future performance of the firm. The firm also faces challenges with respect to the evaluation of the credit performance of receivables owed by consumers who have acquired these assets over the Internet and other digital channels. In the private label credit operations, five largest retail partners accounted for over 65% of the outstanding private label credit receivables by the end of year 2021. Diversification of retail partners is desirable from the risk perspective angle.

The auto finance segment faces other challenges such as difficulty in obtaining funding for automobile lending at a cheaper rate, dependence on referrals from dealers, and liquidation of repossessed automobiles.

With respect to macro-environmental risk, the potential for the growth of receivables faces challenges in the context of disruption and volatility in the capital market. During the 2009 economic crisis, the capital market faced significant challenges such as illiquidity in debt capital markets, write offs in the financial service sector, and repricing of credit risk in the syndicated credit market. The company operates in a heavily regulated industry. The business practices of the firm with respect to terms of products, servicing, and collection practices are dependent on periodic and special reviews by regulatory and enforcement authorities. The changes in bankruptcy or consumer protection laws may adversely affect the operations of receivable collections.

Risk Mitigation Strategies

The dealer portfolios across the auto finance segment are monitored and compared against expected collection and peer dealer performance. The company uses techniques such as monitoring of dealer pool vintages, delinquencies, and loss ratios to analyze past and future performance, and the results are used to adjust pricing and reserve requirements.

The collectors monitor and adapt collection strategies, techniques, and technology in order to reduce delinquencies and charge-offs. The adoption of these collection strategies is aimed to lower bad debt losses and operating expenses. The collection strategy also involves re-aging the accounts which are consistent with

FFIEC guidelines. The main characteristics for re-aging an account is that it must have been opened for at least 9 months and may not be re-aged more than once in a 12-month period or twice in a 5-year period. The company is focusing on further investments in artificial intelligence to strengthen the customer-centric approach to the collection process. The business of the company is regulated directly and indirectly under various federal and state consumer protection, collection, and other laws such as the Federal Credit Card Accountability, Responsibility, and Disclosure Act of 2009, Dodd Frank Act, the Federal Truth in Lending Act, and the Federal Equal Credit Opportunity Act. The various statutes in these laws limit the liability of consumers for the unauthorized use, prohibit discriminatory practices in consumer transactions, impose limitations on the type of charges, and restrict the use of consumer credit reports and other account-related information. Most of the lending partners' products are designed for customers at the lower end of the credit score range. The company has taken numerous measures to ensure the security of the hardware and software systems as well as customer information.

Corporate Governance

The Board of Directors (the "Board") of Atlanticus Holdings Corporation together with its subsidiaries ("Atlanticus" or the "Corporation") has adopted this Code of Business Conduct and Ethics (the "Code"), in connection with Rule 4350(n) of the National Association of Securities Dealers' Listing Standards (the "NASD Listing Standards") and Sect. 406 of the Sarbanes-Oxley Act of 2002. An employee of the corporation is expected to be honest and ethical in dealing with all corporation employees, customers, vendors, and third parties. The various committees are the audit committee, compensation committee, nominating committee, and social impact committee. The social impact committee oversees and provides advice on company social responsibility or other public policy initiatives.

The audit committee is comprised of at least three directors designated by the Board who meet the independence and qualification requirements of the Nasdaq stock market and the rules and regulation of the SEC. The members of the nominating and corporate governance committees shall be designated by the Board annually and each member shall serve until such member's successor is duly designated or until such member's earlier resignation or removal.

Stock Purchase Plans

The company implements two stock-based employee compensation plans – the employee stock purchase plan (ESPP) and equity incentive plan. Under the ESPP employees can elect to have 10% of their annual wages withheld to purchase common stock in Atlanticus up to a fair market value of $10,000. The price of the stock purchased under the ESPP is approximately 85% of the fair market value per

Table 1 Shareholding pattern

Individual stakeholders	81.04%
Mutual fund	10.54%
Other institutional holders	5.94%

Table 2 Stock market performance

Year	2016	2017	2018	2019	2020	2021
Atlanticus Holdings	100	84.53	128.21	317.34	867.5	2511.98
Russell 2000	100	114.65	102.02	128.06	153.62	176.39
Nasdaq Financial-100	100	115.14	105.24	136.07	141.13	179.58

Data Source: Atlanticus Annual Report 2021

Table 3 Excess value

Year	2019	2020	2021
Book value of equity	335	76,510	287,499
Market value of equity	143,100	396,900	1,055,900
BV as percent of MV	0.23%	19.28%	27.23%
Average	15.58%		

share of the stock on the purchase date. Table 1 gives the ownership pattern of the company.

Stock Market Performance

The following table shows the cumulative total stockholder return for Atlanticus in comparison with the stock market index, the Russell 2000 Index and Nasdaq Financial-100 Index. The comparative analysis assumes that $100 was invested in the year 2016 (Table 2).

The Atlanticus stock has given a total return of over 2400% in total during the 5-year investment period. The Russell 2000 and Nasdaq Financial-100 Indexes have given returns of 76% and 80%, respectively. The average 5 yearly return for the Atlanticus stock was 109%, while that for Russell 2000 and Nasdaq Financial-100 was 13%.

Table 3 highlights the excess value in terms of market value. The average book value as percent of market value was approximately 15.58%. In other words, approximately 84% of value was not found in operating books reflecting the excess value created during the period 2019–2021.

Stock Return Analysis for the 5-Year Period

The data for the analysis was taken from Yahoo Finance.

During the 5-year period, May 2017–May 2022, the company registered an average yearly growth rate of 77%. During the same period, the Nasdaq Composite Index had registered a yearly return of 15% only. The total monthly cumulative return for the entire 5-year period was 378% for Atlanticus. The Nasdaq Composite Index had a total monthly cumulative return of 75%. Thus, Atlanticus stock market

Table 4 Five-year holding period return

Year	Atlanticus	Nasdaq Composite	Excess return
2017	−10%	12%	−22%
2018	64%	−10%	74%
2019	134%	23%	111%
2020	76%	41%	36%
2021	177%	20%	157%

Table 5 Financial highlights in '000s

	2018	2019	2020	2021
Total assets	582,608	936,266	1,207,214	1,943,863
Cash and cash equivalents	60,968	135,379	178,102	409,660
Total equity	−22,129	335	76,510	287,499
Total revenue	196,085	406,555	403,314	445,757
Total expenses	192,603	374,792	288,923	226,184
Net income	7612	26,210	93,917	177,789
Market cap	56,700	143,100	396,900	1,055,900
Enterprise value	493,900	846,700	1,181,700	2,112,300

performance was much superior compared to the market as a whole during the 5-year period.

Table 4 estimates the 5-year holding period return for the firm. The holding period return was estimated with the assumption that the stock was bought in January and sold in December of each year. The year 2021 witnessed the best performance for Atlanticus stock with excess returns of 157% over the market Nasdaq Composite Index. Except in the year 2017, Atlanticus had superior returns compared to the market in the period 2018–2021.

Financial Performance

Table 5 shows the important financial parameters of the firm during the period 2018–2021.The average growth rate of total assets and cash equivalents during the period 2018–2021 were 50% and 95%, respectively. The average growth rate of revenues is 39% during the period 2018–2021. The total expenses increased by 17% during the above period. The net income of the company increased by 197% on an average basis during the period 2018–2021. The market capitalization of the company increased by 165% and the enterprise value increased by 63% on an average basis during the period 2018–2021. The data was collected from annual reports.

Table 6 highlights the profitability and leverage measures of the company. The company registered significant healthy operating performance. The average net profit margin was 21.16% during the period 2018–2021. The average ROE during the period 2019–2021 was 143.96%. The average ROA was 6.28% during the period 2018–2021.The debt equity ratio is showing a steep declining trend reflecting the healthy leverage position of Atlanticus company.

Table 6 Performance measures

Ratios	2018	2019	2020	2021
Net margin%	5.06	7.41	27.66	44.5
ROE%		264.61	97.42	69.86
ROA%	1.56	3.48	8.78	11.29
DER	−22.89	19.54	7.88	4.35

Table 7 Estimation of economic value

Year	2020	2021
Profit before income and tax	114	219.6
Income tax	20	41.79
Net operating profit after tax (NOPAT)	94	178
Stockholder equity	116.5	327.5
Long-term debt	923.7	1426.7
Total capital employed	1040	1754
WACC	6.75%	8.59%
Capital charge	70.21	150.68
Economic value	24	27

Table 7 shows the estimation of economic value for the company in millions of dollars.

Table 7 illustrates the estimation of economic value for the firm. The data given are in millions of dollars. The weighted average cost of capital estimation value is taken from www.gurufocus.com. The economic value has increased from $24 million to $27 million in the year 2021 compared to the previous year.

References

1. https://www.atlanticus.com
2. Atlanticus Annual Report 2021
3. https://investors.atlanticus.com/news-market-information/press-releases/news-details/2021/Atlanticus-Announces-Leadership-Transition-Discussion-of-Operational-Achievements/default.aspx
4. https://money.cnn.com/quote/profile/profile.html?symb=ATLC
5. https://www.gurufocus.com/stock/ATLC/definition
6. www.yahoofinance.com

Case 2 B. Riley Financial, Inc.

Riley Financial, Inc. is a diversified financial services company which provides a full range of investment banking, corporate finance research, sales and trading, advisory, valuation, and wealth management services.

The company was founded in year 1997 and headquartered in Los Angeles. B. Riley was ranked number 2 by Fortune in the 100 fastest-growing companies list 2021 based on revenue growth rate, EPS growth rate, and 3-year total return for the period which ended June 30, 2021. The company has over 50 capabilities in nine expertise areas. There are 2000 professionals associated with the company. B Riley has over 200 offices throughout the United States. Over a period of 25 years, the company has created a competitive diversified financial service platform by offering a diverse suite of business capabilities beyond the traditional financial service offerings. The company has leveraged cross-platform expertise to provide full-service collaborative solutions in every stage of the business life cycle. As of March 2022, the company had total assets of $5.3 billion and total revenues of $1.35 billion. The market capitalization of the company stood at $1.41 billion dollars. The total 3-year stock return amounted to 250%. The company had over 580 million worth of dividend payment/share repurchases since the year 2017. By December 2021, the company had 1406 full-time employees.

The company has $30 billion client assets under administration and approximately 650 registered representatives. The company engaged in about 500 average advisory matters per year. The company had 2000 plus retail store closures since the year 2020. The equity research services of the company are provided to over 400 companies. B Riley has 1000 plus institutional clients. Over 1000 companies are appraised per year.

The major business lines of Riley Financial, Inc. were B. Riley Securities, B. Riley Wealth Management, National Holdings Corporation, B. Riley Capital Management, B. Riley Advisory Services, and B. Riley Retail Solutions. B Riley Securities was formed by the merger of B. Riley & Co. and FBR Capital Markets & Co. in the year 2017. In B. Riley Securities, the full-service investment bank provides corporate finance, lending, research, securities, sales, and trading services

© The Author(s), under exclusive license to Springer Nature Switzerland AG 2024

B. R. Kumar, *Rising Stars*, Management for Professionals,
https://doi.org/10.1007/978-3-031-50032-9_2

Table 1 Major business segment

Advisory services	Investment banking and capital markets	Real estate solutions	Wealth management	Retail solutions	Principal investments
Appraisal and valuation services	Investment banking	Sales and disposition	Individual client services	Dispositions	
Compliance risk and resilience services	Equity research	Lease restructuring	Business client services	Appraisal and valuation services	
Operations management services	Sales and trading	Real estate advisory services	Tax services		
Restructuring and turnaround management		Financial advisory services			
Transaction support		Capital solutions and acquisitions			

to corporate, institutional, and high net worth individual clients. B. Riley Wealth Management was formed by the acquisition of Wunderlich Securities, Inc. in the year 2017. National Holding Corporation, which was acquired in the year 2021, provides wealth management, brokerage, insurance, tax preparation, and advisory services. B. Riley Capital Management which includes B. Riley Asset Management provides investment advisory services. B. Riley Advisory Services provides expert witness, bankruptcy, financial advisory, forensic accounting, valuation, and operations management services to companies and financial institutions. Riley Retail Solutions is a major provider of asset disposition, liquidation, and auction solutions to retail and industrial firms. B. Riley Real Estate provides advisory services for global real estate projects to companies. This division is also involved in the restructuring of lease obligations of distressed and non-distressed institutions. B. Riley Principal Investments focusses on investment opportunities for its portfolio of companies.

United Online Communications (UOL), the communication company of B. Riley, offers consumer subscription services and products under the banner of NetZero and Juno brands. UOL was formed by the acquisition of magicJack VocalTec, Lingo Management and Marconi Wireless. MagicJack is a voice-over IP cloud-based technology and services and wireless mobile communications provider. Lingo is a global cloud/UC and managed service provider. Marconi Wireless is a mobile virtual network operator. The company owns major holding in BR Brand Holding which holds licenses in six brands.

Table 1 highlights the major business segments of B. Riley Financial.

Basically, the businesses of the company are classified into six operating segments: (1) capital markets, (2) wealth management, (3) auction and liquidation, (4) financial consulting, (5) principal investments, and (6) brands.

The capital market segment provides a full range of investment banking, corporate finance, financial advisory, research, securities lending, and sales and trading services to corporate, institutional, and individual clients. The corporate and investment banking services offered include merger and acquisitions and advisory services to public and private companies. The wealth management segment offers comprehensive wealth management services such as investment strategies, executive services, retirement plans, lending and liquidity resources, and settlement solution to corporate businesses. The auction and liquidation segment offers services to a multitude of clients facing distressed circumstances. The auction and liquidation segment operates through main divisions of retail store liquidations and wholesale and industrial asset dispositions. The financial consulting segment offers services such as bankruptcy advisory, financial advisory, forensic accounting, litigation support, operations management consulting, real estate consulting, and valuation and appraisal services. The principal investment segment consists of communication segment businesses which have been acquired for high investment returns. The brand segment consists of brand investment portfolio which generates revenue through the licensing of trademarks.

The sales and trading professionals of the company are involved in the distribution of B. Riley Securities' proprietary research products to institutional investor clients and high net worth individuals. B. Riley Securities also act as underwriter and execute equity trades on behalf of clients. The equity and fixed income traders of the company make markets in over 1000 securities. The appraisal teams of B. Riley provide independent appraisals to financial institutions, lenders, and private equity firms. Riley Retail Solutions provides services to clients on a guarantee, fee, or outright purchase basis. The Riley Real Estate segment involves in a variety of acquisition strategies which include purchase of real estate and mortgages.

Business Environment

The capital market segment faces intense competition from consolidated US and global financial institutions such as investment banks, bank holding companies, brokerage firms, merchant banks, and financial advisory firms. Many of these financial institutions offer a wide range of products which includes loans, deposit taking, and insurance along with brokerage, asset management, and investment banking services. These financial institutions have the ability to support investment banking and securities product with commercial banking, insurance, etc. in order to widen the market shares. The trend in equity underwriting business of multiple book runners and co-managers has created a stiff competitive environment for B. Riley's capital market segment. In the asset management business, the company faces challenges with respect to identification and completion of investments in an attractive portfolio of securities and retention of skilled asset management professionals.

The retail solution and real estate market division faces challenges from other qualified service providers in terms of discount offering or other preferred pricing arrangements. The competitors of the company may be in a position to secure alliances with clients and affiliates on better terms. The company faces competition for its retail services from traditional liquidators as well as Internet-based liquidators such as overstock.com and eBay. The company also faces competition for its retail solution businesses from large accounting, consulting, and other professional service firms. B. Riley faces competition from different providers of broadband services and other dial-up Internet access providers.

Risk Analysis

The general conditions in the economic and financial market in the midst of the ongoing COVID-19 pandemic affect the ability of the company to generate business and revenues. The strategic investments in terms of acquisitions and alliances made by the company have potential risks. The company faces credit risk on account of its activities related to loans, lines of credit, guarantees, and backstop commitments. Conditions in financial markets would adversely affect the business performance of the company in terms of underwriting or M&A transaction services. The firm may experience losses or write-downs in the realizable value of the proprietary investments on account of the inability of the invested companies to repay their borrowings. The company faces significant legal risk in its businesses on account of potential liability under securities laws and regulations related to capital markets, asset management, and other businesses. The company basically monitors and controls the risk exposure through operational and compliance reporting systems, internal controls, management review processes, etc. The firms in the financial service industry had been operating in a difficult and stringent regulatory environment in the context of failures to detect and prevent fraud. The reforms implemented as a result of Dodd Frank Wall Street Reforms and Consumer Protection Act (Dodd Frank Act) have impacted financial service industry and firms like B. Riley with respect to aspects such as capital and liquidity requirements. A significant portion of the revenues of investment banking operations of the firm is derived from the sales and trading business which has witnessed intense price competition and trading volume reduction in the business. Risks in the principal investment activity arise due to investments in high-risk illiquid assets. The primary clients of the financial consulting business of the firm are the financial institutions and loss of any of these clients will have an adverse impact on the company's businesses.

Corporate Social Responsibility Activities

B. Riley Financial and its associates support several charitable organizations at local and national levels with emphasis on corporate giving, employee engagement, and education. The company supports over 50 charitable organizations towards its commitment for CSR activity. B. Riley supports Toigo Foundation towards the development of leadership skills among underrepresented talent involving minority groups. B. Riley has partnered with Sugar Ray Leonard Foundation to fund research and create awareness for type 1 and 2 diabetes. Riley Financial supports the Memorial Sloan Kettering Cancer Center through charity rides across the United States. The company also supports the "Meals on Wheels America": a program to eradicate hunger and isolation among disadvantaged people. Riley Financial participates in the Malibu Triathlon to raise funds for the Children's Hospital, Los Angeles.

Governance at B. Riley Financial

The Company's business shall be conducted by its officers, managers, and employees, under the direction of the Chief Executive Officer and the oversight of the Board. The directors may be nominated for election by the Board or by stockholders in accordance with the bylaws of the company. The Board of Directors of B. Riley Financial (the "Company") have set high standards for the Company's employees, officers, and directors. The code of Business Conduct and Ethics summarizes the basic guiding principles and standards of conduct to guide employees to maintain business and ethical standards as well as compliance with laws and regulations. The audit committee must review and approve in advance all material-related party transactions or business or professional relationships. Stockholders and other stakeholders can communicate directly with the Board or the nonmanagement directors in writing through the channel of the Company's corporate secretary.

The Board will have three committees consisting of the audit committee, a compensation committee, and a corporate governance committee. The environmental, social, and corporate governance (ESG) committee identifies qualified members to become Board members, recommends the composition of the Board and its committees, and monitors its effectiveness. The ESG committee develops and recommends to the Boards the guidelines related to ESG.

The Board does not limit the number of terms for which an individual may serve as a director. The Board has not established a mandatory retirement age. Alternatively, the corporate governance committee and the Board will review each director's continuation on the Board upon reaching the age of 75 years and each year thereafter. It is stipulated that majority of the Board and all of the members of the audit committee, the compensation committee, and the corporate governance committee must be comprised of independent directors. The Board shall have at least four regularly scheduled meetings each year. The nonmanagement directors of the Board will meet in an executive session at least two times per year and will have an opportunity to meet in an executive session at each regular meeting of the Board.

Table 2 lists the major acquisitions undertaken by the company during the period 2012–2022.

Table 3 shows the revenue trends of the company during the past years.

Table 2 Timelines of major acquisitions

Year	Target company	Business segment
2012	Great American Group	Appraisal and liquidation
2016	United Online	Principal investment
2017	FBR & Co.	Investment banking, capital markets
2017	Wunderlich Securities	Wealth management
2018	GlassRatner	Financial consulting
2018	MagicJack	Principal investment
2019	Brands: Catherine Malandrino, English Laundry, Joan Vass, Kensie Girl, Limited Too, Nanette Lepore	Brand portfolio
2020	Anchor Resource Mgmt.	Operations management
2020	Alderney Advisors	Automotive restructuring
2021	National Holdings	Wealth management
2021	272 Capital	Asset management
2021	Marconi Wireless	Principal investment
2022	FocalPoint Securities	Investment bank

Table 3 Revenues

Year	Revenues
2014	$77.1 million
2015	$112.5 million
2016	$190.4 million
2017	$322.2 million
2018	$423 million
2019	$652.1 million
2020	$902.7 million
2021	$1.74 billion
March 2022	$1.35 billion

Table 4 Ownership

Ownership	Percentage
Institutional holding	51%
Insiders	30%
Others	19%
Total	100%

Table 4 gives the ownership details of the company.

Table 5 gives the segment mix of different divisions of the company.

Table 6 compares the cumulative total return of stock of B. Riley with respect to the Russell 2000 Index during the 5-year period from December 31, 2016, to December 31, 2021. It is assumed that $100 was invested in the beginning of the period and the dividends were invested.

Table 5 Segment mix

Segment	Percentage
Wealth management	30%
Capital markets	48%
Principal investments	8%
Auction and liquidation	5%
Brands	1%

Table 6 Stock performance

	2016	2017	2018	2019	2020	2021
B. Riley Financial	$100	$196	$160	$302	$563	$1432
Russell 2000	$100	$135	$119	$147	$174	$198

Source: B. Riley Financial, Inc. 10 K 2022

Table 7 Excess value

Year	2018	2019	2020	2021	2022 TTM
Book value of equity	258	361	513	661	654
Market value of equity	378	679	1140	2452	1249
BV as percent of MV	68.25%	53.17%	45.00%	26.96%	52.36%
Average	55.47%				

The 5-year (2017–2021) holding period return for B. Riley stock was 1332%, while for the Russell 2000 was 98%. On the basis of average returns, the 5-year average returns for B. Riley Financial was 81%, while that of the Russell 2000 Index was 16%.

Table 7 highlights the excess value created in terms of market value of the firm. The data for analysis is taken from Yahoo Finance and gurufocus.com. The book value and market value of Riley stock are stated in millions of dollars. The given data for year 2022 is the trailing 12-month data. The 5-year average book value of Riley Financial, Inc. was 55.47% of the market value of the company.

Five-Year Stock Return Analysis

The data for analysis is taken for GuruFocus and Yahoo Finance. The total cumulative stock returns for Riley stock during the 5-year period (June 22, 2017, to June 22, 2022) was approximately 188%. The 5-year average return for the stock was 38%. The total cumulative returns for S&P500 was 49% during the above-stated 5-year period. The 5-year average return for the S&P500 Index was 10%.

Table 8 highlights the holding period return of Riley Financial, Inc. in comparison to S&P500 during the 5-year period.

The excess return for Riley Financial, Inc. was highest in the year 2021. The holding period return for Riley Financial, Inc. was 76%, 74%, and 121% for the period 2019–2021.

Table 8 Holding period return

Year	Riley	SP500	Excess returns
2017	−6%	8%	−14%
2018	−21%	−11%	−10%
2019	76%	19%	57%
2020	74%	16%	58%
2021	121%	28%	93%

Table 9 Financial performance

	(In millions)			
Financial highlights	2018	2019	2020	2021
Total assets	1958	2318	2663	5852
Cash and cash equivalents	179	104	104	279
Total equity	258	361	513	661
Total revenue	423	652	903	1741
Total operating expenses	311	385	429	906
Net income	16	82	205	445
Market cap	378	679	1140	2452
Enterprise value	739	1471	2124	4664

Table 10 Performance and leverage measures

Ratios	2018	2019	2020	2021
Net margin%	3.67	12.51	22.73	25.57
ROE%	5.92	26.3	45.91	74.56
ROA%	0.93	3.82	8.24	10.45
DER	2.09	2.4	2.07	3.18

Financial Performance

Table 9 highlights the financial performance of Riley during the period 2018–2021.

The 3-year growth rate in total revenues and total assets during the period 2019–2021 was 62% and 51%, respectively. The average increase in operating expenses amounted to 49%. The average growth rate of net income during the above period was 227%. The average increase in market capitalization and enterprise value was 88% during the period 2019–2021. The cash and cash equivalents increased by 42% on an average basis.

Table 10 highlights the performance and leverage measures for the firm.

The average net margin during the period 2018–2021 was 16.12% for B. Riley Financial, Inc. The average ROE and ROA were 38.17% and 5.86%, respectively. The average debt equity ratio was 2.43 for the period 2018–2021. The ROE for the company was 74.56% in the year 2021.

Table 11 estimates the economic value for the firm during the 2-year period 2020–2021.The values are given in millions of dollars.

The economic value for B. Riley has increased by 1.94 times in the year 2021 compared to the year 2020.

Table 11 Economic value

Year	2020	2021
Profit before income and tax	345	707
Income tax	75	164.00
Net operating profit after tax (NOPAT)	270	543
Stockholder equity	116.5	327.5
Long-term debt	1000	1953
Total capital employed	1117	2281
WACC	7.41%	7.88%
Capital charge	82.7327	179.703
Economic value	187	363

References

1. https://ir.brileyfin.com/
2. B. Riley Financial, Inc., 10 K Report 2022.
3. https://ir.brileyfin.com/governance
4. https://ir.brileyfin.com/events-and-presentations

Case 3 The Joint Corp

The Joint Corp was incorporated in the year 2010 and is headquartered in Scottsdale, Arizona. The Joint Corp was originally founded in the year 1999 by a doctor of chiropractic. The joint was refounded with the acquisition of the original eight franchised clinics. The company operates through direct ownership, management arrangements, franchising, and regional developers. By March 2022, the company has 700 plus clinics located across 37 states in the United States. The company has also executed 38 letters of intent for 38 future clinic licenses. The company has revolutionized the chiropractic care via a model to make the treatment affordable and accessible. This franchisor and operator of chiropractic clinics uses a private pay, on-insurance, cash-based model. This model facilitates Joint Corp to price services below most competitors' pricing for similar services and below most insurance co-payment levels. During the year 2021, the franchise system has registered approximately 10.9 million patient visits and generated system-wide sales of $36.1 million. Joint Corp has a community of more than 1700 fully licensed chiropractic doctors.

Business Environment and Competition

Chiropractic care is widely applied with a variety of medical conditions particularly back pain. Chiropractic care is recognized as an effective treatment for pain conditions. According to an IBIS market research report 2021, the value of chiropractic non-acute treatment market is estimated to be $18 billion. The chiropractic industry in the United States is large and highly fragmented with an estimated amount of $90 billion being annually spent on back pain treatment. Most chiropractic services are provided by sole practitioners generally in medical office settings. According to the Chiropractic Economics survey report 2021, Joint Corp had received an average of 1422 new patients per clinic for the year ended 2021 compared to the average of 291 new patients per year for traditional insurance based on non-multidisciplinary or integrated practices. According to the IBIS market

© The Author(s), under exclusive license to Springer Nature Switzerland AG 2024
B. R. Kumar, *Rising Stars*, Management for Professionals,
https://doi.org/10.1007/978-3-031-50032-9_3

research report in June 2021, the three largest industry companies were each expected to generate less than 1% of total industry revenue in 2021. According to the 2021 Kentley Insights market research report, there are 41,300 independent chiropractic offices in the United States. Joint Corp faces competition from traditional medical practices, outpatient clinics, physical therapists, med-spas, massage therapists, and sellers of devices to manage back and joint discomfort. The three major competitors for Joint Corp are Airrosti, HealthSource Chiropractic, and Chiro One Wellness Centers. Most of the competitors follow insurance-based models. Joint Corp has competitive advantage due to its first-mover advantage, proprietary operation systems, and strong unit-level economics.

Strategy

The growth strategy of the company focusses on the development of franchise base through the sale of additional franchises and development of robust regional developer network. The company also focusses on an expansion strategy in both the organic way of development of new clinics and inorganic way of acquisition of select operating clinics. The patients arrive at the clinics at times convenient to their schedules. The model offered does not focus on the treatment of severe or acute injury and hence does not provide expensive and invasive diagnostic tools such as MRIs and X-rays. The company uses a retail, consumer-driven approach to stimulate brand awareness and attract patients to the clinics. Joint Corp creates awareness of its brands by locating clinics basically at retail centers and convenience points. The clinics offer extended hours of operations including during weekends. The model offered by the company provides an attractive alternative for chiropractic doctors to spend more time on treating patients compared to traditional practices which involve greater overhead, personnel, and administrative expenses.

During the period 2012–2021, the gross sales of the clinics increased from $22.3 million to $361.1 million. The number of clinics increased from 33 to 706 during the above period. The company supports the continued growth of system sales and royalty income. The company gives importance for the development of company-owned or managed clinics often referred to as greenfield in clustered geographies. It was estimated that the United States alone could support at least 1900 clinics. Despite the ongoing pandemic, the Comp Sales (same store) growth for the Joint business model was approximately 29% in the year 2021. With the support of mass media advertising, the increased brand awareness has resulted in revenue growth supplemented with developing and refining management systems, operating standards, training materials, etc. The company was able to leverage technology and existing support infrastructure and control costs over time to improve margins. The company has plans to introduce complementary branded products such as nutraceuticals and dietary supplements along with related additional services.

Regulations

The company has to comply with different healthcare regulations to combat healthcare fraud and protect patient confidentiality measures. The company is also subject to the rules and regulations of the Federal Trade Commission and various state laws regulating the offer and sale of franchises. The company is also mandated to adhere to state regulations related to the corporate practice of chiropractic. The company is also liable for certain employment law and other labor-related claims with respect to franchisees.

Revenue Model

Joint Corp generates revenues basically through company-owned and managed clinics and through franchise fees, royalties, advertising fund contributions, IT-related income, and software fees from the franchisees. Joint Corp receives a royalty of 7% from franchised clinics. The company pays 3% royalty to its regional developers based on the gross sales of franchises opened within certain regional developer-protected territories. The firm also collects a national marketing fee of 2% of gross sales of all franchised clinics. The company receives a franchise sales fee of $39,900 for each direct sale of franchise. The firm also offers a veteran discount and multiple location franchise purchases. In the scenario of purchase of additional franchise licenses, the initial franchise fee for franchises is reduced by $10,000 per additional licenses. The regional developer typically receives up to 50% of the respective franchise fee for each franchise sold through the network of regional developers. The company requires that the entire nonrefundable initial franchise fee to be paid upon execution of a franchise agreement with initial term of 10-year period. Joint Corp collects monthly fees from franchisees for the use of proprietary chiropractic software, computer, and Internet service support. Through the regional developer program offered by Joint Corp, the regional developers are granted an exclusive geographical territory with the mandate for minimum development obligation within that defined territory. Regional developer fees are nonrefundable and are recognized as revenue ratably on a straight-line basis over the term of the regional developer agreement.

IPO Listing

The company was listed on November 14, 2014, and raised net proceeds of approximately $17.1 million. The underwriters of the IPO issue exercised their option to purchase 450,000 additional shares under the over-allotments and raised an amount of $2.7 million.

Risk Analysis

The labor shortage problem in the United Sates has impacted the ability to recruit chiropractors and qualified personnel and hence reduced revenues. The clinic sales depend on factors such as consumer preferences, discretionary spending, clinic traffic, availability of attractive sites, changes in government regulations, etc. Managing growth involves planned expansion whereby the existing clinic management systems, administrative staff, financial and management controls, and information systems required to be enhanced. The company faces challenges with respect to locating and securing new clinic sites in target markets. The ability to open new clinics depends on factors such as negotiating leases with acceptable terms, attracting qualified chiropractors, recruitment of qualified employees, feasibility of management agreements with suitable PCs in target markets, and regulatory issues. The regional developers are independent operators over whom the company has limited control. The failure by regional developers to sell the specified minimum number of franchises within the time limits set forth in their license agreement would reduce the franchise fees and delay the receipt of royalty payments. Joint Corp operates in a highly competitive chiropractic service environment where the primary factors determining competition are quality of care, prices of services, marketing strategy, and visibility of office locations among others. The company is obliged to comply with data privacy, security, and breach notification requirements of the US Department of Health and Human Service.

Governance

There are seven board members. The three committee charters are audit, compensation, and nominating and corporate governance. The committees normally consist of three or more members of the board. The primary purpose of the audit committee of the Board of Directors is to oversee the company's accounting and financial reporting processes and the audits of the company's financial statements. The compensation committee evaluates and approves compensation plans, policies, and programs of the company. The company's executive compensation policies seek to coordinate executive officers' compensation with the company's performance objectives and business strategy. The major function of the nominating and governance committee in to identify individuals qualified to become directors and recommend their selection by the Board of Directors as nominees for election, and recommend to the Board director assignments to the Board's committees and develop, recommend to the full Board, and oversee the implementation of the company's corporate governance policies and practices.

Table 1 gives the value of revenue components during the year 2020 and 2021.

The revenues attributed to company-owned or managed clinics increased by 39.6%, whereas the revenues from royalty and franchise fees increased by 38.9% and 26.6%, respectively, in the year 2021 compared to the previous year. The growth rate of advertising fund revenue and software fees increased by 39.8% and 25.6%,

Table 1 Segment-wise revenues

	2020	2021
Company-owned or managed clinics	31,757,207	44,348,234
Royalty fees	15,886,051	22,062,989
Franchise fees	2,100,800	2,659,097
Advertising fund revenue	4,506,413	6,298,924
Software fees	2,694,520	3,383,856
Regional developer fees	876,804	848,640
Other revenues	861,181	1,257,913
Total revenues	58,682,976	80,859,653

Table 2 Excess value

Year	2018	2019	2020	2021
Book value of equity	0.73	5.72	21.13	29.57
Market value of equity	114.34	224.07	371.76	947.23
BV as percent of MV	0.64	2.55	5.68	3.12
Average	3%			

respectively, in the year 2021 compared to the previous year. The regional developer fees decreased by 3.2% in 2021 compared to the previous year. The other revenues increased by 46% during the above period. The corporate clinic segment had income from operations of $4.4 million for the year ended December 31, 2021.

There were about 584,000 new patients in 2020 and 807,000 new patients in year 2021. Approximately 36% of those new patients of Joint Corp have never been to a chiropractor before.

Acquisitions

During March 2019, the company entered into an asset and franchise purchase agreement under which the company repurchased from the seller one operating franchise in West Covina, California. In July 2019, the company repurchased from the seller one operating franchise in Phoenix, Arizona. The company had acquired three operating franchises in Savanah, Georgia, and Bluffton. During August 2019, the company repurchased from seller one operating franchise in Sayebrook, South Carolina, and one operating franchise in Chula Vista, California. In October 2019, the company repurchased from the seller one operating franchise in Redlands, California.

Stock Performance Analysis

Table 2 illustrates the estimation of book value as percent of market value of the company.

The data given are in millions of dollars. The market value of the company has increased by 8.28 times over the 4-year period, 2018–2021.The book value as percent of market value was only 3% suggesting that 97% of value was not attributed to books, but excess value created in the market. This suggests the superior performance of stock in the market.

Five-Year Return Analysis

The 5-year (2017–2021) monthly return analysis for Joint Corp company reveals that the total monthly cumulative return for Joint Corp stock was 225%, while that of the Nasdaq Composite index was approximately 70%. The 5-year (2017–2021) average yearly return for Joint Corp was 46% compared to 14% yearly return for the Nasdaq composite index. Hence, the performance of the stock was far superior compared to the market index in the stock market. However, the stock value fell by half during months May–June of 2022. The stock was trading in the range of $15–$16 during May–June 2022 compared to $30 during April 2022. The 52-week range for the stock was $13.10–$111.06 during June 2022.

Table 3 analyzes the holding period return for Joint Corp stock during the 5-year period, 2017–2021.

The holding period return analysis assumes a 1-year holding period. The maximum return for Joint Corp was registered in year 2021 with a holding period return of 102% and excess return of 82% over the market NASDAQ Composite index. In the year 2018, Joint Corp had a return of 64% when the market index had loss of 10%. Joint stock had beaten the market index in terms of returns in all the 5 years of analysis.

Table 4 gives the details of major financial parameters of Joint Corp during the 4-year period, 2018–2021.

The financial data values are given in millions of dollars. Joint Corp witnessed an average growth rate of 56% in total assets during the 3-year period, 2019–2021. The corresponding average growth rate in cash and cash equivalents for the company was 45% during the period 2019–2021. Joint Corp saw the average revenue increase in the above period to be 30%. The total operating expenses increased by 29% during the above 4-year period. The average net income growth rate amounted to 787% during the period 2019–2021.The average growth rate of market capitalization and enterprise value was approximately 106% and 111%, respectively, during the period 2019–2021.

Table 3 Holding period returns

Year	Joint Corp	Nasdaq Composite	Excess returns
2017	31%	9%	22%
2018	64%	−10%	75%
2019	97%	23%	74%
2020	57%	41%	16%
2021	102%	20%	82%

Table 4 Financial highlights

Financial highlights	(In millions of dollars) 2018	2019	2020	2021
Total assets	23.43	43.71	65.88	85.45
Cash and cash equivalents	8.72	8.46	20.55	19.53
Total equity	0.73	5.72	21.13	29.57
Total revenue	36.66	48.45	58.68	80.86
Total operating expenses	31.61	39.36	46.73	66.97
Net income	0.15	3.32	13.17	6.58
Market cap	114.34	224.07	371.76	947.23
Enterprise value	106.72	229.89	369.69	951.35

Table 5 Performance and leverage measures

Ratios	2018	2019	2020	2021
Net margin%	0.4	6.86	22.44	8.13
ROE%	15.63	103.1	98.09	25.96
ROA%	0.7	9.9	24.03	8.69
DER	1.51	2.5	0.88	0.8

Table 5 shows the profitability and leverage ratio of Joint Stock during the period 2018–2021.

The year 2020 registered the best performance measures in terms of profitability measures. The net margin was 22.44%, whereas the ROE and ROA were 98% and 24%, respectively, in the year 2020. The average net profit margin was 9.46% during the period 2018–2021. The average ROE and ROA was 60.70% and 10.83%, respectively, during the above period. The average debt equity ratio representing the leverage position of the company was 1.42 during the 4-year period 2018–2021.

References

1. https://ir.thejoint.com/annual-reports
2. https://finance.yahoo.com/quote/JYNT?p=JYNT
3. https://www.gurufocus.com/stock/JYNT/financials?search=Joint%20Corp#_stock-financial-table-header-2
4. https://ir.thejoint.com/corporate-governance
5. https://ir.thejoint.com/company-information

Case 4 PennyMac Financial Services

PennyMac Financial Services, Inc. (PFSI) is a specialty financial service firm with a comprehensive mortgage platform with focus on the production and servicing of US mortgage loans and management of investments related to the US mortgage market. The company has synergistic partnership with PennyMac Mortgage Investment Trust which is a publicly traded mortgage real estate investment trust (REIT). The operating subsidiaries of the company was founded in year 2008. The company was publicly listed in the year 2013. The company had over 6900 employees as of the end of fiscal year 2021. PennyMac Financial had registered a strong performance with revenue and net income of $3.2 billion and $1.0 billion, respectively, in 2021. The diluted EPS was $14.87 in the period. In 2021, approximately 25% of PennyMac Financial Services originated in the higher margin consumer and broker direct lending channels. The market value of PFSI as of June 24, 2022, was $2436.26 million.

Business Segments

PFSI operates and controls all the business operations of Private National Mortgage Acceptance Company, LLC (PNMAC) and its subsidiaries. The principal mortgage banking subsidiary, PennyMac Loan Services LLC (PLS), is a nonbank producer and servicer of mortgage loans. PLS is the servicer for the Fannie Mae and Freddie Mac. PLS also serves as an approved issuer of securities of Ginnie Mae. PLS also performs its role as a lender of the Federal Housing Administration (FHA) and lender/servicer of the Veterans Administration (VA) and the US Department of Agriculture (USDA). The investment management subsidiary PNMAC Capital Management manages PennyMac Mortgage Investment Trust (PMT) which is a mortgage real estate investment trust listed on the NYSE. The production segment performs functions related to loan origination, acquisition, and sale activities. The servicing segment performs functions related to loan servicing for newly originated loans, whereas the investment management segment performs activities related to

© The Author(s), under exclusive license to Springer Nature Switzerland AG 2024

B. R. Kumar, *Rising Stars*, Management for Professionals,
https://doi.org/10.1007/978-3-031-50032-9_4

investment asset acquisitions and dispositions such as sourcing, due diligence, negotiation, and settlement.

Mortgage Banking: The loan production segment sources new prime credit quality first lien residential conventional and government-insured or guaranteed mortgage loans through the three channels of correspondent production, consumer direct lending, and broker direct lending. In correspondent production, PFSI manages the purchase from nonaffiliates of mortgage loans which have been underwritten based on investor guidelines. The correspondent loans are insured or guaranteed by FHA, VA, or USDA. PMT's production focus in terms of correspondent loans are on those loans which can be sold into MBS guaranteed by Fannie Mae or Freddie Mac. In correspondent production activities, PFSI earns origination fees from correspondent sellers and interest income on loans held for the period. PFSI has mortgage servicing rights to retain and recognize the fair value of the contractual rights to service the loans on behalf of the purchaser of the loans other than PMT. For supporting the correspondent production activities of PMT, the company earns fulfillment fees and tax service fees. PFSI originates mortgage loans on a national basis using the consumer direct lending channel. The company obtains loan application packages from nonaffiliated mortgage loan brokers and underwrites and funds the resulting loans for sale through the broker direct lending channel.

Loan Servicing: The loan servicing segment performs the function of loan administration, collection, and default management activities. The company service loans both as the owner of mortgage servicing rights and mortgage servicing liabilities.

Investment Management: The company serves as the investment manager for the subsidiary PCM which provides investment management services to PMT. The company earns management fees as a percentage of PMT's net assets.

Business Environment and Challenges

The US residential mortgage market is stated to be one of the largest financial markets in the world valued at $14.1 trillion as of September 30, 2021. The volume of the first lien mortgage loan origination market was valued at $4.8 trillion in the year 2021. It has been observed that many of the largest financial institutions like banks have reduced their participation in the mortgage market thereby creating opportunities for nonbank participants. There are high barriers to entry in the residential mortgage industry. Regulatory challenges include getting approvals for selling and servicing loans for agencies and state licensing requirements for nonfederally chartered banks. There are significant challenges related to infrastructure, technology, risk management, and processes for successful operations and capital requirements. The industry is facing excess capacity and increased competition for a smaller population of loan among market participants on account of overall reduction in demand for mortgages. The regulatory requirements are increasing for nonbank mortgage lenders and services.

In the loan production and servicing segments, the company faces competition from large financial institutions which includes cash windows of the GSEs and other independent residential mortgage loan producers and servicers such as Wells Fargo, JP Morgan Chase, Rocket Mortgage, Mr. Cooper, and United Wholesale Mortgage.

Strategy of Growth

PennyMac Financial Services focusses on the growth of consumer direct lending business by servicing portfolio through the recapture of existing customers for refinance and purchase money loans. PFSI also focusses on the growth of non-portfolio originations. By 2021, the company has serviced 2.1 million loans. PennyMac is a leader in the mortgage industry. Another potential growth segment involves the broker lending channel. The broker lending channel is involved in the underwriting and funding of mortgage loans sourced by mortgage loan brokers and other financial intermediaries. The company has plans to increase mortgage loan volume by building broker relationships and offering technology access to mortgage loan brokers through dedicated portal. The broker lending channel represents approximately 15% of US residential mortgage origination market according to Inside Mortgage Finance estimations. In 2021, PFSI has funded $16.8 billion worth mortgage loans through broker direct channel. The company also aims to increase correspondent production market share by increasing the number and type of sellers from whom loans are purchased. The company aims to improve the mortgage loan servicing portfolio. The company also evaluates opportunities for expansion into new markets and provides additional services to customers directly or through external partnerships.

The company focusses on investment in the infrastructure and technology for growth of long-term mortgage banking. In 2021, the company invested $100 million on transformational technology projects for strengthening its direct lending channels. The national call center model and technology initiatives enable the company to drive origination process efficiencies and customer services. The growth objectives of the company depend on factors such as disciplined capital, liquidity, and enterprise risk management along with proper hedging of mortgage servicing rights. PennyMac had introduced the "Greatness Lives Here" campaign to bring awareness to PennyMac's history.

Risk Factor Analysis

The COVID-19 pandemic may have adversely affected business and results of operations. The firm operates in a highly regulated industry and the continually changing federal, state, and local laws and regulations could have an adverse effect on the business and results of operations. Pricing changes by US government–sponsored agencies could materially affect the business and results of operations of the firm. Mortgage banking revenues are highly dependent on macroeconomic

Table 1 Comparative performance

Year	2016	2017	2018	2019	2020	2021
PFSI	$100	$134	$130	$209	$408	$440
Russell 2000	$100	$115	$102	$128	$154	$176
S&P 600 Thrifts and Mortgage (Industry) Index	100	122	106	144	137	175

Source: Annual Report PFSI 2022/S&P Global Market Intelligence

factors and real estate market, mortgage market, and financial market conditions. Government intervention has led to lowering of federal fund rates and government has purchased assets in financial markets including the mortgage-backed securities. The CARES act and other forbearance requirements have negatively impacted the fair value of the servicing assets. The failure to modify, resell, or refinance early buyout loans or defaults of the early buyout loans beyond expected levels may adversely affect business, financial condition, liquidity, and operation results. The ongoing COVID-19 has significantly increased the number of Ginnie Mae loans which are seriously delinquent in the Ginnie Mae MSR portfolio. The company has an early buyout repurchase option for loans for 3 months' delinquent in the firm's Ginnie Mae MSR portfolio. During the year end of 2021, the company has repurchased $20.1 billion delinquent Ginnie Mae loans from the Ginnie Mae MSR portfolio. The substantial amount of indebtedness may negatively impact the financial and operating activities in the context of increases in costs due to interest rate fluctuations. By December 31, 2021, the company had $10.9 billion of total outstanding indebtedness. The ability of the firm to refinance existing financial obligations and borrow additional funds depends on factors like restrictive covenants on the firm's financing agreements, restrictions by regulatory agencies, liquidity in the credit market, and interest rate environment. PFSI also considers the risk associated with the discontinuation of the London Interbank Offered Rate (LIBOR). Uncertainty with respect to the nature of alternative reference rates may adversely impact the availability and costs of borrowings. Hedging for interest rate exposure is viewed by the company as expensive during periods of rising and volatile interest rates. PFSI faces related party risks due to its association with PMT which is the counterparty which acquires all of the newly originated mortgage loans in connection with the correspondent production activities. Investment management segment faces risks on account of market conditions which could reduce the fair value of the assets which in turn affect the management and incentive fees.

Table 1 shows the cumulative total return for the common stock of PennyMac compared to the cumulative total returns for Russell 2000 Index and the S&P 600 Thrifts and Mortgage (Industry) Index.

The comparison period is from Dec 31, 2016, to Dec 31, 2021.The assumption made is that $100 was invested in the stock and indexes in the beginning of year 2016. The holding period (2016–2021) return for PennyMac stock was 340%. The corresponding holding period return for Russell 2000 and S&P600 Thrifts & Mortgage Indexes was 76% and 75%, respectively. The 5 yearly average return

Table 2 Segment-wise net revenues ('000s)

Year	2019	2020	2021
Production	993,884	2,824,999	2,306,764
Servicing	440,784	840,762	817,295
Investment management	42,736	39,836	43,302
Total	1,477,404	3,705,597	3,167,361

Source: PFSI Annual Report 2022

Table 3 Loan production activities (in '000s)

Year	2019	2020	2021
Investment trust	47,937,306	60,540,530	64,774,728
Consumer direct channel	9,752,500	23,491,465	43,060,266
Broker direct channel	3,841,289	12,168,106	16,759,314
UPB of conventional loans fulfilled for PennyMac Mortgage Investment Trust	56,033,704	100,389,252	110,003,574
Total loan production	117,564,799	196,589,353	234,597,882

Table 4 Ownership pattern

Institutional holding	40
Insiders	6
Others	54
Total	100

for PFSI was 39%, while that for Russell 2000 and S&P600 Thrifts and Mortgage Indexes was 13% and 14%, respectively, during the period 2017–2021.

Table 2 shows the segment-wise revenues for PFSI for the past 3 years. The revenues attributed to the production and servicing segment peaked in the year 2020. Investment management revenue was highest in the year 2021.

Table 3 highlights the loan production activities of different channels of PFSI.

Table 4 shows the ownership composition at PFSI.

Corporate Sustainability Initiatives at PennyMac

The company's COVID-19 pandemic response was guided by the principles of assisting borrowers, supporting employees, and engagement with local communities. The Coronavirus Aid, Relief and Economic Security (CARES) Act allowed borrowers with federally backed loans to access temporary payment forbearance with respect to borrower hardships during the pandemic period. PFSI provided various types of forbearance options during the period including those under the CARES Act. Customers who were not able to resume monthly payment at the end of their forbearance plans were given an extension up to 180 days. Additional extensions were also provided for some cases after the 180-day period. During the pandemic period, the employees were provided with remote work environment.

The company provided funding to several charitable organizations which support missions such as sustainable homeownership, mortgage and rental assistance, food insecurity, and community empowerment. The company supports charitable organizations such as Rebuilding Together, LA Family Housing, Adopt-A-Family LA, St. Mary's Food Bank Alliance, and Tunnel to Towers Foundation. For environmental sustainability, the company focusses on waste reduction and management with the focus on improving the energy efficiency of the office sites and water conservation. Waste reduction is a central theme of the company's business model and low-cost operations. Printing from centralized locations in the office building is encouraged and personal printers from all workstations and individual offices were removed to reduce waste. The company also encourages customers to use online platforms for effective delivery of documents and statements. In 2021, the use of electronic statements by approximately 42% of customers have resulted in saving of over 44.7 million sheets and 26.1 million envelopes. Approximately 95% of customers of the consumer direct lending channel provide eConsent and electronically signed upfront disclosures. During 2021, PennyMac participated in the USPS BlueEarth Secure Destruction program which was aimed to reduce carbon footprint, improve recycling efforts, and reduce handling costs. In 2021, under the confidential waste recycling program, PennyMac recycled more than 445,000 pounds of paper and other confidential materials. PennyMac recycled approximately 20,000 pounds of e-waste in year 2021 which represented a 100% increase compared to the year 2020. For promoting environmental sustainability, PennyMac has partnered with One Tree Planted and has plans to plant 45,000 trees in critical habitats throughout North America. For energy efficiency, the company has installed new energy-efficient HVAC units and prioritized the use of energy-efficient LED lighting in its office buildings. PennyMac has appointed a mortgage and climate risk analytics firm to provide consulting services as a part of its initiatives to identify, assess, and manage climate and environmental risks to its mortgage loan and servicing portfolio.

With respect to social sustainability, PennyMac focusses on responsible lending initiatives. The company believes that transparency of information in loan products and services is a critical component for borrowers to arrive at effective decisions. The company has adopted a strict lending criterion to ensure that lending is done to customers who can afford to repay. The focus is also on responsible and transparent marketing of products and services. Dedicated complaint response teams are in place as a part of the proactive complaint management system which are governed by corporate policy requirements and executive management oversight. PennyMac offers a number of loan products for first-time homebuyers, homebuyers with compromised credit, and low-income buyers. The company has curated a First-Time Homebuyer Guide to provide guidelines on the home buying process. In 2021, PennyMac joined the Home for All Pledge, a Mortgage Bankers Association (MBA) for the promotion of greater racial equity and inclusion in housing. PennyMac supports sustainable homeownership for veterans and military family members through the VA Home Loan Program. In 2021, PennyMac provided over $50 billion in financing to veterans. The company had also serviced approximately 400,000 loans for veterans and their dependents in the year 2021. The company was

Table 5 Book and market value performance

Year	2018	2019	2020	2021
Book value of equity	1654	2062	3389	3418
Market value of equity	1648	2673	4653	3968
BV as percent of MV	100.36%	77.14%	72.83%	86.14%
Average	84.12%			

ranked as the no 4 VA lender by the Inside FHA/VA Lending report 2021. PennyMac has also partnered with Freddie Mac to provide loans that meet the eligibility requirements of their GreenCHOICE Mortgages® program which focusses on providing finances for energy and/or water efficiency home improvements. In 2021, about 99.5% of the workforce were employed in full-time positions. The PennyMac Corporate University (PCU) Rotational Program is aimed at talent acquisition for next-generation mortgage industry professionals. The company had launched the Diversity, Equity and Inclusion (DEI) Council with the goal to provide strategic guidance on enterprise-wide diversity, equity, and inclusion initiatives to enhance social impact in workplace and communities. In 2021, PennyMac established a leadership and key performance indicator (KPI) to increase the representation of women and underrepresented minorities in management positions. PennyMac offers an employee assistance program with work-life benefit features where licensed counselors support employees and family members without any charge. The corporate philanthropy program consists of three components: employee matching gifts, charitable donations, and corporate sponsorships. The five philanthropic focus areas of PennyMac for charitable activities consists of community development and equitable housing, financial literacy and economic inclusion, human and social services, health and medical research, and environmental sustainability.

With respect to governance statistics, 82% of board members are independent members. The board diversity is 45% characterized in terms of race/ethnicity, gender, or sexual orientation. The company has a robust process to identify, evaluate, and select qualified director candidates and assess the size and composition of the board. The nominating and corporate governance committee sponsors an annual self-assessment of the Board's performance as well as the performance of each committee of the Board. Three women serve on the Board of the company representing 27% of the board members. The committees of the Board include the audit committee, compensation committee, finance committee, and nominating and corporate governance committee. The nominating and corporate governance committee has specific oversight responsibility related to corporate sustainability and ESG practices.

Table 5 shows the book value as percentage of market value. The values are given in millions of dollars.

The average book value as percentage of market value was 84% during the 4-year period, 2018–2021.The company had created a market value of $4.653 billion during the year 2020.

Five-Year Stock Return Analysis

The total cumulative monthly return for PFSI stock was 133% during the period June 2017 to June 2022. During the same period the market Russell 2000 Index registered a total cumulative return of 34%. The average 5-year return for the PFSI stock was 27%, while that for the Russell 2000 Index was a mere 7%.

Table 6 shows the holding period return for PFSI compared to the market Russell 2000 Index. PFSI had the highest holding period of 97% in year 2020. In the year 2018, the holding period return was negative for the company. The market Russell 2000 Index had worse performance in 2018. The excess return analysis shows that PFSI had superior performance compared to the market Russell 2000 Index.

Table 7 shows the performance ratios and leverage ratio of the company.

The profitability position of PFSI was strongest in the year 2020 with ROE of 60.43%. The most debt-intensive period for the company was year 2020. The average debt equity ratio for the 2018–2021 period was 4.61. The average net margin, ROE, and ROA for PFSI was 25.2%, 29.8%, and 4.37%, respectively, during the 4-year period.

Table 6 Holding period return

Year	PFSI	Russell 2000	Excess returns
2017	28%	8%	21%
2018	−2%	−14%	12%
2019	65%	11%	54%
2020	97%	22%	75%
2021	22%	8%	14%

Table 7 Performance and leverage measures

Ratios	2018	2019	2020	2021
Net margin%	7.71	23.39	41.67	28.2
ROE%	8.26	21.15	60.43	29.48
ROA%	1.18	4.44	7.88	3.98
DER	2.95	3.45	7.93	4.09

Table 8 Financial highlights

	(In millions of dollars)			
Financial highlights	2018	2019	2020	2021
Total assets	7479	10,204	31,598	18,777
Cash and cash equivalents	165	210	548	347
Total equity	1654	2062	3389	3418
Total revenue	1137	1680	3953	3559
Total operating expenses	157	153	225	368
Net income	88	393	1647	1003
Market cap	1648	2673	4653	3968
Enterprise value	6359	9583	31,000	17,610

Table 9 Estimation of economic value

Year	2020	2021
Profit before income tax	2241	1359
Income tax	594	356.00
Net operating profit after tax (NOPAT)	1647	1003
Stockholder equity	3389	3418
Long-term debt	26,789	13,875
Total capital employed	30,178	17,293
WACC	2.18%	1.71%
Capital charge	657.88	295.71
Economic value	989	707

Table 8 gives the financial highlights of the company during the 4-year period, 2018–2021.

The data is obtained from financial reports and gurufocus.com. The average growth rate of revenues and net income was 58% and 209% during the period of analysis. The market capitalization of the company increased by 41% on an average basis though the market value fell by 14% in year 2021.The enterprise value also increased by 77% on an average basis. The average total operating expenses increased by 36% during the period. The total assets grew by 69% during the period 2019–2021.The total equity increased by 30% on an average basis. The average increase in cash and cash equivalents amounted to 51% during the period 2019–2021.

Table 9 estimates the economic value for PFSI in year 2020 and 2021.

The values are given in millions of dollars. The economic value for the company has declined in year 2021 compared to the year 2020.

References

1. https://www.pennymac.com/about-us#investors
2. 2021 Corporate Sustainability and ESG Report, https://s23.q4cdn.com/545760634/files/doc_governance/2021/PFSI-Corp-Sustainability-and-ESG-Report-(FINAL)-(1).pdf
3. PFSI Annual Report 2022

Case 5 Etsy

Etsy operates two-sided online marketplaces termed "House of Brands" which connect millions of passionate and creative buyers and sellers around the world. Etsy.com, the marketplace, is the global destination for unique and creative goods made by independent sellers. The Etsy marketplace connects creative artisans and entrepreneurs to consumers and provides tens of millions of buyers with a range of seller tools and services. The House of Brands, in addition to the main Etsy marketplace, consists of Reverb Holdings, Inc., Depop Limited, and Elo7 Serviços de Informática S.A. Reverb Holdings, Inc.is the musical instrument marketplace which was acquired in year 2019. Depop Limited (Depop) is the fashion resale marketplace. Depop deal was valued at $1.493 billion. Elo7 Serviços de Informática S.A is the Brazil-based marketplace for handmade and unique items. Depop and Elo7 were acquired in year 2021. This deal was valued at $212.1 million. The institutional holding of the company is 97.75%.

Etsy is a marketplace where sellers run their own shops, create, sell, and ship their own products and are responsible for complying with the company's robust seller policy. Items on Etsy do not have barcodes or SKUs, and Etsy does not ever touch or possess the items for sale in their marketplace.

Etsy has a large assortment of handmade, customized, personalized, vintage, and craft supply products from different regions of the globe. By end 2021, there were nearly 100 million such items listed on the Etsy marketplace. Custom or made-to-order merchandise accounted for 23% of the GMS in year 2021.

In 2021, Etsy had generated $13.5 billion of gross merchandise sales (GMS). Etsy marketplace accounted 90.6% of the GMS, while Reverb, Depop, and Elo7 accounted for 7%, 2.2%, and 0.2%, respectively, of GMS. Collectively, the Etsy group connected a total of 7.5 million active sellers to 96.3 million active buyers in the year end 2021. As of December 31, 2021, Etsy marketplaces had over 120 million items of sale.

The top six retail categories on the Etsy marketplace were homewares and home furnishings, jewelry and personal accessories, apparel, craft supplies, paper and party supplies, and beauty and personal care. These categories accounted for 87%

© The Author(s), under exclusive license to Springer Nature Switzerland AG 2024
B. R. Kumar, *Rising Stars*, Management for Professionals,
https://doi.org/10.1007/978-3-031-50032-9_5

of GMS of 2021. Approximately 64% of the consolidated GMS were accounted from purchases made on mobile devices. The mobile app is the fastest-growing device for Etsy marketplace.

In 2021, Etsy had 90 million active buyers. Approximately 53% of all active buyers and 37% of new buyers who made a purchase in 2020 bought again in 2021. In 2021, 49% of active buyers made two or more purchases. In 2021, Etsy outgrew the ecommerce industry with GMS growing by 31% to $13.5 billion, revenues grew by 35% to $2.3 billion and net income grew by 41% to $494 million. In 2021 the company had more than $1 billion in cash.

Etsy have superior advantage in terms of global reach. Statistics reveal that 42% of consolidated GMS was generated when a seller or buyer or both were located outside of the United States. The platform offered by Etsy uses innovative machine translation technology to translate listings, reviews, and Etsy advertisements and facilitate interaction between buyers and sellers when they do not use the same language. In 2021, over 70% of GMS in the United Kingdom and Germany was from domestic sales. Approximately 81% of the company's GMS was generated through organic channels which included a large proportion from buyers directly visiting Etsy and other nonpaid channels such as search, social, email, and push notifications.

The Reverb marketplace, which is headquartered in Chicago, connects buyers and sellers of new, used, and vintage musical gear around the globe. By 2021, the Reverb marketplace had 847 thousand active buyers and 210 thousand active sellers. Approximately 65% of Reverb's active sellers also bought on Reverb. It has one of the largest sellers' inventory with 1.6 million listing as of the year 2021.

The Depop marketplace headquartered in London is stated to be the world's most diverse and progressive home of fashion. Depop, established in 2011, is a community-powered fashion marketplace to buy and sell unique fashion with approximately 26 million registered users. By the end of 2021, Depop had approximately 3.7 million active buyers and 2.0 million active sellers. Apparel category accounted for 90% of Depop's GMS. By December 2021, Depop had approximately 16.6 million listing. Majority of Depop's users are Gen Z Millennial shoppers.

Elo7, known as the "Etsy of Brazil," is headquartered in São Paulo, Brazil. The company specializes in custom and made-to-order merchandise. By end 2021, Elo7 had approximately 55 thousand active sellers and 1.8 million active buyers. During the period the company had approximately 9.9 million items for sale. Approximately 70% of Elo7's GMS were comprised of repeat buyers. Items in Elo7 marketplace are comprised of over 40 retail categories with items such as paper and party supplies, housewares and home furnishings, baby and kids apparel, and weddings and craft supplies. Elo7 was ranked among the top 10 e-commerce site in Brazil in 2021.

Around 56% of Etsy sellers are multichannel sellers and Etsy represents their largest sales channel.

Business Environment and Competition

The nature of commerce is undergoing transformational changes with people preferring to purchase goods online. The COVID-19 pandemic has led to a surge in e-commerce and accelerated digital transformation. According to eMarketer, e-commerce's share of global retail trade was 19.6% in the year 2021.The factors which drive shoppers to shop online include the trend of rapid growth of mobile devices and new shopping habits among others. Consumers are increasingly going digital and purchasing more goods and services online. Etsy market study finds that its seven core geographic markets represent a $466 billion market opportunity and a $2 trillion market opportunity when offline is included.

Operating e-commerce marketplaces is highly competitive in every sense. The company faces competition from a wide range of online and offline competitors. Etsy competes for sellers with marketplaces, retailers, social media commerce, and companies which offers software and services to small businesses. From the seller perspective, the competitors include big companies such as Amazon, eBay, Google, or Alibaba. Sellers can also use mediums such as local consignment and vintage stores and commerce channels on social networks like Facebook, Instagram, and TikTok. Depop, Reverb, and Elo7 face competition from online retailers such as Vinted, ThredUp, or Poshmark.

Growth Strategy

The strategy of Etsy involves creation of an environment of building sustainable competitive advantage. The main essence of Etsy.com's competitive advantage is its sellers' collection of millions of unique items. Etsy group focusses on three elements – search and discovery, human connections, and trusted brand – to provide a best-in-class marketplace experience. Etsy is leveraging artificial intelligence and machine learning as part of world-class search and discovery technology to enable Etsy buyers to easily browse, filter, and find items according to their needs. Etsy's differentiation strategy is to foster and elevate the quality of human connections to drive buyer engagement, loyalty, and purchase frequency. The mission is to facilitate Etsy buyers to work with Etsy sellers to personalize or customize items to their exact specifications. Etsy focusses on seven core geographies of the United States, United Kingdom, Germany, Canada, Australia, France, and India as a part of its growth strategy. These regions provide the most attractive buyer GMS opportunities for Etsy. Etsy has created cross-functional, cross-marketplace initiatives to create value creation in terms of onsite customer experiences, efficient payment platforms, value-added seller services such as advertising platforms, and effective shipping options. Etsy's strategy also involves selectively pursuing acquisition of businesses or technologies which complement the marketplaces or align with its strategic pursuit for growth. These acquisitions are aimed to expand the geographic reach or expand the portfolio of technology offerings. The acquisition of Reverb facilitates the Etsy group to increase its presence in the musical instrument market. The acquisition of

Depop was to extend the group's space into apparel resale space. With the acquisition of the local brand Elo7, Etsy expanded its geographic footprint in Brazil. Etsy aims to offer connected experiences across all devices. Its mobile website and Etsy mobile app for Etsy buyers ("Buy on Etsy") offer search and discovery, curation, personalization, augmented reality, and social shopping features. Approximately 64% of Etsy.com GMS was generated on a mobile device during the year 2021. The strategy of the company aims to provide a personalized search experience to Etsy buyers by developing algorithms to deliver personalized results to buyers. In 2021, the company launched a proprietary capability called "XWalk" which is a real-time graph retrieval engine whose function is to expand and process the data to capture semantic meaning and improve the conversion rate by showing more relevant inventory to buyers. Reverb's growth strategy is focused on becoming the best destination for special gear and expand globally. Depop's growth strategy is based on its strong user engagement metrics, leading resale market position with the "Generation Z" consumer demographic and strong brand awareness in its core markets of the UK and United States. Elo7's strategy focusses on optimizing conversion rate and leveraging Etsy's investment for product and marketing.

By 2020 Etsy completed its migration to Google Cloud and increased its engineering efficiency. The subsidiary marketplaces of Reverb, Depop, and Elo7 also operate their marketplaces in the cloud and make similar technical development investments with Amazon Web Services. The company uses go-to market strategies such as deep research, A/B testing, exploratory analysis, product management, design, engineering, and product marketing to find solutions for customer problems. Approximately 67% of sellers' items on the Etsy marketplace offered free shipping to US buyers and 46% of global orders were delivered with free shipping.

All Etsy marketplace brands adopt the capital light business model characterized by the absence of inventory management, planning future styles or trends, manufacturing facilities, fulfillment centers along with sellers' share in marketing/promotion, and loyal and engaged customer cohorts.

ESG Initiatives

Etsy is committed to grow sustainably by aligning its business strategy for economic impact through entrepreneurship. In 2021, Etsy sellers contributed $14.3 billion to the US economy. In addition, Etsy sellers created 3.8 million jobs in independent worker economy.

The company's commitment for building resilience for long-term environmental sustainability is reflected in its resolve to set ambitious net-zero targets by a carbon-neutral company and sourcing 100% renewable electricity. The company had launched sustainable packaging for Etsy marketplace US sellers. The company ensures equitable access to opportunity as part of its social initiative objectives. There have been an increase of percentage of Etsy and Reverb leadership-level employees from underrepresented community. Etsy collected over 6.8 million donations for the Uplift Fund which focusses on eliminating barriers to creative entrepreneurship. As a part of governance initiatives, the company appointed two new directors. The company has also updated certain board practices to enhance oversight of cyber-related risks. In year 2021, the company invested over $ 2.9 million in philanthropic donations which included COVID-19 relief to Asian American– and Pacific Islander–led organizations. Etsy-enabled employees donated 2490 h of paid volunteer time for community service through Etsy's Impact Hours program. With a goal towards social innovation, Etsy established the Uplift Fund to support creative entrepreneurs and have received over 6.8 million contributions from US buyers on the Etsy marketplace. The company had also launched the Uplift Makers program to help create opportunities for economic empowerment for heritage artisans by bringing their products online. About 35 participating shops have made sales over $550,000.

Strategic Risk Analysis

The success of the company depends upon the trustworthiness of the marketplaces and the connections within community stakeholders. The growth of business and financial performance depend on the critical element of the ability to attract and retain active communities of buyers and sellers. The business success depends on unhindered access to third-party services, platforms, and infrastructure. The company faces risk due to technology vulnerabilities, service interruptions, security breaches, or other technological disruptions. The software underlying the platforms is highly interconnected and complex and faces challenges of undetected errors or vulnerabilities. Etsy faces regulatory compliance and legal risks with respect to compliance for privacy and data protection laws, tax laws, antitrust laws, product liability laws, and intellectual property. The company faces risk with respect to integration of Depop and El07. The company also faces risk related to adverse economic and market conditions which include those related to the current COVID-19 pandemic, currency fluctuations, rising inflation, and adverse global events. The financial performance of the company is significantly determined by the success in attracting and retaining active buyers and sellers in the market. Etsy is dependent on widely adopted third-party platforms to reach out to its customers. These platforms include popular mobile, social, search, and advertising offerings. The effectiveness of these platforms is critical for the success of the marketplaces of Etsy.

Table 1 gives the revenue details in '000s.

Table 2 highlights the performance of Etsy in terms of book value and market value of equity stated in millions of dollars.

Table 1 Revenues (in '000s)

Year	2019	2020	2021
Marketplace	593,646	1,303,126	1,745,824
Services	224,733	422,499	583,290
Total	818,379	1,725,625	2,329,114

Table 2 Book value and market value comparison

Year	2018	2019	2020	2021
Book value of equity	401	407	742	629
Market value of equity	5698	5243	22,387	27,810
BV as percent of MV	7%	8%	3%	2%
Average	5%			

Table 3 Comparative stock market performance

Year	2016	2017	2018	2019	2020	2021
ETSY	$100	$172.14	$400.42	$372.90	$1497.56	$1842.93
SP500	$100	$118.42	$111.03	$143.09	$166.36	$211.10
Dow 30	100	124.33	$117.33	$143.54	$153.94	$182.77

Source: Annual Report 2021

Table 4 Profitability and leverage measures

Ratios	2018	2019	2020	2021	Average
Net profit margin%	12.84	11.72	20.24	21.19	16.50
ROE%	19.42	23.75	60.79	71.99	43.99
ROA%	10.28	7.85	17.7	15.83	12.92
DER	0.85	2.08	1.5	3.8	2.06

The average book value of Etsy was only 5% of the market value during the period 2018–2021. In the year 2021, the book value was only 2% of the market value of the company. In other words, 98% of the value was created on account of intangibles. The analysis shows high valuation for the Etsy stock in the stock market.

Table 3 shows the performance of the Etsy stock compared with that of the market S&P500 and Dow 30 Indexes.

The estimation assumes that $100 was invested at the market close on December 31, 2016, in the common stock of Etsy, Inc. The analysis assumes reinvestment of any dividends. Etsy stock's superior performance is reflected in fact that it had beaten the market index by manifold times. The 5-year holding period return for Etsy stock was 1743% during the period 2017–2021 compared to 111% return of SP500 and 83% return of Dow 30. The 5 yearly average return for Etsy was 105%, while that for SP500 and Dow 30 was 17% and 13%, respectively.

Table 4 examines the profitability and leverage position of the firm during the period 2018–2019.

In terms of profitability ratios, Etsy had the best performance in the year 2021 during the period 2018–2021.The company's ROE was approximately 72% in year 2021. The average net profit margin was 16.5% during the period 2018–2021. The average ROE and ROA during the above period were 43.99% and 12.92%, respectively. The average debt equity ratio was 2.06 during the period 2018–2021.

Table 5 gives the details of important financial elements of Etsy company during the past years.

Table 5 Financial highlights

	(In millions of dollars)			
Financial highlights	2018	2019	2020	2021
Total assets	902	1542	2404	3832
Cash and cash equivalents	367	443	1244	780
Total equity	401	407	742	629
Total revenue	604	818	1726	2329
Total operating expenses	338	459	837	1209
Net income	77	96	349	494
Market cap	5698	5243	22,387	27,810
Enterprise value	5416	5272	21,834	29,214

Source: Annual reports

Table 6 Estimation of economic value

Year	2020	2021
Profit before income tax	366	472
Income tax	16	22.00
Net operating profit after tax (NOPAT)	350	450
Stockholder equity	742	629
Long-term debt	1062	2275
Total capital employed	1804	2904
WACC	11.51%	12.37%
Capital charge	207.64	359.225
Economic value	142	91

The values are given in millions of dollars. The data was collected from annual reports and gurufocus.com. The 3-year period (2019–2021) growth rate in total assets on average was 62%. The total revenues and net income grew by 60% and 110%, respectively, during the above period. The cash and cash equivalents grew by 55% during the above period. The total equity increased by 23% on an average basis. The average growth rate in market capitalization and enterprise value during the above period were 114% and 115%, respectively.

Table 6 illustrates the calculation of economic value for the company in the year 2020 and 2021. The values are given in millions of dollars.

The economic value has declined in the year 2021.

References

1. Etsy Annual Report 2021.
2. https://investors.etsy.com/events-and-presentations/default.aspx
3. https://investors.etsy.com/home/default.aspx

Case 6 The Trade Desk

The Trade Desk, Inc. is a global technology industry leading media-buying platform for data-driven marketers. The self-service cloud-based platform offered by the Trade Desk supports advertisement buyers to create, manage, and optimize expressive data-driven digital advertising campaigns across different advertising formats and channels which include display, video, and audio on devices such as computers, mobile devices, and connected TV. Trade Desk's platforms are integrated with major inventory, publisher, and data partners and enable advertisement (ad) buyers to reach the scale and develop effective decision-making capabilities. The enterprise application programming interfaces (APIs) offer competitive benefits for the ad buyers. The Trade Desk is a Delaware corporation which was established in Ventura, California, in the year 2009. In 2011, the company had officially launched the platform. The clients of the company are basically the advertising agencies and other service providers. Trade Desk enters into continuous master service agreements ("MSAs") with the clients. Trade Desk charges the client a platform fee which is estimated on the basis of a percentage of a client's total spend on advertising. The other sources of revenue are obtained by means of providing data and other value-added services and platform features. Trade Desk invoices their clients for the cost of advertising inventory purchased, plus data, and any add-on features purchased through the platform.

The company provides a self-service platform to agencies to pick from over 500 billion digital advertisement opportunities a day. The company is an omnichannel which provides CTV, mobile, video, audio, and display.

The clients of Trade Desk consist of purchasers of programmatic advertising inventory and data. By the end of 2021, the company had 980 clients consisting of advertising agencies or independent groups within advertising agencies. The company has a client retention rate of over 95% during the 3-year period, 2019–2021. By the end of 2021, Trade Desk had 1967 full-time employees in 19 countries with North America representing 65% of the workforce. The Asia Pacific and EMEA regions account for 17% and 18% of the workforce, respectively. The year 2021 revenue amounted to $1196 million.

© The Author(s), under exclusive license to Springer Nature Switzerland AG 2024

B. R. Kumar, *Rising Stars*, Management for Professionals,
https://doi.org/10.1007/978-3-031-50032-9_6

Industry Trends

The advertising industry is witnessing different trends and transformational changes are observed in the field of programmatic advertising which involves the selling and buying of advertising inventory electronically. On account of advances in technology and changes in consumer behavior, media is becoming increasingly digital in nature. This significant shift has created plenty of options for advertisers to target and measure their advertising campaigns across different media channels and devices. Digital advertising contributes significantly towards the total advertising market. The trend observed is that decisions based on consumer and behavioral data are becoming more relevant in the modern context. Audience fragmentation is another trend observed on account of growth of digital media. TV content distribution is substantially impacted by audience fragmentation. This phenomenon has changed the way how advertising inventory is monetized. On account of content fragmentation, the number of devices used by individual consumers has also increased. The fragmentation phenomena have provided opportunities for technology companies to consolidate and simplify media-buying options for advertisers and their agencies. The world is witnessing the mega generational shift from TV to CTV which is reflecting the convergence of the Internet and television programming. New technologies facilitate the process of allowing more video content to the Internet. The worldwide rollout of 5G is facilitating faster data transfer speeds with less latency. These technologies will feed consumer demand for CTV and provide new opportunities for content owners and advertisers to connect with consumers. Developments in software and hardware technologies have enabled the generation of user data which are collected by data vendors across a wide range of Internet properties. Advertisers can integrate this targeting data with their own or an agency's proprietary data which are related to client attributes. Use of this data sources along with real-time feedback on consumer reactions will lead to increase in the value of impressions for advertisers and inventory owners. Automation of advertisement buying has become essential in the context of growing complexity of digital advertising. Programmatic inventory buying tools facilitate advertisers to automate their campaigns and provide them with better price discovery on an impression by impression basis. Through this mechanism, advertisers are able to bid on and purchase the most valued advertising inventory. The digital advertising ecosystem can be divided into buyers, sellers, and marketplaces which can again be segmented on the basis of its participants providing services or technology. The total global advertising spending market is estimated to be $750 billion in year 2021.

Business Model of Trade Desk

Trade Desk provides a self-service omnichannel software platform to advertisement buyer clients to purchase and manage data-driven digital advertising campaigns. The platform allows clients to manage integrated advertising campaigns across various advertising channels and formats which include display, video, audio, native, and social on a variety of devices which include computers, mobile devices, and CTV. The company focusses on the buyer side of the ecosystem. The business model platform was founded on the principle that data-driven decisions would be the future of advertising. The platform provided by Trade Desk is an open platform where the clients use the APIs to design their own user interface, bulk manage advertising campaigns, and link other systems which include advertisement servers or reporting tools. The open platform approach enables the advertising agency and service provider clients to provide differentiated offerings to their client. The bid factor-based architecture system of the platform allows users to define desirable factors and compute in real time the value of impressions. On account of the granularity of bid factors, the platform can rapidly create billions of different bid permutations with only a few clicks. This mechanism facilitates better targeting, pricing, and campaign results. The platform of Trade Desk provides auto-optimization features which allow buyers to automate their campaigns and assist them with computer-generated modelling and decision-making. The platform has advanced reporting and analytics tools to provide a complete view of consumers' interactions with the advertisements purchased. The platform offered by Trade Desk enables a media planner or buyer at an advertising agency to purchase digital media programmatically on various media exchanges and sell-side platforms. It facilitates the acquisition and use of third-party data to optimize, measure, and manage digital advertising campaigns on a real-time basis. The clients can also access other services such as data management platform and publisher management platform marketplace. The core critical features of the platform are scalable architecture, predictive models, performance optimization, and real-time analytics.

Growth Strategy and Competitive Environment

Trade Desk basically focusses on increasing its share of client's digital advertising spend. The trend of moving a greater proportion of advertising budgets to programmatic channels will provide ample opportunity for Trade Desk to capture a larger share of overall advertising spend by the clients. The company also aims to provide additional services and data to its clients. On account of the decentralized nature of the advertising industry, the company aims to grow its client base by leveraging its extensive relationship with many advertising agencies and service providers. Trade Desk is also focusing its attention to expand its omnichannel capabilities by offering client capabilities across all media channels. Investment in innovation across different channels is promoted for integration of new inventory sources within CTV, digital radio, social, native, and digital out-of-home channels. The company also has targeted towards expanding its international presence outside of the United States. The markets of China, India, and Indonesia are markets of good potential for the company. The focus is also on building industry-wide collaboration and support for developing Unified ID 2.0 which is a new open-source identity framework to promote advertising on the open Internet without reliance upon third-party cookies. To facilitate training of clients, suppliers, and digital media participants, Trade Desk has created an e-learning program called the Trade Desk Edge Academy for onboarding integration to the platform.

The industry is highly competitive and fragmented. Trade Desk competes with demand-side platform providers including small privately held companies and large players such as Google and Adobe. The differentiated strategy of Trade Desk is based on the following factors. Trade Desk is an independent technology company which focuses on serving advertising agencies and others on the buy side of the industry. The client relationships of the company are based on master supply agreement (MSA) as opposed to campaign-specific insertion orders. Another differentiation factor is that the platform provides comprehensive access to a wide range of inventory types and third-party data vendors. The platform of the company facilitates clients to build proprietary advantages by integrating custom features and interfaces through APIs.

Risk and Challenges

The sustainability of revenues in the long run is a function of addition of new clients and the extent to which the existing clients maintain or increase the amount of advertising inventory purchased through the company's platform. The ability to provide services to new or existing clients might be impaired if competitors introduce lower cost or differentiated offerings. The loss of advertising agencies as clients could significantly harm the business, financial condition, and results of operations of the company. The success of the business model depends on the investments made for technological innovations to meet the client demand and evolving industry standards. The use of the firm's APIs by clients to build their own media-buying and data management interface will increase the security and operational risks of Trade Desk.

Governance

The Board comprises of a majority of directors who qualify as independent directors as required under Nasdaq rules. The independent directors will meet in executive session without nonindependent directors or management present on a regularly scheduled basis, but no less than twice per year. The Board will meet at least four times annually. The Board currently has three standing committees: (i) the audit committee, (ii) the compensation committee, and (iii) the nominating and corporate governance committee. The governance policy also includes guidelines with respect to the whistleblower hotline. The audit committee consists of at least three members. Each committee member must satisfy the independence requirements of the NASDAQ Stock Market LLC. The compensation committee and the nominating and corporate governance committee must consist of at least two directors.

Stock Performance

The company had a total holding period return of 3211.9% during the 5-year period, Dec 31, 2016, to Dec 31, 2021. An initial investment of $100 on December 31, 2016, would have resulted in total investment value of $3311.89 by the end of December 2021. The initial stock price was $2.77. By the end of the stated period, the end price was $91.64. The compound annual growth rate amounted to 101.32% during the 5-year period.

Table 1 highlights the excess value created by the company during the period 2018–2021. The values are given in millions of dollars.

The average book value as percent of market value was 5% during the period 2018–2021. The book value as percent of market value was only 3% during the period 2020–2021.Thus, the market value was exceptionally high compared to the book value of the firm.

Five-Year Return Analysis

The total cumulative monthly average return for the Trade Desk during the 5-year period 2017–2021 was 340%, while the cumulative monthly average return was 7% for the market index Nasdaq Composite. The average yearly return for Trade Desk for the period 2017–2021 was 69%, while that for the Nasdaq Composite was 14% during the above period.

Table 2 shows the holding period return for the Trade Desk in comparison to the holding period return for the market index Nasdaq.

The peak holding period return for Trade Desk was registered in year 2018 and 2020. The above analysis shows that Trade Desk has superior returns compared to the Nasdaq Composite market index in all years except in year 2017.

Table 3 shows the profitability ratios and leverage ratio of debt to equity during the period 2018–2021.

Table 1 Excess value

Year	2018	2019	2020	2021
Book value of equity	395	613	1013	1527
Market value of equity	5091	11,814	37,919	44,303
BV as percent of MV	8%	5%	3%	3%
Average	5%			

Table 2 Holding period return

Year	Trade desk	NASDAQ	Excess returns
2017	−8%	15%	−24%
2018	154%	0%	154%
2019	36%	21%	15%
2020	167%	53%	114%
2021	20%	8%	12%

Table 3 Performance and leverage measures

Ratios	2018	2019	2020	2021	Average
Net margin%	18.47	16.39	28.98	11.51	18.84
ROE%	27.54	21.51	29.81	10.85	22.43
ROA%	9.21	7.61	10.81	4.35	8.00
DER	0.31	0.29	0.19	0.17	0.24

Table 4 Financial highlights

	(In millions of dollars)			
Financial highlights	2018	2019	2020	2021
Total assets	1118	1729	2754	3577
Cash and cash equivalents	207	131	437	754
Total equity	395	613	1013	1527
Total revenue	477	661	836	1196
Total operating expenses	256	393	513	850
Net income	88	108	242	138
Market cap	5091	11,814	37,919	44,303
Enterprise value	4884	11,748	37,588	43,628

The average net margin was 18.84% during the period 2018–2021. The average ROE and ROA during the above period were 22.43% and 8%, respectively, during the above period. The average debt equity ratio was 0.24 for the above period.

Table 4 provides the financial highlights of the company during the period 2018–2021.

The source of data was annual reports. The average growth rate of total assets during the period 2019–2021 was 48%. The cash and cash equivalents and total equity increased by 90% and 57%, respectively, during the above period. The total revenues increased by 36% on an average basis during the period 2019–2021.The net income of the company grew by 35% during the above period. The total expenses increased by 50% on an average basis during the period 2019–2021. The market value and enterprise value increased by over 120% during the above period of analysis.

References

1. https://investors.thetradedesk.com/stock-info/default.aspx#calculator
2. https://investors.thetradedesk.com/governance/governance-documents/default.aspx
3. https://investors.thetradedesk.com/financials/annual-reports/default.aspx
4. https://www.gurufocus.com/stock/TTD/financials#_stock-financial-table-header-6

Case 7 Quidel Corporation

Introduction

Quidel Corporation was incorporated in the year 1979 as monoclonal antibodies. The company is a California-based leading diagnostic healthcare manufacturer which has expanded its product base through internal development and acquisition with a focus on developing and manufacturing innovative technologies to enhance the performance of diagnostic testing. QuidelOrtho was created in business combination of Quidel and Ortho Clinical Diagnostics in 2022. QuidelOrtho is ranked among the world's largest in vitro (IVD) providers in the world. In 1987 the company was reincorporated as Quidel Corporation. Quidel Corporation is involved in the mission to advance diagnostics to improve human health. Quidel holds leadership position in the development, manufacturing, and marketing of rapid diagnostic testing solutions. The company sells its products directly to end users and distributors. In 1983, the company introduced its first products, dipstick-based pregnancy tests. The products are targeted towards professional end users in physician offices, hospitals, clinical and reference laboratories, urgent care clinics, leading universities, retail clinics, pharmacies, and wellness screening centers. The diagnostic solutions offered by the company are utilized for the detection and diagnosis of critical diseases which include infectious diseases, cardiovascular diseases, gastrointestinal diseases, and autoimmune and thyroid diseases. Quidel's portfolio of products are categorized into four product categories: rapid immunoassay, cardiometabolic immunoassay, molecular diagnostic solutions, and specialized diagnostic solutions. The products are directly sold by the company to end users and distributors for professional use in physician offices, hospitals, clinical laboratories, urgent care clinics, retail clinics, pharmacies, and wellness screening centers. In 2021, the company had an income of $1.69 billion. Quidel focuses on the delivery of a chain of diagnostic solutions from advanced lateral flow and direct fluorescent antibody to molecular diagnostic tests to improve the quality of healthcare.

The company's current product portfolio can be categorized into (a) lateral flow wherein the company is the market leader in the infectious disease and reproductive

© The Author(s), under exclusive license to Springer Nature Switzerland AG 2024
B. R. Kumar, *Rising Stars*, Management for Professionals,
https://doi.org/10.1007/978-3-031-50032-9_7

health segment, (b) direct fluorescent antibodies (DFAs) with expertise in infectious disease and virology, (c) microtiter production with a focus on bone and complement pathway markets, (d) fluorescent immunoassay products (Sofia), and (e) molecular diagnostic products which include the world's first FDA-cleared handheld molecular device. During the COVID-19 period, the company introduced the QuickVue® At-Home OTC COVID-19 test for reopening schools and for health departments, employers, and entertainment centers.

Strategies for Growth

In the year 2017, Quidel acquired the Triage ® MeterPro® cardiovascular and toxicology business ("Triage Business") and B-type natriuretic peptide ("BNP") assay business run on Beckman analyzers from Alere Inc. This acquisition resulted in the addition of cardiovascular and toxicology products to the medical diagnostics portfolio of the company. During the end of 2021, Quidel entered into a business combination agreement with Ortho, Coronado Topco, Orca Holdco Inc., and Laguna Merger Sub, Inc. Ortho is being acquired for $4.3 billion by the company. The deal involves $1.75 billion of cash. The company provides diagnostic testing solutions under various brand names which are classified into four product categories of rapid immunoassay, cardiometabolic immunoassay, molecular diagnostic solutions, and specialized diagnostic solutions. The company had been a leader for the development and production of high-quality lateral flow diagnostics since the early 1990s and offers a wide range of products to diagnose a variety of infectious diseases. The company's offering of the QuickVue At-Home OTC COVID-19 test became a leading at-home COVID-19 product for home use. InflammaDry and Adenoplus products are rapid, lateral flow–based, point-of-care products for the detection of infectious and inflammatory diseases and conditions of the eye. The portable testing platform of Triage MeterPro aids in the diagnosis, assessment, and risk stratification of patients having critical care issues. In 2021, the company had launched Savanna multiplex molecular analyzer system and Savanna RVP4 assay. This Savanna system is a low-cost fully integrated sample to result automated in vitro molecular diagnostic platform which enables analysis of up to 12 pathogens or targets, plus controls from a single assay run in less than 25 min.

The Specialized Diagnostic Solutions Virology department offers a wide variety of traditional cell lines, specimen collection devices, and controls for use in laboratories that test human viruses. The company provides cell-based products under the FreshCells brand in multiple formats which include tubes, shell vials, and multi-well plates. The virology product category provides the FDA-cleared bioassay, Thyretain, which is used for the differential diagnosis of autoimmune diseases. The cell culture and DFA detection solutions such as D3 FastPoint technology offered by Quidel are used by reference laboratories, public health laboratories, and acute care hospitals to detect eight major viral respiratory pathogens. The proprietary cell culture platform R-Mix™, combined with the D3

Ultra DFA antibody kit, detects influenza A and B, RSV, adenovirus, and parainfluenza types 1, 2, and 3, with turnaround times between 16 and 48 h.

The acquisition of the Triage and BNP businesses has positioned Quidel as a market leader in the cardiology diagnostic market. With the development of biomarkers for bone health, Quidel produces both clinical and research products for the assessment of osteoporosis and the evaluation of bone resorption/formation. In 2019, the company launched the new Triage TOX Drug Screen which uses distinct immunoassays for the simultaneous detection of drug and/or urinary metabolites for multiple drug classes. Quidel focusses on the expansion plans to further expand its digital and telehealth solutions from the at-home testing and identity verification and reporting functions to the telehealth setting where patients can use Quidel's digital testing and reporting functions to further interact with healthcare professionals for diagnosis and treatment. The company's strategy is to target market segments with differentiated technologies and products. The company also focusses on the development of innovative products and markets and leverage core competency in new medical and wellness product development for QuickVue, Sofia, and Triage immunoassay brands and next-generation products. The company focusses on wireless connectivity and data management systems and capabilities for the promotion of clinical efficacy and economic efficiency of the diagnostic tests for the professional market. The company focusses on pursuing potential acquisition for expansion into the diagnostics market. The research and development expenses amounted to $95.7 million, $84.3 million, and $52.6 million for the years December 31, 2021, 2020, and 2019, respectively. The company adopts a mix of direct and indirect distribution strategies to sell products globally and market and distribute products. The manufacturing sites of the company are located in San Diego, California, Athens, Ohio, and Europe. The ESG strategy of the company focusses on innovation in the diagnostic market to provide affordable testing for customers and maintain the highest ethical standards for suppliers, stockholders, and collaborators.

Risks and Challenges

The company faces potential challenges from large pharmaceutical and diversified healthcare competitors such as Abbott Laboratories, Beckman Coulter Primary Care Diagnostics, Thermo Fisher Scientific, Becton Dickinson and Company, Meridian Bioscience, Inc., and Danaher Corporation.

The company faces operational and strategic risks on account of the development of new technologies, products, and markets. The company relies on a limited number of key distributors. The firm faces international risk due to compliance issues in terms of product registration requirements, legal requirements, tariffs, and exposure to currency exchange fluctuations. The intense competition would adversely affect the sales and margins for the company. The business and products of the company are highly regulated by various governmental agencies and the success of operations of the company depends on regulatory approvals and authorizations.

ESG Initiatives

The ESG strategy of the company focusses on three pillars of fostering a culture of happy people, operating responsibly and driving equitable healthcare. Quidel has developed a comprehensive compliance program (CCP) that is designed to ensure the company and its employees operate in accordance with all applicable federal and state laws and industry standards relating to the marketing and promotion of its products and relationships with the medical community. Sales and marketing employees receive responsible marketing training. Quidel is required to have a robust responsible marketing audit process as regulated by the FDA. Quidel promotes diversity and inclusion in the workplace through a variety of policies, procedures, and programs such as the tuition reimbursement program available to all employees. Quidel's supplier code of conduct (SCOC) outlines the basic requirements that must be met by suppliers, vendors, and other third-party providers in order to do business with Quidel. Suppliers must adhere to the zero-tolerance policy for anti-bribery, anti-corruption, competition, and unfair business practice laws. Quidel focuses on minimization of environmental impacts by reducing greenhouse gas emissions, protecting water resources, and maximizing the recovery of resources in the waste management process. The company consults with stakeholders and periodically publishes updates on the mitigation of any identified environmental or safety issues. In 2020, 60.9% of waste have been recycled by the company. The company has received Quality Management Certification such as ISO 13485:2016 and MDSAP. Quidel maintains health and safety programs conforming to best practices in the industry. Quidel maintains a comprehensive and multifaceted cybersecurity program. Quidel's cybersecurity program leverages industry standard NIST 800-53 and ISO-27002 risk management frameworks led by certified cybersecurity professionals. Quidel's Total Recordable Cases Incident Rate is below industry average for the year 2020 and 2021.

Quidel's ownership data is presented in Table 1.

Table 2 compares the stock performance of Quidel with that of indexes such as Nasdaq Composite Index, Nasdaq US Benchmark Medical Supplies Index, and Nasdaq Healthcare Index. The assumption made involves investment of $100 on December 31, 2016, in indexes and company along with reinvestment of dividends. The performance is evaluated by December end of each year.

The 5-year holding period return for Quidel stock was 530%. The comparative indexes registered inferior performance in terms of returns compared to Quidel stock. The 5-year holding return for Nasdaq Composite and Nasdaq US Benchmark Medical Supplies was 191% and 176%, respectively. Nasdaq Healthcare had a holding period return of 83% during the 5-year period Dec 31, 2016, to Dec

Table 1 Ownership data

Institutional holding	86.08
Insiders	6.94
Others	6.98
Total	100

Table 2 Comparative stock performance of Quidel corporation

Company/Index	31/12/2016	31/12/2017	31/12/2018	31/12/2019	31/12/2020	31/12/2021
Quidel Corp	$100	$202.38	$227.92	$350.28	$855.46	$630.21
Nasdaq Composite	$100	$128.24	$123.26	$166.68	$239.63	$290.63
Nasdaq US Benchmark Medical Supplies	$100	$130.54	$123.68	$182.74	$230.76	$275.85
Nasdaq Healthcare	$100	$121.30	$116.25	$146.27	$191.72	$183.47

Source: Annual Report 2021

Table 3 Excess value in millions of dollars

Year	2018	2019	2020	2021
Book value of equity	426	560	1333	1929
Market value of equity	1923	3141	7597	5627
BV as percent of MV	22%	18%	18%	34%
Average	23%			

31, 2021. The average return for Quidel stock for the period 2017–2021 was 57%. The three comparative indexes had an average return of 25%, 24%, and 14%, respectively, during the above period of analysis. Hence, it can be concluded that Quidel stock had outperformed the market indexes during the last 5-year period.

Table 3 highlights the comparative book value and market value performance of Quidel Corporation. The data for analysis is sourced from Gurufocus.com.

The average book value as percent of market value was 23%. In the year 2019 and 2020, the book value of Quidel stock accounted for only 18% of the market value of the company.

Five-Year Return Analysis

The cumulative total return for Quidel stock for the 5-year period 2017–2021 was 158%, while that for the Nasdaq Healthcare Index was 31% reflecting the superior performance of Quidel stock compared to that of the Healthcare Index. The average yearly returns based on the 5-year monthly analysis for Quidel Corp was 32% compared to yearly returns of 6% for the Healthcare Index. The data for stock return analysis was sourced from Yahoo Finance.

Table 4 documents the holding period return for the Quidel stock in comparison with Nasdaq Healthcare Index for the 5-year period.

Quidel stock registered the best performance in the year 2020 with excess return of 99% compared to the performance of the Nasdaq Healthcare Index. The stock did poorly in the year 2021 and 2022.

Table 5 shows the profitability and leverage ratios during the period 2018–2021.

The average net margin, ROE, and ROA during the 4-year period 2018–2021 were 29.51%, 41.59%, and 27%, respectively. The profitability ratios peaked during

Table 4 Holding period return

Year	Quidel	IXHCNASDAQ	Excess returns
2017	6%	2%	4%
2018	7%	−11%	17%
2019	29%	12%	18%
2020	134%	35%	99%
2021	−46%	−8%	−38%
2022 till Sept	−17.3%	−7%	−10%

Table 5 Performance and leverage ratio

Ratios	2018	2019	2020	2021	Average
Net margin%	14.20	13.63	48.76	41.46	29.51
ROE%	22.73	14.80	85.63	43.18	41.59
ROA%	8.52	8.49	58.25	32.74	27.00
DER	0.25	0.20	0.08	0.07	0.15

Table 6 Financial highlights

	(In millions of dollars)			
Financial highlights	2018	2019	2020	2021
Total assets	806.00	911.00	1871.00	2430.00
Cash and cash equivalents	44.00	53.00	490.00	829.00
Total equity	426.00	560.00	1333.00	1929.00
Total revenue	522.00	535.00	1662.00	1699.00
Total operating expenses	206.00	216.00	285.00	355.00
Net income	74	73	810	704
Market cap	1923.00	3141.00	7597.00	5627.00
Enterprise value	1987.00	3201.00	7216.00	4937.00

the year 2020. The ROE and ROA during the year 2020 were 85.63% and 58.25%, respectively. The average debt equity ratio was 0.15 during the period 2018–2021.

Table 6 shows the operating performance highlights of the company along with the market performance.

The values are given in millions of dollars. The total revenues grew by 72% on an average basis during the 3-year period 2019–2021. The average growth rate of total assets and total equity during the above period was 49% and 71%, respectively. The net income and cash equivalents increased by 332% and 305%, respectively, during the 3-year period of analysis. The market capitalization and enterprise value increased by an average of 60% and 52%, respectively, during the 3-year period. The data is sourced from annual reports.

Table 7 estimates the economic value of the company.

The economic values are estimated in millions of dollars. The WACC is taken from gurufocus.com. The economic value of Quidel is estimated to be $782 million and $655 million in year 2020 and 2021, respectively.

Table 7 Estimation of economic value

Year	2020	2021
Profit before income tax	1040	900
Income tax	230	196.02
Net operating profit after tax (NOPAT)	810	704
Stockholder equity	1333.00	1929.00
Long-term debt		
Total capital employed	1333	1929
WACC	2.13%	2.53%
Capital charge	28.3929	48.8037
Economic value	782	655

References

1. https://www.quidel.com/
2. Quidel Annual Reports
3. https://ir.quidel.com/home/default.aspx

Case 8 ACM Research

ACM Research was established in the year 1998 in Silicon Valley. ACM Research Inc. develops wet processing technology and products for the semiconductor industry. In September 2006, ACM expanded its operations into Asia and established the subsidiary ACM Research (Shanghai). ACM Research provides advanced wafer cleaning and wet processing equipment for semiconductor manufacturing. In the year 2003, the company began to design an innovative new single-wafer cleaning equipment which was aimed at the emerging generations of IC chips. The company is headquartered in Fremont, California, and employs more than 875 employees in different regions.

ACM Research is involved in the business of supply of advanced innovative capital equipment for the global semiconductor industry. ACM provides wet cleaning and other front-end processing tools to fabricators of advanced integrated circuits and chips. These tools have been designed for usage in fabricating foundry, logic, memory, and compound semiconductor chips. ACM also develops and sells advanced packaging tools to wafer assembly and packaging customers. ACM Research offers two principal models of wet wafer cleaning equipment based on SAPS technology, Ultra C SAPS II, and Ultra C SAPS V. These models are a single-wafer serial processing tool which can be configured to customer specifications. The company has developed the TEBO technology for application in wet wafer cleaning for fabrication of 2D and 3D wafers.

The revenues from wet cleaning and other front-end processing tools amounted to 84.6%, 87%, and 77.9% in the year 2019, 2020, and 2021, respectively.

Since 2009, ACM has delivered more than 225 wet cleaning and other front-end processing tools. Majority of the sales of single-wafer wet cleaning equipment were attributed to the Asian region. The company has received 411 patents from the United States, China, Japan, Singapore, South Korea, and Taiwan. By Dec 31, 2021, 38 patents were issued from United States. Majority of the product development, manufacturing, support, and services are conducted in China with additional product development and subsystem production in South Korea. In 2021, approximately

© The Author(s), under exclusive license to Springer Nature Switzerland AG 2024

B. R. Kumar, *Rising Stars*, Management for Professionals,
https://doi.org/10.1007/978-3-031-50032-9_8

49% of the revenues were accounted by two customers, Shanghai Huali Microelectronics Corporation and Hua Hong Semiconductor Ltd.

During November 2021, ACM's operating subsidiary, ACM Shanghai, was listed on the Shanghai Stock Exchange. By December 2021, the company had 877 full-time employees of whom 85 were in administration, 200 were in manufacturing, 371 were in research and development, and 221 were in sales and marketing and customer services.

Industry Environment

The rapidly changing chip equipment industry is highly competitive. The Gartner study 2021 on major equipment segment points that worldwide the semiconductor wafer fab equipment market has a value of $88.1 billion. ACM Research faces competition globally and also from new competitors from emerging markets like China. The principal competitors include wafer cleaning and electrical plating product manufacturers such as Lam Research Corporation; NAURA Technology Group Co., Ltd.; Mujin Electronics Co., Ltd.; SCREEN SPE USA, LLC; Tokyo Electron Ltd.; and Kokusai Semiconductor Equipment Corporation. The principal competitive factors in the industry include particle removal efficiency, rate of damage to wafer structures, high-temperature chemistry, waste treatment, and environmental impact. The company possesses competitive advantage related to the above factors compared to many competitors and the focus is on the high-end fabrication market with advanced nodes.

Strategy for Growth

The company focusses on building a strategic portfolio of intellectual property to support its key innovations. The tools offered by ACM Research are developed using its key proprietary technologies. Examples include the Space Alternated Phase Shift (SAPS) technology for flat and patterned wafer surfaces which employs alternate phases of megasonic waves for creating megasonic energy uniformly on a microscopic level. Timely Energized Bubble Oscillation (TEBO) technology for patterned water surfaces at advanced process nodes provides effective damage-free cleaning for 2D and 3D patterned wafers. Tahoe technology has competitive advantage in terms of cost and environmental savings. Electrochemical plating (ECP) technology for advanced metal plating is used for front-end wafer fabrication processes. In 2020, the company has introduced product extensions such as the Ultra SFP app tool for advanced packaging solutions, the Ultra C VI 18-chamber single-wafer cleaning tool for advanced memory devices, and the Ultra ECP 3D platform for through-silicon via, or tsv, application.

ACM has focused on selling efforts for establishing a referenceable base of leading foundry, logic, and memory chip makers whose usage of products can influence decision by other manufacturers. ACM Research focuses on providing custom-made differentiated equipment for its back-end wafer assembly and packaging customers. ACM focusses on leveraging local presence in Asia by collaborating with regional semiconductor chip makers to deliver specific requirements. The company continues to focus on investment in research and development to support and enhance existing cleaning products and develop future product offerings. The research and development team of the company is comprised of highly skilled engineers and technologists with vast experience in megasonic technology, cleaning processes and chemistry, mechanical design, and control system design. The company also has collaborations with external research agencies such as International SEMATECH, Shanghai Integrated Circuits Research and Development Center (ICRD), and IMEC for semiconductor technology research. The research and development expenses amounted to 12%, 12.2%, and 13.4% of revenues during the years 2019, 2020, and 2021, respectively.

The company is the best-in-class multiproduct semiconductor capital equipment supplier to leading global semiconductor manufacturers. The differentiated technology used by ACM improves customer production processes with better yields and reduced chemical consumption. State-of-the-art production facilities are established in Shanghai. The growth strategy is focused on new products, customers, capacity, and M&A. In terms of new product development, the company focusses on next-generation TEBO, Tahoe, and other new products. ACM Research is also focusing on plating for front- and back-end, furnace, and semicritical tools. For adoption of new customers, dedicated sales teams are placed in the United States, Europe, and Asia. In terms of new capacity, ACM is targeting to reach $625 million of capacity by the end of year 2022. The company also aims to use selective mergers and acquisitions to broaden product portfolio and add complementary technologies.

Risk Factors

The cyclicality in the semiconductor industry that may lead to substantial variations in demand for the products of the company could adversely affect operating results. The success of the company is determined by the widespread market acceptance of its technologies such as SAPS, TEBO, ECP, and furnace by the chip manufacturers. The business depends upon the capital spending of chip manufacturers, which, in turn, depends upon the current and anticipated market demand for chips. Future success depends on new product development which requires significant investments in engineering hours, third-party development costs, prototypes and sample materials, and sales and marketing expenses. The development of the TEBO technology took 8 years for successful product launch. The chip manufacturing industry is highly concentrated and the company derives the revenues from a limited number of customers. For example, in the year 2021, two customers accounted for 48.9% of the revenues. A significant reduction in orders from these major customers would adversely affect the revenue and operation results of the company. The dual-class structure of common stock has the effect of concentration of voting control.

Ownership Structure

The company has a dual-class structure of ownership. Class B common stock has 20 votes per share and class A common stock has one vote per share. Stockholders who hold shares of class B common stock are basically executive officers, employees, directors, and their respective affiliates and hold approximately 65.5% of the voting power of the outstanding capital stock. The class A common stock has traded on the Nasdaq Global Market under the symbol "ACMR" since November 3, 2017. The class B common stock is not listed or traded on any stock exchange. As of February 23, 2022, there were 17,833,192 shares of class A common stock outstanding held of record by 46 stockholders. As of February 23, 2022, there were 1,695,604 shares of class B common stock held of record by 18 stockholders. The company has not paid any cash or stock dividends so far.

Market Performance

Table 1 highlights the stock performance of ACM Research in comparison to the market indexes of Russell 1000 and Nasdaq Composite.

The analysis assumes $100 investment in the stock of ACM Research in comparison with the Russell 1000 Index and Nasdaq Composite Index. The 5-year holding period return for ACM Research was 1309%, whereas that for Russell 1000 Index and Nasdaq Composite was 57% and 131%, respectively. The 5-year average return for ACM Research was 102%, while for Russell 1000 Index and Nasdaq Composite index was 10% and 20%, respectively. This analysis reflects the superior performance of the company compared to standard benchmark indexes.

Financial Performance

Table 2 shows the revenues realized by the company during the period 2017–2021.

The CAGR for revenues during the period 2017–2021 was 63%. The gross margin for the company was 44.4% in the year 2020 and 44.2% in year 2021.

Table 1 Five-year stock performance

Year	Nov 17	Dec 17	Dec 18	Dec 19	Dec 20	Dec 21
ACM Research	$100	$87.00	$180	$305	$1343	$1409
Russell 1000 Index	$100	$103	$97	$124	$148	$157
Nasdaq Composite Index	$100	$102	$98	$133	$191	$231

Source Annual Report 2022

Table 2 Revenue timeline

Fiscal year	Values in million US dollars
2017	37
2018	75
2019	108
2020	157
2021	260

Table 3 Holding period return and excess return

Year	ACM	Russell 1000	Excess returns
2018	107%	2%	105%
2019	98%	10%	88%
2020	134%	5%	129%
2021	−5%	27%	−32%
2022 till Sept	−53%	−11%	−42%

Table 4 Excess value in millions of dollars

Year	2018	2019	2020	2021
Book value of equity	52.3	97.3	141.2	676.2
Market value of equity	174.2	332.9	1519.3	1668.4
BV as percent of MV	30.0%	29.2%	9.3%	40.5%
Average	27.3%			

Stock Performance Analysis

The 5-year stock return analysis for ACM research suggests that on average the returns generated by the stock during the 5-year period were 77%. The average yearly return for the Russell 1000 Index was 11% during the last 5-year period. The cumulative monthly return for ACM Research for the 5-year period was 335.5% during the period Jan 2017 to September 2022. The cumulative 5-year monthly return for the Russell 1000 Index was 54% during the above period of analysis.

Table 3 shows the holding period return for ACM stock and the excess return in comparison with Russell 1000 Index during the period 2018–2022. The analysis is covered till the end of September 2022. The assumption for the holding period is based on a 1-year period.

The ACM stock registered huge returns during the period 2018–2020 registering excess returns of 105%, 88%, and 129%, respectively. However, the stock has performed poorly during the 2-year period 2021–2022 registering excess negative returns. The stock had the worst stock market performance in the year 2022.

Table 4 analyzes the excess market value over the book value of the company during the past 5-year period. The data for analysis was sourced from gurufocus.com.

The average book value as percent of market value was 27.3%. In 2020, the book value was 9.3% of the market value.

Operating Performance Analysis

Table 5 highlights the performance ratios of profitability and leverage ratio of the company during the period 2018–2021.

The average net margin, ROE, and ROCE were 13.23%, 16.13%, and 12.82%, respectively, during the 4-year period, 2018–2021. The average debt equity ratio during the above period was 0.19. The debt intensity peaked during the year 2020 and then fell drastically in the year 2021.

Table 6 shows the financial highlights of the company during the period 2018–2021.

The average growth rate of total assets, cash and cash equivalents, and total equity was 125%, 274%, and 163%, respectively, during the period 2018–2021. The revenues grew by 52% on an average basis during the period of analysis. The average growth rate of net income was 96%. The market capitalization and enterprise value increased by 152% and 165%, respectively, on an average basis. The source of data is annual reports.

Table 7 gives the estimation of economic value for the period 2020–2021. The WACC estimation is obtained from gurufocus.com

The values are given in millions of dollars.

Table 5 Profitability and leverage ratios

Ratios	2018	2019	2020	2021
Net margin%	8.81	17.57	11.99	14.54
ROE%	14.26	25.25	15.75	9.24
ROCE%	15.3	17.81	10.07	8.08
DER	0.18	0.18	0.35	0.06

Table 6 Financial highlights

	(In millions of dollars)			
Financial highlights	2018	2019	2020	2021
Total assets	103	217.7	341.3	1052.2
Cash and cash equivalents	27.1	58.3	71.8	563.1
Total equity	52.3	97.3	208.2	811.7
Total revenue	74.6	107.5	156.6	259.8
Total operating expenses	28	32.9	48.1	76.2
Net income	6.6	18.9	18.8	37.8
Market capitalization	174.2	332.9	1519.3	1668.4
Enterprise value	156.5	292.3	1536.3	1250.4

Table 7 Estimation of economic value

Year	2020	2021
Profit before income tax	19	43.1
Income tax	2.1	1.00
Net operating profit after tax (NOPAT)	17	42
Stockholder equity	208.2	811.7
Long-term debt	18	23
Total capital employed	226	835
WACC	6.20%	5.71%
Capital charge	14.0244	47.6614
Economic value	3	−6

References

1. ACM Research Website
2. Annual Reports, ACM Research
3. www.gurufocus.com

Case 9 Victory Capital Holdings

Victory Capital is a diversified global asset management firm with $159.1 billion in asset management as of August 31, 2022. The company is headquartered in San Antonio. The company employs approximately 450 employees across 13 offices in the United States and abroad. The operations of the company are based on a next-generation business model which is characterized by boutique investment qualities along with the benefits of a fully integrated, centralized operating and distribution platform. Victory Capital Holdings was named as one of the top fastest-growing companies in Fortune list 2021.Victory Capital consists of 12 autonomous investment franchises which focusses on independent investment approach. Victory Capital Holdings was formed in the year 2013 by acquiring Victory Capital Management and Victory Capital Services from KeyCorp. Victory Capital provides specialized investment strategies to institutions, intermediaries, retirement platforms, and individual investors. Victory Capital offers a diverse array of investment vehicles to manage actively managed mutual funds, rule-based ETFs, separately managed accounts, rule-based ETFs, private funds, and a 529 Education Savings Plan. The employees have personal investments valued at $250 million in the company's investment products. By December 31, 2021, Victory Capital's franchises and solutions platform collectively managed a diversified set of 130 investment strategies for a wide range of institutional and retail clients and direct investors.

Investment Franchises

The company owned 100% ownership of the 12 investment franchises. These franchises are well diversified and are independent from one another with separate brands and logos. Each franchise is integrated with the centralized operating platform to optimize the investment process.

INCORE Capital Management manages convertible bond strategies, short-term US government securities, and customized fixed-income strategies. As of Dec 31, 2021, INCORE has managed $7.5 billion in AUM. Integrity Asset Management

© The Author(s), under exclusive license to Springer Nature Switzerland AG 2024
B. R. Kumar, *Rising Stars*, Management for Professionals,
https://doi.org/10.1007/978-3-031-50032-9_9

utilizes a dynamic value-oriented approach to manage investments in US mid- and small-capitalization companies. By the end of 2021, Integrity Asset Management has managed assets worth $5.3 billion. Munder Capital Management focusses on "growth-at-a-reasonable-price" strategy in the US equity markets and has managed AUM worth $1.9 billion as of December 31, 2021. NEC manages investments in private closed-end funds which focus on clean energy infrastructure projects and companies. NewBridge Asset Management follows a growth-oriented strategy with the focus on large-capitalization companies in the US market. By December 2021 the company had managed $1 billion in AUM. RS Investments focus on value and growth-oriented strategies in the US market. By Dec 2021, the company has managed $11.8 billion in AUM. RS Global focusses on core-oriented global and international equity strategies using a highly disciplined quantitative approach. Sophus Capital manages funds in emerging equity markets based on a quantitative approach. Sycamore Capital follows a value-oriented approach to manage funds' investments in US-based mid- and small-capitalization companies. This franchise has managed $32.3 billion in AUM as of December 31, 2021. The other franchises are THB Asset Management, Trivalent Investments, USAA Investments, and WestEnd Advisors.

Solution Franchise

The solution platform franchise offers multi-asset, multi-manager, quantitative, rule-based, factor-based, and customized portfolios. The company offers a solution platform through different vehicles which include separate accounts, mutual funds, UMA accounts, and active ETFs. By 2021, the solution platform has managed $66.3 billion in AUM.

The trend reveals that approximately 77% of the Victory Capital's AUM had returns in excess of their respective benchmarks over a 10-year period.

Table 1 illustrates the timeline of growth of the company during the past 100 years.

In 2021, Victory Capital launched its mobile app for direct investors and has approximately 120,000 users. In 2021, the total AUM increased by 25% compared to the previous year. The company had a revenue of $890 million in the year 2021.

The company received four US Refinitiv Lipper Awards for the period ending November 30, 2021, for its funds. In 2021, 37% of the AMU was accounted by direct investor clients, 36% by retail clients, and 27% by institutional clients.

Table 2 gives the asset class composition in year 2021.

Table 3 shows the vehicle mix composition in year 2021.

Table 1 Timeline of growth

Year	Event
1894	The predecessor Victory Capital is organized as Cleveland Trust in Ohio and starts managing tax exempt assets in 1912
1993	The trust company becomes a registered investment advisor (RIA) under the parent company Society Corporation
1994	Society Corporation merges with KeyCorp, and the RIA is renamed Key Asset Management Inc. (KAMI).
2001	Victory Capital Management Inc. is established by renaming KAMI
2013	Victory Capital completes management-led buyout with Crestview Partners from KeyCorp
2014	Undertook acquisition of Munder Capital Management and its wholly owned subsidiary Integrity Asset Management
2015	Acquired Compass EMP. Established unique brands like Sycamore Capital, Newbridge Asset Management, INCORE Capital Management, and Trivalent Investments
2016	Acquires RS Investments. RS emerging market team is rebranded as Sophus Capital
2017	ETF business is rebranded as VictoryShares by Victory Capital. VictoryShares platform later became part of Victory Capital Solutions business
2018	Victory Capital is listed on Nasdaq Global Select Market under the symbol VCTR
2019	Victory Capital acquired USAA® Asset Management Company
2020	Victory Capital becomes signatory to United Nations-supported Principles for Responsible Investment (PRI)
2021	Acquires THB Asset Management, New Energy Capital, and WestEnd Advisors

Source: www.vcm.com/about-victory

Table 2 Asset class mix in 2021

Asset class	Composition
Solutions	33%
Fixed income	19%
US mid-cap equity	17%
US small-cap equity	11%
US large-cap equity	9%
Global equity	9%
Money market	2%
Commodity	<1%
Alternate investments	<1%

Source: Annual Report 2021

Strategy of Growth

The company focusses on diversification strategy by offering an array of equity, fixed-income, alternative investments, and close-end private funds representing a diverse spectrum of industry sectors, investment styles, and approaches. The company has grown organically by distributing a diverse product platform through a variety of business channels and inorganically through acquisitions. Victory Capital

Table 3 Vehicle mix composition in 2021

Asset class	Composition
Mutual funds	67%
Separate funds	16%
UMA	10%
ETF	3%
Other pooled vehicles	2%
WRAP	1%
VIP	1%

Source: Annual Report 2021

grows organically by offering strategies which are value added and solution oriented for investment portfolios. One of the key strategies involves strengthening of the existing franchises by providing the franchises access to its operating platforms, technology, centralized distribution, marketing, and other support functions.

The company evaluates potential M&A opportunities in terms of specialized investment capabilities, new technologies, or distribution channels. The company has the potential to achieve synergies in its M&A deals due to its ability to provide access to multiple distribution channels.

Ever since its management-led buyout with Crestview Partners II GP from Keycorp, the company has completed seven deals which include seven acquisitions and two minority investments. As a result of these deals the AUM has increased more than tenfold from $17.9 billion to $183.7 billion.

In the year 2014 Victory Capital acquired Munder Capital Management and its wholly owned subsidiary Integrity Asset Management with the aim of acquiring product capabilities in the growth and value equity, international equity, and fixed-income asset classes. In the same year the company implemented a new business model wherein autonomous and branded investment franchises were given leverage to operate a centralized operating and distribution platform. Victory Capital acquired Compass EMP to expand its range of investment vehicles to include ETFs. In 2016, Victory Capital acquired RS Investments to leverage growth in global and international equities. Victory Capital expanded its distribution network in Asia through a distribution partnership with Bayview Asset Management. In 2019, Victory Capital acquired USAA® Asset Management Company and diversified its asset base by adding the portfolios of mutual fund, ETF, and 529 college savings plan. In 2021, Victory Capital had three significant acquisitions of THB, New Energy Company, and WestEnd Advisors. The company acquired THB Asset Management which specializes in the US and global micro-cap, small-cap, and mid-cap asset class portfolios. THB is also known as an early adopter of socially responsible investment practices. New Energy Company is an alternative asset management company which focusses on debt and equity investments in clean energy infrastructure projects. WestEnd Advisors is a third-party ETF model strategist which provides financial advisors with turnkey, core model allocation strategies. In December 2021, Victory Capital completed the acquisition of its 12th investment franchise, WestEnd

Advisors. WestEnd Advisors offers four primary ETF strategies and one large-cap core strategy.

In 2021, with the acquisition of New Energy Capital, Victory Capital diversified its product offering by entering into an alternative investment platform consisting of private markets thereby adding a new growth vertical.

The company also focusses on product growth and innovation. In 2021, the company introduced the innovative Victory Hashdex Nasdaq Crypto Index Fund for accredited US investors to track the performance of the Nasdaq Crypto Index (NCI). This fund which focuses on broad-based exposure to crypto assets was incorporated as part of an agreement between Nasdaq and global crypto-focused asset manager Hashdex Ltd.

The integrated model of providing centralized distribution, marketing, and support function to investment franchises facilitates the company to derive benefits from a substantial scale and focus on specialized investment managers. The company has created an ownership culture to structurally align the employees' interest with those of other stakeholders of the company and create a collective alignment for success. As of December 2021, the employees beneficially owned approximately 20% of the shares of the company. Moreover, by this period, employees have invested approximately $250 million in products managed by Victory Capital. The company faces competition from other investment firms which operate in the traditional institutional segments via intermediary and retirement distribution platforms.

Business Risk Analysis

The firm basically earns all of its revenues from AUM and any reduction in AUM reduces the revenues and profitability. The COVID-19 pandemic had affected the normal activity of the company. The loss of key investment professionals, termination of contracts, and redemption of assets by investors without prior notice are some of the potential business risks faced by the company. The sustainability of growth is a function of the ability of the firm to integrate new strategic acquisitions made by the company. Another risk factor is that a large proportion of the existing assets under management (AUM) is managed in long-term investments. The failure to comply with regulatory guidelines and investment guidelines set by the clients which include the boards of registered funds is also a source of business risk which may result in punitive damages and loss of AUM. The phasing out of LIBOR is perceived to have a negative impact on the Victory Capital funds. The relative concentration of a large percentage of common stock with a small number of stockholders would potentially increase the volatility of the stock.

ESG Initiatives

In 2021, the company published its first CSR report. In 2021, as part of refinement of corporate governance initiatives, the company eliminated the dual-class stock structure. The company implemented mandatory inclusive cultural eLearning and hosted multiple sustained learning activities to enhance diversion and inclusion in the workplace. As part of ESG Investment initiatives, the company launched three new VictoryShares ESG ETFs. As part of its commitment towards CSR, the company established the Victory Capital Scholars Program in collaboration with Xavier University of Louisiana. Victory Capital uses the Sustainability Accounting Standard Board (SASB) framework to report on the ESG issues of the company. Approximately 84% of the employees of the company work in buildings which are LEED-certified. Victor Capital is a member of the SASB Alliance network which supports best practices to integrate material sustainability information for cost-effective sustainability disclosure. The company also joined the Ceres Investor Network on Climate Risk and Sustainability which promotes investment practices, corporate engagement strategies, and regulatory solutions. Over 180 institutional investors with more than $30 trillion in assets are members of the network.

Financial Highlights

The total revenue for the year ending December 31, 2021, was $890.3 million compared to $775.4 million in the previous year. In 2019, the company had announced the initiation of quarterly cash dividends. In 2020, the dividend was increased by 20% and in November the dividend was increased by 17%.

Table 4 gives the segment-wise revenues of Victory Capital during the period 2019–2021. The values are given in thousands of dollars.

Stock Return Analysis

The 5-year stock return analysis during the period 2018–2022 (up to September 2022) shows that the Victory Capital Stock had a cumulative monthly return of 120%, whereas S&P 500 Index returns amounted to only 47.8% during the above period of analysis. Thus, the S&P 500 Index did not generate even half of the returns registered by Victory Capital. The average monthly return during the 5-year period

Table 4 Revenues in thousands of dollars

Year	2019	2020	2021
Total investment fees	466,802	562,036	674,539
Fund administration and distribution fees	145,571	213,315	215,726
Total revenues	612,373	775,351	890,265

Source: Annual Report 2021

Table 5 Holding period returns

Year	Victory	S&P 500	Excess returns
2018	−17%	10%	−27%
2019	93%	0%	93%
2020	20%	18%	2%
2021	74%	34%	40%
2022 till Sept	−20%	−8%	−12%

Table 6 Profitability and leverage

Ratios	2018	2019	2020	2021
Net margin%	15.41	15.1	27.41	31.27
ROE%	18.55	18.62	34.13	34
ROA%	7.99	7.24	12.2	12.92
DER	0.59	1.72	1.09	1.21

2018–2022 for the Victory stock was 26%, whereas the average monthly S&P 500 returns was 10%.

An investment of $10,000 in the Victory stock during February 2018 would have grown to $ 21,974 by October 2022.

Table 5 illustrates the holding period return for Victory Capital stock for the period 2018–2022. The analysis period is January–September for the year 2022. It is assumed that the stock is purchased in January of each year and held till the end of that particular year.

Victory Holdings registered very high stock returns of 93% and 74% in year 2019 and 2021, respectively. In 2019, the excess returns were 93% which reflected that the stock gained immensely during this period. In 2019 the index has a poor performance record. In 2018 and 2022, the stock was not performing well as reflected from the negative returns of the company.

Operating Performance Analysis

Table 6 compares the profitability position and leverage ratio of the company during the period 2018–2021.

The profitability position of the company has steadily improved over the period 2018–2021. The ROE almost doubled in the year 2020 compared to the year 2018. The net margin doubled in the year 2021 compared to the year 2018. The average net margin, ROE, and ROA during the period 2018–2021 were 22.29%, 26.32%, and 10.08%, respectively.

The debt intensity of the company has increased over the 4-year period 2018–2021. The average debt equity ratio during the above period was 1.15.

Table 7 highlights the important financial variables of the company during the period 2018–2021. The values are given in millions of US dollars.

The market capitalization and enterprise value grew on an average by 58% and 69%, respectively, during the period 2019–2021. The total assets and total equity

Table 7 Financial highlights

	(In millions of US dollars)			
Financial highlights	2018	2019	2020	2021
Total assets	801.5	1753.3	1730.7	2579.7
Cash and cash equivalents	51.5	37.1	22.7	69.5
Total equity	455.5	537.9	707.5	929.9
Total revenue	413.4	612.4	775.4	890.3
Total operating expenses	53.3	70.4	67.6	72.6
Net income	63.7	92.5	212.5	278.4
Market cap	690.5	1419.6	1675.7	2508.3
Enterprise value	907.2	2306.2	2422	3566.6

Table 8 Estimation of economic value

Year	2020	2021
Profit before income tax	278.5	350.6
Income tax	66.0	72.3
Net operating profit after tax (NOPAT)	212.5	278.4
Stockholder equity	707.5	929.9
Long-term debt	769.0	1127.9
Total capital employed	1476.5	2057.8
WACC	0.1	0.1
Capital charge	89.3	110.3
Economic value	123.2	168.1

grew by 56% and 37% on average basis during the period 2019–2021.The total revenues and net income grew by 30% and 69%, respectively, on an average basis during the above period. The cash and cash equivalents declined by 27.9% and 38.8% in year 2019 and 2020, respectively, and then increased by 206% in year 2021. The average increase in operating expenses was 12% during the period 2018–2021. The data source is annual reports.

Table 8 illustrates the estimation of economic value of the company in year 2020 and 2021. The values are given in millions of dollars. The weighted average cost of capital (WACC) is sourced from gurufocus.com.

The economic value has increased from $123.2 million to $168.1 million.

References

1. Victory Capital Annual Report 2021.
2. https://www.gurufocus.com/stock/VCTR/financials#_stock-financial-table-2
3. https://www.vcm.com/
4. https://ir.vcm.com/home/default.aspx

Case 10 Advanced Micro Devices

Advanced Micro Devices (AMD) was founded in the year 1969 as a Silicon Valley startup. It became a publicly held company in the year 1972. The common stock is currently listed on the Nasdaq Global Select Market (Nasdaq) under the symbol "AMD." AMD is a global semiconductor company which services the computing and graphics market with CPU, GPU, APU, system on chip, and chipset product offerings. The performance of a microprocessor in central processing unit (CPU) is a critical factor which impacts the performance of computing and entertainment platforms such as desktop PCs, notebooks, and workstations. Graphical processing unit (GPU) is a programmable logic chip which creates images, animations, and video and is used to handle general computing tasks. Accelerated processing unit (APU) is a processing unit which integrates a CPU and GPU onto one chip and basically facilitates computing devices to improve end user experience, system performance, and energy efficiency. System-on-chip (SoC) represents a complete computing system on a single chip which improves system performance and energy efficiency. Chipsets perform essential logic functions and operate in concert with the microprocessor to manage system control and power management functions of all devices in the system. AMD offers one of the broadest portfolios of high-performance and adaptive processor technologies and leadership computing platforms for cloud, edge, and end devices.

Product Offerings

Computing and Graphics Products

The microprocessors of AMD are incorporated into computing platforms which represent a portfolio of technologies to offer a complete computing solution. AMD bases its microprocessors and chipsets on the x86 instruction set architecture and the AMD Infinity Fabric™, which connects an on-chip memory controller and input/output (I/O) channels directly to one or more microprocessor cores. AMD focuses on

© The Author(s), under exclusive license to Springer Nature Switzerland AG 2024
B. R. Kumar, *Rising Stars*, Management for Professionals,
https://doi.org/10.1007/978-3-031-50032-9_10

continually improving the energy efficiency of its products through design principles and innovations in power management technology.

The microprocessors for desktop platforms offered by the company include the AMD Ryzen™ series processors and AMD Athlon™ processors. The company expanded its third-gen AMD Ryzen desktop processor family by adding AMD Ryzen 3 3,100 and AMD Ryzen 3 3,300X processors with "Zen 2" core architecture for usage by business users, gamers, and other creators. In the year 2020, the company introduced the AMD Ryzen 4000 series desktop processors and the AMD Athlon 3000 series desktop processors with built-in Radeon™ graphics for the consumer market. In the same year the AMD Ryzen 5000 Series desktop processor family powered by "Zen 3" core architecture was introduced to enhance the performance for gamers and content creators. The company invests in designing and developing high-performing and low-power APUs for notebook PC platforms. The company also delivered AMD Ryzen and AMD mobile processors for consumer and commercial markets. The company offers enterprise class desktop and notebook PC solutions which are sold as AMD PRO mobile and AMD PRO desktop processors with Radeon graphics for the commercial market.

AMD offers a full suite of chipset products which include the X570 chipset which supports PCIe® 4.0 (fourth-generation peripheral component interconnect express motherboard interface) designed for desktop platforms.

The semiconductor graphics market caters to the need for improved visual and data processing in various computing devices. On account of core product differentiation elements of visual realism and graphical display capabilities, the semiconductor graphics market has witnessed the increased creation and use of processing intensive multimedia content for playing games, capturing media, viewing online videos, and managing digital content on computing devices. This trend has led to higher consumer demand for performance graphics solutions. There has also been a growing demand for features in modern graphic markets such as accelerated computing which are powered by graphics processors in high-performance computing (HPC), artificial intelligence, and cloud visualization (virtual desktop infrastructure and cloud gaming). The graphics products are developed by AMD for use in different computing devices and entertainment platforms such as desktop PCs, notebook PCs, 2-in-1s, all-in-ones (AIOs), professional workstations, and the data center. The company's discrete GPUs for desktop and notebook PCs support current-generation application program interfaces (APIs). AMD Radeon Pro family of professional graphics products included multiview graphics cards and GPUs designed for integration in mobile and desktop workstations. AMD offers two families of products related to the data center. The visual cloud data center GPUs offer a range of solutions for workloads with features for remote visualization such as desktop-as-a-service, workstation-as-a-service, and cloud gaming. The software solutions offer certification for a number of professional vendor applications and modern gaming titles.

Enterprise, Embedded, and Semi-Custom Product

AMD services the enterprise, embedded, and semi-custom markets with its CPU, GPU, APU, and customized designed system on chips products. Embedded products address computing needs in enterprise class telecommunications, networking, security, storage systems, etc. The embedded products of AMD are used in applications which require high to moderate levels of performance characterized by key features such as relatively low power, small form factor, and 24x7 operations. AMD leverages its graphics and processing technologies to develop semi-custom solutions for the PC and gaming markets. The microprocessor-based server platforms of AMD include the AMD EPYC™ Series processors and AMD Opteron™ X and A-Series processors. The AMD products for embedded platforms include AMD Embedded EPYC CPUs, AMD Embedded V-Series APUs, CPUs and SoCs, AMD Embedded R-Series APUs, CPUs and SoCs, AMD Embedded G-Series SoC platform, and AMD Embedded Radeon GPUs. AMD has developed the semi-custom SoC products used in the Sony PlayStation® 4 and Sony PlayStation 5. AMD semi-custom products are used in the Microsoft Xbox One X, Microsoft Xbox One S, Microsoft Xbox Series X™, and Xbox Series S™ game consoles.

AMD products are sold through direct sales force and through independent distributors and sales representatives in both domestic and international markets. The microprocessor customers basically consist of original equipment manufacturers (OEMs), large public cloud service providers, original design manufacturers (ODMs), system integrators, and independent distributors.

Competitive Analysis

The microprocessor and chipset market are dominated by Intel Corp. Intel has been the market leader for microprocessors in the semiconductor industry for decades. Intel has significant competitive advantage due to its superior market share, margins, and financial resources. Intel is able to drive de facto standards and specifications for x86 microprocessors. Nvidia is AMD's principal competitor in the discrete graphics market. The competitors for AMD in the graphic market include suppliers of discrete graphics, embedded graphic processors, and IGP chipsets. Intel is again a dominant competitor for AMD in this market segment. In the server market, Intel is the main competitor for CPU server products and Nvidia is the main competitor for GPU server products. Nvidia is the main competitor for AMD with respect to the data center. AMD is the market leader in semi-custom game console products.

Growth Strategy

AMD aims to contribute towards high-performance computing technology, software, and product leadership. The AMD strategy is to create and deliver the world's leading high-performance CPUs and GPUs and to integrate them with hardware and software to build differentiated solutions. The company also invests in high-performance GPUs and software for markets such as gaming, compute, artificial intelligence, cloud gaming, and virtual and augmented reality.

AMD focusses on research and development to improve product performance and enhance product design. The major focus of the R&D strategy is to develop the next generation of CPU and GPU IP. The major aim is to design IP into the SoCs for the next generation of products with the intent to improve system performance. AMD has research initiatives in place for improving the battery life of APU products for notebooks and enhancing the performance and power efficiency of its discrete GPUs and microprocessors for servers. Research is also directed towards delivering a range of low-power integrated platforms to serve key markets that include commercial clients, mobile computing, and gaming. AMD also has initiatives to develop machine intelligence. AMD has collaborations with industry consortia to conduct early-stage research and development related to process technology and software.

In the year 2020, AMD entered into an agreement to merge two of its wholly owned subsidiaries Thrones Merger Sub Inc. and Xilinix Inc. with Xilinx being the acquirer. The transaction was valued at $35 billion.

Risk Factors

The dominance of the microprocessor market by Intel Corporation is one of the main challenges faced by AMD. Intel also dominates the computer system platform consisting of core logic chipsets, graphics chips, networking devices, nonvolatile storage systems, etc. The pandemic had a material adverse effect on the company. The semiconductor industry is highly cyclical and downturns had adversely affected the business. Fluctuations in demand for the products or market decline would have material adverse effect on the result of the operations. The company faces operational and technological risks as they have to rely on third parties to manufacture their products. AMD relies on third-party wafer foundries to fabricate the silicon wafers for its products. AMD also relies on third-party manufacturers to assemble, test, mark, and pack (ATMP) products. The competition continues to be intense on account of rapid technological changes and frequent product introductions. Government actions and regulations such as export administration regulations, tariffs, and trade protection measures would affect the business of AMD. The failure to integrate acquired businesses could disrupt the acquired businesses of the company. The company relies on a number of internal business processes and information systems to support key business functions and the efficient operation of these processes is vital to the business success.

ESG Initiatives

The concept of corporate responsibility at AMD is managed through the lens of environmental, social, and governance (ESG) issues. The focus of AMD is on creation of the next generation of products to benefit society and the planet. The mission of AMD is to promote environmental sustainability across its businesses and ensure safe and responsible workplaces in its global supply chain. For over 50 years AMD has driven innovation in high-performance computing, graphics, and visualization technologies. Leading Fortune 500 businesses and scientific research institutions rely on AMD technology to improve their performance measures. Product energy efficiency is one critical focus area for the company in terms of development of the world's most advanced processors. The 2022-year trend suggests that AMD powers the fastest and most energy-efficient supercomputer in the world termed the Frontier supercomputer along with 17 of the top 20 most efficient supercomputers. AMD is on track to achieve its goal to deliver 30 times increase in energy efficiency in AMD processors powering servers in AI training and high-performance computing applications by 2025. In the year 2022, the company expanded the scope of its AMD High Performance Compute Fund to provide researchers with access to more than 20 petaflops of supercomputing power to advance research in areas including climate change, healthcare, and transportation. It is expected that 100 million people will benefit from AMD Foundation philanthropy and partnership programs on STEM education by the year 2025. AMD also aims for absolute reduction in GHG emissions from AMD operations by year 2030. It is also aimed that 100% of AMD manufacturing suppliers will have a public GHG emission reduction goal by the year 2025. It is also envisaged that about 80% of AMD manufacturing suppliers will source renewable energy by 2025. In April 2020, AMD announced an initial US$ 15 million to establish the AMD HPC Fund to provide research institutions with computing resources to accelerate medical research on COVID-19 and other diseases. In its pursuit for minimizing environmental impacts, the company has achieved 12% reduction in energy consumption, 25% reduction in GHG emissions, 50% reduction in water use, and 14% reduction in waste generated in year 2021 compared to the base year 2020. The firm's product cutting-edge chip architecture, design and power management features have resulted in improving the energy efficiency gains of 31.7 times increase in performance per watt for processors in mobile devices during the period 2014–2021. With respect to supply chain sustainability goals, the company has stipulated that its supplier manufacturing units must complete Responsible Business Alliance (RBA) or equivalent by 2025. Another requirement is that 80% of AMD manufacturing supplier by spend have to participate in a capacity building activity by year 2025. In 2021 AMD co-sponsored the RLI Supplier Training on Responsible Recruitment Due Diligence. AMD is a signatory to the United Nations Global Compact mission. By means of industry initiatives and collaboration with supply chain partners, the firm supports responsible sourcing of minerals from CAHRAs. The Responsible Minerals Policy (Conflict Mineral Policy) of the firm governs responsible mineral sourcing initiatives at AMD. As a part of its diversity initiatives, the goal is to ensure participation of

70% of employees in AMD employee resource groups and/or other AMD inclusion initiatives by 2025. The company also focusses on increasing the percentage of global female hires in engineering roles and percentage of underrepresented group hires.

Stock Performance Analysis

Table 1 shows the 5-year comparison of the performance of the AMD stock in relation to the S&P 500 and S&P 500 Semiconductors Index through the period December 31, 2016, to December 25, 2021. The assumption is based on an investment of $100 in December 2016.

On the assumption of the holding period of 5 years, the holding period return for AMD stock was 1189%, whereas for the S&P 500 Index and S&P500 Semiconductors was 131% and 303%, respectively. The average returns for the AMD stock were 76%, while the comparative returns for the S&P 500 Index and S&P 500 Semiconductor Index were 19% and 34%, respectively, during the 5-year period 2017–2021.

Table 2 shows the excess market value of AMD in terms of book value. The analysis shows the book value of AMD share as a percentage of market value during the period 2018–2021.The values are given in millions of US dollars.

The average book value as percent of market value of AMD was 5.4% during the period 2018–2021. The book value as percent of market value was only 4.3% in the year 2021.

Stock Return Analysis

The AMD stock had a cumulative monthly return of 250% during the 5-year period 2018–2022. The period covered for the year 2022 was up to September. The market

Table 1 Five-year stock performance return

Year	2016	2017	2018	2019	2020	2021
Advanced Micro Devices, Inc.	$100	$91.00	$157	$407	$810	$1289
S&P 500 Index	$100	$122	$115	$154	$179	$231
S&P 500 Semiconductors Index	$100	$136	$127	$188	$264	$403

Table 2 Comparison of book value and market value

Year	2018	2019	2020	2021
Book value of equity	1266	2827	5837	7497
Market value of equity	18,552	53,656	111,061	173,687
BV as percent of MV	6.8%	5.3%	5.3%	4.3%
Average	5.4%			

Table 3 Holding period returns

Year	AMD	SP500	Excess returns
2018	34%	−11%	46%
2019	88%	19%	68%
2020	95%	16%	79%
2021	68%	28%	40%
2022 till Sept	−51%	−21%	−30%

Table 4 Financial highlights

	(In millions of dollars)			
Financial highlights	2018	2019	2020	2021
Total assets	4556	6028	8962	12,419
Cash and cash equivalents	1156	1503	2290	3608
Total equity	1266	2827	5837	7497
Total revenue	6475	6731	9763	16,434
Total operating expenses	1996	2237	2978	4281
Net income	337	341	2490	3162
Market cap	18,552	53,656	111,061	173,687
Enterprise value	18,646	52,838	109,302	170,740

Source: Gurufocus/Annual Reports

index S&P 500 registered a cumulative monthly return of approximately 38% during the above period. The average yearly returns for AMD during the above period were 61%, whereas the returns for the S&P 500 Index were only 8% during the period 2018–2022. The data for analysis was sourced from Yahoo Finance.

Table 3 gives the holding period returns for AMD stock in comparison to the S&P 500 Index over the period 2018–2022.

The holding period analysis reveals that AMD stock performed extremely well in the year 2019 and 2020 with excess returns of 68% and 79%, respectively, over the S&P 500 Index. In year 2022, the stock and index registered negative returns.

Table 4 shows the financial parameters of the company during the period 2018–2021. The values are given in millions of US dollars.

The average growth rate of total assets and revenues during the period 2018–2021 was approximately 40%. The total equity grew by 86% on an average basis. The cash and cash equivalent increased by 47% during this period. The total revenues increased by 39% and total expenses increased by 30%. The net income increased by 219% on an average basis. The market capitalization and enterprise value increased by 118% and 115% on an average basis during the period 2018–2021.

Table 5 details the estimation of the economic value for the company during the year 2019 and 2020. The values are given in millions of dollars.

The economic value has increased from $512 million in 2020 to $1740 million in year 2021.

Table 5 Estimation of economic value

Year	2020	2021
Profit before income tax	1369	3648
Income tax	31	1210
Net operating profit after tax (NOPAT)	1338	2438
Stockholder equity	5837	7497
Long-term debt	486	330
Total capital employed	6323	7827
WACC	13.07%	8.92%
Capital charge	826.42	698.17
Economic value	512	1740

References

1. https://www.amd.com/system/files/documents/2021-22-global-cr-report-summary.pdf
2. AMD Annual Report 2021.

Case 11 AppFolio

AppFolio was founded in the year 2006. AppFolio is the leading provider of cloud business management solutions for the real estate industry. AppFolio solutions are designed for the ecosystem of users such as property managers, property owners, real estate, and investment managers. The solution provided by AppFolio facilitates customers to digitally transform their businesses, automate, and streamline critical business operations. The solutions provide services related to real estate life cycle, screening potential tenants, sending and receiving payments, and insurance-based risk mitigation services. The intuitive interface coupled with streamlined and automated workflows helps customers to eliminate redundant and manual processes. The platforms and mobile-optimized solutions offered by AppFolio can be used across multiple devices and operating systems. By 2021 end, the company had 1600 employees of which approximately 45% were women.

Core Solutions

Platform

The platform of AppFolio covers critical aspects of workflows related to property management and is constantly revised to respond to market trends and customer needs. The focus is on partnering and integrating with curated third-party solutions.

AppFolio Property Manager

AppFolio property manager provides the platform for property managers to run their business. Property management companies use the platform to leverage the benefits of process automation and optimization of common workflows. Customers consist of third-party property managers and owner operators who manage single and multi-family residential properties and those who are involved in the management of

© The Author(s), under exclusive license to Springer Nature Switzerland AG 2024

B. R. Kumar, *Rising Stars*, Management for Professionals,
https://doi.org/10.1007/978-3-031-50032-9_11

community associations and commercial properties. All critical transactions are completed and recorded in the system. AppFolio property manager also acts as the system of engagement which customers use to interact with residents living in their properties.

AppFolio Property Manager Plus

This solution provides customers with deeper business insights, automation, and advanced customer experiences. The Plus solution is designed to serve customers having a more diverse mix of property types, wider geographical dispersion of properties, and larger teams to manage these types of portfolios. The solution offers customizable workflows that allow customers to digitize existing processes.

Value-Added Services

The value-added services are designed to enhance, automate, and streamline business-critical processes and workflows. The value-added services are provided for marketing and leasing, electro-payment services, business optimization, and risk mitigation (insurance) services. The value-added services can be categorized into electronic payment services, tenant screening services, and insurance. The online payment services help property managers to streamline receivables and payables through different online payment options. Customers can use services to collect funds through a secure online portal, mobile application, and electronic cash payments from users such as applicants, residents, and property owners. Different types of funds such as rental application fees, security deposits, rent payments, tenant charges, and contributions from property owners can be collected through these value-added services. The tenant screening services include background screening, credit checks, income verification, and a streamlined rental verification process. Risk mitigation services are also provided through some partnerships and wholly owned subsidiaries.

Growth Strategy

The company aims to provide valuable business management solutions to new and existing customers in the real estate industry. The company uses this competitive advantage to expand its footprint in the property management market as well as in adjacent markets that have both real estate and non-real estate characteristics. The company is making significant investments in research and new product development to expand its platform capabilities. The company have adopted inorganic growth strategy of acquisitions and partnerships to maintain its product and technology leadership. The company focuses on product innovation and new customer acquisition for long-term success. To expand the usage of solutions by larger customers, the company focuses on increasing the utilization of partnerships and integration with select third parties. AppFolio also has plans to evaluate and expand into adjacent markets based on a market validation strategy. As a part of this strategy, AppFolio introduced AppFolio Investment Management in the year 2019. This solution was designed to enable real estate investment management organizations to better manage investor relationships by increasing transparency and streamlining certain business processes. The products offered by AppFolio are powered by a highly scalable computing platform and are designed with a strong focus on data security and availability. The computing platform and cloud infrastructure offered by the company are primarily powered by the Amazon Web Services Elastic Compute Cloud (EC2) platform. By 2021, AppFolio had 17,215 property management customers. According to the Rental Housing Financing Survey 2022, 51 million residential units and 28 million community association units are part of the market for AppFolio products.

Environment Analysis

The overall market for business management solutions in real estate is global and highly competitive. The primary competitors of AppFolio are cloud-based real estate and cloud-based horizontal management service providers. The cloud-based real estate service providers serve companies of all sizes whereas cloud-based horizontal management service providers offer broad solutions across multiple industries. AppFolio also faces competition from different cloud-based solutions providers who focus on one or more-point solutions in the real estate industry.

Financial Performance

Table 1 shows the excess market value expressed in terms of book value as a percent of market value. The analysis covers the period 2018–2021. The book value and market values are given in millions of dollars.

The average book value as a percent of market value was approximately 5% during the period 2018–2021. The market value of the company in 2018 was approximately 22 times that of book value. In 2021, the market value was 14 times that of book value in the year 2021. During the period 2018, the book

Table 1 Excess market value

Year	2018	2019	2020	2021
Book value of equity	91.8	131.9	285.9	297.4
Market value of equity	2007.40	3754.40	6191.20	4215.90
BV as percent of MV	4.6%	3.5%	4.6%	7.1%
Average	4.9%			

value increased by approximately 224% whereas the corresponding market value increase was 110% during the period 2018–2021.

Stock Performance Analysis

In this section, the stock return analysis is carried out for a period of 5 years. The data is taken for a period of 5 years. The total monthly cumulative returns for the AppFolio stock was 126% during the 5-year period 2018–2022 (up to October 15, 2022). During the same period, the S&P500 cumulative monthly return was 41.5%. The average yearly return for AppFolio was 27% while that for the S&P 500 was 8% during the above period of analysis. The source of data was Yahoo Finance.

Table 2 documents the holding period return for AppFolio stock for each year during the period 2018–2022 compared with that of returns for the S&P 500 index. The analysis assumes 1 year holding period.

The AppFolio registered an excess return of 51% compared to negative returns documented by the market index in the year 2018. The best performance of the stock was registered in the year 2019. In the years 2021 and 2022, the stock performed badly in the market.

Operating Performance Analysis

Table 3 shows the profitability and leverage ratio of the company during the period 2018–2021.

The profitability position of the company deteriorated in the year 2021. The net margin which reached 51.09% in year 2021 declined drastically to 0.29% in the year 2021. The return on capital employed (ROCE) declined from 16.81% in 2018 to 5.13% by 2021. The average net margin during the period 2018–2021 was 19.02%.

Table 2 Holding period returns

Year	AppFolio	S&P 500	Excess returns
2018	40%	−11%	51%
2019	74%	19%	54%
2020	37%	16%	21%
2021	−21%	28%	−49%
2022 till Oct	−11%	−18%	7%

Table 3 Profitability and leverage position

Ratios	2018	2019	2020	2021	Average
Net margin%	10.51	14.17	51.09	0.29	19.02
ROE%	22.57	32.42	75.81	0.35	32.79
ROCE%	16.81	3.59	3.54	−3.42	5.13
DER	0.54	0.62	0.14	0.19	0.37

Table 4 Financial highlights

	(In millions of dollars)			
Financial highlights	2018	2019	2020	2021
Total assets	175.7	260.1	389.5	408
Cash and cash equivalents	90.7	38.7	168.5	122.4
Total equity	91.8	131.9	285.9	297.4
Total revenue	190.1	256	310.1	359.4
Total operating expenses	96.9	147.9	181.2	227.3
Net income	20	36.3	158.4	1
Market cap	2007.40	3754.40	6191.20	4215.90
Enterprise value	1966.50	3797.60	6062.80	4149.20

Table 5 Estimation of economic value

Year	2019	2020
Profit before income tax	4.8	196.8
Income tax	−0.4	31.5
Net operating profit after tax (NOPAT)	5.2	165.3
Stockholder equity	131.9	285.9
Long-term debt	47.4	
Total capital employed	179.3	285.9
WACC	9.92%	7.89%
Capital charge	17.79	22.56
Economic value	−13	143

The average ROE and ROCE were 32.79% and 5.13%, respectively. The average debt-equity ratio during the period 2018–2021 was 0.37.

Table 4 gives the financial highlights of the AppFolio during the period 2018–2021.

The source of data is gurufocus.com. On an average basis, the total assets, total equity, and total revenue grew by 34%, 55%, and 24%, respectively, during the period 2018–2021. The market capitalization and enterprise value of the company increased by an average of 40% during this period. The total expenses increased by approximately 34% during the period 2018–2021. The year 2021 witnessed a decline in market capitalization and enterprise value by 32% compared to the previous year. The cash and cash equivalent increased by 84% on average basis during the period 2018–2021. The cash and cash equivalents have shown many fluctuations during the period of analysis. The net income declined by approximately 99% in the year 2021 compared to the year 2020. The cash equivalents and net income increased by 335% and 336%, respectively, in the year 2020 compared to the previous year 2019.

Table 5 shows the estimation of the economic value of the company during the period 2020 and 2021. The values are estimated in millions of dollars. The Weighted Average Cost of Capital (WACC) estimates are taken from gurufocus.com.

The economic value increased from −$13 million in 2019 to $143 million in the year 2020.

References

1. Annual Report 2021, AppFolio
2. https://www.appfolio.com/
3. https://ir.appfolioinc.com/

Case 12 Kinsale Capital Group

Kinsale Capital Group was founded in the year 2009. The company is a property and casualty specialty insurance company that is focused on the excess and surplus (E&S) market in the United States. The company offers underwriting expertise to cover small business risks and personal lines risks. These insurance products are sold throughout the United States through a network of independent insurance brokers. The company has delivered attractive underwriting profits and has leveraged its proprietary technology platform to gain entrepreneurial efficiency. As of December 31, 2021, we had 375 employees, of which 364 were full-time employees.

In 2010, Kinsale acquired American Healthcare Specialty Insurance Company and renamed it as Kinsale Insurance Company. In 2013, Aspera Insurance Services was established as an insurance broker. In 2018, Kinsale Real Estate was incorporated as a wholly owned subsidiary to acquire and hold real estate.

Products

Kinsale writes a wide array of insurance coverage for risks that can be categorized as unique or hard to place in the standard insurance market. These types of excess and surplus (E&S) risks are applicable to newly established companies, firms with high-risk operations, firms insured in litigious venues, or poor-performing companies with historic losses. The underwriters of the company specialize in individual lines of business. The company focusses on small to medium-sized client accounts. In the year 2020, the average premium per policy was approximately $9100. In 2020, the gross written premiums increased by 41.9 percent. With the exception of personal insurance lines, the average premium per policy written was approximately $11,800 in the year 2020. The average premium per policy written by the company in 2021 was $10,400.With the exclusion of personal lines, the average premium per policy written was $12,900 in 2021. In 2021, the gross written premiums increased by 38.3% to $764.4 million. In 2021, the casualty sector and property sector premiums constituted approximately 85 percent and 15% of the total gross written premiums.

© The Author(s), under exclusive license to Springer Nature Switzerland AG 2024

B. R. Kumar, *Rising Stars*, Management for Professionals,
https://doi.org/10.1007/978-3-031-50032-9_12

Table 1 Gross premium data

Year	2019	2020	2021
Commercial:			
Small business	63,181	83,289	112,142
Excess casualty	51,225	76,715	109,464
Construction	71,035	87,206	103,540
Commercial property	29,115	51,789	78,722
Allied health	23,962	37,562	59,208
Products liability	26,333	38,306	55,070
Life sciences	17,821	31,027	41,297
General casualty	20,931	24,591	36,042
Professional liability	20,029	27,051	33,226
Management liability	14,820	24,061	32,163
All other commercial lines	34,582	49,507	76,497
Total commercial	373,034	531,104	737,371
Personal insurance	16,660	21,710	27,002
Total gross written premium	389,694	552,814	764,373

Source: Annual Report

The commercial lines offerings by the company included small business, construction, commercial property, allied health, products liability, life sciences, general casualty, professional and management liability, inland marine, and commercial insurance. Homeowners' insurance also constituted a small part of the personal lines market.

Kinsale Capital received the Euro Hedge Global Equity Fund award in the year 2013.

Table 1 shows the summary of gross premiums during 2019–2021. The values are in thousands of dollars.

Growth Strategy

The company focusses on the excess and surplus line (E&S) market. Kinsale Capital has underwriting expertise across a broad spectrum to place risks. The underwriting team of the company is equipped with specialized skills to appropriately price and structure solutions. The company manages its broad risk appetite by maintaining a diversified book of smaller accounts with strong pricing and well-defined coverages. The company believes that technology is the core competency that drives best-in-class expense ratio. The company's competitive strength lies in its proprietary technology platform which helps the company to analyze trends across different functions in the business operations. This integrated digital platform embedded with a data warehouse collects an array of statistical data for meaningful analysis. This customized proprietary system can also reduce the risk of administrative errors in the policy forms and simplify the process of handling claims in an efficient manner. The systems enable rapid response to the brokers' submission within 24 h. The use of a proprietary technology platform along with low-cost operations is a distinct competitive strength for Kinsale for processing quotes, underwriting policies, and operating at lower cost compared to its direct competitors. The company has a fully integrated claims management system. It manages all its claims in-house and does not delegate claims management authority to third parties. The company focusses on expansion in the E&S market. According to A.M Best statistics, the total E&S market was estimated to be $66.1 billion in terms of direct written premium as of the year 2020. In 2021, Kinsale Capital had gross written premiums of $764.4 million representing approximately 1.2% of the market share. The company's strategy focusses on concentrating on hard-to-place risks and enhancing its underwriting profitability irrespective of market cycles. The company markets its product through a broad group of independent insurance brokers. Kinsale also sells policies through its wholly owned broker Aspera. Kinsale does not grant its brokers any underwriting or claims authority. The brokers are selected through management's review of experience, knowledge, and business plan of each broker. In 2021, the largest broker for the company was RSG Specialty, LLC which accounted for 17.9% of the gross written premiums. In 2021, the company paid an average commission of 14.6% of gross written premiums to its brokers. The company promotes entrepreneurial business with a close alignment of owners and employees.

The underwriting department received approximately 520,000 new business submissions in the year ended December 31, 2021. Out of this submission, the company issued approximately 347,000 quotes and bound 36,000 policies for a new policy which represented a new submission ratio of 6.9%. Kinsale Capital also gives importance to the effective management of the claims adjusting process. The claim process is characterized by the extension of low reserve and settlement authority levels to front line claim examiners, greater supervision through keeping the adjuster-to-supervisor ratios low and monitoring the number of claims handled by each claims examiner. The company monitors and adjusts reserves on a continuous basis using new information on reported claims and the usage of statistical techniques. The company uses sophisticated computer models to analyze the risk of severe losses from natural catastrophes.

Kinsale has entered into reinsurance contracts basically to limit its exposure to potential large losses. The reinsurance program of the company is primarily contracted under quota share reinsurance contracts and excess of loss treaties. The property-per-risk reinsurance policy of the company reduces the financial impact of a large loss on a single commercial property or inland marine policy. In terms of investment strategy, the company invests its cash and invested assets in fixed-maturity securities, short-term investments, cash equivalents, exchange-traded funds, and preferred stock.

The Property and Casualty industry is highly competitive. The company faces competition from domestic and international insurers. The primary competitors for the company in the E&S sector include Alleghany Corporation, Arch Capital Group, Ltd., Argo Group International Holdings, Ltd., James River Group Holdings, Ltd., Lloyds of London, Markel Corporation, RLI Corp., and W. R. Berkley Corporation.

Regulation

Kinsale Capital is regulated by the insurance regulatory authorities in different states in the United States where the company has operations. State insurance laws and regulations generally are designed to protect the interests of policyholders, consumers, and claimants. Kinsale Insurance is authorized (licensed) in the State of Arkansas to transact certain lines of P&C insurance. Kinsale Insurance currently operates on an excess and surplus lines basis in all 50 states of the United States. Kinsale Company operates as an insurance holding company system and is subject to the insurance holding company laws of the State of Arkansas.

Risk Analysis

The company faces risks related to business, industry, and operations. The loss reserves may become inadequate to cover actual losses and would have a material adverse effect on financial conditions. The nature of uncertainty of models employed to evaluate risk might result in actual losses that are materially different from the estimates. The probability of failure of any of the loss limitations which are employed or changes in other claims or coverage issues will have a material adverse effect on the operations or financial conditions of the firm. The availability and cost of reinsurance which are dependent on current market conditions in terms of price and available capacity can affect the company's business volume and profitability. Severe weather conditions and catastrophes adversely affects property line businesses and result in both an increase in the number of claims incurred and an increase in the dollar amount of each claim asserted. The business of the firm is exposed to the risk of pandemics, outbreaks, public health crises, and geopolitical and social events. The growth and profitability of the company could be affected by adverse economic factors such as recession, inflation, and high rate of unemployment and could result in the sale of fewer policies or increase in the frequency or severity of claims and premium defaults. The reliance on a select group of brokers to distribute products also have risk implications. In 2021, approximately 56 percent of gross written premiums were distributed through 5 brokers out of the 159 brokers which the company was associated with. Kinsale faces intense competition from other specialty insurance companies, standard insurance companies, underwriting agencies, and diversified financial services companies. The company is also subject to reinsurance counterparty credit risk. The failure of the information technology and telecommunication systems could adversely affect the operations of the company. The company faces extensive regulation and failure to comply with regulations may result in penalties which include fines and suspensions. The business of the firm could be adversely affected by changes in state laws like changes related to asset and reserve valuation requirements, surplus requirements, limitations on investments and dividends, enterprise risk, and risk-based capital requirements.

Financial Performance

Table 2 gives the highlights of premiums written in the year 2020 and 2021. The values are given in thousands of dollars.

The gross written premiums have increased by 38% approximately in 2021 compared to the previous year. The net written premiums have registered a growth rate of 39.6% in 2021 compared to the previous year.

Table 3 gives the key insurance performance ratios during the period 2020–2021.

Loss ratio, expressed as a percentage, is the ratio of losses and loss adjustment expenses to earned premiums, net of the effects of reinsurance. Expense ratio, expressed as a percentage, is the ratio of underwriting, acquisition, and insurance expenses to net earned premiums. Combined ratio is the sum of the loss ratio and the expense ratio. A combined ratio under 100% indicates an underwriting profit. A combined ratio over 100% indicates an underwriting loss.

Market Performance Analysis

Table 4 shows the wealth generated by the Kinsale Capital stock in comparison with a market index of the Nasdaq Composite and Nasdaq Insurance Index during the 5-year period Dec 2016–Dec 2021. It is assumed that an initial investment of $100 is made in the stock and indexes at the beginning of the investment period and reinvested along with dividends.

Table 2 Premium statistics

Year	2020	2021
Gross written premiums	552,814	764,373
Ceded written premiums	74,595	104,164
Net written premiums	478,219	660,209

Source Annual Report 2021

Table 3 Key insurance metrics

Year	2020	2021
Loss ratio	63.90%	55.70%
Expense ratio	22.80%	21.40%
Combined ratio	86.70%	77.10%

Source: Annual Report 2021

Table 4 Comparative wealth

Year	2016	2017	2018	2019	2020	2021
Kinsale Capital	$100	$133.20	$165	$304	$599	$714
Nasdaq Composite Index	$100	$129.64	$125.96	$172.17	$249.51	$304.85
Nasdaq Insurance Index	$100	$116.95	$110.34	$133.15	$132.39	$170.09

Source: Annual Report 2021

Table 5 Excess value

Year	2018	2019	2020	2021
Book value of equity	264	405.9	576.2	699.3
Market value of equity	1180.2	2257.4	4554.4	5432.1
BV as percent of MV	22.4%	18.0%	12.7%	12.9%
Average	16.5%			

Table 6 Holding period return

Year	Kinsale	Nasdaq Composite	Excess returns
2018	16%	−10%	27%
2019	75%	23%	52%
2020	75%	41%	34%
2021	27%	20%	7%
2022 till Oct	56%	−22%	78%

The 5-year holding period return for Kinsale Capital was 614% whereas for the Nasdaq Composite Index was 205% and 70% for the Nasdaq Insurance Index. Hence, the excess returns for Kinsale Capital stock was over 500% compared to the industry insurance sector index. The average returns for Kinsale share was 51 percent for Kinsale stock during the period 2016–2021. The Nasdaq Composite and Insurance Index had registered average returns of 26% and 12%, respectively, during the above period.

Table 5 shows the estimation of book value as a percent of market value of the company. The book value and market value are given in millions of dollars.

The average book value of equity of Kinsale as a percent of the market value of equity is only 16.5%. In 2020, the market value of the company was 7.9 times the book value of the company.

Five-Year Stock Performance Analysis

The total monthly cumulative returns for Kinsale Capital during the period Nov 2017 to Oct 2022 was approximately 225%. The Nasdaq Composite index had documented total cumulative monthly returns of 59% during the above period of analysis. The average 5 year return for Kinsale shares were 43% compared to 12% accounted by the market index Nasdaq Composite. Kinsale Capital stock has performed extremely well compared to the market index Nasdaq Composite. Kinsale Capital's share which was trading at $44 in November 2017 was trading at $313 per share by October end 2022 reflecting an increase of price by approximately 7 times.

Table 6 shows the year-wise holding period return for Kinsale Capital share compared to the market index Nasdaq Composite during the 5-year period Nov 2017–Oct 2022.

Kinsale stock had excess returns of 78% in 2022, 52% in 2019, and 34% in 2020. In the year 2021, Kinsale had marginally performed better than the market index. In rest of the years, the Kinsale Capital share had superior performance compared to the market index.

Operating Performance Analysis

Table 7 gives the important operating performance highlights of the company. The values are given in millions of dollars.

The average growth rate of total assets and equity was 38% and 39%, respectively, during the period 2018–2021. The short-term investments increased by 40% on average basis during the period of analysis. The average total revenue and net income grew by 42% and 67%, respectively, during the above period. The market capitalization and enterprise value of the company increased by 71% and 74% on average basis. The total expenses increased on an average by 36% during the period. The data source is annual reports.

Table 8 shows the profitability ratios of Kinsale during the period 2018–2021.

The average Net margin, ROE, and ROA during the period 2018–2021 were 19.59%, 18.58%, and 6.68%, respectively.

Table 9 illustrates the estimation of the economic value of Kinsale during the years 2019 and 2020. The values are given in millions of dollars. The WACC estimation is sourced from Gurufocus.com.

The economic value has increased from $33 million in 2019 to $44 in 2020.

Table 7 Operating performance highlights

	(In millions of dollars)			
Year	2018	2019	2020	2021
Total assets	773.1	1090.50	1546.90	2025.70
Short-term investments	510.3	729.5	1081.80	1392.10
Total equity	264	405.9	576.2	699.3
Total revenue	222.1	315.9	459.9	639.8
Total operating expenses	181.6	239.8	359.5	451
Net income	33.8	63.3	88.4	152.7
Market cap	1180.20	2257.40	4554.40	5432.10
Enterprise value	1105.20	2173.80	4519.90	5353.70

Table 8 Profitability ratios

Ratios	2018	2019	2020	2021
Net margin%	15.21	20.04	19.23	23.86
ROE%	13.46	18.90	18.01	23.94
ROA%	4.69	6.79	6.70	8.55

Table 9 Economic value

Year	2019	2020
Profit before income tax	76.1	100.4
Income tax	5.05	7.04
Net operating profit after tax (NOPAT)	71.05	93.36
Stockholder equity	576.2	699.3
Long-term debt		
Total capital employed	576.2	699.3
WACC	6.64%	7.02%
Capital charge	38.26	49.09
Economic value	33	44

References

1. www.gurufocus.com
2. Kinsale Capital, Annual Report 2021
3. https://ir.kinsalecapitalgroup.com/overview/default.aspx

Case 13 Freedom Holding Corporation

Freedom Holding Corp. (FRHC) is a corporation originally incorporated in the State of Utah in the United States in the year 1981. Later the company was domiciled in the State of Nevada. FRHC is a holding company that owns and operates diversified financial services businesses through its various subsidiaries. The subsidiaries undertake operations related to securities dealing, market making, retail securities brokerage, investment research, investment banking, and underwriting services. In 2022, FRHC completed the acquisition of two insurance companies operating in Kazakhstan. The principal executive office is located in Almaty, Kazakhstan. In November 2015, the company entered into a reverse acquisition agreement to acquire 100% ownership interests in FFIN Securities, Freedom EU, Freedom RU, and its wholly owned subsidiary, Freedom KZ. The subsidiary Freedom RU owns approximately 90% of Kazakhstan's securities brokerage, Freedom KZ.

The Russia/Ukraine Conflict, with its consequent sanctions and countersanctions, has adversely impacted the operations of the company in Russia. The company have decided to divest its interest in two wholly owned Russian subsidiaries, Freedom RU and Freedom Bank RU. These subsidiaries had 43 offices and branches and employed about 1717 people in Russia. The institutional holding for the company is 0.57% whereas the insider ownership is 3.56%. As of March 31, 2022, the company had 3421 employees.

Products and Services

FRHC provides a comprehensive range of securities brokerage services to individuals, businesses, and financial institutions. The brokerage services offered include securities trading, margin lending, investment research, and investor education tools. Clients are provided with online tools and retail locations to establish accounts and conduct securities trading on transaction-based pricing. The securities brokerages segment also involve in proprietary investment activities, and facilitates repurchase and reverse repurchase agreements. The revenues generated by the

© The Author(s), under exclusive license to Springer Nature Switzerland AG 2024
B. R. Kumar, *Rising Stars*, Management for Professionals,
https://doi.org/10.1007/978-3-031-50032-9_13

brokerage segment accounted for 70% and 69% of the total revenues in the years 2021 and 2022. With respect to retail brokerage, FRHC offers full-service brokerage services which cover investment alternates such as exchange traded, over-the-counter equity and debt securities, money market instruments, options and futures contracts, government bonds, and mutual funds. By March 31, 2022, FRHC had 94,000 active retail brokerage accounts. For investment research related to equity and debt, the company employs around 30 research and securities analysts. The Tradernet platform of FRHC facilitates investment education and training courses for retail brokerage customers and the public. The investment banking division provides strategic advisory services in certain sectors such as consumer and business services, energy, financial institutions, real estate, technology, media, and communications. The investment banking activities are concentrated in Kazakhstan and Uzbekistan. FRHC provides capital raising solutions for corporate customers through initial public offerings and seasoned equity offerings. The company also offers a range of debt capital markets solutions for structuring debt, buyouts, acquisitions, recapitalizations, and venture capital funding. These solutions are provided for emerging growth and small market companies. The company has historically offered commercial banking services through subsidiaries in Kazakhstan and Russia. FRHC is the authorized Visa and MasterCard issuer and also issues multi-currency cards. In Kazakhstan, Freedom Bank KZ has developed the first "invest card" in the region which enables the customers to manage their investment accounts both online and in person. In the year 2021, Freedom Bank KZ launched a first-in-market digital mortgage product that facilitate processing of the residential mortgage loan process online.

In May 2022, FRHC acquired two insurance companies in Kazakhstan, a life insurance company, Freedom Life, and a direct insurance carrier. Many of the services are provided online through the company's proprietary Tradernet software platform.

Table 1 highlights the important milestones for the company.

Growth Strategy

The company aims to establish itself as a leader in the financial services industry in domestic and international capital markets. The company has expanded through adoption of non-organic growth strategies such as mergers and acquisitions. Through the acquisition strategy, the company acquired talented personnel and technology assets. The company intends to acquire financial technologies and financial services-related companies in the future. The company also aims to create a digital fintech ecosystem characterized by innovative and integrated financial technologies in its pursuit of growth strategy. The technology platform integrates many of the services for state-sponsored mortgages and other lending programs. On account of digitalized services, the company is able to market and scale the services into new regions on a cost-effective basis.

Table 1 Company milestones

Year	Events
1986	The company was established in the United States
2008	The company made entry in Moscow
2010	Branches were established in 12 cities in Russia
2011	Link at MOEX and LSE
2012	IPO offered to customers
2013	Company makes acquisition in Kazakhstan; Freedom 24 Start Up initiated
2014	IPO in Kazakhstan
2015	Expansion in Kazakhstan; license acquisition by FFIN bank
2017	Ukraine subsidiary opened; expands into Uzbekistan
2018	Asyl invest, Nettrader companies start operations
2019	Freedom Holding starts trading on Nasdaq Capital Markets
2020	Freedom Holding acquires NYSE Floor Brokerage Firm

Source: Company website

The company also focusses on organic growth through expansion of the network of retail financial advisers, volume of analyst reports targeted toward customer base, and increase of trading volume. The company has expanded operations in countries such as the United Kingdom, Greece, Spain, France, UAE, Armenia, and Azerbaijan. The investment strategies of the firm give importance to capital preservation and liquidity management. Freedom Holding typically follows the strategy of investment in investment-grade securities. For effective implementation of a regulatory mechanism, the company has a compliance department based in Cyprus to oversee compliance for group companies. The department is responsible for the establishment of compliance controls and policies. The company employs robust know your customer, anti-money laundering and countering terrorist financing (AML/CTF), and sanctions screening platforms. This process is facilitated by integration of Freedom Holding's trading platform with various standard third-party data providers. The company is focusing its efforts on a number of technology-related acquisitions. FRHC is in the process of completing the acquisition of Paybox Technologies LLP and its subsidiaries ("Paybox"). The company has also initiated steps to acquire Rekassa PCI Reader which is a mobile and web application to replace traditional cash registers. To create an e-commerce infrastructure, the company is also in the process of acquiring Ticketon Events LLP.

Segments

The company has 20 subsidiaries operating in countries such as Greece, Cyprus, Germany, the United Kingdom, Kazakh, Uzbekistan, Azerbaijan, Ukraine, the United States, Armenia, UAE, and Russia. The Central Asian region consists of operations in Kazakhstan, Kyrgyzstan, Uzbekistan, and Ukraine. The Central Asian region accounted for 21% of the total revenue made by the company during the year

2021. This region accounts for 46 offices that provide brokerage and financial services, investment consulting, and education. The Europe segment consists of operations in Cyprus, the United Kingdom, Germany, Spain, Greece, and France. The Cyprus securities brokerage firm oversees the European region operations. The Europe region generated 78% of the total revenue in the year 2021. Of these, approximately 70% of the revenues was received from FFIN Brokerage. The company made a foray into the US market through the acquisition of an NYSE broker–dealer in the year 2020. The US region generated 2% of the total revenues. In the year 2022, the company entered into the Caucasus and Middle East markets. The Russia segment consisted of securities brokerage and complementary banking operations in Russia.

ESG Initiatives

The company has been focusing on the implementation of ESG initiatives through subsidiaries in different countries. The company implemented schemes with respect to humanitarian efforts related to Russian/Ukraine conflict. During the year 2022, the company has developed programs for green bond underwriting in Kazakhstan. The company has underwritten the placement of Eurasian Development Bank bonds in the ESG segment. The funds raised through this method were utilized to finance ESG projects in Kazakhstan. Freedom Finance Academy provides free online and in-person training courses and webinars in financial literacy related to the general public.

Risk Analysis

Freedom Holding operates in highly regulated industries across several legal jurisdictions. The securities, banking, and other financial business activities of the company are subject to extensive regulation and oversight by the stock exchanges, central/national banks, government, and self-regulatory authorities in foreign jurisdictions. The company faces risks as the countries in which it operates have changing regimes and regulatory policies. The economic sanctions related to Russia/Ukraine conflict had a material adverse impact on the business and operations of FRHC. The operations of subsidiaries of the company will be adversely impacted due to failure to meet capital adequacy and liquidity guidelines. Future prospects may be adversely affected by disruptions or lack of liquidity in the credit markets. The business operations of FRHC in emerging markets are subject to significant political, economic, and legal risks. Global anti-offshore measures and frequent tax law changes could affect the business and value of investments of FRHC. Being a diversified holding company with few operations, the company has to rely more on the operations of its subsidiaries to fund holding company operations. The company also faces data security risks and liabilities. The company depends on third-party US registered securities broker–dealer and clearing firms to receive and transmit securities and funds internationally.

Performance Analysis

Stock Performance

Table 2 shows the cumulative 5-year total shareholder return for FRHC in comparison with important market indexes. It is assumed that an initial investment of $100 is made in the stock and indexes for return analysis. The investment period is from March 31st, 2017 to March 31st, 2022.

The 5-year holding period return for Freedom Holding was exponential at 18,972% while for S&P 500 and S&P diversified financials, the 5-year holding period was 110% and 106%, respectively. The wealth in terms of stock investment increased by 3.75 times in the year 2021 compared to the year 2020. The average 5-year return for FRHC stock was 494% whereas for S&P 500 and S&P 500 diversified financials was 18%.

Table 3 highlights the book value and market value of the company for the past 5 years. The values are given in millions of dollars.

The average book value as percent of market value of the equity during the period 2019–2022 was only 15.7%. The stock registered excellent performance in the year 2021 wherein the market value of the company increased by 276% compared to the increase of book value by 111%.

The data for analysis is sourced from guru focus, yahoo finance and annual report of the company.

Table 2 Five year cumulative stock returns

Year	2017	2018	2019	2020	2021	2022
Freedom Holding Corp	$100	$2192.00	$2774	$4544	$17,075	$19,072
S&P 500	$100	$114.00	$125.00	$116.00	$182.00	$210.00
S&P 500 Diversified Financials	$100	$122.00	$116.00	$105.00	$170.00	$206.00

Source FRHC Annual Report 2022

Table 3 Comparative book value and market value

Year	2019	2020	2021	2022
Book value of equity	117.6	131.3	277.3	514.7
Market value of equity	503.2	828.7	3118.5	3548.7
BV as percent of MV	23.4%	15.8%	8.9%	14.5%
Average	15.7%			

Five-Year Stock Return Analysis

The cumulative monthly return for the stock during the 5-period year Jan 2018–Nov 2022 was 245.6% whereas the cumulative monthly return for the market index S&P500 during the above period was 47%. The 5-year monthly average return for the stock was 53% compared to a 10% gain accounted by the market index S&P500 during the above period. The stock which was trading at $6.85 on 3/1/2018 increased by approximately 8 times during Nov 2022.

Table 4 shows the holding period return for the stock during the period 2018–2022. The analysis is done based on the assumption of 1 year holding period.

The FRHC stock performance was at its best in the year 2020 when the stock had registered excess returns of 227% compared to the market index S&P 500. In 2020, the stock returns were 70% compared to Index Holding period return of 10%. Both the stock and market index had negative returns in the year 2022.

Operating Performance Analysis

Table 5 provides the operating performance highlights of the company during the period 2018–2021. The values are given in millions of dollars.

The total assets increased by 140% on an average basis during the period 2018–2021. The average growth rate of total equity was 69% during the above period. The total revenue and net income grew by 104% and 259% on average basis during the above period. The investments in cash and marketable securities

Table 4 Holding period return

Year	FRHC	SP500	Excess returns
2018	21%	9%	12%
2019	70%	10%	60%
2020	238%	11%	227%
2021	38%	31%	7%
2022(till Oct)	−14%	−15%	1%

Table 5 Operating performance highlights

	(In millions of dollars)			
Financial highlights	2018	2019	2020	2021
Total assets	350.9	453.5	2018.6	2921
Short-term investments	217.9	226.2	1435	1829
Total equity	117.6	131.3	277.3	514.7
Total revenue	74.3	121.9	352.6	564.7
Total operating expenses	43.1	60	77.4	161.6
Net income	7.1	24.8	142.3	217.9
Market cap	503.2	828.7	3118.5	3548.7
Enterprise value	391.5	735.1	2193.7	2605.8

Table 6 Profitability and leverage position

Ratios	2018	2019	2020	2021	Average
Net margin%	9.62	20.37	40.36	38.6	27.24
ROE%	5.84	19.96	69.64	55.03	37.62
ROA%	2.04	6.17	11.51	8.82	7.14
DER	0.9	1.03	1.85	1.74	1.38

Table 7 Enterprise value

Year	2021	2022
Profit before income tax	173	236.9
Income tax	30.10	25.51
Net operating profit after tax (NOPAT)	142.90	211.39
Stockholder equity	277.3	514.7
Long-term debt	71.8	102.6
Total capital employed	349.1	617.3
WACC	8.13%	9.06%
Capital charge	28.38	55.93
Economic value	115	155

increased by 189% during the said period. The average increase in market capitalization and enterprise value was 118% and 102%, respectively, during the period 2018–2021.

Table 6 shows the profitability and leverage position of the firm during the period 2018–2021.

The profitability ratios of net margin and ROE were 40.36% and 69.64%, respectively, in the year 2020. The stock market returns for FRHC was also the highest during this period of time. The average net margin, ROE, and ROA were 27.24%, 37.62%, and 7.14%, respectively, during the period 2018–2021. The average debt-to-equity ratio was 1.38 during the period 2018–2021.

Table 7 shows the estimation of enterprise value of the firm in millions of dollars. The WACC calculation is sourced from gurufocus.com

The economic value has increased from $115 million in 2021 to $155 million in year 2022.

References

1. https://www.freedomholdingcorp.com/about
2. https://ir.freedomholdingcorp.com/

Case 14 STAAR Surgical Company

STAAR designs, develops, manufactures, and markets implantable lenses for eyes with companion delivery systems. These lenses eliminate the reliance on glasses or contact lenses for patients. These lenses are foldable and facilitate surgical placement in the eye through a small incision. The company has been operational in the field of ophthalmic surgery for over 30 years. The company is the exclusive manufacturer of the proprietary EVO Visian® Family of Implantable Collamer® Lenses (EVO ICL) used worldwide to correct refractive errors. The company's goal is to improve its leadership position in the segment of refractive lenses meant as the primary solution for patients with preference for not using eyeglasses or contact lenses. The company also makes lenses for use in surgery which treats cataracts. The products of STAAR are sold in more than 75 countries. Approximately 96% of total sales of the company in the year 2021 were accounted from outside the United States. The global administrative offices and principal manufacturing facility of STAAR are located in Monrovia, California. The operational and administrative facilities of STAAR are located in the United States, Switzerland, and Japan. The Visian implantable Collamer lens product family, preloaded silicone cataract intraocular lenses, and injector systems are developed in the Monrovia manufacturing facility. The technology center of the company located in Tustin, California houses its Research and Development team. All of the company's sales are generated from the ophthalmic surgical product segment. Most of the raw materials and components used for the production process are sourced from external suppliers. By December 2021, the company owned approximately 65 United States and foreign patents and had 27 patent applications. The proprietary technology is protected in part through confidentiality and non-disclosure agreements with employees, consultants, and other involved stakeholders. By December 31, 2021, the company had approximately 806 employees of which 278 were employed outside of the United States. The shares of the company are traded on the Nasdaq Global Market (NASDAQ) under the symbol "STAA." As of February 2022, there were approximately 288 record shareholders. The company has not paid any cash dividends on the stock since its inception. Table 1 lists the major milestones of the company.

© The Author(s), under exclusive license to Springer Nature Switzerland AG 2024

B. R. Kumar, *Rising Stars*, Management for Professionals,
https://doi.org/10.1007/978-3-031-50032-9_14

Table 1 Major milestones

Year	Events
1991	The first version of the foldable IOL made of silicone was introduced. It became the benchmark of care for cataract surgery globally
1996	The product Visian ICL® was marketed outside the United States
1997	CE Mark was received by ICL and sales were initiated in European Union countries
2005	STAAR received FDA approval for treatment of myopia in the United States
2020	Publishes the first sustainability report
2021	EVO Visian ICL and Visian ICL family of lenses are available in more than 75 countries

Source: STAAR Sustainability Report 2022

Products

The principal products of STAAR are ICLs used in refractive surgery and IOLs used in cataract surgery. The ICL (Implantable Collamer Lens) family consists of products such as EVO Visian ICL, EVO Viva ICL, and Visian ICL. The ICL family product line is used to treat a range of refractive errors with known vision disorders such as myopia, hyperopia, astigmatism, and presbyopia. This type of lens is generically termed "phakic IOLs" as they operate along with the patient's natural lens or phakos rather than replacing it. These lenses are implanted by the surgeon using topical anesthesia on an outpatient basis. The company's ICL is the world's largest selling phakic IOL and is the only posterior chamber phakic IOL (PIOL) approved by the Food and Drug Administration (FDA) for marketing and sale in the United States. Statistics show that ICL have been implanted into more than 1 million eyes worldwide. The ICL is available globally in multiple models, powers, and lengths totaling hundreds of different types of inventoried lenses. ICL sales accounted for 86%, 87%, and 92% of the company sales in the years 2019, 2020, and 2021, respectively.

The company also sells IOLs (Intraocular Lens) for use in cataract surgery. In most of the countries where STAAR sells cataract IOLS, the government agencies reimburse most of the cost of cataract surgery and IOLs. The sales of cataract IOLs accounted for 11%, 8%, and 6% of the total sales in the years 2019, 2020, and 2021, respectively. The company also sells injector parts to its acrylic lens suppliers for their preloaded acrylic cataract IOL. The products are marketed to different healthcare providers which include ophthalmic surgeons, vision centers, hospitals, government facilities, and distributors.

Market Scenario Analysis

According to Market Scope, LLC publisher of ophthalmic industry data, approximately 4.2 million refractive procedures like laser vision procedures were performed globally in the year 2021. According to statistics, myopia will affect nearly 5 billion people by the year 2050.[1] This will result in greater demand for ICL products. Research have provided clinical data for the safety, effectiveness, and visual quality of the ICL.

Competition and Growth Strategy

STAAR focusses on developing and launching innovative products to support clinical needs. The company invests in market development, practice support, healthcare professional training, and patient outreach. The marketing strategy of the company aims to position ICL as a premium and primary option for patients in the clinic via digital and social media. There exists intense competition in the ophthalmic surgery product market which is driven by technological innovation and regulatory approval. In the refractive market, the ICL technology faces competition from elective surgical procedures such as laser vision correction. In the cataract surgery market, the IOLs compete based on technology quality. Big multinationals such as Alcon, Johnson & Johnson, Bausch Health Companies, and Carl Zeiss MediTec AG market lasers for corneal refractive surgery. The company also faces competition from low-cost versions of posterior chamber implantable contact lenses from Asian Players. ICL has a clinical advantage over the other lenses which is reflected in the strong market share of the global phakic IOL market.

The company focuses on enhancing the technological advancements in the ophthalmic industry through the development of innovative premium ophthalmic products such as lenses, materials, and designs. The company has an active research agenda for the development of presbyopia corrective ophthalmic medical devices and preloaded injector systems for ophthalmic medical devices. The R&D investments are also directed toward the development of a new generation of ophthalmic medical devices and materials.

As a part of its strategic vision plan, the company aims to achieve strategic goals such as positioning EVO Implantable lenses as a Special and Transformational Pathway to Visual Freedom; Innovate and develop a pipeline of next generation premium Collamer based Intraocular lenses and support the transformation of the refractive surgery paradigm to lens based through Clinical Validation and Medical Affairs Excellence.

Regulation

The products sold by STAAR require premarket clearance, approval of medical devices from governmental or regulatory authorities from almost all the countries where the products are sold. The company is subject to healthcare fraud and abuse

[1] Global Prevalence of Myopia and High Myopia and Temporal Trends from 2000 through 2050, Ophthalmology, Vol. 123, No. 5, May 2016.

and patient privacy regulation by the federal government, the states, and the international jurisdictions in which the businesses are conducted.

Risk Analysis

The revenues of the company grew by approximately 41% in the year 2021. It is uncertain whether the future profitability will be maintained. Compliance issues may adversely impact the operations of the firm. The quality system and other deficiencies observed by the FDA will result in delays for product approvals. In many countries, the products are sold through independent distributors whose certain negative actions could result in declining sales or cause harm to the firm's reputation or result in product or legal liability. Approximately 92% of the revenues of the company were derived from ICL lenses used in refractive procedures. Factors such as economic slowdown, lack of consumer confidence can slow ICL sales growth. Disruptions in the supply chain or failure to forecast product demand could result in significant delays or lost sales. Foreign currency fluctuations contribute to significant risks as 96% of total sales were accounted from regions outside the United States. Public health crises such as COVID pandemic impact the business model adversely. Compliance with regulations is a huge risk factor. Obtaining clearance or approval can be a long and expensive process, and clearance or approval is never certain.

Sustainability Initiatives

In the year 2021, the company undertook major sustainability initiatives. The company started the work on the installation of solar photovoltaic (PV) panels in its three manufacturing locations in California. The company also conducted its first greenhouse gas inventory to establish a baseline understanding of the United States, Swiss, and Japanese operational emissions. STAAR Surgical also installed electric vehicle chargers at its California and Switzerland facilities. The company further strengthened its sponsorship and partnership with "Beyond Blindness" organization to empower children with visual impairments and other disabilities. The company also expanded its global cross-functional ESG steering committee and created Diversity, Equity, and Inclusion (DEI) committee. The goal of the company is to design, manufacture, and offer safe and effective implantable ophthalmic products for improving the patient's quality of life. The ICL lenses are developed in accordance with the international ISO standards. The Quality Management Systems of the company is compliant with Global Quality standards which include ISO 13485 for medical devices. The critical suppliers, processes, materials, and products of the company basically comply with stringent quality system requirements for medical devices. The Supplier Code of Conduct adopted by the company stipulates business ethics, human rights, quality assurance, and legal compliance for suppliers. About 97% of the critical suppliers were audited by a third party in the year 2021. Approximately 92% of suppliers had shared information with the company about

Table 2 Comparative wealth analysis

Year	2016	2017	2018	2019	2020	2021
STAAR Surgical	$100	$142.86	$288.12	$316.87	$730.15	$841.49
Nasdaq Composite	$100	$129.64	$124.98	$173.12	$249.51	$304.85
Peer Group	$100	$128.58	$149.79	$174.19	$211.96	$226.23

Source Annual Report 2021

Table 3 Book value and market value comparison

Year	2018	2019	2020	2021
Book value of equity	132.4	159.9	197.2	258.6
Market value of equity	1410.3	1576.4	3679.6	4356.5
BV as percent of MV	9.4%	10.1%	5.4%	5.9%
Average	7.7%			

their sustainability initiatives. STAAR's ecofriendly initiatives include waste reduction through digitization and resource conservation through optimization of utility consumption. In the year 2021, the company had invested approximately $800,000 in energy efficiency upgrades for Switzerland operations. Over the past 2 years, the company was able to decrease its energy and greenhouse gas emissions per dollar of revenue. The GHG Intensity which measures the amount of carbon dioxide was reduced from 6.67 in 2019 to 4.38 in 2021. In 2021, the company had zero waste-related environmental compliance incidents.

Stock Performance Analysis

Table 2 shows the comparative performance of STAAR stock in relation to market index Nasdaq Composite and a group of peer companies. The stock performance of 16 companies in the sector (for example, Angio Dynamics and Anika Therapeutics) was taken for the peer group analysis (Annual Report 2021). The data assumes that $100 was invested on December 30, 2016, in STAAR stock and in each of the composite indices and any dividends (if any) were reinvested.

The holding period return for STAAR Surgical was 741% compared to 205% for the Nasdaq Composite and 126% for the peer group companies. In terms of average returns for the period 2016–2021, STAAR Surgical had made returns of 60% while Nasdaq Composite and Peer Group had returns of 26% and 18% respectively.

Table 3 shows the book value and market value of the company during the time period 2017–2022. The values are given in millions of dollars. The data source is gurufocus.com.

The average book value as percent of market value during the period 2018–2021 was 7.7%. In 2020, the book value was just 5.4% of the market value reflecting the superior value created by the stock in the market.

Five-Year Stock Return Analysis

The 5-year monthly return analysis was done for the STAAR stock and the market index Nasdaq Composite Jan 1, 2018–Nov 2, 2022. The total monthly return for the stock amounted to 256% whereas for market index, the total monthly return for the Nasdaq index was 58%. The average yearly return was 52% for the STAAR stock while for the market index Nasdaq Composite it was 12% during the 5-year period of analysis. The stock was trading at $15.5 on Jan 1, 2018. The price of stock increased to $154 by Aug 1, 2021, and then further fell to $70 by Nov 2, 2022.

Table 4 lists the holding period return for stock, the index, and excess returns. The analysis is based on the assumption of a holding period of 1 year.

The STAAR stock performed very well in the year 2018 and 2020 with excess returns of 114% and 95%. In the year 2022, both the stock and the market index had negative returns.

Operating Performance Analysis

Table 5 shows the profitability ratios and leverage position of the company during the period 2018–2021.

The average net margin, ROE, and ROA during the period 2018–2021 were 6.90%, 7.34%, and 5.60%, respectively. The average debt-equity ratio was 0.07. The company has low leverage indicating that the company has less debt intensity and the capacity to borrow is quite high.

Table 6 gives the financial highlights of STAAR Surgical during the period 2018–2021. The values are given in millions of dollars.

The analysis based on average during the period shows that the total assets, total equity, and total revenues increased by 27%, 25%, and 24%, respectively. The average growth rate of net income was 146% while the short investments increased

Table 4 Holding period return

Year	STAAR	Nasdaq Composite	Excess returns
2018	103%	−10%	114%
2019	−2%	23%	−25%
2020	135%	41%	95%
2021	−11%	20%	−31%
2022(till Oct)	−3%	−26%	23%

Table 5 Profitability ratios and leverage

Ratios	2018	2019	2020	2021
Net margin%	4.01	9.35	3.62	10.63
ROE%	5.67	9.61	3.31	10.75
ROA%	4.22	7.5	2.54	8.12
DER	0.04	0.06	0.06	0.12

Table 6 Financial highlights

	(In millions of dollars)			
Financial highlights	2018	2019	2020	2021
Total assets	167.3	207.5	257.4	345.8
Short-term investments	103.9	120	152.5	199.7
Total equity	132.4	159.9	197.2	258.6
Total revenue	124	150.2	163.5	230.5
Total operating expenses	84.9	100.1	111.6	145.3
Net income	5	14	5.9	24.5
Market cap	1410.30	1576.40	3679.60	4356.50
Enterprise value	1311.70	1466	3538	4188.80

Table 7 Economic value

Year	2020	2021
Profit before income tax	8.3	31.3
Income tax	2.36	6.80
Net operating profit after tax (NOPAT)	5.94	24.50
Stockholder equity	197.2	258.6
Long-term debt	0	0
Total capital employed	197.2	258.6
WACC	6.49%	4.79%
Capital charge	12.80	12.39
Economic value	–7	12

by 25%. The total expenses grew by 20% on an average basis. The market capitalization and enterprise value increased by 55% and 57%, respectively. The source of data is annual reports and gurufocus.com

Table 7 gives the estimation of economic value for the company during the years 2020 and 2021. The values are given in millions of dollars.

The economic value of the company in the year 2021 was estimated at $12 million.

References

1. https://www.staar.com/
2. https://investors.staar.com/investor-resources-and-faqs/financials/default.aspx#financial-year
3. https://s24.q4cdn.com/405935222/files/doc_downloads/gov_docs/2022/04/2022-Sustainability-Report-(final).pdf

Case 15 Neurocrine Biosciences

Neurocrine Biosciences is a neuroscience-focused, biopharmaceutical company that focusses on development of novel mechanisms to treat intractable diseases related to neurological, neuroendocrine, and neuropsychiatric disorders. The diverse portfolio of the company includes FDA-approved treatments for tardive dyskinesia (TD), Parkinson's disease, endometriosis, uterine fibroids, and late-stage clinical programs in multiple therapeutic areas of neurology, neuroendocrinology, and neuropsychiatry. The company is also focusing on research trials related to schizophrenia and major depressive disorders. Neurocrine Biosciences has marketed INGREZZA® (valbenazine) as the first FDA-approved drug for the treatment of tardive dyskinesia in the United States since 2017. There is a significant opportunity for growth for the company as the estimation suggests that there are 500,000 undiagnosed and untreated patients with Tardive Dyskinesia in the United States.

In 2020, the company launched ONGENTYS® (opicapone) in the United States to treat Parkinson's disease. The strategy of the company involves commercialization of the product portfolio, research efforts toward discoveries related to segments such as neurology, neuroendocrinology, and neuropsychiatry along with acquiring rights for commercial products and drug development molecules. A significant portion of total net product sales of the company is accounted by INGREZZA which amounted to $1.1 billion in the year 2021. The company also receives royalties at tiered percentage rates on products launched by collaborative partners AbbVie (formerly Abbott).

The company has 12 clinical development programs which are in the mid-to-late stages of clinical trials. The disease schizophrenia, which affects up to 3.5 million people in the United States, is one of the leading causes of disability worldwide. There is a clear unmet need for improved pharmacological approaches as approximately 30% of patients with schizophrenia do not properly respond to antipsychotic therapy. The organization has grown from 100 people in 2015 to 1110 people in 2022 and all employees are based in the United States.

© The Author(s), under exclusive license to Springer Nature Switzerland AG 2024

B. R. Kumar, *Rising Stars*, Management for Professionals,
https://doi.org/10.1007/978-3-031-50032-9_15

Product Pipelines

INGREZZA(valbenazine) is the first FDA-approved drug for the treatment of tardive dyskinesia. Tardive dyskinesia is a movement disorder which is characterized by uncontrollable abnormal and repetitive movements of the face, torso and or other body parts. The net product sales from INGREZZA totaled $752.9 million in the year 2019, $993.1 million in the year 2020, and $1.1 billion in the year 2021. In 2015, the company out-licensed the rights of valbenazine to Mitsubishi Tanabe Pharmaceutical Company in Japan and select Asian markets.

ONGENTYS (Opicaone) was launched as an FDA-approved add-on treatment drug to levodopa/carbidopa in patients with Parkinson's disease. ONGENTYS is a once daily peripheral COMT inhibitor that is utilized to prolong the duration of effect of levodopa, the primary treatment option for Parkinson's disease. ONGENTYS is the first and only FDA-approved once daily COMT Inhibitor for Parkinson's disease. ORILISSA (elagolix tablets) is a royalty-bearing product for the company. This oral medication product is used for the management of endometriosis pain in women. The company had out-licensed the global rights of elagolix to AbbVie in the year 2010. Endometriosis affects nearly 200 million women worldwide, including more than 10 million women in the United States. ORIAHNN is the first FDA-approved non-surgical, oral medication drug used for the management of heavy menstrual bleeding associated with uterine fibroids in pre-menopausal women and the company had out-licensed the global rights to Abbvie. The company also has a pipeline of investigational therapies related to Neurology, Neuroendocrinology, and Neuropsychiatry.

Strategic Growth Perspectives

The business strategy of the company is centered around commercialization of the product portfolio. The company has invested in distribution and reimbursement capabilities in order to commercialize its marketed products and product molecules. The specialty salesforce of the company consisting of 350 experienced sales professionals is involved in educating healthcare professionals, psychiatrists, and neurologists. These sales professionals are divided into three dedicated sales teams which focus on psychiatry, neurology, and long-term care. The company focusses on retaining commercial rights for certain products with a concentrated prescriber base and well-defined patient population. Neurocrine Biosciences has multiple programs in different stages of research and development. The focus areas are Neurology, Neuroendocrinology, and Neuropsychiatry. The company takes a portfolio-based approach to manage its pipeline of molecules. For technical and commercial success, the company also focuses on internal resources for development of innovative therapies. The company is placed in a strong financial position with $1.2 billion in cash and investments as of September 2022. The company also selectively acquires rights to commercial products and programs in all stages of clinical development to capitalize on commercial and drug development capabilities. The company also

Table 1 Strategic alliances

Year	Partnerships and collaborations
2010	Neurocrine Biosciences entered into an exclusive worldwide collaboration with AbbVie to develop and commercialize elagolix for women's health. Under the terms of the agreement, AbbVie is responsible for future development and commercialization.
2015	Neurocrine Biosciences entered into an exclusive collaboration and licensing agreement with Mitsubishi Tanabe Pharma Corporation for the development and commercialization of valbenazine in Japan and other select Asian markets.
2017	Neurocrine Biosciences acquired the exclusive US and Canadian rights to ONGENTYS® (opicapone) from Portela & CA, S.A.
2018	AbbVie received US FDA approval for ORILISSA® (elagolix) to treat pain associated with endometriosis.
2019	Neurocrine Biosciences entered into a strategic collaboration with Voyager Therapeutics focused on the development and commercialization of Voyager's gene therapy programs.
2019	Neurocrine Biosciences entered into a license and collaboration agreement with Xenon to identify, research, and develop sodium channel inhibitors.
2020	Neurocrine Biosciences acquired the global rights to NBI-827104 from Idorsia. NBI-827104 is a potent, selective, orally active, and brain penetrating T-type calcium channel blocker to treat patients with, being developed to treat pediatric patients with pediatric epileptic encephalopathy.
2020	Neurocrine Biosciences entered into a strategic collaboration with Takeda Pharmaceutical Company Limited to develop and commercialize compounds in Takeda's early-to-mid-stage psychiatry pipeline.
2021	Neurocrine Biosciences entered into a strategic collaboration and licensing agreement with Sosei Group Corporation to develop novel muscarinic receptor agonists for the treatment of schizophrenia, dementia, and other neuropsychiatric disorders.

Source: https://www.neurocrine.com/investors/partners-and-collaborators/

entered into collaboration and license agreements for enhancing drug development and commercial capability. The company owns a portfolio of the United States and other patents and patent applications. The company relies on third-party manufacturers for the production of INGREZZA and other product candidates. In 2022, the company entered into a strategic partnership with Heptares Therapeutics to expand the clinical pipeline for psychiatry disorders. In the year 2021, Mitsubishi Tanabe Pharma Corporation received approvals for marketing authorization for valbenazine for the treatment of tardive dyskinesia in Indonesia, Singapore, South Korea, and Thailand.

Table 1 highlights the partnerships and collaborations of the company.

Competition

The company faces competition in the development and marketing of its products from academic institutions, government agencies, research institutions, biotechnology, and pharmaceutical companies. The competitors might have greater financial resources, expertise in R&D, manufacturing, preclinical testing, conduct of trials, and obtaining regulatory approvals. New drug development or improved treatment options by competitors also have competitive effects on the company. The competitor product for INGREZZA (for disease Tardive Dyskinesia) is AUSTEDO marketed by Teva Pharmaceuticals. There are several clinical development stage programs that target tardive dyskinesia and other movement disorders. The drug for the treatment of Parkinson's-ONGENTYS competes with FDA-approved COMT inhibitors. The products ORILISSA and ORIAHNN compete with several FDA-approved products for treatment of endometriosis and uterine fibroids.

Risk Perspectives

The ability to produce revenues from products such as INGREZZA depends on the ability to continue to successfully commercialize INGREZZA and secure adequate third-party reimbursement. The commercial success of INGREZZA or ONGENTYS will depend upon the acceptance of those products as safe and effective by the medical community and patients. The sustainability of profitability will be a factor as government and third-party payers impose sales and pharmaceutical pricing controls on the products or limit coverage. Health pandemics or epidemics can cause significant disruption in the operations of third-party manufacturers, CROs, and other third parties. The company currently has no manufacturing capabilities and depends on third-party manufacturers. If the performance of third-party manufacturers is below expectations, then the clinical trials and product introductions may be delayed and result in cost escalation. Some of the core technologies and drug candidates are licensed by third parties. The company might lose the rights for those technologies or drug candidates if any terms of these licenses are violated. Changes in tax laws or regulations may have a material adverse effect on the company's business, cash flows, financial condition, or results of operations. The success of the firm also depends on the company's ability to protect its intellectual property trade secret preservation and prevention of infringement on proprietary rights from third parties. Healthcare reform measures and other legislative initiatives could adversely affect the business of the company.

ESG Initiatives

The Board of Directors and its committees oversee risk in the business with a focus on financial risk, legal/compliance risk, scientific/clinical development risk, and strategic risk. The percentage of women on board is 33%. The Board of Directors annually reviews the independence of each of the directors. The Nominating & Corporate Governance Committee of the Board of Directors has oversight of the Compliance Program. The success of the human capital investments is evidenced by the low employee turnover. The 1 and 3-year voluntary turnover rates were 10% and 6%, respectively. As a part of its Diversity, Equity, and Inclusion Initiatives, Neurocrine Biosciences hired its first Director of Diversity, Equity, and Inclusion. The goals of Biosciences DEI initiatives include focus on recruitment of

Table 2 Acquired in process research and development expenses

Year	2019	2020	2021
R&D expenses	$154.3	$164.5	$105.3

Table 3 Comparative wealth creation

Year	2018	2019	2020	2021
Book value of equity	481	637	1126	1374
Market value of equity	6484	9918	8962	8083
BV as percent of MV	7.4%	6.4%	12.6%	17.0%
Average	10.9%			

underrepresented communities and implementation of mentoring and internship programs for Neurocrine Biosciences employees and students. The company conducts annual outreach programs to promote more inclusive hiring practices for veterans and disabled members of society. The company also sponsors local youth programs. The company is the corporate sponsor of SD Squared and the Ocean Discovery Institute. In the year 2021, the company donated $2 million to a local San Diego food bank. The company has developed and implemented a comprehensive Quality System that focuses on product safety and quality aspects of Good Manufacturing Practices (GMP), Good Laboratory Practices (GLP), and Good Clinical Practices (GCP). These are essential systems required by the regulatory authorities. As part of the company's commitment toward the ethical use of animals in biomedical research, all animal studies are carefully reviewed by an Institutional Animal Care and Use Committee. Neurocrine Biosciences is a member of the American Chemical Society Green Chemistry Institute Pharmaceutical Roundtable whose mission is to catalyze the implementation of green chemistry and green engineering in the global pharmaceutical industry. By applying green chemistry principles in developing the second generation of INGREZZA manufacturing, the company reduced cycle time spent in production and achieved a 65% reduction in waste and water use. In 2021, over 92% of the hazardous waste was recycled via fuel blending prior to recovery or by recovery/reclamation for reuse. In 2021, the company will be shifted to a new San Diego-based campus which will be LEED Silver eligible.

Table 2 gives the R&D expenses for the company in recent years. The values are in millions of dollars.

Stock Performance Analysis

Table 3 highlights the book value and market value of the company along with the excess value created. The values are given in millions of dollars.

The market value peaked in the year 2019. The average book value as a percent of market value was only 10.9% during the period 2018–2021. The market value was approximately 15.5 times the book value in the year 2019. In 2021, the market value was 5.88 times the book value of the company.

Five-Year Stock Return Analysis

The 5-year return analysis during the period Jan 2018–Oct 2022 shows that stock had a total monthly cumulative return of 81% compared to 31% accounted by the NASDAQ biotechnology index. The average annual return for the Neurocrine Biosciences was 17% compared to 6% for NASDAQ biotechnology index for the 5-year period, 2018–2022. The stock which was trading at $77 in Dec 2017 increased to $124 by Oct end 2022 signifying an increase of 1.38 times.

Table 4 shows the holding period return for Neurocrine stock and biotechnology market index during the period 2018–2022. The analysis is based on the assumption of holding period of 1 year during the past 5 years.

The Neurocrine stock performed extremely well compared to the market index in the year 2022 with excess return of 59%. In 2019 too, the excess holding period return for stock over market index was 12%. In the years 2018, 2019, and 2022, both the stock and index registered negative returns.

Financial Performance Analysis

Table 5 gives the financial highlights of the Biosciences during the period 2018–2021. The values are given in millions of dollars.

Table 4 Holding period returns

Year	Neurocrine Biosciences	NASDAQ Biotech Index	Excess returns
2018	−16%	−15%	−1%
2019	22%	10%	12%
2020	−4%	33%	−37%
2021	−22%	−6%	−16%
2022(till Oct)	57%	−2%	59%

Table 5 Financial highlights

	(In millions of dollars)			
Financial highlights	2018	2019	2020	2021
Total assets	993	1306	1735	2073
Short-term investments	651	671	801	711
Total equity	481	637	1126	1374
Total revenue	451	788	1046	1134
Total operating expenses	405	554	708	911
Net income	21	37	407	90
Market cap	6484	9918	8962	8083
Enterprise value	6221	9743	8573	7812

Table 6 Profitability and leverage ratio

Ratios	2018	2019	2020	2021
Net margin%	4.68	4.69	38.94	7.9
ROE%	4.95	6.62	46.2	7.17
ROA%	2.33	3.22	26.79	4.71
DER	0.81	0.78	0.37	0.32

The average growth rate analysis during the period 2018–2021 reveals that the total assets, total equity, and total revenues increased by 28%, 44%, and 39%, respectively. The total expenses increased by 39% during the period of analysis. There was a huge fluctuation in the growth rate of net income. The market capitalization and enterprise value increased by 11% and 12%, respectively.

Table 6 gives the profitability ratios and leverage ratio of Biosciences during the period 2018–2021.

The average net margin, ROE, and ROA during the period 2018–2021 were 14%, 16.24%, and 9.26%, respectively. The average debt-equity ratio was 0.57.

References

1. https://www.neurocrine.com/
2. https://www.neurocrine.com//assets/2022/11/NBIX-Q3-2022-Earnings-Presentation-Final-10.31.22-1.pdf
3. https://neurocrine.gcs-web.com/static-files/6033a874-ed8c-479b-8aa0-32ae8142a5d5

Case 16 Fortinet

Fortinet is a global leader in cybersecurity and networking solutions which provides services for enterprises, communication and security service providers, government organizations, and small businesses. Fortinet was founded in the year 2000 by Ken Xie, the former president and CEO of NetScreen. The company is headquartered in Sunnyvale, California. For over 20 years, Fortinet has been the driving force in the evolution of cybersecurity, networking, and security convergence. The network security solutions of the company are the most deployed, patented, and validated in the industry. The proprietary FortiOS operating system provides the foundation for the operation of FortiGate network security appliances. In 2002, Fortinet established the FortiGuard Labs as the elite cybersecurity threat intelligence and research segment of the company. FortiGuard labs maintain real-time threat intelligence and innovative prevention tactics and tools across the Fortinet Security Fabric.

The Fortinet Security Fabric platform provides broad, integrated, and automated protections against the digital attack. The company is ranked one in terms of the most security appliances shipped worldwide with more than 615,000 customers. The Fortinet NSE Training Institute offers one of the largest and broadest training programs for cyber training and career opportunities. Fortinet is the market leader involved in the development of the custom security processing unit (SPU). Each day Fortinet FortiGuard Labs uses proven Artificial Intelligence (AI) and Machine Learning (ML) systems to process and analyze more than 100 billion events daily related to real-time intelligence for customers. Fortinet has made a mark in cybersecurity innovation through the combination of FortiOS purpose-built SPU technology and AI-powered threat intelligence. The Fortinet flagship enterprise firewall platform, FortiGate provides a broad array of next-generation security and networking functions. Majority of the Fortune 500 companies are customers of Fortinet. It is the only cybersecurity company that is included in the NASDAQ 100 and S&P500.

The company generated revenues of $3.34 billion and a net income of $606.8 million in the year 2021. The market capitalization of the company was $38.3 billion as of September 2022. Its technological leadership in the market is evident through

© The Author(s), under exclusive license to Springer Nature Switzerland AG 2024

B. R. Kumar, *Rising Stars*, Management for Professionals,
https://doi.org/10.1007/978-3-031-50032-9_16

the fact that the company has nearly 3X times more patents than comparable network security companies. The R&D investments of the company amounted to $341.4 million in the year 2020 and $424.2 million in the year 2021. As of December 31, 2021, the company had 1255 US and foreign-issued patents and 254 pending US and foreign patent applications. The company employees are spread over the regions of the Americas, EMEA, and APAC. The APAC region consists of Japan, India, and other regions in Asia. By December 31, 2021, the company employed 10,195 people of which 30% were employed in the United States and the rest 70% outside of the United States.

Business Focus Areas

Convergence/Security-Driven Networking

The security-driven networking solutions facilitate convergence of networking and security to provide next-generation firewall, software defined wide area network, LAN edge (Wi-Fi and switch), and secure access service edge. The majority of the product sales of the company are accounted from the FortiGate network security appliances. FortiGate network security appliances have a broad set of built-in security and network features and functionalities which include firewall, next-generation firewall, secure web gateway, data leak prevention, virtual private network, and wireless controller and wide area network.

Zero Trust Access

Zero Trust Access solutions provide visibility, control, and automated event responses to secure Internet of Things ("IoT") and operational technology (OT) devices. Zero Trust Access solutions include FortiNAC, FortiAuthenticator, FortiClient/EDR, and FortiToken.

Adaptive Cloud Security

The virtual firewall and other software products of the company provide security to individual, hybrid cloud, multi-cloud, and virtualized data center environments. The secure SD WAN of the company automates the deployment of an overlay network across different cloud networks. The cloud security portfolio of the company secures applications which include email and web. Fortinet cloud security products are deployed in major cloud environments such as Alibaba Cloud, Amazon Web Services, Google Cloud, IBM Cloud, Microsoft Azure, Oracle Cloud, and VMWare Cloud. Fortinet also offers managed IPS and Web application firewall rules delivered by FortiGuard Labs.

AI-Driven Security Operations

Fortinet offers a range of products and services that help security operations center (SOC) teams to identify, investigate, and remediate potential incidents whereby cybercriminals bypass prevention-oriented controls. Fortinet Security Fabric cybersecurity mesh platform solutions automatically provide security intelligence which enables organizations to protect against cyber security threats.

Security as a Service

FortiGuard security subscription services are provided as an add on to products and solutions to customers by FortiGuard Labs. The FortiGuard services provide protection for users and applications which include services for IPS, web, video, domain name system filtering, audio/visual, and cloud sandbox along with IoT and OT security.

Support and Professional Services

Fortinet offers technical support, FortiOS updates, and extended product warranty through its FortiCare support services. The company also offers a range of advanced services which include premium support, professional services, and expedited warranty replacement.

Products

The core product offerings consist of FortiGate firewall product family and non-FortiGate products. The non-FortiGate products consist of Fortinet Security Fabric cybersecurity mesh platform, email security, cloud security, endpoint protection, and other products. The FortiGate hardware and software licenses are sold with a set of FortiGate broad security services and enabled by FortiGuard Labs.

FortiGate

FortiGate offers a broad set of security and networking functions which include firewall, intrusion prevention, anti-malware, VPN, application control, web filtering, anti-spam, and WAN acceleration. FortiGate is available as hardware or virtual appliance. There are over 35 models in the FortiGate product family.

Fortinet Security Fabric Cybersecurity Mesh Platform and Non-FortiGate Products

The Fortinet Security Fabric cybersecurity mesh platform offers products that provide network security, endpoint security, cloud security, web-based application security, identity and access management, sandbox protection, and email security. The Fortinet Security Fabric cybersecurity mesh platform consists of products such as FortiAnalyzer, FortiAP, FortiClient, FortiEDR/XDR, FortiGate-VM, FortiMail, FortiManager, FortiSandbox, FortiSwitch, FortiToken, and FortiWeb.

Services

FortiGuard Security Subscription Services and FortiCare Technical Support Services are the main service providers. The company also sells FortiGuard and FortiCare services as bundles which consolidate security services into packages such as Advanced Threat Protection, Unified Threat Protection, and Enterprise Protection.

The company outsources the manufacturing of security appliance products to different contract manufacturers and original design manufacturers. Approximately 83% of the hardware is manufactured in Taiwan. Some of the components in the products like specific CPUs are sourced from Intel Corporation, network chips from Broadcom Inc., Marvell Technology Group and memory devices from Intel, Adata Technology Co Ltd., etc.

Competitive Advantage

The company focusses on providing sustainable security technologies, diversifying cybersecurity talent, and aims to promotion of sustainable business across the value chain. The Security fabric is organically developed, highly integrated, and automated cybersecurity platform. In the traditional method, the networking or security problem is solved by finding a solution for a specific challenge. In the context of network expansion, the problems are complex. Fortinet addressed this challenge by converging networking and security features in a single operating system. Its operating system termed FortiOS is the most deployed and mature OS in the industry. This system reduces complexity, improves operational efficiency, and lowers TCO. The marketing strategy of the company focusses on the criticality of cybersecurity platform adoption and convergence of security and networking solutions.

Competition

The principal competitive factors in the markets include product security performance, technological expertise, compliance with standards and certifications, and price of products and services. The major competitors for Fortinet include Barracuda Networks, Inc., Check Point Software Technologies Ltd., Cisco Systems, CrowdStrike Holdings, F5 Networks, Forcepoint LCC, Juniper Networks Inc., Palo Alto Networks Inc., and Sophos Group Plc.

Risk Analysis

The profitability of the company depends upon the ability to attract and retain new end customers and sell additional products and services to existing end customers. The risk factors include component shortages, product inventory shortages, pandemics, supply chain disruptions, international trade disputes, power outages, labor disruption, and international conflicts. Fortinet is subject to regulation by various federal, state, regional, local, and foreign governmental agencies with respect to environmental laws, consumer protection laws and data privacy laws, and others. Fortinet depends on third-party channel partners for all its revenues. Moreover, a small number of distributors account for a large percentage of revenues and gross accounts receivable. The underperformance of partners will adversely impact the performance of the company. The company relies significantly on revenues from FortiGuard and other security subscription and FortiCare technical support services and the company faces revenue risk if the sources of income from these services decline. The company faces a number of risks associated with international sales and operations as majority of revenue from sales to distributors, resellers, and end customers originated from outside of the United States. The growth of the company depends on its ability to increase sales of its products to large and medium-sized businesses and service providers. The market for network security products is intensely competitive and the company faces competition from different cybersecurity markets. The company is susceptible to manufacturing delays as it depends on several third-party manufacturers to build its products. The business of the firm is subject to the risks of warranty claims, product returns, product liability, and product defects.

Sustainability Initiatives

Fortinet is a founding member of the Cyber Threat Alliance (CTA) and the World Economic Forum (WEF) Center for Cybersecurity. The company also works with public, private, and industry partners worldwide, including Europol, NATO, and INTERPOL, to share intelligence, stop threats, and combat cybercrime. The company aims to reduce the cybersecurity skills gap with the aim to train 1 million people by the year 2026. Through leveraging the latest technologies such as Artificial Intelligence (AI), Machine Learning (ML), and Deep Learning technologies, Fortinet have developed product and services which analyze millions of malware samples per day and provide intelligent threat detection. Fortinet has formed a strategic partnership with Schneider Electric to provide cybersecurity solutions to address the unique needs of OT networks. Fortinet has partnered with Linksys to provide enterprise-class network security for work from home employees. Fortinet solution also contributes toward the educational goals of students through its partnership with Linksys Homework for education initiatives. For innovative initiatives, the company has partnered with industry associations and groups such as 5GACIA, European Telco Standards Institute (ETSI), International Society of Automation (ISA), MEF, and Wi-Fi Alliance. In the year 2021, 87% of employees completed 2021 Infosec-Awareness Compliance training for data privacy. In the year 2021, the company published its first environmental policy to establish a global standard for Fortinet's approach to managing environmental impacts. Fortinet aims to achieve carbon neutrality by 2030 using renewable energy, energy, and carbon efficiency methodologies. The company's owned facilities are run on 100% renewable electricity. In 2021, the company has initiated steps to track water usage and waste in its sites. The radiant cooling system used in Fortinet's new headquarters, for example, saves 76,800 gallons per year compared to a standard cooling tower.

In 2021, the company appointed an external corporate sustainability consultancy to conduct the first material assessment for evolving a methodology to understand the requirements of ESG reporting standards. The sustainability reporting is guided by the GRI and SASB standards. The sustainability strategy is guided by UN SDGs. Fortinet's internal CSR Committee was created to assist the Social Responsibility Committee of the Board in overseeing Fortinet's corporate social responsibility, including ESG matters. As of December 31, 2021, one-third members of the board of directors were women. Approximately 56% of the board of directors was from underrepresented communities as defined by California's Assembly Bill 979. The cross-functional Ethics Committee meets quarterly and promotes initiatives to ensure a culture of ethics and integrity.

Stock Performance Analysis

Table 1 shows the comparative cumulative returns for Fortinet stock and comparative indexes S&P500 index and the Nasdaq Computer Index during the period 2016–2021. The analysis assumes that $100 was invested on December 31, 2016, in the stock or index including reinvestment of dividends.

Fortinet stock's holding period wealth increased by 1093% compared to 113% increase in S&P 500 Index and 315% in NASDAQ Computer index. The average growth rate of returns for Fortinet stock was 68% compared to 17% and 35%, respectively, for the market index S&P 500 and NASDAQ Computer.

Table 1 Comparative cumulative returns

Year	2016	2017	2018	2019	2020	2021
Fortinet	$100	$145.00	$234.00	$354.00	$493.00	$1193.00
S&P 500 Index	$100	$119.00	$112.00	$144.00	$168.00	$213.00
NASDAQ Computer	$100	$139.00	$134.00	$201.00	$301.00	$415.00

Table 2 Comparative book and market value

Year	2018	2019	2020	2021
Book value of equity	1010	1342	856	782
Market value of equity	11,959	18,331	24,136	58,223
BV as percent of MV	8.4%	7.3%	3.5%	1.3%
Average	5.2%			

Table 3 Holding period returns

Year	Fortinet	NASDAQ Computer Index	Excess returns
2018	53%	−10%	63%
2019	39%	38%	1%
2020	29%	44%	−16%
2021	148%	36%	112%
2022(till Oct)	−21%	−33%	12%

Table 2 shows the comparative book value and market value of the company during the period 2018–2021. The values are given in millions of dollars.

The average book value was 5.2% of the market value of the company. In 2020 and 2021, the market value was 28 times and 74 times that of book value of the firm.

Five-Year Stock Return Analysis

The period of analysis is from Jan 2018 to Nov 4, 2022. The stock which was trading at $8 per share in Dec 2017 increased by approximately 5 times to trade at $47 per share by Nov 4, 2022. The total monthly cumulative returns for the Fortinet stock during the period 2018–2022 was approximately 209% compared to the 75% return generated by market index NASDAQ Computer Index (IXCO). The average annual returns for the stock was 43% compared to 15% accounted by the NASDAQ Computer Index.

Table 3 shows the holding period return for the Fortinet stock, market index NASDAQ Computer Index, and the excess returns. The holding period is assumed to be 1 year.

The stock had the best performance in the year 2020 where the excess return over the market index was 112%. The market index performed better compared to the stock in the year 2020. Both the stock and market indexes registered negative returns in the year 2022.

Financial Performance

Table 4 shows the financial highlights of the company during the period 2018–2021. The values are given in millions of dollars.

Table 4 Financial highlights

	(In millions of dollars)			
Financial highlights	2018	2019	2020	2021
Total assets	3078	3879	4045	5919
Short-term investments	1650	2066	1837	2552
Total equity	1010	1342	856	782
Total revenue	1805	2163	2594	3342
Total operating expenses	1120	1306	1533	1913
Net income	335	332	489	607
Market cap	11,959	18,331	24,136	58,223
Enterprise value	16,265	22,299	56,676	36,399

Table 5 Profitability and leverage ratio

Ratios	2018	2019	2020	2021
Net margin%	18.56	15.34	18.83	18.16
ROE%	41.87	28.2	44.44	74.1
ROA%	12.55	9.54	12.33	12.18
DER				1.26

Table 6 Economic value

Year	2020	2021
Profit before income tax	542.00	628.00
Income tax	53.22	14.07
Net operating profit after tax (NOPAT)	488.78	613.93
Stockholder equity	856.00	782.00
Long-term debt		988.00
Total capital employed	856.00	1770.00
WACC	5.89%	4.39%
Capital charge	50.42	77.70
Economic value	438.36	536.23

The average growth rate analysis for the period 2018–2021 reveals that total assets, cash, and short-term investments grew by 26% and 18%, respectively. The total revenues and net income grew by 23% and 24% on average basis. The market capitalization and enterprise value increased by 75% and 76%, respectively. The total expenses increased by 20% during the above period. The data was sourced from gurufocus.com and annual reports.

Table 5 analyses the performance and leverage ratio of the company during the period 2018–2021.

The 4-year average net margin, ROE, and ROA for Fortinet were 17.72%,47.15%, and 11.65%, respectively.

Table 6 illustrates the estimation of the economic value for Fortinet in the years 2020 and 2021. The WACC calculation is taken from gurufocus.com. The values are given in millions of dollars.

The economic value increased from $438.36 million to $536.23 million in 2021 compared to the previous year.

References

1. https://www.fortinet.com/
2. https://www.fortinet.com/content/dam/fortinet/assets/brochures/FortinetBroch.pdf
3. https://investor.fortinet.com/
4. Annual Report 2022
5. https://www.fortinet.com/content/dam/fortinet/assets/reports/fortinet-sustainability-report-2021.pdf

Case 17 Jefferies Group

Jefferies is a major independent US headquartered global full-service integrated investment banking and securities firm. Jefferies Group LLC ("Jefferies Group"), the largest subsidiary, was established in 1962. The year 2022 marked Jefferies Group's 60th anniversary. The company own a legacy portfolio of businesses and investments. Jefferies is involved in the business of investment banking, capital markets, and asset management. Jefferies is ranked eighth globally and seventh in the United States across all investment banking product. The company is ranked seventh globally in equity underwriting and eighth globally in equities cash trading. Jefferies is ranked No. 1 in market share in 2021 for secondary market trading of Investment Companies. In 2021, the company registered $4.4 billion record in investment banking net revenues which marked an 84% increase compared to the previous year.

Over the period 2018–2021, the company has generated significant excess liquidity from operations and sales of merchant banking businesses. Over a period approximately $3.9 billion was returned to shareholders. This included 127 million shares repurchased at an average price of $21.55 per share. The net income increased by 118% to $1.7 billion in the year 2021 up from the prior year. In 2021, approximately $490 million including share repurchases of $267 million was returned to shareholders. The company owns about 56% of Linkem, the largest fixed wireless broadband service provider in Italy with approximately 650,000 subscribers. Vitesse Energy is the company's 97% owned consolidated subsidiary which acquires, invests, and monetizes non-operated oil and gas interests and royalties. By November 30, 2021, the net book value of the company's investment in real estate businesses was $476.9 million. By 2021, the company employed 5556 employees throughout the world.

Table 1 provides a snapshot of the comparative growth of the company in over two decades.

Table 2 gives the net earnings trend during the period 1990–2021.

© The Author(s), under exclusive license to Springer Nature Switzerland AG 2024

B. R. Kumar, *Rising Stars*, Management for Professionals,
https://doi.org/10.1007/978-3-031-50032-9_17

Table 1 Growth trend

Values in million dollars	2000	2021	Growth	CAGR
Investment banking net revenues	$91	$4423	47.7x	20.30%
Jefferies group net revenues	$617	$7044	10.4x	12.30%
Net earnings of Jefferies Group	$55	$1619	28.4x	17.50%
Jefferies group period number of employees	1014	4508	3.4x	7.40%

Source: Annual Report 2021

Table 2 Net earnings trend

Values in million dollars	1990	1995	2000	2005	2010	2015	2020	2021
Net earnings	$7	$29	$55	$157	$240	$183	$879	$1619

Source: Annual Report 2021

Strategies

The future growth of Jefferies will be propelled by the segments of investment banking, capital markets businesses, and Leucadia Asset Management alternative asset management platform. Jefferies group have meaningful operating leverage as reflected by its net earnings growth trend. The Group's net revenues increased by 126% in 2021 compared to the year 2019.

Jefferies Group has made a substantial investment in human capital. In 2022, the number of Managing Directors was 278 representing an increase of 24% from the previous year. The Group headcount increased by 15% in the year 2021. The investment banking business market share has grown exponentially from 0.1% in 2000 to 4% of the market by 2021. In 2021, the Investment Banking business was approximately $4.4 billion.

Jefferies has a flat structure and an entrepreneurial culture that encourages employee stakeholders to find innovative ways to serve the clients. The company has entered into key partnership with different institutions such as MassMutual, Berkshire Hathaway, and Sumitomo Mitsui Financial Group (SMFG). Jefferies Group have strengthened its wealth/asset management, insurance/reinsurance, and equity underwriting businesses and established a strategic equity transaction and private capital advisory group. The company has also expanded outside the United States in regions such as France, Spain, Central and Eastern Europe. The Joint Venture of Jefferies Finance (JFIN) with MassMutual facilitated gains for the company in terms of record-setting underwriting volumes and corresponding fees. The strategic alliance with SMFG enabled JFIN to increase the scale of transactions. Jefferies Finance (JFIN) is in the process of transforming its direct lending business model to a third-party fund management to offer customized solutions to investors.

In July 2021, Jefferies entered into a strategic alliance with Sumitomo Mitsui Financial Group, Inc., Sumitomo Mitsui Banking Corporation, and SMBC Nikko Securities Inc. These together are referred to as SMBC Group. This alliance is expected to assist in highly accretive growth in corporate and investment banking sectors. This partnership is expected to help the company to expand the US leveraged finance business and explore M&A opportunities in Japanese market.

Business Segments

Investment Banking and Capital Markets

This segment primarily serves institutional investors, corporations, and government entities and focus on investment banking, equities, and fixed income. Investment banking provides a full range of financial advisory, equity, and debt underwriting services. The company has over 1200 investment banking professionals operating in regions of Americas, Europe, and Asia Pacific. The industry coverage groups of the segment consist of sectors such as Consumer; Energy; Financial Services; Healthcare; Industrials; Technology, Media and Telecommunications; Real Estate, Gaming and Lodging; Financial Sponsors; and Public Finance. The product coverage groups of the business segment include advisory involving M&A and other corporate restructuring such as divestitures, strategic ventures, and corporate defense equities along with equity and debt underwriting. The company also focus on structuring, underwriting, and distributing public and private debts which includes investment-grade debt, high-yield bonds, leveraged loans, municipal debt, mortgage-backed and other asset-backed securities, and liability management solutions.

Corporate Lending

Jefferies Finance is a 50–50 joint venture partnership between Jefferies Group and Massachusetts Mutual Life Insurance Company which structures, underwrites and syndicates senior secured loans to corporate borrowers and manages third-party investments for syndicated and direct lending loans. Jefferies Finance operates through the two business lines of Leveraged Finance Arrangement and Portfolio and Asset Management. The Portfolio and Asset Management collectively is referred to as Jefferies Credit Partners is composed of three registered Investment advisors namely Jefferies Finance, Apex Credit Partners LLC, and JFIN Asset Management LLC which act as a private credit platform to manage proprietary and third-party capital related to comingled funds, separately managed accounts, and collateralized loan obligations.

Equities Segment

The equity segment services are organized across the three geographical regions of Americas, EMEA and Asia Pacific. The clients are institutional market participants such as mutual funds, hedge funds, investment advisors, pension and profit-sharing plans, and insurance companies. The company earn commissions or income by executing and clearing transactions related to equity and equity-related products, including common stock, American depository receipts, global depository receipts, exchange-traded funds and over-the-counter equity derivatives, convertible, and other equity-linked products and closed-end funds. The equity research segment covers 2800 global companies.

The Equity Finance business segment provides financing, securities lending, and prime brokerage services. The prime brokerage services are provided to hedge funds, money managers, and registered investment advisors. The finance segment provides finance to clients' securities positions through margin loans which are collateralized by securities, cash or other acceptable liquid collateral.

Wealth Management

The wealth management services are provided to meet the needs of high net worth individuals, private equity, and venture funds.

Fixed Income

In fixed income capital markets, the company assists clients with sales and trading of investment-grade corporate bonds, the US and European government and agency securities, municipal bonds, mortgage-backed and asset-backed securities, leveraged loans, consumer loans, high yield and distressed securities, emerging markets debt, interest rate, and credit derivative products. Jefferies LLC is a primary dealer in fixed income market designated by the Federal Reserve Bank of New York. Through repurchase agreements, the company act as an intermediary between borrowers and lenders of short-term funds. The company also makes principal investments in private equity and hedge funds managed by third parties.

Real Estate

The real estate services are provided through Real Estate Berkadia Commercial Mortgage Holding LLC ("Berkadia") which is Jefferies Group's 50/50 joint venture with Berkshire Hathaway, Inc. Berkadia provides capital solutions, investment sales advisory and mortgage servicing for multifamily and commercial real estate. It is also involved in the origination of commercial real estate loans for multifamily housing units on behalf of Fannie Mae and Freddie Mac, the government mortgage agencies in the United States. Berkadia also facilitate origination and provide brokerage services for non-government agency programs related to commercial/ multifamily mortgage loans.

Asset Management

Through the Leucadia Asset Management (LAM) arm, Jefferies manages and provide services to a diverse group of alternative asset management platforms across a wide range of investment and asset classes. Affiliated managers of LAM offer a range of investment strategies to institutional clients. LAM products are offered to pension funds, insurance companies, sovereign wealth funds, and other institutional investors worldwide. The investment products offered consists of multi-manager products, niche equity long/short strategies, and credit strategies.

CSR Initiatives

The company has taken initiatives for the promotion of employee engagement, diversity, equity, and inclusion. The company has implemented a number of policies and measures focused on non-discrimination, sexual harassment prevention, health and safety, and training and education. The company has internal partnership with eight Employee Resource Groups for promoting a diverse, and inclusive workplace. In July 2021, the company appointed two new female directors to the Board of Directors. The Board of Directors have established an Environmental, Social and Governance ("ESG") Oversight Committee to oversee the sustainability matters related to company's businesses. Approximately 30% of board became diverse by the year 2021. The company is committed to net zero energy across the businesses and achieved 100% carbon neutrality for its operations by purchasing carbon offsets and RECs equivalent. By purchasing carbon offsets, Jefferies was able to fund carbon-reduction initiatives associated with reforestation, wind farms, and landfill gas-capture programs. The company has conducted firm-wide ESG training program led by a global ESG working group. During 2021, the company supported nearly 400 non-profit organizations with charitable donations amounting to approximately $30 million. Jefferies has a Whistle Blower Policy in place that includes procedures for receiving and investigating complaints as well as the protection of whistleblowers.

Risk Factors

The business operations of the company involve significant credit risk. The company is involved in the execution, settlement, and financing of different customer and principal securities and derivative transactions. The company faces counterparty or customer non-performance risks as these activities are transacted on a cash, margin, or delivery versus payment basis. The company manages counterparty risks by establishing and monitoring credit limits, collateral, and transaction levels daily. Maintenance of credit ratings is critical for the group's businesses. The company is also exposed to market risk as the value of assets and liabilities will be adversely affected by changes in market conditions. The company may be adversely affected by changes in or the discontinuance of Interbank Offered Rates. Any adverse changes in the businesses or investments in a particular industry will negatively impact the financial operations of the company. The company also faces economic environment risks, legal, legislation, and regulation risks.

Stock Performance Analysis

The data for analysis was taken from yahoo finance and gurufocus.com.

Table 3 gives the comparative book and market value of the company during the period 2018–2021. The values are given in millions of dollars.

The average book value as percent of market value was approximately 140%. The market value was only 0.59 times and 0.85 times of market value in the years 2020 and 2021.

Five-Year Stock Return Analysis

The 5-year stock return was compared with the S&P 500 financial index returns during the period Nov 2017–Nov 2022. Jefferies stock which was trading at $24.8 during Nov 2017 was trading at $37.5 by Nov 2022.The stock price increased by 1.5 times during the above period of analysis. The cumulative monthly returns for Jeffery stock was 73.2% during the period 2017–2022 whereas for the S&P 500 financial index, the cumulative monthly returns were approximately 33%. The 5-year average return for the Jefferies stock was 15% whereas for S&P 500 financial index, the return was 7% approximately.

Table 4 highlights the holding period return for the stock and index.

Table 3 Book and market value comparison

Year	2018	2019	2020	2021
Book value of equity	10,231	9705	9529	10,679
Market value of equity	8834	6095	5677	9152
BV as percent of MV	115.8%	159.2%	167.9%	116.7%
Average	139.9%			

Table 4 Holding period return

Year	Jefferies	S&P 500 financial index	Excess returns
2018	−36%	−20%	−16%
2019	10%	19%	−9%
2020	14%	−1%	15%
2021	66%	35%	31%
2022(till Oct)	2%	−8%	11%

In year 2021, the excess return for the stock was 31%. In most of the years of analysis, the market index registered negative returns.

Operating Performance Analysis

Table 5 gives the financial highlights of the company during the period 2018–2021. The values are given in millions of dollars.

The average growth rate of total assets, revenues, and net income was 9%, 22%, and 186%, respectively. The market capitalization increased by 8% while the enterprise value increased by 87%, respectively.

Table 6 shows the profitability and leverage position of Jefferies during the period 2018–2021.

The average net margin, ROE, and ROA was 12.77%, 9%, and 1.71%, respectively, during the period 2018–2021. The average debt equity ratio was 1.93.

Table 7 illustrates the calculation of the economic value for the company. The values are given in millions of dollars.

The economic value has increased from $540.25 million in 2020 to $1293.05 million in 2021.

Table 5 Financial highlights

	(In millions of dollars)			
Financial highlights	2018	2019	2020	2021
Total assets	47,169	49,460	53,118	60,404
Short-term investments	22,075	7679	9055	10,755
Total equity	10,231	9705	9529	10,679
Total revenue	5049	5359	6956	9040
Total operating expenses	888	1163	1237	1436
Net income	172	965	775	1674
Market cap	8834	6095	5677	9152
Enterprise value	7171	16,505	16,635	18,441

Table 6 Profitability and leverage position

Ratios	2018	2019	2020	2021
Net margin%	3.4	18	11.14	18.52
ROE%	1.68	9.68	8.06	16.57
ROA%	0.37	2	1.51	2.95
DER	1.94	1.85	2.08	1.86

Table 7 Estimation of economic value

Year	2020	2021.00
Profit before income tax	1067.00	2254.00
Income tax	298.65	576.80
Net operating profit after tax (NOPAT)	768.35	1677.20
Stockholder equity	856.00	782.00
Long-term debt	10163.00	10651.00
Total capital employed	11019.00	11433.00
WACC	2.07%	3.36%
Capital charge	228.09	384.15
Economic value	540.25	1293.05

References

1. https://www.jefferies.com/CMSFiles/Jefferies.com/Files/Sustainability/Jefferies-2022-ESG-Report.pdf
2. https://www.jefferies.com/

Case 18 Medpace Holdings

Medpace Holdings is a global full-service clinical contract research organization (CRO), which offers all phases of clinical development services to the biotechnology, pharmaceutical, and medical device industries. Medpace is involved in the mission of development of safe and effective medical therapeutics across major segments such as oncology, cardiology, metabolic disease, endocrinology, central nervous system, and antiviral. Medpace is headquartered in Cincinnati, Ohio. By September 2022, the company employed about 5000 people across 40 countries. The company is one of the world's leading clinical contract research organizations by revenue. The company offers an operating model of full-service Phase I–IV clinical development services. CROs provide a comprehensive range of product development services for Phase I–IV clinical trials. The company generate fees through the performance of services specified in the customer contracts. The contract scope and pricing are based on either a fixed fee or unit of service model which includes services offered by third parties.

The company aims to expand the market share in the growing Phase I–IV CRO market. The company conduct clinical trials across all major therapeutic areas such as Oncology, Metabolic Disease, Cardiology, Antiviral and Anti-infective (AVAI), and Central Nervous System (CNS). The solutions provided by Medpace are for Early Phase Clinical Research, Phase II-III Clinical Research, RWE-Late Phase Clinical Research, and Medical Device and Diagnostics.

Markets and Clinical Development Services

The medical department of the company focus on therapeutic leads and provide strategic direction for study design and planning, train operational staff, work with primary investigators, provide medical monitoring and undertake regulatory obligations. The clinical trial managers (CTMs) lead all aspects of study execution and coordinate functional team members. The CTMs use the Clin Trak, the proprietary information system for clinical trials with its standard operating procedures

© The Author(s), under exclusive license to Springer Nature Switzerland AG 2024
B. R. Kumar, *Rising Stars*, Management for Professionals,
https://doi.org/10.1007/978-3-031-50032-9_18

(SOPs) and enable CTMs to access real time study metrics. The global study start up staff conducts trial start up activities such as study documentation, submission processes to institutional review boards or ethics committees. The patient recruitment and retention department identify patients. The clinical research associates (CRAs) provide site management services which include in house, onsite, and virtual monitoring. The CRAs receives comprehensive hands on training, field-based training based on clinical research department core rotations and specific training. Medical writers use the services of the company's medical experts, biostatisticians, and other members of the study team to develop study protocols, clinical, and statistical study reports. With respect to biometrics and data sciences, the company provide high quality data collected during clinical trials which supports regulatory submissions for NDAs or Biologics License Application for approval by FDA. The safety and pharmacovigilance group of the company collects, evaluates, analyzes, and reports safety information. The core laboratory services offer imaging and cardiovascular core laboratory services. The Bioanalytical laboratory delivers method transfer, development, validation, sample analysis, and metabolite screening and identification of pre-clinical and clinical biological samples. The company employ an integrated sales and marketing team to sell the services to biotechnology, pharmaceutical, and medical device companies.

Competitive Environment

The CRO industry is fragmented and consists of several narrowly focused service providers with global capabilities. The challenges are in terms of cost involved to develop strong therapeutic areas, expertise to manage complex clinical programs, infrastructure to support global programs and expertise to deal with regulatory approvals in various jurisdictions. The major CRO competitors are Laboratory Corporation of America Holdings, ICON plc, Syneos Health, Inc., PAREXEL International Corporation, PPD Inc., and IQVIA Holdings.

Regulatory Aspects

The development of drugs, biologics, and medical devices is highly regulated in the United States. The services offered by CRO are subject to varying regulatory requirements to ensure the quality and integrity of the pre-clinical and clinical trial processes. FDA has the primary authority to regulate these activities in the United States. The manufacturer or sponsor of the clinical product candidate must file an Investigational-10-New Drug Application (IND) with the FDA before the commencement of human clinical trial in the United States. The application must give the results of pre-clinical tests along with other analytical data. Clinical trials conducted outside the United States are subject to the laws and regulations of the country where the trials are conducted. Within the EU, these requirements are enforced by the EMA and requirements may vary slightly from one-member state to another. With reference to health information privacy, the confidentiality of personal health information, for example, patient-specific information collected for clinical trails is heavily regulated in the United States and other countries. CROs are also subject to laws and regulations related to protection of environment and human health and safety in different regions for disposal of hazardous substances and wastes, the cleanup of contaminated sites. The company uses a combination of confidentiality policies, non-disclosure agreements and other contractual arrangements to protect intellectual property rights related to its proprietary methodologies, analytics, systems, and other technologies.

Risk Factors

On account of clinical trials, the company could be held liable for injury or death claims. The company faces business and economic risks as potential loss, delay, or non-renewal of contracts would adversely affect the business results of the company. Medpace faces technical and cybersecurity risks for its information systems. The business is subject to international economic, political, and other risks which would adversely affect the operations of the company. The company has challenges due to industry risks as outsourcing trends in biopharmaceutical industry would affect the operating results. The company may be adversely impacted by healthcare reform and potential additional regulatory reforms. The company also faces structural and organizational risks as the Chief Executive Officer controls a substantial amount of outstanding common stock (17.2%) and conflict of interests might arise.

Corporate Social Responsibility Initiatives

The company's code of business conduct and ethics serves as the foundation of its global compliance and ethics program. The company have a zero-tolerance policy with respect to human trafficking, child labor, or modern slavery. The company also conducts business in accordance with anti-bribery/anti-corruption policies. The company follows in letter and spirit Good Clinical Practice (GCP) in its operations which is the common benchmark for clinical trials globally. The company also comply with all standards applicable to conduct clinic trials ethically. Approximately 64% of management globally are women and 67% of all associates globally are women.

Performance Measures

The key financial and performance metrics used are net new business awards and backlog. New business awards represent the value of anticipated future net revenue that has been recognized in backlog during the period. In 2021 and 2022, the net new business awards amounted to $1610.4 million and $1175.0 million, respectively.

Backlog represents anticipated future net revenue from net new business awards that have been initiated but not yet completed. The backlog amounted to $1541.7 million and $1997.1 million in years 2020 and 2021, respectively.

Stock Performance Analysis

Table 1 shows the book value and market value trend during the period 2018–2021. The values are given in millions of dollars.

The average book value was only 20.9% of the market value of Medpace during the period 2018–2021. The market value was 6x and 8x of the book value during the years 2020 and 2021.

Five-Year Stock Price Performance

The data source was Yahoo Finance. The period of analysis was taken as Dec 2017–Nov 14, 2022. The stock traded at $36.25 on Dec 1 2017. By Nov 11, 2022, the stock price was $221 representing an increase of 6x. The total cumulative monthly return for Medpace Holding was approximately 232% while for the market index-Nasdaq Health care index, the total return was 32%. The average yearly return for the Medpace stock during the period Dec 2017–Nov 2022 was 47%. During the same period, the Nasdaq health index had registered average yearly return of 7%.

Table 2 analyzes the holding period return for Medpace Holding and Nasdaq Healthcare index during the period 2018–Nov 2022. The analysis assumes holding period of 1 year.

The Medpace stock registered its best performance in the year 2021 when the stock had holding period return of 64% compared to −9% returns received by the

Table 1 Book value and market value trends

Year	2018	2019	2020	2021
Book value of equity	590	726	806	953
Market value of equity	1888	3032	4944	7837
BV as percent of MV	31.3%	23.9%	16.3%	12.2%
Average	20.9%			

Table 2 Holding period returns

Year	Medpace	NASDAQ Healthcare index	Excess returns
2018	44%	−11%	55%
2019	31%	12%	19%
2020	63%	35%	27%
2021	64%	−9%	72%
2022(till Nov)	2%	−5%	6%

NASDAQ Healthcare index. In 2020, the excess return for stock over the index returns was 27%.

Operating Performance

Table 3 highlights the growth trend of the financial variables of the company during the period 2018–2021.The values are given in millions of dollars.

The total assets and total equity increased by 20% and 17%, respectively, on average basis during the period 2018–2021. The average growth rate of revenues and net income was 18% and 36%, respectively, during the above period. The market capitalization and enterprise value increased by 61% and 55%, respectively, on average basis during the period of analysis. The short-term investments in the form of cash and cash equivalents increased by an average of 217% during the period of analysis. The total expenses were fluctuating with an average increase of 5%.

Table 4 shows the performance ratios and leverage of the company.

The average net margin, ROE, and ROA for Medpace Holding was 13.42%, 17.08%, and 10.14%, respectively, during the period 2018–2021. The average debt equity ratio was 0.12.

Table 5 illustrates the estimation of economic value of Medpace Holding in the year 2020 and 2021. The values are given in millions of dollars. The weighted average cost of capital (WACC) values are taken from gurufocus.com.

The economic value has increased from $59.48 million in 2020 to $84.64 million in 2021.

Table 3 Operating performance highlights

	(In millions of dollars)			
Financial highlights	2018	2019	2020	2021
Total assets	968	1143	1391	1660
Short-term investments	23	132	278	461
Total equity	590	726	806	953
Total revenue	705	861	926	1142
Total operating expenses	114	118	112	130
Net income	73	100	145	182
Market cap	1888	3032	4944	7837
Enterprise value	1944	2945	4782	7506

Table 4 Profitability and leverage

Ratios	2018	2019	2020	2021	Average
Net margin%	10.39	11.67	15.7	15.92	13.42
ROE%	13.39	15.27	18.98	20.68	17.08
ROA%	7.63	9.52	11.48	11.92	10.14
DER	0.14	0.06	0.14	0.14	0.12

Table 5 Economic value

Year	2020	2021
Profit before income tax	169	202
Income tax	23.22	20.02
Net operating profit after tax (NOPAT)	145.78	181.98
Stockholder equity	806	953
Long-term debt	115	131
Total capital employed	921	1084
WACC	9.37%	8.98%
Capital charge	86.30	97.34
Economic value	59.48	84.64

References

1. https://www.medpace.com/
2. https://investor.medpace.com/financial-information/annual-reports
3. https://investor.medpace.com/static-files/2f6112e6-cbcc-4dbc-bc70-f8fa9971fea7

Case 19 Green Brick Partners

Green Brick is a diversified homebuilding and land development company which operates in the US states of Texas, Georgia, and Florida. Green Brick Partners Inc. is Fortune Magazine's 2021 fastest growing public homebuilder and land developer in the United States. Green Brick is a Delaware corporation incorporated in year 2006. The company commenced operations as a publicly held homebuilding company in year 2014. Green Brick encompasses eight homebuilder brands across four states in the United States. This publicly traded company is listed on NYSE. The core markets of the company are located in the high growth US metropolitan areas of Dallas Forth Worth (DFW), Texas and Atlanta, Georgia, treasure coast area in Florida. Green Brick also own a non-controlling interest stake in a builder in Colorado Springs. The company is involved in all the aspects of the homebuilding process which includes land acquisition and development, entitlements, design, construction, title and mortgage services, marketing and sales, and the creation of brand images at residential neighborhoods and master planned communities. The company manage land risk through underwriting. The subsidiary homebuilders are provided with centralized state of the art operational support. By December 2021, Green Brick Partners owned or controlled approximately 28,600 home sites in high growth submarkets in DFW, Atlanta metropolitan areas and Treasure Coast, in Florida. By December 2021, the company had approximately 540 full-time employees.

In the year 2021, the company completed a $100 million tranche of 8 year privately placed unsecured notes in a club deal structured by Prudential Capital at 3.25% interest rate. In 2021, with a debt to total capital of 27.7%, Green Brick has become one of the lowest leveraged public builders.

© The Author(s), under exclusive license to Springer Nature Switzerland AG 2024
B. R. Kumar, *Rising Stars*, Management for Professionals,
https://doi.org/10.1007/978-3-031-50032-9_19

Brands and Services

The Green Brick Partners subsidiary homebuilder network is composed of seven consolidated homebuilders and in another homebuilder, the company have 49.9% ownership interest.

Table 1 gives the number of units sold, revenues, and price range in the year 2021 under different brands of Green Brick.

Table 2 highlights the product mix of each brand.

Table 1 Brand volume

Brand	No. of units	Revenues in 2021	Price range
Trophy Signature Homes	1053	$472.3 million	$300,000 to $930,000
CB JENI Homes	593	$205.9 million	$240,000 to $550,000
Normandy Homes	202	$105.9 million	$430,000 to $880,000
The Providence Group of Georgia	501	$257.2 million	$360,000 to $1,000,000
Southgate Homes	158	$117.6 million	$590,000 to $1,390,000
Centre Living Homes	76	$36.0 million	$370,000 to $750,000
GHO Homes	251	$110.6 million	$240,000 to $1,620,000
Challenger Homes	484	$196.0 million	$270,000 to $770,000

Source: Annual Report 2021

Table 2 Product mix

Brand	Single family homes	Town homes	Condominiums
Trophy Signature Homes	✓		
CB JENI Homes		✓	
Normandy Homes	✓		
The Providence Group of Georgia	✓	✓	✓
Southgate Homes	✓		
Centre Living Homes	✓	✓	
GHO Homes	✓	✓	
Challenger Homes	✓	✓.	

Source: Annual Report 2021

Brands

Trophy Signature Homes

The brand of Trophy Signature Homes was established in the year 2018 to cater to the need for high quality affordable homes with unique blend of functionality and design in the Dallas Fort Worth market. In early 2022, Green Brick made its debut into Austin market through the Trophy Signature Homes.

CB JENI Homes

CB JENI Homes has built new townhomes in the Dallas Fort Worth location since 2009 for lifestyle conscious homebuyers who look to buy moderately sized home with elegant architecture, low maintenance, and level of service. This brand has grown to become DFW's largest townhome builder.

Normandy Homes

Normandy Homes were first built in 2012.These homes are characterized by traditional design and enduring value. Green Brick have earned over 20 home building awards for this brand.

Southgate Homes

Southgate Homes is known for its generous features and upgrade options. It is recognized as one of the top luxury production homebuilders in the Dallas Fort Worth metroplex.

Providence Group of Georgia

This brand is the leading lifestyle builder of Green Brick partners based in Atlanta and offers a variety of home styles which include single family homes, townhomes, and midrise condominiums. These homes are built at desirable locations which offer home owners great access to major interstates, dining, shopping, and recreation.

Centre Living Homes

Centre Living Homes brand is a premier, single family, and townhome builder in DFW, Texas. The high-density housing developments offers world class architecture with smart home technology and its rooftop decks offers panoramic view of the city.

In 2021, Centre Living Homes expanded its product offering to include suburban areas of DFW metroplex and different regions in Texas.

GHO Homes

GHO Homes has been involved in construction of homes for over 25 years. This brand offers homes to communities on Florida's Treasure coast. GHO has built award winning homes through their St. Lucie Collection series of homes. The GHO Tailor Made program facilitates home buyers to customize their homes with numerous plan options and upgrades. All GHO Homes are characterized by time tested quality materials, latest design features, and energy efficient components.

Challenger Homes

Challenger Homes is the major new homebuilders offering home site in Colorado Springs and Fort Collins. Challenger Homes have features such as elegant floorplans with large open spaces, quality craftsmanship, and energy efficient solutions.

Services

Green Brick Mortgage offers finances to homebuyers through their preferred lender referral program in Dallas Fort Worth, Texas, and Atlanta. BHome Mortgage is a full-service mortgage banking company which associate with REALTORS®, homebuilders and its clients. It was launched in the year 2020. Bhome offers a wide array of mortgage products including conventional, fixed-rate, ARMs, FHA, VA, Texas Veteran Housing Assistance Program, and first-time homebuyer program. Green Brick Title help with finances for new homeowners to close on their new homes and works closely with REALTORS®, banks, land brokers, builders, developers, and mortgage companies. Green Brick Partners have an equity stake of 49.99% equity interest in Green Brick Mortgage LLC, a 49% equity interest in BHome Mortgage LLC, and 100% ownership stake in Green Brick Title LLC.

Growth Strategy

The company focusses on the strategies to deliver superior designs, broad product ranges, and enhanced homebuying experience. The homebuilding projects offered by Green Brick include townhomes, patio homes, single family homes, and luxury homes. The company focuses on growth through acquisitions of builders and organic growth. The company acquired 80% majority ownership of GHO Homes.

The company have scaled up its business through the growth of Trophy Signature Homes. In 2021, the Signature brand homes increased by 53% compared to the previous year and had constructed 1281 homes in 2021. In 2022, the company announced plans to expand Trophy into Austin and Texas markets with development of over 850 homesites. The current strategy focusses on disciplined investment strategy with the prudent use of leverage for investment in land acquisition, development, and homebuilding businesses. The target debt to total capitalization ratio is in the range of 30%–35%. By December 31, 2021, the debt to total capitalization ratio was 27.7%. The land strategy of the company involves a hybrid model of desirability and affordability of homesites in the market. In DFW and Atlanta, Green Brick Partners leverages its relationship with land sellers and municipalities to get lot positions in attractive markets. Green Brick also focuses on acquiring lots in affordable outskirt communities to cater to the need of entry level buyers to purchase quality homes at value-oriented pricing. The strategic plan in 2022 aims to spend over $285 million to develop lots for about 4700 finished homesites to subsidiary homebuilders across 43 communities. The company is focusing on markets in sunbelt and sunbelt adjacent states which offer attractive residential real estate investment characteristics in terms of economic growth rate, population growth, migration patterns, and housing affordability. Green Brick Partners gives importance for creating sustainable products and enhancement of green features in its home portfolio. The land inventory strategy aims to provide the company with multiyear supply of lots for all the brands for future home building with the focus on limiting any excess supply. Green Brick also stresses the importance of the development of entitled parcels in communities where the sales of lots and homes is completed within 24–60 months from the initiation period of sales. This limits the exposure to land development and land risks. The Green Brick partners offer a preferred lender referral program for home buyers. Homeowners are offered an 8 to 10-year warranty for structural concerns; 2 years for electrical, plumbing, heating, and air conditioning; and 1 year for defects and products used. Advertising is basically done through digital channels which include real estate listing sites, paid search, display advertising, social media, and email marketing.

Land Acquisition and Development

Sustainability Development Strategy

Sustainability initiatives are adopted for the land development strategy ranging from site selection to design and development. The company conducts environmental impact studies and take different sustainable approaches to protect the environment. Some of the measures include stormwater management measures, earthwork strategies to minimize slope and soil disturbance and initiatives to protect wildlife and natural landscape. With a goal to reduce carbon emissions, the company-initiated action plan to benchmark its homes against the Home Energy Rating System (HERS) index. The company has also implemented strategies to increase operational efficiencies and minimize impact on environment. Many of its homes feature fully encapsulated spray foam insulation, tankless water heaters, and low-flow fixtures. 100% of the Green Brick Homes across all brands use double pane E insulated windows. One-hundred percent of the homes utilize LED lighting. The company's Operation FINALLY HOME provides mortgage free home and home modifications to wounded, ill, and injured military veterans and their dependents. The company is subject to various local, state, and federal statutes, ordinances, rules and regulations with respect to zoning, building design, construction, and local regulations which impose restrictive zoning and density requirements. The company is also subject to a variety of local, state, federal statutes, rules and regulations related to protection of environment.

Risk Factors

The residential homebuilding industry is cyclical and highly sensitive to changes in general economic conditions. The COVID-19 pandemic has negatively impacted the global economy and disrupted global supply chains. Adverse changes in financial conditions of buyers and sellers of properties, competition from other real estate operating companies, unanticipated increases in expenses, insurance costs and real estate assessment, changes in the enforcement of laws, regulations and government policies, environmental, zonaling, and tax laws are risk factors for Green Brick Partners. Building sites have inherent dangers. Land development and homebuilding industries have significant health and safety risks. The specific environmental laws which apply to any given homebuilding or development site vary according to different factors such as site's location, its environmental condition and uses of the site. Actions for compliance of these environmental laws may result in delays and incur substantial costs. Any failure in health and safety performance may result in penalties for non-compliance with relevant regulatory requirements. Information technology failures and data security breaches could affect the businesses. Product liability claims, litigation, and warranty claims could adversely affect the business of the company.

Stock Price Performance

The common stock of the company is traded on the New York Stock Exchange under the symbol "GRBK." The company has not paid any dividends since its inception. The stock which was trading at $11.3 in November 2017 was valued at $23 by early November 2022. The stock price increased by 2.05 times during this period. The historical stock data was taken from Yahoo Finance. The total monthly cumulative return for Green Brick stock was 121% during the 5-year period November 18, 2017–November 18, 2022. The average yearly return for the Green Brick stock was 25% during the period November 2018–November 2022. The total cumulative monthly return for the market index Russell 3000 was 46% during the above period. At the same time, the average yearly returns for the market index Russell 3000 was 9% during the above period.

Table 3 Holding period return

Year	Green Brick Partners	Russell 3000	Excess returns
2018	−35%	−7%	−28%
2019	36%	19%	17%
2020	98%	19%	79%
2021	52%	25%	28%
2022(till Nov)	−2%	−13%	11%

Table 4 Comparative market and book value trends

Year	2018	2019	2020	2021
Book value of equity	486	536	663	911
Market value of equity	366	580	1163	1540
BV as percent of MV	132.8%	92.4%	57.0%	59.2%
Average	85.3%			

Table 5 Financial highlights

	(In millions of dollars)			
Financial highlights	2018	2019	2020	2021
Total assets	784	876	989	1422
Short-term investments	38	33	19	79
Total equity	468	523	640	875
Total revenue	624	792	976	1403
Total operating expenses	80	98	112	134
Net income	52	59	114	190
Market cap	366	580	1163	1540
Enterprise value	546	801	1389	1884

Table 3 shows the holding period return for the stock and index Russell 3000 for the 5-year period 2018–2022. The holding period return calculation assumes holding period of 1 year.

Green Brick Partner stock had the best performance in the year 2020 with excess returns of 79% over the market index Russell 3000. In 2021, the Green Brick partners return was twice as compared to the market index Russell 3000. In 2019, the excess return for the stock was 17%.

Table 4 shows the comparative book and market value trend of equity of the company during the period 2018–2022. The values are given in millions of dollars.

The average book value as percentage of market value was approximately 85%. In 2020 and 2021, the market value was 1.75 times and 1.69 times that of book value of the company.

Financial Performance

Table 5 gives the financial highlights of the company. The values are given in millions of dollars.

The average growth rate of total assets and total equity during the period 2018–2021 was 23% and 24%, respectively. The total revenues and net income increased by 31% and 58%, respectively. The cash investments increased by 87% during the above period of analysis. The market capitalization and enterprise value increased by 64% and 56%, respectively, during the above period of analysis. The operating expenses increased by 19% during the above period.

Table 6 shows the profitability ratios and leverage ratio of the company during the period 2018–2021.

The average net margin, ROE, and ROA for the period 2018–2021 was 10.23%, 17.04%, and 10.61%, respectively. The average debt equity ratio for the company was 0.41.

Table 7 illustrates the estimation of economic value for the company. The values are given in millions of dollars.

The economic value has increased from $67.19 million to $96.37 million dollars.

Table 6 Profitability and leverage ratios

Ratios	2018	2019	2020	2021
Net margin%	8.28	7.41	11.65	13.56
ROE%	11.67	11.83	19.55	25.11
ROA%	7.4	7.07	12.2	15.78
DER	0.43	0.46	0.35	0.39

Table 7 Economic value

Year	2020	2021
Profit before income tax	143.00	257.00
Income tax	25.05	52.61
Net operating profit after tax (NOPAT)	117.95	204.39
Stockholder equity	640.00	875.00
Long-term debt	113.00	336.00
Total capital employed	753.00	1211
WACC	6.74%	8.92%
Capital charge	50.75	108.02
Economic value	67.19	96.37

References

1. file:///C:/Users/Admin/Downloads/2021-Annual-Report-Web.pdf
2. https://greenbrickpartners.com/
3. https://investors.greenbrickpartners.com/overview/default.aspx

Case 20 JD.com Inc

The company was incorporated in the British Virgin Islands (BVI) in November 2006 and was redomiciled in the Cayman Islands in January 2014 as an exempted company registered under the laws of Cayman Islands.JD.com Inc. is a major supply chain-based technology and service provider which provides products and services to consumers, third-party merchants, suppliers, and other business partners through its subsidiaries, consolidated variable interest entities (VIEs) and consolidated VIEs subsidiaries. The Group basically operates e-commerce business which include online retail and online market place through its retail mobile apps and www.jd.com website (collectively, JD Platform). JD.com offers services to consumers through online retail for product selection, price, and convenience. The company also facilitate third-party merchants to sell their products on JD Platform. The third-party merchants can fulfill the orders either by themselves or through the Group's logistics services. The Group provides a variety of marketing services to business partners through its proprietary advertisement technology platform. The JD Group also offers integrated supply chain solutions and logistics services which include warehousing and distribution services, express and freight services and other value added services to third parties. These value added services are offered to both third-party merchants and suppliers on JD Platform and other business partners through the company's logistics subsidiary JD Logistics. The company generated total net revenues of RMB576.9 billion, RMB745.8 billion, and RMB951.6 billion (US$149.3 billion) in 2019, 2020, and 2021, respectively. The JD company have a network of 1300 warehouses with an aggregate gross floor area of 24 million square meters. By December 2021, the company had a strength of 298,717 warehouse and delivery personnel. The research and development expenses amounted to US$ 2.563 million in year 2021.

The e-commerce business of the company offers the customers a wide selection of authentic products at competitive prices. The company offers a great online shopping experience through its content rich, user friendly, and highly personalized mobile apps and website www.jd.com. The online market place was introduced in the year 2010 and is continuously expanding its third-party merchants and new

© The Author(s), under exclusive license to Springer Nature Switzerland AG 2024
B. R. Kumar, *Rising Stars*, Management for Professionals,
https://doi.org/10.1007/978-3-031-50032-9_20

products which included premium international brands. The company provides an array of digital marketing services to marketers on its e-commerce platforms like digital branding and performance-based marketing solutions which are powered by AI technology.

The company had 362 million, 471.9 million, and 569.7 million annual active customer accounts in 2019, 2020, and 2021, respectively. The company operates online retail and marketplace e-commerce businesses. The company purchase products from suppliers and sell directly to customers through its online retail business. The firm offer diversified range of product categories through its online retail business which includes electronics products, home appliances, and other general merchandise categories. By December 2021, JD have sourced products from over 40,000 suppliers.

In 2020, the company shares were listed on the Stock Exchange of Hong Kong Limited. During the same period, JD Health International, the Group's Health subsidiary had its initial public offering and were listed on the Stock Exchange of Hong Kong Ltd. In 2021, JD Logistics completed its IPO and got listed on Hong Kong stock exchange. In 2018, the Board of Directors of the company authorized a share repurchase program to buy back US$ 1000 million worth of its ADSs.

Major Subsidiaries

The company have 30 subsidiaries, 5 Consolidated VIEs (Variable Interest Entities) and 6 Consolidated VIEs' Subsidiaries. Consolidated VIEs means those franchise agreements and operator agreements with franchisees that the Parent Borrower had to consolidate in its consolidated financial statements.

JD Logistics is operating as a stand-alone business segment of the company since April 2017. It offers a full spectrum of supply chain solutions and high-quality technology enabled logistics services which ranges from warehouses to distribution which spans across manufacturing to end customers. JD Health focusses on building Internet enabled healthcare ecosystem consisting of providing Internet-based healthcare services to customers. JD Property is the infrastructure asset management and integrated service platform for JD Logistics. In 2021, JD acquired CNLP which is involved in the leasing of storage facilities and related management services in China. JD Industrial Technology Inc. is the subsidiary that gives emphasis for industrial development through supply chain, technology, and services. In 2019, the company acquired 46% stake in Jiangsu Five Star Appliance Co Ltd. which is one of the leading offline retailers of home appliances and consumer electronics in China.

Growth Strategy

The company aims to strengthen its market leadership in e-commerce business by enhancing its supply chain-based technology service capabilities along the principles of sustainable and quality growth. The growth objectives are propelled through investments in logistics infrastructure and supply chain platforms. The company also gives importance to develop innovative online retail channels. In 2019, the company launched Jingxi, an online marketplace channel which addresses the demand of customers in lower tier cities for rich social attributes and curated products. The company gives importance for investment in holistic smart supply chain technology platform based on technology initiatives such as AI, big data, and cloud computing.

The company gives emphasis for strategic alliances and partnership as a part of its growth strategy. JD have strategic collaboration with Walmart on e- commerce and have Walmart and Sam's Club Flagship stores on its platform. The Dada Group had strategic partnership with JD Logistics to provide customers with on demand and last mile delivery services for grocery and fresh products through JD Daojia. The offline fresh food markets arm of the company 7FRESH is experimenting on the omni channel model. In 2014, JD had acquired certain e-commerce businesses and assets from Tencent and established a strategic partnership with Tencent. Tencent, the leading Internet firm in China offers a wide array of Internet services such as social communications, online games, and digital content and payment to online community in China. As of December 31, 2021, Tencent had 1268 million monthly active user accounts for its mobile apps Weixin and Wechat. Tencent offers prominent access points to JD in its mobile apps Weixin and Mobile QQ and provides with traffic and other support system from its key platforms. JD acquired 100% stake in Tencent's Paipai (C2C online marketplace) and QQ Wanggou (B2C online marketplace). In 2016, JD entered into a strategic partnership with Walmart. Walmart subscribed approximately 5% of the total issued and outstanding shares of JD. com. Through the strategic alliance with Walmart, JD acquired the ownership of the Yihaodian marketplace platform assets such as the Yihaodian brand, mobile apps, and websites. JD launched Walmart's Sam's Club Flagship Store and Walmart Flagship, Walmart Global Flagship store, ASDA Flagship Store, etc. on www.jd. com website and JD Worldwide.

In August 2020, JD Logistics acquired a controlling stake in the Kuayue Express Group Co Ltd., the integrated express transportation firm in China. In 2022, JD Logistics entered into agreement to acquire 99.99% stake in the Deppon Logistics Co Ltd. In 2020, the company acquired 36.8% stake in JD Technology. JD formed a strategic partnership deal with Yonghui to strengthen supply chain management capability. By 2021, JD held 13% stake in Yonghui Superstores Co Ltd. In 2018, JD entered into a strategic alliance with Wanda Commercial Properties, the leading developer, owner, and operator of commercial properties in China.

The competitors for JD include major e-commerce companies in China such as Alibaba Group which operates Taobao.com and tmall.com and other traditional retailers in China such as Suning Appliance Company Ltd. which operates suning.com.

By December 31, 2021, the company owned 3300 computer software copyrights in China and had maintained approximately 18,900 trademark registrations inside China and approximately 3200 trademark registrations outside China.

Corporate Responsibility

The company have adopted Digitally Intelligent Social Supply Chain as the technology driver for its sustainability initiatives. The company have focused upon sustainability initiatives to improve rural revitalization, improve social efficiency, and support supply side structural reforms. The company focusses on creating a low-carbon enterprise through environmentally friendly logistics, procurement and facilities. As a part of low carbon and green supply chain initiatives, the company have replaced traditional fuel combustion trucks with new energy vehicles in more than 50 cities in China. As a result, the company was able to reduce about 400,000 tons of carbon dioxide emissions per year. In order to optimize the efficiency of logistics transportation in terms of reduction in the number of vehicles in transit or increase in the full load rate of return vehicles, the company uses big data to carry out real time optimal route and storage network planning. In 2019, the company collaborated with the World Wide Fund for Nature (WWF) to launch the "Giant Panda Friendly Enterprise Alliance." As a part of its poverty alleviation project, the company introduced supportive measures for the development of brands such as Suqian King crabs and increased the transaction volume of local agricultural products by more than 200% in year 2021.

Risk Factors

The revenues and growth prospects of the company depends on the growth of the retail industry sector in China. The company faces intense competition from other players in the ecommerce market. As the business operations are predominantly based in China, the company's operations are subject to complex and evolving PRC laws and regulations. The quality of customer service depends on the safe operations of the regional fulfillment centers, front distribution centers, warehouses, delivery, and pickup stations. The company don't have much control over the storage and delivery of products sold on its online marketplace. Many third-party merchants use their own facilities to store their products and uses their own or third-party delivery systems to deliver their products to customers. The Cayman Islands based holding company do not have equity ownership in its variable interest entities with whom the company maintain contractual arrangements. The failure on part of the variable interest entities to perform its contractual obligations would have a material and adverse effect on businesses of the company.

Stock Market Performance

The stock price performance was analyzed for the 5-year period Dec 1, 2017–Nov 18, 2022. The analysis was based on monthly returns. The data was collected from Yahoo Finance. The JD stock was trading at $49.23 on Jan 1, 2018. By Nov 1, 2022, the stock price increased to $56 reflecting an increase of 1.14 times. The total cumulative monthly return for JD stock during the 5-year period Dec 1, 2017–Nov 1, 2022, was 77%. The market index Nasdaq Composite registered a return of 59% during the above period. The 5-year average return for the JD share was 16% while for the Nasdaq Composite index, the average yearly return was 12%.

Table 1 shows the holding period return for the JD stock and the market index Nasdaq Composite during the period 2018–2022. The analysis is based on 1 year holding period.

The stock registered best performance in the year 2022 with holding period return of 133%. The market index Nasdaq Composite had superior performance compared to JD stock in year 2020. In years 2018, 2021, and 2022, the stock had negative returns.

Table 2 gives the comparative book and market value of the company in millions of dollars during the 5-year period 2017–2021.

The book value was only 27.6% of market value on average basis during the 5-year period 2017–2021. In 2017 and 2020, the market value was seven and four times that of the book value of the company.

Table 1 Holding period return

Year	JD.com Inc	Nasdaq Composite	Excess returns
2018	−57%	−10%	−47%
2019	42%	23%	19%
2020	133%	41%	92%
2021	−21%	20%	−41%
2022(till Nov)	−25%	−22%	−3%

Table 2 Comparative book and market value

Year	2017	2018	2019	2020	2021
Book value of equity	7945.87	11160.88	14346.81	33890.32	38745.86
Market value of equity	59411.61	30427.62	51735.96	136398.83	108986.88
BV as percent of MV	13.37%	36.68%	27.73%	24.85%	35.55%
Average	27.6%				

Financial Performance

Table 3 gives the profitability ratios and debt-equity ratio during the 5-year period 2017–2021.

The average net margin, ROE, and ROA are 1.57%, 9.73%, and 3.62%, respectively, during the period 2017–2021. The average debt equity ratio was 0.25.

Table 4 highlights the financial performance of the company. The values are given in millions of dollars.

The source of data was gurufocus.com. The total assets and total equity increased by 31% and 55% on average basis during the 5-year period 2017–2021. The cash and cash equivalents grew by 63% during the 5-year period 2017–2021. The average growth rate of revenues was 29%. However, the growth rate of net income was highly fluctuating during the 5-year period 2017–2021. The market capitalization increased by 164% in the year 2020 compared to the previous year. The market capitalization decreased for the company in year 2018 and 2021. The growth rate of enterprise value was 36% during the period 2017–2021.

Table 3 Profitability and leverage position

Ratios	2017	2018	2019	2020	2021
Net margin%	0.04	−0.54	2.11	6.62	−0.37
ROE%	0.31	−4.37	17.07	37.45	−1.82
ROA%	0.08	−1.24	5.15	14.87	−0.78
DER	0.46	0.24	0.23	0.17	0.16

Table 4 Financial highlights

	(In millions of dollars)				
Financial highlights	2017	2018	2019	2020	2021
Total assets	27915.88	30385.53	37030.91	64576.94	77953.15
Short term investments	5198.72	5273.04	8779.13	22427.78	29097.55
Total equity	7945.87	11160.88	14346.81	33890.32	38745.86
Total revenue	54955.37	67117.94	82251.59	114049.21	149402.92
Total operating expenses	7705.96	9869.08	10991.2	14660.44	19344.35
Net income	19.53	−361.96	1737.17	7555.09	−558.93
Market cap	59411.61	30427.62	51735.96	136398.83	108986.88
Enterprise value	57876.57	29727.22	48308.74	124007.13	91195.6

References

1. https://ir.jd.com/annual-reports
2. Annual Report 2021

Case 21 Kornit Digital

Kornit Digital was incorporated under the laws of the State of Israel in the year 2002. In 2015, the company had its IPO and shares traded on the Nasdaq Global Select Market under the symbol “KRNT.” Kornit is the leading player in the fast-growing, industrial and mass production, digital direct-to-garment industry. The company has operations in six countries. The company develops, designs, and markets innovative digital printing solutions for the global printed textile industry. The major aim of the company is to become the operating system for on-demand sustainable fashion-the theme for self-expression through textiles in terms of anyone, anywhere, and anytime. The solutions offered by the company are complemented by additional layers of product and services offerings to serve fulfillers and demand generators with the focus on fashion, apparel, and home décor segments of the industry. The company’s business models are based on digital methods of garment, apparel, and home décor finished goods production and decoration. Kornit Digital connect demand generators such as fashion brands, e-commerce platforms, marketplaces, designers, and licensors to the most advanced production capabilities through its operating system for on demand, sustainable fashionX. By December 31, 2021, the company had approximately 1200 active customers around the world. By December 31, 2021, the company had 882 employees. The revenues generated in 2021 amounted to $322 million which represented an increase of 66% compared to the previous year. In 2021, approximately 68% of the revenues were accounted from Americas region and 24.5% were obtained from Europe, Middle East, and Asia region (EMEA). The capital expenditures for the company amounted to $5.4 million, $13.5 million, and $14.5 million in 2019, 2020, and 2021, respectively. By the year 2026, it is estimated that Kornit’s technology will leverage the production of approximately 2.5 billion apparel items in an environmentally sustainable manner. By the end of December 31, 2021, Kornit owned 37 issued patents in the United States and 43 provisional or pending US patent applications. The company also had 29 patents issued in non-US jurisdictions.

© The Author(s), under exclusive license to Springer Nature Switzerland AG 2024

B. R. Kumar, *Rising Stars*, Management for Professionals,
https://doi.org/10.1007/978-3-031-50032-9_21

Industry Environment

The global printed textile industry offers activities in different stages along the value chain for the production of goods for fashion, apparel, home decoration, and soft signage applications. These activities consist of printing on fabric rolls, finished garments, and unsewn pieces of cut fabric. According to Statista, the market value of the global apparel industry is expected to be $1.8 trillion by 2023.The primary drivers for demand in the apparel market is attributed to factors such as increasing per capita, favorable demographics, and changing consumers' shopping habits. The Future of Digital Textile Printing Report 2021 published by Pira suggest that the global value of digital printed textile output is estimated to be $7.9 billion by the year 2026. The pandemic had impacted the fashion industry through unprecedented disruption in supply chain activities. The fashion industry which is heavily reliant on extensive supply chains faced disruptions such as increased shipping costs, shortages in commodities, and materials and long lead times. The two primary methods of screen printing in textile are rotary screen printing and automated carousel screen printing. The modern trend involves consumers seeking new ways to express their identities through unique customized or personalized impressions, styles, and messages. The Facebook data suggest that about 72% of US fashion shoppers believe that at least one form of personalization increases the likelihood of making a purchase. On account of the explosive growth of technology and mobile applications usage, another trend observed is that modern consumers seek solution in a faster time period. The Future of Commerce Trend Report 2022 states that about 68% of online shoppers are influenced by estimated time of delivery and expect either same, one or two-day delivery. According to Statista Report, the same day shipping market in the United States is forecasted to exceed $10.6 billion in the year 2022. The change in consumer behavior trend with respect to instant gratification have led retail brands to leverage the capacity of third-party online stores to meet customer demand for delivery speed and product availability. Fashion influencers are using sustainable bloggers and green living influencers to promote ethical fashion brands and spread ecoconscious messages. According to the Global Web Index study report approximately 60% of the Millennials in the age group of 22–35 years are ready to pay extra for ecofriendly or sustainable products. Digital fashion industry has to evolve sustainable strategies and achieve ever faster speed to market. The industry has to develop innovative solutions to connect with consumers for self-expression via unique graphical and text designs. The industry sector has to invest in an omni channel strategy to enhance their manufacturing productivity, supply chain resilience, and lean inventory management. According to McKinsey's 2022 report, the logistics challenges in fashion industry will intensify in the coming years with global surges in demand conflicting with pressures on freight services, ports, and terminals.

Products

Direct-to-Garment (DTG) Systems is one of the major offerings of the company. In 2019, the core DTG products portfolio was consolidated using the HD technology which enabled the clients of the company to produce retail quality prints with competitive cost per print. In 2019, the company introduced Specialty DTG solutions. In the same year, the company introduced a new and innovative process for printing on dyed polyester. This new solution was introduced to market on a new system from the Avalanche platform—the Avalanche Poly Pro. The Avalanche Poly Pro enabled the production of on-demand customized polyester products without any minimum order quantity requirement. In 2021, Kornit launched a new industrial DTG platform—the Kornit Atlas MAX which is the next generation direct-to-garment printing platform. Direct-to-Fabric (DTF) Systems consists of Presto and Presto Max. The Presto system offers one step DTF printing through a full end-to-end manufacturing process by the combination of a printing system and a drying and curing module. The Presto MAX is the first digital print system to offer white printing on colored fabrics and also decoration capabilities for dark colored fabrics. This system is the most sustainable solution available for direct-to-fabric printing. Kornit NeoPigment™ inks are water based, non-toxic, phthalate free, and free of heavy metals and follow the highest international sustainability standards. DTG systems also have software solutions such as QuickP production software which manages the system operation and prepares image files for print. Kornit services consist of maintenance and support, consulting, and professional services.

Business Analysis

The company develop, design, and market innovative digital printing solutions for the global printed textile industry. The company services the high throughput, Direct-to-Garment (DTG), Direct-to-Fabric (DTF) segments of the printed and decorated textile industry. The solutions provided include proprietary digital printing systems, ink, and other consumables for software and value-added services which enable large scale printing of short runs of complex images and designs on finished garments and fabrics. The solutions offered by Kornit is unique in the sense that they eliminate the need to pretreat fabrics prior to printing and enable to digitally print high quality images and designs on a variety of fabrics in a streamlined and environmentally friendly manner. The industrial and mass production DTG solutions are suited to the needs of mass producers with complex manufacturing requirements. The patented NeoPigment ink and other consumables have enhanced the quality of impressions of digital printing. In 2019 and 2021, Kornit supplemented its original DTG printing technology with Kornit NeoPoly Technology and Kornit MAX technology. In 2021, Kornit introduced the Presto MAX, the first digital print system to offer white printing on colored fabrics to enhance decoration capabilities for dark colored fabrics. Kornit Presto Max offer a sustainable Eco Factory to decrease their carbon footprint, improve productivity, and generate less waste. In 2021, KornitX was established as an operating system for on-demand sustainable fashion. KornitX provides end-to-end solution to connect demand generators and ecommerce channels to global fulfillment network of on-demand manufacturers and fulfillers. KornitX provides solutions for print service providers and demand generators such as brands, creators, retailers, and online commerce platforms.

Strategy

Kornit is digitizing its production floor by investments in technology leadership and solution offering. The company focuses on ongoing investments in research and development, product management solutions, and application development areas to drive innovation and automation. In 2016, Kornit initiated the implementation of a long-term strategy for supporting its installed base with upgrade paths to more advanced systems. In 2019, the company implemented a product refurbishment strategy based on the Avalanche and Storm platforms which enabled the company to expand its product offerings with latest technology capabilities. The company have developed a strong portfolio of intellectual property to cover wet printing methodology, ink formulations, printing processes, and related methods and systems. The company has established KornitX as the virtual layer of the on-demand production workflow which connects the front end with the back end. The company have taken initiatives to expand into different markets. In 2017, it entered into a Master Purchase Agreement with an affiliate of Amazon.com to supply different systems, large quantities of inks and consumables. In 2020 and 2021, Amazon-related revenues were \$21.1 million and \$ 87 million, respectively. The company have competitive advantage to penetrate markets by offering start up brands, private labels, and DTG and DTF printing solutions. The company aims to increase its sales to existing customers by introduction of new digital printing applications and developing new features and functionality of its systems. The company also focusses on investments in its go to market infrastructure across geographies. Since February 2019, Kornit adopted a full direct sales model with the acquisition of customer business assets from Hirsch, the company's primary distributor in the United States and Canada. In 2016, Kornit acquired the digital DTG printing assets of SPSI. The company focusses on development of strategic accounts.

Acquisitions

Inorganic growth is a part of the growth strategy of Kornit Digital. In 2020, Kornit acquired Custom Gateway which is a provider of cloud-based software workflow solutions for on-demand B2B and B2C business models. This acquisition helped Kornit's Konnect platform to improve its visibility and control of print operations in the context of market dynamics and pandemic disruption. The value of the deal was estimated to be $16.9 million. In 2021, the company acquired the assets of Voxel8 which had competitive advantage in terms of advanced additive manufacturing technology for textiles. Voxel8's technology facilitated digital fabrication of functional features with zonal control of material properties. Voxel8 also possess high-performance elastomers adhering to inkjet technology. This deal was valued at $15 million. In 2022, the company announced plans to acquire Germany-based Tesoma which provided cutting edge textile curing solutions. This all cash deal was valued at Euro 11 million.

Risk Analysis

The performance of the company depends on the adoption of digital textile printing to replace the existing methods of printing. The success of the company depends on the capability of the company to introduce new products. The company places heavy reliance on large number of customers including Amazon. The company faces risk due to significant reliance on single source suppliers coupled with global supply chain delays and reliance on third-party manufacturers. The company faces risk with respect to acquisition and integration of companies. The expansion of the company's international operations is accompanied by costs, operational risks, and required regulatory compliance in many jurisdictions.

ESG Initiatives

The company focuses on 22 ESG priorities. The company have set forth sustainability goals like reducing overproduction by1.1 billion apparel items, reduction of greenhouse gas emissions by 17.2 billion kilograms and saving 4.3 trillion liters of water by the year 2026. Another KPI for the achieving sustainability goals is to build and innovate a richer suite of products and tools for expansion of on-demand production. By 2025, the company would establish an evaluation index to enable the clients to track and monitor their water conservation impact. The company aims to perform ESG audits for 20% of the material suppliers by the year 2027. It is planned that by 2030, 70% of all customers will undergo safety training through designated digital portal. By the year 2030, the company will develop and implement a Kornit index for inclusiveness in all partnership with fashion designers. The Supplier Code of Conduct for the three pillars of ESG came into effect in the year 2021. Approximately 63% of the procurement in Israel was made from local sources in the year 2021. With Kornit's on-demand technology, the customers in fashion industry can customize and personalize products more efficiently. The company focusses on diversity of ideas and approaches to promote progress in the fashion industry. Supporting inclusivity is a major sustainable goal for the company.

Stock Performance Analysis

The 5-year monthly return analysis was done for the Kornit stock and market index Nasdaq Composite for the period December 1 2017–November 1, 2022. The data was sourced from Yahoo Finance. The stock which was trading at $16.15 on December 1, 2017 increased to $25.19 representing an increase of 1.68 times. The total cumulative monthly return for Kornit stock was 122% and the average yearly return was 25%. The total cumulative monthly return for market index Nasdaq Composite was half (60%) compared to Kornit stock. The average yearly return for Nasdaq Composite index during the above period of analysis was 12%.

Table 1 shows the holding period return for Kornit stock and Nasdaq Composite market index during the 5-year period 2018–2022. The analysis is based on holding period assumption of 1-year period.

Kornit Digital had superior stock performance in all years in the period of analysis except in the year 2022 when both Kornit stock and market index registered negative holding period return. In 2020, Kornit Digital had an excess return of 72% compared to the market index Nasdaq Composite.

Table 2 gives the comparative book and market value of Kornit during the period 2017–2021. The values are given in millions of dollars.

The average book value as percent of market value was only 20.8% during the 5-year period 2017–2021. In the years 2020 and 2021, the market value was 7.89 and 8.21 times of the book value of the firm.

Financial Highlights

Table 3 shows the financial highlights of the company during the 5-year period 2017–2021. The values are given in millions of dollars.

Table 1 Holding period return

Year	Kornit Digital	Nasdaq Composite	Excess returns
2018	25%	−10%	36%
2019	79%	19%	60%
2020	113%	41%	72%
2021	68%	20%	48%
2022(till Nov)	−76%	−21%	−55%

Table 2 Comparative book and market value

Year	2017	2018	2019	2020	2021
Book value of equity	150.7	179.14	338.3	519.02	919.55
Market value of equity	551.11	656.42	1392.62	4098.96	7554.61
BV as percent of MV	27.34%	27.29%	24.29%	12.66%	12.17%
Average	20.8%				

Table 3 Financial highlights

	(In millions of dollars)				
Financial highlights	2017	2018	2019	2020	2021
Total assets	178.37	214.82	405.47	628.99	1040.88
Short-term investments	18.63	74.13	40.74	125.78	611.55
Total equity	150.7	179.14	338.3	519.02	919.55
Total revenue	114.09	142.37	179.87	193.33	322.01
Total operating expenses	55.69	63.94	74.48	94.53	139.12
Net income	−2.02	12.43	10.17	−4.78	15.53
Market cap	551.11	656.42	1392.6	4098.96	7554.61
Enterprise value	522.44	573.31	1247.5	3757.31	6932.74

Table 4 Profitability and leverage position

Ratios	2017	2018	2019	2020	2021
Net margin%	−1.77	8.73	5.65	−2.47	4.82
ROE%	−1.56	7.54	3.93	−1.12	2.16
ROA%	−1.27	6.32	3.28	−0.92	1.86
DER			0.07	0.04	0.03

The growth trend is analyzed for the 5-year period 2017–2021. The total assets and total equity increased by 57% and 60%, respectively, on average basis during the above period. The total cash investments increased by 212% on average basis though the total cash investments decreased by 45% in 2019 compared to the year 2018. The total revenues increased by 31% on average basis. However, the net income growth rate was highly fluctuating with negative growth rate throughout the period. The market capitalization and enterprise value increased by 102% and 103% on average basis during the above period. The total expenses increased by 26% during the period 2017–2021. The source of data was gurufocus.com.

Table 4 shows the profitability ratios and leverage ratio during the period 2017–2021.

The average net margin, ROE, and ROA were 2.99%, 2.19%, and 1.85%, respectively. All the profitability ratios were highly fluctuating with negative values in 2017 and 2020. The average debt equity ratio was 0.05 during the period of analysis.

References

1. www.kornit.com
2. www.kornit.com/sustainability
3. Kornit Annual Report 2021.
4. https://kornit.com/lp/esg/y2022/kornit_impact_report/

Case 22 Medifast Inc.

Medifast Inc. is one of the fastest growing global company which offers health and wellness services for communities. The holistic approach of the company focusses on offering Lifelong Transformation, One Healthy Habit at a Time. The company offers services through its direct-to-consumer business model.

The OPTAVIA brand of the company offers effective lifestyle solution which focusses on innovative healthy habits through smaller, foundational changes called micro habits. The four pillars of the OPTAVIA program involve Independent OPTAVIA Coaches, OPTAVIA Community, The Habits of Health® Transformational System, and Products and Plans. The OPTAVIA Coaches provide individualized support and guidance to clients for optimal health and wellbeing. The goal of the community is to provide each other with real time connection and support. The Habits of health initiative is a proprietary system which offers guidelines for sustainable healthy lifestyle. The products and plans component provide clinically proven plans and scientifically developed products called "Fuelings" which are recommended by dietitians and physicians. The company have facilitated over 2 million clients to achieve their health goals through a network of approximately 59,800 independent OPTAVIA Coaches who themselves were associated with Medifast initially as clients. OPTAVIA Coaches offer clients advisory with respect to set of healthy eating habits and offer exclusive OPTAVIA branded nutritional products or Fuelings. Fuelings are prepared with high-quality ingredients and are fortified with probiotic cultures, vitamins and minerals. The OPTAVIA client centric coaching model goal is to create an energized health and wellness community. OPTAVIA Coaches are independent contractors who market company's products and services through word of mouth, email, and via social media channels. The operations of the company are carried out through wholly owned subsidiaries such as Jason Pharmaceuticals, Inc., OPTAVIA, LLC, Jason Enterprises, Inc., Jason Properties, LLC, Medifast Franchise Systems, Inc., Seven Crondall Associates, LLC, Corporate Events, Inc., OPTAVIA (Hong Kong) Limited, OPTAVIA (Singapore) PTE. LTD, and OPTAVIA Health Consultation

© The Author(s), under exclusive license to Springer Nature Switzerland AG 2024

B. R. Kumar, *Rising Stars*, Management for Professionals,
https://doi.org/10.1007/978-3-031-50032-9_22

(Shanghai) Co.. The company enhanced safety protocols to comply with guidelines from health officials related to COVID pandemic.

Medifast also develop and market products for weight loss. The market for weight loss was valued at $20 billion in 2021 with an annual growth rate of 6%. According to OPTAVIA estimates, the total potential pool of OPTAVIA clients is estimated to be 175 million people. In 2016, the World Health Organization estimated that approximately 1.9 billion people 18 years and older were overweight worldwide, triple the rate since 1975. The National Centre for Chronic Disease Prevention and Health Prevention Division report suggest that consumers in the United States spend an estimated $147 billion on obesity-related medical conditions. The average annual medical costs for obese people are more than $1400 higher than those of people in a normal weight range. A 2020 study commissioned by Market Data Enterprises in US estimates that the US weight loss market is estimated to be roughly $61.9 billion per year which includes consumer spending on diet foods, drinks, health clubs, fitness centers, workout videos, commercial weight loss programs with medical supervision, etc.

During the year 2021, the company launched two integrated digital apps to facilitate Coaches support their current and future clients to manage their OPTAVIA relationship for health and wellness journey. By end 2021, more than 300,000 users are using these apps in the OPTAVIA community.

In 2021, Medifast launched a pilot called Experience OPTAVIA: Employees on Plan which enables selected team members to participate in health journey supported by Coach and free Fuelings. In 2020, Medifast was awarded a Gold Wellness at Work Award from the Maryland Department of Health Center for Chronic Disease Prevention and Control. The United States is the principal market for the company. In 2019, the company commenced its international operations with entry into the Asia Pacific markets of Hong Kong and Singapore. The demand for weight management products and programs are typically seasonal in nature. Jason Pharmaceuticals Inc., the wholly owned subsidiary is the primary manufacturers of the powder-based products.

OPTAVIA Branded Products and Plans

OPTAVIA branded nutritional products include OPTAVIA essential Fuelings which contain 24 vitamins and minerals with complete protein and no colors or flavors from artificial sources. OPTAVIA Select Fuelings is composed of the Non-GMO line of products with unique flavor profiles and same suite of optimal weight plans. OPTAVIA Coach business kit is another branded product. OPTAVIA branded health and wellness plan facilitate clients to achieve their health goals. OPTAVIA premier service help clients to stay on plan and provides them with discounts on purchased products and free shipping.

Competitive Strength

Medifast support consumers through independent OPTAVIA Coaches of which 90% were clients first. The innovative model of OPTAVIA is client centric and has one sales price to both OPTAVIA Coaches and clients. There is no tiered pricing. The coaches promote holistic wellness program and are not exclusively focused on product sales. The coaches do not hold inventory or manage cash. The coach compensation plan is carefully structured to incentivize coaching. Another competitive advantage for the company is its focus on a unified training system with a common mission.

Competitors

The weight loss industry is competitive in nature and encompasses various weight loss products and programs which include pharmaceutical products, books, self-help diets, dietary meal replacements, app-based health, and wellness monitoring solutions. Med fast's competitors in the general health and wellness diet industry include USANA Health Sciences Inc., WW International, Inc., Nature's Sunshine Products Inc., Herbalife Nutrition Ltd., Simply Good Foods Co., The Hain Celestial Group, Inc., BellRing Brands, Inc., and Beyond Meat, Inc.

Risk Analysis

The company faces challenges from government regulators on account of its direct selling model. The legal and regulatory requirements for direct selling industry are inherently fact based and are subject to interpretation. The future growth depends on Medifast's ability to maximize operational efficiencies across distribution center network. The company rely on third parties for manufacturing and distribution of majority of its products. The company depend on deliveries of ingredients and other products from domestic and foreign suppliers for its non-powder product. Any disruption to its supply chain could materially adversely affect its business operations. The weight management industry is highly competitive and entry of new competitors may significantly affect the business operations of the company. The ability to attract and retain clients depend upon the effectiveness of the OPTAVIA Coaches' advertising and marketing practices.

Social and Environmental Responsibility

The independent OPTAVIA Coaches actively support the communities for healthy wellbeing. In 2018, Medifast launched the philanthropic initiative, Healthy Habits For All to bring healthy habits among people. This initiative also provides free education for children in underserved communities. Through this initiative, the

Table 1 Five-year growth analysis

Year	2016	2017	2018	2019	2020	2021
Medifast	$100	$172.35	$313.84	$283.33	$527.35	$576.87
S&P 500	$100	$121.83	$116.49	$153.17	$181.35	$233.41
2021 peer group	$100	$140.31	$155.90	$132.01	$145.89	$151.63

Source Medifast Annual Report 2021

company had pledged to donate more than $2.5 million to local and national non-profit organization through the year 2023.The company has donated up to 10 million meals for children in underserved communities through its partnership with the nonprofit campaign No Kid Hungry®. The company have ensured that its manufacturing and warehouse locations operate in an environmentally efficient manner. The company utilize cardboard recycling programs and do not use Styrofoam products. In 2019, Medifast established a Vendor Code of Conduct as a part of its environmental sustainability policies. The company ensure that its third-party suppliers and their subcontractors within the supply chain comply with applicable laws, rules, and regulations.

Stock Performance

A $10,000 invested in Medifast during August 2003 would have amounted to $109863.26 by December 2022 registering a growth of approximately 998%.[1]

Five-Year Cumulative Return Analysis

Table 1 illustrates the growth of $100 investment in Medifast stock and S&P 500 Index along with select peer group companies in year 2021. The investment is assumed to be made on December 31st, 2016.The peer group companies include 15 select companies including Blue Apron Holdings, Duluth Holdings Inc., and Farmers Brothers Company.

The 5-year holding period return for Medifast stock was 477% whereas for S&P 500 stock and for peer group the holding period return was 133% and 52%, respectively. The annual 5-year average returns for the Medifast stock was 48% compared to 19% and 10% returns for S&P500 index and peer group based on the wealth created during the period 2016–2021.

[1]https://ir.medifastinc.com/calculator.

Table 2 Holding period returns

Year	Medifast	S&P 500	Excess returns
2018	82%	−11%	93%
2019	−14%	19%	−33%
2020	103%	16%	87%
2021	−11%	28%	−39%
2022(till end Nov)	−39%	−10%	−30%

Table 3 Book and market value

Year	2017	2018	2019	2020	2021
Book value of equity	108.58	109.11	104.83	157.25	202.47
Market value of equity	835.7	1483.74	1289.1	2311.31	2427.92
BV as percent of MV	12.99%	7.35%	8.13%	6.80%	8.34%

Comparative 5-Year Stock Market Performance

The data for analysis was sourced from Yahoo Finance. The stock which was trading at $68 on 1/1/2018 rose to $120 per share by December 1, 2022, registering an increase of over 1.88 times. The total monthly cumulative returns for the Medifast stock was 147% while for S&P 500 Index it was 45% during the period 2018–2022. The average yearly returns for the stock was 30% for the stock during the above period. At the same time, the S&P 500 Index had an average yearly return of 9% during the period 2018–2022.Table 2 gives the holding period returns for the stock and the comparative market index S&P 500 during the 5-year period. The holding period assumes 1 year.

Medifast shares had the best performance in terms of returns during the year 2018 and 2020. Market index S&P 500 registered better performance than Medifast stock in 2019 and 2021. The performance of market index S&P 500 was better than of the stock in year 2022, though both stock and index had negative returns.

Table 3 give the comparative book and market value of Medifast during the period 2017–2021 in millions of dollars.

The book value was only 8.7% of the market value on average basis during the 5-year period 2017–2021. In 2020, the market value was approximately 14.69 times of the book value of the firm.

Financial Performance

Table 4 gives the financial highlights of the company during the period 2017–2021. The values are given in millions of dollars. The data for analysis was taken from gurufocus.com.

The growth rate analysis in terms of averages observe that the total assets and total equity increased by 29% and 19% during the period 2017–2021.The total cash investments increased by 20% during the period 2017–2021. The total revenues and

Table 4 Financial highlights

	(In millions of dollars)				
Financial highlights	2017	2018	2019	2020	2021
Total assets	145.93	169.43	194.65	276.08	398.33
Short-term investments	75.08	81.36	76.97	163.72	104.18
Total equity	108.58	109.11	104.83	157.25	202.47
Total revenue	301.56	501	713.67	934.84	1526.09
Total operating expenses	188.18	310.84	445.82	563.66	911.36
Net income	27.72	55.79	77.92	102.86	164.03
Market cap	835.7	1483.74	1289.1	2311.31	2427.92
Enterprise value	736.86	1382.7	1210.02	2148	2350.92

Table 5 Performance measures

Ratios	2017	2018	2019	2020	2021
Net margin%	9.19	11.14	10.92	11	10.75
ROE%	27.1	51.26	72.84	78.49	91.2
ROA%	20.75	35.38	42.8	43.7	48.64
DER			0.13	0.07	0.16

Table 6 Economic value

Year	2020	2021
Profit before income tax	134.27	216.13
Income tax	31.41	52.11
Net operating profit after tax (NOPAT)	102.86	164.02
Stockholder equity	157.25	202.47
Long-term debt	–	–
Total capital employed	157.25	202.47
WACC	11.07%	11.39%
Capital charge	17.41	23.06
Economic value	85.46	140.96

net income grew by 51% and 58% during the period 2017–2021.The total expenses increased by 49% during the above period. The market capitalization and enterprise value increased by 37% and 41%, respectively.

Table 5 gives the profitability and leverage position of the company during the period 2017–2021

The average net margin, ROE, and ROA during the 5-year period 2017–2021 was 10.60%, 64.18%, and 38.25%, respectively. The average debt-equity ratio was 0.12 during the 3-year period 2019–2021.

Table 6 illustrates the estimation of enterprise value of the company in millions of dollars during the period 2020 and 2021.

The economic value has increased from $85.46 million to $140.96 million.

References

1. https://ir.medifastinc.com
2. Medifast Annual Report 2021.

Case 23 Vertex Pharmaceuticals

Vertex Pharmaceuticals is a global biotechnology company which focusses on specialty markets to create innovative medicines for treating serious diseases like cystic fibrosis. Vertex have a pipeline of investigational therapies to find cure for diseases like sickle cell disease, beta thalassemia, APOL1-mediated kidney disease, type 1 diabetes, pain, alpha-1 antitrypsin deficiency, and muscular dystrophies. The four medicines TRIKAFTA/KAFTRIO, SYMDEKO/SYMKEVI, ORKAMBI, and KALYDECO are used to treat over 83,000 people for cystic fibrosis in regions of North America, Europe, and Australia. As of December 31, 2021, the company had approximately 3900 employees. The common stock of Vertex is traded on Nasdaq Global Select Market under the symbol "VRTX." The company has headquarters in Boston and London.

Strategy for Growth

Vertex focusses on investment in R&D to discover and develop innovative medicines by combining transformative advances in the field of human diseases and the science of therapeutics. The central theme of the R&D strategy is to focus on developing multiple compounds from each program into early clinical trials and evaluate the patient data from the results for the discovery and development of additional products. The strategic objective is to develop best-in-class therapies to patients. The company have a pipeline of programs across multiple disease areas and modalities. The major focus is to address diseases like Cystic Fibrosis(CF), Sickle Cell Disease and Beta Thalassemia, APOL1-Mediated Kidney disease, and Type 1 Diabetes. Vertex Pharma is evaluating Phase 3 clinical trials for diseases like Cystic Fibrosis and Sickle Cell Disease and Beta Thalassemia. The company have positive Phase 2 data for treatment related to APOL1 medicated kidney disease. Vertex is also evaluating a stem cell derived islet therapy for potential treatment of type 1 diabetes. The company is also evaluating VX-548, a NaV 1.8 inhibitor for the non-opioid treatment of acute pain in two Phase 2 clinical trials. Over the years, the

© The Author(s), under exclusive license to Springer Nature Switzerland AG 2024

B. R. Kumar, *Rising Stars*, Management for Professionals,
https://doi.org/10.1007/978-3-031-50032-9_23

company have expanded its capabilities to include additional innovative therapeutic modalities with the focus on cell and genetic therapies. The company have made substantial investment in cell and genetic therapies. Vertex focusses on strategic alliances and M&A as a part of its growth strategy. The strategic plan involves acquiring businesses and technologies and establishing collaboration with biopharmaceutical and technology companies, leading academic, research institutions, and foundations. Vertex have collaborations with CRISPR to develop therapeutics based on the CRISPR gene editing technology. The agreement with CRISPR also authorize Vertex to lead the worldwide development, manufacturing, and commercialization of CTX001. Vertex acquired Semma for the establishment of cell therapy programs. The acquisition of Exonics facilitated Vertex to establish genetic therapy programs. Vertex also have collaborations with Moderna for the discovery and development of lipid nanoparticles and mRNAs which can deliver gene editing therapies. The internal programs of the company are directed toward development of transformative treatments for life-threatening diseases and innovative therapeutic approaches to develop targets. The company's strategic goals also include development of biological assays and clinical biomarkers which are designed to predict clinical responses. Vertex are developing autologous, fully differentiated stem cell derived islet cell therapies which are designed to replace insulin producing islet cells which are destroyed in people with T1 Diabetes. The company have discovered multiple inhibitors of NAV1.8 in three clinical pain models of acute pain, neuropathic pain, and musculoskeletal pain. In 2019, Vertex acquired Semma Therapeutics for approximately $950 million. The privately held Semma focused on the use of stem cell-derived human islets as a potentially curative treatment for type I diabetics. The acquisition of Semma provided synergistic benefits for Vertex for advancing its cell therapy capabilities and development of transformative therapies for type 1 diabetics. In the same year, Vertex acquired Exonics which focuses on creation of transformative gene editing therapies to repair mutations that cause DMD and other severe neuromuscular diseases. The acquisition enhanced Vertex's gene editing capabilities and potential development of novel therapies for DMD and DM1. The acquisition deal included an upfront payment of $245 million plus working capital adjustments in cash and potential future payments based on the success of the programs and compliance of regulatory milestones for DMD and DM1 programs.

Vertex has also entered into various in-license agreements to obtain access to technologies from third parties and conduct research and development activities with collaborators. Pursuant to these in-license agreements, Vertex have received development and commercialization rights for the resulting product candidates. On the basis of the arrangements, Vertex have responsibility with respect to the cost incurred for research activities and required to make upfront payments or milestone payments upon the achievement of certain research development objectives.

Table 1 highlights the In-License Agreements of Vertex Pharma.

Vertex also have entered into out license agreements for certain product candidates with third-party collaborators. In 2017, Vertex entered into a strategic collaboration and license agreement with Merck to grant an exclusive worldwide

Table 1 In-license agreements

Sl	Year	Company	Objectives
1	2015	CRISPR Therapeutics AG	For discovery and development of potential new treatments aimed at the underlying genetic causes of human diseases using CRISPR/Cas9 gene editing technology
2	2016	Moderna Inc	To identify and develop mRNA therapeutics for the treatment of CF
3	2018	Arbor Biotechnologies	To focus on the discovery of novel proteins, including DNA endonucleases, to advance the development of new gene editing therapies
	2018	Genomics plc, Merck KGaA, Darmstadt, Germany, and X-Chem, Inc.	R&D efforts
4	2019	Kymera Therapeutics, Inc.	For the research and development of small molecule protein degraders.
5	2019	Ribometrix, Inc	R&D efforts
6	2020	Affinia Therapeutics, Inc.	To gain access to a novel library of AAV capsids to support R&D initiatives in genetic therapies, including DMD, DM1, and CF
7	2020	Moderna Inc	To discover and develop lipid nanoparticles and mRNAs which can deliver gene editing therapies to lung cells for the treatment of CF
8	2020	Skyhawk Therapeutics, Inc.	For the discovery and development of novel small molecules that modulate RNA splicing for the treatment of serious diseases
9	2021	Arbor Biotechnologies	To develop ex vivo engineered cell therapies for multiple serious diseases using Arbor's proprietary CRISPR gene editing technology
10	2021	Mammoth Biosciences, Inc	To develop in vivo gene editing therapies for two diseases using Mammoth's next-generation CRISPR systems
11	2021	Obsidian Therapeutics, Inc	For the discovery of novel therapies that regulate gene editing for the treatment of serious diseases

Source: Vertex Annual Report 2021

license to research, develop, and commercialize four oncology research and development program. In 2004, Vertex entered into a collaboration agreement with the Cystic Fibrosis Foundation to support research and development activities. In 2021, the total R&D investment amounted to $3.05 billion.

The company market its products mainly to the EU and the United States. In addition, the products are marketed to countries like Australia, Switzerland, Israel, and Canada. The products are marketed through personal interactions with physicians and allied healthcare professionals. The sales of the products are reimbursed by third-party payees such as government health programs, commercial insurance, and managed health care organizations. Vertex participate in the

Medicaid Drug Rebate program, Medicare, and other governmental pricing programs. The company have established own manufacturing capabilities in Boston for clinical trial and commercial supplies. The sourcing of raw materials and other supplies are made from multiple sources including contract manufacturers. The company have developed systems and processes to track, monitor, and oversee third-party manufacturers' activities which includes a quality assurance program. Vertex rely on third-party manufacturers to produce or process cell culture reagents, gene editing components such as Cas9 protein and guide RNA molecules and also for generation of gene edited cells to supply CTX001 for clinical trials.

Competitive Environment

The company faces competition from pharmaceutical and biotechnology companies which are having similar R&D activities in therapeutic areas and drug development. A number of companies such as AbbVie, Inc. are involved in the identification and development of product candidates for the treatment of CF. Nucleic acid therapies are under development by companies such as Arcturus Therapeutics Holdings, Inc., ReCode Therapeutics, Inc., Krystal Biotech, Inc., Spirovant Sciences, Inc., and 4D Molecular Therapeutics, Inc. There are multiple approved treatments for SCD and beta thalassemia, including products from Novartis International AG, or Novartis, Global Blood Therapeutics, Inc., and Bristol Myers Squibb in partnership with Acceleron Pharma.

Risk Factors

The future growth of the company depends on the successful commercialization of therapies for which Vertex have invested significant resources in the research and development of therapies. Major chunk of product revenues for the company is derived from the sale of medicines related to the treatment of CF. Hence the business would be adversely affected if the company is unable to increase sales of medicines related to treatment of CF. Vertex faces risk if the company fail to comply with US and foreign regulations or have safety issues. The revenue stream of the company would be adversely affected if government or other third-party payees fail to provide coverage and adequate reimbursement rates for the products of the company. Incremental pricing pressures would negatively impact the future profitability of the company. Vertex also faces risks related to development and clinical testing of its products and product candidates. The company faces risks related to government regulations related to applicable healthcare laws, disclosure laws and other regulatory laws. Vertex depend on third-party manufacturers to manufacture products and materials required for clinical trials. The company also depend on third parties to conduct pre-clinical work and clinical trials. The company faces various risks related to supply, manufacturing, and reliance on third parties.

Sustainability Initiatives

In 2015, Vertex established its goal to reduce greenhouse gas emissions by 35% by 2020. The company exceeded the target by the year 2019 and have resolved to reduce global carbon emissions by an additional 20% by the year 2024. The major offices and research facilities of the company are certified by LEED or BREEAM. In 2021, over 60% of total waste was diverted from landfill globally. In 2017, the Vertex Foundation was established to provide a long-term source of charitable giving to communities through education, innovation and health. In 2021, the charitable giving amounted to $9 million. Through the focus area of STEM education, the company works with local educators and community organizations to create opportunities for young women and students in the field of biotechnology. In 2021, together Vertexians and the Foundation donated nearly $3.9 million dollars to 1971 organizations worldwide.

Wealth Creation

An investment of $100 in the Vertex Pharma stock on July 24,1991 would have led to the invested amount accumulated to $7141.56 by December 3, 2022, reflecting a return of 7041.56%.[1]

Comparative 5-Year Stock Return Analysis

The monthly stock return was analyzed for the period Jan 1, 2018–Dec 2, 2022. The Vertex share was trading at $166.86 on Jan 1st, 2018. By Dec 2, 2022, the stock price increased to $321.36 which reflected an increase of 1.93 times. The total cumulative monthly return for Vertex stock was 82.6% during the period 2018–2022. The average yearly return for Vertex share was 17% during this period. During the same period, the NYSE pharma index gave total cumulative monthly return of 40%. The average yearly return for market index NYSE pharma index was 8% during the period 2018–2022.

Table 2 shows the holding period return for Vertex stock and the pharma index during the period 2018–2022. The analysis is based on holding period of 1 year.

Vertex stock had the best performance in the year 2022. The market pharma index had superior performance compared to the stock in years 2020 and 2021.

Table 3 shows the comparative book value and market value of equity of Vertex Pharma during the 5-year period, 2017–2021, in millions of dollars.

The average book value as percent of market value was 11.8% during the period 2017–2021. In 2017, the market value was 18.58 times of book value and it decreased to 5.53 times in year 2021.

[1] https://investors.vrtx.com/stock-information/investment-calculator.

Table 2 Holding period return

Year	Vertex	NYSE Pharma Index	Excess returns
2018	−1%	1%	-1%
2019	15%	15%	0%
2020	4%	7%	−3%
2021	−4%	9%	−13%
2022(till Nov)	32%	−2%	34%

Table 3 Comparative book and market value

Year	2017	2018	2019	2020	2021
Book value of equity	2042.31	4435.2	6085.24	8686.8	10,100
Market value of equity	37952.49	42284.55	56706.52	61422.4	55883.59
BV as percent of MV	5.38%	10.49%	10.73%	14.14%	18.07%

Table 4 Financial highlights

	(In millions of dollars)				
Financial highlights	2017	2018	2019	2020	2021
Total assets	3546.01	6245.9	8318.47	11751.8	13432.5
Short-term investments	2088.67	3168.24	3808.29	6658.9	7524.9
Total equity	2042.31	4435.2	6085.24	8686.8	10,100
Total revenue	2488.65	3047.6	4162.8	6205.7	7574.4
Total operating expenses	1820.7	1974.09	2413	2600	3891.2
Net income	263.48	2096.9	1176.8	2711.7	2342.1
Market cap	37952.49	42284.55	56706.52	61422.4	55883.59
Enterprise value	36483.99	39703.13	53559.89	55695.4	49292.79

Table 5 Profitability and leverage ratio

Ratios	2017	2018	2019	2020	2021
Net margin%	10.59	68.8	28.27	43.7	30.92
ROE%	16.54	64.88	22.37	36.71	24.93
ROA%	8.18	42.83	16.16	27.02	18.6
DER	0.13	0.3	0.11	0.11	0.09

Financial Performance

Table 4 shows the financial highlights of the company in millions of dollars.

The average growth rate analysis during the 5-year period 2017–2021 reveal that total assets, total equity, and total cash investments increased by 41%, 53%, and 40%, respectively. The total revenues and net income increased by 33% and 192%, respectively, during the period 2017–2021.The total expenses increased by 22%. The market capitalization and enterprise value increased by 11% and 9%, respectively, during the 5-year period on average.

Table 5 gives the profitability and leverage position of the firm during the period 2017–2021.

Table 6 Estimation of economic value

Year	2020	2021
Profit before income tax	3116.9	2730.4
Income tax	405.20	388.26
Net operating profit after tax (NOPAT)	2711.70	2342.14
Stockholder equity	8686.80	10100.00
Long-term debt	–	–
Total capital employed	8686.80	10,100
WACC	4.78%	4.82%
Capital charge	415.23	486.82
Economic value	2296.47	1855.32

The average net margin, ROE, and ROA for the company was 36.46%, 33.09%, and 22.56%, respectively, during the period 2017–2021. The average debt-equity ratio was 0.15 during the period 2017–2021. Vertex company had the highest profitability ratios in the year 2018.

Table 6 illustrates the estimation of the economic value of the company for the year 2020 and 2021 in millions of dollars.

The economic value for Vertex declined from $2.296 billion in 2020 to $1.855 billion in the year 2021.

References

1. https://www.vrtx.com/
2. Annual Report 2021
3. https://www.vrtx.com/responsibility/

Case 24 Enstar Group

Enstar is a major global reinsurance group which provides innovative insurance solutions through its network of group companies. The company was founded in Bermuda in the year 1993. Through acquisitions, the company became the largest stand-alone run-off consolidator in the year 2013.In the same year, the company diversified by investments in leading specialty insurance companies. The company also have made high-quality strategic investments. Enstar's diversified portfolio of companies is positioned across major insurance hubs spanning different regions like Bermuda, the United States, London, Continental Europe, and Australia.

Enstar manages (re)insurance companies and portfolios of (re) insurance and other liability business in run off for portfolio returns. Enstar acquire legacy liabilities and (re) insurance reserves from companies and provide retroactive reinsurance coverage for portfolios of (re) insurance business primarily via loss transfer contracts (LPTs). Enstar provide reinsurance contracts to other (re) insurers to mitigate some of their risk of future adverse development (ADC) on insurance risk related to prior accident years. A run-off portfolio is a group of insurance policies which is characterized by the accident year and line of business based on the classification as discontinued business by the insurer which initially underwrote the risks. For example, an owner of a company with direct exposure to asbestos and environmental liabilities would desire to dispose their exposure to such liabilities. Enstar receive premium for its retroactive insurance solutions and invest the funds to generate investment earnings. Enstar has to negotiate the investment class type, fixed income duration, and minimum asset quality for each portfolio with the reinsured as basically these investments are pledged as collateral in the context of reinsurance contract.

As of end September 2022, the total assets of the insurance major amounted to $21.6 billion. The company have made over 110 acquisition transactions since it was established. In 2021, Enstar completed seven high-quality acquisitions and assumed related assets of $3.8 billion. The company have completed $942 million of share repurchases in year 2021. Enstar had also completed the sale and issuance of $500 million of 3.1% notes due 2031 for raising capital.

© The Author(s), under exclusive license to Springer Nature Switzerland AG 2024

B. R. Kumar, *Rising Stars*, Management for Professionals,
https://doi.org/10.1007/978-3-031-50032-9_24

The majority of the acquisitions made by the company have been in the run-off business which includes property and casualty, worker's compensation, asbestos, motor, marine, aviation, closed and discontinued blocks of business, and others. Since 2000, the company have completed 110 plus transaction deals with value of acquired liabilities of $32.4 billion which includes gross loss reserves and defendant A&E liabilities. As of December 31, 2021, the company had 832 employees.

Table 1 gives the major acquisition timeline of the company.

Business Strategy

Enstar focusses on consolidating its position as a leading run-off acquirer. The company follows a detailed due diligence process to identify potential acquisition targets by analyzing risk exposures, claims practices, reserves, and return objectives. Enstar manages assumed liabilities and (re) insurance assets in a cost-effective manner. This process involves negotiation with policyholders and reinsurers using claims analysis and actuarial projects with the aim to settle existing (re) insurance liabilities and monetization of (re) insurance assets. In 2021, Enstar completed the strategic exit from its active underwriting platforms with the sale of Northshore Holding Ltd. Enstar acquired (re) insurance companies and legacy manufacturing companies with direct exposure to asbestos and environmental liabilities. The company employ strategies such as claims management, commutations, and policy buyback and reinsurance recoverables to manage its acquired companies and portfolios of business in run-off segments. The claims management processes focus on leveraging extensive relationships and developing protocols to manage third parties in an efficient way to reduce expenses. Enstar have also entered into agreements with third-party administrators to manage and pay claims on subsidiaries and advise them on case reserves. The company also negotiate with third-party (re)insureds to commute their (re)insurance agreement for an agreed upon upfront payment to manage (re)insurance claims in more efficient manner. The company manage reinsurance recoverables by collaborating with reinsurers, brokers, and professional advisors. With respect to investment strategy, the company invest in investment grade fixed maturity securities as a part of core assets investment portfolio. These asset investments are held against reserves as specified in contractual obligations with counterparty insurers and in accordance with statutory liquidity and solvency regulations. These fixed maturity assets are duration and currency optimized. The fixed maturity asset investment includes US government and agency investments, highly rated sovereign and supranational investments, high-grade corporate investments along mortgage and asset backed investments. The company also focuses on non-core asset strategy to provide diversification and enhance return. The non-core asset investments include below-investment grade fixed income securities, bank loans, hedge funds, private equity funds, collateralized loan obligation, real estate funds, and private credit funds. The Run-off segment of the company faces competition in the global insurance market from domestic and international reinsurance companies.

Table 1 Major deals

Sl	Year	Major run-off deal highlights
1	2001	Two reinsurers, River Thames Ins. Co. Ltd. (UK) and Overseas Re. Corp. Ltd. (Bermuda), were purchased by Enstar for $15.2 million
2	2002	Acquired Hudson Re. Co. Ltd. (Bermuda) for $4.1 million
3	2003	Acquired 50.1% of Hillcot Re. Ltd. for $46.4 million
4	2004	UK based reinsurers Mercantile Indemnity Co. Ltd., Harper Ins. Ltd. and Swiss re/insurer Longmynd Ins. Co. Ltd. were acquired for $4.5 million
5	2005	Enstar acquired reinsurer Fieldmill Ins. Co. Ltd. for $1.4 million
6	2006	Enstar acquired reinsurer Unione Italiana(UK),Cavell Holding Ltd. (UK) and Norwegian reinsurers for $17.4 million, $60.9 million and $108.9 million, respectively
7	2007	Enstar acquired UK reinsurer Marlon Ins. Co. Ltd. and Marlon Management Services Ltd. for $31.2 million
8	2008	Unionamerica Holdings Ltd., the run-off London Market business of St. Paul Fire and Marine Ins. Co., was acquired for $343.3 million. Enstar bought the remaining 49.9% of Hillcot Re Ltd. In two stages, Enstar acquired 99.45% of Goshawk Ins. Holdings plc. for $86.7 million
9	2009	Danish run-off reinsurer Copenhagen Re. Co. Ltd. was acquired from Alm. Brand Forsikring for 29.9 million. Enstar bought New York run-off reinsurer Constellation Re. Co. Ltd. for $2.5 million
10	2010	California run-off insurer Claremont Liability Ins. Co. was purchased for $13.9 million. Enstar acquired New Castle Re. Co. Ltd., a Bermuda run-off insurer, for $22.0 million. Enstar bought, from Shinsei Bank Ltd., the remaining 49.9% of Hillcot Holdings Ltd. Enstar purchased the remaining 55.6% of Seaton Ins. Co. Enstar acquired P.W. Acquisition Co., which owns Rhode Island run-off insurer Providence Washington Ins. Co., for $25.0 million. A portfolio of run-off business underwritten by Japan's Mitsui Sumitomo Ins. Co., Ltd. was transferred to 50.1%-owned Enstar subsidiary Bosworth Run-off Ltd. Enstar acquired Swedish run-off reinsurer Forsakringsaktiebolaget Assuransinvest MF for $11.0 million. The United Kingdom run-off reinsurer Knapton Ins. Ltd. was purchased from RSA Ins. Group plc for $44.0 million
11	2011	Enstar through Gordian acquired an inward reinsurance portfolio from Insurance Australia Group Ltd. Enstar purchased then New Jersey-domiciled run-off insurer Clarendon National Ins. Co for $219.1 million. Enstar acquired Irish run-off life insurer Laguna Life Ltd.$21.2 million
12	2013	Enstar and the Trident V funds acquired Lloyd's Atrium Underwriting Group Ltd., for $158.0 million. Enstar and the Trident V funds acquired Bermuda-based Arden Re. Co. Ltd. through North shore for $79.6 million. Enstar purchased Sea Bright Holdings an Illinois insurer commercially domiciled in California involved in workers' compensation business, for $252.1 million
13	2014	Enstar and the Trident V funds acquired Torus Insurance Holdings Ltd. through Bayshore Holdings Ltd. The deal involved Enstar's contribution of cash of $41.6 million and 2.6 million shares
14	2015	Enstar purchased Companion Property and Casualty Ins. Co. from Blue Cross and Blue Shield of South Carolina for $218 million. Enstar acquired Belgian life and non-life insurer Nationale Suisse Assurance S.A. from Helvetia Group for $35.2 million
15	2016	Enstar acquired Dana Companies, LLC from Dana Incorporated for a total purchase price of $88.5 million

(continued)

Table 1 (continued)

Sl	Year	Major run-off deal highlights
16	2017	Enstar sold its subsidiary Pavonia Holdings (US), Inc. for a total purchase price of $120 million to an affiliate of Global Bankers Insurance Group
17	2018	Enstar acquired the remaining shares in KaylaRe, a Bermuda Class 4 reinsurer
18	2019	Enstar acquired Borgwarner Morse TEC from BorgWarner Inc. Morse TEC
19	2020	Enstar completed a transaction with Great Lakes Insurance SE and HSB Engineering Insurance Limited. Enstar completed an adverse development cover reinsurance transaction with Aspen Insurance Holdings Limited
20	2021	Enstar completed an adverse development cover ("ADC") with RSA. The ADC provides cover losses incurred on or prior to December 31, 2020, within a diversified portfolio of commercial and personal insurance lines risks for certain the United Kingdom, Irish, and other business of RSA and its subsidiaries

Source: https://www.enstargroup.com/acquisitions/

Business Segment

The results of the operations of the Enstar are presented through four reportable segments.

Run-off segment consists of acquired property and casualty and other (re) insurance business. Enhanzed Re includes life and catastrophe business. Investment segment deals with investment activities. Legal underwriting focusses on businesses which the company have exited via the sale of the majority of its interest. The Run off and Enhanzed Re businesses offer a variety of capital release solutions such as LPTs and ADCs. LPTs are offered to clients who wish to divest themselves of a portfolio of non-core insurance business. ADCs are offered when the clients are concerned about loss deterioration on selected books of business. In this scheme, the company offer ADCs whereby the company reinsure certain losses in excess of the clients' established reserves up to a pre-determined limit.

Risk Factors

The acquisition of appropriate run-off business is highly competitive and depends on different factors such as proposed acquisition price, collateral arrangements, and financial resources. The company may not be able to sustain its growth through acquisitions in future as the evaluation and negotiation of potential run-off acquisitions and integration of acquired businesses can be complex and costly along with integration challenges.

The adequacy of loss reserves and the need to adjust such reserves as claims develop over time is a significant risk factor for Enstar. The company faces risks with respect to its evaluation of acquisitions and deal payments. The Enhanzed Re's life and annuity business faces the risk of mismatch in asset/liability duration. The company also faces risks related to variability of statutory capital requirements. The reinsurance subsidiaries may not be able to provide the required collateral to the ceded companies. The value of reinsurance subsidiaries' investment portfolios may decline due to market and economic conditions. The business of (re)insurance is regulated in most countries. The company may face regulation in new jurisdictions or additional regulations in existing jurisdictions based on the location and nature of acquired companies. The company is a holding company and depend on its subsidiaries to distribute funds. The company have adopted a comprehensive risk management framework to identify, measure, manage, monitor, and report risks.

Stock Market Performance

Table 2 shows the growth of value of $100 invested in the Enstar stock in comparison to same investment of $100 made in market index S&P 500 and S&P Property & Casualty Insurance index during the 5-year period 2016–2021. It is assumed that $100 is invested initially in stock or index, including reinvestment of dividend on December 31, 2016.

The 5-year holding period return for Enstar stock was 25% while for S&P 500 and S&P Property & Casualty index, it was 133% and 82%, respectively. The 5-year average returns for Enstar was 6%. S&P 500 and S&P Property & Casualty index had average returns of 19% and 13% during the 5-year period 2017–2021.

Five-Year Stock Return

The stock was trading at $ 207 in Nasdaq on January 1, 2018. By December 1st, 2021, the stock price increased by 1.04 times to trade at $217.77. The cumulative monthly return for the Enstar share was 19% during the period Jan 2018–Dec 2022. The 5-year average return for the stock was just 4% during the above period. During the above period, the market index S&P 500 index had registered cumulative return of 42% and average 5-year return of 8%. Hence, the market index S&P 500 had superior performance compared to the stock Enstar.

Table 3 gives the holding period return of the stock and market index S&P 500 during the period 2018–2022. The holding period is assumed for a period of 1 year.

The market index had superior returns compared to Enstar stock during the 5-year period 2018–2022.

Table 2 Wealth generation

Year	2016	2017	2018	2019	2020	2021
Enstar	$100	$101.54	$84.76	$104.63	$103.64	$125.24
S&P 500	$100	$121.83	$116.49	$153.17	$181.35	$233.41
S&P Property & Casualty	$100	$121.82	$113.52	$143.28	$152.90	$182.48

Source: Enstar Annual Report 2021

Table 3 Holding period return

Year	Enstar	S&P 500	Excess returns
2018	−19%	−11%	−8%
2019	16%	19%	−3%
2020	5%	16%	−12%
2021	24%	28%	−5%
2022(till Dec)	−18%	−13%	−5%

Table 4 Comparative book and market value

Year	2017	2018	2019	2020	2021
Book value of equity	3625.55	4372.53	5295.14	7053	6505
Market value of equity	3895.9	3596.05	4449.87	4525.04	4511.98
BV as percent of MV	93.1%	121.6%	119.0%	155.9%	144.2%

Table 5 Financial highlights

Financial highlights	(In millions of dollars)				
Year	2017	2018	2019	2020	2021
Total assets	13606.42	16556.27	19826.1	21,627	24,429
Short-term investments	955.15	602.1	624.47	901	1646
Total equity	3625.55	4372.53	5295.14	7053	6505
Total revenue	1060.81	582.39	2132	2501	686
Operating expenses	752.3	841.99	1255	1005	264
Net income	311.46	−150.22	938	1755	473
Market cap	3895.9	3596.05	4449.87	4525.04	4511.98
Enterprise value	4076.69	4836.48	5979.95	5886.04	5475.98

Table 4 shows the excess value created by the Enstar stock during the 5-year period 2017–2021 in millions of dollars.

The average book value as percent of market value was 126.7% during the period 2017–2021.

Financial Performance

Table 5 highlights the important financial parameters of Enstar during the period 2017–2021. The values are given in millions of dollars. The data source was sourced from gurufocus.com.

The total assets, total equity grew by 16% and 17% on average basis during the period 2017–2021. The total cash and net income had shown high fluctuating trend during above period. The market capitalization and enterprise value increased by 4% and 8% on average basis during the above period. The total revenue growth rate had been fluctuating during the above period.

Table 6 observes the profitability and leverage position of the company.

Table 6 Profitability and leverage

Ratios	2017	2018	2019	2020	2021
Net margin%	29.36	−25.79	44	70.17	68.95
ROE%	10.49	−4.27	21.45	30.48	7.41
ROA%	2.35	−1	5.16	8.47	2.05
DER	0.21	0.22	0.25	0.21	0.28

Table 7 Economic value

Year	2020	2021
Profit before income tax	1496	422
Income tax	23.936	25.32
Net operating profit after tax (NOPAT)	1472.06	396.68
Stockholder equity	7053.00	6505.00
Long-term debt	1188.00	1691.00
Total capital employed	8241.00	8196
WACC	4.71%	5.05%
Capital charge	388.15	413.90
Economic value	1083.91	−17.22

The average net margin, ROE, and ROA for Enstar during the 5-year period 2017–2021was 37.34%, 13.11%, and 3.41%, respectively. The average debt-equity ratio during the above period was 0.23.

Table 7 illustrates the estimation of economic value for Enstar in millions of dollars.

References

1. https://www.enstargroup.com/enstar-group-operations/
2. Annual Report 2021

Case 25 EPAM Systems Inc.

EPAM is one of the most important global digital transformation service providers which delivers end-to-end value to customers through its advanced software engineering and consultancy expertise. The company focusses on advanced technology software solutions, intelligent enterprise services, and digital engagement. The service offerings of the company focus on providing customized integrated solutions to customers. EPAM also provides services for business consulting, design and physical product development, artificial intelligence, robotics, and virtual reality.

Service Offerings and Solutions

Engineering

The engineering expertise facilitates the company to build and scale next-generation software solutions and agile delivery teams. EPAM focusses on building enterprise technologies which improve business processes, offer smarter analytics, and achieve operational excellence through requirement analysis, platform selection, cross-platform migration, implementation, and integration. EPAM uses its custom tools and specialized knowledge to integrate customers' selected application platforms with their internal systems and processes. The infrastructure management services of the company provide enterprise integration between software development, testing, and maintenance with private, public, and mobile infrastructures for its customers. The engineering solutions of EPAM cover the full lifecycle of infrastructure management which includes application, database, network, server, storage, and systems operations management. The company offers maintenance and support services through its proprietary distributed project management processes and tools. EPAM offers a complete set of software product development services which include product research, customer experience design, prototyping, program management, full lifecycle software testing, product deployment, and end-user customization.

© The Author(s), under exclusive license to Springer Nature Switzerland AG 2024

B. R. Kumar, *Rising Stars*, Management for Professionals,
https://doi.org/10.1007/978-3-031-50032-9_25

Operations

The proprietary platforms, integrated engineering practices, and smart automation of the company facilitate the transformation of customers' operations into intelligent enterprise hubs.

Optimization

The company has in place a dedicated team of testing and quality assurance professionals with experience across a wide range of technology platforms and industry verticals to perform software application testing, test management, automation, and consulting services. The company employs standard proprietary defect tracking tools and frameworks to provide a comprehensive range of testing services to identify threats and protect the customers' business systems.

Consulting

The company offers consulting services across business, experience, technology, and data. The technical advisory group helps customers to be equipped with the knowledge of current trends in technology changes.

Design

The digital and service design segment of the company provides design strategy, creative, and program management services for customers to improve the user experience. In order to enhance its physical design and product development capabilities, EPAM has undertaken a couple of acquisitions. In 2018, EPAM acquired Continuum Innovation LLC and Think Ltd. In 2021, the company acquired Emakina Group to improve its ability to deliver creative solutions and develop next-generation digital products.

Industry Focus

The customers of the EPAM operate in five main industry verticals: Financial Services, Travel and Consumer, Software and Hi-Tech, Business Information and Media, Life Sciences, and Healthcare. EPAM provides services for global investment banks, commercial and retail lending institutions, credit card and payment solution companies, and insurance companies. The company offers a range of platforms, applications, and solutions to travel and hospitality sectors like airlines, global hotel chains, and online travel agencies. EPAM provides complex software product development services for software and technology companies. For business information and media customers, EPAM builds products and solutions for modern platforms such as web media streaming, mobile information delivery, print-to-digital transformations, and information discovery. In the Life Sciences category, the company has collaborated with global pharmaceutical, medical and scientific technology, biotechnology companies, and retail pharmacies to deliver sophisticated scientific informatics and innovative enterprise technology solutions. The top ten customers account for 29.1%, 30.9%, and 25.7% of the total revenues in the years 2019, 2020, and 2021, respectively.

Strategy

One of the key competitive advantages for the company is its focus on a robust global delivery model. The focus is on the growth of its delivery platform both organically and strategically through strategically acquired locations and personnel. By December 31, 2021, the company had 52,617 delivery personnel consisting of core IT professionals, designers, consultants, and scientists. The company had 36,739, 41,168, and 58,824 employees in the years 2019, 2020, and 2021. EPAM invests significant resources in training and development and the employees had spent over 3.7 million learning hours in 2021 and were awarded LinkedIn's Best Culture of Learning Talent Award for the year 2021. The company has not declared or paid any cash dividends on its common stock.

Risk Factors

Many foreign and US federal and state agencies regulate various aspects of the business of EPAM. COVID-19 pandemic has contributed toward significant volatility in the price of the stock of the company which leads to uncertainty in customer demand and economic disruption. The rapid growth of the company through organic and strategic acquisitions has created challenges for the company in terms of administrative, operational, and financial infrastructure. Strategic acquisitions result in significant risks for the company in terms of integration challenges. Economic, civil, military, and political uncertainties pose significant risks for the company. More than half of the global delivery and support personnel in emerging market economies of Eastern Europe are located in Ukraine, Belarus, and Russia. The company also faces intense competition from onshore and offshore IT services and other consulting companies. The global operations of the company have to comply with a wide variety of foreign laws and regulations. Changes in the general economic or political conditions in the United States could adversely affect the business operations of the company. The company normally does not have long-term commitments from customers. The company faces risk in revenue generation if customers terminate contracts before completion or choose not to renew contracts or are not guaranteed payment for services performed under a given contract. The business growth of the company is largely dependent on demand for its services from customers in select industry verticals and a downturn in these industry sectors will have a material effect on the business operations of the company. A significant failure in the systems, telecommunications, or IT infrastructure of the company would disrupt the business service model of the company. Security breaches and disruptions to network security would adversely affect the business operations of the company.

Corporate Social Responsibility

In terms of innovation, EPAM focuses on social value and machine learning. The company has been chosen as a top 10 App in Google's Android Development Challenge. The company reuses, recycles, and upcycles end-of-life electronics and computers in partnership with Sims Recycling Solution. The company was named a 2021 Top 100 Tech Culture Champion in the United Kingdom. In 2021, EPAM employees have dedicated 30,000 plus volunteer hours in 27 locations for global mentorship, training, and teaching programs. They have dedicated more than 750,000 h to mentorship, training, and teaching. The company has pledged to empower about 5000 students with high-tech skills and global opportunities by the year 2025. The company helped the Raspberry Pi Foundation to provide over 60,000 young people with access to free learning resources related to technology and coding skills.

Comparative Stock Wealth Creation

Table 1 shows the comparative stock wealth creation for EPAM, Peer Group, and S&P 500 index. It is assumed that $100 is invested in the stock in the period beginning December 31, 2016, and ending December 31, 2021.

The 5-year holding period return for EPAM systems stock was 939% while the holding period return for the Peer Group Index and S&P 500 index was 104% and 133%, respectively. The 5-year average returns for EPAM stock was 63% while for Peer Group and S&P 500, the average returns were 20% and 19%, respectively.

The EPAM stock was trading at $117.47 on 1/1/2018. By December 1st, 2022, the stock price increased by 2.94 times to $345.89. The monthly cumulative returns for the stock during the period Jan 2018–Dec 2022 was 178.7% while for the S&P 500 index, the monthly cumulative returns were 43%. The average yearly returns for

Table 1 Comparative wealth creation

Year	2016	2017	2018	2019	2020	2021
EPAM	$100	$167.05	$180.30	$329.90	$557.22	$1039.42
Peer Group Index	$100	$153.51	$110.09	$107.82	$159.25	$204.45
S&P 500	$100	$121.83	$116.49	$153.17	$181.35	$233.41

Source: Annual Report 2021

Table 2 Holding period returns

Year	EPAM	S&P 500	Excess returns
2018	−1%	−11%	10%
2019	50%	19%	30%
2020	57%	16%	41%
2021	94%	28%	66%
2022(till first Dec)	−27%	−12%	−16%

Table 3 Book and market value

Year	2017	2018	2019	2020	2021
Book value of equity	974.95	1262.6	1596.15	1983.02	2495.84
Market value of equity	5692.04	6273.84	1170.62	20106.3	38000.71
BV as percent of MV	17.1%	20.1%	136.4%	9.9%	6.6%

Table 4 Financial highlights

	(In millions of dollars)				
Financial highlights	2017	2018	2019	2020	2021
Total assets	1250.26	1611.8	2244.21	2721.33	3523.23
Short-term investments	582.59	770.56	936.56	1382.15	1446.63
Total equity	974.95	1262.6	1596.15	1983.02	2495.84
Total revenue	1450.45	1842.91	2293.8	2659.48	3758.14
Total operating expenses	356.15	410.23	502.75	547.63	732.13
Net income	72.76	240.26	261.06	327.16	481.65
Market cap	5692.04	6273.84	1170.62	20106.3	38000.71
Enterprise value	5134.49	5528.32	11035.53	18990.55	36801.97

the EPAM stock was 36% during the above period whereas for the index it was just 9%.

Table 2 highlights the holding period return for the stock and S&P 500 index for the period 2018–2022.

EPAM Systems has the best stock market performance in the year 2021 with excess returns of 66%. In the years 2019 and 2020, EPAM registered returns of 50% and 57%, respectively, compared to S&P 500 returns of 19% and 16%, respectively. In the years 2018 and 2022, the stock had registered negative returns. The data is taken from Yahoo finance.com.

Table 3 shows the comparative book and market value of EPAM during the 5-year period 2017–2021. The values are given in millions of dollars.

The average book value was 38% of the market value during the 5-year period 2017–2021. In 2021, the book value was only 6.6% of the market value of the company. In 2020, the market value was 10 times as that of the book value of the company. In the year 2019, the book value was higher compared to the market value of EPAM Systems.

Table 4 highlights the financial performance of the company. The values are given in millions of dollars.

Table 5 Profitability and leverage position

Ratios	2017	2018	2019	2020	2021	Average
Net margin%	5.02	13.04	11.38	12.3	12.82	10.912
ROE%	8.29	21.47	18.26	18.28	21.55	17.57
ROA%	6.69	16.79	13.54	13.18	15.43	13.126
DER	0.03	0.02	0.17	0.13	0.1	0.09

Table 6 Estimation of economic value

Year	2020	2021
Profit before income tax	378.48	533.39
Income tax	51.32	51.74
Net operating profit after tax (NOPAT)	327.16	481.65
Stockholder equity	1983.02	2495.84
Long-term debt	25.07	25.04
Total capital employed	2008.09	2520.88
WACC	4.71%	5.05%
Capital charge	94.58	127.30
Economic value	232.58	354.35

The average growth rate of total assets and total equity was 30% and 27% during the period 2018–2021. The cash and cash equivalents grew by 27% on an average basis during the period 2018–2021. The total revenues increased by 27% and net income increased by 78% during the 5-year period of analysis. The enterprise value increased by 68% during the period 2018–2021.

Table 5 shows the profitability ratios and leverage position of the company during the 5-year period 2017–2021.

The average net margin, ROE, and ROA were 10.91%, 17.57%, and 13.13% during the period 2017–2021. The average debt-equity ratio during the period was 0.09.

Table 6 illustrates the estimation of the economic value of EPAM Systems during the period 2020 and 2021 in millions of dollars.

The economic value has increased from $232.58 million in 2020 to $ 354.35 million in 2021.

References

1. https://www.annualreports.com/HostedData/AnnualReports/PDF/NYSE_EPAM_2021.pdf
2. https://www.epam.com/

Case 26 Veeva Systems

Veeva is a major global provider of industry-specific cloud-based software solutions for the life sciences industry. The solutions provided by Veeva support pharmaceutical and life sciences firms to implement cloud-based architectures and mobile applications for its most important business functions. The solutions span cloud software, data, and business consulting which involve strategic business functions such as research and development to commercialization. The commercial solutions offered by the company facilitate life science companies to have better engagement with healthcare professionals and healthcare organizations across different communication channels. The R&D solutions for clinical, regulatory, and safety solutions facilitate life sciences firms to streamline their end-to-end product development processes to improve operational efficiency and maintain regulatory compliance in the product life system. The company also provides content and data management solutions to customers in the consumer products and chemical industries.

The industry cloud solutions offered by Veeva Systems for life sciences industry can be classified into two major segments—Veeva Commercial Cloud and Veeva Development Cloud.

Veeva Commercial Cloud offers a suite of software, data, and analytics solutions to support the sales, medical affairs, and marketing functions of life sciences companies. Veeva CRM and Veeva Medical CRM provide single integrated solution to manage, track, and optimize services for healthcare professionals. Veeva CRM MyInsights and Veeva CRM Approved Email provide tailored CRM user experience. Veeva CRM Engage platform provides digital engagement through compliant video meetings, phone calls, contactless in-person interactions, or chat. Veeva CLM provides sales professionals with digital marketing content on mobile devices such as iPad for in-person interactions. Veeva Align enables life sciences companies to perform fast, accurate territory alignments. Veeva Digital Events facilitates planning, management, and execution of group meetings with healthcare professionals. Veeva Vault for Commercial Content Management is a unified suite of cloud-based, enterprise content, and data management applications. Veeva Vault PromoMats is an end-to-end content and digital asset management (DAM) solution

© The Author(s), under exclusive license to Springer Nature Switzerland AG 2024

B. R. Kumar, *Rising Stars*, Management for Professionals,
https://doi.org/10.1007/978-3-031-50032-9_26

which facilitate life sciences companies to collaborate, review, distribute, and update commercial content and manage assets. Veeva Vault MedComms helps to streamline the creation, approval, and delivery of medical content for life sciences companies in order to maintain a single validated source of medical content across multiple channels and geographies. Veeva Data and Analytics solutions include Veeva Link, Veeva Crossix, Veeva Data Cloud, Veeva Open Data, Veeva Nitro, and Veeva Network. Veeva Link provides strategic market insights and real-time customer intelligence on key scientific experts. Veeva Crossix provides a standard best-in-class analytics platform to maximize media investments. Patented Crossix SafeMine technology performs the function of connecting health and non-health data for US patients. Veeva Data Cloud provides longitudinal US-based patient data for retail and specialty distribution channels and prescriber data for patient segmentation, commercial analytics, and artificial intelligence. Veeva OpenData provides healthcare professionals and healthcare organizations with relevant information related to demographics, licenses, specialty information, etc. Veeva Nitro is a data science and analytics platform which enables life science companies to unify data sources such as prescription, sales, formulary, and claims data. Veeva Network is an industry-specific customer master software solution for maintaining customer master record.

Veeva Development Cloud solutions consist of platforms such as Veeva Digital Trials, Veeva Vault Clinical Suite, Veeva Vault Clinical Data Management Suite, Veeva Vault Clinical Operations Suite, Veeva Site and Patient Engagement Applications, Veeva Vault RIM, Veeva Vault Quality, and Veeva Vault Safety. Veeva Digital Trials Platform provides the technological ecosystem for clinical trial execution. Veeva Vault Clinical Suite provides the most comprehensive suite of clinical solutions on a single cloud platform. Veeva Vault Clinical Data Management Suite provides sponsors and CROs design and run trials with tools. Veeva Vault Clinical Operations Suite offers fit-for-purpose solutions for clinical research sites. Veeva Vault RIM is a suite of applications which provides fully integrated regulatory information management (RIM) capabilities on a single cloud platform. Veeva MedTech Suite is composed of unified and connected cloud software solutions that offer faster delivery of medical devices and diagnostics to patients. The Cloud Solutions also offers consumer products and chemical industries. Veeva QualityOne is a robust quality management, document management, and training solution. Veeva RegulatoryOne supports firms in managing regulatory submission content.

Veeva Business Consulting provides strategic consulting services and solutions for different industry sectors.

By January 31st, 2022, the company has served 1205 customers. The company had a world wide employee population of 5482 employees as of January 31, 2022. Veeva adheres to ISO9001 standards to ensure process controls across its regulated product offerings. Veeva maintains a global privacy program which is aligned to laws such as the California Consumer Privacy Act (CCPA), the California Privacy Rights Act (CPRA), the European Union's General Data Protection Regulation (GDPR), and the US Health Insurance Portability and Accountability Act (HIPAA).

Competitors

The principal competitor for Veeva Commercial Cloud applications is IQVIA Inc. which offers CRM applications built on the Salesforce Platform.IQVIA, Dassault Systèmes, OpenText Corporation, Oracle Corporation, and Honeywell International Inc., offer applications that compete with certain Veeva Vault applications. The Commercial cloud and development cloud application suites also compete to replace client server-based legacy solutions offered by companies such as Oracle, Microsoft, and other smaller application providers.

Risk Factors

The company may face significant liabilities if the security measures are breached and if the customers stop the use of its solutions. The business of the company may be negatively impacted if the third-party providers of healthcare professional and healthcare organization data do not allow customers to use data in the company's solutions. The company also relies on third-party providers for computing infrastructure, securing network connectivity, and technology-related services. The company also depends on the Salesforce platform for multichannel CRM applications. The markets in which the firm participates are highly competitive in nature. The revenues of the firm are dependent on factors in the life sciences industry and any changes in the industry would affect the revenues of the firm.

A critical factor for the success of the firm is the renewal and expansion of existing subscription agreements. The subscription services revenue retention rate was 119% in the year 2022. The company focusses on the expansion of its product portfolio through acquisitions. Veeva Systems also invests in research and development to expand existing solutions and build new solutions. For the fiscal year 2022, subscription service revenues constituted 80% of the total revenues and the rest was accounted by professional services and other revenues. The company enters into master subscription agreements with the customers.

Table 1 Comparative 5-year cumulative return

Year	2017	2018	2019	2020	2021	2022
Veeva Systems	$100	$148.50	$257.64	$346.35	$653.06	$558.80
S&P 500	$100	$126.41	$123.48	$150.26	$176.18	$217.21
S&P 1500 Application Software Index	$100	$148.30	$178.97	$241.85	$318.66	$352.87

Source: Annual Report

Stock Market Performance

Table 1 shows the growth performance of the stock and index during the period 2017–2022. It is assumed that $100 was invested in stock Veeva, index S&P 500, S&P 1500 Application Software Index on 31/1/2017. The wealth generation assumes reinvestment of dividends.

The 5-year holding period return for Veeva Systems was 459% while the S&P 500 and S&P 1500 Application Software Index had holding period returns of 117% and 253%, respectively. The 5-year average returns for Veeva Systems during the period 2018–2022 was 46% while for S&P 500 and S&P Application Software Index, the average returns were 17% and 29%, respectively.

Stock Return Analysis

The stock return analysis is done for the period Jan 1,2018–Dec 1, 2022. The stock which was trading at $62.86 on Jan 1st, 2018, increased by 2.6 times to $163.91 by Dec 1, 2022. The cumulative monthly return for the Veeva stock during the above period was 126% whereas for the S&P 500 Index the cumulative return was 39%. The 5-year average annual return for the stock was 26% whereas for the S&P500 Index the average annual return was 8%.

Table 2 shows the holding period return for the Veeva stock during 2018–2022 in comparison with the S&P500 Index. The analysis involves assumption of a holding period of 1 year.

The stock registered its best performance in the year 2020 with holding period return of 86%. The stock had negative returns in the years 2021 and 2022.

Table 3 shows the comparative book and market value of the company during the period 2017–2021. The values are given in millions of dollars.

Table 2 Holding period return

Year	Veeva	S&P 500	Excess returns
2018	42%	−11%	53%
2019	29%	19%	9%
2020	86%	16%	69%
2021	−8%	28%	−36%
2022	−31%	−15%	−15%

Table 3 Book and market value

Year	2018	2019	2020	2021	2022
Book value of equity	906.24	1237.75	1665.59	2266.32	2911.64
Market value of equity	8930.46	15943.48	21858.96	42034.64	36473.76
BV as percent of MV	10.1%	7.8%	7.6%	5.4%	8.0%

Table 4 Financial highlights

	(In millions of dollars)				
Financial highlights	2018	2019	2020	2021	2022
Total assets	1230.33	1653.77	2271.78	3046.07	3816.47
Short-term investments	761.96	1090.16	1086.75	1663.63	2376.1
Total equity	906.24	1237.75	1665.59	2266.32	2911.64
Total revenue	690.56	862.21	1104.08	1465.07	1850.78
Total operating expenses	321.21	394.06	514.49	678.35	841.6
Net income	151.18	229.83	301.12	380	427.39
Market cap	8930.46	15943.48	21858.96	42034.64	36473.76
Enterprise value	8168.5	14853.32	20827.04	40434.13	34152.24

Table 5 Profitability and leverage ratio

Ratios	2018	2019	2020	2021	2022
Net margin%	21.89	26.66	27.27	25.94	23.09
ROE%	19.4	21.44	20.74	19.33	16.51
ROA%	14.08	15.94	15.34	14.29	12.46
DER			0.03	0.03	0.02

The average book value as a percent of market value was only 7.8% during the period 2018–2022. In 2021, the market value was 18.58 times the book value of the firm.

Table 4 gives the financial highlights of the company during the past 5 years. The values are given in millions of dollars.

The average growth rate analysis for the period 2018–2022 suggests that the total assets, short-term investments, and total equity increased by 33%, 35%, and 34%, respectively. The revenues and net income increased by 28% and 30% on an average basis. The total expenses increased by 27% during the above period. The average growth rate of market capitalization and enterprise value was 49% and 50%, respectively, during the above period of analysis. The data source is www.gurufocus.com.

Table 5 shows the profitability and leverage position of the company during the period 2018–2022.

The average net margin, ROE, and ROA during the period 2018–2022 were 23.09%, 16.51%, and 12.46%, respectively. The average debt-equity ratio was 0.02 during the period 2018–2022.

Table 6 illustrates the estimation of economic value of Veeva Systems during the period 2021–2022. The values are given in millions of dollars.

The economic value of Veeva Systems increased from $257.85 to $282.72 million dollars.

Table 6 Economic value

Year	2021	2022
Profit before income tax	393.99	512.31
Income tax	13.99	81.97
Net operating profit after tax (NOPAT)	380.00	430.34
Stockholder equity	2266.32	2911.64
Long-term debt		
Total capital employed	2266.32	2911.64
WACC	5.39%	5.07%
Capital charge	122.15	147.62
Economic value	257.85	282.72

References

1. https://www.veeva.com/
2. Veeva Annual Report 2022
3. www.yahoo finance.com

Case 27 Logitech International

Logitech is a world leader in designing, manufacturing, and marketing products and facilitates people to connect to digital and cloud experiences. Logitech is a multi-brand and multi-category company. The Logitech brands include Logitech, Logitech G, ASTRO Gaming, Streamlabs, Blue Microphones, and Ultimate Ears.

Logitech was established in Switzerland in 1981. Logitech International SA is the parent holding company of Logitech which conducts its business through subsidiaries in the Americas, EMEA, and Asia Pacific. Logitech is listed on the Nasdaq Global Select Market under the symbol LOGI and on the Six Swiss Exchange under the symbol LOGN. As of March 31, 2022, Logitech employed over 8200 people of which 3000 were employed in the firm's Suzhou manufacturing operations. In 2020, Logitech announced a share buyback program for an amount of USD 250 million. In 2021, the share buyback program was amended to increase the amount to US $1 billion and further to US $1.5 in the year 2022. In 2022, Logitech paid an aggregate gross dividend of approximately $172.1 million.

Products

Logitech designs, manufactures, and markets products that facilitate people to connect through computing, gaming, video, music, and other digital platforms. Logitech offers a variety of pointing devices, corded and cordless keyboards, and living room keyboards. The PC Webcams offered by Logitech primarily is aimed at video conferencing users. The Logitech HD Pro Webcam C920 and C922 are the key products offered in this category. The Tablet and other Accessories category include keyboards for tablets and smartphones and accessories for mobile devices. Logitech G provides gamers with industry-leading keyboards, mice, headsets, and simulation products such as steering wheels and flight sticks. In the Video collaboration segment, Logitech's video collaboration segment includes conference cams that combine enterprise quality audio and high-definition 4 K video. The key products in this category include Logitech Rally Bar which is an all-in-one video

© The Author(s), under exclusive license to Springer Nature Switzerland AG 2024

B. R. Kumar, *Rising Stars*, Management for Professionals,
https://doi.org/10.1007/978-3-031-50032-9_27

bar purpose-built for a midsize room with characteristics such as room-filling audio. The mobile speakers' category includes a portfolio of portable wireless Bluetooth and Wi-Fi-connected speakers for music. The audio and wearables category consists of PC speakers, PC headsets, in-ear headphones, and premium wireless audio wearables. Logitech's blue microphone product line which offers a range of audio tools for recording or broadcasting applications has a 25-year legacy of innovative design and premium performance in the professional and consumer market.

Industry Environment and Growth Strategy

Logitech's growth has been driven by similar trends related to adoption of desktop and laptop PCs for consumers and businesses. The factors that contributed to the growth trends include affordable processing power, communications bandwidth along with increased accessibility of digital content through Internet penetration. The other factors that contributed toward Logitech's business growth include increase in remote and hybrid work and learning, rise in gaming, and growth in streamers. The growth of cloud-based experiences in gaming, video, and music has created market opportunities for Logitech. Logitech offers peripherals and accessories to facilitate the use of cloud-based content platforms. Logitech has made investments for the development of research and development capabilities in the area of PC peripherals to develop industry-leading gaming gear systems. The company works closely with esports athletes to improve the quality of its gaming products. The growing trend of video conferencing by organizations and the adoption of remote work, learning, and telemedicine is a significant driver for long-term growth of Logitech's businesses of collaborative video products. The company is well poised to offer innovative, affordable, and easy-to-use video collaboration products suited for meeting rooms lacking video facilities. In the music category, the innovation in wireless headphones provides a growth opportunity for Logitech. Consumers are increasingly focusing on streaming and broadcasting using microphones and other peripherals. The company faces challenges such as well-financed competitors, short product life cycles, and rapid adoption of technological and product advancements by competitors in the retail markets.

Logitech's growth strategy is based on the core capabilities of design, engineering, Go to market, and operations. Logitech has improved its design capabilities by building a world-class team of internal designers. During the past 3 years, the company has earned about 202 design awards. The focus on design has helped the company to reduce product costs through increased collaboration between design, engineering, and manufacturing teams. The key design centers of the company are located in Switzerland, Ireland, the United States, and Taiwan. One of the key competitive strengths of Logitech lies in its expertise in key engineering aspects such as sensors, acoustics, optics, wireless, and power management. The company has extended its engineering capabilities into more advanced technologies such as software, apps, cloud, data analytics, and machine learning. Logitech has built an extensive go-to-market network in order to enter new market categories and optimize the value of its existing products. The company has numerous cross-selling opportunities across its broad product portfolio. Logitech has positioned itself as a neutral technology supplier that associates with leading technology vendors and platforms. The company has enhanced its marketing capabilities with respect to brand strategy, digital marketing, and marketing technology. The firm also focusses on increasing its leverage of digital media channels and programs along with maintaining relationships with creators to drive brand engagement and purchase across B2B and B2C. Logitech's operations expertise is based on the hybrid model of in-house manufacturing and third-party contract manufacturers.

The company incurred R&D expenses of $177.6 million, $226 million, and $291.8 million in the years 2020, 2021, and 2022, respectively. Logitech's manufacturing operations consist principally of final assembly and testing. The new product launches, process engineering occur in China, Taiwan, Hong Kong, Malaysia, and Vietnam.

Risk Perspectives

The success of the company depends on its ability to innovate and develop new products in a timely and cost-effect manner. The success of the product portfolio depends on the ability of Logitech to anticipate technology changes, market trends, and consumer preferences. The company purchases key components and products from a limited number of sources and the business of the firm would be adversely affected if Logitech faces supply constraints or shortages of required components. The firm also faces risks related to potential tariffs, adverse trade regulations, and tax factors as its principal manufacturing operations and third-party contract manufacturers are located in China and Southeast Asia. The disruption in relationship with channel partners, changes in distribution partners, and practices are potential risk factors for the firm. Being a global company, changes in trade policy and regulations and imposition of tariffs in countries where the firm operates may have adverse impact on the business of Logitech. Significant disruptions or breaches in security of websites or information technology systems would adversely affect the business operations of Logitech.

Competitors

In the pointing devices category, the main competitors are Apple, Microsoft, Lenovo Group, and HP. In the PC keyboard and combo product category, Microsoft and Apple are the main competitors for Logitech. For PC webcams, the primary competitors are Microsoft and other manufacturers such as Razer Inc. The competitors in the tablet keyboard market are Apple, Zagg Inc., Kensington, and Belkin International Inc.. The competitors for gaming products include Razer, Corsair Gaming, Inc., SteelSeries, Turtle Beach Corporation, and HyperX. The competitors for Bluetooth wireless speakers include Bose Corporation and Harman

International Industries. For PC speakers, the competitors include Bose, Cyber Acoustics, and Philips Consumer Lifestyle among others.

Sustainability Initiatives

The sustainability standards set forth in the Responsible Business Alliance (RBA) code of conduct are the guiding principle for the sustainability initiatives of the company. In 2021, Logitech mapped its sustainability programs with the United Nations Sustainable Development Goals (SDGs). The design-with-People approach is applied to sustainability initiatives at Logitech. The company participates in third-party audits to evaluate its management approach and performance related to RBA code requirements. The company focusses on eliminating its carbon footprint through Reduce, Renew, and Restore levers. The company has 14 products with certified carbon footprint labels and has plan to carbon label for 100% of its products by 2025. The company has reduced its carbon intensity by more than 20% since 2019 and in 2021 became certified carbon neutral across its entire corporate carbon footprint.

The carbon reduction programs adopted by Logitech have resulted in Logitech being listed as number 1 in the FT European Climate Leader index. The company has made a positive impact toward carbon footprint reduction through the focus on 160 plus product lines through recycled plastics, Printed Circuit Boards size reduction, lower weight, lower power electronics, and better packaging. The company has eliminated or replaced 29 million bags and substituted 11.2 million plastic PET labels with bio-based cellulose sea labels. Logitech has replaced plastic-based hang tabs with 7.6 million paper pulp hang tabs. The responsible minerals programs have resulted in 100% engagement and audit of its direct suppliers. The company achieved an Ecovadis platinum rating and continues to maintain its European listing on the Dow Jones Sustainability Index and FSTE4Good. In 2020, Logitech launched a Renewable Electricity Portal and Buyers Club for the purchase of high-quality and third-party certified renewable electricity. The company has made a financial contribution toward the Henan Fangcheng and Tanghe Afforestation project. The Design for Sustainability (DfS) framework combines the DfS goals into key focus areas of Breakthroughs, New Products, Existing Portfolio, and Data and Insights. As a part of DfS, the company has shifted focus to post-consumer recycled plastic across majority of its product lines. In the year 2022, the company has initiated steps to implement new greener Primary Circuity Board (PCB) technologies. The company aims to implement optimized architecture. For example, the company introduced the 163-gram weighted G435 as the lightest ever gaming headset which uses less material and fewer components compared to any other Logitech headset. The A10 Gen 2 is one of the first product lines to use Low Carbon Aluminum which results in an avoidance of projected 33 ton CO_2 per 100,000 units compared with the use of traditionally produced aluminum products. All the major suppliers were trained with respect to green procurement standards. In 2020, the company introduced a new voluntary paint policy with the target of having a 70% reduction in annual solvent-based paints. The key program of circular design focuses on the development of longer-lasting more energy-efficient products. The company uses best practice tools and processes to promote responsible sourcing and avoidance of conflict minerals through its global supply chain. In the year 2022, STREAMLABS Charity helped to raise over US$ 18 million through its platform. In 2022, the LogiCares program connected employees to more than 1100 non-profit organizations and more than US$285,000 in employee giving.

Stock Market Performance

An investment of $10,000 in July 2000 in stock would have amounted to $4289 only by April 2020.

Table 1 shows the cumulative return on the stock, the Nasdaq Composite Index, and the S&P 500 Information and Technology Index during the recent 5-year period. It is assumed that $100 was invested on March 31, 2017, in the stock or index including reinvestment of dividends till the fiscal year ending on March 31, 2022.

The 5-year holding period return for Logitech stock was 142% while for Nasdaq Composite and S&P 500 IT index the holding period return were 152% and 228%. The average annual returns for Logitech stock was 30% while for Nasdaq Composite and S&P 500 IT Index the average returns were 23% and 28%, respectively.

Five-Year Stock Return Analysis

The stock which was trading at$42.29 a share on Jan 1, 2018, increased by 1.45 times to trade at $61.63 by Dec 23, 2022. The total monthly cumulative return for the Logitech stock was 61.8% while for Nasdaq Composite Index, the monthly cumulative return was 46%. The average 5 yearly return for Logitech stock was 13% while for Nasdaq Composite, the return was 9%.

Table 2 gives the holding period return for the stock and Nasdaq Composite Index for the recent 5-year period. The analysis assumes a holding period of 1 year.

The stock registered its best performance in the year 2020 with holding period returns of 118%. The stock registered negative returns in the years 2018, 2021, and 2022.

Table 1 Cumulative stock returns

Year	2017	2018	2019	2020	2021	2022
Logitech International	$100	$117.00	$126.00	$139.00	$341.00	$242.00
Nasdaq Composite Index	$100	$121.00	$134.00	$135.00	$233.00	$252.00
S&P 500 Information and Technology Index	$100	$128.00	$147.00	$163.00	$271.00	$328.00

Source Annual Report

Table 2 Holding period returns

Year	Logitech	Nasdaq Composite Index	Excess returns
2018	−26%	−10%	−16%
2019	30%	23%	6%
2020	118%	41%	77%
2021	−21%	20%	−41%
2022	−26%	−26%	0%

Table 3 Book value and market value

Year	2018	2019	2020	2021	2022
Book value of equity	1050.56	1176.34	1489.27	2261.79	2398.74
Market value of equity	6044.99	6525.01	7164.85	17588.08	12192.22
BV as percent of MV	17.4%	18.0%	20.8%	12.9%	19.7%

Table 4 Financial highlights

	(In millions of dollars)				
Financial highlights	2018	2019	2020	2021	2022
Total assets	1743.16	2024.12	2363.47	4142.38	4035.41
Short-term investments	641.95	604.52	715.57	1750.33	1328.72
Total equity	1050.56	1176.34	1489.27	2261.79	2398.74
Total revenue	2566.86	2788.32	2975.85	5252.28	5481.1
Total operating expenses	684.53	762.52	822.5	1181.95	1483.34
Net income	208.54	257.57	449.72	947.26	644.51
Market cap	6044.99	6525.01	7164.85	17588.08	12192.22
Enterprise value	5403.04	5920.5	6479.76	15872.17	10905.4

Table 3 gives the book value and market value of the company during the recent 5-year period. The values are given in millions of dollars.

The average book value as a percent of market value was 17.7% during the period 2018–2022. In 2021, the market value was 7.78 times that of the book value of the company.

Financial Performance

Table 4 gives the highlights of the financial performance of the company during the period 2018–2022. The values are given in millions of dollars.

The growth rate of total revenue and net income in the year 2021 was 76% and 111%. The total assets and cash investments increased by 75% and 145% during the fiscal year 2021. On average basis the total assets, cash investments, and total equity increased by 26%, 33%, and 24%, respectively, during the period 2018–2022. The total revenues and net income increased by 24% and 44%, respectively, during the

Table 5 Profitability and leverage position

Ratios	2018	2019	2020	2021	2022
Net margin%	8.12	9.24	15.11	18.04	11.76
ROE%	21.88	23.13	33.74	50.51	27.66
ROA%	12.87	13.67	20.5	29.12	15.76
DER			0.02	0.02	0.02

Table 6 Economic value

Year	2021	2022
Profit before income tax	1148.12	775.82
Income tax	200.81	131.27
Net operating profit after tax (NOPAT)	947.31	644.55
Stockholder equity	2261.79	2398.74
Long-term debt		
Total capital employed	2261.79	2398.74
WACC	17.49%	16.92%
Capital charge	395.59	405.87
Economic value	551.73	238.68

above period of analysis. The market capitalization and enterprise value grew by 33% on an average basis.

Table 5 shows the profitability and leverage position of the firm during the period 2018–2022.

The average net margin, ROE, and ROA were 12.45%, 31.38%, and 18.38% during the period 2018–2022. The average debt-equity ratio was 0.02.

Table 6 illustrates the estimation of the economic value of Logitech in the years 2021 and 2022.

The economic value has declined from $551.73 million in the year 2021 to $238.68 million in the year 2022.

References

1. https://ir.logitech.com/stock-info/share-repurchase-history/default.aspx
2. https://www.logitech.com/en-us/sustainability/reports-and-resources.html
3. https://ir.logitech.com/stock-info/stock-quote-and-charts/default.aspx#module_tab%2D%2Dsix
4. Annual Report 2022

Case 28 PJT Partners

PJT Partners was formed by merger and spin-off transactions between PJT Partners and Blackstone Inc. The combined business was distributed to Blackstone's unitholders to create PJT Partners Inc. as a stand-alone independent publicly traded company. PJT Partners is a premier global advisory-focused investment bank. The firm offers strategic advisory, capital markets advisory, restructuring services, shareholder advisory services to corporations, financial sponsors, and institutional investors. PJT Partners Inc. is a holding company. The company offers private fund advisory services for private equity, real estate, hedge funds, and private credit. The company started trading on the New York Stock Exchange under the symbol PJT on October 1, 2015. The company advises clients on transactions which include mergers and acquisitions, spin-offs, joint ventures, minority investments, and divestitures. The company provides advisory services related to debt financings, acquisition financings, structured product offerings, IPO, and private capital related to early-stage financing. PJT Park Hill is the leading global alternative asset advisory and fundraising business which provides private fund advisory and fundraising services for a diverse range of investment strategies. PJT Park Hill's secondary advisory business is the leading advisor to global alternative asset managers. PJT also provides advisory services related to liquidity and structured solutions. By December 31, 2021, the company employed 833 individuals. The company has 10 offices in five countries with 105 global partners and clients across 58 countries.

Growth Strategy

The company focuses on providing clients with creative solutions for complex strategic problems. The Restructuring and Special Situations Group is a global market leader. The PJT Park Hill Platform has a leading market position in sectors such as private equity, real estate, hedge funds, private credit, and secondary advisory. PJT Camberview has advised over 55 Fortune 100 companies. The company follows an asset light business model in which it operates in an asset

© The Author(s), under exclusive license to Springer Nature Switzerland AG 2024

B. R. Kumar, *Rising Stars*, Management for Professionals,
https://doi.org/10.1007/978-3-031-50032-9_28

light, cloud-based environment devoid of constraints of heavy infrastructure, legacy systems, and processes. The company relies on limited embedded infrastructure to serve clients. The company aims to expand into new industry verticals to serve a broader range of clients. The company focusses on global expansion through talent additions and strategic alliances. The company operates on a scaled diversified global advisory franchise which consists of highly synergistic businesses. By undertaking operations in a more integrative manner, the firm is able to offer clients a comprehensive and differentiated suite of advisory services.

The competitors for PJT are other investment banking and financial advisory firms consisting of brokers and dealers, investment banking, and commercial banks.

Regulation

The financial services industry is subject to extensive regulation in the United States and across the globe. PJT Partners' LP as a registered broker dealer is subject to regulation and oversight by the Securities Exchange Commission. State securities regulators have regulatory oversight authority over registered broker dealers. Being a registered commodity trading advisor, PJT is regulated by the Commodity Futures Trading Commission and the National Futures Association.

Risk Factors

The business of the firm is subject to risks due to catastrophic events such as pandemic disease. The revenues of the firm are materially affected by conditions in the global financial markets and economic conditions. During period of unfavorable market or economic conditions, the demand for M&A advisory services may decline and result in increased price competition among the financial services companies. PJT Park Hill's ability to source business and earn fees related to private fund advisory and fundraising services depends on the availability of private and public capital for investments in illiquid assets such as private equity, real estate, hedge funds, and private credit.

The company had 159 clients with generated fees equal to or greater than $1 million for the year 2021. The reduction in the number of clients will adversely affect the revenues of the firm. The general economic conditions cost of debt and equity financing, and changes in laws and regulations may affect the company's restructuring and special situations businesses. The company faces the risk of foreign currency exchange rate fluctuations as approximately 12% of the total revenues are earned from international operations. The company may face increased litigation and regulatory risks due to its new entry into certain lines of business, joint ventures, strategic investments, etc. The company faces intense competition from financial services firms. PJT competes on both a global and regional basis. In this context, the company faces a number of risk factors such as strength and depth of client relationships, industry knowledge, and transaction execution skills. The company faces the risk of significant intervention by regulatory authorities which includes extended investigation and restrictive new regulations and its non-compliance may result in substantial penalties. The cost of compliance with international broker dealer, employment, labor, benefits, tax laws, and regulations may adversely affect the business operations of the firm.

Sustainability

In August 2022, PJT partnered with Sunrise Association for Sunrise Day Camp. Sunrise is a non-profit organization that supports local children with cancer and their families through zero-cost summer camps and hospital programs. In December 2021, PJT partnered with the River Fund to volunteer and help distribute food donations to over 2000 families. In May 2022, PJT hosted a ride for colleagues and clients in support of the David Riddell Memorial CIO (Charitable Incorporated Organization). The David Riddell Memorial CIO was established to destigmatize mental illness and reduce the risk of suicide by raising awareness, particularly among people working in the financial services sector and associated industries. PJT partnered with an independent third party to conduct the first inventory of Scope 1, Scope 2, and Scope 3 (business air travel) global greenhouse gas (GHG) emissions for the period 2019–2021. The corporate headquarters in New York, NY is LEED® (Leadership in Energy and Environmental Design) certified gold-rated and all of the leased office spaces in the United States are LEED® certified.

Stock Market Performance

The stock which was trading at $47.34 on January 1st, 2018, increased by 1.57 times to trade at $74.4 by December 2022. The cumulative monthly return for the PJT stock during the 5-year period Jan 2018–Dec 2022 was 61.2% while for the Nasdaq Composite index, the total monthly return was 44%. The average yearly returns for the stock during the period 2018–2022 was 12% while for the Nasdaq Composite Index, the return was 9%.

Table 1 provides the holding period return for PJT Partners stock during the period 2018–2022. The holding period return analysis is based on the assumption of a holding period of 1 year.

Table 1 Holding period return

Year	PJT Partners	Nasdaq Composite	Excess returns
2018	−18%	−10%	−8%
2019	4%	23%	−19%
2020	64%	41%	23%
2021	7%	20%	−12%
2022	7%	−28%	36%

Table 2 Book and market value

Year	2017	2018	2019	2020	2021
Book value of equity	422.45	487.75	574.52	687.85	637.57
Market value of equity	845.38	875.46	1041.46	1792.18	1801.82
BV as percent of MV	50.0%	55.7%	55.2%	38.4%	35.4%

Table 3 Financial highlights

	(In millions of dollars)				
Financial highlights	2017	2018	2019	2020	2021
Total assets	558.97	671.82	952.78	1171.61	987.63
Short-term investments	145.62	106.11	215.95	299.51	200.48
Total equity	422.45	487.75	574.52	687.85	637.57
Total revenue	499.28	580.25	717.64	1052.3	991.95
Total operating expenses	78.7	93.64	106.9	94.37	104.78
Net income	−32.55	27.17	29.56	117.55	106.17
Market cap	845.38	875.46	1041.46	1792.18	1801.82
Enterprise value	1279.5	1313.56	1573.06	2198.55	2275.7

Table 4 Profitability and leverage ratio

Ratios	2018	2019	2020	2021	2022
Net margin%	−6.52	4.68	4.12	11.17	10.7
ROE%			1198.3	126.64	77.36
ROA%	−5.66	4.42	3.64	11.07	9.83
DER		−1.13	6.51	1.12	1.31

The Holding period return for PJT was highest in the year 2020. The market index Nasdaq Composite had superior returns compared to the stock in the years 2019 and 2020.

Table 2 gives the book and market value of the stock during the period 2017–2021. The values are given in millions of dollars.

The book value as a percent of market value was 46.9%. In the year 2017, the market value was twice that of book value of the firm. By 2021, the market value increased by 2.83 times compared to the book value of the firm.

Table 3 gives the financial highlights of PJT Partners during the 5-year period 2017–2021. The values are given in millions of dollars.

The total assets, cash, and total equity grew by 17%, 21%, and 11%, respectively, on average basis during the period 2017–2021. The total revenue and net income grew by 20% and 28%, respectively, on average basis. The market capitalization and enterprise value increased by 24% and 16% on average basis during the above period of analysis. The total expenses grew by 8% on average basis during the above period.

Table 4 gives the profitability and leverage position of the company during the period 2017–2021.

Table 5 Estimation of economic value

Year	2020	2021
Profit before income tax	247.96	219.45
Income tax	35.53	29.49
Net operating profit after tax (NOPAT)	212.43	189.96
Stockholder equity	687.85	637.57
Long-term debt		
Total capital employed	687.85	637.57
WACC	5.66%	5.34%
Capital charge	38.93	34.05
Economic value	173.50	155.91

The average net margin, ROE, and ROA were 4.83%, 467.43%, and 4.66%, respectively, during the period 2018–2022. The average debt-to-equity ratio was 1.95.

Table 5 illustrates the estimation of economic value of PJT Partners during the years 2020 and 2021.

The economic value has declined from $173.50 million in 2020 to $155.91 million in the year 2021.

References

1. https://ir.pjtpartners.com/sec-filings/annual-reports/content/0001564590-22-007189/0001564590-22-007189.pdf
2. https://d1io3yog0oux5.cloudfront.net/pjtpartners/files/pages/corporate-sustainability/PJT_Corporate_Sustainability_Report_2022_Final.pdf
3. https://pjtpartners.com/

Case 29 MVB Financial Corporation

MVB Financial Corp is a financial holding company incorporated in the year 2003 and operates principally through its wholly owned subsidiary MVB Bank. The consolidated subsidiaries of the bank include MVB Insurance LLC and MVB Community Development Corporation.

MVB Financial Corporation is involved in a range of commercial and retail (CoRe) banking services and Fintech banking. The products and services offered to customers under CoRe banking include different demand deposits, savings account, money market accounts, certificates of deposits, commercial, consumer and real estate mortgage loans, and lines of credit. Debit cards, cashier's checks, and safe deposit rental facilities are also offered. Non-deposit investment services are offered through an association with a broker dealer. The bank provides banking services to corporate Fintech clients with a focus on operational risk management and compliance. The bank provides client services for payments, digital savings, cryptocurrency, crowdfunding, and gaming industries. The revenues from CoRe banking activities consist of interest earned on loans and investment securities and service charges on deposit accounts. The core banking segment consists of the Fintech banking division, MVB insurance, and MVB CDC. The revenues from the mortgage banking activities consist of interest earned on loans and fees from the mortgage loan origination process. The revenues from financial holding company are sourced from intercompany service income and dividends. By December 2021, commercial loans represented 80% of the total aggregate loan. Commercial loans include commercial and industrial, commercial real estate, and financial loans. The consumer loans consist of installment loans used by clients to purchase automobiles, boats, and recreational vehicles.

MVB Financial Corp is publicly traded on the Nasdaq Capital Market under the ticker "MVBF." MVB Financial was ranked as number 29 on Fortune's 100 fastest-growing companies list for the year 2021. MVB's services are provided to clients in the Mid-Atlantic region as well as to Fintech, Payment, and Gaming clients throughout the United States. MVB Bank was named Bank of the Year 2021 United States by the Banker magazine.

© The Author(s), under exclusive license to Springer Nature Switzerland AG 2024

B. R. Kumar, *Rising Stars*, Management for Professionals,
https://doi.org/10.1007/978-3-031-50032-9_29

MVB in its 20-year-plus history, has grown from a community bank with just 35 employees to Nasdaq listed Russell 2000 company with over 500 team members based throughout the United States.

Growth Strategy

The growth strategy of MVB focusses on strategic components such as building fintech, strategic acquisition, resource allocation, efficient capital structure, and introduction of new business lines. The strategic aim is to have strong loan growth and increase a diverse client base. By 2021, the loan-to-deposit ratio increased to 78.6% reflecting low-cost funding and diverse loan growth. The bank has a focused strategy for reallocation of resources. MVB is in a competitive position with a robust capital base and low credit risk profile. The low-cost deposit growth from the Fintech business has reduced the need for the bank to build infrastructure to attract adequate funding. MVB has undertaken a couple of acquisition and divestiture activities during recent years. In 2021, the Bank entered into an agreement to acquire an 80% interest in Flexia which possesses a proprietary license that allows users to access a reloadable account that combines a debit card account and casino gaming accounts into one card for non-cash transactions.

In 2021, MVB acquired Trabian Technology Inc. which is a software firm involved in the servicing of financial institutions and Fintech companies. Trabian builds digital products and web and mobile applications for community banks, credit unions, digital banks, and Fintech companies. With respect to divestiture activity, the bank completed the sale of certain assets and liabilities of four banking centers in West Virginia in the year 2021.

MVB established a wholly owned subsidiary MVB Edge Ventures as a management company that manages Fintech companies of MVB. During 2021, MVB established a new partnership agreement with NYDIG a leading technology and financial services firm which offers Bitcoin services to Fintechs. The company has a strategic plan to build and invest in the entire Fintech ecosystem along with providing banking services to Fintechs. MVB Technology is a 93.4% owned subsidiary of Edge Ventures. The primary product of MVB Technology-GRAND facilitates cost-effective payment from modern bank accounts. This product facilitates significant savings for online merchants through a streamlined process for transfers of customer funds. In the year 2021, Victor was established as a wholly owned subsidiary of Edge Ventures to offer a broad spectrum of Fintech solutions for gaming, payments, banking as a service, and digital asset sectors.

In 2021, MVB made strategic investments of $3.8 million as a part of its Fintech investment portfolio. This investment portfolio has generated an IRR of 185% since its initiation in the year 2016. The proportion of stakeholder investments consists of 43% institutional investors, 42% retail, and 15% insiders.

Competitive Factors

The major competitors for MVB are commercial banks, savings associations, insurance companies, governmental agencies, credit unions, brokerage firms, and pension funds. Interest rates, loan terms, and overall lending services are the primary factors that determine the competitiveness of loans. The major competitors for deposits are commercial banks, savings associations, money market funds and credit unions, insurance companies, and brokerage firms. The competitive factors for deposits are deposit interest rates, technology offerings, etc. Fintech companies that operate in partnership with financial service providers are also competitors for the company. The strategic approach adopted by the company provides integrated banking services to offer an array of banking products and services. The company offers a need-based selling approach to meet the financial needs of customers.

Risk Factors

MVB is subject to extensive regulation under federal and state banking laws. The earnings of the company are affected by general economic conditions, management policies, and changes in state and federal laws and regulations. There has been a significant increase in regulation and regulatory oversight on account of enactment of the Dodd–Frank Wall Street Reform and Consumer Protection Act. Approximately 63% of the total loans are based on real estate sector. Declining real estate values could negatively impact the value of real estate collaterals that are used for securing such loans. The non-residential real estate loans expose MVB to greater risks of non-payment and loss than residential mortgage loans which might affect net income as provisions for loan losses could increase. By 2021, the loan portfolio comprised $41.5 million subprime automobile loans. The loan portfolio may be adversely affected if the firms experience delinquencies or non-payment related to subprime automobile loans. The ICM's profitability depends on its ability to originate high volume of mortgage loans and sell them in the secondary market. The bank's earnings depend primarily on its net interest income which is significantly affected by interest rate risks. The competitive pressures to pay higher interest rates on deposits to gaming customers might increase funding costs and compress net interest margins. The transition from LIBOR mechanism may adversely impact the bank as the return on the financial instruments are indexed to LIBOR. There are substantial risks associated with adoption of new product lines and services. Investments made in evolving businesses like Fintech lead to increased business, reputational, and operational risks along with complex legal, regulatory, and compliance costs. Investments in Fintech companies are subject to financial, reputational, and strategic risks. Interruption in information systems or security breaches could adversely affect the operations of the firm. The bank's engagement with clients in the cryptocurrency market creates uncertainties with respect to risks.

Sustainability

MVB has focused on three key projects involving community service, technical assistance, and leadership to community organizations as part of its sustainability initiatives. In 2021, MVB became a corporate sponsor of Knoble, the non-profit network of experts with the aim of human and financial prevention, child exploitations, and scams. MVB is a founding corporate sponsor of the West Virginia Game Changer program which is an initiative designed to combat opioid and substance misuse. In September 2021, virtual game changer programs were introduced across 125 high schools and 160 middle schools in the United States. In the year 2021, Team MVB performed 1626 h of community service. MVB partners with United Ways, non-profit agencies, local community foundations, local schools, and economic development groups. In 2021, MVB group conducted a financial literacy impact program for 3217 students and businesses. MVB has established a Diversity, Equity, and Inclusion Team Member Resource Group, composed of 28 company volunteers across the organization.

Five-Year Stock Performance

Table 1 shows the cumulative total shareholder return including the reinvestment of dividends for MVB stock in comparison to the KBW index and the Russell 2000 index. The stock performance is measured based on the assumption that $100 was invested on December 31, 2016, and the cumulative return is measured as of each subsequent fiscal year end.

The 5-year holding period return for MVB Financial Corp stock was 234% whereas for KBW Bank index and Russell 2000, the returns amounted to 44% and 65%, respectively. The average yearly return during the period 2017–2021 was 32% for the MVB Financial Corp while for KBW Bank Index and Russell 2000, the average returns were 10% and 11%, respectively.

Five-Year Stock Return Analysis

The return analysis is based on the 5-year period 1/1/2018–30/12/2022. The stock was trading at $19.37 on January 1, 2018, increased by 1.13 times to trade at $22.02 on December 30, 2022. The MVB stock had a cumulative monthly return of 45%

Table 1 Five-year stock performance

Year	2016	2017	2018	2019	2020	2021
MVB Financial Corp.	$100	$157.81	$142.58	$197.85	$183.16	$334.34
KBW Bank Index	$100	$116.25	$93.46	$123.50	$106.67	$144.05
Russell 2000	$100	$113.14	$99.37	$122.94	$145.52	$165.45

Source: Annual Report 2021

Table 2 Holding period return

Year	MVB	Russell 2000	Excess returns
2018	−7%	−14%	7%
2019	48%	11%	37%
2020	14%	22%	−9%
2021	85%	8%	77%
2022	−45%	−13%	−32%

Table 3 Book and market value

Year	2017	2018	2019	2020	2021
Book value of equity	150.19	176.77	211.94	239.48	275.3
Market value of equity	209.94	209.4	297.65	261.42	501.85
BV as percent of MV	71.5%	84.4%	71.2%	91.6%	54.9%

Table 4 Financial highlights

	(In millions of dollars)				
Financial highlights	2017	2018	2019	2020	2021
Total assets	1534.3	1750.97	1944.11	2331.48	2792.45
Short-term investments	35.08	37	40.55	275.7	310.16
Total equity	150.19	176.77	211.94	239.48	275.3
Total revenue	81.8	87.14	120.96	134.75	122.33
Net income	7.58	12	26.99	37.41	39.12
Market cap	209.94	209.4	297.65	261.42	501.85
Enterprise value	368.38	412.64	491.44	36.46	265.7

while the index registered a cumulative monthly return of 25% during the period 2018–2022. The 5-yearly average return for the MVB stock was 9% while for the index Russell 2000 the average return was 5%.

Table 2 shows the holding period return for the stock and the market index Russell 2000 during the period 2018–2022. The analysis assumes a holding period of 1 year. The data for analysis was taken from Yahoo Finance.

MVB stock registered its best performance in the year 2021 with holding period returns of 85%. In 2019, the stock had a holding period return of 48%. The market index Russell 2000 had superior returns compared to stock returns in the years 2020 and 2022.

Table 3 gives the book value and market value of MVB during the period 2018–2022. The values are given in millions of dollars.

The average book value as percent of market value was approximately 75% during the 5-year period 2017–2021. In 2021, the market value was 1.82 times that of the book value of MVB Financials.

Table 4 gives the financial highlights of the company during the period 2017–2021. The values are given in millions of dollars.

The total assets, cash investments, and total equity increased by 16%, 152%, and 16% on average basis during the period 2017–2021. During the above period, the

Table 5 Profitability and leverage position

Ratios	2017	2018	2019	2020	2021
Net margin%	9.26	13.77	22.31	27.76	31.98
ROE%	5.12	7.34	13.89	16.57	15.23
ROA%	0.51	0.73	1.46	1.75	1.53
DER	1.24	1.32	1.07	0.18	0.27

Table 6 Economic value

Year	2020	2021
Profit before income tax	46.94	48.58
Income tax	9.53	9.88
Net operating profit after tax (NOPAT)	37.41	38.70
Stockholder equity	239.48	275.30
Long-term debt	43.41	73.03
Total capital employed	282.89	348.33
WACC	6.81%	8.02%
Capital charge	19.26	27.94
Economic value	18.14	10.76

growth rate of revenues and net income was 12% and 57% on average basis. The market capitalization and enterprise value increased by 30% and 142%, respectively, during the above period of analysis. The data was sourced from gurufocus.com

Table 5 gives the highlights of the performance indicators for MVB during the period 2017–2021.

The net margin, ROE, and ROA during the period 2017–2021 were 21.02%, 11.63%, and 1.20%, respectively. The average debt-equity ratio during the above period was 0.82.

Table 6 illustrates the estimation of economic value for MVB Corporation.

The economic value has declined from $18.14 million in 2020 to $10.76 million in the year 2021.

References

1. https://mvbbanking.com/
2. MVB Annual Report 2021

Case 30 Amazon

Amazon is the leading online retailer and one of the highest-grossing e-commerce aggregators positioning as the e-commerce leader. In 2021, the company had $386 billion in net sales and approximately $578 billion in estimated physical/digital online gross merchandise volume. Retail-related revenues comprise approximately 80% of the total revenues. Amazon through Amazon Web Services (AWS) is also a market leader in public cloud services.

During the pandemic, millions of people relied on Amazon for PPE, food, clothing, and other items. Amazon stores are designed to offer millions of unique products to consumers which are sold by Amazon and third parties across dozens of product categories. Customers can access the offerings through websites, mobile apps, Alexa, devices, streaming, and physical visits to its stores. The company also manufactures and sells electronic devices such as Kindle, Fire tablet, Fire TV, Echo, and Ring. Amazon also develops and produces media content. Amazon offers subscription services such as Amazon Prime whose membership program facilitates fast free shipping on millions of items, access to award winning movies and series. The company satisfies customer orders through online and physical stores. Amazon has organized its operations into three segments: North America, International, and Amazon Web Services. The company fulfills customer orders through North American and International fulfillment networks, co-sourced and outsourced arrangements, digital delivery, and physical stores. The company serves developers and enterprises which include startups, government agencies, and academic institutions through AWS which offers a broad set of on-demand technology services such as analytics and machine learning. Through Kindle Direct Publishing and its own Amazon publishing arm, Amazon serves authors and independent publishers by making their books available in the Kindle Store. Amazon also offers programs for musicians, filmmakers, and Twitch streamers to publish and sell content. The company also provides advertising services to sellers, vendors, and publishers through programs such as sponsored advertisements, display, and video advertising. Amazon works with more than 2 million independent partners in the United States which include sellers, developers, content and delivery providers.

© The Author(s), under exclusive license to Springer Nature Switzerland AG 2024

B. R. Kumar, *Rising Stars*, Management for Professionals,
https://doi.org/10.1007/978-3-031-50032-9_30

Amazon has a presence in more than 130 countries around the world. The company has more than 3000 independent delivery service partners. Amazon has delivered more than 2.2 billion packages and has generated over $12 billion in revenues. Millions of organizations in over 190 countries are powered by Amazon Web Services (AWS). Thousands of startups, non-governmental agencies are powered by AWS's reliable, scalable, and low-cost cloud technology. Innovations are happening at unprecedented pace to offer real-world sustainability solutions using AWS. There are over 900,000 developers building for Alexa. Amazon had introduced the Appstore Small Business Accelerator and the Alexa Skill Developer Accelerator aimed at helping small-scale developers to grow their app and skill businesses. Amazon Appstore is also involved in curating apps for the Windows 11 storefront which enables functioning of mobile apps and games on Windows.

By December 31, 2021, the company employed 1608,000 full-time and part-time employees. Amazon also uses independent contractors and temporary personnel to supplement its workforce.

Growth Strategy

The company aims to be the most customer-centric company in the world. The focus is on to serve the primary customer sets consisting of consumers, sellers, developers, enterprises, content creators, and advertisers.

The company focusses on its strategy to offer customers low prices, fast and free delivery, and timely customer service. Amazon had spent the first 25 years since its establishment to build a very large fulfillment network. By the end of 2021, the company have 253 fulfillment centers, 110 sortation centers, and 467 delivery stations in North America. Moreover, the global network includes 157 fulfillment centers, 58 sortation centers, and 588 delivery stations. There are more than 100 aircraft in the Amazon air cargo fleet. The delivery network consists of 260,000 drivers worldwide. Over the last one and a half decade, the company has made a capital investment of over $100 billion. The company has built its infrastructure to manage its shipments efficiently.

In 2007, the firm made its entry into devices through Kindle which offered customers the ability to download over 90,000 books which has improved over to millions of downloads. Amazon introduced Alexa, the first Echo device resourceful personal assistant for customers. Amazon devices such as Ring and Blink provide leading digital home security solutions. The company started Prime Video in 2006 where customers could download movies from major studios. In 2011, Amazon started offering over 5000 streaming movies as part of customers' Amazon Prime subscriptions. Many large entertainment companies have prime video channels as partners.

The primary source of revenue for Amazon is the sale of a wide range of products and services offered to customers through its stores which include merchandise and content which the company has purchased for resale and products offered by third-party sellers. The company focusses on increasing unit sales across its stores through increased product selection across numerous product categories. The company focuses on increasing all aspects of customer experience such as lowering prices, improving availability, offering faster delivery, and performance times. Amazon aims for variable cost reduction through direct sourcing, increasing discounts from suppliers, and reducing defects in the processes. In its technological focus, Amazon invests in AWS which offers a broad set of on-demand technology services which include compute, storage, database, analytics, and machine learning.

Competition

Amazon has many competitors in different industries which include physical, e-commerce, and omni channel, retail, e-commerce, web and infrastructure computing services, digital content, advertising, grocery, transportation, and logistics services. The competitive factors in the retail businesses include selection, price, and convenience.

Risk Factors

The businesses of Amazon are rapidly evolving and intensely competitive. The competitors may secure better terms from vendors, adopt more aggressive pricing and devote more resources to technology, infrastructure, fulfillment, and marketing. Hence Amazon may face business risks. Amazon's expansion into new products, services, technologies, and geographic regions leads to additional risks. International sales and operations are subject to a number of risk factors such as local economic and political factors, restrictive government regulations such as trade protection measures, restrictions on foreign ownership, regulations with respect to physical and digital distribution of media products, and enforcement of intellectual property rights. Limitations on the repartition and investment of funds and foreign currency exchange restrictions can create risks for operations of Amazon's businesses. Amazon has significant suppliers which include content and technology licensors. Violations by suppliers and vendors with respect to regulations, contractual terms, and intellectual property rights may expose Amazon to reputational damages and affect the operations of the firm. Amazon may face risks if the company is not able to implement, maintain, and develop commercial relationships related to web services, fulfillment, tax collection, payment processing, etc. The company also faces inventory and payment-related risks.

Sustainability Initiatives

The Climate Pledge undertaken by Amazon aims to be net zero carbon by the year 2040. Amazon is the world's largest corporate buyer of renewable energy with over 247 projects globally. Amazon aims to power its operations with 100% renewable energy by the year 2025. The Climate Pledge has been signed by Amazon and other companies which account for over $3.5 trillion in global annual revenues and have more than 8 million employees across 51 industries in 29 countries. The climate pledge program would cover more than 200,000 products which will enable customers to shop for products that have one or more of 37 different sustainability certifications. Amazon has mobilized $1 billion as a part of the ambitious public–private partnership initiative designed to protect tropical forests. Amazon has partnered with automakers as a part of its decarbonization goals. Amazon also has long-term programs to support communities in different ways. Amazon Future Engineer is the global childhood-to-career computer science program to help students from underserved and underrepresented communities. The Amazon web services designed programs provide free cloud skills training aimed at 29 million people around the world by the year 2025. Amazon launched the $10 million AWS Artificial Intelligence and Machine Learning Scholarship, for preparing underrepresented and underserved students globally for careers in machine learning. Amazon Housing Equity Fund has initiated plans for providing over 8000 affordable houses at an estimated cost of $1.2 billion. Amazon donates its logistics network to support food banks and community organizations. In 2021, over 20 million meals were delivered in the United States, Australia, Japan, Singapore, Spain, and the United Kingdom. Amazon also leverages its operational excellence, technologies, and worldwide logistics network to support management of large-scale natural disasters. In 2021, Amazon donated more than 300,000 emergency aid items to support communities that were affected by natural disasters in the United States, India, British Columbia, and Canada. Amazon has created more jobs in the last decade than any other company. These jobs pay an average of $18 per hour more than double the federal minimum wage.

Amazon has launched a $12 million, 5-year partnership with the US National Safety Council to research musculoskeletal disorders.

In May 2021, the company released Amazon's Sustainable Bond Framework and issued a $1 billion Sustainability bond and allocated the net proceeds to clean transportation projects. The company has custom orders for delivery of 100,000 electric delivery vehicles by the year 2030 in partnership with Rivian Stellantis. Amazon has aims to deliver 50% of all shipments with net zero carbon by the year 2030.

As a part of the Responsible Minerals Initiative of Amazon, the company identifies and assesses risk in the supply chain through conflict minerals due diligence which is based on survey information from in-scope product suppliers. AWS aims to be water positive by 2030 by returning more water to communities than it uses in direct operations through special projects. Amazon focuses on sustainable packaging options using science-based approach that combines lab testing, machine learning, materials science, and manufacturing partnerships. Since 2015, Amazon was able to reduce the weight of outbound packaging per shipment by more than 36%. The company has eliminated over 1 million tons of packaging material which is equivalent to 2 billion shipping boxes.

In 2021, Amazon invested in companies such as Amogy, BETA Technologies, CMC Machinery, and Hippo Harvest to accelerate sustainability initiatives across sectors such as transportation, aviation, freight, packaging, farming, and technology. Amogy's technology facilitates decarbonization of long-distance transportation such as cargo shipping. Amazon's investment in BETA Technologies is aimed at zero-emissions package delivery. CMC's technology could reduce the cubic volume of boxes for package deliveries by 24% on average basis and reduce usage of 1 billion plastic air pillows. Hippo Harvest's technology addresses the emissions and waste that result from traditional produce farming. In 2021, Amazon partnered with The Nature Conservancy to launch the Agroforestry and Restoration Accelerator to restore native rainforests to naturally trap and store carbon and mitigate climate change.

By the end of 2021, Amazon has announced 274 global renewable energy projects, 105 utility-scale wind and solar projects, and 169 solar rooftops on facilities and stores.

Political Engagement Policy

Amazon's policy is to participate in public policymaking by engaging in lobbying in the context of existing and proposed laws, legislation, regulation, and policy initiatives which includes commerce, intellectual property, trade, data privacy, transportation, web services, sustainability, and other areas. The Company's Vice President of Public Policy reviews and approves each campaign contribution made with company funds or resources.

Stock Market Performance

The stock market performance of Amazon was analyzed in comparison with the market index S&P500 index during the period Jan 2018–Jan 2023. The Amazon stock which was trading at$75.6 on January 2nd, 2018, increased by 1.12 times to trade at $85.13 by January 1st, 2023. The total cumulative monthly return for Amazon during the period Jan 2018–Jan 2023 was 38% whereas the cumulative monthly return for S&P 500 Index was 44%. The average yearly return for Amazon stock was 8% while for the index the return was 9%.

Table 1 Holding period return

Year	Amazon	S&P 500	Excess returns
2018	−1%	−8%	7%
2019	8%	19%	−12%
2020	62%	16%	46%
2021	4%	28%	−24%
2022	−44%	−15%	−29%

Table 2 Book and market value trends

Year	2017	2018	2019	2020	2021
Book value of equity	27,709	43,549	62,060	93,404	138,245
Market value of equity	566023.48	737467.27	920224.32	1638230.7	1697179.06
BV as percent of MV	4.9%	5.9%	6.7%	5.7%	8.1%

Table 3 Financial highlights

	(In millions of dollars)				
Financial highlights	2017	2018	2019	2020	2021
Total assets	131,310	162,648	225,248	321,195	420,549
Short-term investments	30,986	41,250	55,021	84,396	96,049
Total equity	27,709	43,549	62,060	93,404	138,245
Total revenue	177,870	232,890	280,520	386,060	469,820
Total operating expenses	13,957	18,446	24,282	28,601	41,436
Net income	3030	10,070	11,590	21,330	33,360
Market cap	566023.48	737467.27	920224.32	1638230.7	1697179.06
Enterprise value	572963.48	729362.27	928408.32	1638223.76	1717525.06

Table 1 shows the holding period return for Amazon stock and S&P 500 during the period Jan 2018–Dec 2022. The source of data was Yahoo finance.com. The analysis assumes a holding period of 1 year.

The market index S&P 500 Index had superior performance compared to the stock in the years 2019, 2021, and 2022. Amazon stock had superior returns compared to S&P 500 Index with excess returns of 46%.

Table 2 gives the market value and book value of Amazon during the period 2017–2021. The values are given in millions of dollars.

The average book value as percent of market value was 6.3% during the period 2017–2021. In 2017, the market value was 20 times that of the book value of Amazon. In 2021, the market value of Amazon was 12 times that of the book value of the firm.

Operating Performance Highlights

Table 3 gives the financial highlights of Amazon during the period 2017–2021. The values are given in millions of dollars. The data source is Morningstar, Yahoo Finance, and gurufocus.com.

On an average basis, the total assets, cash investments, and total equity grew by 34%, 33%, and 50%, respectively, during the period 2017–2021. The total revenues and net income increased by 28% and 97%, respectively, during the period 2017–2021. The total operating expenses increased by 32% on average basis. The

Table 4 Profitability and leverage ratios

Ratios	2017	2018	2019	2020	2021
Net margin%	1.71	4.33	4.13	5.53	7.1
ROE%	12.91	28.27	21.95	27.44	28.81
ROA%	2.83	6.85	5.97	7.81	9
DER	1.37	0.91	1.02	0.9	0.84

Table 5 Estimation of economic value

Year	2020	2021
Profit before income tax	24,178	38,151
Income tax	2862.68	4791.77
Net operating profit after tax (NOPAT)	21315.32	33359.23
Stockholder equity	93404.00	138245.00
Long-term debt	31816.00	48744.00
Total capital employed	125220.00	186989.00
WACC	7.69%	6.64%
Capital charge	9629.42	12416.07
Economic value	11685.91	20943.16

market capitalization and enterprise value increased by 34%, respectively, during the above period.

Table 4 gives the performance indicators for Amazon in terms of profitability and leverage position.

The average net margin, ROE, and ROA during the period 2017–2021 were 4.56%, 23.88%, and 6.49%. The average debt-equity ratio was 1.01.

Table 5 shows the estimation of the economic value of Amazon during the period 2020 and 2021. The values are given in millions of dollars.

The economic value has increased from $11.685 billion dollars in 2020 to $20.943 billion dollars in the year 2021.

References

1. https://ir.aboutamazon.com/overview/default.aspx
2. aboutamazon.com/impact/community
3. Amazon 2022 Proxy Statement.
4. 2021 US Political Engagement and Policy Statement
5. Amazon Sustainability Bond Allocation Report 2022
6. 2021 Amazon Mineral Conflict Report
7. https://www.aboutamazon.com/planet/improving-packaging
8. https://sustainability.aboutamazon.com/2021-sustainability-report.pdf

Case 31 Scotts Miracle-Gro

The company Scotts Miracle-Gro (SMG) was established in the year 1968 when its founder O M Scott opened a storefront in Marysville, Ohio. SMG is the leading manufacturer and marketer of branded consumer lawn and garden products in North America. SMG also has a presence in similar branded consumer products in China. SMG is also the exclusive agent of the Monsanto company, the subsidiary of Bayer AG for the marketing and distribution of certain Monsanto's consumer Roundup®1 branded products within the USA and certain other specified countries. The company has an equity interest in Bonnie Plants, a joint venture with Alabama Farmers' Cooperative, Inc. which is involved in planting, growing, and selling live plants. The US Consumer segment consists of consumer lawn and garden business in the USA. The Hawthorne segment consists of indoor and hydroponic gardening business. The other segment consists of consumer lawn and garden business outside of the USA.

The major consumer lawn and garden brands include Scotts® and Turf Builder® lawn and grass seed products; Miracle-Gro® gardening and landscape products; Ortho® and Home Defense® insect control and weed control products; and Tomcat® branded rodent control products. SMG also owns the company AeroGarden that manufactures hydroponic gardening products for consumers. The subsidiary Hawthorne Gardening is a leading manufacturer and distributor of nutrients, advanced indoor growing products, lighting and ventilation systems, and accessories for hydroponic gardening. The key brands in this segment include General Hydroponics®, Gavita®, Botanicare®, Agrolux®, Can-Filters®, Sun System®, Luxx Lighting®, GroPro®, Mother Earth®, Hurricane®, Grower's Edge®, and Hydro-Logic.

In 2021, Scotts Miracle-Gro (SMG) owned or leased 94 manufacturing properties, 28 distribution properties, and four research and development properties in the USA and Canada.

© The Author(s), under exclusive license to Springer Nature Switzerland AG 2024

B. R. Kumar, *Rising Stars*, Management for Professionals,
https://doi.org/10.1007/978-3-031-50032-9_31

Principal Products and Services

SMG manufacture, market, and sell lawn and garden products in the following categories.

Lawn Care

This segment is designed specifically for lawn users. The products included in this category include lawn fertilizer products and lawn-based weed, pest, and disease control products under different brands like Scotts and Turf Builder. The lawn category also includes spreaders, other durables, and market outdoor cleaners.

Gardening and Landscape

This segment is designed to facilitate cultivation of flowers and vegetable gardens and beautify landscaped areas. Products offered in this category consist of water-soluble plant foods, continuous-release plant foods, potting mixes, garden soils, ground cover, etc. These products are mainly offered under the Miracle-Gro brand. Plant-related pest and disease control products are sold under the Ortho® brand. Hydroponic and indoor gardening-focused growing media and nutrient products are marketed under the Mother Earth®, Botanicare®, General Hydroponics®, Vermicrop®, and Cyco® brand names.

Hydroponic Hardware and Growing Environments

The products offered under this category include growing systems, trays, fans, filters, humidifiers, timers, water pumps, irrigation supplies, and hand tools.

Lighting

The products offered consist of lighting systems and components for use in hydroponic and indoor gardening applications. The products offered include lighting sensors, controls, fixtures, reflectors, and lamps and are marketed majorly under the Gavita®, Agrolux®, and Titan® brand.

Controls

The products offered consist of insect, rodent, and weed control products. These products are marketed under brands such as Ortho, Tomcat, and Groundclear.

Hydroponic gardening-focused control products are marketed under the Alchemist® and General Hydroponics® brand names.

Growth Strategy

In the early 1900s, the company began selling grass seed to consumers. In the late 1920s, SMG started manufacturing and selling quality fertilizers for usage in the lawns. In the 1990s, SMG expanded its product offering with three powerful leading brands in the US home lawn and garden industry. In 1995, the company acquired the Miracle-Gro brand through a merger with Stern's Miracle-Gro Products Inc. which was a leader in water-soluble garden plant foods. In 1999, SMG acquired the Ortho® brand in the USA and obtained exclusive rights to market Monsanto's consumer Roundup® brand within the USA and other contractually specified countries. Through this restructuring, SMG diversified its portfolio by adding industry leading weed, pest, and disease control products. Through a series of acquisitions and investments, the Hawthorne subsidiary of the company was catapulted as the market leader of indoor and hydroponic gardening products in North America. In 2021, Hawthorne acquired the assets of Luxx Lighting Inc. for a purchase price of $213.2 million. SMG had also acquired the assets of True Liberty Bags, a leading provider of liners and storage solutions to dry and cure plant products, for $10.1 million. In the year 2022, Hawthorne segment completed the acquisition of all assets of S J Enterprises PTY Ltd., an Australian based provider of premium nutrients, additives, and media products for indoor gardening for a purchase price of $37.3 million. SMG made an additional investment in Toronto-based RIV Capital Inc. which is a cannabis investment and acquisition firm listed on the Canadian Securities Exchange. The company sells its products through direct sales force, e-commerce website, and network of brokers and distributors to home centers, mass merchandisers, large hardware chains, nurseries, garden centers, indoor gardening and hydroponic product distributors, etc.

The company's North America consumer lawn and garden business is highly seasonal with approximately 75% of the annual net sales accounted in the second and third fiscal quarters. Home Depot and Lowe's are the two largest customers and represent more than 10% of reported consolidated net sales during the recent fiscal years.

By September 30, 2022, the company had employed approximately 6100 employees.

Competitors

The markets in which SMG operates are highly competitive in nature. The primary competitors are Spectrum Brands Holdings, Central Garden & Pet Company, Enforcer Products, Kellogg Garden Products, Oldcastle Retail, Inc., Reckitt Benckiser Group plc, and Hydrofarm Holdings Group. Research and Development expenses amounted to $39.7, $45.3, and $45.3 million in the year 2020,2021 and 2022 respectively.

Regulations

Laws and regulations in the USA and other countries affect the manufacture, sale, and distribution of products of the company. The pesticide products are required to be registered with the US Environmental Protection Agency and must comply with the Federal Insecticide, Fungicide, and Rodenticide Act (FIFRA). Fertilizer and growing media products are subject to different laws and regulations which require registration, mandate labeling requirements, etc. The grass seed products are regulated by the Federal Seed Act and various state regulations.

Risk Factors

The unpredictability of demand for products and non-maintenance of appropriate inventory could negatively impact the operations of the firm. Increase in price of raw materials or transportation costs could adversely affect the business operations. The recurrence of pandemics like COVID will have a material adverse effect on the company's businesses. The two top retail customers of Home Depot and Lowe's together accounted for 43% and 46% of net sales and outstanding accounts receivable as of September 2022. The loss or significant reduction in orders from top customers will adversely affect the financial results of the firm. Acquisitions, other strategic alliances, and investments could result in operating difficulties and adversely affect the business operations. The company sell certain products over the internet through online store and other e-commerce retail platforms. The success of the firm's e-commerce business depends on investment in these platforms, consumer preferences, and buying trends related to e-commerce. The company faces risks if the information technology systems fail to perform or are subject to data breach or cyber-attack. The international operations of the firm are subject to risks in foreign countries such as fluctuations in currency exchange rates, restrictions on the remittance of dividends, and additional costs of compliance with local regulations. By September 2022, the company had $2992.1 million of debt and $1185.5 million in available borrowings under credit facility. The inability of the firm to meet restrictive financial and non-financial covenants with respect to debt or generate sufficient cash flow to repay debt could adversely affect the financial condition of the firm.

ESG Initiatives

The Innovation and Technology Committee in consultation with the Nominating & Governance Committee oversees the company's product-related ESG policies and practices. SMG through the Supplier Code of Conduct has mandated that all labor must be voluntary and no supplier shall support or engage in slavery or human trafficking in its supply chain activities. The company engages with different stakeholders at local, state, national, and international organizations to align with ESG-related goals and priorities. The company have partnered with over 25 organizations for maintaining its interest across diverse aspects of its businesses. The company engages in public policy which affects the company through educating and lobbying elected and appointed officials at all levels of government. The company is a member of the Council of State Governments (CSG), State and Agriculture Rural Leaders (SARL), and National Association of State Departments of Agriculture (NASD). As an industry leader in lawn and garden products, the company actively advocates pesticide stewardship by providing consumers with effective pest control products. With respect to water conservation, the company focuses on evolving formulations, application devices, and education for consumers as part of its environmental protection initiatives. The company supports the government's initiatives to develop responsible and effective regulation which governs legalized cannabis. In 2019, the company retained the services of an outside consulting firm specializing in ESG to prioritize its most important ESG opportunities and risks through a robust, third-party materiality assessment. In 2021, the company developed an assessment tool to assess all new ingredients in its product development process using enhanced product design standards with the focus on environmental and safety impacts. More than 35% of the company's total active ingredient portfolio was assessed during this period. To optimize packaging design, the firm focuses on making 3% reduction goal through multiple redesign projects. The company has plans to introduce new flexible packaging that uses less plastic material in the near future. To support packaging recycling, the company added the How2Recycle label to more than 100 products to optimize the recycling communications with consumers. By 2025, the company aims to convert 20% of sales fleet to hybrid vehicles. By 2025, the company aims to reach 145 million Americans through environmental partnerships. In 2021, the company established the first Hawthorne Social Justice Fund grantees to provide $600,000 over 2 years to support research related to cannabis policy and social justice reform. For product innovations, the company invests approximately $40 million in research and development. In 2020, the company launched 1868 ventures to find innovative ways to meet the needs of gardeners and growers. As part of sustainable material sourcing, the company's paper fiber-based packaging is certified as sustainably sourced by the Sustainable Forestry Initiative (SFI) or Forest Stewardship Council (FSC). Over a 10-year period, the company focused on creating a phosphorous free high-performance lawn fertilizer which resulted in the removal of over 1000 metric tons of phosphorous across lawn maintenance fertilizers.

Stock Market Performance

The stock market performance of SMG was analyzed during the period 2018–2022 in comparison with the market index Russell 2000. The period covered 2/1/2018–1/1/2023. The cumulative monthly return for the stock was 2%, while for the market index the cumulative return was 31%. The average yearly stock return was 1%, while the yearly return for market index was 6%.

Table 1 gives the holding period return for the stock and market index Russell during the last 5-year period. The holding period is assumed to be 1-year period.

SMG had superior market performance compared to the index Russell 2000 in the year 2019 and 2020.

Table 2 gives the market and book value of SMG during the past 5 years. The values are given in millions of dollars.

The average book value as percent of market value was 18% during the period 2018–2022. In 2018, the market value was 12 times that of book value. In 2022, the market value declined to 2 times that of book value of SMG.

Financial Highlights

Table 3 shows the financial highlights of the company during the period 2018–2022. The data source was gurufocus.com. The values are given in millions of dollars.

The total assets, short-term investments, and total equity grew by 11%, 312%, and 39% on an average basis during the period 2018–2022. The total revenues and net income grew by 12% on an average basis during the above period. The net income witnessed fluctuating growth trends. The total operating expenses increased by 5% on an average basis. The growth rates of market capitalization and enterprise value had been highly fluctuating during the above period of analysis.

Table 4 shows the profitability and leverage trend of the company during the period 2018–2022.

Table 1 Holding period yield

Year	SMG	Russell 2000	Excess returns
2018	−32%	−11%	−21%
2019	43%	11%	32%
2020	62%	22%	40%
2021	−27%	8%	−36%
2022	−68%	−13%	−55%

Table 2 Comparative market and book value

Year	2018	2019	2020	2021	2022
Book value of equity	359.6	723.2	702.9	1013.3	1147.7
Market value of equity	4353.77	5681.56	8532.38	8137.62	2372.63
BV as percent of MV	8.3%	12.7%	8.2%	12.5%	48.4%

Table 3 Financial highlights

	(In millions of dollars)				
Financial highlights	2018	2019	2020	2021	2022
Total assets	3054.5	3028.7	3380.5	4800	4296.8
Short-term investments	33.9	18.8	16.6	244.1	86.8
Total equity	359.6	723.2	702.9	1013.3	1147.7
Total revenue	2663.4	3156	4131.6	4925	3924.1
Total operating expenses	540.1	601.3	761	741.7	613.8
Net income	63.7	460.7	387.4	512.5	–437.5
Market cap	4353.77	5681.56	8532.38	8137.62	2372.63
Enterprise value	6341.27	7318.86	10203.8	10488.82	5555.73

Table 4 Profitability and leverage

Ratios	2018	2019	2020	2021	2022
Net margin%	2.39	14.6	9.38	10.41	−11.15
ROE%	12.7	85.85	54.72	59.92	−75.37
ROA%	2.2	15.15	12.09	12.53	−9.62
DER	5.69	2.3	2.41	2.56	22.14

Table 5 Economic value

Year	2020	2021
Profit before income tax	510.6	677.1
Income tax	123.72	159.80
Net operating profit after tax (NOPAT)	386.88	517.30
Stockholder equity	702.90	1013.30
Long-term debt	1455.10	2236.70
Total capital employed	2158.00	3250.00
WACC	7.04%	8.10%
Capital charge	151.92	263.25
Economic value	234.96	254.05

In terms of profitability, the company had worst performance in the year 2022 where all profitability ratios were negative. In the year 2022, the company's leverage had significantly increased compared to the previous years. Excluding the year 2022, the company had average net margin, ROE, and ROA of 9.19%, 53.29% and 10.49%, respectively.

Table 5 shows the estimation of economic value of Scotts Miracle-Gro during the period 2020 and 2021. The values are given in millions of dollars.

The economic value has increased from $234.96 million in the year 2020 to $254.05 million in the year 2021.

References

1. https://scottsmiraclegro.com/wp-content/uploads/2022/06/ScottsMiracle-Gro-2022-CSR-report.pdf
2. Scotts Miracle-Gro Annual Report 2022
3. www.gurufocus.com

Case 32 Virtu Financials

Virtu Financials is a leading provider of financial service and products. Virtu had been in the market making business for more than 15 years. The company conducts its business through Virtu Financial LLC and its subsidiaries. In 2015, the company had its IPO listing.

Virtu offers a robust suite of product offerings related to execution, liquidity, sourcing, analytics, and broker-neutral, multi-dealer platforms in workflow technology. Virtu's product offerings enable clients to trade on hundreds of venues across 50 plus countries in multiple asset classes like global equities, ETFs, foreign currencies, fixed income, and other commodities. Virtu's integrated multi-asset analytics platform offers a range of pre- and post-trade services, data products, and compliance tools. Virtu offers market making, execution services, and analytics to a diverse client base of retail and institutional capital market participants in 235 plus venues. In 2021, the company had made $2.8 billion in revenues. Market making and execution services are the two operating segments of the company.

The market making segment consists of market making in the cash, futures, and options markets across global equities, fixed income, currencies, cryptocurrencies, and commodities. As a market maker, the company offers to buy or sell securities to broker dealers, banks, and institutions. Virtu undertakes principal trading in the market making segment directly to clients and also through electronic market making sources such as electronic communications networks (ECNs) and on alternative trading systems (ATSs). The cash trading business handles specialized orders and transactions on the OTC link. The company's transaction processing is automated over the full life cycle of a trade. Virtu's market making platform generates and publicizes continuous bid and offer quotes. Virtu offers direct-to-client market making services across multiple asset classes basically to sell-side clients which include international, national, and regional broker dealers and banks. The market making services are also offered to buy-side clients consisting of mutual funds, pension plans, plan sponsors, hedge funds, endowments, and trusts based in North America, Europe, and Asia. Virtu trades over 25,000 listed and over-the-counter securities on US SEC registered exchanges and market centers such as the

© The Author(s), under exclusive license to Springer Nature Switzerland AG 2024
B. R. Kumar, *Rising Stars*, Management for Professionals,
https://doi.org/10.1007/978-3-031-50032-9_32

NYSE, Nasdaq, TSX IN Canada, Bovespa in Brazil, BMV in Mexico, and also in more than 20 private liquidity pools. Virtu Financials is also the authorized participants of exchange traded products and can create and/or redeem ETPs. The fixed income market making activity of Virtu is in US treasuries, corporate bonds, and other debt instruments. These products are traded on a variety of specialized exchanges, trading arenas such as BrokerTec, eSpeed, Dealer Web, Bloomberg, Tradeweb, MarketAxess, and BGC's Fenics UTS. Virtu offers market making in spot, forward, and futures currency market in over 80 currencies. The company is a leading participant in major foreign exchange venues such as LSEG, Currenex, Chicago Board of Exchange, and Chicago Mercantile Exchange. Commodity market making is offered on the CME, ICE, and Nasdaq futures exchanges for crude oil, natural gas, heating oil, and gasoline futures. Virtu trades over 100 energy products and futures on the ICE, CME, and TOCOM. The company also trades on precious metals such as gold, silver, platinum, palladium, and base metals such as aluminum and copper. The company undertakes market making in option exchanges such as CBOE, ISE, and NYSE Arca. The cryptocurrency market making includes spot, perpetuals, futures, and ETFs.

Virtu offers agency execution services to financial institutions, banks, and broker dealers in global equities, ETFs, fixed income, currencies, and commodities. The company earns commission for providing agent services to clients. The company provides agency-based execution-only trading done through a variety of access points such as algorithmic trading and order routing. Virtu offers integrated broker-neutral trading tools meant for workflow technology such as order and execution management systems, order management software applications, and network connectivity. The company offers trading analytics for portfolio managers to improve pre-trade and real-time execution performance and post-trade analysis. The company offers execution services across different product classes to buy-side clients such as mutual funds, pension plans, hedge funds, trusts, and endowment and to sell-side clients which include dealers and banks. By February 2022, the company employed 973 employees in nine countries.

The company conducts its US equities and options market making and provides execution services through SEC registered broker dealer VAL which is regulated by SEC. VAL is also registered as a floor trader firm with the Commodity Futures Trading Commission. The energy, commodities, and currency market making and trading activities are primarily conducted through Virtu Financial Global Markets LLC. The European, Middle Eastern, and African (EMEA) market making activities are done from Dublin through the subsidiary Virtu Financial Ireland Limited (VFIL). APAC market making is done mainly through the Singapore subsidiary.

Growth Strategy

The company has adopted technology and operational efficiency as the central focus of its business. The focus is on market making and order routing technology as the tools for competitive advantage. Virtu Financials Inc. has developed a scalable and modular proprietary, multi-asset, multi-currency technology platform which is integrated with exchanges, liquidity centers, and clients. Different modules such as the market data, order routing, transaction processing, risk management, and market surveillance manage the market making and institutional agency activities. The company uses its latest technology to deliver liquidity to global markets and innovative trading solutions and analytics tool to its clients. The company is a leading low-cost market maker which aims to provide critical market functionality and robust price competition across multiple asset classes. The team of in-house software engineers develops software and applications for integration of optimized infrastructure with exchanges and trading venues. The technology adopted has enabled Virtu to emerge as one of the lowest cost providers of liquidity in the global electronic trading market. The core operations team across offices in North America, APAC, and Europe monitors the full technology platform systems all throughout the year. Virtu aims to utilize high-speed, efficient connections to all registered exchanges and market centers. The company has expanded its electronic trading and market making business through two major acquisitions during the past 5 years. In 2017, the company completed the all-cash acquisition of KCG Holdings. In 2019, the firm completed the acquisition of Investment Technology Group in an all-cash deal. ITG is a global financial technology company which offered a suite of trading and financial technology products.

Risk Factors

The revenues and profitability of the firm depend on the magnitude of trading activity of securities and derivatives which depends on economic and political factors. The businesses of the firm provide two-sided liquidity to market participants across asset classes. In the event of large price movements, some market participants may not be able to meet their obligations to their other trading counterparties which could lead to major defaults by one or more market participants. There are chances of losses in the market making activities and execution service businesses due to failures of customized trading platform. The operating results may be negatively impacted by changes which adversely affect the US equity as the market making business is heavily concentrated toward US equity market. The loss of one or more larger clients could have an adverse effect on the revenues and profitability in the future. The firm is subject to liquidity risks as the company requires liquidity to fund various ongoing obligations which include operating expenses, margin requirements, and capital expenditures. The use of open-source software may expose Virtu to additional risks.

Risk Management

The market making activities and execution services business expose the company to market, counterparty, operational, and regulatory risks. Virtu aims to mitigate these risks through prudent risk management practices. These risk management practices include pre-trade risk controls, model restrictions, aggregate exposure monitoring, and operational controls. In pre-trade risk control setup, the messages which go through the trading environment initially pass through a series of preset risk controls which are aimed to minimize the likelihood of unwanted activities by algorithms. Trading strategies are designed to automatically reduce exposures when limits are reached and are monitored by the trading team and risk managers. The automated MIS monitor in real time exposures related to risk profiles, statistical risk measures such as value at risk, equity betas, stress and scenario analysis, concentration measures, etc. The trading assets and liabilities are marked to market daily for financial reporting purposes by reference to official exchange prices. The assets and liabilities are revalued continuously throughout the day for risk management and asset/liability management purposes. Virtu Financials has a series of automated controls for managing the operations. The technical operations system continuously monitors the network and proper functioning of the trading centers across the world. The market making system evaluates the listed securities and financial products in which bid and offer quotes are made in order to minimize exposure to directional price movements. Traditional notional limits for customers and counterparts are monitored throughout by trading support and risk professionals. The company faces cyber threats due to its heavy reliance on technology. Cybersecurity risk is managed as part of overall information technology risk framework under the direction of chief information security officer. The company has a Chief Risk Officer who reports to the Board Risk Committee. The business, financial conditions, and operating results of the company may be adversely affected due to new or revised legislation or regulations.

Competition

The institutional securities brokerage business in the financial services industry is highly competitive. The individual products offered by Virtu compete with different firms. In the market making segment, firm faces competition from sole proprietors to large integrated broker dealers. The major competitors in this segment include market participants such as Citadel Securities, Susquehanna International Group LLP, Two Sigma, Jane Street, DRW Holdings, etc. In the execution services segment, the algorithmic and smart routing products compete with sell side affiliated firms.

Stock Market Performance

The stock performance analysis compares the performance of an investment in Class A common stock in comparison with the S&P 500 Index and NYSE Acra Securities Broker/Dealer Index during the period from December 31, 2016, to December 31, 2021. The analysis is based on the assumption of investment of $100 in the stock and indexes. Table 1 shows the wealth created through investment in stock in comparison with similar investment in market indexes.

The 5-year holding period return for Virtu Financials was 118%, while for S&P 500 and NYSE Acra Securities, the holding period return was 111% and 137%, respectively. In terms of average returns, Virtu Financials had average returns of 22%, while for S&P 500 and NYSE Acra Brokers and Dealers, the corresponding return was 17% and 20%, respectively.

Five-Year Stock Return Analysis

The following section analyzes the Virtu Financials' stock return during the past 5-year period. The source of data was Yahoo Finance. The Virtu stock was trading at $29.70 on 2/1/2018. By 12/1/2022, the stock price declined to $21.62. The cumulative monthly return for Virtu stock was −7% during the 5-year period 2018–2022. At the same time, the market index S&P 500 registered cumulative monthly return of 45%. The average yearly return for Virtu stock was −1%, while that for market index S&P 500, the average yearly return was 9%.

Table 2 highlights the holding period yield for the stock and market index S&P 500 during the period 2018–2022. The holding period assumption is for 1-year period.

The market index S&P 500 outperformed the stock Virtu in all years except in 2020 when Virtu share had an excess return of 34%.

Table 1 Stock wealth creation

Year	2016	2017	2018	2019	2020	2021
Virtu Financials	$100	121.52	177.36	115.52	189.94	217.5
S&P 500	$100	118.42	111.03	143.09	166.36	211.1
NYSE Acra Securities. Brokers/ Dealers	$100	129.21	115.62	141.46	183.94	237.17

Source: Annual Report 2021

Table 2 Holding period yield

Year	Virtu	S&P 500	Excess returns
2018	−13%	−8%	−6%
2019	−37%	19%	−57%
2020	51%	16%	34%
2021	4%	28%	−25%
2022	−34%	−15%	−19%

Table 3 Book and market value

Year	2017	2018	2019	2020	2021
Book value of equity	1151.58	1494.7	1228.94	1855.04	1863.62
Market value of equity	1643.31	2750.55	1890.93	3071.04	3262.72
BV as percent of MV	70.1%	54.3%	65.0%	60.4%	57.1%

Table 4 Financial highlights

	(In millions of dollars)				
Financial highlights	2017	2018	2019	2020	2021
Total assets	7320.01	7380.98	9609.37	9965.8	10319.97
Short-term investments	532.89	729.55	732.16	889.56	1071.46
Total equity	1151.58	1494.7	1228.94	1855.04	1863.62
Total revenue	1027.98	1878.72	1517.49	3239.33	2811.49
Total operating expenses	152.62	154.05	239.88	235.55	225.63
Net income	2.94	289.44	−58.6	649.2	476.88
Market cap	1643.31	2750.55	1890.93	3071.04	3262.72
Enterprise value	3993.2	4797.87	5753.88	5996.78	6107.25

Table 5 Performance indicators

Ratios	2017	2018	2019	2020	2021
Net margin%	0.29	15.41	−3.86	20.04	16.96
ROE%	0.6	30.75	−5.91	54.1	31.6
ROA%	0.05	3.94	−0.69	6.63	4.7
DER	3.08	2.22	4.61	2.34	2.33

Table 3 shows the comparative book and market value of Virtu Financials during the 5-year period 2017–2021. The values are given in millions of dollars.

The average book value as percent of market value was 61.4%. In 2017, the market value was 1.43 times that of book value. By 2021, the market value was 1.75 times that of the book value of the firm.

Table 4 gives the financial highlights of Virtu Financials during the 5-year period 2017–2021. The values are given in millions of dollars. The source of data was gurufocus.com and annual reports.

The average growth rate of total assets, short-term investments, and total equity were 10%, 20%, and 16%, respectively. The revenues declined by 13% in 2021 compared to the previous year. The average growth rate of revenues and net income was 41% and 21% approximately. The total operating expenses declined by 2% and 4% in the year 2020 and 2021. The total operating expenses increased by 13% on an average basis during the period of analysis. The market capitalization and enterprise value increased by 26% and 12%, respectively.

Table 5 highlights the profitability and leverage ratio of the company during the period 2017–2021.

Table 6 Economic value

Year	2020	2021
Profit before income tax	1382.84	996.9
Income tax	261.91	169.67
Net operating profit after tax (NOPAT)	1120.93	827.23
Stockholder equity	1855.04	1863.62
Long-term debt	2587.54	2747.18
Total capital employed	4442.58	4610.80
WACC	0.54%	1.86%
Capital charge	23.99	85.76
Economic value	1096.94	741.47

The net margin, ROE, and ROA during the period 2017–2021 were 9.77%, 22.23%, and 2.93%, respectively. The average debt equity ratio during the above period was 2.92.

Table 6 shows the estimation of economic value of Virtu Financials during the year 2020 and 2021, respectively. The values are estimated in millions of dollars.

References

1. https://ir.virtu.com/investor-relations/default.aspx
2. Virtu Financial Annual Report 2021.

Case 33 Repligen

Repligen Corporation is a global life science company which develops and commercializes highly innovative bioprocessing technologies and systems which facilitate the manufacturing of biological drugs. Repligen was founded in the year 1981 by two distinguished scientists Prof Alexander Rich and Prof Paul Schimmel who pioneered breakthrough advances in the field of molecular biology. Repligen offers a comprehensive suite of products in its bioprocessing business which are used for upstream and downstream processes in biological drug manufacturing. The product portfolio offered by Repligen consists of filtration, chromatography, process analytics, and proteins. The proteins business focuses on affinity ligands and growth factor solutions.

The company is headquartered in Massachusetts with 16 manufacturing sites predominantly located in the USA and the rest in Estonia, France, Germany, Ireland, Netherlands, and Sweden. The company became a publicly traded company in the year 1986. The common stock is listed on the Nasdaq Global Market under the symbol "RGEN." The company has over 1850 employees with 12 offices in the USA, Europe, and Asia.

Products

The bioprocessing business comprises four main franchise segments of filtration chromatography, process analytics, and proteins. The company has built a highly diversified portfolio of products offered under these franchises. The majority of the revenue for the company is derived from consumable and/or single-use product sales in comparison to sales of associated equipment.

© The Author(s), under exclusive license to Springer Nature Switzerland AG 2024

B. R. Kumar, *Rising Stars*, Management for Professionals,
https://doi.org/10.1007/978-3-031-50032-9_33

Filtration

Filtration is the largest franchise with diversified product offering which covers upstream and downstream technologies. The filtration products are used in process development and clinical and commercial production and offer significant advantages to manufacturers of biologic drugs. XCell Alternating Tangential Flow ("ATF") systems are used in upstream perfusion (continuous) and N-1 (intensified fed-batch or hybrid perfusion) cell culture processing. XCell ATF is based on a cell retention technology. The TangeX product line offers a portfolio of flat sheet tangential flow filtration (TFF) cassettes used in downstream biological drug concentration and formulation processes. The other portfolio of filtration business includes Spectrum HF filtration solutions, fully integrated KrosFlo TFF systems with Konduit sensing, and ProConnex Flow Path single-use assemblies. The company also gained the Spectra/Por portfolio of laboratory and process dialysis products and launched the SpectraFlo™ Dynamic Dialysis Systems. The Spectrum product line of HF filters is used in bench tops through commercial scale processes basically for filtration, purification, and concentration of biologics and diagnostic products. Through the acquisition of PolyMem, Repligen expanded its HF membrane and module production capabilities and added core R&D, engineering, and production expertise in HF technology for both industrial and bioprocessing markets. The acquisition of Engineered Molding Technology LLC (EMT) added EMT's silicone-based, single-use components.

Chromatography

The chromatography franchise consists of products used in downstream purification, development, manufacturing, and quality control of biological drugs. The main determinant of growth of this portfolio is the OPUS pre-packed column (PPC) product line. Through the acquisition of ARTeSYN, the company added chromatography systems to its offerings along with single-use components and flow path assemblies for fluid management. The company has a wide range of OPUS columns that can be used as single-use or campaign-use disposable columns for downstream purification.

Process Analytics

The process analytics products support the filtration, chromatography, and protein franchises which allow end users to make absorbance measurements for determining protein concentration in filtration, chromatography formulation, and fill-finish applications. The process analytics devices are SoloVPE® Device, FlowVPE® Device, and FlowVPX® System.

Affinity Ligands

Affinity Ligands are a leading provider of Protein A affinity ligands to life sciences companies. Protein A ligands are an essential binding component of Protein A affinity chromatography resins which are used in the purification of all mAb-based drugs on the market or in development. The company manufactures multiple forms of Protein A ligands under the long-term supply agreements with major life sciences companies.

Growth Factors

Growth factors such as insulin are added to the cell culture media by biopharmaceutical firms to stimulate cell growth and maximize overall yield from a bioreactor. Repligen produces insulin-like growth factor LONG® R3 IGF 1 which is found to be biologically superior than insulin.

In 2021, COVID-19 and cell and gene therapy related revenue constituted 40% of the total revenue. In the same year, the company added 70 new cell and therapy accounts. In 2021, Repligen generated nearly $190 million in revenue from COVID-19 programs. The company introduced 12 new products in the year 2021.

Table 1 lists the revenues by biological type.

Market Environment and Strategy

The global market for bioprocessing products which include therapeutic antibodies, recombinant proteins, and vaccines is estimated to be over $22 billion. Repligen's addressable market opportunity is estimated to be $8.1 billion as of year-end 2021. Antibody-based biologics accounted for $130 billion of global biopharma revenue in the year 2020. The mAbs market is expected to grow in the range of 10%–12% annually through 2025. Repligen has the competitive positioning in the segments of both originator and follow-on biologics manufacturing process. Cell and gene herapy market is a rapidly growing area of biological drug development with over 1200 clinical trials underway as of year-end 2020. The company focuses on the development, production, and commercialization of highly differentiated technology leading systems and solutions in the biologics manufacturing process. Through continuous innovation, the company capitalizes on the internal technological expertise to develop products in upstream and downstream bioprocessing. A key element

Table 1 Revenue by biological type in the year 2021

Type	Revenues
Monoclonal antibodies	$405 million
Cell and gene therapy	$76 million
Covid related	$190 million

Source: Annual Report

Table 2 Strategic acquisitions

Year	Acquisitions
2011	Acquired Novozymes Biopharma
2014	Acquired Refine ATF Technology
2016	Acquired Atoll OPUS process development; TangenX Cassettes
2017	Acquired Spectrum HF Systems
2019	Acquired CTech Technologies
2020	Acquired EMT, NMS BioSolutions; Artesyn BioSolutions
2021	Acquired Avitide; PolyMem; BioFlex Solutions

of strategy adopted by the company for enhancing the market adoption of its products is through delivery of enabling technologies which emerge as the standard technology in markets where Repligen competes. The company focuses on winning early-stage technology evaluations through direct interaction with key biomanufacturing decision makers in process development lab. The company also pursues acquisitions of innovative technologies and products. The company also focuses on global geographical expansion through building global sales, marketing field applications, and services infrastructure. The company also aims to enhance operating margins through capacity utilization and process optimization. The company has Ligand Supply Agreements with large life sciences companies such as Cytiva, MilliporeSigma, and Purolite.

Table 2 lists the strategic acquisitions made by Repligen.

The company focuses on both organic growth initiatives and targeted acquisitions as strategies for growth. The company is focusing on sustainable innovation and has introduced disruptive new products to offer solutions to customers' bioprocessing challenges. The growth strategy basically aims for expansion of geographic scope, customer base, and application of technologies.

Through the process of internal innovation, the company has developed and launched the single-use formats of the original stainless steel XCell ATF devices for satisfying the industry demand for single-use sterile systems with "plug and play" technology. The single-use format of ATF technology reduces the implementation time by elimination of time-intensive workflow related to autoclaving and facilitates accelerated evaluation of the products with lower costs.

The use of single-use products used for biological manufacturing processes addresses the contamination risk which is a major concern for customers. The single-use products are advantageous in terms of customization, scalability, and plug and play convenience.

On the M&A front, Repligen made three major acquisitions in the year 2021. PolyMem based in France was acquired and is a leading industrial expert in the development of hollow fiber membranes and modules. This acquisition strengthened the filtration franchise and expanded the hollow fiber membrane and module production capacity of Repligen. The acquisition of Avitide—an affinity ligand technology leader based in Lebanon—expanded the protein franchise business of Repligen, thereby addressing the purification needs of gene therapies. The acquisition of New Jersey-based BioFlex Solutions bought high precision injection molding and design capabilities to Repligen's single-use portfolio of flow paths and assemblies. This acquisition aided the company's fluid management and systems strategy. The acquisition of EMT, NMS, and ARTeSYN addresses the need for single-use flow paths and brought best in class filtration and chromatography systems to Repligen's portfolio. The acquisition of BioFlex Solutions LLC and Newton T&M expanded the filtration franchise as these companies possessed single-use fluid management components which included clamps, adapters, end caps, and hose assemblies.

Risk Factors

The bioprocessing market is intensely competitive. The company competes with several medium and small firms in each of its product categories. Repligen competes with life sciences, pharmaceutical, and biotechnology companies which are capable of developing new approaches. Recently much of the firm's revenues are accounted from commercialization of bioprocessing products which the company sells directly to end users. As a result, the company has to invest additional resources in sales and marketing capabilities. The company has historically depended on a limited number of customers for a high percentage of the revenues. The loss of, or a significant reduction in, orders from large customers due to termination or failure to renew a long-term supply contract would affect the results of the operations of the company. Unforeseen adverse events, negative clinical outcomes, or increased regulatory scrutiny of cell and gene therapy affects customers' ability to conduct business and may have an adverse effect on the performance of the company. The COVID pandemic or similar health crises have a material adverse impact on the business of the company. The acquisitions made by the firm involve numerous risks and operational, financial, and integration challenges related to operations, technologies, products, and personnel. The company depends on a limited number of suppliers for certain products, and inability to find replacements or transition to alternative suppliers would have a material adverse effect on the operations of the businesses. Healthcare reform initiatives by government to reduce the healthcare costs may adversely affect the business and financial condition of pharmaceutical and biotechnology companies.

Sustainability

In the year 2020, Repligen joined the United Nations Global Compact (UNGC) for supporting its ten principles related to human rights, labor, the environment, and anti-corruption. The company has become an active participant in the sustainability reporting ecosystem by taking membership with the Sustainability Accounting Standards Board (SASB) which is a part of the Value Reporting Foundation and Global Reporting Initiative.

The principles adopted by the company for sustainability are based on the framework for business ethics and compliance, enterprise risk management, financial integrity, cybersecurity and data privacy, supplier ethics, and compliance. As a part of diversity initiatives, the internal management team of the company comprises 47% women and people of mixed race. In the year 2021, Repligen established a Diversity, Equity and Inclusion (DE&I) council composed of ten senior leaders to have a greater focus on DE&I initiatives. Repligen complies with all occupational health and safety (OH&S) regulations and reports recordable incidents at each manufacturing sites. Repligen promotes safety via in-person and online safety training programs. The company focuses on product innovation with a pioneering mindset and aims to achieve these goals by adding new products through R&D, acquisitions, and product design and life cycle management. The company has adopted initiatives to re-engineer the packaging of key products to reduce weight and waste which significantly impacts material use, volume, and energy consumption without affecting product quality. The company is involved in the introduction of disruptive new products to face customers' bioprocessing challenges through internal R&D and acquisition. Repligen's global packaging engineering team is involved in the improvement of the environmental profile of all Repligen products across the full product life cycle. Repligen adopts different approaches to reduce potential supply chain risks such as disruption and quality concerns through quality agreements with important suppliers and auditing of Tier 1 suppliers. Approximately 13% of the total revenues in year 2020 came from COVID-19 vaccine and therapeutic developers. The company reduced the total carbon emissions by 12.35% in the year 2020 compared to the previous year 2019.

Wealth Creation

An amount of $1000 invested in Repligen share in 2003 would have amounted to $58,270 by 2023 representing total return of 5728%. This includes reinvestment of dividends.

In the next section, the stock returns of Repligen were compared to market index Nasdaq Biotechnology Index (NBI) during the 5-year period 2/1/2018–4/1/2023. The stock was trading at $34 on 2/1/2018 increased by approximately five times to trade at $175.06 on 1/1/2023. The cumulative monthly returns for Repligen during the 5-year period 1/1/2018–1/1/2023 were 204%. The 5-year average returns for the Repligen stock were 42% during the period 2018–2022. The cumulative monthly returns for the Nasdaq Biotechnology index (NBI) were 36% during the 5-year period of analysis. The 5-year average returns for the Nasdaq Biotechnology index were only 7% during the 5-year period of analysis.

Table 3 gives the holding period yield for the Repligen stock and market index NBI for the 5-year period 2018–2022. The analysis assumes holding period of 1 year.

Table 3 Holding period yield

Year	Repligen	NBI	Excess returns
2018	54%	−10%	64%
2019	62%	10%	53%
2020	91%	33%	58%
2021	32%	−6%	39%
2022	−15%	1%	−16%

Table 4 Comparative market and book value

Year	2017	2018	2019	2020	2021
Book value of equity	591.55	615.57	1059.77	1529.15	1750.07
Market value of equity	1581.34	2316.2	4817.24	10493.81	14651.35
BV as percent of MV	37.4%	26.6%	22.0%	14.6%	11.9%

Table 5 Financial highlights

	(In millions of dollars)				
Financial highlights	2017	2018	2019	2020	2021
Total assets	743.52	774.62	1400.11	1902.89	2358.35
Short-term investments	173.76	193.82	528.39	717.29	603.81
Total equity	591.55	615.57	1059.77	1529.15	1750.07
Total revenue	141.24	194.03	270.25	366.26	670.53
Total operating expenses	60.18	81.51	115.06	139.8	218.14
Net income	28.35	16.62	21.41	59.93	128.29
Market cap	1581.34	2316.2	4817.24	10493.81	14651.35
Enterprise value	1506.83	2225.87	4552.17	10051.94	14413.59

The Repligen stock had superior market performance compared to the market index Nasdaq Biotechnology Index (NBI) in all years except in 2022. The positive excess returns for the stock had a range of 39%–64% during the period 2018–2021.

Table 4 shows the comparative book and market value of Repligen share during the 5-year period 2017–2021. The values are given in millions of dollars.

The average book value as percent of market value during the period 2017–2021 was 22.5%. In 2017, the market value was 2.67 times that of the book value of the company. By the year 2021, the market value was 8.37 times of the book value of the firm. The source of data was annual reports and guru focus.com.

The next section discusses the operating performance of Repligen during the period 2017–2021. Table 5 shows the financial highlights of the company during the period 2017–2021. The values are given in millions of dollars.

On an average basis, the total assets, short-term investments, and total equity increased by 36%, 51%, and 34%, respectively. The total revenues and net income grew by 49% and 70% respectively during the above period of analysis. The market capitalization and enterprise value increased by 78% and 79% on an average basis. The total expenses increased by 39% on an average basis during the period 2017–2021.

Table 6 Profitability and leverage

Ratios	2017	2018	2019	2020	2021
Net margin%	20.07	8.56	7.92	16.36	19.13
ROE%	7.46	2.75	2.56	4.63	7.82
ROA%	5.49	2.19	1.97	3.63	6.02
DER	0.17	0.17	0.25	0.18	0.21

Table 7 Estimation of economic value

Year	2020	2021
Profit before income tax	59.22	153.54
Income tax	−0.71	25.26
Net operating profit after tax (NOPAT)	59.93	128.28
Stockholder equity	1529.15	1750.07
Long-term debt		
Total capital employed	1529.15	1750.07
WACC	6.49%	5.55%
Capital charge	99.24	97.13
Economic value	−39.31	31.15

Table 6 displays the performance indicators of Repligen during the period 2017–2021.

The average net margin, ROE, and ROA for the 5-year period 2017–2021 were 14.41%, 5.04%, and 3.86%, respectively. The average debt equity ratio was 0.20 during the above period.

Table 7 shows the estimation of economic value for the company during the years 2020 and 2021. The values are given in millions of dollars.

References

1. https://www.repligen.com/company/investors
2. https://repligen.q4ir.com/stock-information/investment-calculators/default.aspx
3. https://repligen.q4ir.com/financial-information/annual-reports/default.aspx
4. https://www.repligen.com/company/sustainability-report-2020

Case 34 Jacobs (Engineering Group)

The company was established by Joseph J. Jacobs in the year 1947. The company is publicly traded as a Fortune 500 company. This American international technical professional services firm provides a full spectrum of professional services which includes consulting, technical, scientific, and project delivery for government and private sector. The company had approximately $15 billion in revenues during the year 2021. Jacobs Group has a talent force of approximately 60,000 people worldwide. In 2022, the company repurchased $281.9 million in shares.

Business Segment

The major business lines of the company are Critical Mission Solutions (CMS), People & Places Solutions (P&PS), and investment in PA Consulting (PA). The company is also in the process of creating a new enabling platform Divergent Solutions (DVS) to support its lines of businesses to develop and deliver innovative, next-generation cloud, cyber, data, and digital technologies.

Critical Mission Solutions (CMS)

CMS offers the entire spectrum of cyber, data analytics, systems and software application integration services and consulting; enterprise level IT operations and maintenance; and mission IT services along with other highly technical consulting solutions to government agencies and commercial customers in US and international markets. The CMS line of business is also involved in engineering and design, software development, testing and mission integration, enterprise operations and maintenance, program management, research, development, test, and evaluation services, specialized training and mission operations, environmental remediation, etc. The clients of CMS segment include government clients such as US Department of Defense, the US Intelligence Community, NASA, the US Department of Energy,

© The Author(s), under exclusive license to Springer Nature Switzerland AG 2024
B. R. Kumar, *Rising Stars*, Management for Professionals,
https://doi.org/10.1007/978-3-031-50032-9_34

UK Ministry of Defense, the UK Nuclear Decommissioning Authority (NDA), and the Australian Department of Defense. The private sector clients include customers from basically aerospace, automotive, energy, and telecom sectors. In 2022, approximately 73% of CMS revenue was derived from US governmental agencies such as DoD, Intelligence Community, DoE, and other US Federal civilian governmental entities. International customers accounted for 18% of the revenues in the year 2022. Approximately 9% of CMS's revenues were accounted from various US commercial sectors such as telecommunication sector which expects large cellular infrastructure investment due to the transition from 4G to 5G technology. Many clients in the commercial aerospace and automotive segment rely on CMS for advanced research and development systems for facilities to enable product development.

People & Places Solutions (P&PS)

The P&PS line of business provides end-to-end solutions for climate change, energy transitions, connected mobility, integrated water management, smart cities, and vaccine manufacturing. The P&PS sector provides services for transportation, water, cities and places, environmental, energy and power, health and life sciences, and advanced manufacturing. This line of business is involved in providing services related to consulting, planning, science, architecture, design and engineering, infrastructure delivery services, and long-term operation of facilities. The clients include national, state, and local government in the USA, Europe, the UK, the Middle East, Australia, New Zealand, and Asia. The clients also include multinational and local private sector players. P&PS have advised transit agencies for services related to decarbonization of vehicle fleets and electrification of New York City's bus fleet. The P&PS segment also designs and delivers battery and vehicle manufacturing facilities for private clients across North America and Europe. The firm also offers services for enabling infrastructure to support the development of offshore wind assets in the Northeast USA.

PA Consulting

Jacobs holds a 65% stake in PA Consulting which provides services across seven sectors such as consumer and manufacturing, defense and security, energy and utilities, financial services, government, health and life sciences, and transport. PA Consulting has offices in the UK, Ireland, the USA, the Nordics, and the Netherlands. PA Consulting offers end-to-end innovation for new growth ideas.

Market Environment

The government sector faces an evolving external threat environment related to information and cyber warfare, digital transformation and IT modernization, national security, and defense infrastructure modernization. Global green energy transition challenges, decommissioning, and remediation of legacy nuclear sites are other significant trends which are of concern for governments. All these factors are driving demand for the firm's highly technical solutions. There has also been an increase in the space exploration initiatives primarily from US government. Strategic trend drivers such as infrastructure modernization, climate action, urbanization, water food, and energy security are driving demand for solutions offered by the P&PS line of business of the company. City master planning requires advanced analytics to plan for climate adaptation, equitable inclusion, and next-generation mobility services. The future of major utilities such as water, power/energy, and telecommunications has become highly technology enabled with the focus on predictive analytics and smart metering as strategies for environmental protection. The business model of the company aims to develop proprietary software and analytics to solve these challenges.

Strategy for Growth

The company focuses on innovation and inorganic growth as a part of its strategic pursuit for becoming the leading solutions provider for high valued government services and other clients. In the year 2021, the company acquired a 65% stake in PA Consulting Group Ltd. The company had also acquired the John Wood Group's nuclear business, the Buffalo Group, Black Lynx, and Streetlight. The current focus is on building leadership position in sustainable high growth sector. In March 2022, Jacobs launched a new 3-year strategy to focus on three growth accelerators of climate response, consulting and advisory, and data solutions. Jacobs stresses on leadership on climate response and social value. The company aims to align positive societal impact with long-term business growth. Jacobs has established an Office of Global Climate Response and ESG to deliver climate action commitments through innovative solutions for clients and stakeholders. The company aims to achieve net zero greenhouse gas emissions across the value chain by the year 2040. The company focuses on maintaining carbon neutrality status in its operations and 100% low carbon electricity for its operations.

In January 2023, a consortium comprising Westinghouse Electric Spain, Jacobs, and the Lithuanian Energy Institute was selected to plan dismantling and waste management at the Ignalina Nuclear Power Plant (INPP) in Lithuania. The company also has a contract with Norsk Nukleaer Dekommisjonering as a part of its strategy to grow the decommissioning and regeneration solutions business in continental Europe. In 2022, Jacobs Engineering Group Inc. (the predecessor parent company) created a new holding company, Jacobs Solutions Inc. which became the new parent of Jacobs Engineering Group. The company is one of the world's first companies with net zero targets approved by the science-based targets initiatives.

Jacobs pursues acquisitions, divestitures, and strategic investments to create long-term value. In 2007, Jacobs acquired planning, engineering, and design firm Edwards and Kelcey. In 2008, Jacobs acquired Carter and Burgess for an amount

Table 1 Recent restructuring activities

Year	Activities
December 2017	Jacobs acquired CH2M, a provider of consulting and other services in the water, environmental, transportation, and nuclear remediation sectors
April 2019	The company completed its divestiture of energy, chemicals and resources (ECR) business to Worley Ltd. based in Australia. Through this restructuring, the company exited direct hire construction and fixed price lump-sum energy-related construction
June 2019	Jacobs acquired US-based KeyW Holding Corporation (KeyW). KeyW is a US-based national security technology solutions provider to the intelligence, cyber, and counterterrorism organizations
March 2020	Jacobs acquired the nuclear consulting, remediation, and program management business of UK-based energy services company John Wood Group
Nov 2020	Jacobs acquired Buffalo Group, the leader in advanced cyber and intelligence solutions
March 2021	Jacobs completed the strategic investment of 65% interest in UK-based innovation and transformation consulting firm, PA Consulting
Nov 2021	Jacobs acquired BlackLynx which is a provider of high-performance software. This acquisition was basically to support the company's portfolio of cyber, intelligence, and digital solutions
Feb,2022	Jacobs acquired StreetLight Data Inc., a pioneering firm in the field of mobility analytics which offers solutions for complex transportation problems

Source: Annual Report 2022

of $264 million. The company had also acquired 60% stake in Zamel and Turbag Consulting Engineers. In 2010, Jacobs acquired TechTeam, Tybrin, and Jordan, Jones and Goulding for the total amount of $259.5 million. In 2014, Jacobs completed the merger transaction with Australia-based Sinclair Knight Merz (SKM) for an amount of US$ 1.1 billion. In 2017, Jacobs acquired the global engineering firm CH2M Hill which provided professional services for key infrastructure and government service sectors. The deal was valued at $3.27 billion (cash and stock deal).

Table 1 lists the recent corporate restructuring activities undertaken by the firm.

Risk Factors

The company operates in a highly competitive business environment to provide technical, professional, and construction management services to clients. The results of the operation depend on the award of new contracts and the timing of the award of these contracts and economic conditions. The competition can place downward pressure on the contract prices and profit margins. Delays in the timings of the awards or its cancellations on account of economic conditions, material and equipment pricing, etc., can impact the long-term performance of the company. Uncertainty related to global economic, socioeconomic, and political conditions will impact clients' ability to proceed on with their projects. In such a scenario, the clients may reduce their capital expenditures, alter the mix of services purchased, and seek more favorable pricing and other contract terms. The rising inflation, interest rates, and construction costs would reduce the demand for the services offered by the company. The failure to implement the corporate strategy would have a material adverse effect on the business of the company. Project sites are inherently dangerous workplace which expose employees and other workers with large pieces of mechanized equipment, moving vehicles, chemicals, and highly regulated materials. The company are also subject to regulations with respect to occupational health and safety. The nature of contracts particularly fixed price contracts is subject to risks of cost overruns. The company may have reduced profits or losses if costs increase above budgets or the project experiences delays. The failure to meet performance requirements or contractual schedules would adversely affect the business, financial condition, and results of operations. Contracts with the US federal government and other agencies pose addition risks compared to contracts with private sector clients. Some of the government contracts are only funded on an annual basis. Moreover, public supported financing such as state and local municipal bonds may be only partially raised to support existing infrastructure projects. The contracts with governmental agencies are subject to audit, investigations which would result in adjustments to reimbursable contract costs. Most government contracts are awarded through rigorous competitive process which emphasizes price over other qualitative factors.

ESG Initiatives

Jacobs ESG Reporting is aligned to the Sustainability Accounting Standards Board (SASB) and Global Reporting Initiative Standards. As set forth in Jacobs Climate Action Plan, the company achieved 100% low carbon electricity and became carbon neutral for its operations and business travel from the year 2020 onward. Jacobs is the first consultancy firm globally with net zero targets approved by Science Based Target initiative (SBTi). The company reduced its carbon emission by 52% during the period 2019–2021. The company has committed to reduce absolute scopes 1, 2, & 3 GHG emissions 90% by 2040. Jacobs is a member of US EPA Green Power Partnership, a voluntary program which supports the development of new renewable generation capacity in the USA.

In 2022, the company donated $3.2 million to 3000 plus charities across 26 countries. The employees had tracked approximately 23,000 volunteer hours and completed 8000 volunteer activities. The company could visualize business risks of $10–$100 million due to disruption to major revenue streams and losses accounted from reduced services for fossil fuel-related projects. However, this loss is offset by greater opportunities from emergency management and national security, environmental planning, waste management, and clean energy. In the year 2022, Jacobs introduced an internal carbon price of $50 USD per metric ton of $CO2$ applied to non-billable business travel at Jacobs. Over 97% of employees have completed Advocate & Ally inclusion learning program. The company aims to realize its aspirational goal of 40% men, 40% women, and 20% any gender to be achieved by the year 2025. In the year 2021, approximately 2000 employees were covered by collective bargaining agreements which constituted approximately 3.6% of the global workforce. In the same year, the company introduced paid volunteering time for STEAM education outreach activities globally. In 2021, 99% of the employees completed the online code of conduct training program. The representation of board members who are ethnically diverse or female is 50%.

Stock Market Performance

The following section analyzes the changes in the wealth created through an investment of $100 in the stock and market indexes during the 5-year period ending September 30, 2022. The values of each investment are based on share price appreciation with reinvestment of all dividends. The investments are assumed to have occurred at the beginning of the period presented. Table 2 shows the changes in the wealth generated for the company and market indexes.

The 5-year holding period return for Jacobs was 94%, whereas for S&P 500 and S&P 1500 IT Consulting, the holding period return was 56% and 30%, respectively. The average yearly return for Jacobs and market indexes S&P 500 and S&P 1500 IT Consulting were 16.39%, 10.30%, and 7.27% during the period 2018–2022.

The following section analyzes the stock returns for Jacobs and market index based on monthly returns data during the recent 5-year period. The data is taken from Yahoo Finance. Jacobs share which was trading at $61.05 on January 2, 2018, increased by approximately 2 times to trade at $124 on January 2, 2022. The cumulative monthly return for Jacobs stock was 87% during the time window Jan 2018–Dec 2022. The average yearly return for the stock was 17% during the recent 5-year period. The cumulative monthly return for the market index S&P 500 during the same period was 47%, while the average yearly return was 10%.

Table 2 Wealth creation

Year	2017	2018	2019	2020	2021	2022
Jacobs	$100	132.8	159.9	163.55	235.25	194.31
S&P 500	$100	117.91	122.93	141.05	184.02	155.55
S&P 1500 IT consulting	$100	116.79	135.05	116.64	157.29	130.09

Source Annual Report 2022

Table 3 Holding period return

Year	Jacobs	S&P 500	Excess returns
2018	−4%	−8%	3%
2019	39%	19%	19%
2020	18%	16%	1%
2021	38%	28%	10%
2022	−8%	−15%	7%

Table 4 Comparative book and market value

Year	2018	2019	2020	2021	2022
Book value of equity	5944.35	5768.66	5855.67	6632.56	6736.91
Market value of equity	10879.68	12158.43	12036.72	17082.19	13820.87
BV as percent of MV	54.6%	47.4%	48.6%	38.8%	48.7%

Table 5 Financial highlights

	(In millions of dollars)				
Financial highlights	2018	2019	2020	2021	2022
Total assets	12645.8	11462.71	12354.35	14632.61	14660.42
Short-term investments	634.87	1082.2	1209.93	1014.25	1140.48
Total equity	5944.35	5768.66	5855.67	6632.56	6736.91
Total revenue	10579.77	12737.87	13566.98	14092.63	14922.83
Total operating expenses	1771.11	2072.18	2050.7	2355.68	2409.19
Net income	163.43	847.98	491.85	477.03	644.04
Market cap	10879.68	12158.43	12036.72	17082.19	13820.87
Enterprise value	12482.16	12531.34	13443.2	20584.62	17522.53

Table 3 shows the holding period return for the stock and market index S&P 500 during the period 2018–2022. The holding period is assumed to be 1-year period.

Jacobs' share had significant superior returns compared to market index S&P 500 during the year 2019 and 2022.

Table 4 displays the comparative book and market value of the company during the period 2018–2022. The values are given in millions of dollars. The data source was from gurufocus.com and Morningstar.

The average book value as percent of market value of Jacobs was 47.7%. In 2021 and 2022, the market value was 2.58 and 2.05 times that of book value of the firm.

Table 5 shows the financial highlights of the company during the period 2018–2022. The data was sourced from annual reports, guru focus, and morning star. The values are given in millions of dollars.

The average growth rate of total assets, cash investments, and total equity during the period 2018–2022 was 4%, 20%, and 3%, respectively. The total revenues and net income increased by 9% and 102% during the period 2018–2022. The total expenses increased by 8% on an average basis. The market capitalization and enterprise value of firm increased by 8% and 11% respectively on an average basis during the period 2018–2022.

Table 6 shows the profitability and leverage position of the firm during the period 2018–2022.

The average net margin, ROE, and ROA during the recent 5-year period were 3.91%, 9.04%, and 4.15%, respectively. The average debt equity ratio for the company was 0.48.

Table 7 estimated the economic value for Jacobs during the period 2021–2022. The values are given in millions of dollars.

Table 6 Performance ratios

Ratios	2018	2019	2020	2021	2022
Net margin%	1.54	6.66	3.63	3.38	4.32
ROE%	3.18	14.66	8.53	8.12	10.73
ROA%	1.63	7.03	4.13	3.54	4.4
DER	0.37	0.25	0.44	0.64	0.69

Table 7 Economic value

Year	2021	2022
Profit before income tax	695.6	876.35
Income tax	146.08	160.90
Net operating profit after tax (NOPAT)	549.52	715.45
Stockholder equity	6632.56	6736.91
Long-term debt	2839.93	3357.26
Total capital employed	9472.49	10094.17
WACC	5.42%	7.05%
Capital charge	513.41	711.64
Economic value	36.12	3.81

References

1. https://www.jacobs.com/
2. https://invest.jacobs.com/overview/default.aspx
3. https://invest.jacobs.com/news/news-details/2023/Jacobs-to-Plan-Dismantling-of-Soviet-era-Nuclear-Reactors/default.aspx
4. https://jacobs.foleon.com/planbeyond20v1/planbeyond-20-719/esg-disclosures/
5. Annual Report 2021

Case 35 National MI

National Mortgage Insurance Corporation (National MI) is an approved primary mortgage insurance company which offers private mortgage insurance to low down payment borrowers and protects lenders and investors against losses related to defaulters. NMI Holdings Inc. was incorporated in May 2011. The company provides mortgage insurance through the wholly owned insurance subsidiaries, National Mortgage Insurance Corporation (NMIC) and National Mortgage Reinsurance Inc One. NMIC is the primary insurance subsidiary which is approved as an NMI provider by the GSEs and has license to write MI coverage in all the states in the USA. Re One provides reinsurance coverage to NMIC. NMI Services Inc. (NMIS) provides outsourced loan review services to mortgage loan originators.

By December 2021, the NMI had issued master policies for 1732 clients consisting of mortgage banks, credit unions, community banks, builder-owned mortgage lenders, credit unions, and community banks. By year-end 2021, National MI had $153.6 billion of total insurance-in-force (IIF). During this period, the company had generated new insurance written (NIW) of $85.6 billion. As of December 31, 2021, the company had 247 full-time and part-time employees.

Market Environment

The US residential mortgage market is one of the largest in the world with $12 trillion of mortgage debt outstanding based on data published by US Federal Reserve in the year 2021. The primary market is composed of lenders originating home loans to borrowers, loans for home purchases (purchase originations), and loans for refinance of existing mortgages (refinancing originations). The secondary market is composed of financial institutions engaged in securitization (buying and selling of mortgages in the form of whole loan or securitized assets such as mortgage-backed securities). Government-sponsored enterprises (GSEs) such as Fannie Mae and Freddie Mac are the largest participants in the secondary mortgage market. On account of being the largest participants, these GSEs are the principal purchasers

© The Author(s), under exclusive license to Springer Nature Switzerland AG 2024
B. R. Kumar, *Rising Stars*, Management for Professionals,
https://doi.org/10.1007/978-3-031-50032-9_35

of mortgages insured by mortgage insurers such as NMIC. Hence the performance of the private mortgage insurance industry in the USA is basically driven by GSEs' demand for high-LTV loans, mortgage insurance requirements, and business practices. Mortgage Insurers (MI) play a pivotal role in the US housing market. MI provides protection to lenders and investors from default-related losses on the unpaid principal balance portion of a covered mortgage. Both government MIs and private MI firms such as NMIC provide mortgage insurance. Mortgage insurance is heavily skewed toward high-LTV loans where borrowers make downpayment which is less than 20% of the value of a home. MI supports secondary market sales of mortgages which are related primarily to GSEs and facilitate lenders and investors to diversify and mitigate their exposure to mortgage credit risk.

The company faces risks from other private mortgage insurers, government MIs, and other financial institutions which offer piggyback loans or front-end risk sharing arrangements which do not require MI on loans sold to the GSEs. The five major competitors for the company in the private MI sector in the USA are Arch Capital Group Ltd., Essent Group Ltd. (Essent), Enact Holdings, Inc. (Enact), MGIC Investment Corporation (MGIC), and Radian Group Inc. (Radian). The main factors determining competition in the sector are based in terms of coverage, underwriting guidelines, pricing, customer service, use of technology, and innovation for delivery and servicing of insurance products.

Product and Services

1) Mortgage Insurance

The company offers primary and pool mortgage insurances. Primary mortgage insurance provides default protection on individual mortgage loans at specified coverage percentages. In this category, the mortgage insurance is written on a flow basis wherein mortgages are insured on an individual, loan by loan basis at the time of origination. Primary mortgage insurance can also be offered on an aggregated basis wherein after the point of origination, each mortgage in a given loan is individually insured in a single transaction. National MI's primary insurance is written on first-lien mortgage loans. These are secured by owner-occupied single-family homes such as one to four family homes and condominiums. National MI also offers primary insurance on first-lien mortgages secured by vacation properties, second homes, and investment properties. The premium rates of the company generally increase as coverage levels increase. Basically, premiums are calculated as a percentage of the original principal balance of an insured loan. The company offers four premium plans—single, annual, monthly, and monthly advantage. In the single plan, the entire premium is paid upfront at the time coverage is placed. In the annual plan, the premiums are paid in advance for a subsequent 12-month period over the life of a policy. In monthly plan, the premiums are paid in advance on a monthly basis over the life of the policy. In the monthly advantage plan, the premiums are billed initially on receipt of notice of a mortgage close and then paid in arrears over a monthly basis during the policy life. The RIF across all policies written by National MI is expected to approximate 25% of the primary IIF. However, the coverage levels will vary on an individual loan basis between 6% and 35%. IIF is the unpaid principal balance of all insured loans at a specified date, and RIF is the product of coverage percentages multiplied by the IIF on such date. With respect to a claim, the maximum obligation is generally determined by multiplying the selected covered percentage by the loss amount on an insured loan.

2) Pool Insurance

Pool insurance provides additional credit enhancement for certain secondary market mortgage transactions. It covers the excess of loss on a defaulted mortgage loan which exceeds the claim payment under the primary MI coverage.

Loan Review Services

The subsidiary company NMIS offers outsourced loan review services to mortgage originators. NMIS performs the function of assessing whether the individual loan applications comply with the originator's and/or GSEs' underwriting guidelines. The loan review services are provided for all mortgages irrespective of mortgage insurance requirement. NMIS offers clients with limited indemnification against losses for certain material loan review errors as a part of the terms of loan review agreement.

The customers of National MI are classified into national accounts and regional accounts. National accounts are the most significant residential mortgage originators as determined by the combined volume of retail originations and insured business. National account lenders may also retain loans which they originate or purchase in their portfolios. The regional account lenders typically originate loans on a local or regional level.

Underwriting

The company has established underwriting and risk management guidelines which influence the performance of mortgage credit. The company evaluates loans and issues policies through the underwriting platforms, namely non-delegated and delegated. In non-delegated submission, the company reviews the information, documentation, and data provided by the lender to underwrite the MI application. The company offers delegated underwriting to lenders who have a track record of originating quality mortgage loans and meeting approval requirements. The delegated eligibility rules are programmed into the company's insurance management system which enables the company to automatically reject policies which don't meet threshold requirements. The company has a team of experienced underwriters who review and evaluate its non-delegated loan submissions. The company also engages third-party underwriting service providers.

Policy Pricing

In 2018, the company introduced Rate GPS, a proprietary risk-based pricing platform to offer individualized premium rates for new loans insured based on risk perception and expected performance of each loan. Different factors such as property type, type of loan product, credit characteristics of borrowers, and lender and market factors are considered in the Rate GPS. The Rate GPS offers a granular and analytical approach to evaluate and price risk for offering mortgage insurance portfolio with attractive risk-adjusted returns.

The policy servicing department carries out servicing activities related to master policies and certificate administration, premium billing, and payment processing. It is the responsibility of the policy servicing department to interface with the insured mortgage loan servicers. National MI is currently integrated with the two largest third-party mortgage service systems—Black Knight Financial Services and Fiserv.

3) Reinsurance

This segment consists of internal reinsurance and third-party insurance. NMIC and Re One had reinsurance agreement with Re One in which Re One provided reinsurance to NMIC on certain insured loans with coverage levels in excess of 25% after accounting for third-party insurance. With the repeal of state coverage limits, the reinsurance coverage provided by Re One to NMIC has been reduced. Active insurance exposures are not currently maintained by Re One. The company also has reinsurance agreement with third-party insurance providers such as Oaktown Re Ltd. Under the terms of agreement, NMIC retains the first layer of aggregate loss exposure on covered policies and the third-party insurer provides second layer loss protection up to a defined reinsurance coverage amount. Finally, NMIC retains losses in excess of the respective reinsurance coverage amounts. Under the terms of a quota share reinsurance agreement, the ceding insurer pays a premium in exchange for coverage on an agreed-upon portion of incurred losses.

Enterprise Risk Management

National MI has well-established enterprise-wide policies, procedures, and processes for identifying, monitoring, and managing credit market and operational risks in businesses. To manage credit risk in its businesses, National MI has established prudential underwriting standards and loan level eligibility matrices. These eligibility matrices deal with factors such as maximum LTV, minimum FICO, maximum borrower DTI ratio, maximum loan size, property type, and occupancy status of loans. The company also conducts due diligence of lender customers and implements quality control process to ensure ongoing adherence with underwriting guidelines and eligibility criteria. Concentration limits are also set to regulate the aggregation of loan level risks in overall portfolio. The company also underwrites individually significant majority of loans through non-delegated platform. National MI deploys Rate GPS, the proprietary risk-based pricing platform to manage risk in its policy pricing process. National MI manages operational exposures through a variety of standard risk management practices such as purchasing hazard and cyber insurance coverage, maintaining oversight of third-party vendors, and establishing IT system redundancy and disaster recovery practices.

Sustainability Initiatives

The company has facilitated 13 million people to achieve homeownership. The company offers educations services through online courses, webinars, and podcasts to educate potential borrowers on low down payment options. The company has adopted a "Total Rewards" strategy which includes programs and practices to motivate the employees. The 5-year average voluntary turnover rate for the company is 6.6%. The company received Fortune magazine's recognition as one of the "Best Workplaces" in the years 2015, 2017, 2019, and 2021, respectively. The company has adopted integrated recruitment strategies such as targeted job postings and diversity partnerships. National MI is a member and sponsor of the National Association of Minority Mortgage Bankers of America (NAMMBA). The company hosts mandatory ethics and compliance training for employees all through the year. The company has well-established compliance-related policies such as Anti-Fraud Policy Business Conduct and Ethics Policy, Compliant Handling Process, Conflicts of Interest Policy Document, and Retention and Destruction Policy Employee Handbook. The company has implemented comprehensive information security program which governs cybersecurity and data management services.

Table 1 lists the primary portfolio statistics during the 3-year period 2019–2021. All values except default rates are given in millions of dollars.

Table 1 Portfolio statistics

	2019	2020	2021
Net insurance written	45,141	62,702	85,574
New risk written	11,715	15,602	21,607
Insurance-in-force	94,754	111,252	152,343
Risk-in-force	24,173	28,164	38,661
Loans in default	1448	12,209	6227
Default rate	0.4%	3.06%	1.22%

Source: Annual Report, Values in millions of dollars

Stock Performance

Table 2 compares the cumulative stock wealth created for National MI's common stock with the cumulative stock wealth created for market indexes such as Russell 2000 Index, S&P Small Cap 600 Index, and an index representing select mortgage insurance companies such as Essent, MGIC, and Radian. The period of analysis is from December 31, 2016, until December 31, 2021. The analysis assumes an investment of $100 in stock and indexes in 2016.

The 5-year holding period return for National MI was 105%. The comparative holding period return for Russell 2000, S&P Small Cap 600, and PeerIndex was 76%, 80%, and 42% respectively. The yearly average returns for National MI were 23.05%, whereas for Russell 2000, S&P Small Cap 600, and PeerIndex, the average returns were 12%, 13%, and 11% approximately during the period of analysis.

Five-Year Stock Return Analysis

The return analysis was done for the National MI stock and market index Russell 2000 for the 5-year period Jan 2018–Jan 2023. The National MI stock price which was trading at $19.85 on 2/1/2018 increased by 1.11 times to trade at $22.05 on 19/1/2023. The total monthly cumulative returns for National MI during the above period were 65%, whereas the average yearly return for the stock during the 5-year period was 13%. During the same period, the total monthly cumulative returns for Russell 2000 index were 33% and the average 5 yearly returns were 7%.

Table 3 shows the holding period return for the stock and market index Russell 2000 for the 5-year period 2018–2022. The holding period return analysis is based on the assumption of holding period of 1 year. The data for analysis was taken from Yahoo Finance.

Table 2 Comparative stock wealth

Year	2016	2017	2018	2019	2020	2021
National MI	$100	160	168	312	213	205
Russell 2000	$100	115	102	128	154	176
S&P Small Cap 600	$100	113	104	127	142	180
PeerIndex	$100	$129	$102	$157	$135	$142

Source: Annual Report 2021

Table 3 Holding period return

Year	National MI	Russell 2000	Excess returns
2018	−10%	−11%	1%
2019	51%	11%	40%
2020	−29%	22%	−51%
2021	3%	8%	−5%
2022	−16%	−13%	−2%

Table 4 Book and market value comparison

Year	2017	2018	2019	2020	2021
Book value of equity	509.8	701.5	930.42	1369.59	1565.79
Market value of equity	1028.8	1183.79	2268.12	1928.94	1874.57
BV as percent of MV	49.6%	59.3%	41.0%	71.0%	83.5%

Table 5 Financial highlights

	(In millions of dollars)				
Financial highlights	2017	2018	2019	2020	2021
Total assets	894.85	1092.04	1364.82	2166.67	2450.58
Short-term investments	19.2	23.88	38.43	121.38	73.48
Total equity	509.8	701.5	930.42	1369.59	1565.79
Total revenue	178.64	273.63	370.11	436.19	485.64
Net income	22.05	107.93	171.96	171.57	231.13
Market cap	1028.8	1183.79	2268.12	1928.94	1874.57
Enterprise value	1153.48	1306.67	2375.46	2200.86	2195.71

Table 6 Performance indicators

Ratios	2017	2018	2019	2020	2021
Net margin%	12.34	39.44	46.46	39.33	47.59
ROE%	4.48	17.83	21.07	14.92	15.75
ROA%	2.54	10.86	14	9.72	10.01
DER	0.28	0.21	0.16	0.29	0.25

National MI has superior returns compared to market index Russell in the year 2019.

Table 4 shows the excess value created based on the market and book of National MI during the period 2017–2021. The values are given in millions of dollars.

The average book value as percent of market value was 60.9% during the time period 2017–2021. In 2017, the market value was twice that of book value of the company. By 2021, the market was 1.2 times that of the book value of firm. The data source was gurufocus.com.

The following section discusses the operating highlights of the company during the period 2017–2021.

Table 5 gives the financial highlights of the company during the period 2017–2021.

The average growth rate of total assets, short-term investments, and total equity during the period 2017–2021 was 30%, 65%, and 33%, respectively. The average growth rate of revenue and net income was 29% and 121%, respectively. The market capitalization and enterprise value increased by 22% on an average basis during the above period.

Table 6 gives the profitability and leverage position of the firm during the period 2017–2021.

Table 7 Economic value

Year	2020	2021
Profit before income tax	218.11	296.73
Income tax	46.54	65.61
Net operating profit after tax (NOPAT)	171.57	231.12
Stockholder equity	1369.59	1565.79
Long-term debt	393.30	394.62
Total capital employed	1762.89	1960.41
WACC	10.62%	11.17%
Capital charge	187.22	218.98
Economic value	−15.65	12.15

The average net margin, ROE, and ROA during the period 2017–2021 was 37%, 14.81%, and 9.43%, respectively. The average debt equity ratio during the period 2017–2021 was 0.24.

Table 7 shows the estimation of economic value of National MI during the year 2020 and 2021.

The economic value is given in millions of dollars.

References

1. https://ir.nationalmi.com/
2. Sustainability At National MI – National MI

Case 36 Ubiquiti Inc.

The company was established by Robert Pera in the year 2005. The company is headquartered in New York. Ubiquiti Inc. sells equipment and its related software platforms through a network of over 100 distributors, online retailers, and customers directly through its webstores. The company specializes in providing networking infrastructure in over 200 countries globally. These networking products are driven by UISP and UniFi OS software platforms to facilitate high-capacity distributed internet access and unified information technology management for consumer electronics. The solutions can be categorized into high-performance networking technology for corporates, service providers, and consumers. The company focuses on enterprise and service provider markets through its Ubiquiti community consisting of service providers, distributors, value-added resellers, webstores, system integrators, and IT professionals. The consumers are basically targeted through digital marketing efforts. The company also offers a portfolio of networking products and solutions for operator-owners of wireless internet services (WISP) and smart homes. Carrier class infrastructure for wireless broadband, wireless backhaul systems, and routing are provided by operator-owner-service-provider to control, track, and bill their respective customers. For simplified user software interface, Ubiquiti's enterprise product platforms provide wireless LAN infrastructure, video surveillance products, switching and routing solutions, security gateways, and door access systems. By 2022, the company had employed 1377 full-time equivalent employees.

The company had revenues of $1.3 billion, $1.9 billion, and $1.7 billion in the years 2020, 2021, and 2022, respectively. By 2022, the research and development team of the company consisted of 978 employees in different countries such as the USA, Taiwan, China, and European countries. The R&D expenses of the company amounted to $89.4 million, $116.2 million, and $137.7 million in the years 2020, 2021, and 2022, respectively. The company uses contract manufacturers located in China and Vietnam to manufacture its products. In 2022, the company sold its products globally to over 100 distributors and direct to customers through its webstores based in 75 countries.

© The Author(s), under exclusive license to Springer Nature Switzerland AG 2024

B. R. Kumar, *Rising Stars*, Management for Professionals,
https://doi.org/10.1007/978-3-031-50032-9_36

Technology Platforms and Products

The service provider and carrier solutions offered include airMax technology, EdgeMax, airFiber, and UFiber GPON. The airMax technology platform includes proprietary protocols consisting of advanced technologies for minimizing signal noise. EdgeMAX platform is software and systems routing platform which is powered by full featured USIP operating system with features such as firewall, dynamic routing, and virtual private network functionality. airFiber platform is a wireless backhaul point to point radio system which is designed to offer low latency with high throughput. UFiber GPON platform is based on plug and play fiber network technology which facilitates passive optical network deployment. This platform is designed to enable internet providers to build high-speed fiber internet networks for users.

The enterprise provider solutions include UniFi WLAN, UniFi Protect, UniFi Switch, UniFi Console, and UniFi Access. WLAN is designed as an enterprise Wi-Fi system to facilitate on-site or remote management through the cloud and allows for the configuration of network system. UniFi Protect platform is a video surveillance system accessible from any web browser and performs the functions of detailed statistical reporting and advanced analytics. It provides management console with multiple views, camera settings, and customizable event recordings. UniFi Console is an enterprise class router and security gateway device which provides cost-effective reliable routing and advanced network security. UniFi Access is the state-of-the-art door access system offered by Ubiquiti. The company also offers Wi-Fi system product solutions for consumers such as AmpliFi and Alien.

Business Environment and Strategy

The internet traffic growth has been unprecedented, driven by the usage of high bandwidth applications such as video, audio, cloud-based applications, online gaming, and social networking. It is estimated that the proportion of internet users as a percentage of global population would be 66% by the year 2023 (Cisco Annual Internet Report). According to this report, the number of networked devices per capita will be increased from 2.4 in 2018 to 3.6 in the year 2023. Consumer and enterprise bandwidth needs can be addressed by wired networking solutions. The broadband access needs in underpenetrated markets through the world can be addressed by wireless networks. The products offered by Ubiquiti can be differentiated in terms of proprietary software, firmware expertise, and hardware design capabilities. The consumer products are basically targeted toward smart home and highly connected consumers.

Risk Factors

The market for wireless broadband networking and enterprise network equipment is emerging and is characterized by rapid technological change, evolving industry standards, new product introductions, and short product life cycles. The company may face constraints for offering products with respect to keeping pace with technological and market developments while offering products at competitive prices. The markets in which the company operates such as networking, enterprise WLAN, routing, switching, video surveillance, wireless backhaul, and machine to machine communications are highly competitive in nature.

The company has limited visibility with respect to end customer demand and channel inventory levels. The products and solutions are primarily sold through the network of distributors and resellers and the company doesn't employ a traditional direct sales force. The distributors don't make long-term purchase commitments and don't provide information about market demand for the products. Hence the future sales cannot be adequately forecasted. The markets in which the company operate can become volatile and future results of operation may be affected. The company also faces business risks associated with distributors' inventory management practices. The company also faces business risks in terms of the need to build inventory for new product announcements and shipments or decisions related to maintaining higher levels of inventory which may lead to inventory write-downs. The company relies on a limited number of distributors, and relationship changes may disrupt the sales of the company. Undetected defects or bugs could result in unforeseen delays or expenses. Security vulnerabilities in the products, services, and systems or distribution channel may lead to reduced revenues. The company also relies upon a limited number of contract manufacturers to produce its products. Shortage of components or manufacturing capacity may lead to cost escalation or results in delay to fulfill future orders, thereby leading to a material adverse impact on the firm's business.

Stock Performance

The following section compares the stock returns of Ubiquiti with returns of market index Nasdaq Composite during the recent 5-year period. The Ubiquiti closing stock price on 2/1/2018 was $63.59. By December 1, 2022, the stock price increased by 4.5 times to trade at $288.26. The total cumulative monthly return for Ubiquiti stock was 201% during the 5-year period 2018–2022. The average yearly return for the stock for the same period was 41%. The total cumulative monthly return for the market index Nasdaq Composite was 48%, while the average yearly return for the index was 10%.

Table 1 shows the holding period returns for Ubiquiti stock and market index Nasdaq Composite during the 5-year period 2018–2022.

Ubiquiti's stock had superior performance compared to market index Nasdaq Composite during the 3-year period 2018–2020. In 2021, the performance of stock

Table 1 Holding period returns

Year	Ubiquiti	Nasdaq Composite	Excess returns
2018	56%	−9%	65%
2019	75%	23%	51%
2020	70%	41%	30%
2021	0%	20%	−20%
2022	−6%	−26%	21%

Table 2 Performance indicators and leverage

Ratios	2018	2019	2020	2021	2022
Net margin%	19.3	27.78	29.61	32.48	22.38
ROE%					
ROA%	19.68	34	47.14	75.73	43.63
DER	1.54	4.99	−2.3	197.22	−2.23

Table 3 Financial highlights

	(In millions of dollars)				
Financial highlights	2018	2019	2020	2021	2022
Total assets	1022.58	875.87	737.45	890.99	844.71
Short-term investments	666.68	308.01	143.54	250.74	136.65
Total equity	315.75	99.28	−295.46	2.7	382.88
Total revenue	1016.86	1161.73	1284.5	1898.8	1691.69
Total operating expenses	117.45	125.31	129.97	169.68	207.55
Net income	196.29	322.69	380.3	616.58	378.66
Market cap	6275.42	9135.65	11117.36	19537.76	14996.97
Enterprise value	6093.52	9323.01	11651.91	19819.32	15713.58

was below that of market index. In 2022, both the stock and index registered negative returns.

Table 2 gives the performance ratios of the company and leverage ratios.

Table 3 gives the financial highlights of the company. The values are given in millions of dollars.

The average growth rate of total assets, cash and cash equivalents, and total equity was highly fluctuating. The average growth rate of total revenues and net income was 15% and 26%, respectively. The market capitalization and enterprise value increased by 30% and 32% on an average basis.

References

1. https://ir.ui.com/
2. SEC Filings | Ubiquiti Networks Inc

Case 37 Salesforce

Salesforce founded in the year 1999 is the largest customer relationship management (CRM) platform in the world which offers CRM applications for sales, services, and marketing. The CRM platform of Salesforce is used by more than 150,000 companies globally. This American cloud-based software company is headquartered in San Francisco. Approximately 90% of the Fortune 500 are Salesforce customers. Salesforce is the fastest growing among the top five enterprise software companies in the world. Salesforce empowers companies around the world to adopt technologies such as cloud, mobile, social, blockchain, and artificial intelligence to connect customers in the digital world. The Customer 360 platform enables digital transformation for companies by means of connecting customer data across systems, apps, and devices to facilitate companies sell, service, market, and conduct commerce from anywhere in the world. Customer 360 service offerings are configured easily and can be integrated with other platforms and enterprise applications. Through direct sales and partners, the company sells the products primarily on a subscription basis. Salesforce also allows third parties to use its platform and developer tools to create additional functionality and new applications which can be run on salesforce platform.

By January 2022, the company had 73,541 employees of which 55% were located in the USA. The principal executive offices are located in San Francisco, California. In the year 2022, the company made $26.5 billion in revenue which was 25% higher compared to the previous year. Every year the company completes a corporate V2MOM, which is an internal management tool used to align the firm on its vision, values, methods, obstacles, and measures for the upcoming year.

Offerings

The leading AI-powered Customer 360 platform covers functional areas of sales, service, marketing, and other areas. Sales offering facilitates the automation of entire sales process from lead generation to billing with speed and efficiency. The sales

© The Author(s), under exclusive license to Springer Nature Switzerland AG 2024

B. R. Kumar, *Rising Stars*, Management for Professionals,
https://doi.org/10.1007/978-3-031-50032-9_37

offering facilitates storage of data, monitors leads, forecasts opportunities, offers other functions related to analytics and relationship intelligence, and delivers quotes, contracts, and invoices. The sales offering facilitates teams to work from anywhere in the office. The service offerings enable companies to connect its service agents with customers anytime across any touchpoint from the phone to digital channels and self-service portals. Routine issues related to predictions, recommendations, and chatbots across digital channels can be resolved using the service offerings. The field service solution offered by the service offering of Salesforce enables firms to connect agents, dispatchers, and mobile employees through one centralized platform. This platform facilitates scheduling and dispatch of work intelligently and allows tracking and managing jobs in real time.

Platform offers built-in compliance, integrated platform services, and automatic upgrades. Trailhead is the free online learning platform which facilitates people to learn in-demand salesforce skills. Marketing offering enables integrated customer experience with real-time personalization. The marketing offering allows companies to plan, personalize, and optimize one-to-one customer interactions across email, mobile, social, web, and connected products. The commerce offering facilitates personalized shopping experiences and robust partner ecosystem. The commerce offering delivers click-to-code tools which facilitate customers to build and deploy solutions when the market environment demands changes. The data analytics offering such as Tableau offers customers advanced end-to-end analytics solutions with intelligent analytics capabilities to understand data. The integration offering powered by MuleSoft enables customers to unlock, unify, and secure data for exploring new revenue opportunities and create differentiated customer experiences. The service offerings of the company basically address the needs of customers in specific industries such as financial services, healthcare, life sciences, and manufacturing.

Growth Strategy

Salesforce is the industry leading CRM integrated platform for business to business, business to consumer, business to employee, and enterprise application market place. The company focuses on strengthening existing customer relationships through cross selling and upselling and adoption of multiple offerings among small and large enterprise customers. The company aims to expand all editions of its offering through new features, functions, and enhanced security using internal development, acquisitions, and partnerships. Armed with the go-to-market capabilities globally, the company aims to grow its business by selling to new customers in new areas. The aim is to increase the number of direct sales professionals and develop indirect distribution channels. The company focuses on developing innovative solutions in new segments such as analytics, e-commerce, collaboration, integration, and workforce management. In the fiscal year 2022, Salesforce introduced Health & Safety Solution or Dreampass which enabled companies safely return to work after the COVID pandemic through managing contact tracing. The solution also enabled healthcare organizations to distribute vaccines around the world. Salesforce also introduced NetZero Cloud which provides insights on emission data related to carbon footprint as a part of sustainability initiatives. The company also focuses on strengthening its partner ecosystem. The company has well-strategized plans to strengthen its partner ecosystem. The Customer 360 platform facilitates customers, independent software vendors, and third-party developers to create, test, and deliver cloud-based apps. The Customer 360 platform is the growth engine for the company which connects every customer touchpoint through interaction across sales, service, marketing, and commerce. The AI platform Einstein has become the benchmark of industry standard with delivery of more than 150 billion predictions every day. Hyperforce, the new public cloud infrastructure, facilitates the scaling of the apps and integration across any platform. The free curated resources such as Trailhead help firms to adopt innovation programs.

M&A and Strategic Investments

In terms of inorganic growth strategy, the company evaluates opportunities to acquire complementary businesses and technologies. Acquisitions are made to complement existing products or accelerate development of features which result in new service offerings. The company also makes strategic investments in privately held or publicly traded companies such as enterprise cloud companies, technology startups, and system integrators. The investments are made in early- to late-stage companies as well as participation in IPO offerings. The Salesforce solutions are offered as highly scalable cloud computing application and platform services on a multi-tenant technology architecture. This strategic approach enables the company to spread the cost of delivering the services across the user base and scale its business faster than the traditional software vendors and offer new functionality and innovative existing offerings. The company also offers its services through cloud computing partners who offer Infrastructure-as-a-Service which includes servers, storage, databases, and networking. In 2022, the company launched Hyperforce, the reimagination of platform architecture to deliver Customer 360 platform on major public clouds in select regions.

Table 1 lists the major acquisitions undertaken by Salesforce during 2008–2021.

Risk Factors

The company faces operational and execution risks, strategic and industry risk, legal and regulatory risk, and financial and general risks. Operational and execution risks are accounted by security breaches in the security measures or those of third-party data center hosting facilities, cloud computing platform providers, or third-party service partners. Any defects or disruptions in services would diminish demand for the firm's services. Time-consuming and expensive sales cycle, pricing pressure, and

Table 1 List of acquisitions

Year	Acquisitions
2008	InStranet, the AppExchange partner, was acquired. The target firm was the producer of customer service knowledge technology
2011	Acquired Radian6, the industry leading social media monitoring platform used by more than half of Fortune 100 companies. This acquisition enhanced all salesforce products and added social intelligence across sales cloud, service cloud, chatter, and force.com platform
	Salesforce completed its acquisition of Heroku, a leading cloud application platform for writing Ruby-based applications
	The acquisition positioned salesforce.com to take a greater share in the public cloud services market.
2012	Salesforce completed its acquisition of Buddy Media, the world's leading social media marketing platform
2013	Salesforce completed its acquisition of Exact Target, a leading cloud marketing platform
2016	Salesforce acquired SteelBrick, which has tools that take care of orders, contracts, billing, and payments
	Salesforce completed its acquisition of Metamind, a deep learning artificial intelligence platform
	Salesforce acquired Demandware, the industry leading provider of enterprise cloud commerce solutions
	Salesforce completed its acquisition of Krux, a CRM traffic and data management platform
2018	Salesforce completed its acquisition of CloudCraze, a leading B2B commerce platform built natively on Salesforce
	Salesforce acquired MuleSoft, a major leading platform for building application networks that connect enterprise apps, data, and devices, across any cloud and on-premise
	Salesforce acquired Datorama, the leading cloud-based, AI-powered marketing intelligence and analytics platform for enterprises, agencies, and publishers
2019	Salesforce completed its acquisition of Map Anything, a pioneer in location-based intelligence software built natively on the Salesforce Platform
	Salesforce.org was integrated into Salesforce
	Salesforce acquired Tableau Software, the world's largest analytics platform
	Salesforce acquired ClickSoftware, a leader in field service management solutions
2020	Salesforce completed its acquisition of Evergage, the leading software platform for real-time 1:1 personalization
	Salesforce acquired Vlocity, a leading provider of industry-specific cloud and mobile software for the world's major companies
2021	Salesforce completed its acquisition of Acumen Solutions, a leading professional services firm with deep Salesforce knowledge and extensive industry expertise across public sector, manufacturing, financial services
	Salesforce acquired Slack Technologies, Inc., and created the digital HQ for success from anywhere

configuration challenges are also potential risk factors. The inability to compete effectively in the intensely competitive market and the failure to expand services and integrate existing services to keep pace with technological developments are examples for strategic and industry risks. Evolving regulation of cloud computing, restrictions of cross-border data transfers, unfavorable industry-specific regulations, and lawsuits against the company by third parties for various claims reflect potential legal and regulatory risks. Fluctuations in the rate of anticipated growth and failure to balance expenses with revenue forecasts, fluctuations in currency exchange rates, and debt service obligations constitute financial risks.

Sustainability Initiatives

The company has achieved net zero emission. The company has allotted 6 million plus hours to the community since its inception. Around 4 million people have used the Trailhead learning platform to upgrade the skills for jobs. Free streaming service, Salesforce+, is empowering millions of people around the world with live, on-demand content. During the pandemic, the company has delivered more than 60 million pieces of personal protective equipment and distributed over 150 million vaccine doses using the Salesforce Platform. Over 50% of the US employees are members of underrepresented groups. The company follows the 1-1-1 model of philanthropy wherein 1% of profits, employees' time, and product are utilized to serve communities. Over the past 23 years, the company has donated over $500 million in grants to communities which included donation of $107 million to public schools. Salesforce employees have volunteered nearly 7 million hours and over 54,000 nonprofits and NGOs run on Salesforce. The company has achieved net zero residual emissions across its entire value chain and has used 100% renewable energy for its global operations. Salesforce has committed $100 million and 2.5 million volunteer hours to fight for climate action over the next 10 years. The company is half way through its commitment toward the mission of planting 100 million trees as part of the global movement 1t.org, to conserve and grow 1 trillion trees. The platform UpLink which Salesforce created through partnership with the World Economic Forum has empowered more than 30,000 ecopreneurs and innovators to develop cutting-edge climate solutions. The company's sustainable bond framework was released in the year 2020 and the company issued $1 billion of 2028 Senior Sustainability Notes. Salesforce intended to allocate an amount equal to the $990 million net proceeds from the offering to finance or refinance in whole or in part projects which meet the eligibility criteria under the framework related to nine green and social eligible project categories. Salesforce has committed to pursuing LEED Platinum and ILFI Zero Carbon certification for all new major offices by the year 2030.

Stock Wealth

An amount of $1000 invested on December 22, 2014, in the stock would have grown to an amount of $2215 by December 30, 2022. The analysis for the 8-year period assumes reinvestment of dividends.

Table 2 Comparative wealth creation

Year	2017	2018	2019	2020	2021	2022
Salesforce.com	$100	144	192	230	285	294
S&P 500	$100	124	119	142	163	198
Nasdaq Computer	$100	141	138	199	291	365
Nasdaq 100	$100	$136	$135	$176	$253	$292
Dow Jones Industrial Average	100	105	$100	$113	$126	$141

Source Annual Report 2022

Table 3 Holding period return

Year	Salesforce	Nasdaq 100	Excess returns
2018	18%	−8%	25%
2019	7%	26%	−19%
2020	22%	43%	−21%
2021	13%	26%	−14%
2022	−43%	−27%	−16%

Table 2 compares the cumulative total stock return for Salesforce with the cumulative total return for market indexes of S&P500 Index, Nasdaq Computer & Data Processing Index, the Nasdaq 100 Index, and the Dow Jones Industrial Average (DJIA) for each of the recent five fiscal years ending January 31, 2022. The analysis assumes an initial investment of $100 and reinvestment of dividends.

The holding period return for Salesforce was 194% for the Salesforce.com while the holding period return for market index S&P 500, Nasdaq Computer, Nasdaq 100, and Dow Jones Industrial Average were 98%, 265%, 192%, and 41%, respectively. The 5-year average return for the stock was approximately 25%, while for S&P 500, Nasdaq Computer, Nasdaq 100, and Dow Jones Industrial Average, the 5-year average returns were 15%, 31%, 25%, and 7%, respectively.

The next section analyzes the recent 5-year return for Salesforce.com in comparison to the market index Nasdaq 100. The Salesforce stock which was trading at $116.25 on 2/1/2018 increased by 1.3 times to trade at $132.58 by 1/12/2022. The total cumulative monthly return for Salesforce stock was 52% and 58% for the market index Nasdaq 100 during the period 2018–2022, while the 5-year average returns for the stock were 11% and 12% for market index Nasdaq 100.

Table 3 shows the holding period return for Salesforce and Nasdaq 100 during the recent period 2018–2022. The stock return analysis assumes holding period of 1 year.

The market index Nasdaq 100 had superior returns compared to the stock in all years except in 2018. The source of data was Yahoo Finance.

Table 4 shows the comparative book and market value of Salesforce during the period 2018–2022. The values are given in millions of dollars. The data source is gurufocus.com.

The average book value as percent of market value during the 5-year period 2018–2022 was approximately 18%. In 2018, the market value was almost eight

Table 4 Market and book value comparison

Year	2018	2019	2020	2021	2022
Book value of equity	10,376	15,605	33,885	41,493	58,131
Market value of equity	83137.56	117016.9	162802.83	207289.64	230071.07
BV as percent of MV	12.5%	13.3%	20.8%	20.0%	25.3%

Table 5 Financial highlights

	(In millions of dollars)				
Financial highlights	2018	2019	2020	2021	2022
Total assets	21,984	30,737	55,126	66,301	95,209
Short term investments	4521	4342	7947	11,966	10,537
Total equity	10,376	15,605	33,885	41,493	58,131
Total revenue	10,540	13,282	17,098	21,252	26,492
Total operating expenses	7313	9296	12,400	15,359	18,918
Net income	360	1110	126	4072	1444
Market cap	83137.56	117016.9	162802.83	207289.64	230071.07
Enterprise value	80336.56	115847.9	160723.83	201604.64	233515.07

Table 6 Profitability and leverage trends

Ratios	2018	2019	2020	2021	2022
Net margin%	3.42	8.36	0.74	19.16	5.45
ROE%	4.03	8.54	0.51	10.8	2.9
ROA%	1.82	4.21	0.29	6.71	1.79
DER	0.17	0.2	0.17	0.15	0.24

times of book value which declined by approximately four times that of book value by the year 2022.

Table 5 gives the financial highlights of Salesforce in millions of dollars.

The average growth rate of total assets, total cash investments, and total equity during the period 2018–2022 was 46%, 29%, and 58%, respectively. The total revenues increased by 58% on an average basis. The net income was showing highly fluctuating trend. The total expenses increased by 27% on an average basis. The market capitalization and enterprise value grew by 30% and 31%, respectively.

Table 6 gives data related to profitability and leverage position of the company.

The average net margin, ROE, and ROA were 7.43%, 5.36%, and 2.96%, respectively, during the period 2018–2022. The average debt equity ratio during the above period was 0.19.

References

1. https://investor.salesforce.com/stock-information/default.aspx

2. https://www.salesforce.com/uk/news/
3. https://investor.salesforce.com/stock-information/default.aspx
4. Annual Report 2022
5. https://www.salesforce.com/news/stories/salesforce-acquisitions/
6. https://investor.salesforce.com/environmental-and-social-practices/default.aspx

Case 38 Newmont Corporation

Newmont Corporation is primarily a gold producer with operations and assets spread out in different countries such as the USA, Canada, Mexico, the Dominican Republic, Peru, Suriname, Argentina, Chile, Australia, and Ghana. By December 2020, Newmont had attributable proven and probable gold reserves of 94.2 million ounces. The company also possessed an aggregate land position of approximately 58,900 square kilometers. The company is also involved in the production of copper, silver, lead, and zinc. Newmont Corporation was incorporated in the year 1920 and completed its 100th year in 2021.

In 2021, Newmont produced 6 million attributable ounces of gold and 1.3 million attributable gold equivalent ounces from other metals. It is estimated that the portfolio of operations and projects accounted by Newmont will produce nearly 8 million attributable gold equivalent ounces per year during the next 10 years. Newmont has reserves of nearly 93 million gold mineral ounces and 65 million gold equivalent resources. The gold resources reserves are estimated to be 68.3 million ounces and inferred gold resources of 33.2 million ounces. In 2021, the company generated $4.3 billion in cash from continuing operations and $2.6 billion in free cash flow. In 2021, the company paid $1.8 billion as dividends to shareholders with a dividend of $2.20 per share. Newmont is among the top 10% of S&P 500 large cap dividend payers. The company is the only gold producer listed in the S&P 500 Index. Approximately 14,400 people were employed by Newmont Corporation by 2021. Around 16,600 contractors are associated with the company's operations.

Table 1 lists the regions and segments in which the company operates.

© The Author(s), under exclusive license to Springer Nature Switzerland AG 2024

B. R. Kumar, *Rising Stars*, Management for Professionals,
https://doi.org/10.1007/978-3-031-50032-9_38

Table 1 Segment information

Region	Segment
North America	Cripple Creek & Victor ("CC&V") in the USA, Musselwhite, Porcupine and Éléonore in Canada, and Peñasquito in Mexico
South America	Yanacocha in Peru, Merian in Suriname, Cerro Negro in Argentina, and 40% equity interest in the Pueblo Viejo mine
Australia	Boddington and Tanami in Australia
Africa	Ahafo and Akyem in Ghana
Nevada	Carlin, Phoenix, Twin Creeks, and Long Canyon

Source Annual Report 2021

Products

Gold

The consolidated gold production from continuing operations of the company amounted to 6.4, 5.8, ad 5.9 million ounces in the years 2019, 2020, and 2021, respectively. In 2021, North America, South America, Australia, Africa, and Nevada accounted for 27%, 16%, 20%, 15%, and 22% of the total consolidated gold production. Approximately 93%, 90%, and 86% of the sales of the company were attributed to gold (refined gold) in the years 2019, 2020, and 2021, respectively. The end product of the firm's gold operations is an alloy named dore bars consisting primarily of gold along with silver and other metals. The refiners produce bullion from dore bars which is made up of 99.95% gold. Gold is basically used for fabrication or investment. Fabricated gold is used in jewelry, electronics, dentistry, industrial and decorative uses, medals, and official coins. Gold investors buy gold bullion, official coins, and jewelry. During the period 2018–2020, mine production has averaged approximately 70% of the annual gold supply. Gold is extracted from naturally oxidized ores by either milling or heap leaching depending on the amount of gold found in the ore.

Co-Product Metals

If the metal mined has more than 10–20% of the life of mine sales value in terms of all metal mined, then the metal is considered as a co-product metal by the company. The consolidated co-product copper production of the company amounted to 56 million pounds and 71 million pounds in the years 2020 and 2021, respectively. The co-product silver production amounted to 27.8 million ounces and 31.4 million ounces in the years 2020 and 2021. The co-product lead production amounted to 179 million pounds and 177 million pounds in the years 2020 and 2021. The co-product zinc production amounted to 381 million pounds and 435 million pounds in the years 2020 and 2021.

Environment

It is estimated that the top 10 producers of gold constitute approximately 30% of the globally mined gold production. Newmont has the largest market share of approximately 6% of the estimated total worldwide mined gold production. The company has a diverse portfolio of mining operations with varying ore grades and cost structures. The metal markets are cyclical in nature and the ability to remain competitive in the field depends upon the firm's ability to acquire and develop quality deposits along with the capability to maintain a skillful workforce and focus on cost optimization.

Strategy

In 2019, Newmont acquired Goldcorp Inc. The company also acquired 38.5% stake in Nevada Gold Mines. The company focuses on an integrated operating model and has the best portfolio of long-life operations and organic project pipeline.

The company has entered into a strategic alliance with Caterpillar Inc. to introduce a comprehensive mining system consisting of all electric zero emitting autonomous haulage fleet for optimizing underground and open pit operations.

Newmont has achieved $814 million in cost and productivity improvements in the year 2021. The Full Potential program which was initiated in the year 2014 had generated $4 billion in savings. The company focuses on advancing projects of Tanami Expansion 2 in Australia and Pamour in Canada. These projects are estimated to add 3 million ounces of gold production over an initial 13-year mine life. The company has also expanded its project portfolio with the acquisition of GT Gold and the Saddle project in the Golden Triangle district of British Columbia in Canada.

ESG Sustainability Initiatives

ESG initiatives have been a priority for the company for the past 30 years. All ESG standards are maintained in all Newmont operations. Since 2007, the company has assessed its environmental management systems against International Standards Organization 14,001:2016 stipulations.

In 2021, Newmont had issued a $3 billion sustainability-linked revolving credit facility with an interest adjustment based upon third-party assessment of the company's ESG performance. The company became the first firm in the industry to issue a sustainability-linked bond with the public offering of $1 billion aggregate principal amount of 2.6% sustainability-linked senior notes which is due by 2032. Since its inception in 2014, the Global Community Support Fund of the firm has provided $14 million in relief in the form of critical medical supplies, testing equipment, educational support, micro credits, and other financial support. In the year 2020, the company launched an integrated global compliance audit program to assess environment and social obligations as stipulated in regulations and agreements. The company aims to achieve 30% reduction in greenhouse gas emissions by the year 2030 with the aim of achieving net zero carbon emissions by the year 2050. During the period 2021–2025, the company has plans to invest $500 million as part of climate change initiatives. The company is recognized as the second most transparent reporter related to ESG practices in the S&P 500 as measured by the Bloomberg ESG Disclosure score. Newmont has been listed consistently on the Dow Jones Sustainability World Index since the year 2007. With respect to diversity and inclusion, the Board of company has been recognized as the leader in board diversity and inclusive leadership. By 2020, the board representation achieved gender parity with 50% female members and 70% of the independent directors belonging to either gender or ethnically diverse categories. The company is also an active participant in the Paradigm for Parity framework which emphasizes equal power, status, and opportunity for men and women with respect to senior leadership by the year 2030. ESG would comprise 30% of the company's short-term incentive plan payout with 20% allocated to health and safety metrics and 10% to sustainability performance based on key public indices.

Risk Factors

Health epidemics like COVID outbreak have the potential to materially and adversely affect the business and financial condition of the company. The business of the company is dependent on the prices of gold, silver, zinc, and lead. A significant decline in gold, silver, copper, zinc, or lead prices would have a material adverse effect on the operations of the firm. Factors which tend to affect prices include gold sales, purchases or leasing by governments, speculative short positions taken by significant investors in metals, exchange rates, taxes, inflation, reduced economic activity, changes in consumer or investor activity, etc. The producers of metals must continually replace reserves depleted by production to maintain production levels in future and provide sustainable return on investment. All the future exploration programs may not result in new mineral producing operations. The estimates of proven and probable reserves and mineralized material are uncertain in nature. The volume and grade of ore actually recovered may fluctuate from the estimated values. There exist risks related to implementation, upgrade, operation, and integration of the firm's information technology and operational technology systems. Foreign exchange fluctuations and capital controls may adversely affect the firm's earnings and value of its specific assets. Potential future investments such as projects, acquisitions, and investments which require funds for capital expenditure may place constraints on Newmont's cash flows. There are also chances that the company may experience increased costs or losses which result from hazards and uncertainties related to mining. Extractive industries are increasingly required to meaningfully engage in order to satisfy significant increases in stakeholder expectations. Mining companies are required to provide more welfare initiatives to communities and countries in which they operate for maintaining operations. The company's exploration, mining, and processing operations are subject to extensive laws and regulations related to land use and protection of the environment. Producing gold is an energy-intensive business which results in significant carbon footprint. In general, mining industry is subject to continued geotechnical challenges which would adversely impact the production and profitability of the company.

Stock Performance Analysis

The return analysis was done for Newmont stock and market index for the recent 5-year period 2018–2022. The Newmont stock was trading at $38.2 in NYSE on February 2, 2018. By January 1, 2023, the stock price increased by 1.4 times to trade at $53.63. The total cumulative monthly return for the Newmont stock was 59% while the returns for S&P 500 index were 48% during the period 2018–2022. The 5-year average return for the Newmont stock was 12%, while for market index S&P 500, the average yearly return was 10% during the above period. The data was taken from Yahoo Finance.

Table 2 gives the holding period return for the Newmont stock and market index S&P 500 during the period 2018–2022. The holding period return analysis assumes holding period of 1 year.

Newmont stock performed better compared to market index S&P 500 in the years 2019 and 2020, respectively.

Table 3 compares the book value and market value of the company during the period 2017–2021. The data is sourced from gurufocus.com. The values are given in millions of dollars.

The average book value as percent of market value was 55.6% during the period 2017–2021. In 2021, the market value was 2.25 times of the book value of the firm.

Table 2 Holding period return

Year	Newmont	S&P 500	Excess returns
2018	−9%	−8%	−2%
2019	27%	19%	8%
2020	33%	16%	16%
2021	4%	28%	−24%
2022	−23%	−15%	−8%

Table 3 Book and market value

Year	2017	2018	2019	2020	2021
Book value of equity	11,519	11,512	22,417	23,879	21,861
Market value of equity	20001.35	18468.45	35107.6	47,912	49119.84
BV as percent of MV	57.6%	62.3%	63.9%	49.8%	44.5%

Operating Performance

Table 4 highlights the financial highlights of Newmont Corporation during the period 2017–2021. The values are given in millions of dollars.

The total assets, short-term investments, and total equity grew by 24%, 24%, and 23%, respectively, on an average basis during the period 2017–2021. The total revenues and net income increased by 14% and 66% on an average basis. The total expenses increased by 41%. The market capitalization and enterprise value increased by 30% and 29%, respectively.

Table 5 gives the profitability and leverage position of the firm during the period 2017–2021.

The profitability ratios were highly fluctuating during the period 2017–2021. The average net margin, ROE, and ROA during 2017–2021 were 13.22%, 7.53%, and 4.03%, respectively. The average debt equity ratio was 0.34.

Table 4 Financial highlights

	(In millions of dollars)				
Financial highlights	2017	2018	2019	2020	2021
Total assets	20,646	20,715	39,974	41,369	40,564
Short-term investments	3321	3445	2480	5830	5074
Total equity	11,519	11,512	22,417	23,879	21,861
Total revenue	7379	7253	9740	11,497	12,222
Total operating expenses	751	757	1008	1122	2476
Net income	−114	341	2805	2829	1166
Market cap	20001.35	18468.45	35107.6	47,912	49119.84
Enterprise value	21729.35	20294.45	40533.6	49,655	50186.84

Table 5 Performance indicators

Ratios	2017	2018	2019	2020	2021
Net margin%	−1.54	4.7	28.8	24.61	9.54
ROE%	−1.07	3.24	17.57	12.74	5.18
ROA%	−0.55	1.65	9.24	6.96	2.85
DER	0.39	0.41	0.32	0.29	0.29

References

1. https://www.newmont.com/investors/reports-and-filings/default.aspx
2. Newmont Annual Report 2021

Case 39 HarborOne Bancorp

HarborOne Bancorp is a bank holding company and the parent of HarborOne Bank, the state-chartered savings bank. HarborOne Bank is headquartered in Massachusetts. The bank has 31 branches in eastern Massachusetts and Rhode Island with commercial lending offices in Boston and Providence. The bank was established in the year 1917 as a state-chartered credit union which was converted to a state-chartered cooperative bank during 2013. HarborOne became a state-chartered savings bank on March 17, 2020. The bank provides a variety of financial services to individuals and businesses online through its 30 full service branches located in Massachusetts and Rhode Island. The bank also provides a range of educational services through "HarborOneU" with classes on small business and financial literacy. HarborOne Mortgage LLC, the wholly owned subsidiary of the bank, is a residential mortgage company headquartered in New Hampshire with offices in Massachusetts, Rhode Island, and New Hampshire. By December 31, 2021, the company had 635 full-time equivalent employees. In 2021, the bank made a record in terms of $3.6 billion in new loans and approximately $900 million in commercial originations.

Table 1 shows the performance highlights of the company during the period 2018–2021.

Competition

HarborOne faces significant competition for deposits and loans. The major competitors in the deposit market are banking institutions which operate in the primary market area and from financial services firms such as securities brokerage firms, credit unions, insurance companies, financial technology companies, etc. The competition for loans comes from financial institutions such as credit unions and other financial service providers such as mortgage companies and mortgage brokers. The company also faces competition from money market and mutual funds.

© The Author(s), under exclusive license to Springer Nature Switzerland AG 2024

B. R. Kumar, *Rising Stars*, Management for Professionals,
https://doi.org/10.1007/978-3-031-50032-9_39

Table 1 Performance highlights

	2018	2019	2020	2021
Total deposits	2,685,061	2,942,873	3,506,209	3,682,649
Commercial construction, commercial real estate loans	1,368,858	1,628,601	2,114,989	2,258,048
Net interest and dividend income	88,930	109,062	120,066	131,370

Source: Annual Report 2021

Lending Activities

The commercial real estate loans are focused on small and mid-size owner occupants seeking loans between $350,000 and $30 million. In December 31, 2021, the commercial real estate loans accounted for 47.1% of the total loans. The total commercial real estate loans in 2021 amounted to $1.7 billion of which fixed-rate loans were of $898 million and adjustable rate loans amounted to $801.9 million. The commercial real estate loans have terms of 5 to 10 years. Some loans may extend to 20 years. The bank also originates commercial and industrial loans and lines of credit for professionals, sole proprietorships, and small to medium-sized privately held businesses. The small business lending team generates small business loans which consist of loans originated through the US Small Business Administration. As of December 31, 2021, the commercial and industrial loans accounted for 11.7% of the total loans. HarborOne Bank originates commercial construction loans for commercial development projects which include industrial building, retail and office building, and speculative residential real estate. By the end of 2021, the commercial construction loan portfolio consisted of $52.5 million in loan balances and accounted for 3.8% of the total loans. HarborOne provides one-to-four-family residential real estate loans through HarborOne Mortgage for home purchase or refinancing of existing homes. By December 31, 2021, residential mortgage loans accounted for 29% of the total loans. The residential mortgage loans were of value $1.05 billion during this period. One-to-four-family residential mortgage originations are generally underwritten to conform to federal mortgage associations' (Fannie Mae and Freddie Mac) underwriting guidelines. HarborOne originates one-to-four-family residential mortgage loans with loan-to-value ratio up to 80%. The private mortgage insurance for residential loans is secured by a first mortgage with a loan-to-value ratio over 80%. The majority of the conforming fixed-rate-one-to-four-family residential mortgage loans originated by HarborOne are sold on the secondary market to Freddie Mac, Fannie Mae, and private investors. The bank also offers second mortgages and equity lines of credit which are secured by owner occupied residences. By the end of 2021, second mortgages and equity lines of credit accounted for 3.8% of the total loan. HarborOne offers professional developers, contractors, and builders residential real estate construction loans through HarborOne Mortgage. Till 2019, HarborOne provided auto lease loans for the leasing of new or used automobiles through Credit Union Leasing of America.

The securities portfolio of the bank consists of US government and government-sponsored mortgage-backed and collateralized mortgage obligations or "CMOs." GSE securities and mortgage-backed securities accounted for 10.5% and 88.5% of the bank's securities portfolio. The residential mortgage-backed securities issued by US government agencies and GSEs are more liquid than individual mortgage loans due to the presence of an active trading market for such securities.

Sources of Funds

The major sources of funds for the bank are deposits, borrowings, and loan repayments. The factors which influence deposit inflows and outflows and loan repayments are general interest rates and money market conditions. By December 2021, the total deposits amounted to $3.68 billion. Different types of deposit instruments such as non-interest-bearing demand deposits, interest bearing demand accounts, savings account, and term certificates of deposit are offered by the bank. The business banking deposit products include commercial checking account, sweep accounts, money market accounts, etc. The bank's municipal department provides core depository services to local municipalities. The bank also participates in a reciprocal deposit program which provides access to deposit products insured by the Federal Deposit Insurance Corporation.

The total borrowings amounted to $89.9 million in the year 2021. The borrowings consist of short-term and long-term obligations from FHLB and subordinated mortgages. In 2018, the bank issued $35 million in fixed to floating rate subordinated notes. HarborOne being a bank holding company is subject to regulation, examination, and supervision by the Board of Governors of the Federal Reserve System.

Risk Factors

The bank has loan underwriting risks with respect to different types of loans. Normally loans secured by commercial real estate have larger balances and have a greater degree of risk than residential mortgage loans. Repayment of real estate loans may be subject to adverse conditions in the real estate market or economy. Commercial loans also have a greater degree of risk than residential mortgage loans. Construction financing also involves a higher degree of risk of loss than long-term financing such as real estate loans. Consumer loans also entail greater risk than do residential mortgage loans. The profitability of the bank could be affected as additional provisions or charge-offs are required due to changes to the estimates of collectability of commercial real estate and commercial loan portfolio on account of its unseasoned nature. The commercial and residential construction loans are subject to different lending risks which depend on the nature of borrower's businesses and cash flows. The environmental liability associated with commercial lending may result in losses for the bank. The bank's business may be adversely affected by credit risks associated with residential property. Residential mortgage lending is sensitive to regional and economic conditions, and these factors impact the creditworthiness of borrowers to meet their loan payment obligations. Changes in the secondary mortgage market or increases in interest rates may lead to reduction in the bank's mortgage banking revenues which would adversely impact its non-interest income. The bank's portfolio of indirect auto lending and auto lease lending exposes the bank to increased credit risks. Hedging activities against interest rate exposure like purchase and sale of futures contracts and purchase of put and call options may adversely affect the earning of the bank. The financial services industry is witnessing frequent introduction of new technology-driven products and services. The business of the bank would be adversely affected if the bank is unable to introduce products and services based on evolving industry standards and consumer preferences. The banking business is highly regulated, which limits or restricts the activities for the conduct of business.

Sustainability Initiatives

In 2021, the bank donated $1.7 million in community support to 175 organizations across Massachusetts and Rhode Island. In the same year, HarborOne Foundation made 42 grants of $387,000 to nonprofit organizations to address education, housing, and basic human needs. The bank had also provided over $997,684 in financial and in-kind support to local nonprofit and civic organizations. The ONECommunity Scholarship program awarded $100,000 in college scholarships to outstanding high school senior students. The Caring Crew Member initiative program offered more than 3630 h of volunteer service. HarborOne U focuses on providing virtual and online delivery of education content. Over a decade, HarborOne U has provided financial education, small business, and life skills training to over 20,000 individuals for economic mobility. HarborOne has made $20 million commitment to promote home ownership to low- and moderate-income borrowers. The bank has made over $66.7 million in community development loans to fund affordable housing and solar power generation and support the credit needs of nonprofit organization and healthcare providers.

Stock Performance

The following section analyzes the stock wealth generated by the bank as compared against the wealth generated by the market index Russell 2000 Index and the S&P 600 Thrift and Mortgage Finance Index from December 31, 2016, to December 31, 2021. The analysis assumes an initial investment of $100 in the stock and market indexes and reinvestment of dividends during the above period.

Table 2 shows the cumulative return for the HarborOne stock and market indexes.

The holding period return for HarborOne during the above period was 41%, while for Russell 2000 index and S&P 600 Thrifts & Mortgage Finance Index, the holding period return was 76% and 75%, respectively. The average yearly returns for

Table 2 Wealth generation

Year	2016	2017	2018	2019	2020	2021
HarborOne Bancorp, Inc.	100	99.07	82.16	102.02	101.82	140.62
Russell 2000 Index	$100	114.65	102.02	128.06	153.62	176.39
S&P 600 Thrifts & Mortgage Finance Index	$100	121.8	106.22	143.5	136.75	175.02

Source: Annual Report 2021

Table 3 Holding period return

Year	HarborOne	Russell 2000 Index	Excess returns
2018	−17%	−11%	−7%
2019	30%	11%	19%
2020	0%	22%	−23%
2021	37%	8%	28%
2022	−2%	−13%	11%

Table 4 Book and market value

Year	2017	2018	2019	2020	2021
Book value of equity	343.48	357.57	665.79	696.31	679.26
Market value of equity	625.42	517.41	642.01	621.25	777.48
BV as percent of MV	54.9%	69.1%	103.7%	112.1%	87.4%

HarborOne, Russell 2000 Index, and S&P 600 Index during the period 2016–2021 was 8.85%, 12.29%, and 13.48%, respectively.

The following section analyzes the returns for HarborOne and market index Russell 2000 during the period 2018–2022. The HarborOne stock which was trading at $10.72 on January 2, 2018, increased by 1.29 times to trade at $13.91 by December 1, 2022. The total cumulative monthly return for HarborOne share and market index Russell 2000 was 40% and 36% during the period 2018–2022. The average yearly return for HarborOne and Russell 2000 index was 8% and 7% during the above period. The data was taken from Yahoo Finance.

Table 3 provides the holding period return for HarborOne and market index Russell 2000 during the period 2018–2022.

HarborOne had superior market performance compared to market index Russell 2000 in the years 2019 and 2021.

Table 4 gives the book value and market value of HarborOne during the period 2018–2022. The values are given in millions of dollars.

The average book value as percent of market value was 85.4% during the period 2017–2021.

The next section analyzes the financial condition and operating performance of HarborOne during the period 2017–2021. Table 5 shows the financial condition of the HarborOne bank during the period 2017–2021.

The total assets, cash and cash equivalents, and deposits increased by 15%, 31%, and 17%, respectively, during the period 2017–2021. The non-interest income

Table 5 Financial condition and operational highlights

	(In millions of dollars)				
Highlights	2017	2018	2019	2020	2021
Total assets	2684.92	3653.12	4058.92	4483.62	4553.41
Cash and cash equivalents	80.79	105.52	211.62	205.87	194.72
Deposits	2013.74	2685.06	2942.87	3506.21	3682.65
Total equity	343.48	357.57	665.79	696.31	679.26
Net interest income	74.35	88.93	109.06	120.07	131.37
Interest expense	15.94	26.78	45.72	28.49	12.53
Total non-interest expense	101.18	108.3	134.83	154.24	150.25
Market cap	625.42	517.41	642.01	621.25	777.48

Source Annual Report 2021

Table 6 Performance measures

Ratios	2017	2018	2019	2020	2021
Performance ratios					
Return on average assets %	0.4	0.39	0.49	1.05	1.29
Return on average equity%	3.09	3.27	3.82	6.55	8.45
Net interest margin%	3.04	3.22	3.14	3.06	3.12
Efficiency ratio%	84.75	86.35	82.4	63.48	67.94
Asset quality ratio					
Non-performing assets to total assets%	0.69	0.51	0.76	0.77	0.79
Capital ratios					
Common equity tier 1 to risk-weighted assets%	15.1	9.9	18.7	17.7	16.4
Total capital to risk-weighted assets	16	11.8	20.6	19.9	18.5

Source Annual Report 2021

increased by 15% on an average basis during the above period. The interest expense and total non-interest expense increased by 11% on an average basis during the period 2017–2021. The market capitalization had increased by 7% on an average basis during the above period.

Table 6 shows the performance ratios along with asset quality and capital ratios for HarborOne during the period 2017–2021.

The average of return on average assets and average equity were 0.72% and 5.04% during the period 2017–2021. The average net interest margin and efficiency ratio were 3.12% and 76.98%, respectively. The average non-performing assets to total assets were 0.704% during the above period. The average capital ratios for HarbonOne Bancorp were 15.56% and 17.36%, respectively.

References

1. https://www.harborone.com/home
2. https://www.harboronebancorp.com/corporate-profile/default.aspx

Case 40 Netflix

Netflix Inc., the American subscription video on-demand over-the-top streaming service and production company, is based in Los Gatos, California. The company was founded by Reed Hastings and Marc Randolph. Netflix offers a film and television series library through distribution deals as well as through its own production known as Netflix Originals.

Netflix Inc. is one of the world's major entertainment service companies with approximately 222 million paid subscribers in over 190 countries. Netflix provides programs such as TV series, documentaries, feature films, and mobile games in different genres and languages. The members are provided with the ecosystem of internet-connected screens to engage as much they want, anytime and anywhere. Netflix launched its streaming service in the year 2007 and has become a pioneer in the delivery of streaming entertainment. In 2012, Netflix expanded to Europe with its launch in the UK and Ireland. During March 2012, Netflix acquired the domain name DVD.com. In 2013, Netflix signed an agreement with Turner Broadcasting System and Warner Bros. Television to distribute Cartoon Network, Warner Bros. Animation, and Adult Swim content along with TNT's Dallas. In 2015, Netflix expanded to Australia, New Zealand, Japan, Italy, Portugal, and Spain. In 2016, Netflix announced plans to expand to additional 130 countries. In 2016, Netflix released about 126 original series or films. In 2017, Netflix signed a music publishing deal with BMG Rights Management wherein BMG will oversee rights for music associated with Netflix original content outside of the USA. In the same year, Netflix signed a licensing deal with IQivi, a Chinese video streaming platform of Baidu, to allow selected Netflix original content to be distributed in China. In 2017, Netflix made its first acquisition by acquiring Millarworld, a publishing company owned by comic book writer Mark Millar. In 2018, Netflix entered into a partnership with Telltale Games to port its adventure games to the service in a streaming video format. In 2019, Netflix entered into a multiyear agreement with Nickelodeon for production of several original animated feature films and television series based on Nickelodeon's library. In 2021, Night School Studio, an independent video game developer, was acquired by Netflix. In the same year, Netflix officially launched

© The Author(s), under exclusive license to Springer Nature Switzerland AG 2024

B. R. Kumar, *Rising Stars*, Management for Professionals,
https://doi.org/10.1007/978-3-031-50032-9_40

Table 1 Performance highlights

Year	2019	2020	2021
Streaming revenues	19,859,230	24,756,675	29,515,496
DVD revenues	297,217	239,381	182,348
Total revenues	20,156,447	24,996,056	29,697,844
Global streaming memberships			
Paid net membership additions	7831	36,573	18,181
Paid memberships at end of period	167,090	203,663	221,844
Average paying memberships	152,984	189,083	210,784
Average monthly revenue per paying membership	10.82	10.91	11.67
Operating income	2,604,254	4,585,289	6,194,509
Operating margin	13%	18%	21%

mobile games for Android users throughout the world. In 2021, Netflix announced plans to acquire Scanline VFX, a visual effects and animation company.

The company has focused on adding programming mix of new content over the years for the delivery of streaming entertainment. The company continuously enhances its user interface and extends its streaming service to more internet-connected screens.

In 2021, Netflix achieved several milestones. Netflix had the biggest TV show of the year "Squid Game" and two biggest film releases of all time (Red Notice and Don't Look Up). Netflix also had the most Emmy-winning and the most Oscar-winning and nominated movies studio in the year 2021.

The revenues for the company are derived primarily from monthly membership fees for offering services related to streaming content to members. In 2021, the annual revenue for the company was approximately $30 billion which represented 19% year-over-year growth.

Video entertainment industry is highly competitive. The company faces intense competition from several providers such as multichannel video programming distributors (MVPDs), streaming entertainment providers, and video gaming providers. Netflix also competes with streaming entertainment providers and content producers for licensed content and original content projects. Seasonal pattern is observed in membership growth. For the company, the fourth quarter represents the greatest streaming membership growth. As of December 31, 2021, the company had approximately 11,300 employees located globally in 60 countries. The company maintains a website known as www.netflix.com.

Table 1 lists the performance highlights of Netflix during the period 2019–2021. The values are given in thousands except revenue per membership and percentages. The source of data is annual reports.

Risk Factors

The success of Netflix's businesses depends on the ability to attract and retain subscription members. The market for entertainment video is intensely competitive, and changes in the competitive offerings for entertainment video could adversely impact Netflix's businesses. Consumers have increased options to access entertainment videos through new and existing distribution channels. These channels have the option to use various economic models such as subscription, transactional, ad-supported, and piracy-based models. The traditional providers of entertainment video such as broadcasters, cable network operators, internet-based e-commerce, or entertainment video providers are adding different streaming video offerings to their portfolio. The COVID-19 pandemic has caused disruption to the company's business, increased cost, and led to delay in content releases. The company may face potential liability for negligence, copyright, and trademark infringement when the company acquires, produces, licenses, and/or distributes as producer and distributor of content. The company may face potential liability for content used in promoting its service which includes marketing materials. The businesses of Netflix could be adversely impacted by costs and challenges related to its strategic acquisitions and investments. Netflix has agreements with various cable, satellite, and telecommunications operators to make its services available through the TV set-top boxes of the service providers. The business would be adversely impacted if Netflix could not maintain or create new relationships with these partners. The company faces payment processing risk as members pay for the service through different payment methods such as credit and debit cards, gift cards, prepaid cards, direct debit, online wallets, and direct carrier and partner billing. The company depends on internal systems and third parties to process payment. The rise in the number of litigation or claims could negatively affect the business and financial operations of Netflix. The company faces risks related to intellectual property if studios, content providers, or other rights holders refuse to license streaming content or other rights upon terms acceptable to Netflix. The company also faces risk related to information technology. For example, Netflix depends on Amazon Web Services to operate certain aspects of its services and any disruption would impact the operations of Netflix. The long-term and predominantly fixed cost nature of content commitments may adversely affect the liquidity and results of operations of the firm. The company is subject to economic, political, regulatory, and other risks arising from its international operations. The company is subject to taxation-related risks in multiple jurisdictions.

ESG Initiatives

Netflix has reduced or avoided more than 14,000 MT of greenhouse gas emissions. Through this, Scope 1 and 2 carbon footprint has been reduced by 10% and the company is on track to meet its goal of cutting 45% of the Scope 1 and 2 emissions by the year 2030. Netflix has set and implemented its science-based target (SBT) of

46.2% absolute emissions reduction below 2019 levels across Scopes 1 and 2 by 2030. The company had purchased 40,000 gallons of sustainable aviation fuel for its corporate aviation fleet and 75,000 gallons of renewable diesel for use on productions. In the year 2021, the company matched its global operations with 100% renewable electricity in all its offices and self-managed productions. On the basis of five screening criteria, 17 projects were selected for implementation for the company's 2021 carbon credit portfolio. These projects basically focus on climate initiatives, habitat restoration, biodiversity protection, and sustainable livelihoods. In 2021, the company conducted climate risk assessment as part of Netflix's risk assessment process and was led by internal audit and sustainability teams. Netflix co-launched Business Alliance for Scaling Climate Solutions with Disney, Google, Microsoft, Amazon, Workday, Salesforce, the WWF, and the United Nations to share best practices and insights to improve climate solutions. In 2020, Netflix created Netflix Fund for Creative Equity valued at $100 million to help create new opportunities for underrepresented communities within the entertainment industry. Women constitute about 51.7% of the global workforce. The senior leadership team consists of 45% women. The Global anti-corruption policy requires employees and contractors to abide by global anti-corruption and anti-bribery laws. Netflix has employed a VP of Leadership Programs whose mission is to design programs such as seminars and lectures to foster leadership culture at Netflix, Inc.

Stock Performance

The next section analyzes the stock returns for Netflix and market index Nasdaq Composite during the most recent period of 5 years. Netflix stock was trading at $291.38 on January 2, 2018. The stock price increased by 1.25 times to trade at $ 364.86 on January 1, 2023. The total monthly cumulative return for Netflix stock and market index Nasdaq Composite was 73% and 58% during the period 2018–2022. The average yearly return for Netflix and market index Nasdaq Composite was 15% and 12%, respectively, during the period 2018–2022. The source of data is Yahoo Finance.

Table 2 shows the holding period return for Netflix and the market index Nasdaq Composite during the period 2018–2022. The holding period is assumed to be 1-year period.

The market index had better performance than Netflix stock in all years except in the year 2020.

Table 2 Holding period return

Year	Netflix	Nasdaq Composite	Excess returns
2018	−8%	−9%	1%
2019	−5%	23%	−28%
2020	57%	41%	16%
2021	13%	20%	−7%
2022	−31%	−26%	−4%

Table 3 Book value and market value of equity

Year	2018	2019	2020	2021	2022
Book value of equity	5238.77	7582.16	11065.24	15849.25	20777.4
Market value of equity	116860.09	141984.78	239486.61	267461.07	131227.5
BV as percent of MV	4.5%	5.3%	4.6%	5.9%	15.8%

Table 4 Financial highlights

	(In millions of dollars)				
Financial highlights	2018	2019	2020	2021	2022
Total assets	25974.4	33975.71	39280.36	44584.66	48594.77
Short-term investments	3794.48	5018.44	8205.55	6027.8	6058.45
Total equity	5238.77	7582.16	11065.24	15849.25	20777.4
Total revenue	15794.34	20156.45	24996.06	29697.84	31615.55
Total operating expenses	4221.58	5111.98	5134.45	6170.65	6814.43
Net income	1211.24	1866.92	2761.4	5116.23	4491.92
Market cap	116860.09	141984.78	239486.61	267461.07	131227.5
Enterprise value	123425.66	151725.6	247590.04	276826.16	139522.12

Table 5 Performance indicators

Ratios	2018	2019	2020	2021	2022
Net margin%	7.67	9.26	11.05	17.23	14.21
ROE%	27.46	29.12	29.62	38.02	24.53
ROA%	5.38	6.23	7.54	12.2	9.64
DER	1.98	1.95	1.47	0.97	0.69

Table 3 shows the market value and book value trends of the company during the period 2018–2022. The values are given in millions of dollars.

The average book value as percent of market value was 7.2% during the period 2018–2022. In 2018, the market value was 22.31 times of the book value of equity. By the year 2022, the market value was only six times that of book value of Netflix.

Table 4 shows the financial highlights of Netflix during the period 2018–2022. The values are given in millions of dollars. The source of data is annual reports and gurufocus.com.

The total assets, cash investments, and equity of Netflix increased by 17%, 17%, and 41%, respectively, during the period 2018–2022. The average revenue and net income increase during the above period was 19% and 44%, respectively. The average increase in total expenses was 13%. The market capitalization and enterprise value of Netflix increased by 13% and 12% on an average basis during the period 2018–2022.

Table 5 highlights the profitability and leverage position of Netflix during the period 2018–2022.

Table 6 Estimation of economic value

Year	2020	2021
Profit before income tax	5840.1	5263.93
Income tax	723.59	772.22
Net operating profit after tax (NOPAT)	5116.51	4491.71
Stockholder equity	15849.25	20777.40
Long-term debt	14693.07	14353.08
Total capital employed	30542.32	35130.48
WACC	6.51%	5.16%
Capital charge	1988.31	1812.73
Economic value	3128.21	2678.98

The average net margin, ROE, and ROA during the period 2018–2022 were 11.88%, 29.75%, and 8.20%, respectively. The average debt equity ratio for Netflix during the period 2018–2022 was 1.41.

Table 6 illustrates the estimation of economic value for Netflix in millions of dollars for the years 2021 and 2022.

References

1. "Netflix buys Scots comic book firm Millarworld". BBC News. *August 7, 2017*
2. https://ir.neflix,Netflix - Overview - Profile
3. Netflix Sustainability Accounting Standards Board (SASB) Report, ESG Report 2021
4. Annual Report 2021

Case 41 CapStar Financial Holdings

CapStar Financial Holdings Inc., a Tennessee corporation, is a bank holding company headquartered in Nashville, Tennessee, USA. The company operates primarily through its wholly owned subsidiary, CapStar Bank. CapStar Bank was incorporated in the State of Tennessee in the year 2007 and acquired a state charter in the year 2008. The products and services offered by the bank include commercial and industrial loans to small and medium-sized companies, mortgage banking products and services, private banking and wealth management services, correspondent banking services, retail and consumer products, etc. By December 2021, the bank had total assets of $3.1 billion and total deposits and total net loans of $2.7 billion and $1.9 billion, respectively. As of December 31, 2021, the company had employed 397 employees.

Product and Services

CapStar offers a broad range of commercial lending products to small and medium-sized businesses and high net worth individuals. The commercial and industrial lending products consist of commercial loans, business term loans, equipment financing, and lines of credit targeted for both small and medium-sized business firms. Commercial real estate loans offered by CapStar are collateralized by owner- and non-owner-occupied properties as well as interim construction loans. First mortgage loans are the major consumer lending products which are typically thereafter sold on the secondary market. CapStar offers second mortgage home equity mortgage loans and consumer-related loans such as loans for automobiles. Lines of credits are offered to consumer clients to facilitate investment opportunities. Lending products and services are marketed to existing clients through the bank's client service and new lending clients are approached through specialized banking teams with industry-specific knowledge and local market expertise. The company adheres to thorough underwriting standards to deliver customized and creative loan

© The Author(s), under exclusive license to Springer Nature Switzerland AG 2024

B. R. Kumar, *Rising Stars*, Management for Professionals,
https://doi.org/10.1007/978-3-031-50032-9_41

solutions. The bank's underwriting processes involve collaborative engagement with bankers and credit underwriters for the analysis of each loan request.

CapStar offers a full range of deposit products and services which include demand deposits, interest bearing transaction accounts, money market accounts, saving deposits, certificates of deposit, and CDARS® reciprocal products. The largest sources of deposits are NOW, demand deposit accounts, money market, and savings accounts. CapStar offers correspondent banking services to community banks by offering settlement, Fed Funds lines of credit, depository products, wire transfer services loans for bank holding company, and loan syndication for large commercial and commercial real estate exposures. By December 31, 2021, correspondent banking constituted 15% of the bank's total deposits.

In 2013, CapStar initiated correspondent banking as a valuable funding source for bank as there was a potential need for correspondent banking market in Tennessee due to reasons such as the instability of larger correspondent banks, diversification of funding base, the demand for doing business with a Tennessee-based correspondent bank, and the ability to license a low-cost proprietary settlement platform. In 2021, mortgage banking generated $0.9 billion in mortgage loan originations. Mortgage loans are typically sold in the secondary market and are underwritten by the bank. CapStar offers a range of products and services which include 24-h telephone and online banking, direct deposit, mobile banking, safe deposit boxes, remote deposit, and cash management services for individuals and small and medium-scaled businesses.

Strategic Perspective of Growth

The four strategic pillars of growth are based on enhancement of profitability and earning consistency, organic growth, sound risk management, and disciplined capital allocation. The company focuses on the significance of maintaining the drivers of performance in terms of four key ratios representing the" algebra of banking." In this context, the benchmark standards are maintaining 5% revenue growth, net margin of greater than or equal to 3.60, efficiency ratio of 55%, and net charge-off less than 0.25%. The bank is situated in an advantageous position in attractive market. The bank is located in the three fastest growing and most dynamic markets in the Tennessee state. CapStar is the fourth largest bank in the State of Tennessee. In 2021, the loans and deposits for the bank amounted to $2 billion and $2.7 billion, respectively. The bank had increased the institutional ownership to 42.6%. As a part of its strategy, the bank maintains a broadly diversified loan portfolio with respect to type of loan product, client, and industry sectors.

The company has focused on acquisitions as a part of its strategy for growth. In 2018, CapStar acquired Athens Bancshares Corporation, the holding company for Athens Federal Community Bank, which is headquartered in Athens, Tennessee. During the period of acquisition, Athens Federal had eight banking locations in Tennessee. In 2020, CapStar acquired FCB Corporation, the bank holding company for the First National Bank of Manchester. In the same year, CapStar acquired the

Bank of Waynesboro through stock acquisition by offering 0.7 million shares of common stock of CapStar to the shareholders of target bank, Bank of Waynesboro. Bank of Waynesboro had six banking locations throughout Southern Tennessee. CapStar also focuses on organic expansion after identification and buildup of a strong banking team with attractive economic characteristics and market demographics. The bank is a relationship-oriented bank rather than transaction based as approximately 73% of loans in its loan portfolio were offered to borrowers located in its target market as of December 31, 2021. Credit risk management strategy of the bank involves disciplined underwriting process which is subject to prudent standards, risk monitoring, and review processes for all loan exposures. In order to promote core deposit growth, deposit rates are reviewed periodically by pricing committee.

Competitive Environment

The financial services industry is highly competitive in the target market segment of Tennessee. By June 30, 2021, this target market segment comprised 84 financial institutions with over $114 billion in deposits. CapStar accounted for 2.5% of the deposit market share. CapStar competes directly with other banks and non-bank institutions, Internet-based banks, bank holding companies, money market and mutual funds, brokerage houses, mortgage companies, and insurance firms for financial services products. Competition involves aspects such as retention of current clients, obtaining new loans and deposits, offering competitive interest rates on deposits and loans, and enhancing the type of services offered. Many of the competitors have competitive advantages compared to CapStar in terms of greater financial resources, wide geographic coverage, additional service offerings, favorable pricing alternatives, and lower origination and operating costs.

Risk Factors

Global pandemic had adversely affected the business and financial condition of CapStar. CapStar faces credit and interest rate risk. As CapStar targets small and medium-sized businesses as loan clients, there is potential for increased risk of credit defaults. The repayment of leveraged loans depends on cash flows of the borrower which is unpredictable and the secured collaterals may fluctuate in value. The allowances provided for loan losses might be insufficient to absorb losses inherent in CapStar's loan portfolio. The liquidity might be affected due to unique risks on account of correspondent banking activities. Profits may be affected due to interest rate risks. Changes in monetary policy, adverse economic conditions, and government responses to address these concerns may have an adverse effect on the business operations of the bank. Strategic risks also may lead to an adverse impact on the performance of the company. Strategic risks can manifest with respect to regulatory and internal lending limits, strategic acquisitions, and additional capital requirement.

The bank is also subject to operational, regulatory, and compliance risks. CapStar is subject to extensive state and federal regulation which could limit or restrict business activities and impose financial requirements such as minimum capital requirements and could affect the profitability of the bank.

ESG Initiatives

The company offers a competitive compensation package which includes low-cost medical, dental, and vision benefits, paid life, disability, and long-term care insurance along with 401(k) employer contribution. CapStar introduced the Diversity Scholarship in the year 2020 to support individuals who are underrepresented in the financial services industry. In 2020–2021, the bank donated more than $750,000 to nonprofit organizations, charitable causes, and community development initiatives. As a result of Cap Star's 2018 acquisition of Athens Bancshares Corporation, CapStar donated $1.5 million to Athens Federal Foundation and local East Tennessee community. The bank sponsors an exclusive digital interactive Financial Literacy Program in four high schools. Chief Risk Officer is responsible for identifying, analyzing, and mitigating internal and external risk at CapStar. The Information Technology Steering Committee oversees IT strategic and investment priorities and the company's information security program. The company has more than 20% female representation in the board.

Stock Performance

An investment of $1000 made in CapStar Financial Holdings during September 1, 2016, would have become $1066.40 registering a return of 6.6% by January 27, 2022.

Table 1 compares the total shareholders return for CapStar's common stock for the 5-year period beginning at the close of trade on December 31, 2016, until December 31, 2021, with the cumulative total return of the Nasdaq Composite Index and the Nasdaq Bank Index during the same period. The analysis assumes $100 invested on December 31, 2016.

The holding period return for CapStar, Nasdaq Composite, and Nasdaq Bank were 0%, 205%, and 45%, respectively, during the comparative period 2016 and

Table 1 Stock performance

Year	2016	2017	2018	2019	2020	2021
CapStar Financial Holdings	100	95	67	77	69	100
Nasdaq Composite	$100	130	126	172	250	305
Nasdaq Bank (BKX)	$100	106	88	110	101	145

Source Annual Report 2021

Table 2 Holding period returns

Year	CapStar	Nasdaq Composite	Excess returns
2018	−23%	−9%	−14%
2019	4%	23%	−19%
2020	−1%	41%	−42%
2021	45%	20%	25%
2022	−18%	−26%	9%

Table 3 Book and market value of equity

Year	2018	2019	2020	2021	2022
Book value of equity	254.38	273.05	343.49	380.09	354.18
Market value of equity	261.08	305.77	324.33	466.15	467.87
BV as percent of MV	97.4%	89.3%	105.9%	81.5%	75.7%

2021. The average yearly return for CapStar, Nasdaq Composite, and Nasdaq Bank were 3%, 26%, and 9.88%, respectively.

The following section analyzes the stock returns for CapStar and the market index Nasdaq Composite for the recent 5-year period 2018–2022. CapStar stock which was trading at $19.02 on January 2, 2018, declined to trade at $16.95 by January 1, 2023. The cumulative monthly return for CapStar stock during the period 2018–2022 was 13%, while the average yearly return for CapStar was 3%. The cumulative monthly return for Nasdaq Composite index during the period was 59%, while the average yearly return was 12% during the 5-year period 2018–2022.

Table 2 shows the holding period return for the stock and market index Nasdaq Composite for the period 2018–2022. The holding period is assumed to be 1 year.

CapStar stock had superior market performance compared to index in the year 2021.

Table 3 gives the book value and market value of equity CapStar during the 5-year period 2018–2022 in millions of dollars.

The average book value of equity as percent of market value of equity during the period 2018–2022 was 90%. In 2018, the market value was 1.03 times of book value of equity. In 2022, the market value was 1.32 times of the book value of equity.

Table 4 gives the details of the operating and financial highlights of the CapStar during the recent 5-year period of 2018–2022. The values are given in millions of dollars. The data was sourced from annual reports and gurufocus.com.

During the 5-year period 2018–2022, the average growth rate of total assets, cash investments, and deposits were 14%, 39%, and 16%, respectively. The total equity increased by 17% on an average basis during the recent 5 years. The net interest income grew by 25% during the last 5-year period on an average basis. The interest expense and total non-interest expense increased by 13% and 17% during the above period. The market capitalization of the bank increased by 17% on an average basis.

Table 5 shows the performance measures in terms of profitability, asset quality, and capital ratios of CapStar during the recent 5-year period 2017–2021.

Table 4 Financial highlights

	(In millions of dollars)				
Financial highlights	2018	2019	2020	2021	2022
Total assets	1963.88	2037.2	2987.01	3133.05	3117.17
Cash and cash equivalents	94.68	101.09	277.44	395.23	135.31
Deposits	1570.01	1729.45	2568	2684.28	2756
Total equity	254.38	273.05	343.49	380.09	354.18
Net interest income	51.69	67.75	76.32	91.17	96.09
Interest expense	16.09	23.8	15.53	7.29	17.44
Total non-interest expense	43.68	59.34	71.97	73.22	69.37
Market capitalization	261.08	305.77	324.33	466.15	467.87

Table 5 Performance measures

Ratios	2017	2018	2019	2020	2021
Performance ratios					
Return on average assets %	0.11	0.63	1.12	0.94	1.56
Return on average equity%	1.05	5.50	8.49	8.08	13.38
Net interest margin%	3.25	3.55	3.64	3.10	3.16
Efficiency ratio%	63.98	79.65	67.37	64.70	54.94
Asset quality ratio					
Non-performing assets to total assets%	0.2	0.16	0.12	0.18	0.11
Capital ratios					
Common equity tier 1 to risk-weighted assets%	10.7	11.61	12.73	13.52	14.11
Total capital to risk-weighted assets%	12.52	12.84	13.45	16.03	16.29

Table 6 Economic value

Year	2021	2022
Profit before income tax	61.38	48.77
Income tax	12.70	9.75
Net operating profit after tax (NOPAT)	48.68	39.02
Stockholder equity	380.09	354.18
Long-term debt	29.53	29.57
Total capital employed	409.62	383.75
WACC	10.78%	9.09%
Capital charge	44.16	34.88
Economic value	4.52	4.13

The average return on assets and equity during the period 2017–2021 was 0.87% and 7.30%. The average net interest margin and efficiency ratio were 3.34% and 66.13%, respectively. The average non-performing assets to total assets ratio was 0.154%. The average capital ratios were 12.53% and 14.22%, respectively.

Table 6 illustrates the estimation of economic value for CapStar Financial Holdings for the years 2021 and 2022. The values are given in millions of dollars.

References

1. https://ir.capstarbank.com
2. https://ir.capstarbank.com/stock-information/investment-calculator
3. Annual Report 2021

Case 42 Teradyne, Inc.

Teradyne, Inc., is a major global supplier of automation equipment for test and industrial applications. The company was established in the year 1960. Teradyne is involved in the designing, developing, manufacture, and sale of automatic test systems which are used to test semiconductors, data storage, and complex electronic systems. The products of Teradyne are used in different industrial sectors such as consumer electronics, wireless, automotive, industrial, computing, communications, aerospace, and defense industries. The industrial automation products offered by the company include collaborative robotic arms, autonomous mobile robots, and advanced robotic control software. These automation products are used by global manufacturing, logistics, and light industry sector firms to enhance manufacturing and material handling efficiency and to lower manufacturing and logistics costs. The automatic test equipment and industrial automation products and services offered by Teradyne consist of semiconductor test systems, storage, system level test systems, defense/aerospace test instrumentation and systems, circuit board test and inspection systems, wireless test systems, and industrial automation products. The industrial automation segment of Teradyne consists of Universal Robots which is a leading supplier of collaborative robotic arms. Mobile Industrial Robots is a leading manufacturer of autonomous mobile robots (AMRs) for industrial automation. AutoGuide LLC is a manufacturer of high payload AMRs.

The corporate strategy of the company focuses on expanding the market share in the test businesses through the introduction of differentiated products in the industrial automation business segment. The demand for industrial automation segment is dependent on the extent of adoption of new automation technologies by large as well as small and medium enterprises. By December 31, 2021, the company employed 5900 people of whom approximately 2000 were employed in the USA. In 2015, Teradyne acquired Universal Robots. In 2018, the company acquired Energid and MiR. In 2019, Lemsys and AutoGuide were acquired by Teradyne.

© The Author(s), under exclusive license to Springer Nature Switzerland AG 2024
B. R. Kumar, *Rising Stars*, Management for Professionals,
https://doi.org/10.1007/978-3-031-50032-9_42

Product Offerings

Semiconductor

The company designs, manufactures, and supports semiconductor test products and services globally that are used for wafer level and device package testing. These manufactured chips are used for different applications in segments such as automotive, industrial, communications, consumer, smartphones, cloud, computer, and electronic game applications. Semiconductor test products and services are sold to integrated device manufacturers. These companies outsource the manufacturing of silicon wafers to foundries. The FLEX Test Platform architecture manufactures test equipment which is designed for high efficiency multi-site testing. The IG-XL™ software operating system of the platform facilitates efficient and fast program development which includes instant conversion from single to multi-site test. Flex Test Platform is basically purchased by IDMs, OSAT, Foundries, and Fabless clients. FLEX Test Platform family of products provides a diverse range of technologies and instrument coverage to end use markets such as smart phones, cell phones, tablets, set top boxes, HDTVs, game controllers, computer graphics, and automotive controllers. Tetradyne expanded the J750 platform technology to create the IP750 Image Sensor test system to focus on testing image sensor devices used in smartphones, automobiles, and other imaging products. The Magnum platform facilitates the mass production test of memory devices for flash and DRAM memory which has immense application in consumer, industrial, and computing equipment segments. The ETS platform offered by Tetradyne is used by semiconductor manufacturers and assembly and test subcontractors for usage in the analog/mixed signal markets for cost-sensitive applications.

System Test

The system test segment comprises of three business units of storage test, defense/aerospace, and production board test. The storage test business unit provides the high-throughput, automated manufacturing test applications for hard disk drive (HDD) and semiconductor manufacturers. The HDD products facilitate the client market which satisfies the requirement of desktop, laptop, and external HDD products. The HDD products of the company also address the enterprise storage markets which is driven by the requirements of data centers and cloud storage. Tetradyne is a major provider of high-performance test systems, subsystems, instruments, and service for defense and aerospace markets. The demand for high-performance test systems is driven by new programs such as tactical aircraft and missile systems along with upgrade programs. The production board test system of Tetradyne is used by global electronics manufacturing firms to conduct in-circuit test and device programming of printed circuit board assemblies. Tetradyne offers the test station in off-line and automated in-line configurations.

Wireless Test

The company operates the wireless test business segment through the LitePoint brand name. LitePoint offers test solutions for the development of wireless devices and modules. LitePoint technology is used by global manufacturers of smartphones, tablets, notebooks, laptops, peripherals, and Internet of Things devices. LifePoint's platform IQxstream is a multidevice production test optimized solution which facilitates high-speed testing of technologies such as GSM, EDGE, CDMA2000, TD-SCDMA, WCDMA, HSPA+, LTE, and 5G. The system can be used for calibration and verification of devices such as tablets, smartphones, small cell radio units, and embedded cellular modules.

Industrial Automation

The industrial automation segment of Tetradyne consists of three business units—Universal Robots, Mobile Industrial Robots, and AutoGuide. Universal Robots offers low-cost, easy to deploy, and simple-to-program collaborative robots to improve manufacturing efficiency and optimize cost resources. Universal Robots offers a variety of collaborative robot models such as the UR3, UR5, UR10, and UR16 with different weights and arm reach. Universal Robots offers four e-Series collaborative robot models. Mobile Industrial Robots (MiR) offers low-cost, easy to deploy AMRs for enhancing manufacturing and warehouse efficiency. MiR offers seven collaborative autonomous mobile robot models with different payload carrying capacity. Universal Robots and MiR have sold over 60,000 collaborative robots and 6000 collaborative mobile robots respectively for varied production and warehouse environments. AutoGuide manufactures high payload AMRs for the global forklift market. The AMRs manufactured by AutoGuide are used for material transport of payloads up to 4500 kilograms related to manufacturing warehouse and logistics applications. These AutoGuide products complement MiR's lower payload products.

Tetradyne has sales and service offices located in North America, Central America, Asia, and Europe. The products are sold through direct sales force except for industrial automation products which are sold through distributors. The manufacturing activities for test businesses are basically conducted through subcontractors and outsourced contract manufacturers located in China and Malaysia. The industrial automation products are manufactured in production facilities in Denmark and the USA. Non-US sales accounted for 85%, 90%, and 89% of the consolidated revenues in the year 2019, 2020, and 2021, respectively.

Major Competitors

The major competitors for Tetradyne in semiconductor test segment include Advantest Corporation and Cohu. The competitors for the company in the system test segment include Keysight Technologies, Advantest Corporation, Test Research Inc., and SPEA. The major competitors in the wireless test are Rohde & Schwarz GmbH & Co, Anritsu Company Keysight Technologies Inc., etc. The competitors in the industrial automation segment include traditional industrial robots' manufacturers such as KUKA Robotics Corporation, FANUC, and Yaskawa Electric Corporation. The company faces competition from emerging Asian companies and from internal suppliers.

Risk Factors

The COVID-19 pandemic has impacted adversely the operations and cash flows of the company. Capital equipment providers in the semiconductor industries and industrial automation such as Teradyne have been negatively impacted by the global economic slowdown and recurring cyclicality within those industries. The businesses of Teradyne basically depend on the capital expenditures of manufacturers of semiconductors electronics and other industrial products. Teradyne faces significant competition from different competitors with significant resources in all of its segments. The products offered by Tetradyne are purchased by a limited number of customers accounting for a substantial portion of the purchases. The five largest direct customers of Teradyne accounted for 27%, 36%, and 33% of the consolidated revenues in the years 2019, 2020, and 2021, respectively. The future revenue generation depends on the ability of the company to technologically upgrade its products and services. Teradyne faces the risks of operating internationally due to economic factors and unexpected changes in legal and regulatory requirements. The company may not be able to realize the expected synergies and economies of scale from its acquisitions. The company would have reduced revenues if the suppliers do not meet product or delivery requirements. The operations of the company will be adversely impacted due to non-performance of outsourced contract manufacturers and global supply shortage of electrical components. The breach of operational or security systems could negatively affect the business and operations of the company. Teradyne faces risks due to legal and regulatory compliance. The implementation of tariffs on the products may negatively impact the success of business. For example, in 2018, US trade department imposed a 25% tariff on certain Teradyne products which were made in China and imported into the USA. The US government from time to time has issued export restrictions for US companies with more than 25% controlled US content, as well as US origin technology.

Table 1 reports the segment-wise revenue highlight during the year 2021. The values are given in thousands of dollars.

Table 1 Segment-wise revenues

Segment	Revenues
Semiconductor test	
System on a chip	2,246,730
Memory	395,612
System test	467,739
Industrial automation	
Universal Robots	311,182
Mobile Industrial Robots	63,544
AutoGuide	1179
Wireless test	216,895

Source: Annual Report 2021

Table 2 Holding period return

Year	Teradyne	S&P 500	Excess returns
2018	−31%	−8%	−23%
2019	89%	19%	70%
2020	82%	16%	65%
2021	44%	28%	16%
2022	−26%	−15%	−11%

Table 3 Book and market value of equity

Year	2017	2018	2019	2020	2021
Book value of equity	1953.65	1522.35	1480.16	2210.81	2563.96
Market value of equity	8187.59	5507.88	11347.5	19916.49	26532.91
BV as percent of MV	23.9%	27.6%	13.0%	11.1%	9.7%

Stock Performance

An investment of $1000 made in Teradyne stock on January 3, 1975, would have led to wealth creation of $ 265,230.78 by January 29, 2023.

The next section analyzes the stock returns for Teradyne for the recent 5-year period (2018–2022) in comparison to the returns for the market index S&P 500. The Teradyne share which was trading at $45.40 on February 2, 2018, increased by 2.27 times to trade at $103.44 on January 1, 2023. The total cumulative monthly return for Teradyne stock and market index S&P 500 during the period 2018–2022 was 128% and 49%, respectively. The average yearly return for Teradyne stock and market index S&P 500 was 26% and 10%, respectively.

Table 2 shows the holding period return for Teradyne and S&P 500 during the period 2018–2022. The holding period is assumed to be 1-year period.

Teradyne stock outperformed the market index S&P 500 by 70%, 65%, and 16%, respectively, during the years 2019, 2020, and 2021.

Table 3 displays the book and market value of equity of the company during the period 2017–2021 in millions of dollars.

The average book value of Teradyne as percent of market value of the company was approximately 17% during the time period 2017–2021. In 2017, the market value was 4.19 times that of book value. By 2021, the market value increased to 10.35 times that of book value.

Operating Performance

The following section analyzes the operating performance of the firm. Table 4 shows the financial highlights of the company during the period 2017–2021. The values are given in millions of dollars.

On an average basis, the total assets and total equity increased by 6% and 10% during the period 2017–2021. The short-term investments of cash and cash equivalents were fluctuating during the above period. The average growth rate of total revenue and net income were 16% and 44%, respectively. The average increase in operating expenses had been 10%. The market capitalization and enterprise value of firm increased by 46% and 52% on an average basis. The data is obtained from annual reports and gurufocus.com.

Table 5 highlights the performance indicators of profitability ratios and leverage ratio during 2017–2021.

The average net margin, ROE, and ROA during the period 2017–2021 were 21.29%, 31.15%, and 18.58%, respectively. The average debt equity ratio was 0.21 during 2017–2021.

Table 6 illustrates the estimation of economic value of the company during 2020 and 2021. The values are given in millions of dollars.

Table 4 Financial highlights

	(In millions of dollars)				
Financial highlights	2017	2018	2019	2020	2021
Total assets	3109.55	2706.61	2787.01	3652.35	3809.43
Short-term investments	1777.82	1116.85	911.23	1436.4	1366.43
Total equity	1953.65	1522.35	1480.16	2210.81	2563.96
Total revenue	2136.61	2100.8	2294.97	3121.47	3702.88
Total operating expenses	686.75	731.37	800.06	870.54	996.62
Net income	257.69	451.78	467.47	784.15	1014.59
Market cap	8187.59	5507.88	11347.5	19916.49	26532.91
Enterprise value	6775.76	4771.01	10896.28	18952.84	25351.06

Table 5 Performance indicators

Ratios	2017	2018	2019	2020	2021
Net margin%	12.06	21.51	20.37	25.12	27.4
ROE%	13.63	25.99	31.14	42.49	42.5
ROA%	8.78	15.54	17.02	24.35	27.19
DER	0.19	0.25	0.31	0.21	0.07

Table 6 Economic value

Year	2020	2021
Profit before income tax	901.02	1160.96
Income tax	116.86	146.40
Net operating profit after tax (NOPAT)	784.16	1014.56
Stockholder equity	2210.81	2563.96
Long-term debt	376.77	89.24
Total capital employed	2587.58	2653.2
WACC	9.10%	9.49%
Capital charge	235.47	251.79
Economic value	548.69	762.77

The economic value has increased from $ 548.69 million in 2020 to $762.77 in 2021.

References

1. https://investors.teradyne.com/financials-filings/annual-reports-proxies
2. https://investors.teradyne.com/stock-information/investment-calculator
3. Annual Report 2021

Case 43 Century Communities

Century Communities was incorporated in the year 2002. The company is the ninth largest homebuilder in the USA. The company went public in the year 2014. The company is the number one fastest growing public builder during the period 2017–2019. The common shares are traded on New York Stock Exchange under the symbol “CCS.” By 2021, the company has operations in 17 states of the USA and in over 40 markets. The company is involved in different aspects of homebuilding such as acquisition, entitlement, and development of land, construction, and sale of quality houses for different range of home buyers. The subsidiaries of the company such as Parkway Title, IHL Insurance Agency, and Inspire Home Loan subsidiaries offer financial services like insurance and lending services. Inspire originates mortgage loans primarily for the homebuilding customers of Century. The company made 9452 new home deliveries in the year 2020. In 2021, Century delivered 10,805 homes and the net new home contracts were a record 12,017 contracts. Approximately 75% of the deliveries were made to entry-level home buyers and 87% of the homes delivered were built as move-in ready homes. Century Communities have consistently made profits for the past 18 years. The company made $3.2 billion in total revenues in the year 2020. Century’s main focus is on the development and sale of single-family homes along with the construction of townhomes, condominiums, and multifamily housing. The land pipeline of the company amounted to approximately 80,000 lots by 2021.

The homes are built and sold under the Century Communities and Century Complete brands. The Century Communities brand offers entry-level, first- and second-time move-up, and lifestyle homes. The home buyers have the option to personalize their homes and are provided upgrade opportunities. Century Complete brand basically focuses on entry-level home buyers through retail studios and the internet. The company typically takes 4 to 8 months to construct a home. The total number of employees as of December 31, 2021 was 1600.

© The Author(s), under exclusive license to Springer Nature Switzerland AG 2024

B. R. Kumar, *Rising Stars*, Management for Professionals,
https://doi.org/10.1007/978-3-031-50032-9_43

Growth Strategy

Since 2013, Century has expanded geographically through the acquisitions of other homebuilders and organically grown through entry into new markets. In 2017, Century merged with UCP Inc. for transaction value of approximately $356 million. The combined company had operations in 10 states, 17 markets, and 111 communities. Century benefitted from the deal by means of increased scale through a geographically diversified portfolio of attractive homebuilding markets possessed by UCP. In the same year, Century had acquired all assets of Sundquist Homes. In 2018, Century Communities acquired 100% of Wade Jurney Homes. Wade Jurney Homes specializes in providing single-family homes for entry-level buyers with sales prices averaging $150,000. Its asset light business model is streamlined and its product offering is sold online and through retail outlets. This acquisition brought together the number one fastest growing public and number one fastest growing private US home builder. This acquisition enhanced the geographic reach and product diversification through additional exposure to new markets.

The new home communities offered by Century are positioned competitively in growing high demand markets with low availability of resale homes. The constrained supply of available homes coupled with the high demand from millions of Millennials, the largest generational group in the USA for new household formation, provides immense opportunity for driving growth for the company. It is estimated that by 2025, there would be demand for additional 6.4 million new households as the Millennials would age into their home buying years. The company has a high concentration in the entry-level segment with more than 75% of the total deliveries priced below FHA loan limits. The company gives emphasis for providing affordable housing options for home buyer segments such as entry-level, move-up, and lifestyle offerings. The company maintains a strong pipeline of future land holdings with an emphasis on lot option contracts to manage risks related to land holding. The company aims to maintain a strong balance sheet along with prudent use of leverage. The company evaluates opportunistic strategies for the construction of single-family and multifamily rental units. The company focuses on digital marketing for controlling costs. Century gives priority for building move-in ready homes over built-to-order homes as this strategy facilitates the company to speed up the construction process, offer competitive pricing with subcontractors, and shorten time cycle from home sale to home delivery.

The strategic business plan of Century involves acquisition of land based on population growth trends, local markets, entitlement restrictions, and infrastructure development. The company focuses on diversified product strategy to offer an extensive product offering to entry-level to first- and second-time move-up buyers and lifestyle home buyers. This strategy helps the firm to adapt to changing market conditions and optimize returns and minimize portfolio risk. The land acquisition process involves stages such as soil tests, environmental studies, engineering work, and financial analysis to evaluate the profitability of the project. Single-family detached or attached homes for sale are constructed on the acquired land. The company may also sell land to other developers and homebuilders in scenarios of

Table 1 Land pipeline statistics

Year	Owned and controlled lots
2017	30,784
2018	37,919
2019	38,942
2020	49,965
2021	79,856

Source: Annual Report 2021

excess land positions. Century generally acquires land for cash by means of bulk acquisitions of land or through option contract. In 2021, out of 79,856 lot position, 41% were owned and rest 59% were controlled through option contracts.

Table 1 shows the land pipeline trend of the Century for the period 2017–2021.

Risk Factors

Century faces risks related to demand fluctuations in the housing market and general economic conditions. The long-term growth of the company depends on the ability to lead successful acquisitions of land parcels at competitive prices and management of land and lot inventory. The company also has to face risks related to the homebuilding and real estate industries. The success of the company depends on the ability to develop projects within expected timeframes. Century faces risks related to resource optimization in terms of raw materials, labor, and prices. The company has risk challenges related to potential liability for health and safety incidents, product liability, and warranty claims. The homebuilding industry is cyclical, seasonal, and competitive in nature. The real estate investments are risky and depend on the ability to manage the land acquisitions and construction processes. The financial services related to mortgage lending business requires substantial capital. The financial services segment might be adversely affected by reduced demand for homes, slowdown in mortgage refinancing, and inability to sell mortgages in the secondary market. The company is subject to different local, state, federal, and other statutes, rules, and regulations related to concerned zones, development, building design, and construction which impose restrictive zoning and density requirements. Costs are incurred for the homebuilding activities of the company for maintenance of these laws and regulations. The environmental laws applicable to the homebuilding site vary according to site's location and environmental conditions, and the company may have to incur substantial compliance and other costs for homebuilding activity in environmentally sensitive regions. The mortgage, title, and insurance subsidiaries ought to comply with real estate, lending, and insurance laws and regulations. The company has substantial indebtedness with approximately $1.3 billion in debt as of December 31, 2021.

ESG Initiatives

The Board of Century has adopted a code of business conduct and ethics which are applicable to officers, directors, and employees. The ESG reporting of the company is focused on the industry-specific reporting standards of the Sustainability Accounting Standards Board (SASB) which were launched in the year 2018. The SASB reporting is also compliant with the Task Force on Climate-Related Financial Disclosure (TCFD) recommendations. The company has adopted energy-efficient building technologies and eco-products as a part of sustainable practices for addressing environmental concerns. The homes built by the company are certified based on third-party multi-attribute green building standards. In 2020, approximately 84% of home deliveries used WaterSense® Certified fixtures and about 4107 homes received HERS Rating score. The company has also adopted Vendor Code of Conduct to have responsible businesses with vendors and partners. The company offers customers sustainable solutions such as low-VOC paint and improved indoor air quality, energy-efficient HVAC units with whole-home air purification system, and ENERGY STAR® appliances. With respect to social initiatives, all new employees are required to undertake training related to anti-harassment and anti-discrimination. The company focuses on pay-for-performance strategy. The board is responsible for implementing sound corporate governance practices. In 2020, Century Communities through the services of WAP Consulting evaluated the company's first carbon footprint. The results suggest that overwhelming majority of GHG emissions are in the scope 3 category of purchased goods. The total corporate greenhouse gas emissions statistics shows that at company level, the emissions per home sold was 131 MT CO2e/home in the year 2020.

Stock Performance

The following section analyzes the stock returns of Century Communities in comparison with market index S&P 500 for the recent 5-year period. The source of data was Yahoo Finance. Century Communities stock was trading at $29.75 on February 2, 2018. By January 1, 2023, the stock price increased by 1.98 times to trade at $58.91. The total cumulative monthly return for Century stock was 144% compared to 48% monthly returns for market index S&P 500 during the period February 2018–January 2023. The average yearly returns for Century stock were 29% compared to 10% registered by market index S&P during the period February 2018–January 2023.

Table 2 shows the holding period return for the Century stock and market index S&P 500 during the period 2018–2022. The holding period is assumed to be 1-year period.

The Century stock outperformed the market index in the years 2020 and 2021.

Table 3 shows the book and market value of the equity of company during the recent 5-year period 2018–2022. The values are given in millions of dollars.

Table 2 Holding period return

Year	Century	S&P 500	Excess returns
2018	−42%	−8%	−34%
2019	17%	19%	−3%
2020	48%	16%	31%
2021	74%	28%	46%
2022	−24%	−15%	−9%

Table 3 Book value and market value of equity

Year	2017	2018	2019	2020	2021
Book value of equity	735.23	859.36	1061.7	1280.71	1764.51
Market value of equity	917.53	520.47	904.39	1460.09	2761.3
BV as percent of MV	80.1%	165.1%	117.4%	87.7%	63.9%

Table 4 Financial highlights

	(In millions of dollars)				
Financial highlights	2017	2018	2019	2020	2021
Total assets	1735.02	2254.26	2499.97	2845.09	3496.88
Short-term investments	88.83	32.9	55.44	394	316.31
Total equity	735.23	859.36	1061.7	1280.71	1764.51
Total revenue	1423.8	2147.41	2535.91	3161.19	4216.31
Total operating expenses	176.3	263.98	301.53	341.71	389.6
Net income	50.3	96.46	112.99	206.16	498.5
Market cap	917.53	520.47	904.39	1460.09	2761.3
Enterprise value	1653.3	1579.4	2007.76	2236.81	3793.17

The average book value as percent of market value was 102.3% approximately during the 5-year period 2017–2021. In 2021, the market value of equity was 1.56 times that of the book value of the equity.

Table 4 gives the financial and operating highlights of the company in millions of dollars during the period 2017–2021. The data is sourced from annual reports and gurufocus.com.

The total assets and total equity grew by 19% and 25%, respectively, on an average basis during the period 2017–2021. The average growth rate of cash, cash equivalents, and marketable securities of the firm was 149% during the above period, though fluctuations were observed. The total revenue and net income increased by 32% and 83%, respectively. The total expenses increased by 23% on an average basis. The average growth rate of market capitalization and enterprise value was 45% and 26% during the period 2017–2021.

Table 5 gives the performance measures of profitability and leverage position of the firm during the period 2017–2021.

The net margin improved from 3.73% in 2017 to 11.82% in 2021. The ROE and ROA also exhibited consistent increasing trend. The ROE in 2017 increased from 8.32% to 32.74% by 2021. The leverage of the company has shown declining trend,

Table 5 Performance indicators

Ratios	2017	2018	2019	2020	2021
Net margin%	3.53	4.49	4.46	6.52	11.82
ROE%	8.32	12.1	11.76	17.6	32.74
ROA%	3.67	4.84	4.75	7.71	15.72
DER	1.12	1.27	1.09	0.91	0.76

Table 6 Economic value in millions of dollars

Year	2020	2021
Profit before income tax	270.24	641.12
Income tax	64.07	142.65
Net operating profit after tax (NOPAT)	206.17	498.47
Stockholder equity	1280.71	1764.51
Long-term debt	1153.93	1330.81
Total capital employed	2434.64	3095.32
WACC	6.89%	9.34%
Capital charge	167.75	289.10
Economic value	38.42	209.37

suggesting that the firm has become less risky over a period of time. The average net margin, ROE, and ROA for Century had been 6.16%, 16.50%, and 7.34%, respectively during the period 2017–2021. The average debt equity of the company was 1.03.

Table 6 shows the estimation of the economic value for Century Communities during the period 2017–2021.

The economic value has improved from $38.42 million in 2020 to $209.37 million in the year 2021.

References

1. https://investors.centurycommunities.com/ir-home/default.aspx
2. Century Communities ESG Report 2021
3. https://www.businesswire.com/news/home/20170804005433/en/Century-Communities-Completes-Business-Combination-with-UCP
4. https://www.builderonline.com/money/m-a/century-communities-acquires-100-of-wade-jurney-homes_o

Case 44 SSR Mining

SSR Mining Inc. is a leading precious metals mining company with four producing assets located in the USA, Turkey, Canada, and Argentina. SSR Mining Inc. was incorporated in British Columbia, Canada, in the year 2005. The predecessor companies have been incorporated in year 1946. SSR Mining produces gold ore as well as copper, silver, lead, and zinc concentrates. In the year 2021, the company's produced 794,000 gold equivalent ounces. The company has a strong balance sheet with over $ 1 billion in cash and cash equivalents by December 31, 2021. SSR Mining Inc. is listed under the ticker symbol SSRM on the Nasdaq Capital Market and Toronto Stock Exchange and SSR on the Australian Stock Exchange. The operations of the company are based in four operating mine sites—Çöpler Gold Mine, Turkey, Marigold Mine, located in Nevada, USA, Seabee Gold Operations, Canada, and Puna Operations, Argentina. In 2021, 41%, 29%, 15%, and 15% of the revenues were accounted from Çöpler, Marigold, Seabee, and Puna fields, respectively. By December 31, 2021, the company has employed approximately 2429 full-time employees and 1608 contract employees.

Product Offering

The mine fields of Çöpler, Marigold, and Seabee produce gold doré which is unrefined gold bullion bars consisting in excess of 90% gold. The gold doré is subsequently refined by a third party to gold bullion. Gold doré is primarily sold to bullion banks. All the gold doré produced at Çöpler field is delivered to Istanbul Gold Refinery. Puna field produces silver, lead, and zinc concentrates which are further processed for refining by smelters or traders. Gold doré accounted for 84% of revenues in the year 2021. SSR Mining sells lead and zinc concentrate with high silver content through contractual arrangements with smelters and traders in Asia and Europe.

Table 1 lists the revenues proportion by product category for the period 2019–2021.

© The Author(s), under exclusive license to Springer Nature Switzerland AG 2024
B. R. Kumar, *Rising Stars*, Management for Professionals,
https://doi.org/10.1007/978-3-031-50032-9_44

Table 1 Product revenue

Product	2019	2020	2021
Gold	76%	88%	84%
Silver	19%	11%	12%
Lead	2%	1%	2%
Zinc	3%	1%	1%

Source: Annual Report

By December 2021, the company had attributable proven and probable gold reserves of 9154 koz. The precious and base metals mineral exploration and mining business is highly competitive. The company competes with mining and exploration companies for the acquisition of mineral properties.

Risk Analysis

The company's profitability depends upon the market price of gold, silver, copper, lead, and zinc. The market prices of these metals are volatile and are affected by factors such as global or regional consumption patterns, supply and demand of metals, gold sales, purchases or leasing by governments and central banks, and monetary policies. The public health crisis could adversely affect the company's business. The company has to replace its depleted mineral reserves to maintain production levels in the long term by expanding known ore bodies, locating new deposits, or making acquisitions. There exists a risk that depletion of firm's mineral reserves may not be offset by discoveries or acquisitions. There are uncertainties inherent with respect to estimation of quantities of mineral reserves and grades of mineralization. The company's profitability could be affected by increased operating and capital costs. The operations of the company may be adversely affected by rising energy prices or energy shortage. Supply chain disruptions, power outages, labor disputes, and natural disasters are potential risk factors for the company. The mining industry as a whole faces geotechnical challenges which could adversely impact the production and profitability of the company. Production of precious metals is an energy-intensive business which results in carbon emissions. The transition to lower carbon economic regime may entail risks related to extensive policy, legal, technology, and market changes. The firm's mining, exploration, and development activities are subject to different federal, provincial, state, and municipal laws and regulations related to environmental protection.

ESG Initiatives

The company publishes an ESG and Sustainability Report which is developed using the Global Reporting Initiative framework. The company's Board of Directors has established an Environmental, Health, Safety and Sustainability Committee of the Board for review of the company's safety, health, security, risk, and sustainability policies. In 2007, the Marigold field became the first operating gold mine in the world to be certified as fully compliant with the International Cyanide Management Code which is a voluntary industry program for companies involved in the production of gold by the cyanidation process. SSR Mining plans to establish an action plan to achieve net zero emissions by 2050. The company focuses on local development activities to promote sustainable long-term economic and social benefits. The company supports local communities by investment in education, social programs, and infrastructure projects. In the year 2019, SSR Mining became a member of the Catalyst Accord 2022 and the 30% Club Canada. These initiatives focus on acceleration of the advancement of women in the workplace with the target goal of at least 30% representation of women on public company boards. The company has adopted a Human Rights Policy which is aligned with United Nations global impact and OECD guidelines for multinational enterprises. The company has a zero-tolerance approach to bribery and corruption.

Stock Performance

Table 2 shows the performance of the SSR Mining stock in comparison to the market index S&P/TSX Global Gold Index and S&P 500 Gold (Sub Ind) during the period December 31, 2016, and ending December 31, 2021. The analysis involves investment of $100 in SSR Mining shares and in each of the indexes with the assumption of reinvestment of dividends paid on such investments.

The holding period return for SSR Mining Inc. is 101%, while the holding period return for S&P/TSX Global Gold Index and S&P 500 Gold (Sub Ind) is 50% and 87%, respectively. The yearly average return for SSR Mining Inc. was 17.79%, while for the market indexes, the returns were 9.87% and 14.48%.

The next section analyzes the stock returns for SSR Mining Inc. and market index S&P 500 for the recent 5-year period 2018–2022. SSR Mining stock was trading at $8.30 on February 1, 2018. By January 1, 2023, SSR stock price rose to $16.99 which represented an increase of over 2.04 times. The total cumulative monthly return for the stock was 121% compared to 48% for the market index S&P 500 during the recent 5-year period Feb 2018–Jan 2023. The average yearly return for the stock was 25% compared to 10% registered by the market index during the time period Feb 2018–Jan 2023.

Table 2 Comparative wealth generation

Year	2016	2017	2018	2019	2020	2021
SSR Mining Inc.	$100	$98.54	$135.54	$215.92	$225.45	$201.02
S&P/TSX Global Gold Index	$100	$100.62	$96.16	$134.52	$162.38	$150.31
S&P 500 Gold (Sub Ind)	$100	$110.13	$101.70	$130.71	$180.17	$186.58

Source Annual Report 2021

Table 3 Holding period

Year	SSR Mining	S&P 500	Excess returns
2018	46%	−8%	53%
2019	40%	19%	21%
2020	10%	16%	−7%
2021	1%	28%	−28%
2022	−5%	−15%	10%

Table 4 Book and market value of equity

Year	2020	2021
Book value of equity	5109.05	5665.42
Market value of equity	5729.55	5127.47
BV as percent of MV	89.2%	110.5%

Table 5 Financial highlights

	(In millions of dollars)				
Financial highlights	2017	2018	2019	2020	2021
Total assets	2010.99	2121.99	2541.16	6875.51	7285.59
Short-term investments	750.62	626.01	827.79	1178.44	1479.07
Total equity	1339.3	1403.34	1646.5	5109.05	5665.42
Total revenue	587	586.84	881.15	1132.9	2060.93
Total operating expenses	47.46	70.32	77.23	119.79	138.37
Net income	90.67	80.9	149.23	201.24	514.57

Table 3 shows the holding period return for the stock and market index S&P 500 during the 5-year period 2018–2022. The analysis is based on the holding period assumption of 1 year.

On the basis of holding period returns, SSR Mining stock outperformed the market index S&P 500 in the years 2018 and 2019.

Table 4 gives the book and market value of SSR stock in millions of dollars during the 2-year period 2020–2021.

The average book value as percent of market value during the period 2020–2021 was 99.8%.

The next section analyzes the operating and financial performance of the SSR Mining during the 5-year period 2017–2021. Table 5 gives the financial highlights of the company. The values are given in millions of dollars. The data is sourced from Yahoo Finance and gurufocus.com.

The average growth rate of total assets, total cash investments, and total equity were 50%, 21%, and 61%, respectively. The total revenue and net income grew by 40% and 66%, respectively. The total expenses increased by 32% on an average basis.

Table 6 shows the profitability and leverage position of the firm during the period 2017–2021.

Table 6 Profitability and leverage measures

Ratios	2017	2018	2019	2020	2021
Net margin%	15.45	1.52	16.94	17.76	24.97
ROE%	7.15	0.67	9.93	6.62	10.98
ROA%	4.57	0.43	6.4	4.27	7.27
DER	0.23	0.25	0.25	0.17	0.14

The average net margin, ROE, and ROA during the 5-year period 2017–2021 were 15.33%, 7.07%, and 4.59%, respectively. The average debt equity ratio was 0.21.

References

1. https://www.ssrmining.com/company/
2. SSR Sustainability Report 2021

Case 45 Merchants Bancorp

Merchants Bancorp is a diversified bank holding company headquartered in Indiana, USA. The company was founded in 1990 as a mortgage banking company which provides financing for multifamily housing and senior living properties. Merchants Bancorp operates different lines of business such as Federal Housing Administration, multifamily housing, healthcare facility financing, mortgage warehouse financing, retail and correspondent residential mortgage banking, agricultural lending, and community banking. Merchants Bank is also a syndicator of low-income housing tax credit and debt funds.

By September 30, 2022, the Merchants Bancorp had assets worth $12 billion in value and deposits worth $10.3 billion. The main subsidiaries of Merchants Bancorp include Merchants Bank of Indiana, Merchants Capital Corp, Farmers-Merchants Bank of Illinois, Merchants Capital Servicing, and Merchants Mortgage. One of the wholly owned banking subsidiaries, Merchants Bank of Indiana, provides traditional community banking services along with retail and correspondent residential mortgage banking and agricultural lending.

The business operations of Merchants Bancorp mainly consist of funding low-risk loans which sell within 90 days of origination. The source of noninterest income is the gain on sale of loans and servicing fees which are basically generated from the multifamily rental real estate loans service portfolio. The funding source of the Merchants Bancorp is from mortgage, custodial, commercial, and brokered deposits. By year-end 2021, Merchants Bank had 481 full-time employees.

Business Segments

Multifamily Mortgage Banking

The subsidiaries Merchants Capital Corp (MCC) and Merchants Capital Servicing (MCS) offer mortgage banking with specialization in origination and service of loans for multifamily rental housing and healthcare facility. The servicing portfolio

© The Author(s), under exclusive license to Springer Nature Switzerland AG 2024

B. R. Kumar, *Rising Stars*, Management for Professionals,
https://doi.org/10.1007/978-3-031-50032-9_45

consists primarily of Ginnie Mae loans. Merchants Bank also originates and services Fannie Mae and Freddie Mac affordable multifamily products. These origination and servicing portfolio platforms form the major portion of noninterest income and deposits. The bank originates Federal Housing Authority loans (FHA) through the Multi-Family Mortgage Banking segment. These loans are then sold as Ginnie Mae mortgage-backed securities within 30 days. The primary source of funding for the segment is the national secondary mortgage market of federal government and chartered agencies. The major investors in the market are large financial institutions, brokerage companies, insurance companies, and real estate investment trusts. MCC is an approved FHA lender and issues mortgage-backed securities for Ginnie Mae. The loans funded by multifamily mortgage banking segment have 35-year fixed rates with 10-year call protection. These loans are insured by FHA and Rural Housing Service (RHS). The segment also offers customized loan products for independent living, assisted living, memory care, and skilled nursing projects. Loan products are also offered for refinancing of healthcare properties, and these loans are underwritten with the provision to convert into permanent loans within 3 years. MCC through its comprehensive suite of debt offerings and syndication platform offers affordable housing transactions.

Mortgage Warehousing

Merchants Bank offers warehouse lines of credit and loan participation to non-depository financial institutions and mortgage bankers in the industry. The mortgage warehousing segment provides asset-based financing in the form of warehouse facilities to non-depository financial institutions and mortgage bankers. These facilities help these institutions to fund residential and multifamily mortgage loans until they are sold and purchased in the secondary market by an approved investor. Mortgage warehousing funding has grown from over $20 billion in the year 2015 to over $78 billion by 2021.

Banking

The banking segment consists of retail banking, commercial lending, agricultural lending, correspondent residential mortgage banking, and SBA lending. The correspondent banking segment has a well-diversified presence at national level with significant growth prospects.

Commercial Lending and Retail Banking

Merchants Bank provides multifamily construction and bridge loans, owner-occupied commercial real estate loans, commercial and industrial loans, agricultural loans, residential mortgage loans, and consumer loans. Merchants Bank receives deposits from customers located in Indiana and through servicing activities of escrows generated by MCC and MCS.

Agricultural Lending

Merchants Bank offers operating lines of credit for crop and livestock production, intermediate term financing to purchase agricultural equipment and breeding livestock, and long-term financing to purchase agricultural real estate. Merchants Bank also sells agricultural loans in the secondary market through the Federal Agricultural Mortgage Corporation. The bank is also a certified lender with the Farm Service Agency.

Single-Family Mortgage Lending, Correspondent Lending, and Servicing

Merchants Mortgage division of Merchants Bank is a full-service single-family mortgage origination and servicing platform. This division also serves as both retail and correspondent mortgage lender. It offers different mortgages such as agency eligible, jumbo fixed, and hybrid adjustable rate mortgages for purchase or refinancing of single-family residences. The other products offered in this segment include construction, bridge and lot financing, and first-lien home equity lines of credit (HELOC). Merchants Mortgage also involves in origination of loans held for investment and earns interest income over the life of the loan.

SBA Lending

Merchants Bank offers SBA lending through participation in the SBA's 7(a), 504, and Express programs to cater to the needs of small business communities. In 2018, SBA bestowed preferred lender program status on Merchants Bank, and this award enabled the bank to take loan decisions quickly.

Strategy for Growth

The strategy of the bank is to create a diversified financial services company at national level through mortgage banking and related services and locally through community bank. The bank focuses on organic growth. The combination of net interest income and noninterest income which the bank generates from the sale of low-risk profile assets results in a lower expense base which enables the bank to maximize net income and shareholder return. The bank focuses on diversification of segments to provide synergies across segments. The focus is on MCC and MCS for growth opportunities as these segments fund loans and provide Ginnie Mae custodial services. The lending activities of new and existing multifamily mortgages are complemented by low-income tax credit syndication and debt fund offerings. Mortgage Warehousing offers leads to correspondent residential lending in the banking segment. Cross selling opportunities exist between retail and commercial customers within the banking divisions. Merchants Mortgage segment acts as a risk mitigant for Mortgage Warehousing as it provides an organized platform for selling the underlying collateral to secure repayment.

Competition

Merchants Bank faces direct competition for deposits, loans, loan origination, and other financial services from commercial and retail banking, residential mortgages, multifamily FHA, Fannie Mae, and Freddie Mac in the multifamily and healthcare segments. The bank also competes with non-depository financial institutions, community banks, and thrifts and credit unions. Merchants Bank competes with consumer finance companies, brokerage firms, mortgage banking companies, insurance companies, securities firms, mutual funds for different types of loans, and financial services.

Risk Factors

Merchants Bank's profitability may be decreased due to decreases in residential and multifamily mortgage origination, pricing decisions of competitors, and interest rate changes by loan competitors. These factors may adversely affect the demand for mortgage loan products and affect the revenues realized on the sales of loans and servicing the loans. The profits associated with mortgage banking would be adversely affected if the bank is not able to originate and resell a high volume of mortgage loans. It has to be noted that mortgage activity such as refinancing generally falls in periods of high interest rate environment. The origination and sale of residential mortgage loans by the warehouse financing customers is dependent on the availability of an active secondary market for single-family mortgage loans, which in turn depend on programs offered by GSEs along with other investors. The multifamily FHA origination business would be adversely affected if the HUD lending requirements are violated. Real estate construction loans are subject to additional risks since the funds are given based on the security of the project whose value may be uncertain prior to its completion. The company faces strong competition from financial services companies which offer banking, mortgage, leasing, and multifamily agency financing and services. The bank also faces reputational, credit, and financial risks. The business and operations of Merchants Bank are sensitive to general business and economic conditions and any regulatory response to adversary conditions may affect the growth prospects of Merchants Bank. Inefficiencies in credit risk management would lead to increased levels of delinquencies, non-performing loans, and charge-offs. The bank may be adversely impacted on account of transition from LIBOR as a reference rate. Breaches of network security or system failure would lead to increased operating costs as well as litigation and other liabilities. Fluctuations in interest rates may reduce net interest income and negatively impact the financial position of the bank. A major portion of the bank's loan portfolio consists of loans with real estate as primary or secondary component of collateral. Adverse developments with respect to real estate values in market could lead to increase in credit risk associated with real estate loan portfolio. Merchants Bank faces legal, regulatory, and compliance risks. Merchants Bank is subject to heightened regulatory requirements since the bank has assets of value greater than $10 billion.

Stock Performance Analysis

The following section analyzes the stock performance of Merchants Bancorp in comparison to the market index Nasdaq Bank. The data is taken from Yahoo Finance. The time period of analysis is from February 2018–January 2023. Merchants Bancorp was trading at $13.66 on February 2, 2018. By February 2, 2023, the stock price increased 2.19 times to trade at $30.04. The total cumulative monthly return for Merchants Bancorp amounted to 110% compared to cumulative monthly return of 22% accounted by Nasdaq Bank Index. The average yearly return for the Merchants Bancorp stock was 22% compared to 4% yearly returns registered by Nasdaq Bank Index.

Table 1 shows the holding period returns for Merchants Bancorp and Nasdaq Bank Index for the period 2018–2022.

The Merchants Bancorp outperformed the bank index in all years except in 2019.

Table 2 shows the comparative market and book value of the equity during 2018–2022. The values are given in millions of dollars.

Table 1 Holding period returns

Year	Merchants Bancorp	Nasdaq Bank Index	Excess returns
2018	−3%	−19%	17%
2019	1%	9%	−9%
2020	40%	−5%	45%
2021	59%	34%	25%
2022	−17%	−18%	2%

Table 2 Market and book value trends

Year	2018	2019	2020	2021	2022
Book value of equity	421.24	653.73	810.62	1155.41	1459.74
Market value of equity	572.73	565.8	794.28	1362.47	1184.67
BV as percent of MV	73.5%	115.5%	102.1%	84.8%	123.2%

Table 3 Financial highlights

	(In millions of dollars)				
Financial highlights	2018	2019	2020	2021	2022
Total assets	3884.16	6371.93	9645.38	11278.64	12615.23
Cash and cash equivalents	336.52	506.71	179.73	1032.61	226.16
Deposits	3231.09	5478.08	7408.07	8982.61	10071.35
Total equity	421.24	653.73	810.62	1155.41	1459.74
Net interest income	89.97	122.3	224.15	277.99	318.55
Interest expense	50.59	89.7	58.64	33.89	162.28
Total noninterest expense	46.28	58.78	87.34	117.73	131.35
Market cap	572.73	565.8	794.28	1362.47	1184.67
Enterprise value	473.24	453.18	2063.23	1565.96	2015

Table 4 Performance indicators

Ratios	2017	2018	2019	2020	2021
Performance ratios					
Return on average assets %	1.84	1.71	1.47	2.12	2.23
Return on average equity%	22.00	15.86	14.37	25.09	22.07
Net interest margin%	2.32	2.54	2.40	2.69	2.79
Efficiency ratio%	30.32	36.47	37.38	27.42	28.80
Asset quality ratio					
Non-performing assets to total assets%	0.09	0.06	0.08	0.07	0.01
Capital ratios					
Common equity tier 1 to risk-weighted assets%	11.8	10.6	7.4		
Total capital to risk-weighted assets%	13.4	11.9	11.3		

The average book value as percent of market value of equity was 99.8% during the period 2018–2022. The market value which was 1.36 times of book value of equity in 2018 declined to 0.81 times of book value by the year 2022.

Table 3 shows the financial highlights of Merchants Bancorp in millions of dollars during the period 2018–2022.

The data was sourced from annual reports. The average growth rate analysis reveals that the total assets, total cash investments, and deposits increased by 36%, 96%, and 35%, respectively, during the period 2018–2022. The cash and cash equivalents were highly fluctuating during the above period. The net interest income had registered negative growth in both 2020 and 2021. However, the net interest income increased by 379% in the year 2022. The interest and noninterest expenses increased by 30% and 24% during the period 2018–2022. The market capitalization for Merchants Bancorp increased by 24% on an average basis during the period 2018–2022.

Table 4 shows the performance indicators in terms of profitability, asset quality, and capital ratios during the time period 2017–2021.

The average values for return on average assets, return on average equity, and net interest margin were 1.87%, 19.88%, and 2.55%, respectively. The average

Table 5 Economic value

Year	2021	2022
Profit before income tax	304.93	291.14
Income tax	77.82	71.42
Net operating profit after tax (NOPAT)	227.11	219.72
Stockholder equity	1155.41	1459.74
Long-term debt	573.95	930.00
Total capital employed	1729.36	2389.74
WACC	5.41%	6.33%
Capital charge	93.56	151.27
Economic value	133.55	68.45

efficiency ratio was 32.08%. In terms of asset quality, the ratio of non-performing assets to total assets was 0.062%. The average capital ratios were 9.93% and 12.2%, respectively.

Table 5 illustrates the economic value of Merchants Bancorp for the years 2021 and 2022. The values are given in millions of dollars.

References

1. https://investors.merchantsbancorp.com/corporate-profile/corporate-profile/default.aspx
2. https://investors.merchantsbancorp.com/filings/default.aspx
3. Annual Report 2021

Case 46 Boston Beer

The Boston Beer Company along with its subsidiaries is involved in the production and selling of alcoholic beverages mainly in the USA and in select international markets. The Boston Beer operates under different trade names such as "the Boston Beer Company®," "Twisted Tea Brewing Company®," "Hard Seltzer Beverage Company," "Angry Orchard® Cider Company," "Dogfish Head® Craft Brewery," "Dogfish Head Distilling Co.," "Angel City® Brewing Company," "Coney Island® Brewing Company," and "Bevy Long Drink Co." The company produces alcoholic beverages such as hard seltzer, malt beverages, and hard cider. These products are produced in company-owned breweries and its cidery and through contract arrangements at other brewery locations. The company's four primary owned breweries are located in Boston, Massachusetts, Ohio, Delaware, and Pennsylvania. The company also produces distilled spirits and spirits based ready-to-drink beverages in small quantity. The company also owns five smaller local breweries which focuses on brewing and packaging beers for retail sales. Boston Beer's hard seltzers, beers, and hard ciders are basically positioned as high-end category characterized by higher price, quality, image, and taste compared to regular domestic beer. Boston Beer is one of the largest suppliers in the high-end category in the USA. The market share of high-end category is approximately 38% in the beer market, and the company has 11% market share in the high-end category.

The value chain of Boston Beer expands from a network of 150 suppliers to millions of consumers around the world. The network of distributors includes more than 400 US wholesalers and group of foreign wholesalers who sell the products to retailers. The company has more than 70 third-party logistics partners which transport the products to retail customers through road, rail, and intermodal transport methods. The company also has contract manufacturing agreements with third-party breweries and packaging facilities.

Truly Hard Seltzer brand beverages are primarily packaged in sleek cans, and Twisted Tea brand beverages are primarily packaged in standard cans. Over 75% of the company's total volume was packaged in can. The company's beverages are packaged in cardboard wraps, carriers, and cardboard shipping cases. The two row

© The Author(s), under exclusive license to Springer Nature Switzerland AG 2024
B. R. Kumar, *Rising Stars*, Management for Professionals,
https://doi.org/10.1007/978-3-031-50032-9_46

varieties of barley are used in the company's malt. The company uses multiple yeast strains for production of its beverages. Special varieties and origins of apples are used in its hard ciders.

Industry Scenario

By 2008, consolidation in the beer industry led to the emergence of two largest breweries Anheuser—Busch InBev and Molson Coors which controlled over 90% of all US domestic beer production. However, the number of breweries in the USA had increased significantly from over 1500 in 2009 to over 8000 by 2021. The growth of small and independent brewers has now led to decline in the volume of two largest breweries who account for 77% of all the US domestic beer production. The beverages industry predicts that there exists significant potential for the emergence of new category named "Beyond Beer" which includes hard seltzer, flavored malt beverages, cider, spirits RTDs, and other emerging beverages. Boston Beer has a market share of approximately 26% in the Beyond Beer category. In 2021, Boston Beer entered the market for spirits RTDs through its Dogfish Head brand.

Growth Strategy

The company's focus is to become the leading supplier in the "high-end" and "Beyond Beer" categories by offering high-quality alcohol beverages. The company has competitive strength as a trained sales organization with world-class brewers. The company focuses on enhancing brand awareness through traditional media and digital advertising, point of sale, promotional programs, and drinker education and engagement. The company focuses on consumer-responsive hard seltzers, beers, hard ciders, and spirits RTDS. The strategic aim of the company is to offer different varieties of traditional and innovative alcohol beverages.

The primary brands of the company include the Truly Hard Seltzer, Twisted Tea, Samuel Adams, Angry Orchard, and Dogfish Head brands. The national distribution of the Truly Hard Seltzer brand was started in the year 2016, and it became one of the leading brands in the hard seltzer segment by the year 2021. The hard seltzer category comprises approximately 8% of the US beer consumption. Boston Beer offers over 30 styles of hard seltzer in the truly brand family.

The Twisted tea brand was introduced in the year 2001 and became the largest selling flavored malt beverage (FMB) brand by the year 2021. The FMB category accounts for approximately 5% of US beer consumption market. Boston Beer offers over ten styles of flavored malt beverages in the Twisted Tea brand family. The company's Samuel Adams and Dogfish Head beers compete with the craft beer and domestic specialty beer category and account for 6% of US beer consumption. There is intense competition in this category which includes large international, national competitors along with smaller national, regional, and local craft breweries. The Samuel Adams brand was introduced in the year 1984 and is one of the largest craft beer brands in the category of lagers and seasonal beers. The Dogfish Head brand introduced in the year 1995 is one of the most innovative and well-established craft beer and spirits brand. Boston Beer offers over 20 and 25 styles of beer in the Samuel Adams and Dogfish Head brand family. Boston Beer's Angry Orchard ciders compete with the hard cider category which accounts for less than 1% of US beer consumption. The company offers over ten styles of hard cider in the Angry Orchard brand family. The activity related to distilling spirits began in the year 2002 by Dogfish Head brand and is known as one of the original craft distilleries. The company offers over 15 styles of distilled spirits under the Dogfish Head brand. In 2021, the company made entry into the market for spirits RTDs through its Dogfish Head brand.

The two local brewery brands Angel City® and Coney Island® focus on tap rooms and local and regional distribution. In the year 2021, the company entered into separate licensing agreements with PepsiCo Inc., Jim beam Brands Co, and Patagonia Provisions to develop, market, and sell alcohol beverages. Under the Pepsi agreement, the company has the responsibility to develop, manufacture, and market flavored malt beverage products under the Pepsi's MTN DEW® brand.

Boston Beer has a proven track record of innovation. The company focuses on R&D to test new alcohol beverages and sell them under various brand labels for evaluation of taste and preferences. The Boston Brewery and other large breweries of the company focus on ideation, testing, and developing alcoholic beverages for future commercial development and process development for existing beverages. In 2021, the company launched new products such as Truly Fruit Punch Mix Pack and Truly Iced Tea Seltzer Mix Pack. The company also introduced five styles of spirits RTDs under the Dogfish Head brand and two Angry Orchard fruit ciders and two non-alcoholic beers. In 2022, the company planned for new product introductions such as Hard Mountain Dew and Sauza Agave Cocktails. The company announced plans to establish a dedicated research and innovation hub in Canada to focus on non-alcoholic cannabis beverages. The company has made capital investments of $147.9 million in the year 2021. The company had entered into a production agreement with Rauch North America which involves a minimum capacity availability commitment by Rauch and the company has the obligation to meet annual volume commitments.

Competition

The high-end and Beyond Beer categories in the USA are highly competitive due to the presence of large domestic and international beverage companies. The two largest brewers AB InBev and Molson Coors are active participants in both the categories. Another trend observed is the entry of non-alcoholic beverage companies such as Pepsi, Coca-Cola, and Monster Beverage Corporation into the alcoholic segment through licensing agreements with alcoholic beverage companies. Boston Beer's Truly Hard Seltzer beverages compete with companies in the hard seltzer category such as Mark Anthony Brands. The Twisted Tea beverages compete basically with the FMB category of the beer industry with brands such as Mike's Hard Lemonade®, Smirnoff Ice®, and Bud Light Lime® Ritas. The Samuel Adams and Dogfish Head beverages basically compete within the craft beer and domestic specialty beer segment of the beer industry and the major competitive brands are Craft Brew Alliance, Elysian Brewing Company, Golden Road Brewing, etc. The Angry Orchard product line of the company competes with companies such as C&C Group PLC within the hard cider category. The Dogfish Head RTDs product competes with competitors such as E&J Gallo Winery within the spirits RTD category.

Risk Analysis

The company's operations were significantly impacted on account of the global COVID-19 crisis. Boston Beer faces substantial competition in the high-end and Beyond Beer categories on account of the presence of large domestic and international breweries along with craft brewers and craft distilleries in the beverages market. The competitors of the Boston Beer such as AB InBev, Molson Coors, Constellation, Heineken, and Mark Anthony Brands have greater financial resources, marketing strength, and distribution networks than the company. The entry of large non-alcoholic beverage companies such as Pepsi, Coca-Cola, and Monster to develop alcoholic versions of their brands is a potential challenge for the company. The consolidation being witnessed in the industry might reduce the contract brewing capacity available to the firm. Approximately 96% of the beer produced by the company is sold in the USA. Most of the alcohol beverages are sold to independent beer distributors who in turn distribute to retailer and finally to drinkers. The company faces distribution risk as the distribution agreements can be terminated by distributors on short notice. The future growth of the company depends upon its ability to adapt to the challenges of the changing competitive environment. The increased demand for the products may lead to challenges such as production and supply constraints. The production constraints result from canning and variety pack limitations. The company is increasingly depending on third party-owned breweries to meet demand as evident from the fact that the percentage of production volume at its own breweries has decreased from over 90% in 2017 to approximately 56% by 2021. The demand for packaging materials in the beverage industry has led to shortage of capacity. The supply constraints have impacted the company's production schedules and increased costs as the company had to depend on expensive suppliers. Boston Beer enters into limited term supply agreements with certain vendors to receive preferential pricing. Boston Beer purchases a significant portion of the ingredients for beverages such as flavorings, malt, hops, and apples from a limited number of foreign and domestic suppliers. This creates foreign exchange risk exposure for the company. Boston Beer's businesses are highly regulated by federal, state, and local laws and regulations related to licensing requirements, trade and pricing practices, and advertising. Tax and environmental changes or failure to comply with existing regulations could have adverse effect on the financial condition of the company.

ESG Initiatives

The company follows ESG reporting frameworks such as Global Reporting Initiative (GRI) and Sustainability Accounting Standard Board (SASB). The Board of Directors through the nominating/governance committee is responsible for guiding sustainability strategy and initiatives. In 2021, the company made three structural changes such as formation of an executive sustainability committee, appointment of senior manager of sustainability, and establishment of sustainability network group of 200 coworkers. The company through its Rehoboth Beach restaurant is involved in local habitat restoration projects such as living shorelines and oyster gardening to recover the oyster shells and redistribute them into the Delaware Island Bays. In 2017, the company joined the Surfrider Foundation Ocean Restaurants Program to cut out single-use plastics and reduce the impact of restaurant operations on the ocean waters. All coworkers of the company are trained for the Code of Business Conduct and Ethics and are provided with an anonymous hotline to report violations and grievances and maintain regular compliance oversight. The legal team is responsible for legal compliance in matters related to regulatory securities, marketing, employment law, and contractual compliance. The risk management team is involved in assessing enterprise risks such as risks of fraud, corruption, and unethical behavior. Boston Beer undertakes extensive tests, tastings, and evaluations to ensure that each beverage batch conforms to high standards. The company provides comprehensive companywide supply chain quality awareness training courses in line with Food and Drug Administration standards and protocols related to food allergens, hazard analysis for safety, glass and brittle plastic, food defense, and good manufacturing practices. Through the creation of Boston Beer Cybersecurity team, the company has implemented robust software and services to defend against external threats which included approximately 30,000 suspicious emails per month. The company has comanufacturing agreements to produce Twisted Tea and Truly products which enabled the company to produce products closer to its distributors and cut down transportation costs and emissions. The company is also strategizing plans to reduce outsourced warehouse footprint, outsource variety packing to third-party warehouses, and source empty cans from plants which are closer to the production locations. With respect to environmental sustainability, the company is in the process of integrating new data collection and management platform to curate and track KPI metrics such as purchased electricity, fuel, and water. In its two largest production breweries, the company has invested in CO_2 recovery systems which allows for the capture and reuse of CO_2 from the fermentation process for carbonation and other brewery-related processes. This mechanism facilitates the company to recover and reuse more than 50% of the total CO_2 needs. For water conservation stewardship, the largest production breweries of the company have unique water usage targets for water-used-to-barrels-produced ratios based on the site size, product lines, and local water utility infrastructure. With respect to social initiatives, the company has an 80% participation rate in the annual coworker engagement survey. Brewing Change is the company's multiyear strategy for promoting programs for establishment of a baseline directed toward diversity, equity, and inclusion (DEI). By 2021, the company increased hiring of candidates from traditionally underrepresented groups from 17% to 20%. In 2021, the company partnered with Modern Health to expand access to mental health care through coaches and therapist. The company has contributed over $2.34 million to support programs such as Brewing the American Dream (BTAD) and the Dogfish Head's Beer & Benevolence program in year 2021. Since 2008, approximately 13,000 small business owners accessed more than $74 million in food and beverage loans through the support of BTAD. Over 9000 jobs were created through BTAD since 2008. In 2021, approximately $500,000 were invested in nearly 100 nonprofit organizations through Dogfish Head's Beer & Benevolence program.

Stock Performance Analysis

This section analyzes the stock performance of Boston Beer in comparison to market index S&P 500 Beverage Index for the recent 5 years. Boston Beer was trading at $189.05 on March 1, 2018. By February 1, 2023, the stock price increased by 2.13 times to trade at $402.98. The total cumulative monthly return for Boston Beer stock was 131% compared to the cumulative returns of 41% for market index S&P 500 Beverages Index during the period March 2018–Jan 2023. The average yearly return for Boston Beer was 27% compared to 8% returns accounted by market index S&P 500 Beverage Index during the above period. The data source is Yahoo Finance.

Table 1 shows the holding period return for the stock in comparison to the market index during the recent 5 years. The holding period is assumed to be 1-year period.

In terms of holding period returns, the Boston Beer stock had best performance in the year 2020 compared to the market index S&P 500 Beverages Index.

Table 2 analyzes the book value and market value of equity of Boston Beer in millions of dollars during the period 2018–2022. The data source is annual report and gurufocus.com.

Table 1 Holding period return

Year	Boston Beer	S&P 500 Beverages Index	Excess returns
2018	32%	3%	29%
2019	14%	23%	−9%
2020	147%	1%	147%
2021	−59%	24%	−83%
2022	1%	6%	−5%

Table 2 Book and market value of equity

Year	2017	2018	2019	2020	2021
Book value of equity	423.52	460.32	735.64	956.97	983.41
Market value of equity	2220.79	2769.32	4550.64	12113.14	6188.38
BV as percent of MV	19.1%	16.6%	16.2%	7.9%	15.9%

Table 3 Financial highlights

	(In millions of dollars)				
Financial highlights	2017	2018	2019	2020	2021
Total assets	569.62	639.85	1054.06	1378.83	1386.78
Short-term investments	65.64	108.40	36.67	162.28	26.85
Total equity	423.52	460.32	735.64	956.97	983.41
Total revenue	862.99	995.65	1249.82	1736.43	2057.62
Total operating expenses	331.78	395.71	468.34	565.78	740.62
Net income	99.05	92.66	110.04	191.96	14.55
Market cap	2220.79	2769.32	4550.64	12113.14	6188.38
Enterprise value	2155.16	2660.92	4573.07	12017.26	6223.01

Table 4 Performance indicators

Ratios	2017	2018	2019	2020	2021
Net margin%	11.48	9.31	8.8	11.05	0.71
ROE%	22.77	20.97	18.4	22.68	1.5
ROA%	16.71	15.32	12.99	15.78	1.05
DER			0.08	0.07	0.06

The average book value of equity as percent of market value of equity during the period 2017–2021 was approximately 12%. In the year 2020, the market value of equity was 12.66 times that of the book value of equity.

Table 3 gives the financial highlights of Boston Beer during the period 2017–2021. The values are given in millions of dollars.

On an average basis, the total assets and total equity increased by 27% and 25% respectively during the time period 2017–2021. The total cash investments and net income growth rate have been highly fluctuating during the above period. The net income declined drastically in the year 2021. The average growth rate of net income during the period 2017–2020 was 29%. The average growth rate of revenues during the period 2017–2021 was 25%. The total operating expenses increased by 22% on an average basis. The market capitalization and enterprise value increased by 52% on an average basis during the period 2017–2021.

Table 4 gives the profitability and leverage measures of the firm during the period 2017–2021.

The profitability position of Boston Beer was low in the year 2021 compared to the previous years. The company is low levered and the debt equity ratio has been declining indicating stability in leverage. The average net margin, ROE, and ROA

Table 5 Economic value

Year	2019	2020
Profit before income tax	144.37	244.23
Income tax	34.33	52.27
Net operating profit after tax (NOPAT)	110.04	191.96
Stockholder equity	735.64	956.97
Long-term debt		
Total capital employed	735.64	956.97
WACC	5.71%	4.98%
Capital charge	42.01	47.66
Economic value	68.03	144.31

for Boston Beer were 8.27%, 17.26%, and 12.37% respectively during the period 2017–2021. The average debt equity ratio for the firm was 0.07.

Table 5 illustrates the estimation of the economic value of Boston Beer during the year 2019 and 2020. The values are given in millions of dollars.

The economic value has improved from $68.03 million in 2019 to $144.31 million in 2020.

References

1. Boston Beer Annual Report 2021
2. Boston Beer ESG Report 2022
3. http://www.bostonbeer.com/

Case 47 Emergent BioSolutions

Emergent BioSolutions is a global life sciences company involved in providing innovative and responsive solutions for public health threats for nearly 25 years. Emergent BioSolutions manufactures a pipeline of innovative vaccines and therapeutics worldwide. Emergent was established as a private company with a single product and a single location. Over the years, Emergent has transformed itself into a flourishing global company.

The portfolio of solutions provided by Emergent consists of a product portfolio, product development portfolio, and CDMO services portfolio. The public health threats addressed by Emergent can be categorized into five categories of (1) chemical, biological, radiological, nuclear, and explosives (CBRNE), (2) emerging infectious diseases (EID), (3) travel health, (4) public health crisis, and (5) acute, emergency, and community care. The company employs approximately 2400 people as of the year 2021.

Business Segment

The business segment consists of the Government Medical Countermeasures (MCM), the commercial business line, and the CDMO business line. The R&D segment is centralized and has adopted an enterprise-wide governance approach to manage its portfolio of R&D projects. The MCM business line of Emergent focuses on procurement and sale of MCM products and procured product to domestic and international government and nongovernmental organizations in different regions of the world. The commercial line is involved in the sale of nasal spray (naloxone HCI) and travelers' vaccines (Vaxchora® and Vivotif®). The nasal spray is sold commercially through physician-directed or standing order prescriptions at retail pharmacies and to the state and local governments. The travelers' vaccines are primarily sold to private travel clinics, retail pharmacies, and integrated hospital networks. The portfolio of CDMO services delivers "molecule-to-market" offering by using three diverse technology platforms for mammalian, microbial, viral, and plasma segment.

© The Author(s), under exclusive license to Springer Nature Switzerland AG 2024

B. R. Kumar, *Rising Stars*, Management for Professionals,
https://doi.org/10.1007/978-3-031-50032-9_47

The services offered by CDMO can be segregated into development service, drug molecule manufacturing, and drug product manufacturing. All the three phases of the drug development life cycle are supported by CDMO services. The CDMO services are offered to biotechnology and pharmaceutical segment clients, government entities, and nongovernmental organizations (NGOs). The company has over 60 active CDMO customers.

Table 1 lists the primary product and product candidates in its three lines of business segments.

The company had revenues of $1.79 billion in the year 2021. In 2021, the company delivered more than 130 million dose equivalents of COVID-19 vaccine.

Table 2 lists the major milestones of the company.

Growth Strategy

The recent 5-year strategic plan 2020–2024 gives emphasis on leveraging five core competencies which the firm has developed for various segments of the PHT market over a span of 23 years. Emergent BioSolutions focuses on building leadership position in the management of public health threats by strengthening the portfolios of MCMs, travel health, and CDMO services. The company has well-defined strategy in place to leverage its specialized government relations and contracting operations for negotiation of its long-term profitable procurement and development agreements for sustainable business. The company has undertaken a number of mergers and acquisition to expand into new markets and provide a differentiated R&D pipeline. The company has the strategic objective to acquire accretive or clinical stage assets and to form partnerships. The acquisition of Trubion Pharmaceuticals provided Emergent with multiple, advanced stage candidates in the key disease areas of oncology and autoimmunity along with access to novel and versatile protein therapeutic platforms. In 2014, Cangene Corporation was acquired for $222 million in cash. The acquisition was aimed to expand Emergent' s biodefense product portfolio by adding marketed therapeutics which are offered to hospitals and specialty clinics through an established commercial infrastructure. In 2017, the company acquired raxibacumab, a fully human monoclonal antibody from GlaxoSmithKline. In 2018, Emergent BioSolutions acquired PaxVax which focused on development, manufacture, and commercialization of specialty vaccines against infectious diseases. The deal was valued at $270 million. Emergent added two revenue-generating FDA-licensed vaccines for cholera and typhoid and established international manufacturing footprint through this acquisition.

BioSolutions also focuses on strengthening its R&D portfolio by expansion and advancement of its pipeline of vaccines and therapeutic product candidates. These R&D investments are funded by the company by investing its own funds and securing government contracts, grants, and other non-dilutive funding. The company also focuses on building scalable capabilities by investments in infrastructure, internal governance, and capabilities to achieve economies of scale. The focus is on new capital investments for development of manufacturing facilities,

Table 1 Primary product and product candidates

Government-MCM—Products	
Product	Description
ACAM2000®, (smallpox (Vaccinia) Vaccine, Live)	Smallpox vaccine is licensed by the FDA and is the primary smallpox vaccine designated for use in a bioterrorism emergency
Anthrasil®	The only polyclonal antibody therapeutic licensed by the FDA and Health Canada for the treatment of inhalational anthrax
BAT®	The only equine plasma antitoxin licensed by the FDA and Health Canada for the treatment of all seven botulinum neurotoxin serotypes
BioThrax®	BioThrax is the only vaccine licensed by the FDA for pre-exposure prophylaxis of anthrax disease in persons at high risk of exposure
Raxibacumab injection	A fully human monoclonal antibody licensed by the FDA for the treatment and prophylaxis of inhalational anthrax due to Bacillus anthracis
RSDL®	The only medical device cleared by the FDA that is intended to remove or neutralize chemical warfare agents from the skin
Trobigard®	This auto-injector is used for the emergency treatment of exposure to nerve agents or toxic organophosphates. Approved by Belgian Health Authority
VIGIV CNJ-016 ®	It is the only polyclonal antibody therapeutic licensed by the FDA and Health Canada to address certain complications from replicating virus smallpox vaccination
Commercial products	
NARCAN®(naloxone HCl) Nasal Spray	Used for emergency treatment of known or suspected opioid overdose as manifested by respiratory and/or central nervous system depression
Vaxchora® (Cholera Vaccine, Live, Oral)	A live attenuated cholera vaccine for oral administration and the first vaccine approved by the FDA for the prevention of cholera infection
Vivotif® (Typhoid Vaccine Live Oral Ty21a)	A live attenuated vaccine for oral administration to prevent typhoid fever
Product candidates	
AP003	Being developed for the emergency treatment of a known or suspected opioid overdose, as manifested by respiratory and/or central nervous system depression
AP007	This injectable is being developed for the treatment of opioid use disorder
AV7909	Anthrax vaccine product candidate
CGRD-001	Auto-injector is being developed for treatment of poisoning by organophosphorus nerve agents. Aimed for protection of soldiers and first responders
CHIKV VLP	Chikungunya virus (CHIKV) vaccine candidate
COVID-HIG	Fully human polyclonal antibody therapeutic product candidate made from plasma

(continued)

Table 1 (continued)

Government-MCM—Products	
Product	Description
EGRD-001	Used for treatment of status epilepticus and severe recurrent convulsive seizures caused by nerve agent poisoning
SIAN	An antidote candidate for initial treatment of acute poisoning of cyanide
UniFlu	A universal influenza vaccine candidate based on a nanoparticle vaccine

Source: Emergent BioSolutions Annual Report 2021, page 5–12

Table 2 Milestones[a]

Period	Event
1998	Partnered with US government to supply anthrax vaccine
2001	Renovated Lansing manufacturing facility approved by the FDA
2002	Distribution of BioThrax (anthrax vaccine) approved by the FDA
2003–2006	Acquisition of Antex Biologics, Microscience Ltd, and Vivacs GmbH
2006	Investment of $80 million for additional state of industry vaccine manufacturing facility. Emergent BioSolutions stock listed on NYSE
2007	Multiyear contract for BioThrax given by the US government
2008	Anthrax Vaccine adsorbed funded by Biomedical Advanced Research and Development Authority to develop the next-generation anthrax vaccine
2009	BioThrax approved by the FDA for a five-dose intramuscular administration
2010	Trubion Pharmaceuticals is acquired, thereby extending the company portfolio to include novel protein therapeutics in oncology segment
2011–2013	BioThrax license gets approval in India, Germany, and Singapore. Enters chemical countermeasure market and device business by acquiring reactive skin decontamination lotion kit product
2014	Cangene Corporation is acquired. This acquisition broadened the portfolio of government-procured countermeasures and facilitated the establishment of hyperimmune platform for Emergent's mobile manufacturing unit
2015	Rights to auto-injector technology are acquired. The company acquires antibacterial and antiviral platforms to develop broad-based antimicrobials
2017	Small pox vaccine is acquired. Acquires raxibacumab, a fully monoclonal antibody approved by the FDA for treatment and prophylaxis of inhalational anthrax
2018	BioThrax licensure approved in France, Italy, the Netherlands, Poland, and the UK. Investment of $50 million in Camden facility, Baltimore, is undertaken. Acquisition of PaxVax for FDA-licensed travelers' vaccine. Adapt Pharma is acquired, thereby diversifying into commercial markets with addition of nasal spray
2019	Market authorization is granted in five EU countries for Typhoid Vaccine Live Oral. Contract worth $535 million awarded by HHS to deliver vaccinia immune globulin. Ten-year contract awarded by HHS to deliver small pox vaccine into strategic national stockpile

Source: Company Website

[a]https://www.emergentbiosolutions.com/about-us/

strengthening global sales, and procurement models along with technology upgradation.

Risk Factors

The company's business faces risk in terms of reduced demand for or funding for procurement of product candidates and stoppage of funding for USG procurement and development contracts. The company faces manufacturing risks such as compliance risk, disruption or damage of manufacturing facility, and potential liabilities for operations due to use of hazardous materials, chemicals, and microorganisms such as bacteria and viruses. There are a number of product development and commercialization risks which would impact the business of the company. The clinical trials of product candidates are time-consuming, are expensive in nature, and have uncertain outcomes. Competitive and political risks could impact the business and financial condition. Private and public sector competition exists for the development and commercialization of pharmaceutical products. Products such as NARCAN face generic competition and are subject to additional branded and generic competition. Regulatory and compliance risks could impact the business and financial conditions of the company. Failure to comply with complex laws and regulations related to government contracts is a potential risk factor for the company. Failure to comply with healthcare laws will result in severe penalties. Risks arise due to reliance on third parties. The loss of sole source suppliers or nonperformance of third parties as contractually required will affect the operations of the company. Legal and reputational risk may impact the business and financial condition of the firm. Emergent faces risks related to strategic acquisitions and collaboration in terms of synergy realization and integration challenges. Emergent BioSolutions faces government contracting risks as a substantial portion of revenues is derived from US government procurement of AV7909, ACAM2000, and BioThrax. If the government demand for and/or funding for procurement is substantially reduced, then the company's financial condition would be adversely affected.

ESG Initiatives

ESG strategy is guided by the Task Force on Climate-Related Financial Disclosures (TCFD) framework as well as the Sustainability Accounting Standards Board's (SASB) standards which are focused on the healthcare, biotechnology, and pharmaceutical industries. The special committee on manufacturing and quality oversight, all composed of independent directors, oversees all aspects of manufacturing and quality operations which include quality systems, compliance with Current Good Manufacturing Practices (CGMPs), medical device Quality System Regulations (QSRs), and other legal and regulatory requirements. In 2022, the company hired a new executive vice president role with responsibility for quality, ethics, and compliance. Pre-clinical safety and efficacy testing is performed on the product candidates before the initial clinical trials. All medical products are reviewed by a multidisciplinary committee which is led by the global head of safety and pharmacovigilance. The policy is such that employees, contractors, consultants, and third parties are required to report adverse events and product complaints no later than 24 h following the individual's first knowledge. Suppliers are managed through supply agreements, quality agreements, periodic audits, supplier change notifications, and performance monitoring. The supplier diversity program involving small businesses addresses the broader diversity, equity, and inclusion strategy of the company. The company has provided reliable supply of high-quality medical countermeasures (MCMs) such as anthrax, smallpox vaccines, and therapeutics to US government for years. The company has also collaboration on clinical research for Ebola and Zika vaccines. In 2021, the company supplied more than 10 million doses of NARCAN® Nasal Spray and collaborated with opioid overdose awareness organizations to launch the Reverse the Silence campaign. The board and management conducted a rigorous enterprise risk assessment to identify strategic and operational risks. As part of the COVID-19 response efforts, Emergent BioSolutions donated $100,000 to the CDC Foundation to support its Emergency Response Fund for Coronavirus SOS Program.

Stock Performance

The following section analyzes the stock performance of Emergent BioSolutions in comparison with market index Nasdaq Biotechnology Index (NBI) during the recent 5-year period March 2018–February 2023. The stock was trading at $52.65 on March 1, 2018. By February 1, 2023, the stock price declined to $13.97. The total cumulative monthly return for the BioSolutions stock was −68% compared to 36% returns accounted by Nasdaq Biotechnology Index during the period March 2018–February 2023. The average yearly return for Emergent BioSolutions was −14% compared to 7% registered by market index NBI. The data is taken from Yahoo Finance.

Table 3 gives the holding period return for the Emergent BioSolutions stock and market index NBI for the period 2018–2022. The holding period is assumed to be 1-year period.

The stock has outperformed the market index in the years 2018 and 2020.

Table 3 Holding period return

Year	Emergent BioSolutions	Nasdaq Biotech Index	Excess returns
2018	18%	3%	16%
2019	−6%	1%	−6%
2020	82%	41%	41%
2021	−51%	−16%	−36%
2022	−68%	9%	−77%

Table 4 Book and market value of equity

Year	2017	2018	2019	2020	2021
Book value of equity	912.3	1010.9	1088.5	1447	1619
Market value of equity	2295.87	3035.14	2789.22	4757.76	2230.01
BV as percent of MV	39.7%	33.3%	39.0%	30.4%	72.6%

Table 5 Financial highlights

	(In millions of dollars)				
Financial highlights	2017	2018	2019	2020	2021
Total assets	1070.2	2229.4	2327.3	2883.2	2959
Short-term investments	178.3	112.2	167.8	621.3	576.1
Total equity	912.3	1010.9	1088.5	1447	1619
Total revenue	560.9	782.4	1106	1555.4	1792.7
Total operating expenses	248.9	370.3	558.4	597.6	640.9
Net income	82.6	62.7	54.5	305.1	230.9
Market capitalization	2295.87	3035.14	2789.22	4757.76	2230.01
Enterprise value	2131.07	3717.54	3432.72	5011.26	2494.91

Table 6 Performance indicators

Ratios	2017	2018	2019	2020	2021
Net margin%	14.73	8.01	4.93	19.62	12.88
ROE%	10.95	6.52	5.19	24.07	15.06
ROA%	8.1	3.8	2.39	11.71	7.9
DER	0.02	0.79	0.75	0.61	0.52

Table 4 gives the book value and market value of equity of Emergent BioSolutions for the period 2017–2021. The values are given in millions of dollars.

The average book value as percent of market value of equity was 51.5% during the period 2017–2021.

Table 5 gives the financial and operational highlights of Emergent BioSolutions during the period 2017–2021.

The average growth rate of total assets, short-term investments, and total equity were 35%, 69%, and 16%, respectively. The total revenues increased by 34% on an average basis. The growth rate of net income was highly fluctuating with a growth rate of 460% in the year 2020. The market capitalization and enterprise value increased by 10% and 16%, respectively. The data source is annual reports and gurufocus.com.

Table 6 highlights the performance measures of profitability and leverage ratio of the company during the period 2017–2021.

The average net margin, ROE, and ROA during the period 2017–2021 were 12.03%, 12.36%, and 6.78%, respectively. The average debt equity ratio was 0.54.

Table 7 shows the estimation of economic value of Emergent BioSolutions in 2020 and 2021. The values are given in millions of dollars.

Table 7 Estimation of economic value

Year	2020	2021
Profit before income tax	407.20	314.40
Income tax	102.09	83.50
Net operating profit after tax (NOPAT)	305.11	230.90
Stockholder equity	1447.00	1619.00
Long-term debt	841	809
Total capital employed	2288	2428
WACC	6.99%	5.65%
Capital charge	159.93	137.18
Economic value	145.18	93.71

References

1. https://www.emergentbiosolutions.com/
2. https://investors.emergentbiosolutions.com/
3. https://www.emergentbiosolutions.com/press/news-releases-news-release-details-emergent-biosolutions-completes-acquisition-trubion/
4. https://www.globenewswire.com/en/news-release/2018/10/04/1617201/33240/en/Emergent-BioSolutions-Completes-Acquisition-of-Specialty-Vaccines-Company-PaxVax.html
5. Annual Report 2021
6. ESG Report 2021

Case 48 Alarm.com

Alarm.com was established in the year 2000. It is a leading platform for intelligently connected property which offers a complete suite of cloud-based solutions for smart residential and commercial properties consisting of interactive security, video monitoring, intelligent automation, access control, energy management, and wellness solutions. In 2021, the Alarm.com platforms processed more than 200 billion data points which were generated by over 100 million connected devices. The solutions offered by Alarm.com are delivered through a well-established network of over 10,900 trusted service providers. The company receives license revenue from service provider partners for its Software-as-a-Service or Saas. These service partners resell these services and pay Alarm.com monthly fees. The company also receives revenues through the sale of its hardware products such as video cameras, video recorders, gunshot detection sensors, gateway modules, and smart thermostats. The contracts between the company and service providers have an initial term of 1 year with subsequent renewal every year.

The company has generated revenues of $502.4 million, $618 million, and $749 million during the years 2019, 2020, and 2021, respectively. The SaaS and license revenue amounted to $337.4 million, $393.3 million, and $460.4 million in the years 2019, 2020, and 2021, respectively, which represented a compound annual growth rate of 16.8%. The company had 1500 full-time employees of which 837 were in R&D segment as of December 2021.

Solutions and Platforms

The solutions offered by Alarm.com are designed for the efficiency and technology adaption of residential and commercial properties in the connected property market sector. The market environment includes residential and commercial property owners, hardware partners, and service partners. The property owners subscribe to the services offered by Alarm.com. The hardware partners manufacture devices for

© The Author(s), under exclusive license to Springer Nature Switzerland AG 2024
B. R. Kumar, *Rising Stars*, Management for Professionals,
https://doi.org/10.1007/978-3-031-50032-9_48

integration with the company's interactive platform. The service provider partners install and maintain the solutions of the company.

Subscriber Solutions

Interactive Security

The interactive security system is used by smart home and business subscribers. Subscribers are provided with the opportunity to connect to the services offered by Alarm.com to control and monitor their security systems and IoT devices such as door locks, garage doors, thermostats, and video cameras through Alarm.com's family of mobile apps, websites, and engagement platforms. The engagement platforms such as voice control are offered through Siri Shortcuts, Amazon Echo and Google Home, Apple Watch, and TV applications such as Apple TV and Amazon Fire TV. The systems are characterized by real-time alerts and always-on monitoring. The notifications for any type of system event are delivered through push notifications, short message service, or email based on subscriber's preferences. The alarm transmission takes place from monitored properties through the cloud platforms to over 1000 third-party central monitoring stations with live operators throughout the day to initiate emergency responses. Smart signal enhances the overall value of the professional monitoring services associated with Alarm.com systems. Flex IO is a versatile wireless device installation that creates awareness using new technological applications across assets in any location such as backyard gate, detached garage, boat, tractor, or lawn mower. Flex IO triggers activity notifications and video recordings to subscribers when an activity is detected or an asset is moved. The battery-powered cellular Connected Car solution facilitates subscribers to track their vehicle location, view engine status, and analyze fuel efficiency using the Alarm.com mobile app. The Connected Car solution provides more responsive alerts and intelligent automation than standalone solutions. The intelligent technology-based wellness solution monitors the quality of daily wellness through a suite of connected sensors and devices.

Video Monitoring and Video Analytics

Alarm.com provides indoor and outdoor video cameras for residential and commercial properties. The company also offers video management software and cameras for enterprise commercial applications through its OpenEye business. Alarm.com also offers a doorbell video camera solution which supports two-way audio communication with people at the door. The video monitoring solution offers capabilities such as video analytics, video doorbell, intelligent integration, live streaming, secure cloud storage, and video alerts. The video analytics engines offer object classification and tracking technology which can differentiate between humans, animals, and vehicles and also determine the direction and duration of activity. Alarm.com offers a full range of video doorbell options. Alarm.com's video surveillance solution facilitates intelligent integration with devices and sensors installed in the property.

Intelligent Automation and Energy Management

The intelligent automation and energy management solution of Alarm.com focuses on enhanced monitoring and control of large ecosystem of connected devices such as thermostats, lights, locks, and power meters. The capabilities offered by this solution include scenes, video analytics, smart thermostat schedules, responsive savings, precision comfort, energy usage monitoring, HVAC monitoring services, places feature, demand response programs, and whole home water safety solutions. The customizable scenes button offered by Alarm.com can adjust multiple devices in the property using a single command. For example, a person can leave the house arming the security system, lock the front door, close the garage door, and adjust the thermostat with a single command. The robust set of automation rules in video analytics enables subscribers to customize automations for response when a certain activity is detected by the video monitoring solution. The Places feature utilizes a phone's geo location to determine when to notify a subscriber of specific system conditions or automatically adjust system settings.

Commercial Solutions

Alarm.com offers a full range of commercial security services targeted toward small, medium, and enterprise scale business. The security solution, Alarm.com for Business, combines intelligent intrusion detection, video surveillance, access control, and energy management into a single solution through Alarm.com's app and online interfaces. The OpenEye enterprise commercial video management solution complements the Alarm.com for Business platform. The key benefits of the OpenEye solution are in terms of features such as intelligent cloud architecture, enterprise level capabilities, large-scale video deployments, and CloudConnect. CloudConnect is a two-way integration between the OpenEye Cloud Video Platform and the Alarm.com for Business platform which directly connect event data from intrusion sensors and access control readers with Open Eye's VSaaS offering.

Service Provider Solutions

Alarm.com provides a comprehensive suite of enterprise grade business management solutions for the service provider partners. The permission-based online portal offers account management, sales, marketing, training, and support tools. The service dashboard-based partner services platform provides a unified interface which displays key operational and customer experience dimensions such as technician performance, system reliability, and customer engagement metrics. Alarm.com supports end-to-end process for deployment and management of solutions with tools to make installation and support efficient. These tools include mobile tech application and remote toolkit, video health reports, and smart gateway. The powerful business intelligence tools provide service providers with crucial insights into the performance of their Alarm.com subscriber account base.

Home Builder Program of Alarm.com consists of hardware and service plans designed to facilitate partnerships between home builders and the company's service provider partners.

Hardware and Manufacturing

The company is involved in the design and manufacture of different types of hardware such as cellular communication modules, flex IO, image sensor, video cameras, smart thermostat, and smart water valve.

Growth Strategy

The company is a pioneer in the intelligently connected property market and focuses on making investments in innovative research and development. As a result of the technologically competitive differentiated strategy adopted, the company has 597 issued patents as of December 31, 2021.

The cloud-based platforms provided by Alarm.com provide subscribers with a single point of integrated control across a diverse ecosystem of IoT devices. The platform offers a highly scalable data analytics engine with features and capabilities such as aggregate real-time, multi-point data with respect to property activity and system status. The company is a reliable technology provider.

The company focuses on driving SaaS and license revenue growth along with expanding the network of service provider partners. The company leverages its position as a trusted provider by enabling service provider partners to upgrade their legacy security customers to the connected property solutions. The company invests heavily to add additional innovative offerings and broaden its suite of solutions. The company focuses on the growth of its international subscribers in existing markets and expanding to additional markets. Currently, the products of the company are available in approximately 40 countries outside of North America. The company aims to strengthen its presence in the commercial market segment. The company further has plans for channel expansion by developing partnerships with property management companies, utility firms, HVAC installers, and other service companies for expanding opportunities in residential and commercial property sector. The residential subscribers are owners of single-family homes, whereas the commercial subscribers include retail businesses, restaurants, educational institutions, and professional establishments. According to research data published by Strategy Analytics 2021, the global installed base for smart home devices is estimated to grow at a 22.7% compound annual growth during the period 2021–2025. The company focuses on multi-tenant SaaS platform architecture to facilitate rapid innovation in a scalable environment. Cybersecurity is a crucial part of the company's business. The company focuses on acquisitions of assets as a part of its growth strategy. In 2017, Alarm.com acquired certain assets of ObjectVideo consisting of products, technology portfolio, and engineering team. ObjectVideo is a pioneer in the fields of video analytics and computer vision. In the same year, the firm acquired certain assets related to the Connect business unit of Icontrol Networks, Inc., which provides a custom, on-premise interactive security and home automation platform. In 2019, the company acquired 85% stockholding of Open Eye which provides managed video surveillance solutions for the enterprise commercial market. In 2020, the company acquired Shooter Detection System which is a provider of an indoor gunshot detection solution which alerts people against active shooter threat.

Competitors

The competitors include providers of technology platforms for the connected property like Alula, Avigilon Corporation, Brivo Inc., Digital Monitoring Products Inc., Eagle Eye Networks Inc., and Honeywell International Inc. These firms also sell solutions to service providers, cable operators, technology retailers, and residential and commercial automation providers. The company also competes with interactive monitored security solutions providers such as Abode Systems, Arlo Technologies, Cove Smart, and Scout Security Inc. The service provider partners compete with companies such as Comcast Cable Communications, Rogers Communications, and providers of point products such a Google Inc.'s Nest Labs. Amazon.com offers Amazon Home Services security packages with bundled equipment and professional installation.

ESG Initiatives

Alarm.com contributes toward environmental sustainability by developing solutions which can reduce energy waste and facilitate water conservation. These initiatives include the development of demand response programs, smart thermostats, energy management solutions, smart water valve meter device, and advanced functionality within Alarm.com applications. The company's demand response programs manage over 700,000 connected devices to realize clean energy targets for 60 energy utilities in North America. The Smart Water Valve + Meter device is part of the comprehensive water management solution of the company. In 2021, the company created a Sustainability Team for integration of sustainability activities in the company. The company has improved the packaging of the hardware by switching to recyclable materials and eliminating polyethylene bags from user guides. With respect to social initiatives, the company has identified diversity ambassadors to foster communication with respect to diversity and inclusion initiatives with the focus on training to improve team performance. The Nominating and Corporate Governance Committee of Board of Directors oversees the firm's corporate governance mechanism and strategies.

Risk Factors

The COVID-19 pandemic has disrupted the firm's hardware supply chain, increased lead times, and shipping delays and caused restriction on service providers to offer services to residential and commercial property owners. The future profitability depends on different factors such as macroeconomic conditions, the product mix sold, and relative sales of platforms and solutions. The company faces challenges related to retaining and providing incentives to the service provider partners who market, sell, install, and support platforms and solutions. The success of the business depends on the ability of hardware vendors to manufacture high-quality products and supply of adequate components and products to satisfy the demand. The business results also depend on the timing and success of new solution and product introduction, upgrades by competitors, and entrance of new competitors. The company also faces risks in terms of problems related to security, privacy, integrity, reliability, and compatibility of its solutions.

Stock Performance

The following section analyzes the stock returns for Alarm.com in comparison to the market index Nasdaq Composite for the recent 5-year period. Alarm.com stock was trading at $37.74 on March 1, 2018. By February 1, 2023, the stock price increased by 1.47 times to trade at $55.54. The total cumulative monthly returns for Alarm stock were 82%, while for the market index Nasdaq Composite, the cumulative monthly return was 64% during the 5-year period March 2018–February 2023. The average yearly return for Alarm stock and Nasdaq Composite was 17% and 13%, respectively, during the above 5-year period. The stock data is sourced from Yahoo Finance.

Table 1 shows the holding period return for the Alarm stock and market index Nasdaq Composite for the 5-year period 2018–2022. The holding period is assumed to be 1-year period.

Alarm.com outperformed the market index Nasdaq Composite in the years 2018 and 2020 with excess returns of 64% and 40%, respectively.

Table 2 shows the market value and book value of equity of the company in millions of dollars during the period 2017–2021.

The average book value as percent of market value was 12% during the period 2017–2021. In 2020, the market value was 10.70 times of the book value of the firm.

Table 1 Holding period return

Year	Alarm.com	Nasdaq Composite	Excess returns
2018	67%	3%	64%
2019	−33%	21%	−55%
2020	93%	53%	40%
2021	−15%	8%	−23%
2022	−19%	−16%	−3%

Table 2 Book value and market value of equity

Year	2017	2018	2019	2020	2021
Book value of equity	232.83	277.59	366.86	478.44	626.06
Market value of equity	1781.89	2495.06	2092.67	5119.08	4262.5
BV as percent of MV	13.1%	11.1%	17.5%	9.3%	14.7%

Table 3 Financial highlights

	(In millions of dollars)				
Financial highlights	2017	2018	2019	2020	2021
Total assets	371.64	440.99	557.8	731.69	1232.02
Short-term investments	96.33	146.06	119.63	253.46	710.62
Total equity	232.83	277.59	366.86	478.44	626.06
Total revenue	338.94	420.49	502.36	618	748.97
Total operating expenses	189.38	262.58	268.35	334.28	381.5
Net income	29.25	21.52	53.53	77.85	52.26
Market capitalization	1781.89	2495.06	2092.67	5119.08	4262.5
Enterprise value	1756.56	2415.99	2092.13	5033.98	4033.03

Table 4 Performance measures

Ratios	2017	2018	2019	2020	2021
Net margin%	8.63	5.12	10.66	12.6	6.98
ROE%	13.8	8.43	16.91	18.91	9.67
ROA%	9.24	5.3	10.72	12.08	5.32
DER	0.31	0.24	0.3	0.34	0.76

Operating Performance

Table 3 gives the financial highlights of the company during the period 2017–2021.

The data for analysis is taken from annual reports and gurufocus.com. The average growth rate of total assets, short-term investments, and total equity were 36%, 81%, and 28% during the 5-year period 2017–2021. The revenues and net income grew by 22% and 34%, respectively, on average. The total operating expenses increased by 20% during the above period. The market capitalization and enterprise value increased by 38% and 36%, respectively.

Table 4 shows the profitability ratios and leverage performance of the company during the period 2017–2021.

The average net margin, ROE, and ROA were 8.79%, 13.54%, and 8.53%, respectively, during the 5-year period. The average debt equity ratio was 0.39.

References

1. https://investors.alarm.com/investor-overview/default.aspx
2. Annual Report 2021

Case 49 StoneX

StoneX is a global financial services network company which provides digital platforms, end-to-end clearing, and execution services for connecting companies, traders, and investors to the global market ecosystem. FCStone had its origin in the year 1924 when its predecessor Saul Stone & Company was established by a door-to-door egg wholesaler. In 1930, Saul Stone and Company became one of the first clearing members of the Chicago Mercantile Exchange. In 1978, Farmers Commodities Corporation (FCC) is established for the conduct of the grain hedging brokerage services. In 1981, International Assets is established as international boutique brokerage firm. In 1994, International Assets was listed on NASDAQ. In 2000, FCC acquires Saul Stone and Company to become one of the nation's largest commercial grain brokerage. In 2009, International Assets Holding Corporation and FCStone Group, Inc., merged to form StoneX.

The subsidiaries of StoneX connect clients to the global markets' ecosystem with institutional grade market access, end-to-end clearing, and execution. The company earns revenue through client activity over its network involving commissions and spreads on trades and other transactions, fees for access to market intelligence, and interest earned on customer deposits. The company offers vertically integrated product suite. The company is involved in the entire lifecycle of a trade which starts from market expertise and on-the-ground intelligence to best execution and the final stage involves post-trade clearing, custody, and settlement services. The revenue streams are accounted from diversified sources such as asset class, client type, and earning commissions. The company serves more than 54,000 commercial, institutional, and global payment clients and over 400,000 retail accounts located in more than 180 countries. The company is considered as the third largest independent non-bank futures commission merchant in the USA. The company has $6.2 billion in required client segregated assets as of September 30, 2022. The company is involved in making markets in over 16,000 equities on the NYSE, NASDAQ, OTC markets, and exchange traded funds and over 7000 ADRs, GDRs, and foreign securities. StoneX is one among the eight Category One ring dealing members of the London Metals Exchange. The clients include commercial organizations, broker dealers at

© The Author(s), under exclusive license to Springer Nature Switzerland AG 2024

B. R. Kumar, *Rising Stars*, Management for Professionals,
https://doi.org/10.1007/978-3-031-50032-9_49

regional and national level, asset managers, insurance companies, brokers, institutional and individual investors, professional traders, commercial and investment banks, and other NGOs. The company employs 3600 employees in 21 countries as of September 2022.

Business Activities

The financial network of StoneX connects the clients to over 40 derivative exchanges, 185 foreign exchange markets, and over 18,000 over the counter markets. StoneX provides trade execution services to clients via both high touch service and diverse technology platforms for assets related to listed futures, options on futures, equities, mutual funds, ETFs, foreign currencies, government bonds, and unit investment trusts. StoneX provides efficient clearing on all major future exchanges globally. The company acts as an independent full-service provider of clearing, custody, research, and security-based lending products. The company also facilitates multi-asset prime brokerage, outsourced trading, and clearing services for hedge funds, mutual funds, and family offices. The company provides prime brokerage services in major foreign currency and swap transactions to institutional clients. StoneX also clears foreign exchange transactions. StoneX facilitates clients access to the OTC markets for a broad range of traded commodities, global securities, foreign currencies, and interest rate products. StoneX also provides market making and execution in a variety of financial products which include commodity derivatives, unlisted American Depository Receipts (ADRs) and Global Depository Receipts (GDRs), foreign ordinary shares, and foreign currencies. The company is also an institutional dealer in fixed income securities such as US Treasury, US government agency, agency mortgage-backed, emerging market, convertible, and high yield securities. The company has built a scalable platform to provide end-to-end global payment solutions to banks and commercial businesses, charities, NGOs, and government institutions. The company offers payment services in over 140 currencies. The company provides value-added advisory services and high touch trade execution across a variety of financial markets which include commodities, foreign currencies, interest rates, institutional asset management, and wealth management. The market intelligence platform offers clients with access to deep data and detailed intelligence from markets where the company is engaged in trading. StoneX also offers support to clients for physical trading of precious metals, energy commodities, cotton, coffee, edible oils, and feed products. StoneX operates an asset management business in which the company earns fees, commissions, and other revenues for the management of third-party assets and investment gains or losses on its investments in funds and proprietary accounts. SA Stone Wealth Management Inc., the independent broker arm along with SA Stone Investment Advisors Inc., the investment advisor, offers an integrated platform of technology, wealth, and investment management services to registered representatives.

Growth Strategy

The company focuses on technology and digitization as strategic objectives for growth. The company believes that operational leverage and scalability through technological adoption will result in improvement of margins. The company has speeded up investment in technology over the last 5 years. The company owns FOREX.com and City Index which are the top two retail trading brands in the world. The business model of StoneX offers vertically integrated execution, clearing, and custody facilities. The model combines digital trading platforms and high touch service. The company has minimal exposure to directional market risk. The company receives a significant amount of recurring revenues from interest and fees on \$8.6 billion of client balances. The low correlation across asset classes and markets basically leads to stable top line growth for the company. The focus of the company is on earning 15% return on equity as the key metric for sustainable growth. The company enhances the value of its network by focusing on addition of new products, capabilities, markets, and liquidity venues. The product offerings, marketing strategy, and client experience are integrated through the digitization of its platforms. The focus on highly flexible cost structure enables StoneX to protect its bottom line from the inherent cyclicality of the market. The company is in the process of transforming into a fintech business.

StoneX engages in direct sales initiatives to seek new clients in new geographic locations and expand the services in existing locations. The company focuses on digital marketing and brand advertising through its web and mobile sites such as StoneX.com, FOREX.com, and Cityindex.com to attract new clients. The company attracts new clients through indirect channels such as StoneX Marketing Partners and StoneX.com. The strategy of the company is to utilize a centralized and disciplined process for capital allocation, risk management, and cost control. StoneX focuses on mitigation of market risk exposure to ensure adequate liquidity to maintain daily operations.

Mergers and Acquisitions

StoneX has a disciplined focus on strategic acquisitions to complement organic growth. The company undertakes small to medium-sized acquisitions to expand into new asset classes and client segments. Table 1 lists the major acquisitions undertaken by the company during the period 2000–2022.

Table 2 gives some statistical highlights about StoneX.

Risk Factors

StoneX faces different risk factors which could adversely affect the financial condition and operational results of the company. The revenues generated depend on economic factors such as price levels, volatility in the commodities, securities and

Table 1 Major acquisitions

Year	Event
2000	FCC acquires Saul Stone and Company to become one of the nation's largest commercial grain brokerage firms
2004	International Assets acquires global payments business global currencies
2007	International Assets acquires Gainvest group in South America which specializes in asset management and asset-backed securities. FCStone acquires Chicago-based dairy specialist, Downes-O'Neill
2008	FCStone acquires Nashville-based cotton specialist, Globecot
2009	International Assets Holding Corporation and FCStone Group, Inc., merged
2010	Risk Management Inc., an energy risk management specialist, is acquired by StoneX. The company acquires Hanley Group companies to expand the group's OTC trading business. The company acquires the futures division of Hencorp, a coffee, cocoa, and sugar specialist
2011	Ambrian Commodities Limited ("ACL") is acquired to provide commodities execution capabilities in the key LME market. The Metals Division of MF Global is acquired and the company is upgraded to LME Category One ring dealing membership
2012	The company acquires TRX Futures Ltd., a London-based brokerage and clearing firm dealing with coffee, cocoa, energy, and financial products. The institutional accounts of Tradewire Securities LLC were acquired by the firm
2014	The two UK subsidiaries of the company INTL FCStone Ltd. and INTL Global Currencies Ltd. were consolidated into the parent company
2015	The company acquires the acquisition of G.X. Clarke & Co., an institutional dealer in US government securities, federal agency, and mortgage-backed securities
2016	The company acquires the correspondent securities clearing business and independent wealth management business from Sterne Agee LLC. London-based EMEA oils business of ICAP plc was acquired by the firm to strengthen its global energy space
2018	The SWIFT Service Bureau of PayCommerce acquired by StoneX to expand its global payment portfolio. The company acquires Luxembourg-based Carl Kliem SA. Company acquires coinvest GmbH and European Precious Metal Trading GmbH to focus on the expansion of its retail precious metals portfolio. StoneX acquires the futures and options brokerage business of Singapore-based UOB. Through this acquisition, the company becomes a fully regulated FCM in the Asia-Pacific region
2020	The brokerage businesses of Tellimer Group were acquired by INTL FCStone for expansion into frontier and emerging markets. EncoreFX Inc. was acquired by the company. EncoreFX is involved in the foreign currency exchange risk management and global payment solutions to small and medium-sized businesses. The company acquires Giroxx GmbH and IFCM GmbH to expand its business in Europe. StoneX adds FOREX.com and City Index for retail expansion through the acquisition of GAIN Capital Holdings, Inc. This acquisition enabled the company to add a self-directed mobile platform which focused on high net worth retail and small professional trading clients
2021	Chasing Returns Ltd. is acquired to assist expansion of retail portfolio offerings through utilization of its expertise to analyze trends and decision making. Minority equity stake investment in diversity broker Tigress Financial Partners LLC is made by StoneX
2022	The company acquires Cotton Distributors Inc. to expand its cotton trading and hedging businesses

Source: Annual Report 2022

Table 2 Statistical facts

Highlights	Number
Connection with exchanges	40
Number of OTC products	180,000
Dealing with currencies	140
Institutional, commercial, and payments clients	54,000+
Retail clients	400,000+
Client assets	$8.6 billion +
Volume traded	$4.4 trillion
Listed derivative contracts traded	161 million

Source Annual Report 2022

foreign exchange markets, and changes in the volume of market making and trading activities. Changes in the value of financial instruments, currency, and commodity positions along with the volatility of interest rates are risk factors which affect the business performance of StoneX. The ongoing COVID-19 pandemic and conflict between Ukraine and Russia have created significant market volatility, uncertainty, and economic disruption for the company. StoneX also faces risks related to market making and trading activities. Reduction in the volume of equities, commodities, and derivative transactions and in market liquidity may result in lower revenues from market making and trading activities. StoneX functions as a principal in the OTC derivatives markets and hence is exposed to unique risks due to its OTC derivative transactions. The company is also exposed to counterparty credit risks in the context of the failure of counterparties to meet their obligations to the company or other third parties. StoneX is also subject to risk of default by financial institutions which hold its funds and clients' funds. The company is also subject to reputational risk due to broker misconduct or errors. The company's dealing in products linked to cryptocurrencies expose the firm to technology, regulatory, and financial risks. The company is exposed to significant risks related to cybersecurity attacks against its trading platforms, internal databases, and other technology systems. StoneX faces global regulatory risks as the securities and derivatives industries are subject to extensive regulation under federal, state, and foreign law. StoneX also faces competition and organizational risks.

ESG Initiatives

StoneX plays a pivotal role in global carbon reduction efforts. Through its global financial network, the company focuses on providing clients with access to exchange-listed carbon instruments such as carbon credits via its execution, clearing, and custody strength. In the year 2022, the company launched its Carbon Solutions division which provides climate advisory, carbon brokerage, and trading along with financial structuring services to clients for pursuing its decarbonization and climate mitigation initiatives. StoneX actively participates in RenovaBio program in Brazil which focuses on decarbonization initiative under the Paris Agreement. Under this program, the company has helped clients generate more than 1.3 million CO2 credits in the year 2022. The company has also enabled the clients to access physically deliverable environmental futures and options contracts via the Nodal Exchange. StoneX is a leader in the renewable diesel and biodiesel markets in the USA. The manufacturers of these biofuels are provided with physical feedstock consisting of fats, oils, and greases by StoneX and help them to reduce the carbon footprints. The company has 100% origination agreements for 600 million gallons of biodiesel, renewable diesel, and sustainable aviation fuel capacity. StoneX also offers consultancy services related to the production of over 1 billion gallons of ethanol production. In the year 2022, over 850 NGOs used the services of StoneX to transfer over $ 6 billion in funds globally. The Carbon Solutions team of the company is involved in the development of StoneX's own climate mitigation strategy in alignment with the group's approach to ESG. The composition of the company's Board of Directors complies with the board diversity requirements established under NASDAQ guidelines. In the year 2022, the company launched the employee-led, self-directed voluntary group, Philanthropy @StoneX Affinity Group to raise awareness for charitable opportunities.

Stock Performance

The recent 5-year stock performance of StoneX is compared with that of the market index S&P 500 based on the monthly returns. The data is taken from Yahoo Finance.

The stock was trading at $42.68 on March 1, 2018. By February 1, 2023, the stock was trading at $99.75 registering an increase of 2.33 times. The total cumulative monthly returns for StoneX were 115% compared to 53% returns registered by the market index S&P 500 during the period March 2018–February 2023. The average yearly return for StoneX stock was 23% compared to 11% accounted by S&P 500 during the above period.

Table 3 shows the book value and market value of equity trends during the period 2018–2022. The values are given in millions of dollars.

The average book value as percent of market value was 66.4% during the recent 5-year period 2018–2022.

Table 4 shows the financial highlights of StoneX during the period 2018–2022 in millions of dollars.

On an average basis, the total assets, short-term investments, and total equity increased by 27%, 39% and 21%, respectively. The total revenue and net income

Table 3 Book value and market value of equity

Year	2018	2019	2020	2021	2022
Book value of equity	505.3	594.2	767.5	904	1070.1
Market value of equity	913.66	783.24	991.31	1306.4	1684.01
BV as percent of MV	55.3%	75.9%	77.4%	69.2%	63.5%

Table 4 Financial highlights

	(In millions of dollars)				
Financial highlights	2018	2019	2020	2021	2022
Total assets	7824.7	9936.1	13474.9	18839.6	19859.6
Short-term investments	342.3	471.3	952.6	1109.6	1108.5
Total equity	505.3	594.2	767.5	904	1070.1
Total revenue	27622.7	32,897	54139.6	42534.2	66,036
Total operating expenses	140.3	152.1	205.8	309.8	394.5
Net income	55.5	85.1	169.6	116.3	207.1
Market cap	913.66	783.24	991.31	1306.4	1684.01
Enterprise value	3141.16	4915.44	5538.41	7593.5	5991.01

Table 5 Performance indicators

Ratios	2018	2019	2020	2021	2022
Net margin%	0.2	0.26	0.31	0.27	0.31
ROE%	11.62	15.48	24.91	13.92	20.98
ROA%	0.79	0.96	1.45	0.72	1.07
DER	5.09	7.75	7.17	8.18	5.06

Table 6 Economic value

Year	2021	2022
Profit before income tax	154.1	277.2
Income tax	37.80	70.10
Net operating profit after tax (NOPAT)	116.30	207.10
Stockholder equity	904.00	1070.10
Long-term debt	7001.50	1591.80
Total capital employed	7905.5	2661.9
WACC	1.61%	1.95%
Capital charge	127.28	51.91
Economic value	−10.98	155.19

increased by 29% and 50%, respectively, during the period 2018–2022. The total expenses increased by 30% on an average basis. The market capitalization and enterprise value increased by 18% and 21%, respectively. The data source is annual reports and www.gurufocus.com.

Table 5 shows the performance measures in terms of profitability ratios and leverage ratio of debt equity.

The average net margin, ROE, and ROA were 0.27%, 17.38%, and 0.99%, respectively, during the recent 5-year period 2018–2022. The company had a high leverage position with average debt to equity ratio of 6.65.

Table 6 illustrates the estimation of the economic value of StoneX during the period 2021 and 2022. The values are given in millions of dollars.

References

1. https://www.stonex.com/
2. https://ir.stonex.com/

Case 50 Cigna

Cigna is a global health services company with more than 190 million customer and patient relationship and presence in 30 countries. The company is one of the oldest with a history of more than 225 years of existence. The company supports individuals to maintain, improve, or recover their physical or mental health through behavioral and lifestyle changes, affordable and effective medication options, and targeted medical and surgical interventions. The company has over 1000 health coaches to assist people to meet health goals and lifestyle changes. The differentiated set of pharmacy, medical, dental, and supplemental products and services is offered through two brands—Cigna and Evernorth. The company offers a broad portfolio of solutions and services, integrated behavioral, medical and pharmacy management solutions, specialty pharmacy, clinical and care management expertise and advanced analytics for engaging individuals, plan sponsors, and provider partners.

Evernorth is the company's service portfolio launched in the year 2020. The health services capabilities offered by Evernorth consist of pharmacy solutions, benefits management solutions, care solutions, and intelligence solutions. Evernorth offers innovative products such as Healthy Ways to WorkSM, Family Path SM, and MyndSM. Health Ways to WorkSM offers a broad suite of solutions to assist health plans and offers solution to address the COVID-19 pandemic. FamilyPathSM offers comprehensive fertility solution to reduce avoidable costs. MyndSM solution treats and supports mental health conditions of clients. The Evernorth portfolio is offered to health plans, employers, government organizations, and healthcare providers. Cigna's US commercial and US government businesses are represented by US Medical segment which offers complete comprehensive medical and coordinated solutions to customers. US Commercial products and services include medical, pharmacy, behavioral health, dental, vision, and health advocacy programs. The US Government solutions offer Medicare Advantage, Medicare Supplement and Medicare Part D plans for seniors, Medicaid plans, and individual health insurance plans. Supplemental health, life and accident insurance products, and healthcare coverage are covered by international market segment. Group Disability and Life segment offers group long-term and short-term disability, group life, accident,

© The Author(s), under exclusive license to Springer Nature Switzerland AG 2024

B. R. Kumar, *Rising Stars*, Management for Professionals,
https://doi.org/10.1007/978-3-031-50032-9_50

voluntary and specialty insurance products, and related services. This segment was sold off to New York Life during December 2020. Corporate-owned life insurance provides permanent insurance contracts to corporations. The run-off businesses include reinsurance, settlement annuity, individual life insurance, and annuity and retirement benefits businesses. In 2013, the reinsurance business comprising guaranteed minimum death benefit and minimum income benefit was divested through reinsurance with Berkshire Hathaway Life Insurance company.

Principal Products and Services

Pharmacy Solutions

Cigna Healthcare's pharmacy operations consist of ten order processing pharmacies, five patient contact centers, 26 specialty branch pharmacies, and 11 high volume automated home delivery and specialty dispensing pharmacies in the USA. Express Scripts Pharmacy dispenses approximately 1.5 billion prescriptions annually to members of pharmacy plans managed by the company's Express Scripts PBM. Specialty Pharmacy Services provide specialty medications involving high cost for the treatment of rare and complex diseases.

Benefits Management Solution

Cigna Healthcare Solution provides cost-effective care through prescription, drug utilization, and cost management. Through the drug utilization review program, the company reviews the claims submission made for prescription drugs by the pharmacies electronically in real time. The Benefits Design Consultation for clients is designed to structure and leverage the pharmacy benefits to meet plan objectives for access to the prescription medications. myMatrixx is a unique PBM with an exclusive focus on workers' compensation. eviCore Medical Benefits Management is a leading provider of integrated technology-enabled managed solutions in clinical diagnostic segments such as advanced imaging, cardiology, and gastroenterology. In the Medical drug management segment, Cigna offers a comprehensive range of services and guaranteed savings for managing medically billed specialty drugs.

Supply Chain Administration and Network Management

Cigna offers retail network pharmacy administration through negotiating with pharmacies to provide discounts on drug prices to customers and perform network functions related to client preferences. The formulary management services assist clients in establishing formularies which enable customers and physicians to select clinically effective drugs in the context of access, safety, and affordability. Express Scripts operates different group purchasing organizations whose function is to negotiate prices for the purchase of drugs, fees, and formulary rebates with the manufacturers of pharmaceuticals. Cigna's first-to-market innovative copay solutions help patients to protect plan design preferences. Inside Rx is a prescription medication savings program which offers eligible self-paying customers with discounts on brand and generic medications. Cigna also offers value-based programs such as Express Scripts SafeGuardRx and Patient Assurance Program.

Care Solution

Cigna offers care solution-based clinical programs to assist clients for effective health management. The Health Ways to Work Initiative offered a suite of agile solutions to help partners and employees to navigate the COVID-19 pandemic. Mynd mental health solution provides access to expert guidance and support for anxiety, depression, and insomnia. Health Connect 360 is a transformational, outcomes-based, clinical management model to provide healthcare clinical support.

Evernorth Intelligent Solution

Evernorth Labs collaborates with clients, customers, and partners to launch innovative programs for their businesses. Evernorth also uses advanced predictive modeling to develop solutions to improve health outcomes and address challenges such as opioid abuse and emerging health issues.

Provider Services

CuraScript SD is a specialty distributor of pharmaceuticals and medical supplies. The company provides distribution services primarily to office and clinic-based physicians who treat chronic diseases through CuraScript SD.

The customers of the Evernorth segment include clients and patients. The clients consist of managed care organizations, health insurers, third-party administrators, employers, union sponsored benefit plans, workers' compensation plans, government health programs, providers, clinics, hospitals, etc. Patients belong to those target segments which receive the service offerings which are provided to the company's clients. Prescription drugs are provided to the patients.

The company faces competition from managed care PBMs, independent PBMs, pharmacies, third-party benefit administrators, clinical solutions, and healthcare data analytics firms. The main competitors in the managed care PBMs include CVS Caremark, Humana, IngenioRx, OptumRx, and Prime Therapeutics. The competitor independent PBMs include MedImpact, Navitus Health Solutions, and Elixir. The competitor pharmacies are CVS, Walgreens Boots Alliance, Walmart Inc., and Rite Aid. Good is an emergent competitor in the third-party benefit administrator segment. Some examples of clinical solutions players who compete with Cigna are

Anthem, Magellan Health, HealthHelp, and Inovalon. South Korea is the single largest geographic market in its international market segment.

In the Cigna Healthcare portfolio segment, the company caters to the needs of 17.1 million medical customers. As of December 2021, the company employs 73,700 employees with 89% based in the USA. The company made $174.1 billion in revenues and $7.2 billion from cash flow in operations in the year 2021. The company had paid $9 billion to shareholders in the form of dividends and share repurchases. By the end of December 2021, over 67,900 pharmacies had participated in one or more of the company's networks. The ten largest pharmacy chains account for 62% of the total number of stores in the company's largest network. Table 1 lists the major milestones of Cigna over the past 200 years.

Strategy

The strategy of growth adopted by the company is based on the major trends that are changing the healthcare landscape. The healthcare industry is witnessing an increased acceleration of pharmacological innovation which encompasses pharmaceuticals, gene therapies, and vaccines. The trend suggests the biosimilars will become the low-cost alternatives for high-cost biological drugs. Approximately 66 biological drugs covered by patents in the market would expire by 2025. The increased use of biosimilar is expected to decrease healthcare spending by over $100 billion. Cigna expects to capitalize on this market through the platforms of Evernorth's pharmacy. The demand for behavioral health services continues to rise ever since the pandemic outbreak. The behavioral network of Evernorth has doubled in size over the past 5 years. The company focuses on the development of new digital provider relationships for strengthening its behavioral network. Cigna has partnered with Ginger to assist customers with on-demand behavioral health coaching, therapy, and psychiatry services accessible via a mobile app. The company is also focusing on the opportunities due to rise of virtual care and other alternative care delivery options driven by technological innovation and consumer preferences. Through the acquisition of virtual telehealth leader MDLIVE in the year 2021, the company expanded its access to virtual care services in the segments of primary and dermatology care along with behavioral healthcare. The company has also launched an innovative virtual first health plan option for employers. The company has also developed additional digital first pathways to assist patients with musculoskeletal disorders, anxiety, and depression.

For targeted medical and surgical interventions, the company focuses on partnerships and value-based care quality programs which are powered by data and analytics. As a part of its strategy to focus on the health portion of the portfolio, the company sold off its life, accident, and supplemental benefits businesses in seven international markets to Chubb in the year 2021. In 2021, the company made investments of $550 million in the technology-enabled health insurance carrier Bright Health Group.

Table 1 Major milestones

Year	Major events
1792	Insurance Company of North America (INA), the first marine insurance company in the USA, was formed. INA remains the nation's oldest, stockholder-owned insurer in the world
1794	INA is incorporated, and issues its first life insurance policy. This policy provides insurance for a sea captain against death during a voyage. The policy included clauses such as promising benefits if Barbary Coast pirates capture the captain
1871	During the Great Chicago Fire, INA pays $650,000 as claim settlement in full
1926	A syndicate which included INA and Connecticut General initiated aircraft insurance which was a forerunner to modern-day health insurance offered to airline passengers
1942	On the basis of request from US army, INA company writes accident and health insurance for the 30 men working on the Manhattan Project
1946	INA expands foothold to Europe, Asia, Africa, the Near East, and Central and South America
1950	Connecticut General introduces medical catastrophe (major medical) insurance
1964	Connecticut General introduces group dental insurance for organization with at least 35 employees
1970	Connecticut General provides group insurance and pension services to employees of international firms based abroad. INA offers the first medical cost containment business in the USA through the formation of International Rehabilitation Associates (IRA).
1978	INA makes entry into the prepaid health plan business by acquiring HMO International, which operated hospitals in the USA and abroad
1980	INA purchases Ross-Loos, the nation's oldest HMO
1982	Cigna formed by the merger of Connecticut General Corporation and INA Corporation. The merger combined the operations and health insurance businesses
1984	Cigna acquires American Foreign Insurance Association (AFIA), an international insurance underwriting firm with services offered in over 100 countries
1990	Cigna acquires EQUICOR, the sixth-largest provider of employee benefits in the USA
1997	Cigna acquires Healthsource Inc. to expand its network of healthcare plans in new markets
1998	Restructuring of healthcare business. In 1998, the individual life insurance and annuity business sold to Lincoln National Corporation
1999	Cigna sold the property and casualty business to ACE Ltd. of Hamilton, Bermuda
2002	The world's first online physician-led healthcare network for employees on global assignment launched by Cigna. Cigna enters the Chinese life insurance market through joint venture
2004	Cigna divested its financial and retirement business to Prudential Financial Inc.
2005	Cigna International becomes the only US insurer to offer web-based expert second opinion services for expatriates through the e-Cleveland Clinic
2009	Cigna becomes the first health service company in the USA to offer live 24/7/365 access to its call center service representatives
2011	Cigna enters into joint ventures with Finansbank in Turkey and TTK Group in India. Cigna acquires First Assist in the UK; starts operations in Singapore and expands health networks in Brazil and Africa. Cigna acquires Great American Supplemental Benefits which cater to the needs of seniors
2012	Cigna acquires HealthSpring to expand its focus on target segment of senior citizens
2013	Cigna announces a strategic venture with MyFitnessPal, a web-based food log

(continued)

Table 1 (continued)

Year	Major events
2014	Cigna launches a new global campaign and tagline—"Together, all the way"
2017	Cigna acquires Brighter, a leader in digital engagement, to connect healthcare consumers and providers through technology platforms
2018	Cigna completes combination with Express Scripts®, establishing a blueprint to transform the healthcare system through flexible, open, and connected solutions
2021	Acquires virtual telehealth leader MDLIVE

Source: https://www.cigna.com/about-us/company-profile/milestones

Risk Factors

In terms of strategic and operational risks, the future performance of the company's business depends upon its ability to execute strategic and operational initiatives. The ability to execute these initiatives depends upon factors such as introduction of differentiated and innovate products, services and solutions, cost control, and development of analytical solutions to improve the services. The health service industry is dynamic in nature, and shifts in the structure of the industry such as inter-industry merger or industry consolidation, strategic alliances, and new or alternative business models will affect the ability of the firm to attract or retain clients and customers. Cigna faces price competition with respect to service and quality factors. The company faces risk with respect to establishment of medical claims reserve for estimated future payments. The success of Cigna's business depends on how well it maintains relationships with physicians, hospitals, and other health service providers. The contracts of Cigna with pharmaceutical manufacturers are basically nonexclusive and terminable on relatively short notice by either party. Changes in drug or industry pricing benchmarks might impact the financial performance of the company. Being a global healthcare company, the company also faces political, legal, operational, regulatory, and economic risks. Cigna's business is regulated at the federal, state, local, and international levels. New laws or changes in regulations might have a material adverse effect on the business of the company.

ESG Initiatives

The company launched the Building Equity and Equality Program to support diversity, inclusion, and equity for different communities. The company is committed to achieve $ 1 billion in diverse supplier spending by 2025. Cigna Foundation had funded $15.8 million approximately toward its focus areas of health, education, and workforce development. The company occupies number one position on Dow Jones Sustainability Index for the healthcare services industry. Cigna occupies number 33 position on DiversityInc's Top 50 most diverse companies list.

Stock Performance

Table 2 compares the cumulative total stockholder return for Cigna stock for the 5 years ended December 31, 2021, with the cumulative total shareholder return of the S&P 500 Index and S&P 500 Health Care Index. It is assumed that the value of investment in Cigna stock and each index was $100 on December 31, 2016, and the dividends were also reinvested.

The holding period return for Cigna stock was 75%, while for S&P 500 and S&P 500 Health Care Index, the holding period return was 133% and 125%, respectively, during the 5-year period. The average yearly return for Cigna, S&P 500, and S&P 500 Health Care Index were 13.78%, 16.82%, and 15.68%, respectively, during the above period.

Table 3 compares the book value and market value of equity of Cigna during the period 2018–2022. The values are given in millions of dollars.

The average book value as percent of market value of equity was approximately 63% during the period 2018–2022.

Table 4 gives the financial highlights of Cigna Healthcare company in millions of dollars.

Table 2 Wealth comparison

Year	2016	2017	2018	2019	2020	2021
Cigna	$100	$152.00	$142.00	$153.00	$156.00	$175
S&P 500	$100	$122.00	$116.00	$153.00	$181.00	$233
S&P 500 Health Care Index	$100	$122.00	$130.00	$157.00	$178.00	$225

Source Annual Report 2021

Table 3 Book value and market value of equity

Year	2018	2019	2020	2021	2022
Book value of equity	41,072	45,379	50,386	47,184	46,164
Market value of equity	72345.09	76178.86	73856.23	74158.55	84683.84
BV as percent of MV	56.8%	62.7%	66.1%	63.9%	62.3%

Table 4 Financial highlights

	(In millions of dollars)				
Financial highlights	2018	2019	2020	2021	2022
Total assets	153,226	155,774	155,451	154,889	152,630
Short-term investments	3855	4619	10,182	5081	7079
Total equity	41,072	45,379	50,386	47,184	46,164
Total revenue	48,569	153,743	160,577	174,272	180,642
Net income	2637	5104	8458	5365	6668
Market cap	72345.09	76178.86	73856.23	74158.55	84683.84
Enterprise value	111012.09	109007.86	96658.23	102819.55	109274.84

Table 5 Performance indicators

Ratios	2018	2019	2020	2021	2022
Net margin%	5.43	3.32	5.27	3.08	3.69
ROE%	9.63	11.82	17.68	11.01	14.15
ROA%	2.45	3.3	5.44	3.46	4.31
DER	1.04	0.83	0.65	0.72	0.72

Table 6 Economic value

Year	2020	2021
Profit before income tax	10,868	6782
Income tax	2369.22	1367.25
Net operating profit after tax (NOPAT)	8498.78	5414.75
Stockholder equity	50386.00	47184.00
Long-term debt	29545.00	31125.00
Total capital employed	79,931	78,309
WACC	5.05%	5.56%
Capital charge	4036.52	4353.98
Economic value	4462.26	1060.77

On an average basis, the total cash investments increased by 32%. The total revenues and net income increased by 58% and 37%, respectively, during the period 2018–2022. The data source is from annual report and www.gurufocus.com.

Table 5 highlights the performance and leverage measures of Cigna during the period 2018–2022.

The average net margin, ROE, and ROA were 4.16%, 12.86%, and 3.79%, respectively, during the recent 5-year period 2018–2022. The average debt equity ratio was 0.79 during the above period.

Table 6 illustrates the estimation of economic value for Cigna during the period 2020 and 2021. The values are given in millions of dollars.

References

1. https://investors.cigna.com/financials/annual-reports/default.aspx
2. https://www.cigna.com/about-us/company-profile/
3. Annual Report 2021

Case 51 Paylocity

Paylocity is a leading cloud-based provider of human capital management (HCM) and payroll software solutions. The comprehensive platform offered by the company facilitates companies to automate their HR and payroll processes. The company provided its software-as-a-service or SaaS solutions to approximately 33,000 clients across the United States which had an average of 100 employees. The platform offered by Paylocity is basically a single-employee system of record that supports the entire employee lifecycle comprising Talent, Payroll, Core HR, Workforce Management, and Benefits system. The platform centralizes payroll and HCM databases. The platform provides tools to communicate, connect to organizations, and facilitate career development and growth. The dashboards of the company use advanced Artificial Intelligence to improve efficiency and build a healthier workforce. The comprehensive software solutions offered by Paylocity are supplemented with an integrated implementation and client service organization. The software solutions of Paylocity offer clients automated data integration with hundreds of third-party partner systems such as 401(k), benefits, and insurance provider systems. Paylocity uses a direct sales force to market and sell its products. The company uses its extensive referral network of 401(k) advisors, benefits administrators, insurance brokers, third-party administrators, and HR consultants for sales lead generation.

The company's workforce consists of 5300 employees. The company has received significant recognition in terms of being listed in Best-Led Companies list, Fortune's 100 Fastest-Growing Companies list, and Forbes' Best Mid-Size Employers list, Best Employers for Diversity list, and Best Employers for Women list. The main competitors of Palocity are primarily payroll and HR service and software providers such as Automatic Data Processing, NC, Paychex, Inc., Paycom Software, Inc., Paycor, Inc., and Ultimate Kronos Group.

The company generated revenues of $852.7 million in the fiscal year 2022. The research and development costs amounted to $91 million, $108.5 million, and $145 million in 2020, 2021, and 2022, respectively.

© The Author(s), under exclusive license to Springer Nature Switzerland AG 2024

B. R. Kumar, *Rising Stars*, Management for Professionals,
https://doi.org/10.1007/978-3-031-50032-9_51

Products

Paylocity's HCM and payroll software solutions offer a unified platform for the modern workplace.

Payroll

The company's Payroll and Tax services solution simplify payroll, automate processes, and manage compliance requirement within one system. The payroll solution leverages data from Time and Attendance and Human Capital Management solutions to calculate wages, deductions, and withholdings. The integration function of the platform automatically transfers 401(k) information, retirement plans, and benefit files to third-party providers. The tax services solutions facilitate the preparation and filing of tax documents for various jurisdictions. The cloud-based global payroll solution facilitate US-based companies to manage payroll for international employees with respect to specific requirements of countries where the employees provide services. The expense management solution helps mobile applications capture receipts and import transactions from credit cards and minimizes paperwork through automated workflows for payroll reimbursement. On Demand Payment solution enables employees to estimate earned wages between pay cycles on the basis of hours of work. This payment solution also offers financial flexibility to employees to access a portion of their earned wages before the scheduled payday. The Garnishments solution facilitates the calculation, setup, and maintenance of historical deduction records and enables compliance risk management related to state and federal rules.

Human Capital Management

Paylocity's Human Capital Management solutions—Core HR streamlines HR processes using modern mobile-enabled tools that automate administrative tasks and provide data-driven reports. The Employee Self Service module enables employees to view checks, request time off, update personal data, and collaborate with teammates. Through the module, employees can enroll in benefits and access a learning management system which facilitate training. The Document Library functions as a central location to store personal employee files such as performance reviews in an organized way. The Compliance Dashboard provides inputs on new laws and regulations related to employment verification, equal employment opportunity, and compensation. HR Edge offers knowledge resources related to complex compliance requirements, social issues, and HR policies.

Workforce Management

The time and attendance solution speeds up administrative tasks by accurately tracking time and attendance data. The Scheduling solution can automate schedule tracking with features to adjust work schedules, leverage templates, and build policies on the basis of duration and time between shifts. Paylocity's time collection devices include kiosks, state-of-the-art time clocks, mobile, and web applications with advanced features to specify geographic parameters and temperature checks.

Talent Management

Recruiting solutions enable clients to select suitable candidates by using intuitive tools to streamline talent acquisition processes. The platform offers features such as embedded text messaging and instantly tracking conversations. Through the platform, HR professionals can customize job applications and automatically post to online job portals. The onboarding platform enables new employees to perform all pre-hire tasks through digital data collection. The Learning Management Solution (LMS) of Paylocity enables clients to train their employees on new skills, policies, products, diversity, equity, inclusion, and accessibility modules. The course delivery method consists of on-demand and webinars which are made available through mobile apps. Clients can create different contents for employees using a Sharable Content Object Reference Model (SCORM), embedded video, etc. The Performance Management solution facilitates employee reviews. Compensation Management solution enables clients to analyze employee's compensation and benefits.

Benefits Management

The Employee Benefits Management tool facilitates clients to plan and administer competitive benefits packages. This tool's features enable benefit administrators to add enrollment rules, manage benefit offerings for different employee groups, customize user plan limits, and view plan documentation. The Third Party Administrative (TPA) solutions provide clients with a single, unified access point for payroll, HR, and benefits administration.

Employee Experiences

Community platform streamlines communication by optimizing broadcast communications into a single location. The announcements made through the platform can be managed, sent, and tracked with an intuitive dashboard. Premium video enables clients to record, upload, and embed videos across the company's HCM platform to facilitate engagement and productivity. The Survey tools help clients to gather employee feedback and the Peer Recognition tool facilitates employees to recognize colleagues' achievements.

Insights and Recommendations

The Modern Workforce Index (MWI) integrates Artificial Intelligence into an HR intelligence dashboard to provide clients insight into employee sentiment and performance metrics. Using the Data Insights solution, the clients can evaluate the health of their firms in terms of headcount, turnover, labor costs, diversity, and requirements of underrepresented groups.

Growth Strategy

Paylocity focusses on technological innovation of its mobile applications, social features, and analytics capabilities to sustain its technological leadership position. Paylocity offers solutions on a cloud-based platform which are designed with a multi-tenant unified architecture. Mobile-centric principles are used in the solution design and development. Paylocity maintains a comprehensive security program to ensure security and integrity of client and employee data and protect against security threats or data breaches.

The competitive strength of the company's solution over alternative solutions is based on its cloud-based software solutions and database architecture. The intuitive user interface of Paylocity's platforms offers many application experiences. The company focusses on growing its client base. The company focusses on the growth opportunities in target market of over 1.3 million businesses with 10–5000 employees. The company has estimated that its realizable target addressable market is approximately $18.6 billion. Paylocity also focusses on new product development initiatives for new and existing clients. The company focusses on modern workforce solutions such as Community, Surveys, Premium Video, and Learning Management System. The company is known for its investment in product development as it was recognized as an overall leader for all 12 HRIS product categories for the 15th straight quarter by G2 Crowd, an independent product review site. The company believes that SaaS solutions are designed to meet the firm's unique needs and provide value-based engaging experience to the client firms. The platform offered by the company drives HR automation and digital transformation. The company also focusses on the expansion of its referral network to grow its client base and lower client acquisition costs. Paylocity has developed a partner ecosystem of third-party systems such as 401(k), benefits, and insurance provider systems wherein the company provides automated data integration for the clients of the third party.

Risk Factors

The success of Paylocity's business depends on factors such as the ability of the company to maintain market acceptance of its products, new product introductions, and updates to existing products on a timely basis. Competitive pressures and introduction of enhanced products and services from competitors, changes in client budgets, and procurement policies are other factors that affect the firm's business success. The market for HCM and payroll solutions is highly fragmented and competitive. The existing clients may experience service outrage and new clients may experience delays in the deployment of modules if the company fails to manage technical operations infrastructure. The ability to deliver cloud-based modules depends on the development and maintenance of Internet infrastructure by third parties which includes the maintenance of a reliable network backbone with speed, data, and bandwidth capacity. The business of Palocity would be materially adversely affected if the third-party software used in the firm's products is not adequately maintained or updated. The solutions of the company store and transmit the clients' and their employees' proprietary and confidential information. The company faces cybersecurity risks if the firm's security measures are breached. The success of the company depends on the protection of its proprietary technology. Paylocity also faces risks related to legal and regulatory matters.

Sustainability Initiatives

The Sustainability Employee Resource Group and Task Force aims to boost sustainability initiatives in all Paylocity business activities. The Task force aims toward the achievement of zero waste and net-zero carbon emissions. The Phase-I priorities involve increased recycling, centralize office waste stations, incentivize paperless practice and reduce food waste. In 2022, the company lowered print waste by cutting of in office printers by 50%. The company also implemented refillable water stations to reduce plastic bottle output. The company executed carbon offset contracts for shipping activities to have net-zero carbon impact on the environment. The firm also delegated independent third parties to quantify the firm's carbon footprint from air travel. The company has partnered with Stars, Aspire, and YWCA Racial Justice to serve people with disabilities, under-resourced communities, and aging workforce. For community-based outreach programs, the company has partnered with organization such as Blessings in a Backpack, Feeding America, Second Chance Studios, and Red Cross. The company runs campaigns and promotes education related to mental health awareness in partnership with organizations such as the National Alliance on Mental Illness. The company also focusses on education and literacy for underrepresented sections of society in partnership with associations such as Big Brothers Big Sisters of America and Youth Guidance. Employee Resource group supports diversity, equity, inclusion, and accessibility initiatives (DEIA).

Stock Performance

The following section analyzes the return performance of Paylocity's stock in comparison with the market index S&P 500 for the recent 5-year period. The Paylocity stock which was trading at $51.23 on March 1st, 2018, increased by 4.29 times to trade at $220.02 by February 1st, 2023. The total monthly cumulative return for Paylocity stock was 193% compared to 52% registered by the market index S&P 500 during the period March 2018–February 2023. The average yearly return for Palocity and S&P 500 during the above period were 39% and 11%, respectively. Table 1 compares the holding period return for Paylocity stock and market index S&P 500 during the 5-year period 2018–2022. The holding period is assumed to be 1 year.

On the basis of holding period return, the Paylocity stock had outperformed the market index during the 3-year period 2018–2020. The market index outperformed the stock in the year 2021. Negative returns were registered for both stock and index in the year 2022. The data was sourced from Yahoo Finance.

Table 2 compares the book and market value of equity of Paylocity during the recent 5-year period. The values are given in millions of dollars.

The average book value of equity as a percent of market value of equity was 4.5% during the period 2018–2022.

Table 3 shows the financial highlights of Paylocity in millions of dollars.

During the recent 5-year period, the total assets, short-term investments, and total equity of Paylocity increased by 37.62%, 9%, and 31%, respectively, on average basis. The total revenues and net income grew by 23% and 24%, respectively. The total operating expenses increased by 23%. The market capitalization showed volatile trends during the above period and has increased by 52% on an average basis. The data was taken from Nasdaq and annual reports for analysis.

Table 4 gives the profitability ratios of the company during the period 2018–2022.

Table 1 Holding period return

Year	Paylocity	S&P 500	Excess returns
2018	39%	2%	36%
2019	62%	16%	46%
2020	45%	26%	19%
2021	7%	18%	−12%
2022	−2%	−7%	5%

Table 2 Book and market value of equity

Year	2018	2019	2020	2021	2022
Book value of equity	212.824	307.964	392.908	476.93	613.463
Market value of equity	2770	6740	11,180	13,000	10,690
BV as percent of MV	7.7%	11.1%	5.8%	4.3%	4.7%

Table 3 Financial highlights

	(In millions of dollars)				
Financial highlights	2018	2019	2020	2021	2022
Total assets	1507.599	1803.941	1985.648	2414.885	4809.014
Short-term investments	137.193	132.476	250.851	202.287	139.756
Total equity	212.824	307.964	392.908	476.93	613.463
Total revenue	377.527	467.63	561.33	635.627	852.651
Total operating expenses	212.381	257.558	313.148	358.286	481.055
Net income	38.598	53.823	64.455	70.819	90.777
Market cap	2770	6740	11,180	13,000	10,690

Table 4 Profitability ratios

Ratios	2018	2019	2020	2021	2022
Net margin%	10.22	11.51	11.48	11.14	10.65
ROE%	21.42	20.67	18.39	16.28	16.65
ROA%	2.92	3.25	3.4	3.22	2.51

The average net margin, ROE, and ROA during the period 2018–2022 were 11%, 18.68%, and 3.06%, respectively, during the period 2018–2022.

References

1. https://investors.paylocity.com/financials/annual-reports
2. https://www.paylocity.com/who-we-are/about-us/corporate-responsibility/

Case 52 SS&C Technologies

SS&C Technologies Holdings is the world's largest hedge fund and private equity administrator. The company is also the largest mutual fund transfer agent in the world. It was founded in the year 1986 and employs over 24,000 employees globally. The company has 125 offices in 94 cities. The company has over 20,000 clients which spans in the health and financial services industries. The unique model of the company combines end-to-end expertise across financial services operations with software and solutions to customers in the financial services and healthcare industries. SS&C supports the technology-enabled operations related to securities accounting, front-to-back office operations, performance and risk analytics, regulatory reporting, and healthcare information processes. SS&C Technologies provides a multitude of software-enabled outsourcing services and subscription based on demand cloud solutions for the global financial services industry. The proprietary software system offers comprehensive fund administration services to alternative and traditional asset managers such as fund manager services, transfer agency services, funds-of-funds services, tax processing, and accounting. Clients are offered the flexibility to choose from multiple software delivery options which include on-premise applications and hosted, multi-tenant, or dedicated applications. Clients are also offered targeted, blended solutions that are based on a combination of software and software-enabled services. The company also serves the healthcare industry through its SS&C Health services and technology-enabled business. The suite of solutions offered by SS&C basically pans across health plan operations. The options offering includes core claims processing, operational software, and high-value applications meant for value-based payment and total cost management. SS&C apply modern technology to medical and pharmacy claims processing, data, and analytics to its market segments consisting of health plans and pharmacy benefit manager.

The company has high revenue retention rates and cash flows as revenues are generated from high-value software-enabled services. The software-enabled services are basically provided under contracts with initial terms of 1–5 years in which payments are required on a monthly or quarterly basis and are subject to automatic

© The Author(s), under exclusive license to Springer Nature Switzerland AG 2024

B. R. Kumar, *Rising Stars*, Management for Professionals,
https://doi.org/10.1007/978-3-031-50032-9_52

renewal at the end of the initial term. The company generated revenues of $5051 million by the year-end 2021. Approximately 76% of the revenues are accounted from clients in North America.

The financial services clients of the company include investment management firms, alternative investment funds, retail asset managers, insurance companies, registered investment advisors, wealth managers, banks, and brokerage firms. The healthcare clients include both individual and government sponsored health plans and healthcare providers. The company's IPO raised $71 million in year 1995.

Products and Services

Software-Enabled Services

SS&C GlobeOp with over $2.2 trillion in assets under administration (AUM) provides services to hedge funds, private equity funds, managed accounts, and institutions with collective investments in transferable securities. SS&C provides services such as global regulatory compliance, tax reporting, risk reporting, valuation, transfer agency services, and automated support of post-trade activities. The company also offers middle and back office outsourcing services and application hosting for institutional asset managers, insurance firms, and real estate investment trusts. Global Investor and Distribution Solutions (GIDS) using proprietary software applications performs global transfer agency and investor servicing using a single global servicing platform. SS&C Retirement Solutions provides technology-enabled administration and recordkeeping services for organizations with over 12 million participants and approximately 400,000 plan sponsors. Black Diamond Wealth Platform provides cloud-based innovative and dynamic portfolio management and reporting solutions for independent advisors, wealth managers, and independent broker dealers. Bluedoor is an integrated registry system which provides services for wealth managers and fund platforms in the United Kingdom and Australia. Advent Outsourcing offers cloud delivered technology to co-sourcing specific workflows and full outsourcing of operational processes. Advent Data Solutions offers services related to the management of custodial data, corporate actions, portfolio data, and market data. ALPS Advisors offers a comprehensive suite of asset servicing, distribution solutions, and asset management for mutual funds, exchange traded funds, and alternative investment funds. Intralinks Virtual Data Rooms (VDRs) based on SaaS application is designed for M&A, alternative investments, and capital markets.

HealthCare Services

The company uses its proprietary software applications to provide pharmacy health management solutions to support commercial, Medicaid, and Medicare Part D plans. The services provided through pharmacy solutions include pharmacy claims administration, pharmacy network solutions, trend control, quality compliance programs, and discount drug card programs. DomainRx is the cloud native claims adjudication platform of SS&C. Using proprietary software applications, the company offers medical claim administration services and health plan compliance services to clients in the healthcare industry. SS&C also provides health outcomes optimization solutions through integrated care management and population health analytics applications for healthcare sector.

Software Licenses and Maintenance

SS&C provides comprehensive and integrated portfolio/investment accounting and analytics software for accounting process. The fund accounting solutions support global fund managers with respect to multi-asset class and multi-currency strategies. Solutions are also offered for insurance accounting and commercial, consumer, and residential loan accounting. Geneva is a global portfolio management platform designed for global asset managers, hedge funds, fund administrators, private equity firms, and family offices. Advent Portfolio Exchange (APX) is a comprehensive portfolio management solution for asset managers and wealth managers. Axys is a turnkey portfolio management and reporting system for small and medium-sized enterprises. Singularity is the company's pioneer cloud-based solution which uses artificial intelligence, machine learning, robotic process automation, and advanced predictive analytics to support the investment operations, accounting, and analytics systems of financial institutions. Global Wealth Portfolio is a comprehensive cloud-based solution which facilitates wealth managers to manage the entire investment process on a single platform based on a single database. Aloha, the investment operations platform offers asset class and functional support across the front, middle, and back office. HiPortfolio offers investment accounting and asset servicing solutions for third-party administrators, asset managers, and insurance firms in over 35 countries. PORTIA is a comprehensive middle to back-office investment operations platform. CAMRA is a portfolio accounting solution which is tailored for insurance investment operations. Innotrust solution supports the accounting operations of trust companies, banks, private banks, and retirement plan administrators.

Portfolio Management Software

Eze Eclipse is a cloud-native front-to-back investment management platform. Sylvan Insight is the performance measurement, attribution and composite management platform for SS&C. SS&C Vision FI (Financial Insights) offers end-to-end solutions for designing, producing, and distributing client communications. SS&C's Verify is a highly scalable reconciliation and exception management system related to the accounting lifecycle.

Trading Software

Moxy, the SS&C's trade order management system provides centralized platforms for making and managing trade orders. SS&C's multi-broker execution management system is a cloud-based platform which provides trading data and insights for the global equity, futures, and options market. Chorus, the digital process automation product suite with features for business process management, content management, and case management is used in segments such as asset management, life insurance, property and casualty insurance, healthcare, and wealth management.

Banking and Lending Solution

EVOLV offers complete cloud-based end-to-end accounting solutions for financial institutions. Precision LM is a single database application-based solution which provides comprehensive commercial loan management.

Research, Analytics, Risk, and Training

The cloud-based solution, Algorithmics offers risk analytics to address regulatory changes and market, credit, and liquidity risks. Tamale RMS is a purpose-built research management solution for investment analysts and portfolio managers and acts as a centralized repository for research data collection. SS&C's Research, Analytics and Consulting (RAC) group offers advanced analytics, research, and distribution intelligence technologies to firms in the financial services industry to evaluate their business performance. The SS&C Learning Institute is an education, training, and research organization for investment management professionals.

Market Environment

The demand for the company's products and services is shaped by several industry trend drivers. The post-COVID-19 environment necessitates an increased attention on achieving operational efficiency and infrastructural aspects along with the ability to access systems and data through cloud and web-based portals. Diversification of business lines and product proliferation is another trend which shapes the growth of the industry sector. Regulatory changes and directives from governmental and self-regulating organizations increase the complexity of compliance and clients are compelled to develop systems infrastructure and research management process to comply with the regulatory requirements. Clients invest in new technology to achieve higher profit margins and add new products. Moreover, investments in new technology such as artificial intelligence consisting of machine learning and robotic process automation are gaining traction in the financial technology industry. The trend observed is the increasing migration to the cloud in order to achieve operational scalability and lower fixed costs. There has been increased demand for transparency, efficiency, and risk management in the financial service industry after the 2008 economic crisis.

Competitive Strengths and Growth Strategy

The company has focused on the development of proprietary software products and infrastructure to enhance the capability of its software-enabled services and improve operating margins. The company has become a global industry leader with a dominant position to provide software and software-enabled services for the financial services industry. The products and services enabled clients to automate and integrate front-office, middle-office, and back-office functions thereby increasing productivity and reducing costs. The company possesses a highly diversified and growing client base. For the past four decades, the company have developed a large and growing installed client base consisting of some of the largest financial services firms in the world. SS&C is the largest fund administrator for alternative investment managers and the largest third-party mutual fund transfer agent. SS&C owns and operates a global data center footprint to provide high uptime and regional service delivery for its customers. The SS&C Private Cloud delivers software with very high throughput.

The company focuses on enhancing its technological leadership by utilizing its domain expertise to build new software-enabled services and solutions organically and through acquisitions which satisfy the highly specialized needs of the financial services industry. The company has the competitive advantage to satisfy the requirements of high-end clients by providing cloud-based services and related mobility platforms which facilitate automation and integration of functions for productivity improvement, compliance, and bottom-line savings. The company focusses on cross-selling its products and bundling solutions. The company focusses on a highly disciplined and focused acquisition strategy targeted at expansion of its intellectual property portfolio, product and service offerings, and addition of new clients. During the past 27 years, the company made approximately 59 acquisitions. The company acquires targets that provide complementary products or services and have competitive technological strength with an established client base. The company also focusses on expanding into strategic geographic markets. Companies that have their own solutions for software-enabled services are also attractive targets for SS&C.

Table 1 shows the acquisitions made by the company during the period 1995–2022.

In 2015, the company acquired Advent Software, a leading provider of software and services for the global investment management industry. In the same year, the company acquired Varden Technologies, a leading provider of client and advisor communication solutions for investment firms and Primatics Financial, a leader in accounting, forecasting, regulatory reporting, reserving, and stress testing solutions to financial institutions. In 2016, SS&C Technologies acquired Conifer Financial

Table 1 Acquisitions

Year	Acquisitions (deal value)
1995	Acquires Chalke ($10 million)
1997	Acquires Shepro Braun ($16.5 million); Mabel Systems ($2.1 million)
1998	Acquires Quantra ($16.1 million); Savid Group ($0.8 million)
1999	Acquires HedgeWare Inc. ($11.9 million); Brookside Corporation
2001	Acquires Digital Visions($1.3 million)
2002	Acquires Real Time ($4 million); DBC ($4.5 million)
2003	Acquires Amicorp Fund Services ($1.8 million)
2004	Acquires Investment Advisory Network ($3 million), NeoVision Hypersystems ($1.6 million), OMR Systems ($19.7 million)
2005	Acquires Eisnerfast ($25.3 million), FMC ($159 million), Financial Interactive ($12 million), MarginMan ($5.6 million), Open Information System ($24 million), Achievement Technologies ($0.47 million)
2006	Acquires Cogent Management ($12.3 million), Zoologic ($3 million)
2007	Acquires Northport LLC
2008	Acquires Micro Design Services
2009	Acquires Evare LLC, MAXIMIS business from Unisys, The Next Round, Tradeware Global Corp
2010	Acquires Geller Investment, thinklink product from TD Ameritrade, Time Shareware ($30.5 million)
2011	Acquires Benefits, BDO Simpson Xavier Fund Administration, Teledata Communications
2012	Acquires Thomson Reuter's Portia ($170 million), GlobeOp Financial Services ($834.4 million), Gravity Financial, Hedgemetrix
2013	Acquires Prime Management Ltd
2014	Acquires DST Global Solutions ($95 million)
2015	Acquires Primatics Financial ($122 million), Varden Technologies ($25 million); Advent Software ($2.6 billion)
2016	Acquires Conifer Financial Services ($88.5 million), Salentica, Wells Fargo's Global Fund Services ($75.1 million), Citi's alternative investor services business ($321 million)
2017	Acquires Modestspark, Commonwealth Fund Services ($16.4 million)
2018	Acquires Intralinks ($1.5 billion), EZE Software($1.45 billion), DST Systems ($5.4 billion)
2019	Acquires Algorithmics($88.8 million), Investrack
2020	Acquires Millennium Consulting and Seminar Services, Innovest Systems($120 million)
2022	Acquires Complete Financial Ops; Tier1's CRM; O'Shares ETFs, MineralWare($18 million); Hubwise Securities; Blue Prism Group ($1.6 billion)

Source: https://www.ssctech.com/about-us/acquisitions

Services, an independent asset services firm with $110 billion of combined assets and 200 clients. This acquisition strengthened the company's market position with a wider base of services related to foundations, endowments, pensions, and outsourced CIO portfolios. Salentica the leading CRM Solution was acquired and became a platform partner to the firm's Black Diamond® wealth platform. SS&C acquired Wells Fargo's Global Fund Services business which is a leading provider of comprehensive administration, middle office, operations, and cash/collateral management services with over $42 billion under alternative assets administration. SS&C acquired Citi's Alternative Investor Services business which was a top fund administrator in hedge fund and private equity segment with 1400 staff, 265 customers, and $395 billion in assets under administration. In 2017, the company acquired Modestspark, a digital service provider to financial advisors and wealth management firms with over 400 clients. The acquisition of Commonwealth Fund Services Ltd., a fund administrator with Assets under Management of $8 billion enabled SS&C to expand the company's footprint in Canada. In 2018, Intralinks, a financial technology provider for the global banking, deal making, and capital markets communities was acquired by SS&C. Through this acquisition, SS&C added over 800 employees and more than 400 clients including banks, blue chip corporate clients to its portfolio. The company acquired Eze Software, a provider of investment management solutions and through this acquisition added 1050 employees and 2500 clients based globally. SS&C acquired a global strategic advisory, technology, and operations outsourcing company, DST Systems with approximately 13,000 global clients. The company had acquired CACEIS North America, the fund administration business of CACEIS based in Toronto and New York. In the year 2020, SS&C acquired Captricity, the maker of Vidado data transformation platform. The acquisition of Innovest Systems, a web-based technology system provider for trust accounting, payments, and unique asset servicing enabled SS&C to broaden its wealth management technology suit. Millennium Consulting Services and Millennium Seminar Services which offer consulting and training services to insurance companies and regulators was acquired by SS&C. In 2021, the acquisition of CLPSI extended SS&C's business process outsource offerings globally. In 2022, SS&C Technologies acquired the leading UK-based robotics process automation company, Blue Prism which offered services to over 2000 businesses globally. SS&C completed the acquisition of Hubwise, a regulated B2B investment platform, which serves advisers, discretionary wealth managers, and self-directed digital D2C propositions. SS&C acquired MineralWare, a cloud-based asset management platform, which focuses on managing minerals. The deal added around 350 institutional and high net-worth clients, 750,000 mineral assets along with annual recurring revenue of $5.5 million toward the SS&C portfolio. The acquisition of O'Shares ETFs expanded the offerings of SS&C's wholly owned asset manager, ALPS Advisors. The acquisition of the sell side Tier 1 CRM business of Tier 1 Financial Solutions in an all-cash deal expanded SS&C's CRM offerings related to capital markets and investment banks. During December 2022, SS&C Technologies completed the acquisition of Complete Financial Ops which offers fund administration to private equity funds and family offices.

Risk Factors

The company's business prospects depend on changes in the state of general economy, financial markets, financial services, and healthcare industry. The company derives its revenues from the delivery of products and services to clients primarily in the financial services and healthcare industries. The company faces the risk of not achieving the benefits from its acquisitions in terms of revenue and cost synergies. Consolidations in financial services or healthcare industry sectors could lead to a decline in the demand for SS&C's products and services. SS&C generates significant revenues from transaction processing fees which the company earns through products and services sold in the securities market. These revenue sources are determined by the level of activity in the security market. SS&C's business focus on hedge fund industry and developments in the sector have an impact on the business performance of SS&C. The software-enabled services of SS&C may be subject to disruptions and cybercrime attacks which could adversely affect the reputation of the company. The company also faces legal or regulatory risks. SS&C's business is subject to increased US and foreign regulations which include privacy, licensing, processing, record keeping, broker /dealer, retirement, and other related regulations. As a fund administrator, SS&C may be exposed to claims and litigation from clients, investors, and other third parties. SS&C's substantial indebtedness could adversely affect the financial health of the company.

Stock Performance

Table 2 shows the comparison of the cumulative total return of SS&C stock with that of market indexes returns during the period from December 31, 2016, to December 31, 2021. The market indexes used for comparison are the Nasdaq Composite Index and the Nasdaq Technology Dividend TR Index. An initial investment of $100 is assumed along with reinvestment of dividends.

The 5-year holding period return for SS&C stock was 198% compared to Nasdaq Composite and Nasdaq Technology Dividend Index returns of 205% and 148%. The 5-year average returns for SS&C was 25.03% compared to 27.19% and 18.19% returns for Nasdaq Composite and Nasdaq Technology Dividend Index.

Table 2 Comparative wealth creation

Year	2016	2017	2018	2019	2020	2021
SS&C Technologies Holdings, Inc.	$100	$143.00	$160.00	$219.00	$262.00	$298
Nasdaq composite	$100	$130.00	$126.00	$172.00	$250.00	$305
Nasdaq technology dividend TR index	$100	$123.00	$120.00	$161.00	$190.00	$248

Source: Annual Report 2021

Table 3 Book and market value of equity

Year	2018	2019	2020	2021	2022
Book value of equity	4580	5116.1	5716.5	6223.2	6102.9
Market value of equity	11313.59	15632.44	18740.4	20986.88	19115.1
BV as percent of MV	40.5%	45.2%	36.6%	33.2%	29.1%

Table 4 Financial highlights

	(In millions of dollars)				
Financial highlights	2018	2019	2020	2021	2022
Total assets	16107.5	16741.1	15923.6	17,333	16653.3
Short-term investments	166.7	152.8	209.3	564	440.1
Total equity	4580	5116.1	5716.5	6223.2	6102.9
Total revenue	3421.1	4632.9	4667.9	5051	5283
Total operating expenses	843.1	1106.8	1108	1167	1372.4
Net income	103.2	438.5	625.2	800	650.2
Market capitalization	11313.59	15632.44	18740.4	20986.88	19115.1
Enterprise value	19402.89	22982.34	25297.1	26697.78	20049.69

Table 5 Profitability and leverage position

Ratios	2018	2019	2020	2021	2022
Net margin%	3.02	9.46	13.39	15.84	12.31
ROE%	2.84	9.04	11.54	13.47	10.65
ROA%	0.95	2.67	3.83	4.81	3.83
DER	1.8	1.47	1.18	1.01	1.21

Table 3 compares the book value and market value of equity of SS&C in millions of dollars during the period 2018–2022.

The average book value as a percent of market value of equity of SS&C was 31.1% during the period 2018–2022. The data for analysis was taken from gurufocus.com.

Table 4 shows the financial highlights of SS&C during the period 2018–2022.

The data is obtained from annual reports and gurufocus.com. The average growth rate of total assets, short-term investments, and total equity during the period 2018–2022 were 1%, 44%, and 8%, respectively. The total revenues increased by 12% while the total operating expenses increased by 14%. The net income has shown a fluctuating trend during the above period. The market capitalization increased by 15% on an average basis during the period 2018–2022.

Table 5 gives the performance measures during the period 2018–2022.

The average net margin, ROE, and ROA during the period 2018–2022 were 10.80%, 9.51%, and 3.2%, respectively. The average debt-equity ratio was 1.33 during the above period.

References

1. https://www.ssctech.com/about-us/acquisitions#
2. https://investor.ssctech.com/investor-relations/

Case 53 Hibbett, Inc.

Hibbett is a leading athletic fashion retailer with approximately 1100 stores under the Hibbett and City Gear banners. The company was founded in the year 1945 and is headquartered in Birmingham, Alabama. Hibbett offers personalized customer service and access to footwear, apparel, and equipment from top brands such as Nike, Jordan, and Adidas. By January 2022, Hibbett owned approximately 1096 retail stores consisting of 900 Hibbett stores, 179 City Gear stores, and 17 Sports Additions athletic shoe stores. These stores are located in 35 states across the United States. By 2022, the store base of Hibbett consists of 833 stores located in strip centers, 32 free-standing stores, and 231 enclosed mall locations. Consumers can make new purchases, browse, and find new information through its website www.hibbett.com. The purchases can be made online or by visiting the nearest store of the company. By January 2022, Hibbett employed approximately 11,000 team members of which 3600 were full-time team members. Over 92% of the total population work in retail locations. None of the team members were represented by a labor union. The Moonan family has owned the Hibbert and its predecessors since the 1930s.

Table 1 shows the Store brand details of the company. Strip centers include free-standing stores. Approximately 90% of the merchandise in the Sports Additions stores are related to athletic footwear.

Growth Strategy

The stores of Hibbett offer a core merchandising mix of premium athletic branded footwear, accessories, and team sports equipment which are designed for GEN-Z customers within each market. The focus of the company is on meeting the fashion and technical demands of its customers. The company targets the underserved markets with branded products and gives special attention in terms of providing a high level of customer service. The company provides a premium assortment of footwear, apparel, accessories, and team sports equipment. The company

© The Author(s), under exclusive license to Springer Nature Switzerland AG 2024

B. R. Kumar, *Rising Stars*, Management for Professionals,
https://doi.org/10.1007/978-3-031-50032-9_53

Table 1 Store brand details

Location				
Brand	Average Square Footage	Strip Center	Mall	Total
Hibbett	5800	720	180	900
City gear	5100	142	37	179
Sports additions	2900	3	14	17

Source Annual Report 2022

differentiates its store experience through extensive product knowledge, customer service, and convenient locations.

Hibbett is recognized as a leading specialty retailer in these underserved markets. The company distinguishes itself from major national competitors through alignment of its merchandising mix to local preferences and also by means of providing sales opportunities for its vendor partners. The company relies on information systems to maintain checks on inventory and operating costs. Hibbett identifies markets for its stores through a clustered expansion program. This strategy enables the company to open new stores within the close proximity of existing locations thereby consolidating the efficiencies with respect to logistics, marketing, and regional management. Potential markets are evaluated for enhancing return on investment through consideration of factors such as economic conditions, local competitive dynamics, and availability of appropriate real estate. The company also focuses on omni-channel strategy by making investments to enhance the website and apps, fulfillment capabilities, and speed. In the year 2023, the focus of Hibbett is on investment in the next-generation omni-channel capabilities. This would facilitate the company to offer greater shopping flexibility and convenience. In addition to full line wholesale and logistics facility, the company also utilizes a third-party logistics facility to enhance efficiencies and improve time to market. The main products are allocated and shipped to stores through an automatic replenishment system based on inventory levels and sales.

Merchandise is delivered to stores and transferred between stores via small package carriers. The company has increased its delivery frequency to all stores in the chain and improved its store-to-store transfer capabilities to enhance speed to market and in-store product availability. Strong logistics support is a critical element for the growth of the company's business success. The merchandising strategy focuses on a TOE-TO-HEAD approach wherein the company provides a broad assortment of premium brand-name footwear, apparel, accessories, and team sports equipment at competitive prices in a full-service omni-channel environment. The company coordinates with vendors to educate sales staff at store level with respect to new products and trends. The company offers a best-in-class omni-channel experience through physical locations, mobile apps, and website. The company is a pioneer in offering primary retail distribution avenues for brand names in underserved markets. As a result of this strategic initiative, the company was able to establish long-term partnerships with vendors. The company works with vendors to establish favorable pricing and receive cooperative marketing funds. The company uses technology as an enabler of its business strategies. The company implements and maintains systems that are targeted at improving financial control, cost management, inventory control, merchandise planning, logistics, replenishment, and product allocation. Critical business data are processed from stores, third-party cloud providers, and data centers by the company's communication networks. Hibbett attempts to mitigate the risk of cyber security threats and business interruptions by establishing strong security protocols, threat monitoring, regular risk reviews, and a detailed disaster recovery plan.

Competition

Hibbett operates in a highly competitive environment. The athletic specialty merchandise is highly fragmented with the presence of different brick and mortar and online retailers who compete for market share through different formats and merchandising strategies. Hibbett competes with specialty shoe stores, department, and traditional shoe stores, mass merchandisers, e-commerce retailers, and national sporting goods superstores in large and medium-sized markets.

ESG Initiatives

The company stresses upon the use of ecofriendly products as a part of its commitment toward corporate sustainability initiatives. The company provides services based on a strong emphasis with respect to sound environmental practices. The company has entered into a partnership with a third party to develop a science-based methodology for measuring, monitoring, and reporting on sustainability initiatives. The current focus of Hibbert is on reduction of waste and energy consumption along with sustainable product offerings. Hibbert's LED Lighting Initiative which was initiated in year 2016 aims to reduce store energy use by 30% approximately. The company has target plans to divert waste from landfills by increasing focus on existing recycling programs. For waste reduction, the company recycles corrugated boxes and strives to reuse cartons and pallets for its logistics facility. The shopping bags provided by the company contain approximately 15% of recycled materials. With respect to initiatives for promoting sustainable product offerings, the company supports Nike's Move to Zero®, a closed-loop process that uses manufacturing scrap, unsellable products, and worn-out shoes to make new products, by significant marketing and social media efforts and in-store displays.

The company supports different organizations such as the Leukemia and Lymphoma Society, Children's Hospital of Alabama, Alabama Sheriff's Youth Ranch, UAB O'Neal Comprehensive Cancer Center, and the Jefferson County, Alabama Board of Education through financial grants and in-kind giving. Hibbert's retail store members engage with local community partners by hosting events such as free haircuts for back to school and holiday food drives. In the year 2022, the company partnered with over 85 schools through the program SOLE SCHOOL which organized product donations, engagement programs, career coaching, academic incentives, and monetary donations.

Risk Factors

The COVID-19 pandemic has significantly impacted the domestic and international global supply chain of the company and has negatively affected the flow or the availability of certain products. Hibbett is a retailer of manufacturer's branded items and its business performance is dependent on its relationship with vendors and ability to purchase brand merchandise at competitive prices. In 2022, approximately 61% of the inventory was purchased from one vendor, Nike. Approximately 64% of the net sales were accounted from Nike in fiscal year 2022. Any adverse effect on the business of such large vendors will adversely affect the performance of the company. Hibbett cannot control the supply, design, function, or cost of the products which are offered for sale by the company. Factors such as security threats which include physical and cyber security, unauthorized disclosure of sensitive information would harm the business of the company. The online operations of the company depend upon the secure transmission of confidential information over public networks such as information involving cashless payments. Hibbett depends on commercially available systems, software, tools to provide security for processing, transmission, and storage of all data. The competition in the e-commerce market continues to be highly intensive. The sales and profitability of Hibbert would be adversely affected if the company is unable to identify and capitalize on new retail trends or provide an omni-channel experience for its customers as offered by more established e-commerce companies such as Amazon. The business of the company would be adversely affected in case of failure to effectively manage social media and other consumer-oriented technologies related to information dissemination. Direct competition from key vendors who sell directly to consumers through consumer programs may affect the business performance of the company. The business success of Hibbett depends on the ability to identify product trends and respond to changing merchandise trends and consumer demand in appropriate time period. Decreases in customer traffic in malls and shopping centers on account of factors such as the growing preference for online shopping may affect the ability of company to attract customers to the stores and hence profitability may be affected. The imposition of tariffs and export controls on the products might have an adverse effect on the business operations of the company. New emerging technologies such as artificial intelligence and Internet of Things (IoT) may create disruption in the retail industry. In this scenario, the failure of the company to quickly adapt to these changes may affect the supply chain, distribution channels, and point of sale capabilities. The company also faces risks related to governance, regulatory, legislative, and legal matters. The failure to comply with changes in federal, state, or local laws would expose the company to legal risks.

Stock Performance

Table 2 analyzes the cumulative 5-year shareholder return generation for Hibbett stock in comparison with that of cumulative total returns for market indexes Nasdaq Composite index and Nasdaq Retail trade index. The analysis assumes a $100 investment in the stock and indexes with the reinvestment of all dividends from the period January 31, 2017, to January 31, 2022.

Based on the above analysis, Hibbett stock had a holding period return of 89% compared to 166% and 182% returns accounted by market indexes Nasdaq Composite and Nasdaq Retail Trade during the period 2017–2022. However, the average yearly return registered by Hibbett stock was 26.09% while that of the Nasdaq Composite and Nasdaq Retail Trade Index were 22.70% and 6.72%, respectively, during the period 2017–2022.

The following section analyzes the monthly stock returns for Hibbett and Nasdaq Composite during the recent 5-year period March 2018–February 2023. The Hibbett stock which was trading at $23.95 on March 1st, 2018, increased by 2.90 times to trade at $69.48 by February 1st, 2023. The total monthly cumulative return for the Hibbett stock was 188% compared to monthly cumulative returns of 66% accounted by market index Nasdaq Composite during the 5-year period March 2018–February 2023. The 5-yearly average returns for Hibbett and Nasdaq Composite were 38% and 13%, respectively during the above period. The data for analysis is sourced from Yahoo Finance.

Table 3 shows the holding period return for Hibbett stock and market index during the period 2018–2022. The holding period analysis assumes a holding period of 1 year.

The Hibbett stock outperformed the market index Nasdaq Composite in all years except in year 2018.

Table 4 shows the comparative book and market value of equity of Hibbett during the period 2018–2022. The values are given in millions of dollars.

Table 2 Comparative stock wealth

Year	2017	2018	2019	2020	2021	2022
Hibbett	$100	$68.48	$49.52	$75.09	$171.06	$188.53
Nasdaq composite	$100	$133.43	$132.52	$168.35	$242.57	$265.98
Nasdaq retail trade index	$100	$152.24	$161.79	$187.53	$298.48	$281.88

Source Annual Report 2022

Table 3 Holding period return

Year	Hibbett	Nasdaq Composite	Excess returns
2018	−40%	−6%	−34%
2019	72%	23%	48%
2020	86%	41%	46%
2021	27%	20%	8%
2022	11%	−26%	37%

Table 4 Comparative book and market value of equity

Year	2018	2019	2020	2021	2022
Book value of equity	319.6	336.05	328.98	391.04	291.52
Market value of equity	428.33	298.97	417.8	930.23	819.53
BV as percent of MV	74.6%	78.5%	110.0%	93.6%	31.3%

Table 5 Financial highlights

	(In millions of dollars)				
Financial highlights	2018	2019	2020	2021	2022
Total assets	461.85	546.07	769.76	808.17	703.22
Short-term investments	73.54	61.76	66.08	209.29	17.05
Total equity	319.60	336.05	328.98	391.04	291.52
Total revenue	968.22	1008.68	1184.23	1419.66	1691.80
Total operating expenses	256.04	291.19	347.33	386.44	418.24
Net income	35.03	28.42	27.34	74.27	174.31
Market capitalization	428.33	298.97	417.80	930.23	819.53
Enterprise value	357.97	275.23	605.66	969.24	1085.74

Table 6 Performance indicators

Ratios	2018	2019	2020	2021	2022
Net margin%	3.62	2.82	2.31	5.23	10.31
ROE%	10.72	8.67	8.22	20.63	51.08
ROA%	7.61	5.64	4.16	9.41	23.07
DER	0.01	0.11	0.77	0.64	0.97

The average book value as a percent of market value of equity was approximately 62.5% during the period 2018–2022.

Table 5 shows the financial highlights of the company during the period 2018–2022.

On average basis, the total assets and short-term investments increased by 12.80% and 29% during the period 2018–2022. The total revenues and net income grew by 15% and 71%, respectively. The total expenses increased by 13% on average basis. The market capitalization and enterprise value increased by 30% and 42%, respectively, on average basis during the above period. The data is sourced from annual reports and gurufocus.com.

Table 6 shows the profitability measures and leverage ratio of the company during the period 2018–2022.

The average net margin, ROE, and ROA during the period 2018–2022 were 4.85%, 19.86%, and 9.98%, respectively. In the year 2022, the company's ROE and ROA were 51% and 23%, respectively. The average debt-equity ratio was 0.5.

Table 7 shows the estimation of economic value for the company in the years 2021 and 2022. The values are estimated in millions of dollars.

The economic value has increased from $36.84 million in the year 2021 to $141.90 million in the year 2022.

Table 7 Estimation of economic value

Year	2021	2022
Profit before income tax	97.95	227.89
Income tax	23.68	53.58
Net operating profit after tax (NOPAT)	74.27	174.31
Stockholder equity	391.04	291.52
Total capital employed	391.04	291.52
WACC	9.57%	11.12%
Capital charge	37.42	32.42
Economic value	36.84	141.90

References

1. https://investors.hibbett.com/websites/hibbett/English/0/investor-relations.html
2. ESG Report 2021

Case 54 LGI Homes, Inc

LGI Homes, Inc. is a Delaware corporation incorporated in the year 2013. LGI Homes is involved in the design, construction, and sale of new homes in different markets in the United States. The management team of the company has been in the residential land development business from the mid-1990s onward. The company commenced homebuilding operations in the year 2003. Over the past two decades, LGI Homes has constructed and closed over 50,000 homes. By 2021, the company has made 10,442 home closings. LGI Homes had its initial public offering in the year 2013. Over the past decade, the company has expanded its presence from nine markets in four states to 35 markets in 19 states in the United States. The company focusses on geographical expansion as a part of its growth strategy. LGI Homes has a diversified multiple entry-level product offerings such as attached and detached homes, active adult offerings. The active adult offerings are sold under the LGI Homes brand. The luxury series homes are sold under the Terrata Homes brand. The wholesale business unit builds and sells houses to corporates who are looking to acquire multiple homes for rental purposes through bulk sales agreements. LGI Mortgage Solutions facilitates sources of finances for the customers. By 2021, 93 active communities possessed the LGI Homes brand. Eight communities had the Terrata Homes brand. In 2021, the LGI Homes had closed 183 Terrata Homes with an average sales price per home of $482,410. The pricing strategy of the attached townhome product involving entry-level pricing within the reach of new home buyers enables the company to expand into the densely populated markets and insulate the company against rising land and home costs. In the years 2020 and 2021, the company had 850 and 1515 wholesale home closings respectively. By December 31, 2021, the company employed 952 people.

The homebuilding operations are managed by seven operating segments West, Northwest, Central, Midwest, Florida, Southeast, and Mid-Atlantic. In 2019, LGI Homes introduced CompleteHome and CompleteHome Plus packages which featured attractive move-in ready homes with superior quality and more standard features. These packages offered upgraded standard features such as cabinets with crown molding, granite or quartz tops, Kwikset door hardware, and a Wi-Fi-enabled

© The Author(s), under exclusive license to Springer Nature Switzerland AG 2024
B. R. Kumar, *Rising Stars*, Management for Professionals,
https://doi.org/10.1007/978-3-031-50032-9_54

garage door opener. The CompleteHome Plus package includes all features in the CompleteHome package plus 42-inch upper cabinets, 9-foot ceilings, designer paint selections, enhanced landscaping selections, and window blinds. LGI Homes made an average home completion time of approximately 90–130 days in the year 2021. Experienced construction management professionals are employed by LGI Homes to perform the tasks of general contractors for home construction. LGI's own employees provide the purchasing, construction management, and quality assurance for the homes built whereas the third-party subcontractors provide the material and labor components for the houses built by LGI Homes. Construction managers with local market knowledge and expertise are employed for the construction activity.

With respect to land acquisition and development policies, LGI Homes is an active and opportunistic acquirer of land for residential development in different markets. The company sources land from a wide range of landowners, brokers, lenders, builders, and land development firms. LGI Homes maintains a pipeline of land positions for replacement communities and new communities. By December 2021, the lot inventory amounted to 91,845 owned or controlled lots. The allocation of capital for land investment is undertaken at the corporate level based on a portfolio management approach. LGI Homes has purchased larger tracts of land across different markets to build homes with multiple price points in the communities.

Strategy

LGI Homes focusses on a flexible land acquisition strategy of either purchasing/ optioning finished lots at attractive prices or purchase of raw land for residential development. As a land developer, the company has rich experience in converting raw land into residential communities. LGI Homes maintains a pipeline of land portfolio for replacement communities and new communities. Land acquisitions are specially targeted at locations further away from urban centers but with access to centers of business and retail districts. These target areas offer a better value proposition for homeowners in terms of lower prices or larger lot sizes. Projects are evaluated using an elaborate due diligence checklist with parameters such as assessment of permits and regulatory requirements, environmental factors, market conditions, floor plans, pricing, and financial viability in terms of forecasted returns. Demand estimates are also made with respect to potential residents in the market and rental households within driving distance of the proposed projects. The focus of LGI Homes is on entry-level home buyers. The company uses extensive digital and print advertising methods such as interactive online media, social media, direct mail, directional signage, and billboards to attract potential homebuyers. Each customer is provided with a complete introduction to the community and information regarding utilities, educational institutions, local entertainment, and shopping options. The company does not sell a home until the construction has begun on the house. The continuous construction methodology enables the company to build and maintain an inventory of move-in-ready homes that are available for immediate sale.

LGI Homes operates in a highly competitive homebuilding environment. The company competes in each of its markets with numerous national, regional, and local homebuilders for homebuyers, land properties, financing, raw materials, and skilled labor.

Risk Factors

The long-term sustainability and growth of the business of LGI Homes depend on the ability of the company to acquire finished lots and land parcels for undertaking homebuilding at competitive prices. Factors such as risks inherent in controlling, purchasing, and developing land for home construction are immense. As demand for housing decreases and the holding period increases, there is substantial risk in purchasing and developing land parcels on account of realization of profits from such deals. Inventory carrying costs can result in reduced margins or losses in a poorly performing community or market. Development of land and construction of homes involves a significant amount of time and huge cash investment. The residential construction industry experiences raw material shortages, labor shortages, price fluctuations, and supply chain constraints which would lead to increase in the cost of home construction. The labor and raw material shortages are more severe during times of natural disasters or economic disruptions such as COVID-19 pandemic. The business performance of LGI Homes depends on the availability, skill, and performance of subcontractors. LGI Homes being a homebuilder and land developer faces risks related to construction defect, product liability, and home and other warranty claims. Construction defects and warranty matters can result in negative publicity which could damage the reputation of the home and negatively affect the ability to sell homes. Delays with respect to the development of communities and delays on the part of subcontractors to perform development activities would affect the performance of the company. The company faces risks related to sources of financing if the surety providers are reluctant to issue bonds, letters of credit, or guarantees for the completion of housing development projects. In 2021, the company established LGI Mortgage Solutions, a joint venture with third-party lenders. The success of these relationships depends upon the financial stability of the joint venture partners. Disputes with joint venture partners may result in litigation or arbitration which would increase the expenses for LGI Homes. Macroeconomic risk factors such as inflation could adversely affect the financial results due to increase in the costs of land, raw materials, and labor, which is needed to operate the business. The business prospects of the company would be adversely affected due to tightening of mortgage lending standards and mortgage financing requirements as inappropriate mortgage loan originations and rising mortgage interest rates could adversely affect the availability of mortgage loans for potential home buyers of the company. Uncertainty in the financial, credit, and consumer lending markets would impact the growth of homebuilding industry in general. LGI Homes faces stiff competition in the homebuilding industry. Ownership, leasing, or occupation of land and use of hazardous materials might lead to potential environmental risks and liabilities for the company. The company is subject to a variety of local, state and federal statutes, rules and regulations related to easements, land use, and the protection of health and the environment.

Stock Performance

Table 1 compares the cumulative total return for LGI Homes stock with that of S&P 500 Index and S&P's Homebuilders Select Industry Index during the 5-year period 2017–2021. The analysis assumes $100 invested at the close of market on December 31, 2016, in the stock and indexes and reinvestment of any dividends.

The holding period return for LGI Homes was 438% compared to 113% and 152% accounted by the market indexes S&P 500 and S&P 500 Homebuilders Index. The 5-yearly average returns for LGI Homes, S&P 500, and S&P 500 Homebuilders Index were 54.69%, 17.04%, and 23.84%, respectively, during the above period.

The following section compares the total cumulative monthly returns for LGI Homes stock with that of the cumulative monthly returns of S&P 500 during the period March 2018–February 2022. The LGI Homes stock which was trading at $70.57 on March 1st, 2018, had increased 1.65 times to trade at $116.91 by February 1st, 2023. The total monthly cumulative returns for the LGI Homes stock was 113% compared to 52% for the market index S&P 500 during the period March 2018–February 2023. The stock made approximately twice the average yearly returns compared to the S&P 500 Index. The average yearly returns for the stock and index were 23% and 11%, respectively, during the above period. The data source is Yahoo Finance.

Table 2 shows the holding period return for the stock and S&P 500 Index during the period 2018–2022. The holding period return analysis is based on holding period of 1 year.

On the basis of holding period return, the stock performance was better in the years 2020 and 2021 compared to the performance of market index S&P 500.

Table 1 Comparative total returns for stock and market indexes

Year	2016	2017	2018	2019	2020	2021
LGI homes	$100	$261.16	$157.40	$245.91	$368.43	$537.70
S&P 500	$100	$119.42	$111.97	$144.31	$167.77	$212.89
S&P 500 homebuilders index	$100	$130.65	$95.95	$134.45	$169.62	$252.40

Source: Annual Report 2021

Table 2 Comparative holding period return

Year	LGI Homes	S&P 500	Excess returns
2018	−36%	−5%	−31%
2019	19%	19%	0%
2020	33%	16%	16%
2021	45%	28%	16%
2022	−26%	−15%	−11%

Table 3 Value comparison

Year	2017	2018	2019	2020	2021
Book value of equity	413.92	576.57	760.67	936.26	1235.33
Market value of equity	1399.43	892.17	1584.96	2198.56	3157.1
BV as percent of MV	29.6%	41.2%	85.3%	59.1%	56.2%

Table 4 Financial highlights

	(In millions of dollars)				
Financial highlights	2017	2018	2019	2020	2021
Total assets	912.51	1226.62	1499.5	1501.04	2081.4
Short-term investments	57.1	40.98	34.51	29.54	44.7
Total equity	413.92	576.57	760.67	936.26	1235.33
Total revenue	1062.98	1322.37	1654.34	1946.44	2699.38
Total operating expenses	127.27	158.05	188.05	195.95	239.25
Net income	95.74	136.50	160.75	266.24	380.24
Market capitalization	1399.43	892.17	1584.96	2198.56	3157.10
Enterprise value	1743.87	1425.82	2177.04	2615.92	3829.75

Table 5 Profitability and leverage measures

Ratios	2017	2018	2019	2020	2021
Net margin%	9.01	10.32	9.72	13.68	14.09
ROE%	25.51	27.56	24.04	31.38	35.02
ROA%	11.37	12.76	11.79	17.75	21.23
DER	0.97	1	0.82	0.48	0.58

Table 3 evaluates the book and market value of equity of the company during the 5-year period 2017–2021. The values are given in millions of dollars.

The average book value of equity as percent of market value was approximately 57.6% during the period 2017–2021. Table 4 shows the financial highlights of the company in millions of dollars during the period 2018–2022.

On average basis, the total assets and total equity increased by 24% and 32%, respectively, during the period 2018–2022. The total revenues and net income increased by 26% and 42%, respectively. The operating expenses on an average basis increased by 17%. The market capitalization and enterprise value of the company increased by 31% and 25%, respectively, during the above period. The data source is annual reports and gurufocus.com.

Table 5 gives the profitability ratios and leverage position of the company during the period 2017–2021.

The average net margin, ROE, and ROA for LGI Homes during the above period were 11.36%, 28.70%, and 14.98%, respectively. The average debt-equity ratio during the above period was 0.77.

Table 6 shows the estimation of economic value for LGI Homes during the years 2020 and 2021. The values are given in millions of dollars.

Table 6 Economic value

Year	2020	2021
Profit before income tax	302.37	480.36
Income tax	36.13	100.11
Net operating profit after tax (NOPAT)	266.24	380.25
Stockholder equity	936.26	1235.33
Long-term debt	442.56	712.63
Total capital employed	1378.82	1947.96
WACC	7.84%	10.58%
Capital charge	108.10	206.09
Economic value	158.14	174.16

The economic value for LGI Homes has improved from $158.14 million to $174.16 million in 2021 compared to the previous year.

References

1. LGI Homes Annual Report 2021
2. https://www.lgihomes.com/

Case 55 Align Technology Inc

Align Technology is a global medical device company, which is involved in the design, manufacture, and marketing of Invisalign® clear aligners, iTero® intraoral scanners and services for dentistry, and exocad® computer-aided design and computer-aided manufacturing ("CAD/CAM") software for dental laboratories and dental practitioners. Consumer products that are complementary to principal products prescribed by doctors are also sold by the company mainly under the Invisalign brand. The consumer products sold by Align Technology include retainers, aligner cases (clamshells), teeth whitening products, and cleaning solutions. The company is focused on positioning itself as the main treatment provider preferred by orthodontists and general dental practitioners. The products are sold through a specialized sales force to its customers consisting of orthodontists, general practitioner dentists, aesthetic dentists, oral surgeons, and dental laboratories. The products are also sold to Dental Support Organizations. The manufacturing facilities for aligner fabrication and distribution are located in Mexico and China. The digital treatment planning facilities are located globally in regions which includes Costa Rica, China, Germany, Spain, and Japan. By December 2021, the company had approximately 22,540 employees.

The company has two operating Systems-Clear Aligner and Imaging Systems and CAD/CAM Services. Clear Aligner net revenues accounted for 82% of the worldwide net revenues while Systems and Services net revenues accounted for 18% of the worldwide revenues. The products representing clear aligners are sold under the Invisalign brand name. The Invisalign system is basically used for the treatment of malocclusions. The company's iTero intraoral scanner is used by dental professionals and labs and service providers for restorative and orthodontic digital procedures along with Invisalign case submissions. The company have sold over 68,000 iTero scanners by the year end of 2021. Align Technologies' CAD/CAM software products offer restorative dentistry, implantology, guided surgery, and smile design to dental labs and dental practices. The company has over 200 exocad strategic distribution partners and over 47,000 software licenses installed globally.

© The Author(s), under exclusive license to Springer Nature Switzerland AG 2024
B. R. Kumar, *Rising Stars*, Management for Professionals,
https://doi.org/10.1007/978-3-031-50032-9_55

Clear Aligner Segment

Malocclusion and Traditional Orthodontic Treatment

It is estimated that 21 million people are treated by orthodontists for Malocclusion, the most common clinical dental problem. Traditional methods such as metal arch wires and brackets are used for treatment in the normal course of treatment. The Invisalign system is used as post-treatment retainer appliance of 90% of the patients.

The Invisalign System

The Invisalign system is a proprietary method for treating malocclusion based on a proprietary computer-simulated virtual treatment plan and series of custom manufactured, polymer-based removable aligners. The phases of Invisalign system consist of diagnosis and transmission of treatment data, computer-simulated treatment plan, review, and approval of the treatment plan, manufacture of custom aligners, and shipment to the dental professional and patient aligner wear.

Globally more than 85% of Invisalign system case submissions are submitted via digital scan such as Align's iTero scanner or certain third-party scanners.

Clear Aligner Products

Comprehensive Products—Invisalign Treatment Option

The Invisalign Comprehensive Package offers treatment for mild-to-severe malocclusion in adults and teenagers. It also serves the orthodontic needs of younger patients with features such as mandibular advancement, compliance indicators, and compensation for tooth eruption.

Non-Comprehensive Products—Invisalign Treatment Options

Align Technologies also offers low-priced treatment packages for complex orthodontic cases, non-comprehensive relapse cases, and cosmetic treatments. These treatment packages include Invisalign Express, Lite, Go, Go Plus, and Moderate.

New Products

Invisalign G8 with SmartForce® Activation is a new clear aligner biomechanical innovation that is designed to optimize tooth movements. In 2022, Align Technologies introduced Align digital platform consisting of software, systems, and services to integrate users such as doctors, labs, patients, and consumers.

Non-Case Products

The non-case products of Clear Aligner consist of retention products, Invisalign training, tools for dental professionals, and oral health products. Align Technologies offers four sets of custom clear aligners caller Vivera retainers composed of proprietary material for tooth position alignment. In 2021, the company entered into a multi-year supply and distribution agreement with Ultradent Products to facilitate Invisalign system-trained dentists to offer a professional whitening system using Ultradent's Opalescence whitening system with Vivera retainers.

SmartTrack Aligner Material

SmartTrack clear aligner material is a patented and custom-engineered Invisalign system for orthodontic tooth movements.

Systems and Services Segment

Intraoral scanning which has a significant impact on the practice of dentistry is a rapidly evolving technology. The iTero portfolio of intraoral scanners includes the iTero Element 2, the iTero Element Flex, iTero Element 5D Imaging System, and iTero Element Plus Series. The iTero Element 5D imaging system is the first integrated dental imaging system which simultaneously records 3D, intraoral color camera images, and near imaging ("NIRI") technology.

Services and Ancillary Products

The Restorative software for iTero scanners and imaging systems is designed for General Practitioners, prosthodontists, periodontists, and oral surgeons. Orthodontic software for iTero scanners and imaging systems is designed for orthodontists for digital records storage, orthodontic diagnosis, and fabrication of printed models and retainers. The company's exocad CAD/CAM software platform offers end-to-end digital platform workflow for ortho-restorative and comprehensive dentistry. Align Technologies also sells disposal sleeves for the wand and other ancillary products for the iTero scanners.

iTero Applications and Tools

The Invisalign Outcome Simulator is an exclusive chair-side and cloud-based application for the iTero scanner used for the Invisalign system of treatment. The Invisalign Progress Assessment tool is a comparative tool for the Clincheck treatment plan which involves color-coded tooth movement report. The TimeLapse technology allows practitioners to compare patient's historic 3D scans and enables clinicians to identify and measure orthodontic movement, tooth wear, and gingival recession.

Business Strategy

The company focusses on providing digital solutions to assist doctors and lab technicians in offering the best possible treatment experiences for the improvement of overall oral health. The company aims to expand its presence abroad by entering new regions and countries. In 2021, the percentage of global doctors trained to prescribe treatment under the Invisalign system grew by 21% compared to the previous year. By the end of 2021, the company has made its presence in more than 100 countries either selling directly or through authorized distributors. The company fabricates its aligners in China for APAC markets. The company is creating an infrastructure that allows the company to address local and regional needs while providing global operational flexibility and scale to meet global and regional demand. The strategic aim is to drive Invisalign treatment growth by developing innovative technology for digital dental scans, exocad CAD/CAM software for solutions targeted at dental labs. The company focusses on enabling general practitioners to identify potential cases which can be treated using the Invisalign system and refer cases to orthodontist to provide high-quality restorative, orthodontic, and dental hygiene care. Digital tools such as the iTero scanner and products like Invisalign Go treatment focusses on satisfying the distinctive needs of General Practitioner Patients. The company focusses on creating awareness for Invisalign treatment among consumers by using an integrated consumer marketing strategy which involves digital media, social networking, event marketing, and strategic alliances with professional sports teams. Align Technologies supports doctors to adopt digital dentistry through programs such as the Align Digital and Practice Transformation (ADAPT) which is an expert and independent fee-based consulting service to optimize operational workflow and enhance patients' experiences. Recently the company has started offering additional dental-related consumer products in certain e-commerce channels in the United States. Align Technologies also focuses on innovating its Invisalign system through improvements in its Invisalign treatment software and ClinCheck Pro software. Through the innovation of the Align digital platform, the company focusses on enhancing the digital treatment planning experience for orthodontics and restorative dentistry. Align Technologies' R&D activities are focused toward development of next generation of products and solutions for the Align digital platform. By the end of December 2021, Align Technologies had 642 active US patents, 724 active foreign patents, and 736 pending global patent applications. The company had spent $250 million toward R&D investments in the year 2021.

The clear aligner products of the company compete directly against companies that provide orthodontic treatments with metal brackets and wires both in the United

States and at global level. The company also faces competition in the emerging and rapidly evolving markets for intraoral scanners and software solutions which include CAD/CAM.

ESG Initiatives

The Align Foundation has contributed over $4.6 million to charitable causes such as Operation Smile, America's Tooth Fairy, and other non-profit organizations which are dedicated to youth development through educational programs. The company has donated more than $2.5 million to Operation Smile, a global medical non-profit organization, which provide thousands of free surgeries for people born with cleft lip and cleft palate in low- and middle-income countries. In 2018, the company established the Month of Smiles, a dedicated month of giving where all employees are encouraged to contribute toward making a difference in the lives of others. Align Technologies has supported America's Tooth Fairy program by providing approximately $2 million dollars for the operational expenses of the foundation and children's oral health programs. Through the program, the company created awareness in more than 8 million children and their caregivers about prevention of tooth decay and gum disease. The global women@align chapters encourage networking, professional development, leadership mentoring, and educational projects. In 2019, Align was named as one of the best Places to Work in IT by Computerworld. In 2019 and 2020, the Canadian Great Place to Work program has recognized Align as a top workplace in the areas of Giving Back, Managed by Women and in Healthcare. The products and services of the company are broadly used across age groups, gender identities, races, ethnicities, and cultures. In 2021, 54% of the company's employees had engaged in some form of professional development activities.

Risk Factors

The operations of Align Technologies have been materially adversely affected by the pandemic COVID-19. The decline in sales of the company's products and services in the Invisalign ecosystem and iTero scanners may adversely affect the net revenues and gross margin of the company. The company faces aggressive competition from existing competitors or other firms that may use new technologies to create orthodontic appliances and solutions. An increasing portion of the total revenues from international sales are generated through the company's direct and indirect operations. The demand for the company's products depends on different factors such as changing consumer demand and economic conditions. The success of the company also depends upon how successfully the firm introduces, achieves market acceptance, and manages new products and services. The company relies on efficient, uninterrupted, and secure operation of its own complex information technology systems and is dependent on key software of third parties which are embedded in the firm's products and IT systems. Disruption in the operations of the primary freight carrier, higher shipping costs, or delays could disrupt the supply chain and affect net revenues of the company.

Stock Performance Analysis

The common stock is traded on the NASDAQ Global Market under the symbol ALGN. This section compares the stock returns of Align Technologies with that of market index S&P 1500 Healthcare Equipment and Supplies Index during the 5-year period March 2018–February 2023. Align Stock which was trading at $251.31 on March 1st, 2018, increased by 1.21 times to trade at $304 by February 1st, 2023. The total cumulative monthly return for Align Technology stock was 91% compared to the cumulative monthly return of 52% registered by the market index S&P 500 Healthcare Equipment and Supplies Index during the 5-year period March 2018–February 2023. The 5-year average yearly return for Align was 19% compared to 10% average yearly returns of the market index S&P 1500.

Table 1 gives the holding period returns for Align stock and market index S&P 1500 during the 5-year period 2018–2022. The analysis is based on the assumption of holding period of 1 year.

The stock outperformed the market index to a great extent in the year 2020 with excess returns of 92%. The data source is Yahoo Finance.

Table 2 compares the book value of equity with the market value of equity of Align Technologies during the period 2018–2022. The values are given in millions of dollars.

The average book value of equity as percent of market value of equity was 7.8% during the period 2018–2022.

Table 3 shows the financial highlights of the company during the period 2018–2022.

The data source is annual reports and gurufocus.com. The total assets, short-term investments, and total equity increased by 34.5%, 9%, and 40% on average basis

Table 1 Holding period return

Year	Align technologies	S&P 1500	Excess returns
2018	−17%	−6%	−10%
2019	12%	19%	−7%
2020	108%	16%	92%
2021	25%	24%	1%
2022	−57%	−16%	−42%

Table 2 Book value and market value of equity

Year	2018	2019	2020	2021	2022
Book value of equity	1252.89	1346.17	3233.87	3622.71	3601.36
Market value of equity	16707.91	21885.94	42141.21	51726.64	16302.57
BV as percent of MV	7.5%	8.1%	14.8%	8.6%	7.0%

Table 3 Financial highlights

	(In millions of dollars)				
Financial highlights	2018	2019	2020	2021	2022
Total assets	2052.46	2500.7	4829.68	5942.11	5947.95
Short-term investments	735.36	868.63	960.84	1171.34	999.58
Total equity	1252.89	1346.17	3233.87	3622.71	3601.36
Total revenue	1966.49	2406.8	2471.94	3952.58	3734.64
Total operating expenses	981.3	1229.41	1376.06	1958.96	1979.73
Net income	400.24	442.78	1775.89	772.02	361.75
Market capitalization	16707.91	21885.94	42141.21	51726.64	16302.57
Enterprise value	15972.55	21076.52	41266.54	50680.67	15403.32

Table 4 Performance indicators

Ratios	2018	2019	2020	2021	2022
Net margin%	20.35	18.4	71.84	19.53	9.68
ROE%	33.25	34.07	77.55	22.52	10.01
ROA%	20.86	19.45	48.45	14.33	6.08
DER		0.04	0.03	0.04	0.03

during the period 2018–2022. The total revenues declined in the year 2022 compared to the previous year. The average growth rate of revenues was 20% during the period 2018–2022. The net income is showing huge fluctuating trend. The market capitalization and enterprise value declined by approximately 70% in the year 2022 compared to the previous year.

Table 4 shows the profitability and leverage position of the firm during the period 2018–2022.

The average net margin, ROE, and ROA were 27.96%, 35.48%, and 21.83%, respectively, during the period 2018–2022. The average debt-equity ratio for the firm was 0.035.

References

1. https://investor.aligntech.com/financial-information/annual-report
2. Annual Report 2021

Case 56 Adobe

Adobe is involved in the game-changing innovations for enhancing digital experiences by adding millions of new customers, delivering billions of experiences across screens, and processing trillions of data transactions online. Adobe is in the Fortune's Best Companies to Work in list for the past 21 years. Adobe was founded by Charles Geschke and John Warnock in the year 1982. The company had its IPO listing on August 20, 1986. In 2022, the company generated US$ 17.61 billion in revenues. The company employs over 28,000 people globally.

Adobe is one of the largest and most diversified software companies in the world. Adobe offers a line of products and services which are used by professionals like photographers, video editors, designers and game developers, content creators, and knowledge workers. Adobe licenses its products to end users through its own app stores and own website at www.adobe.com. Adobe offers many products via a Software-as-a-Service (SaaS) model or managed services model which could be through hosted or cloud-based through term subscription and pay-per-use models. The company also distributes some products and services through a network of distributors, value-added resellers, systems integrators, software developers, and original equipment manufacturers. The products of the company are run on desktop and laptop computers, other devices, and web depending on the product. The company has operations in the Americas, Europe, Middle East, Africa, and Asia Pacific. By December 2021, the company employed 25,988 people.

Offerings

Digital Media

The company provides products, services, and solutions which facilitate creation, publication, and promotion of creative content. The Digital Media segment consists of Adobe Creative Cloud and Adobe Document Cloud which consists of Creative Cloud Express, Photoshop, Illustrator, Lightroom, Premier Pro, Acrobat, Adobe

© The Author(s), under exclusive license to Springer Nature Switzerland AG 2024

B. R. Kumar, *Rising Stars*, Management for Professionals,
https://doi.org/10.1007/978-3-031-50032-9_56

Sign, etc. The flagship of Adobe's Digital Media business is Adobe Creative Cloud which is a subscription service that facilitates members to use creative products integrated with cloud-delivered services across desktop, web, and mobile devices. Over 90% of the world's creative professionals use Adobe Photoshoot. Adobe Stock offers over 320 million assets. These assets include over 195 million photos, 98 million vectors and illustrations, 24 million videos, 70,000 music tracks, 5.1 million premium assets, and over 850,000 plus free photos, vectors, videos, and templates. Behance, Adobe's online creative community, has over 30 plus million members.

Adobe Document Cloud business is a unified, cloud-based document services platform, which integrates Adobe's pioneering PDF technology with Acrobat and Adobe Sign applications to deliver fully digital document workflows. Within the Adobe Document Cloud business, Adobe Acrobat had a strong leadership in document-intensive industries such as government, financial services, pharmaceutical, legal, aerospace, insurance, and technical publishing. In 2021, it was estimated that more than 400 billion PDFs were opened in Adobe products. Over 8 billion electronic and digital signature transactions were processed through Adobe Document Cloud in the year 2021. Most Fortune 100 companies rely on Adobe Sign for fast and secure e-signatures. Adobe Scan is the leading scanning app on iOS and Android with over 150 million downloads and 2.5 billion documents. Adobe Document Cloud-based documents provide 90% cost savings and 95% reduction in environmental impact compared to paper-based processes. The statistics suggest that every 1 million Adobe Sign transactions would result in the retention of approximately 105 million liters of water, 31,000 trees along with reduction of costs by more than $7.2 million. Trillions of PDF documents are created every year and millions of users engage with PDF files on a daily basis in industries such as legal, financial services, and publishing.

Digital Experience

Adobe provides an integrated platform and set of applications and services through Adobe Experience Cloud to optimize customer experience which spans from analytics to commerce. The customers in the segment include marketers, advertisers, agencies, publishers, merchandisers, web analysts, data scientists, and executives. The Adobe Experience Platform uses insights driven by artificial intelligence to facilitate the delivery of personalized experiences across different channels in milliseconds.

Adobe was named as a leader in the 40 plus analyst reports in content management systems, customer analytics, B2B marketing automation platforms, digital commerce, digital experience, and enterprise marketing suites. The Adobe Experience Cloud is supported by an expansive global ecosystem of 4000 plus active solution integrator, agency, technology, and more than 460,000 developers and community members. Adobe Analytics analyzes one trillion plus visits to retail websites in the United States along with over 100 million product SKUs in

18 categories to offer e-commerce and online inflation insights to businesses, policymakers, and consumer segments. Over 85% of the top 100 retailers in the United States rely on Adobe Analytics to deliver, measure, and personalize shopping experience online.

Publishing and Advertising Segment

The legacy products and solutions are included in the Publishing and Advertising segment. The segment solutions include eLearning solutions, technical document publishing, web conferencing, document and forms platform, web application, high-end printing, and Adobe Advertising Cloud offerings. Adobe PostScript and Adobe PDF printing technologies offer advanced functionality to meet requirements in the market. Adobe Advertising Cloud offers an end-to-end, demand-side platform for managing advertising across different digital formats. Adobe generates revenues in the legacy publishing products and services by licensing the technology to OEMs which manufacture workflow, software, printers, and other output devices. The company generates revenues in advertising through usage-based offerings.

Products and Solutions

Creative Cloud

Adobe Creative Cloud is a cloud-based subscription app that enables creative professionals and others to use apps and services for photography, design, vide, and web to connect devices and platforms. Adobe Photoshop is the world's most advanced digital imaging and design app, with powerful editing and effects tools to transform photos. Adobe Illustrator is the industry-standard vector graphics app for desktops and iPad used worldwide by designers. Adobe InDesign is an industry-leading design and layout app for print and digital media. Adobe Premiere Pro is the leading non-linear video editing app used by filmmakers, TV editors, YouTubers, and videographers. Adobe XD is Adobe's all-in-one experience design ("XD") app for desktop and mobile to build user experiences. Adobe Stock provides designers and businesses with access to millions of high-quality, curated, royalty-free photos, vectors, illustrations, videos, templates, audio, and 3D assets, for creative projects. Substance 3D is an ecosystem of desktop apps, including Substance 3D Stager, Substance 3D Painter, Substance 3D Sampler, and Substance 3D Designer. Creative Cloud Express is a web and mobile app directed toward first-time creators and creative professionals. Adobe After Effects is the industry-standard motion graphics and visual effects app which are used by a wide variety of animators, designers, and compositors to create cinematic movie titles and create animations. Frame.io is the cloud-native video collaboration platform. Behance is the social community for creative work online.

Adobe Document Cloud

Adobe Document Cloud is a cloud-based subscription offering, which consists of Adobe Acrobat, Adobe Sign, Adobe Scan, and other apps.

Digital Experience Offerings

Experience Cloud consists of sets of solutions for customers such as Adobe Experience Platform; Data, Insights, and Audiences; Content and Commerce; Customer Journeys; Marketing Workflow; and Digital Enrollment and Onboarding.

Strategy

Adobe focusses on becoming the leading provider of cloud-based solutions for delivering digital experiences and enabling digital transformation. The aim of Adobe is to become the leading platform for creativity and digital document solutions which offer a wide range of products and services for individuals, small, medium, and large organizations design and deliver content to enhance productivity and creativity. The company aims to achieve this objective by using data-driven customer engagement to drive product lead growth through innovation to focus on creative applications. Adobe aims to advance every creative category across desktop, web, and mobile. The company focusses on empowering content-first task-based creativity through the launch of its Creative Cloud Express, a web and mobile application with a content and template-first experience which allows users such as content creators, communicators, and creative professionals to create, edit, and customize content with ease. Adobe has enabled its flagship applications such as Photoshop, Illustrator, and Lightroom to be available to users for working from anywhere on any device. The company offers a range of creative tools and services such as hobbyist products like Photoshop Elements and Premier Elements, libraries of creative assets such as Adobe Stock and Adobe Fonts, mobile-first apps such as Photoshop Camera and Creative Cloud Libraries. The company uses a data-driven operating model and Digital Experience solution to drive and optimize customer awareness, engagement, and licensing of creative products and services. To serve customers better, the company offers free and premium levels for certain applications such as Creative Cloud Express and targeted packages and sites consisting of Photography Plan and Substance 3D Collection. Adobe also uses data-driven operating model to optimize the conversion of users of free apps and trials to paid subscribers.

The company focusses on acquisitions as a part of strategic growth objectives. Adobe acquired Frame.io to make the creative process more collaborative, efficient, and productive by combining Adobe Creative Cloud with Frame.io's cloud-native collaboration workflows while continuing to facilitate third-party applications. Adobe Experience Cloud offers solutions with a strategic focus on data insights and audiences, content and commerce, customer journeys, and marketing flow. Adobe Solutions such as Adobe Analytics, Adobe Experience Platform, Customer Journey Analytics, Adobe Audience Manager, Real Time Customer Data Platform offer robust customer profiles, and Al-powered analytics to provide relevant experiences across platforms. The solutions also facilitate customers to manage, deliver, and optimize content delivery through Adobe Experience Manager and facilitate shopping experiences for mid-market and enterprise businesses. The solutions facilitate businesses to manage, test, and orchestrate campaigns and customer journeys across B2E use cases which include Marketo Engage, Adobe Campaign, Adobe Target, and Journey Optimizer. The company also offers a work management platform which enables marketers to focus on campaign workflows. Adobe enhances digital experience by the use of AI and machine learning framework through Adobe Sensei. Adobe Experience Cloud facilitates an open platform and ecosystem through Adobe Experience Platform, Al services, and developer services through Adobe I/O. The growth of Adobe Experience Cloud is driven by offering best customer experience management solutions for B2E, enterprise, and mid-market segments through its applications, services, and platform. Adobe has added new services such as Adobe Developer App Builder, Adobe Experience Cloud for Healthcare, and new functionality and features to offerings such as new B2B edition of Adobe Real Time Customer Data Platform, Adobe Experience Manager Screens, and new personalized features in Adobe Experience Cloud.

Table 1 lists the major acquisitions undertaken by the company.

Competition

Adobe focusses on a highly competitive environment worldwide. The Digital Media segment faces competition from large, established companies as well as a variety of point offerings, free products, and downloadable apps. Adobe Experience Cloud solutions face competition from large established companies which include large enterprise software, Internet, and database management companies. The Publishing and Advertising product offerings face competition from large-scale publishing systems and XML-based publishing firms. The web conferencing product faces competition from a number of established products from large software companies. Acrobat web offers single-click tools for users to edit, comment, convert, organize, and sign PDF documents directly within the web browser.

Table 2 displays the recognitions received by the company over a period of time.

Risk Factors

COVID-19 pandemic has affected the business operations of the company. The business performance of Adobe depends upon factors such as severe competition, new industry standards, new distribution models, emergence of disruptive

Table 1 Major acquisitions

Year	Major acquisitions
2005	Acquired Macromedia
2009	Omniture, Inc.
2010	Adobe Systems acquired Day Software Holding AG. The combination created the leading platform for designing, building, and optimizing customer experience across all channels such as web, mobile social, and instore interaction. Solutions of Day Software are used by companies such as Volkswagen, Daimler, BMW, General Motors, McDonald, Newsweek, and World Bank.
2012	Adobe Systems Incorporated acquired privately held Behance, a leading online social media platform with over 1 million members to enhance Adobe's strategy to acquire community features for Creative Cloud. Behance provides showcases for creative work across industries and disciplines. Behance also powers the portfolio display for thousands of other websites around the Web which includes Ad Week, Rhode Island School of Design, and The Smithsonian National Design Awards.
2015	Adobe acquired privately held Fotolia, a leading marketplace for stock content. This acquisition facilitated Creative Cloud members to access and purchase over 35 million images and videos for the design process.
2018	Adobe acquired Magento Commerce, the market-leading commerce will deliver end-to-end digital experience platform which include which includes content creation, marketing, advertising, analytics, and commerce for B2B and B2C customers. The Magento platform brings together digital commerce, order management, and predictive intelligence. The Magento platform is built on scalable technology supported by a community of 300,000 developers.
2018	Adobe acquired Marketo, the market leader for B2B marketing management. This acquisition combined Adobe's experience in cloud analytics, personalization, and content capabilities with Marketo's lead management, account-based marketing, and revenue attributions technology.
2019	Adobe acquired Allegorithmic, makers of substance the industry standard for 3D textures and material creation in game and video post-production. Allegorithmic combined 3D design tools with Adobe's Creative cloud industry-leading imaging, video, and motion graphics tools. This acquisition of Adobe empowered video game creators, VFX artists in digital medium, designers and marketers to deliver the next generation of immersive experiences.
2020	Acquires Workfront, the leading work management platform for marketers with over 3000 customers and 1 million customers. Both companies had a base of 1000 shared customers which included Armour, Nordstrom, Prudential Financial, T-Mobile, and Home Depot.
2021	Acquires Frame.io, a leading cloud-based video collaboration platform. This acquisition accelerated the creative process and delivered an end-to-end video platform for Adobe.
2021	Acquires Contentcal which facilitates users' focus on creativity by automating social media publishing and reporting tasks.

Source: Investor resources I Adobe Investor Relations

technology developments, short product life cycles, and new product introductions. The future success depends on factors such as the ability to innovate and integration of products and services factors in cost-effective manner. The company faces numerous risks with respect to non-realization of the anticipated benefits of an investment or acquisition of a company, division, product, or technology. The

Table 2 Industry recognitions

Next big things in tech	Fast company
World's best workplaces	Forbes
Happiest employees	Comparably
Best global brand	Interbrand
Best places to work	Glassdoor
Best culture	Comparably
Best employers for diversity	Forbes
Most innovative companies	Fast company
Corporate equality index	DEI
JUST100	Forbes & JUST capital
Companies that care	People magazine
Disability equality index	DisabilityIN
CDP A list	Carbon disclosure project
Gender equality index	Bloomberg
Dow Jones sustainability index	S&P Dow jones indices
World's Most admired companies	Fortune
Best workplaces in tech	Fortune

Source: Adobe Website

sales cycles of some of the Adobe's enterprise offerings are multi-phased and complex. The operating results would be affected if the customers fail to renew subscriptions. The company faces different risks such as exchange rate risks, regional economic political risks on account of being a multinational company with approximately 43% of the total revenues from overseas. The company is also subjected to risks associated with compliance with laws and regulations globally.

ESG Initiatives

The innovations introduced by Adobe such as cloud-based software delivery, paperless workflows, and virtual collaboration facilitate reduction of physical waste and cut emissions due to reduced transportation and shipping. Adobe Creative Cloud, Document Cloud, and Experience Cloud eliminate the environmental impact associated with physical software, manufacturing, packaging, and distribution. Adobe Creative Cloud supports creative teams to collaborate across different regions thus reducing the need for business travel. Adobe's 3D design and immersive technologies allowed designers to replace costly photoshoots and physical samples with photorealistic 3D designs thereby reducing carbon footprints. Environmental organizations such as Conservation International uses Creative Cloud to create environmental awareness. Adobe Document Cloud reduces the waste associated with paper document processes. Every 1 million transactions completed via Acrobat Sign in place of paper workflows saves more than 27 million gallons of water, 1.5 million pounds of waste, and 23.4 million pounds of CO_2. The company partners with nonprofits to transform the lives of weaker sections of society. Through the

Employee Community Fund, the company's grant makers awarded $4 million to 200 non-profits in the year 2021.

Stock Performance Analysis

The returns registered by Adobe are compared with the market returns of the Nasdaq Composite during the recent 5-year period March 2018–February 2023. Adobe stock was trading at $216.08 on March 1st, 2018. By February 1st, 2023, the stock price increased by 1.48 times to trade at $320.45. The total cumulative monthly returns for Adobe stock was 65% compared to 60% returns for Nasdaq Composite during the period March 2018–February 2023. The yearly average return for Adobe stock was 13% compared to 12% accounted by market index Nasdaq Composite during the period March 2018–February 2023.

Table 3 shows the holding period return for Adobe during the 5-year period 2018–2022. The analysis assumes investing in a stock during the beginning of January of each year and selling the stock by end December of that year. The data source is Yahoo Finance.

Adobe had superior stock market performance compared to market index Nasdaq Composite during the period 2018–2021.

Table 4 gives the market value and book value of equity of Adobe during the period 2018–2022. The values are given in millions of dollars.

The average book value of equity as percent of the market value of equity was 5.4% during the period 2018–2022. The market value of equity which was 13 times of book value in 2018 increased to 22 times of book value by the year 2022.

Table 5 shows the financial highlights of the company during the period 2018–2022.

On average basis, the total assets, short-term investments, and total equity increased by 9.87%, 19%, and 11%, respectively, during the period 2018–2022. The total revenues and net income increased by 18% and 21% during the period

Table 3 Holding period return

Year	Adobe	Nasdaq Composite	Excess returns
2018	5%	−6%	11%
2019	33%	23%	10%
2020	42%	41%	2%
2021	24%	20%	4%
2022	−37%	−26%	−11%

Table 4 Market value and book value of equity

Year	2018	2019	2020	2021	2022
Book value of equity	9362.11	10,530	13,264	14,797	14,051
Market value of equity	122349.77	149298.39	229187.13	318178.75	159357.66
BV as percent of MV	7.7%	8.6%	8.9%	6.5%	4.4%

Table 5 Financial highlights

	(In millions of dollars)				
Financial highlights	2018	2019	2020	2021	2022
Total assets	18768.68	20,762	24,284	27,241	27,165
Short-term investments	3228.96	4177	5992	5798	6096
Total equity	9362.11	10,530	13,264	14,797	14,051
Total revenue	9030	11,171	12,868	15,785	17,606
Total operating expenses	4995	6230	6909	8118	9343
Net income	2591	2951	5260	4822	4756
Market cap	122349.77	149298.4	229187.13	318178.75	159357.66
Enterprise value	123245.61	149259.4	227903.13	317053.75	157894.66

Table 6 Performance indicators

Ratios	2018	2019	2020	2021	2022
Net margin%	28.69	26.42	40.88	30.55	27
ROE%	29.08	29.67	44.21	34.37	32.97
ROA%	15.56	14.93	23.35	18.72	17.48
DER	0.44	0.39	0.36	0.32	0.33

Table 7 Economic value

Year	2021	2022
Profit before income tax	5705	6008
Income tax	883.1	1252.1
Net operating profit after tax (NOPAT)	4821.9	4755.9
Stockholder equity	14,797	14,051
Long-term debt	4123	3629
Total capital employed	18,920	17,680
WACC	7.81%	11.09%
Capital charge	1477.65	1960.71
Economic value	3344.21	2795.22

2018–2022. On average basis, the total expenses increased by 17%. The market capitalization and enterprise value increased by 16% on average basis during the above period. The data source is annual reports and gurufocus.com.

Table 6 shows the profitability and leverage position of the company during the period 2018–2022.

The average net margin, ROE, and ROA during 2018–2022 were 30.71%, 34.06%, and 18.01%, respectively, during the period 2018–2022. The average debt-equity ratio during the above period was 0.36.

Table 7 shows the estimation of economic value of Adobe in millions of dollars.

References

1. Investor resources | Adobe Investor Relations
2. FastFacts_12152022.indd (adobe.com)

Case 57 Business First Bancshares

Business First Bancshares is the financial holding company and the parent company of Business First Bank (b1BANK), a state banking association and community-based financial institution which provides a full array of banking products and services. The b1 Bank is a commercial bank chartered under the laws of the State of Louisiana and was established in the year 2006 to support entrepreneurs and small community businesses. By December 31, 2021, Business First had total assets of $4.7 billion, total loans of $3.2 billion and total deposits of $4.1 billion. The company is listed on the Nasdaq Global Select Market under the symbol BFST. As of December 31, 2021, Business First had 648 full-time and 18 part-time employees.

Products and Services

Business First Bank offers products such as checking, savings and money market accounts, certificates of deposit, commercial and consumer loans, mortgage loans, real estate loans, and term loans. b1Bank also offers wealth management products, drive-through banking facilities, automated teller machines, night depository, credit and debit cards, Internet banking, electronic funds transfers through ACH services, domestic and foreign wire transfers, cash management, vault services, loan and deposit sweep accounts, and lock box services.

Lending Activities

First Bank provides commercial and industrial (C&I) loans which include commercial lines of credit, working capital loans, term loans, equipment financing, asset acquisition, development loans, borrowing base loans, letters of credit, and other loan products. These loans are underwritten on the basis of the borrower's ability to service debt from income. The bank takes as collateral a lien on general business

© The Author(s), under exclusive license to Springer Nature Switzerland AG 2024

B. R. Kumar, *Rising Stars*, Management for Professionals,
https://doi.org/10.1007/978-3-031-50032-9_57

assets. The C&I loans have variable interest rates and terms typically range from 1–5 years which depend on factors such as the type and size of loan and financial strength of the borrower. First Bank's construction and development loans include loans to small-to-midsized businesses to construct owner–user properties, loans to developers of commercial real estate investment properties, and residential developments. First Bank offers real estate loans for commercial property. The interest rates on the commercial real estate loans are fixed or adjustable. The bank charges an origination fee for its services. The bank also offers first and second lien 1–4 family mortgage loans and home equity lines of credit on owner-occupied primary residences. The retail consumer real estate lending products are offered to customers within the geographic markets of the bank. The bank also offers consumer loans which include secured and unsecured installment and term loans. The credit approval policies provide for various levels of officer and senior management lending authority for new credits and renewals.

Deposits

First Bank provides a complete range of deposit products and services which include checking and savings accounts, certificates of deposits, money market accounts, debit cards, online and mobile banking, e-Statements, and direct deposit services.

Wealth Solution Services

First Bank offers wealth management and private banking services which are targeted toward high net worth individuals like professionals, businessmen, and professional and financial service companies.

Other Products and Services

First Bank also provides a wide array of financial services to customers which include debit and credit card products, treasury, and cash management services, merchant services, employee and payroll benefits solutions, automated clearing house services, lock box services, etc.

Strategy for Growth

The bank has deep market experience which is supported by centralized risk management practices and advanced technology. The bank pursues disciplined growth through the careful selection of markets. The bank's expansion strategy consists of recruiting talented teams of bankers in desirable markets to serve the clients. The bank's commercial and private banking products and services are well suited for small-to-midsized businesses and high-net-worth individuals. The bank focusses on expanding its presence in existing markets. The bank is among the top two or three community banks by deposit market share. The bank aims to add more banking centers or complementary offices in strategic locations in the markets. The company has laid out plans to expand along the I-10/12 and I – 20 corridors, East Texas markets to the west, and into the Jackson and Gulfport/Biloxi, Mississippi markets to the east and in the Dallas/Fort Worth metroplex region. These regions have attractive demographics and a significant concentration of small-to-midsized businesses and high-net-worth individuals which are underserved by the banking industry.

The bank has focused on inorganic growth through a disciplined acquisition strategy. In 2015, the bank acquired the American Gateway Financial Corporation in the home market of Baton Rouge. During the year 2018, Minden Bancorp Inc. was acquired which was located within the second oldest market of the bank-Northwest Louisiana. In the same year, Richland State Bancorp Inc. was acquired. During May 2020, Pedestal Bancshares Inc. which was based in southern Louisiana was acquired. This acquisition added Pedestal Bank's 22 branch locations across southern Louisiana. Pedestal Bank had total assets of $1.4 billion, net loans of $935.8 million, and total deposits of $1.2 billion. The acquisition of Pedestal Bank expanded First Bank's presence in South to Southwest Louisiana markets. In 2021, SmithShellnut Wilson acquired SSW, a registered investment advisor with approximately $3.5 billion in assets under management which manages investment portfolios for corporations, foundations, and individuals. In 2021, SSW had $3.6 million in total assets. The bank completed the acquisition of Texas Citizens Bancorp Inc. (TCBI) in the year 2022 which is the parent bank holding company for Texas Citizens Bank, National Association which is headquartered in Texas. The bank added six banking locations in the Houston Texas market region as a result of this acquisition.

The bank has sophisticated business lending capabilities. The bank basically targets small to medium-sized businesses with credit requirements which range between $1 million and $10 million. The requirements of these types of businesses are too complex for traditional community banks, while at the same time are not attractive for large banking institutions. After the financial crisis in the year 2008, the bank has developed extensive commercial and industrial expertise across markets. The bank has also strengthened its treasury and cash management programs to meet the target customers. The bank focusses on developing credit underwriting expertise which promotes quality loan generation which maximizes efficiency. The focus on asset/liability management facilitates the local banking teams to understand the importance of quality core deposit funding. The bank has followed a disciplined approach to expansion and growth by focusing on locations such as downtowns and suburban centers for optimizing services targeted at small to mid-sized business customers and high-net-worth individuals. Since 2006, the bank has grown rapidly across the state of Louisiana, Dallas/Fort Worth metroplex, and Houston. First Bank has built a strong operational platform to create operational efficiencies across diverse markets with strong underwriting capabilities, networks, asset quality standards, and investments in technology.

Risk Factors

In an economic environment characterized by low-interest rates, the bank faces challenges in attracting deposits and generating earnings through its loan and investment portfolio. The major chunk of loans is provided to borrowers based in regional markets where the bank operates and the loans are secured by collaterals located in these markets. The bank is thereby exposed to risks associated with the lack of geographic diversification as any regional downturn would ultimately affect the profitability of the bank's businesses. Business First Bank operates in the highly competitive banking industry and faces significant competition from regional and national financial services institutions for originating loans, attracting deposits, and providing other financial services. The long-term success of the bank's business strategy depends on factors such as the ability to attract talented bankers, maintain adequate funding sources, attract low-cost deposits, maintenance of commercial banking relationships with clients such as firms, real estate developers, and investors. Investments in new technology to enhance client experience is another critical success factor for the bank. The success of the bank's business depends on its ability to measure and manage credit risk. As of December 2021, approximately 60% of the bank's loan portfolio is secured by commercial real estate. Approximately 22% of the total loans were commercial loans to businesses. These loans are basically collateralized by general business assets which include accounts receivables, inventory, and equipment. These loans have the potential for larger losses on a single loan basis. Adverse changes in commodity prices and real estate values could impair the value of the collateral which secures these loans. The deterioration of the financial condition of large loans would have a significant adverse impact on the asset quality of bank's assets. The allowances for loan losses might prove insufficient to absorb losses inherent in the loan portfolio which in turn would affect the business operations of the bank. The bank is subject to extensive regulation, supervision, and legal requirements.

Stock Performance

The following section analyzes the stock price performance of Business First with that of performance of market index S&P 500 during the recent 5-year period 2018–2022. The total monthly cumulative return for Business First stock was 12.2% compared to the market index S&P 500 returns of 49% during the period March 2018–February 2023. The average yearly return for the stock was 3% compared to the 10% returns accounted by the market index S&P 500 during the period March 2018–February 2023.

Table 1 Holding period return

Year	Business First Bank	S&P 500	Excess returns
2018	3%	3%	1%
2019	8%	10%	-2%
2020	−18%	4%	−22%
2021	39%	27%	12%
2022	−19%	−15%	−4%

Table 2 Book and market value of equity

Year	2018	2019	2020	2021	2022
Book value of equity	260.06	285.1	409.96	433.37	580.48
Market value of equity	320.16	331.06	419.85	577.54	549
BV as percent of MV	81.2%	86.1%	97.6%	75.0%	105.7%

Table 3 Financial highlights

	(In millions of dollars)				
Financial highlights	2018	2019	2020	2021	2022
Total assets	2094.9	2273.84	4160.36	4726.38	5990.46
Cash and cash equivalents	96.07	89.37	149.13	68.38	152.74
Deposits	1733.93	1782.01	3616.68	4077.28	4820.35
Total equity	260.06	285.1	409.96	433.37	580.48
Net interest income	62.23	80.2	127.65	153.88	199.58
Interest expense	13.97	23.27	22.11	16.55	36.54
Total non-interest expense	47.22	58.12	97.02	116.55	144.6
Market capitalization	320.16	331.06	419.85	577.54	549
Enterprise value	304.09	359.68	354.89	677.63	463.11

Table 1 shows the holding period returns for the stock and market index S&P 500 during the period 2018–2022. The holding period for analysis is assumed to be 1 year.

Business First Bank stock outperformed the market index S&P 500 in the year 2021.

Table 2 shows the market value and book value of equity of Business First during the time period 2018–2022. The values are given in millions of dollars.

The average book value as percent of market value of equity was 89.2% during the period 2018–2022. Table 3 shows the financial highlights of the Business First during the period 2018–2022.

The average growth rate of total assets, cash and cash equivalents, and deposits were 33%, 32%, and 34%, respectively, during the period 2018–2022. The total equity grew by 35% during the above period. The net interest income increased by 39% on average basis during the period 2018–2022. The interest expense and total non-interest expense increased by 34% and 16%, respectively. The market capitalization and enterprise value increased by 16% and 19%, respectively, during the period 2018–2022.

Table 4 Performance ratios

Performance ratios	2018	2019	2020	2021	2022
Return on average assets %	0.82	1.09	0.93	1.17	1.01
Return on average equity%	7.54	10.99	10.41	14.74	12.93
Net interest margin%	4.09	4.08	4.37	3.74	4.02

Table 4 shows the performance ratios of the bank during the period 2018–2022. The average return on assets, return on average equity, and net interest margin were 1%, 11.32%, and 4.06% for the bank during the period 2018–2022.

References

1. https://www.nasdaq.com/market-activity/stocks/bfst/sec-filings
2. BFST Annual Report 2022.

Case 58 Take-Two Interactive Software Inc.

Take Two Interactive Software is a global leading developer, publisher, and marketer of interactive entertainment for consumers. The company develops and publishes products basically through Rockstar Games, 2 K, Private Division, and T2 Mobile games. The products offered are designed for console gaming systems for Sony PlayStation®4 ("PS4") and PlayStation5 of Sony Computer Entertainment Inc. and for Xbox One® ("Xbox One") and Xbox Series X|S ("Xbox Series X|S"), and Nintendo's Switch (Switch) of Microsoft. The products are also designed for personal computers, mobile, smartphones, and tablets. The products are offered through physical retail, digital download, online platforms, and cloud streaming services. The company derives revenues mainly from the sales of internally developed software titles and software titles developed by third parties. The company has internal development studios located in Australia, Canada, China, the Czech Republic, Hungary, India, Serbia, South Korea, Spain, the United Kingdom, and the United States. Agreements with third-party developers give the company exclusive publishing and marketing rights and the company makes development payments and pays royalties based on product sales. The company has entered into license agreements with Sony and Microsoft to develop and publish software in Asia, Australia, Europe, North America, and certain Latin American, Middle Eastern, and African countries. By March 2022, the company employed 7799 employees of which 3812 were employed outside of the United States.

Business Offerings

Rockstar Games

Rockstar Games software titles are internally developed. Rockstar Games is a market leader in the action/adventure product category and is the wholly owned publisher of Grand Theft Auto, Pax Payne, Midnight Club, Red Dead Redemption, and other popular franchises. Grand Theft Auto Series is one of the most critically acclaimed

© The Author(s), under exclusive license to Springer Nature Switzerland AG 2024
B. R. Kumar, *Rising Stars*, Management for Professionals,
https://doi.org/10.1007/978-3-031-50032-9_58

brands and has sold in over 375 million units worldwide. Grand Theft Auto V has sold in over 160 million units globally. The title Red Dead Redemption has sold in more than 40 million units worldwide. Rockstar Games has also developed brands in other genres which include LA Noire, Bully, and Manhunt games. Rockstar Game's titles are published across all key platforms which include Mobile.

2 k

The 2 K label has published popular entertainment titles across a range of genres which includes shooter, action, role playing, strategy, sports, and family entertainment. The internally owned and developed franchises of 2 K include BioShock, Mafia, Sid Meier's Civilization, and XCOM series. Externally developed franchises of 2 K include Borderlands. The sports simulation titles such as NBA 2 K series, the WWE 2 K professional wrestling series, and PGA TOUR 2 K provide game experiences. The flagship NBA 2 K series is the top-ranked NBA basketball video game. 2 K publishes mobile titles such as WWE SuperCard. 2 K had secured a multiyear license from the NBA to develop an online version of NBA simulation game in China, Taiwan, South Korea, and Southeast Asia.

Private Division

The Private Division label is the publisher and owner of Kerbal Space Program and OlliOlli World.

T2 Mobile Games

T2 Mobile Games publishes popular free-to-play mobile games which include Socialpoint, Playdots, and Nordeus. T2 Mobile Games' titles include Dragon City, Monster Legends, Two Dots, and Top Eleven.

Business Strategy

Take Two Interactive aims to be the most creative and innovative company in industry by focusing on developing and publishing high-quality interactive entertainment experiences across a diverse range of genres. Take Two focusses on creation of entertainment franchises which publishes a select number of titles where the company can create sequels and have incremental revenue opportunities through virtual currency, add-on content, and in-game purchases. The company possesses a portfolio of proprietary software content for major hardware platforms involving a wide range of genres such as action, adventure, shooter, and sports content. The company has adopted differentiation strategy to offer products that combine advanced technology with unique gameplay experiences for consumers. Take Two has created, acquired, or licensed group of highly recognizable brands for addressing the broad consumer demographic needs. Take Two have used innovative marketing programs and global distribution on platforms to target audiences. The company has also developed World Class Creative Teams. Take Two has 6042 employees associated with game development in its studios located globally. Take Two has also published a number of high-quality titles which are based on internally owned and developed intellectual properties. Take Two and its subsidiaries own intellectual property rights to 30 proprietary brands. The company also develops titles based on licensed properties which include sports leagues and externally developed titles. The company also leverages emerging technologies, platforms, and distribution channels which include digitally delivered content. The company makes a higher gross margin for digitally delivered products and offerings than for physically delivered products. The company also publishes a variety of titles for Mobile which are offered to consumers through digital download. The focus of the company is to expand its business internationally in regions of Asia, Middle East, and Latin America. The focus is on building licensing relationships and expansion of distribution networks. In January 2022, the company entered into a definitive merger agreement to acquire Zynga Inc., a leading developer of mobile games. During June 2021, Take Two acquired Nordeus Ltd. for $289.8 million. Nordeus is a Serbia-based mobile games company with over 240 million registered users. In 2021, Take Two acquired Dynamixyz, the France-based leader in video-based facial animation service provider with proprietary technology. The company also acquired the London-based studio Roll7 which is known for its signature take on action sports and flow-state gaming experiences. Take Two also acquired leading creative studios, elited3D which focuses on innovative 2D and 3D artwork related to video industry. In 2022, the company acquired Zynga, the global leader in mobile games with a diversified portfolio and leading mobile platform.

In its business segment, the company competes with interactive entertainment companies such as Activision Blizzard Inc., Electronics Art Inc., Ubisoft Entertainment, and Embracer Group AB. Take Two faces competition in the interactive entertainment software segment from Microsoft, Sony, and Nintendo. The company also faces competition from software, hardware, entertainment, and media companies for retail shelf space and promotional resources.

Risk Factors

The business operations of the firm were adversely affected by the coronavirus pandemic. The interactive entertainment software industry is highly competitive. The company faces competition from big players such as Sony and Microsoft for licenses to properties and the sale of interactive entertainment software. Factors which might have material adverse effects on the business results of the firm include low market acceptance of new products introduced by the firm, delays in product releases, or disruptions with respect to commercial release of the products. The company is also subject to product development risks which could result in delays and additional costs. The competition for limited shelf space may lead to greater expenses for the company to market its titles. The increased emphasis on digital content delivery increases the potential competition for the company. The business's success depends on the ability of the company to develop commercially successful products for the current video game platforms. The company is required to obtain licenses from certain competitors such as Sony and Microsoft to develop and publish titles for their respective hardware platforms. The business operations of the firm would be adversely affected if the consumer data protection measures are not adequate or if the security measures are breached. The business success of the company also depends on its ability to enter into successful software development arrangements with third parties. The company relies on a limited number of channel partners who have the right to change the fee structures for online distribution of both paid and free content. The company is exposed to the risks of the free-to-play business model as the company is dependent on the ability to develop, enhance and monetize free-to-play games. The company also faces risks from its international operations. Connectivity issues could affect the profitability and the ability to sell and provide online services for the products of the company. The business of the company would suffer if the company were to lose server capacity or lack sufficient Internet bandwidth.

ESG Initiatives

In the year 2020, the company partnered with a third party to perform a materiality assessment with respect to key ESG topics. The company has an organization-wide management committee to give direction for the ESG initiatives. The company offers e-learning and live training sessions to train its employees. The open-door policy facilitates regular interaction between employees and senior executives. The company also offers scholarship programs in association with organizations such as The ESA Foundation, Gay Gaming Professionals, NYU, and USC. The company also partners with Animation Project, Gameheads, Harlem Academy, The Hidden Genius Project, and the School of Interactive Arts to enhance the portfolio of technical and creative offerings. In 2021, the company appointed a sustainability consulting firm to assist it in the calculation and reporting of Scope 1 and 2 GHG footprint across its global portfolio.

Stock Price Performance

Table 1 compares the cumulative stock returns for the stock with that of returns of Nasdaq Composite Index and peer group comprising Activision Blizzard Inc. and Electronics Arts Inc. The time period is from March 31, 2017, to March 31, 2022. The analysis assumes an initial investment of $100 in the stock and indexes on March 31, 2017, and assumes reinvestment of all cash dividends. For the stock, there

Table 1 Comparative wealth creation

Year	2017	2018	2019	2020	2021	2022
Take-two interactive software, Inc	$100	$164.97	$159.22	$200.12	$298.13	$259.39
NASDAQ composite index	$100	$120.76	$133.60	$134.52	$233.26	$252.05
Peer group	$100	$135.75	$101.36	$117.31	$174.69	$155.70

Source: Annual Report 2022

Table 2 Book value and market value of equity

Year	2018	2019	2020	2021	2022
Book value of equity	1488.97	2040.58	2539.24	3331.89	3809.66
Market value of equity	11150.64	10586.52	13462.95	20349.3	17736.52
BV as percent of MV	13.4%	18.3%	24.0%	24.7%	18.7%

Table 3 Financial highlights

	(In millions of dollars)				
Financial highlights	2018	2019	2020	2021	2022
Total assets	3737.84	4243.07	4948.83	6028.22	6546.22
Short-term investments	1424.38	1571.01	2001.67	2731.58	2552.11
Total equity	1488.97	2040.58	2539.24	3331.89	3809.66
Total revenue	1792.89	2668.39	3088.97	3372.77	3504.8
Total operating expenses	744.26	943.04	1121.17	1208.58	1494.96
Net income	173.53	333.84	404.46	588.89	418.02
Market cap	11150.64	10586.52	13462.95	20349.3	17736.52
Enterprise value	9734.32	9015.51	11638.53	17808.99	15434.63

had been no dividend payments and hence cumulative total return calculation is based only on stock price appreciation.

The 5-year holding period return for Take Two stock was 159% while that for the Nasdaq Composite Index and the Peer Group, the holding period return was 152% and 56%, respectively. The 5-year average return for the stock, Nasdaq Composite, and the Peer Group were 24.63%, 22.71%, and 12.84%, respectively.

Table 2 shows the book value and market value of equity of the company during the period 2018–2022. The values are given in millions of dollars.

The average book value as percent of market value of equity was 21.7% during the period 2018–2022. The market value which was 7.49 times of book value of equity in the year 2018 declined to 5.34 times of the book value of equity by the year 2022.

Table 3 shows the financial highlights of the company during the period 2018–2022. The values are given in millions of dollars. The data source is gurufocus.com and annual reports.

During the period 2018–2022, the total assets, short-term investments, and total equity increased by 15%, 17%, and 27%, respectively. The average growth rate in

Table 4 Profitability and leverage

Ratios	2018	2019	2020	2021	2022
Net margin%	9.68	12.51	13.09	17.46	11.93
ROE%	13.92	18.92	17.66	20.06	11.71
ROA%	5.04	8.37	8.8	10.73	6.65
DER	0.01	–	0.07	0.06	0.07

Table 5 Estimation of economic value

Year	2021	2022
Profit before income tax	677.82	465.4
Income tax	88.9	47.4
Net operating profit after tax (NOPAT)	588.9	418.0
Stockholder equity	3331.89	3809.66
Long-term debt		
Total capital employed	3331.89	3809.66
WACC	4.28%	5.23%
Capital charge	142.60	199.25
Economic value	446.29	218.78

revenues and net income were 19% and 33% during the period 2018–2022. The total expenses increased by 19% on average basis. The market value and enterprise value of firm increased by 15%, respectively, during the above period.

Table 4 shows the profitability ratios and leverage position of Take Two during the period 2018–2022.

The net margin, ROE, and ROA were 12.93%, 16.45%, and 7.92%, respectively, during the period 2018–2022. The average debt-equity ratio was 0.05 during the period 2018–2022.

Table 5 illustrates the estimation of economic value of Take Two in millions of dollars.

References

1. https://www.take2games.com/ir
2. 2021 ESG Report

Case 59 MarineMax

MarineMax is the world's largest recreational boat and yacht retailer which sells new and used recreational boats, yachts, and marine-related products and services which include yachts, yacht concierge, and superyacht services. MarineMax was incorporated in January 1998. The company commenced operations with the acquisition of five independent recreational boat dealers on March 1st, 1998. The company is located globally with operations in more than 125 locations. The company has 78 dealerships and 57 marinas. The integrated business division of the company operates luxury marinas in yachting and sport fishing destinations around the world. MarineMax is the largest superyacht service provider with brands such as Fraser Yachts and Northrop & Johnson. Cruiser Yachts is involved in the manufacturing of boats and yachts and sells the products through retail dealership locations and independent dealers. Powerboats are manufactured by Intrepid Powerboats and are sold through a direct-to-consumer model. The wholly owned subsidiaries of MarineMax provide finance and insurance services. The company also owns Boatyard, a well-known digital product company. SkipperBud's is one of the largest boat sales, brokerage, service, and marina/storage groups in the United States. The Retail Operations segment sells new and used recreational boats which includes pleasure and fishing boats with a focus on premium brands. The company also sells related marine products which include engine trailers, parts, and accessories. The company also provides repair, maintenance, and slip and storage services. MarineMax facilitates boat financing, insurance, and extended service contracts along with boat and yacht brokerage sales and yacht charter services. The Product Manufacturing segment includes wholly owned subsidiaries such as Cruisers Yachts and Intrepid Powerboats. Cruisers Yachts is one the world's premier manufacturers of premium sport yachts and yachts. Intrepid Powerboats is a producer of customized boats with a focus on innovation and high-quality craftsmanship. The company is also the largest retailer of Se Ray and Boston Whaler recreational boats which are manufactured by Brunswick Corporation. By September 2022, the company had 3410 employees of which 933 were employed in the yacht manufacturing operations. In the year 2021, the US recreational boating industry had revenues of

© The Author(s), under exclusive license to Springer Nature Switzerland AG 2024

B. R. Kumar, *Rising Stars*, Management for Professionals,
https://doi.org/10.1007/978-3-031-50032-9_59

$56.7 billion in retail sales. The company has never declared or paid cash dividends on its common stock.

Products and Services

New Boat Sales

MarineMax basically sells recreational boats which include pleasure boats and fishing boats. Products sold by the company such as Sea Ray pleasure boats, Boston Whaler fishing boats, and Harris Aluminum boats are manufactured by Brunswick, the world's leading manufacturer of recreational boats and yachts. Some of the company's dealers also sell luxury yachts, fishing boats, and pontoon boats which are manufactured by Italy-based Azimut. Cruisers Yachts manufacturers sport yachts and Intrepid Powerboats manufacturers powerboats. In 2022, new boat sales accounted for approximately 73% of $1.689 billion of revenues of the company.

Product lines owned by MarineMax include E-Power Yachts, Motor Yachts, Pleasure Boats, and Pontoon Boats. H, Fishing Boats T, Ski Boats., Jet Boats. E-Power Yachts manufactures electric yachts which include superyachts, express cruisers, electric catamarans, and wider yachts. The motor yacht product lines include state-of-the-art design with live aboard luxuries. The Sea Ray pleasure boats focus on luxury and family recreational boating markets. Harris is a pontoon industry leader with innovative and luxurious model offerings. The fishing boats include entry level to advanced models such as Boston Whaler, Grady White, Scout, and Sailfish which are designed for fishing and water sports. Yamaha jet boats have high-performing internal propulsion system with superior handling capacity.

Used Boat Sales

The company sells used versions of new makes and models. The company acquires used boat inventory through customer trade ins.

Marine Engines, Related Marine Equipment, and Boating Parts and Accessories

The company sells marine engines and propellers basically to retail customers as replacements for their existing engines or propellers. The company also sells a broad variety of marine parts and accessories through retail locations, offsite locations, and print catalogs. These marine parts and accessories include marine electronics, dock and anchoring products, water sport accessories, corrosion control products, and services along with high-performance accessories such as propellers and instruments.

Maintenance, Repair, and Storage Services

The company provides maintenance and repair services at most of its retail locations.

F&I Products

The company provides financing for the purchase of new or used boats and extended service contracts. The company also arranges insurance coverage for boat property, disability, gel sealant, fabric protection, and casualty insurance coverage. The company also has associations with different marine product lenders through which retail installment contracts are purchased by these lenders based on the retail sales of boats and other marine products which are originated by the company. MarineMax receives a fee for arranging an extended service contract. In 2021, the company partnered with a third-party F&I product provider to offer prepaid maintenance plans for select new models. MarineMax also provides worldwide yacht insurance programs for brokerage houses, yacht management groups, and maritime attorneys. In fiscal 2022, the fee income generated from the F&I products accounted for 3% of the revenues of the company.

Brokerage Sales

MarineMax offers boat or yacht brokerage sales through employees or subcontractors who are licensed boat or yacht brokers. The sales are often co-brokered with the commission split between the buying and selling brokers. Along with revenues from brokerage commissions, the brokerage sales also facilitate the company to offer a broad array of used boats or yachts without increasing related inventory costs. MarineMax offers yacht and superyacht brokerage through the Fraser Yachts Group and Northrop & Johnson. Brokerage sales accounted for 5.8% of the revenues of the company.

Yacht Charter

Yacht Charter business launched in the year 2011 provides charter catamarans in exotic destinations in locations such as the British Virgin Islands. The company sells specifically designed yachts to third parties for inclusion in the yacht charter fleet. The company offers yacht and superyacht chartering, charter management, yacht management, crew placement, new boat build oversight services, and luxury yacht services through the Fraser Yachts Group and Northrop & Johnson segments.

Of Site Sales

The company sells used boats, F&I products, and other parts and accessories at different third-party offsite locations which include marinas.

Strategy

The company focusses on providing a full range of services which offers extensive and high-quality product lines. The company also maintains prime retail locations. The company has opened 35 new retail locations in existing territories.

Ever since its initial acquisitions during the late nineties, the company has acquired 32 independent recreational boat dealers, multiple marinas, five boat brokerage operations, two superyacht service companies, two full-service yacht repair operations, and two boat and yacht manufacturers.

Acquisitions

In 2021, MarineMax acquired Intrepid Powerboats, the manufacturer of powerboats, and Texas Mastercraft, the watersports dealer in Northern Texas. In 2022, the company acquired Superyacht Management based in Golfe-Juan, France. In the year 2022, the company acquired Endeavour Marina and IGY Marinas. IGY Marinas has a network of strategically positioned luxury marinas in yachting and sport fishing destinations around the globe. The acquisition of IGY Marina facilitated the company to offer vertically integrated services to superyacht customers.

Table 1 lists the acquisitions undertaken by the company during the past 10 years.

Table 1 Acquisitions by MarineMax

Sl	Year	Target acquired companies	Sl	Year	Target acquired companies
1	2011	Treasure Island Marina LLC	12	2019	Fraser yachts group
2	2012	Bassett marine LLC	13	2020	Boatyard
3	2013	Parker Boat Company	14	2020	Northrop & Johnson
4	2014	Ocean Alexander yachts	15	2020	Private insurance services
5	2016	Bahia mar marina	16	2020	Skipper Bud's & silver seas
6	2016	Russo marine	17	2021	Cruisers yachts
7	2017	Hall marine group	18	2021	Nisswa marine
8	2018	Island marine center	19	2021	Intrepid powerboats
9	2018	Tera Miranda	20	2021	Texas Mastercraft
10	2018	Bay pointe Marina	21	2022	Superyacht management
11	2019	Sail & ski Center	22	2022	Endeavour marina
			23	2022	IGY marinas

Source: Annual Report 2022

Risk Factors

The business success of the company depends on the reputation and quality of the boating products manufactured by Brunswick's Sea Ray and Boston Whaler boat lines and Azimut products by Azimut Benetti Group. The business of the company would be adversely affected if the company is not able to provide a high quality and desirable mix of competitively priced products based on customer's demand. Any interruption in the operations of manufacturers could lead to shortfalls, disruptions, or delays in inventory for the company. MarineMax has renewable annual dealer agreements with manufacturers. However, these agreements do not contain any contractual provisions with respect to product pricing or required purchasing levels. Changes or termination of these arrangements would adversely affect the product availability and financial performance of the company. The boat manufacturers have substantial control over the business of the firm. The businesses of recreational boating industry are highly seasonal in nature with seasonal variations in different geographic markets. The margins for MarineMax would be affected if the company could not receive rebates and other dealer incentives on inventory purchases or retail sales. The company also operates in a highly competitive environment. Adverse changes in the general economic conditions and consumer spending patterns can negatively impact the operating results of the company. The recreational boats sold by the company are powered by diesel or gasoline engines. Higher energy costs and availability of raw materials, parts, components, and fuel costs are critical factors that affect the business operations of the firm.

Stock Performance

The stock price performance of MarineMax is compared with the performance of the market index Russell 2000 during the 5-year period April 2018–March 2023. The MarineMax stock which was trading at $21.6 on April 1st, 2018, increased by 1.58 times to trade at $34.15 by March 1st, 2023. The total monthly cumulative return for the stock was 98% compared to 37% returns registered by market index Russell 2000 during the period April 2018–March 2023. The average yearly return for the stock was 20% for the stock compared to 7% accounted by the market index during the period April 2018–March 2023. The data source is Yahoo Finance.

Table 2 shows the holding period return of MarineMax and market index Russell 2000 during the period 2018–2023.

Table 2 Holding period return

Year	MarineMax	Russell 2000	Excess returns
2018	−18%	−3%	−15%
2019	2%	2%	−1%
2020	147%	40%	107%
2021	5%	−8%	13%
2022	−32%	−6%	−26%

Table 3 Market and book value

Year	2018	2019	2020	2021	2022
Book value of equity	353.09	368.82	455.4	594.89	782.67
Market value of equity	481.75	330.06	561.23	1058.79	645.63
BV as percent of MV	73.3%	76.6%	138.0%	106.0%	73.9%

Table 4 Financial highlights

	(In millions of dollars)				
Financial highlights	2018	2019	2020	2021	2022
Total assets	640.54	784.08	775.32	1007.82	1352.77
Short-term investments	48.82	38.51	155.49	222.19	228.27
Total equity	353.09	368.82	455.4	594.89	782.67
Total revenue	1177.37	1237.15	1509.71	2063.26	2308.1
Total operating expenses	235.05	262.3	292	449.97	540.55
Net income	39.31	35.99	74.63	154.98	197.99
Market cap	481.75	330.06	561.23	1058.79	645.63
Enterprise value	645.88	603.61	598.31	1019.16	696.92

Table 5 Performance indicators

Ratios	2018	2019	2020	2021	2022
Net margin%	3.34	2.91	4.94	7.51	8.58
ROE%	12	9.97	18.11	29.51	28.74
ROA%	6.14	5.05	9.57	17.38	16.77
DER	0.6	0.85	0.42	0.31	0.36

In the years 2020 and 2021, MarineMax had superior performance compared to the market index Russell 2000.

Table 3 shows the book value and market value of equity of MarineMax in millions of dollars.

The average book value of the equity as percentage of market value was approximately 90% during the period 2018–2022.

Table 4 gives the financial highlights of MarineMax during the period 2018–2022

During the period 2018–2022, the average growth rate of total assets, short-term investments, and total equity were 21%, 82%, and 23%, respectively. On average basis, the total revenues and net income grew by 19% and 59%, respectively, during the period 2018–2022. The total expenses increased by 24% during the above period. The market capitalization and enterprise value increased by 22% and 8%, respectively, during the period 2018–2022. The data is sourced from gurufocus.com and annual reports.

Table 5 shows the performance measures of the company during the period 2018–2022.

The average net margin, ROE, and ROA during the 5-year period 2018–2022 were 5.46%, 19.67%, and 10.98%, respectively. The average debt-equity ratio during the above period was 0.51.

Table 6 Economic value

Year	2021	2022
Profit before income tax	205.79	261.92
Income tax	50.2	64.7
Net operating profit after tax (NOPAT)	155.6	197.3
Stockholder equity	594.89	782.67
Long-term debt	47.5	45.3
Total capital employed	642.39	827.97
WACC	9.48%	11.27%
Capital charge	60.90	93.31
Economic value	94.66	103.94

Table 6 illustrates the estimation of economic value of MarineMax during the period 2021 and 2022. The values are given in millions of dollars.

The economic value has increased from $94.66 million in 2021 to $103.94 million in the year 2022.

References

1. https://investor.marinemax.com/overview/default.aspx
2. https://www.marinemax.com/

Case 60 Fox Factory

Fox Factory Holding Corp. incorporated in Delaware in 2007 is the holding company of Fox Factory which designs and manufactures products and systems that are used on bicycles, trucks all-terrain vehicles (ATVs), snowmobiles, Specialty vehicles, motorcycles, and commercial trucks. Fox Factory, Inc., the operating subsidiary, was incorporated in California in 1978. Some of the products are specifically designed for leading cycling and powered vehicle original equipment manufacturers and the rest of the products are distributed to consumers through a global network of dealers and distributors. The stock is traded on the Nasdaq Global Select Market under the symbol "FOXF." Fox Factory operates in over 20 global locations with state-of-the-art manufacturing facilities, R&D technology centers, administrative offices, and customer support centers. The products of the company are technologically advanced products and offer innovative design, performance, durability, and reliability. The OEM customers of the company include Giant, Merida, Orbea, Kemstone Metal, Canyon Bicycles, Santa Cruz Bicycles, and Yeti Cycles under Specialty Sports segment. In the Powered Vehicles segment BRP, Ford, Polaris, Toyota, 4 Wheel Parts, Kawasaki, Yamaha, and Honda are the major customers of the company. Fox's products for bicycles are basically used for mountain bikes, road bikes, and e-bikes. The products for powered vehicles are used side by side, on-road and off-road vehicles and trucks, ATVs, snowmobiles, specialty vehicles, military vehicles, motorcycles, and commercial trucks. The company offers premium-priced products which are well-designed and performance-focused equipment. By December 2021, the company had employed approximately 4100 employees in the United States, Canada, Europe, Taiwan, and Australia. The total cumulative monthly return for Fox stock was 197% compared to 51% returns accounted for the market index S&P 500 during the 5-year period April 2018–March 2023.

© The Author(s), under exclusive license to Springer Nature Switzerland AG 2024

B. R. Kumar, *Rising Stars*, Management for Professionals,
https://doi.org/10.1007/978-3-031-50032-9_60

Products

The company mainly designs and manufactures suspension products. These suspension products dissipate the energy and force generated by bikes and powered vehicles during their motion. Suspension products allow wheels to move up or down to absorb bumps and shocks while maintaining contact with the ground for better control.

Powered Vehicles

In this powered vehicle category, Fox offers premium products under the FOX BDS Suspension, Zone Off-road, JKS Manufacturing, RT Pro UTV,4*4 Posi–Lok, Ridetech, Tuscany, etc. SCA brands are used for side by sides, on and off-road vehicles and trucks, ATVs, snowmobiles, specialty vehicles, motorcycles, and commercial trucks. In 2021, powered vehicle sales accounted for 55% of the total revenues for the company.

Specialty Sports

The mountain road bike product offerings under this category are offered under the FOX, Race Face, Easton Cycling, and Marzocchi brands. The mountain bike suspension products are sold in five series and under the Marzocchi brand. In 2021, sales of bike-related products accounted for 45% of the total revenues. In the mountain bike market, Fox offers mid-end and high-end front fork and rear suspension products for cross country, trail, all mountain, free ride, and downhill riding.

Growth Strategy and Competitive Strength

The company maintains the reputation of a broad offering of performance-defining products across multiple consumer markets. The attractive features of the company's products such as the use of adjustable suspension, position-sensitive damping, multiple air spring technologies, and other methods facilitate improved performance and control of the vehicles used by consumers in multiple markets. The products offered by the company are premium brands with strong consumer loyalty. The company owns and license premium brands with established trademarks such as FOX, FOXRACING SHOX, and RACE FACE. The Fox logo is prominently displayed on Fox-branded products used on bikes and powered vehicles sold by OEM customers. The company focusses on innovation and new product introductions as key components of its growth strategy. The innovations developed by the company in suspension engineering and design were deployed across multiple markets and led to its success in the high-end ATV category. Over the years, the company has developed multiple new products such as semi-active Live Valve X2 shock, 3.0 internal bypass platform, and sensitive spiral technology. The next generation of Live Valve combined with anodized aluminum shock body is designed to withstand higher internal pressures. The electronically adjustable rear suspension preload features offered by the company enable vehicle users to manage additional weight and facilitate to bring the vehicle back to optimal ride height. The position-sensitive spiral technology uses internal grooves to improve the small bump comfort and bottom-out control for vehicle management. Ridetech RidePro E5 Air Suspension Control System improves comfort and performance of the vehicle. The company focusses on developing new and innovative products to improve ride dynamics and performance. For instance, Fox's patented positive damping system provides terrain-optimized ride characteristics for many of the product lines offered by the company. The evolving market trends such as changes in bike wheel and tire sizes, increases in adoption rates of off-road capable, on-road trucks would increase the demand for the suspension products of the company. Fox has leveraged technology and brand to expand into new categories and end markets. Leveraging technology and scale, Fox has successfully expanded into commercial/RV and street car applications.

The business development group of the company identifies and assesses the potential acquisition opportunities in the ride dynamics platform and other specialty sports technology platforms. In 2020, the company acquired Performing Holdings, Inc., a leading OEM authorized specialty vehicle manufacturer for light-duty trucks and sport utility vehicles. In 2021, the company acquired Shock Therapy LLC, a premier suspension tuning company in the off-road industry. These acquisitions have broadened the company's product offerings in the automotive industry. The company also focusses on aftermarket penetration strategy. The company intends to further penetrate the aftermarket channel by adding new dealers and distributors to existing network of retailer dealers and distributors worldwide. The company also focusses on international expansion by increasing infrastructure investments and focusing on geographic regions with increasing consumer preferences for premium, performance bikes, and powered vehicles. The company aims to increase international viewership of racing and extreme sports and other outdoor events such as the Union Cyclist International Mountain Bike World Cup and X Games. The company also aims to improve operating and supply chain efficiencies.

Competition

The market for performance-defining products such as suspension components, wheels, and cranks are highly competitive. In the market for powered vehicle suspension components, the company competes with several firms in different submarkets. In snowmobile market, the company competes with KYB, Ohlins Racing AB, Walker Evans Racing, Works Performance Products Inc., etc. In the ATV and Side by Side markets, the main competitors are ZF Sachs and Polaris. In the OEM segment, Walker Evan Racing is the major competitor. In the aftermarket business, the main competitors are Elka Suspension, Ohlin Racing, Works Performance Products, and Penske Racing Shocks. In the market for off-road and specialty vehicle suspension segment, the main competitors are ThyssenKrupp Bilstein Suspension, King Shock Technology, and Icon Vehicle Dynamics. In the market for suspension systems, the company competes with TransAmerican Wholesale, Rough Country Suspension Systems, and Rusty's Off Road. In the market for up-fitted vehicles, the main competitors are Roush Performance and DSI Custom Vehicle. In the Specialty sports segment, the main competitors are RockShox, X Fusion Shox, Manitou, etc.

Risk Factors

The company depends on a limited number of suppliers for certain components. The company could experience significant production delays or disruption to the business if the suppliers are unable to timely fulfill orders. The success of the business of the company depends on the continuous development of innovative performance defining products. The new product development requires significant investment in financial, technological, and other resources. The industries in which the company operates are highly competitive. The company competes with a number of manufacturers who sell performance defining products to OEMs and aftermarket dealers and distributors which include OEMs. The performance defining products offered by the company are discretionary products and these businesses are sensitive to economic conditions that impact consumer spending. The company's business may suffer if the company is unable to maintain its brand image. The sales are highly dependent on the demand for high-end bikes and a decline in the demand for these bikes or their suspension components will have adverse effect on the business operations of the firm. Changes in the customer, channel, and product mix may impact the profitability of the business.

Sustainability Initiatives

The company conducted the first materiality assessment to understand the environmental, social, and governance aspects which are of significance for stakeholders. The high-performance products of the company are developed using sustainable processes which include design specifications such as robustness, durability, and longevity. The company has also initiated a life cycle screening to understand the environmental impact of the entire product cycle from raw materials to end product. The company has entrusted an external agency to understand the environmental impact of the high-volume products produced by the company. The company uses high-powered computers to model its designs and test them before making prototypes. To develop an inclusive and diverse workforce, the company have launched initiatives such as ACCELERATE Leadership Development Program, Realizing Inclusion, Diversity & Engagement (RIDE), and signature outreach program such as Trail Trust. The company strives to comply with operational health, safety, and legal requirements in different regions. The company identify work-related hazards and assesses risks through job hazards or job safety analysis. Corporate grant making is offered through partnerships with third-party platforms. The employee giving and voluntary program BOOST was launched in the year 2022. The company conducts environmental audits on a 3-year cycle as part of its ISO 14001 certification.

Stock Performance

The stock returns of Fox Factory are compared with that of the returns of market index S&P 500 during the recent 5-year period April 2018–March 2023. Fox stock which was trading at $33.25 on April 1st, 2018, increased by 3.69 times to trade at $122.74 by March 1st, 2023. The total cumulative monthly return for Fox stock was 197% compared to 51% returns accounted for the market index S&P 500 during the 5-year period April 2018–March 2023. The average yearly return for the stock was 40% compared to 10% returns for S&P 500 Index. The data is sourced from Yahoo Finance.

Table 1 shows the holding period return for the Fox stock and the market index S&P 500 during the recent 5-year period 2018–2022. The holding period return analysis assumes holding period of 1-year period.

The Fox stock registered superior returns compared to market index S&P 500 in the years 2018, 2020, and 2021, respectively.

Table 2 gives the market and book value of equity of Fox stock during the period 2018–2022. The values are given in millions of dollars.

The book value of equity as percent of market value of equity was 17.9% during the period 2018–2022.

Table 3 shows the financial highlights of the company during the period 2018–2022 in millions of dollars.

Table 1 Holding period return

Year	Fox factory	S&P 500	Excess returns
2018	77%	−5%	82%
2019	17%	19%	−2%
2020	61%	16%	44%
2021	42%	28%	14%
2022	−31%	−15%	−16%

Table 2 Book value and market value of equity

Year	2018	2019	2020	2021	2022
Book value of equity	321.21	422.2	719.17	894.08	1121.39
Market value of equity	2236.53	2682.55	4418.89	7164.61	3856.29
BV as percent of MV	14.4%	18.9%	26.8%	20.2%	15.7%

Table 3 Financial highlights

	(In millions of dollars)				
Financial highlights	2018	2019	2020	2021	2022
Total assets	485.25	609.32	1286.56	1515.73	1618.34
Short-term investments	27.96	43.74	245.76	179.69	145.25
Total equity	321.21	422.2	719.17	894.08	1121.39
Total revenue	619.23	751.02	890.55	1299.06	1602.49
Total operating expenses	110.96	129.93	175.4	235.42	284.65
Net income	84.04	93.03	90.67	163.82	205.28
Market cap	2236.53	2682.55	4418.89	7164.61	3856.29
Enterprise value	645.88	603.61	598.31	1019.16	696.92

Table 4 Performance indicators

Ratios	2018	2019	2020	2021	2022
Net margin%	13.57	12.39	10.18	12.61	12.81
ROE%	30.23	25.03	15.89	20.31	20.37
ROA%	18.46	17	9.57	11.69	13.1
DER	0.19	0.18	0.55	0.43	0.19

Table 5 Economic value

Year	2021	2022
Profit before income tax	188.38	233.76
Income tax	24.6	28.5
Net operating profit after tax (NOPAT)	163.8	205.3
Stockholder equity	894.08	1121.39
Long-term debt	360.95	200
Total capital employed	1255.03	1321.39
WACC	11.41%	13.15%
Capital charge	143.20	173.76
Economic value	20.62	31.50

The total assets and total equity grew by 40% and 38% on average basis during the period 2018–2022. The total cash and cash equivalents showed fluctuating trend during this period. The total revenue and net income increased by 27% and 29%, respectively, on average basis. The market capitalization increased by 25% on average basis during the period 2018–2022. The data source is gurufocus.com and annual reports.

Table 4 shows the financial indicators for the firm during the period 2018–2022.

During the period 2018–2022, the average net margin, ROE, and ROA were 12.31%, 22.37%, and 13.96%, respectively. The average debt–equity ratio was 0.31.

Table 5 illustrates the estimation of economic value of Fox Factory during the years 2021 and 2022. The values are estimated in millions of dollars.

The economic value is estimated to have increased from $20.62 million in 2021 to $31.50 million in year 2022.

References

1. https://investor.ridefox.com/investor-relations/default.aspx
2. Fox Sustainability Report 2021

Case 61 Charles River Laboratories

Charles River Lab is a non-clinical Contract Research Organization headquartered in Wilmington, Massachusetts and provides a full suite of products and services that span from target identification and discovery through non-clinical drug development and manufacturing. Charles River Laboratories was founded in the year 1947. The company was incorporated in the year 1994 and completed its IPO in the year 2000. In 2021, Charles River was added to the Standard and Poor's 500 Stock Index (S&P 500). The stock is traded on the New York Stock Exchange under the symbol CRL. The company is also included in the Dow Jones US Health Care Index, the New York Stock Exchange (NYSE) Arca Biotechnology Index, the NYSE, and Russell indexes. The clients of the company include leading pharmaceutical, biotechnology, agricultural and industrial chemical, life science, veterinary medicine, medical device, diagnostic and consumer product companies, contract research and contract manufacturing organizations, commercial entities, leading hospitals, and government agencies.

Charles River Lab is a premier scientific partner for cell and gene therapy (C&GT) development, testing, and manufacturing. The company has operations in 100 plus locations in over 20 countries. The company has over 20,000 employees worldwide. In fiscal 2021, the company made revenues of $3.54 billion. The service areas offered include basic research, discovery, safety and efficacy, clinical support, and manufacturing. The major business segment of Charles River Lab consists of Discovery and Safety Assessment (DSA), Manufacturing Solutions (MFG), and Research Models and Services (RMS) which constitute 60%, 21%, and 19% of the products and services portfolio. Charles River supports the development of novel therapeutics. The company is involved in the evolving area of biomedical research and drug development which focusses on treatment of diseases based on cellular therapy. These therapies extract cells, protein, or genetic material (DNA) from patient or donor and after transformation through altering methods, reinjects them into the patient thereby providing a highly personalized therapy. The company is competitively positioned to become a provider of comprehensive solutions for C&GT research, development, and manufacturing. The company has supported

© The Author(s), under exclusive license to Springer Nature Switzerland AG 2024

B. R. Kumar, *Rising Stars*, Management for Professionals,
https://doi.org/10.1007/978-3-031-50032-9_61

the development of 10 FDA-approved C&GTS. In 2021, the company has conducted more than 1000 C&GT case studies. In 2021, Charles River had researched on 93% of oncology drugs and 87% of the rare and orphan disease drugs approved by FDA. By December end 2022, the company have employed 21,400 employees which included 2600 science professionals with advanced degrees.

Segments

Research Models and Services (RMS)

The RMS segment provides foundational tools for the discovery of new molecules by the supply of research models to drug development industry. RMS segment with over 150 different stocks and strains is a global leader in the production and sale of rodent research model strains. RSM produces the industry's largest used catalog of models and unique research model strains for the development of new drugs, medical devices, and cell therapies. RSM segment offers services to support the clients for breeding, management, and use of research models for the purpose of screening non-clinical drug candidates. The three service offerings in RSM segment are Genetically Engineered Models and Services (GEMS), Insourcing Solutions, and Research Animal Diagnostic Services (RADS). GEMS offerings create, breed, and maintain research models for biomedical research activities for the clients. Insourcing Solutions manages the research operations of government institutions, academic entities, and commercial clients. Charles River Accelerator and Development Lab (CRADL) and Explora BioLabs which offer vivarium space to clients are integral components of the RSM segment. RADS segment monitors and analyzes the health profiles of the clients' research models and research biologics by assessing infectious agents and pathology. The Cell Solutions offer human-derived cellular materials for the development and production of cell therapies.

Discovery and Safety Assessment

Charles River is one of the largest providers of drug discovery and safety testing services worldwide. Discovery and Safety Assessment (DSA) segment comprises Discovery Services and Safety Assessment. Discovery Services offers a full spectrum of discovery services which ranges from the identification and validation of novel targets, chemical compounds, and antibodies to the delivery of preclinical drug and therapeutic candidates. The strategic focus of Discovery Services is on major therapeutic areas of oncology, immunology, and neuroscience. The company offers a full range of safety assessment studies for regulatory approvals in all therapeutic areas including pharmaceutical, biotechnology, industrial, chemical, agrochemicals, consumer products, veterinary medicines, and medical devices industries. The company offers safety assessments for broad specialty toxicology ranging from inhalation and infusion to development and reproductive toxicology. Charles River also offers safety assessments for pathology services and safety pharmacology. The company has safety assessment facilities for bioanalysis, drug metabolism, and pharmacokinetics.

Manufacturing Solutions

The Manufacturing Solutions (MFG) segment consists of Microbial Solutions, Biologics Solutions, and Avian Vaccine Services.

Microbial Solutions is one of the leading global providers of in vitro methods for conventional and rapid quality-control testing of sterile biopharmaceutical products. Microbial Solutions facilitate rapid and efficient testing platforms for microbial detection and identification of sterile and non-sterile applications. The company is a market leader in endotoxin testing products and services for quality-control testing of injectable drugs and medical devices. The Celsis® reagents and instrument systems are used for in-process and product-release testing for the efficient manufacture of pharmaceutical and consumer products. The Accugenix global lab network is an industry leader in contract microbial identification services.

Biologics Solutions (Biologics) business consists of Biologics Testing Services business and CDMO business. Biologics Testing Services business includes process development and quality-control testing to enable the manufacture of biologics. The company performs specialized testing of biologics which are outsourced by global pharmaceutical and biotechnology companies. The testing labs of the company offer regulatory compliant services in the areas of analytical, molecular biology, virology, cell-based bioassays, bioanalysis, immunochemistry, microbiology, cell biology, in vivo, and in vitro studies. The CDMO business focusses on the three major platforms of high-growth advanced therapy which consists of cell therapy, viral vector, and plasmid DNA production.

Avian Vaccine Services which was divested in the year 2022 has been a global leader in the supply of SPF fertile chicken eggs and chickens. SPF chicken embryos are used by vaccine producers as self-contained "bioreactors" for the manufacture of live viruses.

Strategy

Charles River's global portfolio of products, services, and solutions focusses on drug development and early-stage development. As a part of its integrated early-stage portfolio strategy, the company offers research models, discovery research studies, and comprehensive safety assessment studies in both regulated and non-regulated environments. The growth strategy also gives emphasis on a comprehensive biopharmaceutical manufacturing portfolio which facilitates process development, quality control, and production initiatives of the biopharmaceutical industry sector. The company also offers products and services related to the development of clinical stage and commercialized biologics products which include CDMO services to manufacture advanced therapeutics. Charles River offers extensive scientific expertise across a broad range of therapeutic areas consisting of medicinal chemistry, antibody engineering, in vitro biology, in vivo pharmacology, and pathology. The company leverages its expertise embedded in its integrated, non-clinical portfolio to offer customized solutions to address specific needs of clients. The company has deep long-term strategic relationships with its clients and offers support across the non-clinical drug research process. The company offers extensive scientific, technical, and therapeutic area expertise to its clients. By means of digital enhancement, customer centric design thinking, agile-based test, and learning processes in short iterative cycles, the company aims to optimize client experiences. The company aims to deliver fast and high-quality end-to-end integrated solutions to speed up cell and gene therapy development and manufacturing at global level by leveraging its cell and gene therapy strengths and capabilities.

Through focused acquisitions and alliances, the company aims to expand its portfolio and broaden its geographic footprint. In the year 2021, the company acquired Distributed Bio, Retrogenix, Cognate, and Vigene. Through the acquisition of Distributed Bio Inc., after the culmination of an exclusive partnership, the company gained competitive advantage to offer integrated end-to-end solutions for antibody libraries, immune engineering platforms, C&GT discovery, and development services for clients. The acquisition of Retrogenix enhanced Charles River's scientific expertise in large molecule and cell therapy capabilities. Charles River acquired Cognate Bio services, a premier cell and gene therapy contract development and manufacturing organization (CDMO) for its expertise in cellular immunotherapy and immune-oncology, regenerative medicine, and advanced cell therapy. Vigene Biosciences, another CDMO which provides viral vector-based gene delivery solutions was acquired by Charles River. The acquisition of Vigene was a strategic fit for the company to expand its comprehensive cell and gene therapy portfolio. The company has also partnered with leading venture capital firms which basically invest in early-stage life sciences, healthcare, and therapeutics companies. In the year 2022, Explora BioLabs was acquired by Charles River. The acquisition of Explora BioLabs, the provider of contract vivarium research services complemented the Insource Solution business of the company. In 2023, Charles River acquired SAMDI Tech Inc. which is a leading provider of high-quality, label-free high-throughput screening solutions for drug discovery research. This acquisition was aimed to provide Charles River's clients with access to premier label-free HTS MS platform and create a comprehensive industry leading library of drug discovery solutions.

Risk Factors

The businesses of the company bear financial risks for contracts that may be terminated or reduced in scope, underpriced due to cost overrun or delay. Upgradation and integration of business systems could lead to implementation issues and business disruptions. Delays in government funding of R&D would adversely affect the business operations of the company. Contract development and manufacturing services businesses have potential liability risks. The risk of contamination with respect to animal population has the potential to damage the inventory. The industries in which Charles River operates are highly competitive in nature. The company faces legal and regulatory risks related to changes in government regulation, data privacy and security laws, environmental, health and safety laws in different jurisdictions of operations.

Sustainability Initiatives

The company has worked on 80% of the US Food and Drug Administration (FDA) approved drugs since 2017 and has originated 90 novel molecules candidate compounds for clients since the year 1999. Charles River has rigorous genetic standards which include core values of animal welfare, biosecurity, and the 3Rs (Replacement, Reduction, and Refinement) which offer alternatives to animal testing. The company is a trusted global partner for providing industry leading vivarium management, biosecurity, and genetic stability. Charles River is actively engaged with partners such as the American Association for Animal Laboratory Science (AALAS), Diversity Alliance for Science (DA4S), Pharmaceutical Supply Chain Initiative (PSCI), and Science Based Targets Initiative (SBTi) for promoting ESG Initiatives. As a part of its governance initiatives, Charles River implemented a standard proxy access by law in the year 2021 wherein a group of 20 shareholders who have continuously held 3% of Chares River's outstanding shares for 3 years could submit director candidates for inclusion on the proxy ballot. Charles River maintains a robust global Continuity Plan (BCP) program to address issues related to supply chain interruption and loss or damage to critical infrastructure. Charles River maintains a Security Operations Center and conducts threat hunting, ethical phishing tests, and simulated incidents.

Through C&GT investments, Charles River is facilitating the transformation of the global drug development process by changing the way medicines and therapies are discovered, developed, and delivered. The Company publishes the Corporate Citizenship Report in accordance with Global Reporting Initiative (GRI) and Sustainability Accounting Standards Board (SASB) standards. The climate change goal is to reduce the global greenhouse gas (GHG) Scope 1 and 2 emissions from Charles River facilities by 50% and Scope 3 GHG emissions by 15% by the year 2030. To increase focus on renewable energy, Charles River had entered into virtual Power Purchase Agreements to supply solar and wind power based 100% renewable electricity in North American and European regions. Charles River Sustainability Capital Fund provides a $5 million annual commitment to support sustainability projects through 2030. By year end 2021, the company has achieved a 25% reduction in Scope 1 and 2 GHG emissions. The company has launched seven Employee Resource Groups (ERGs) for meaningful employee engagement. The Charles River Humane Care Imperative focusses on initiatives to uphold high standards of humane care and well-being for research animals. Charles River has more than 230 veterinarians and 2000 animal care professionals to ensure the health and well-being of animals for clinical trials. The company also undergoes assessments by AAALAC International, a third-party animal welfare nonprofit organization which conducts rigorous animal welfare assessment and accreditation processes. The compliance Quality Systems program follows Good Laboratory Practices (GLP), Good Clinical Practices, and current Good Manufacturing Practices (cGMP) as required by North American and EU regulations. In 2021, approximately 38% of the hiring in the United States came from underrepresented backgrounds. The company established seven global ERGs which play a central role in talent attraction through partnership with external organizations and local universities. Through the Volunteer Time Off (VTO) program, Charles River employees each receive up to 12.5 h of paid time annually to engage in community service. In 2021, the company made donations to 25 food banks around the globe which resulted in more than 2.5 million meals being offered to underserved sections of society.

Stock Performance

The stock performance of Charles River is compared with that of the performance of S&P 500 Index and S&P 500 Health Care Index during the 5-year period commencing on December 30, 2017, and ending on December 31, 2022. The analysis assumes reinvestment of dividends.

Table 1 shows the comparative stock market performance of Charles River and market indexes.

The 5-year holding period return for Charles River Stock was 99% compared to 57% and 80% return for market indexes S&P 500 and S&P 500 Healthcare. The 5-year average return for Charles River was 21.86% compared to returns of 11.23% and 12.95% accounted by market indexes S&P 500 and S&P 500 Healthcare.

Table 2 gives the book value of equity and market value of equity of Charles River during the period 2018–2022. The values are given in millions of dollars.

Table 1 Comparative stock wealth analysis

Year	2017	2018	2019	2020	2021	2022
Charles River	$100	$102.00	$139.00	$230.00	$337.00	$199.00
S&P 500	$100	$96.00	$126.00	$149.00	$192.00	$157.00
S&P 500 healthcare	$100	$106.00	$129.00	$146.00	$184.00	$180.00

Source Annual Report 2022

Table 2 Book value and market value trends

Year	2018	2019	2020	2021	2022
Book value of equity	1338.3	1666.48	2143.67	2591.99	3023.51
Market value of equity	5456.29	7475.46	12434.78	19019.85	11100.7
BV as percent of MV	24.5%	30.5%	28.7%	20.8%	15.9%

Table 3 Financial highlights

	(In millions of dollars)				
Financial highlights	2018	2019	2020	2021	2022
Total assets	3855.88	4692.79	5490.83	7024.29	7602.77
Short-term investments	196.33	238.96	229.45	241.21	233.91
Total equity	1338.3	1666.48	2143.67	2591.99	3023.51
Total revenue	2266.1	2621.23	2923.93	3540.16	3976.06
Total operating expenses	508.68	607.16	640.81	744.78	811.68
Net income	226.37	252.02	364.3	390.98	486.23
Market cap	5456.29	7475.46	12434.78	19019.85	11100.7
Enterprise value	6948.95	9293.22	14394.45	21788.41	14011.27

Table 4 Performance and leverage measures

Ratios	2018	2019	2020	2021	2022
Net margin%	9.99	9.61	12.46	11.04	12.23
ROE%	19.16	17.07	19.43	16.82	17.65
ROA%	6.67	5.9	7.15	6.25	6.65
DER	1.27	1.24	1.02	1.17	1.04

The average book value as percent of market value of equity was 18.4% during the period 2018–2022.

Table 3 gives the financial highlights of the company during the period 2018–2022. The data source was gurufocus.com

During the period 2018–2022, the average growth rate of total assets, total cash investments, and total equity were 18.72%, 5%, and 23%, respectively. The average growth rate of revenues and net income were 15% and 22% during the period 2018–2022. The total expenses increased by 13% during the above period. The market capitalization and enterprise value increased by 29% and 26%, respectively, during the above period. Table 4 shows the profitability and leverage position of Charles River during the period 2018–2022.

The average net margin, ROE, and ROA during the period 2018–2022 were 11.07%, 18.03%, and 6.52%, respectively. The average debt-equity ratio was 1.15 during the above period.

References

1. Investor Overview | Charles River Laboratories International, Inc. (criver.com)
2. 2021 Corporate Citizenship report 2021

Case 62 Spirit of Texas Bancshares, Inc.

Spirit of Texas Bancshares, Inc. is a registered banking holding corporation with headquarters in Texas. The corporation offers a wide range of commercial and retail banking services through the wholly owned bank subsidiary, Spirit of Texas Bank SSB. The Corporation has operations in 38 locations in Houston, Dallas/Fort Worth, Bryan/College Station, San Antonio-New Braunfels, Corpus Christi, Tyler, Austin metropolitan areas, and North Central Texas. Spirit of Texas offers relationship-driven financial services to small and medium-sized businesses with annual revenues in the range of $3 million to $30 million. The bank offers a wide range of commercial products such as term loans, operating lines of credit to commercial and industrial firms, commercial real estate loans, construction and development loans, SBA loans, commercial deposit accounts, and treasury management services. The retail offerings of the bank include consumer loans, 1–4 single-family residential real estate loans, and retail deposits. Spirit of Texas Bank is the sole banking subsidiary of Bancshares Corporation.

The bank's exposure to dynamic and complementary markets offers it the opportunity for economic diversification and growth. The top four markets for the bank include the Houston-The Woodlands-Sugar Land MSA, Dallas-Fort Worth-Arlington MSA, College Station-Bryan MSA, and San Antonio-New Braunfels MSA. The banking competitors in the target market include various community banks, national and regional banks. The bank also faces competition from savings banks, savings and loan associations, finance companies, credit unions, and other providers of financial services, such as money market mutual funds, brokerage firms, consumer finance companies, asset-based non-bank lenders, and insurance companies. The company's strategy is to compete as a community-oriented bank. The company focusses on relationship and referral-based marketing strategy. In the year 2022, Spirits of Texas Bank SSB was merged into Simmons Bank. Hence the stock was delisted.

© The Author(s), under exclusive license to Springer Nature Switzerland AG 2024
B. R. Kumar, *Rising Stars*, Management for Professionals,
https://doi.org/10.1007/978-3-031-50032-9_62

Lending Activities

The state and federal law stipulates lending limits for the bank. In general, the bank is subject to a legal limit on loans to a single borrower which is equal to 25% of the Bank's tier 1 capital. The credit department of the bank provides in-depth credit administration and reports to the Bank's Asset Quality Committee. The credit department also provides analytical and underwriting services. For loan review, the bank utilizes an internal loan review system called the Relationship Review Process. All loan relationships with a value greater than $500 thousand are reviewed by the loan officer annually. With respect to cases of loan relationships with a value greater than $2 million, the relationship review process is done semiannually. The bank also employs an external third-party loan review team to review up to 70% of the bank's entire loan portfolio on an annual basis. The bank also stringently monitors loans which include nonaccrual loans, loans past due 90 days or more, and renegotiated or restructured loans. The banks also provide allowance for loan and lease losses which is adequate to absorb probable losses on loans that are present in the loan portfolio.

Investments

The bank invests in US Treasury bills and notes, securities of federally sponsored agencies such as Federal Home Loan Bank bonds. The bank also has the option to invest funds in federal funds, negotiable certificates of deposits, banker's acceptances, mortgage-backed securities, corporate bonds, municipal, or other tax-free bonds. The asset/liability /investment committee of the bank periodically reviews the investment portfolio on an ongoing basis.

Sources of Funds

Deposits are the primary source of funds for the investment and lending activities of the bank. Federal Home Loan Bank of Dallas is the primary outside borrowing source. The additional sources of funds are scheduled loan payments, matured investments, loan repayments, retained earnings, income from other earning assets, and loan sales proceeds. The core deposits include checking accounts, money market accounts, savings accounts, certificates of deposit, and individual retirement accounts. The primary sources of core deposits are residents and businesses. The core deposits are obtained through direct mail solicitations, advertisements in the local media, and personal solicitation by lenders, officers, and directors. The core deposits are supplemented by borrowings which consist of advances from the FHLB of Dallas, borrowings under the Paycheck Protection Program Liquidity Facility, long-term subordinated notes, and holding company line of credit with a third-party lender.

Other Banking Services

The bank offers ancillary services such as a full suite of treasury management services, consumer and commercial online banking services, mobile applications, safe deposit boxes, wire transfer services, debit cards, and ATM access. Merchant services and co-branded credit card services are offered through correspondent bank relationships.

Strategy

The company's strategy focusses on both organic and inorganic growth. Organic loan and deposit mobilization are done through the establishment of de novo branches. The company also focusses on strategic acquisitions to expand its presence in existing markets or new markets. In the past decade, the bank has made 11 acquisitions. In 2018, Comanche National Corporation and its subsidiary, The Comanche National Bank was acquired for a total value of $52.9 million. Spirit added eight additional branches in the North Central Texas region as a result of this acquisition. In 2019, Spirit Bank acquired First Beeville Financial Corporation and its subsidiary, The First National Bank of Beeville for a total value of $65.9 million. As a result of this acquisition, Spirit's bank added three additional branches and two loan production offices in Texas to its infrastructure portfolio. The acquisition of Chandler Bancorp Inc. and its subsidiary, Citizens State Bank in 2019 added seven additional branches for Spirit in the Northeast Texas region and the entire transaction was valued at $62.5 million. In 2020, Spirit was involved in Simmons branch acquisition which was valued at $131.6 million. In 2022, Simmons First National Corp completed the acquisition of Spirit, the parent company of Spirit of Texas Bank, SSB. As a result of this acquisition, Spirits of Texas Bank SSB was merged into Simmons Bank.

Risk Factors

COVID pandemic has adversely affected the financial position of the bank. On account of the bank's participation in the SBA's Paycheck protection program, the bank faces operational, and credit risks. The operations of the bank are exclusively focused in Texas region. Any regional or economic downturn may affect the operations of the bank. The bank's focus on acquisition strategy exposes it to financial, execution, and operational risks which will have material adverse impact on performance of the bank. The bank may not be able to generate sufficient new loans and deposits within acceptable risk and expense tolerances. The bank basically focusses on small to medium sized businesses for business development which are more vulnerable to economic downturns. The inability of such borrowers to repay loans would adversely affect the operations of the bank. The commercial loans which comprise a major chunk of the loan portfolio are predominantly secured by receivables, promissory notes, inventory, equipment, or other commercial collateral whose deterioration in value would increase the potential for future losses. Adverse developments that affect real estate values in the primary market could increase the credit risk associated with the real estate loan portfolio. The commercial real estate and construction, land, and development loan portfolios expose the bank to credit risks.

Performance Analysis

Table 1 gives the book value and market value of equity of Spirit during the period 2018–2021. The values are given in millions of dollars.

The average book value as percent of market value of equity was 89.8% during the period 2018–2021.

Table 2 gives the financial highlights of the bank during the period 2018–2021. The values are given in millions of dollars. The source of data was gurufocus.com

The total assets, gross loans, and deposits increased by 32%, 31%, and 35%, respectively, during the period 2018–2021. The total equity increased by 33% during the above period. The interest income grew by 12% on average basis during the above period. The interest expenses and non-interest expenses increased by 20% and 31%, respectively, on average basis. The market capitalization and enterprise value increased by 31% and 17%, respectively, during the above period.

Table 3 shows the performance ratios of the bank during the period 2018–2021.

Table 1 Book and market value of equity

Year	2018	2019	2020	2021
Book value of equity	198.8	345.7	360.8	393.8
Market value of equity	275.7	419.9	287	497.4
BV as percent of MV	72.1%	82.3%	125.7%	79.2%

Table 2 Financial highlights

	(In millions of dollars)			
Financial highlights	2018	2019	2020	2021
Total assets	1476.6	2384.6	3084.8	3266
Gross loans	1106.8	1771.2	2390	2325.6
Deposits	1182.6	1928.1	2459.1	2782.4
Total equity	198.8	345.7	360.8	393.8
Interest income	57.3	95.3	123.5	125.5
Interest expense	10.3	17.4	17.6	11.4
Total non-interest expense	43.4	63	74.8	71.8
Market capitalization	275.7	419.9	287	497.4
Enterprise value	274.2	198.6	126.1	271.2

Table 3 Performance measures

Ratios	2018	2019	2020	2021
Performance ratios				
Return on average assets %	0.8	1.09	1.15	1.32
Return on average equity%	6.7	7.76	8.86	11.15
Net interest margin%	4.3	4.96	4.74	4.27
Efficiency ratio%	75.41	68.19	59.92	
Capital ratios				
Common equity tier 1 to risk-weighted assets%	14.81	14.47	14.47	13.41
Total capital to risk-weighted assets%	15.37	14.85	14.85	14

The average ROA, ROE, and net interest margin for the bank were 1.09%, 8.62%, and 4.57%, respectively, during the period 2018–2021. The average efficiency ratio was 67.84%. The average capital ratios were 14.29% and 14.77%, respectively.

References

1. https://www.simmonsbank.com/about/newsroom/20220411-simmons-first-national-corp-completes-acquisition-and-conversion-of-spirit-of-texas-bancshares
2. https://www.nasdaq.com/press-release/spirit-of-texas-bancshares-inc.-and-chandler-bancorp-inc.-to-merge-2019-07-24
3. Annual Report 2021

Case 63 DuPont

DuPont de Nemours, Inc. is a publicly traded premier global multi-industrial innovation leader with technology-based materials, solutions, and expertise. The company delivers essential innovations in key markets such as electronics, transportation, construction, water, healthcare, and worker safety. In June 2019, DowDuPont Inc. changed its registered name to DuPont de Nemours, Inc. ("DuPont"). In 2015, Dow Chemicals and DuPont merged to form Dow DuPont. In 2019, the Company completed the separation of the materials science business through the spin-off of Dow Inc. The combination of the highly complementary portfolios of Dow and DuPont was intended to create a leadership position for the combined company.

By December end of 2022, the Dupont company owned about 14,000 patents and patent applications globally. The R&D expense of the company in the year 2022 amounted to $536 million. By December 31, 2021, the company had employed 28,001 people across 120 locations globally with 36% of employees located in Asia and 42% in the United States and Canada. The company has subsidiaries in over 60 countries and manufacturing operations in 25 countries. By 2021, DuPont worked with over 100,000 suppliers worldwide and had spent approximately $11.9 billion on supplier front.

Segment Information

Electronics & Industrial

Electronics & Industrial is the leading global provider of differentiated materials and component solutions. This segment of Dupont offers solutions for high-performance computing, 5G, electrical vehicles, a wide range of consumer electronics, and solutions for industry sectors which include aerospace, defense transportation, and healthcare. The major product lines of this segment are classified into Semiconductor Technologies, Interconnect Solutions, and Industrial Solutions. The segment offers materials and solutions for the fabrication of semiconductors and integrated circuits.

© The Author(s), under exclusive license to Springer Nature Switzerland AG 2024

B. R. Kumar, *Rising Stars*, Management for Professionals,
https://doi.org/10.1007/978-3-031-50032-9_63

The segment offers a broad portfolio of semiconductor and advanced packaging materials which provide planarization pads, photoresists, advanced coatings for lithography, and metallization solutions for advanced chip packaging. This segment offers permanent and process chemistries for the fabrication of printed circuit boards, electrolytic metallization solutions, and innovative metallization processes for metal finishing, decorative, and industrial applications. This segment is also the leading global supplier in the packaging graphics industry which provides photopolymer plates and platemaking systems which are used in flexographic printing and digital inks for textile, commercial, and home office printing applications. This segment also offers cutting edge materials for the manufacturing of displays for organic light emitting diode and other display applications. The segment also manufactures high-performance parts, specialty silicone elastomers, and lubricants for applications in automotive, aerospace, electronics, industrial, and healthcare sectors. The segment focusses on providing critical engineering materials and solutions for facilitating the creation of a connected and digital world.

Water & Protection

This segment is a global leader that provides innovative engineered products and integrated systems for worker safety, water purification, transportation, energy, medical packaging, and building materials. The major product lines of Water & Protection segment include Safety Solutions, Shelter Solutions, and Water Solutions. The major innovative brands of the Water & Protection segment include KEVLAR® high-strength material, NOMEX® thermal-resistant material, CORIAN® solid surfaces, TYVEK® selective barriers, FILMTEC™ reverse osmosis elements, STYROFOAM™ insulation, and GREAT STUFF™ insulating foam sealants. Water & Protection is focusing on future innovative initiatives such as water management solutions, construction productivity solutions, high strength and lightweighting composite solutions, and circular ecosystem / zero waste solutions.

Table 1 lists the major milestones of the company.

Corporate Restructuring

The Company acquired Desalitech Ltd., a closed-circuit reverse osmosis (CCRO) company in the year 2020. In the year 2020, the company sold its compound semiconductor solutions business unit to SK Siltron. In 2021, Dupont completed the divestiture of the Nutrition & Biosciences business to International Flavors & Fragrance Inc. In the same year, DuPont acquired Laird Performance Material business from Advent International. In 2022, Dupont decided to divest Mobility & Materials segment to Celanese Corporation. The Board of Directors have approved the divestiture of the Delrin® acetal homopolymer (H-POM) business.

Table 1 Milestones

Year	Events
1802	Du Pont laid the foundation of the first gunpowder mills on the Brandywine River on July 19, 1802.
1900s	DuPont's labs conducted two types of research—Applied research and Basic research. The experimental station did research on problems related to Dupont's product lines while the Eastern Laboratory focused solely on high explosives and achieved success. DuPont established Jackson Laboratory at Deepwater to carry out research related to dyestuffs chemistry.
1910s	Diversified product lines. Product departments such as explosives, paints, and dyestuffs set up their own applied research facilities.
1915	Acquired Arlington Company, the manufacturer of Pyralin®, a nitrocellulose pyroxylin plastic used in combs, collars, cuffs, and automobile side curtains.
1924	Dupont produced 35 mm positive movie film and sold about $4 million worth of film per year.
1925	Acquired Viscoloid which produced pyroxylin plastics for toiletries industry.
1930s	Focus on research and innovation in plastic industry. Basic research initiatives got a boost through the discovery of first true synthetic fiber, Nylon by Wallace Hume Carothers. Agreements with Union Carbide and the Shawinigan Corporation to produce Butacite®, a polyvinyl butyral plastic.
1932	DuPont introduced its X-ray film.
1940s	Acquired two companies to develop X-ray and photographic paper businesses.
1946	DuPont authorized $50 million for construction of new labs.
1950s	Delrin® acetal resin, often called "synthetic stone," was developed which offered both metal-like properties and the ability to be molded into complex shapes.
1960	The Experimental Station's chemical department renewed focus on research breakthroughs in materials and electronics rather than traditional products.
1969	DuPont's first pharmaceutical product, Symmetrel for flu prevention was approved by the Food and Drug Administration (FDA).
1970	DuPont entered the medical/diagnostic instruments with Automatic Clinical Analyzer (ACA) which can perform now up to 67 different tests on blood and other bodily fluids.
1981	Acquired Conoco Oil. DuPont also acquired New England Nuclear Corporation to add radiopharmaceutical tracers to its product line.
1984	Opened $85 million life science research complex. Research mission carried out in 75 labs throughout the world.
1986	DuPont acquired American Critical Care which sold acute care hospital products. The company introduced Dimension analyzer for high-volume diagnostic testing.
1987	Charles Pederson was named a Nobel laureate.
1990	DuPont started manufacturing hydrochlorofluorocarbon refrigerants under the brand name Suva®.
1996	DuPont sold its diagnostic and medical instrument businesses.
2000	Sorona® polymer becomes the advanced DuPont polymer platform.
2003	The world's first integrated bio-refinery was established by DuPont in partnership with the US Department of Energy's National Renewable Energy Laboratory.
2004	DuPont sold off INVISTA, the largest integrated fiber and intermediates business in world to Koch industries for $4.4 billion in cash.
2013	DuPont completed the sale of its coatings business to the private equity firm The Carlyle Group.

(continued)

Table 1 (continued)

Year	Events
2015	DuPont spun off its performance chemicals segment through the creation of the Chemours Company (Chemours).
2015	DuPont and Dow entered into a "merger of equals" for the creation of three independent companies.
2018	DuPont logo updated in more than 100 years with the introduction of a new company purpose focusing on innovation and refreshed brand identity.
2019	The three divisions of DowDuPont are separated and continue its mission which is to build on its rich heritage of scientific discovery.
2021	DuPont divests its nutrition and biosciences business.

. Source: https://www.dupont.com/about/our-history.html

Risk Factors

Dupont faces risks related to the Mobility & Materials (M&M) Divestitures, Nutrition & Biosciences (N&B) Transaction, and the Dow and Corteva Distributions. The company may not be able to realize the anticipated benefits of its share repurchase programs. The company faces significant tax liability risks due to the separation and combination of DuPont's Nutrition & Biosciences business with IFF. The sales and earnings of DuPont would be adversely impacted due to supply chain and operational disruptions, volatility in energy and raw material costs. Interruptions in the company's information technology networks and systems would adversely affect the operations of the company's businesses. The failure of the company to effectively manage acquisitions, divestitures, and alliances would adversely impact the business operations of the company. Risks related to trade disputes, regulations, and policies could adversely impact DuPont's operational results.

Sustainability Initiatives

The sustainability strategies of the company are based on three pillars: Innovate, Protect, and Empower. In terms of business innovation strategies, the company focusses on building science-based competencies such as lifecycle assessment (LCA), circular design, and green chemistry. In terms of environmental initiatives, the company has based its plan on 10% reduction in its GHG emissions, completed Scope 3 inventory, and joined the RE100 Global Initiative. RE100 includes world's leading businesses which have committed to sourcing 100% renewable electricity in their global operations by 2050. The company aims to reduce greenhouse gas emissions by 30% which includes sourcing 60% of electricity from renewable energy by 2030 and deliver carbon-neutral operations by the year 2050. The company focuses on six near-term strategic ESG issues such as sustainable innovation, climate change, circular economy, chemical stewardship, diversity, equity and inclusion, and responsible procurement. As a result of the management review of Dupont's ERM process in 2020, the company formalized an internal governance structure to oversee the annual re-assessment and re-prioritization of enterprise-level risks. In 2021, DuPont has supported more than 450 charitable projects globally through initiatives such as product donations, physical and skills-based employee volunteerism, and provisions for financial resources. The company through partnerships with Habitat for Humanity International, Water.org, etc. supports local and global initiatives. The external initiatives supported by DuPont include the UN Global Compact, World Business Council for Sustainable Development, Responsible Care® Management System, CEO Action for Diversity & Inclusion™, RE100, CEO Water Mandate, and Operation Clean Sweep Blue. The company's new Froth-Pak™ Spray Foam formulation received the American Chemistry Council (ACC)—Sustainability Leadership Award & the Adhesive and Sealant Council (ASC) Innovation Award. The company's B-Free™ technology which is used in reverse osmosis (RO) water treatment systems received the sustainable product of the year award from the Business Intelligence group. The Minimum liquid discharge solution used for industrial water recycling received the Industry Technology and Innovation award from the International Desalination Association. In 2021, DuPont Water Solutions began a collaboration with Vulcan Energy Resources, a lithium and renewable energy project developer, to test and scale up Direct Lithium Extraction technologies for Vulcan's world-first Zero Carbon Lithium® extraction process. Since 2004, the company has installed 204 gigawatts of solar panels with Tedlar®-based backsheets globally. DuPont innovations enable high-frequency connectivity which includes electromagnetic interference shielding products. Integrating circular economy principles, approximately 71% of the company's sites have 4R (reduce, reuse, recycle, and recover) programs. DuPont Second Life Materials (2LM) has unique capabilities to explore, incubate, and accelerate the transition of its businesses from linear to circular models.

Stock Performance

Table 2 illustrates the stock returns of the DuPont in comparison with market indexes of S&P 500, S&P Industrials, and S&P Industrial Conglomerates. The analysis illustrates the cumulative total return for the company stock and market indexes based on the presumed investment of $100 on December 31, 2017, and assumes all dividends received were reinvested.

Table 2 Cumulative stock returns

Year	2017	2018	2019	2020	2021	2022
DuPont	100	$76.84	$66.12	$74.92	$86.45	$74.88
S&P 500	$100	$95.62	$125.72	$148.85	$191.58	$156.89
S&P industrials	$100	$86.71	$112.17	$124.59	$150.89	$142.63
S&P industrial conglomerates	$100	$73.12	$91.49	$100.89	$106.15	$97.23

Source: Annual Report 2022

Table 3 Book and market value of equity

Year	2018	2019	2020	2021	2022
Book value of equity	95,900	41,556	39,070	27,050	27,017
Market value of equity	57548.85	47415.87	52209.25	41342.64	31441.05
BV as percent of MV	166.6%	72.2%	82.4%	51.8%	65.3%

Table 4 Financial highlights

	(In millions of dollars)				
Financial highlights	2018	2019	2020	2021	2022
Total assets	187,855	69,349	70,904	45,707	41,355
Short-term investments	8577	1540	2544	1972	4964
Total equity	95,900	41,556	39,070	27,050	27,017
Total revenue	22,594	15,436	14,338	12,566	13,017
Total operating expenses	5142	3447	3022	2725	2593
Net income	3845	498	−2951	6467	5868
Market cap	57548.85	47415.87	52209.25	41342.64	31441.05
Enterprise value	63218.85	63891.87	65843.25	50769.64	34999.05

Table 5 Performance indicators

Ratios	2018	2019	2020	2021	2022
Net margin%	17.02	23.23	−20.58	51.46	45.08
ROE%	3.95	0.74	−7.42	19.92	22.14
ROA%	2.02	0.39	−4.21	11.09	13.48
DER	0.13	0.43	0.41	0.41	0.3

On the basis of the above analysis, the 5-year holding period return for Dupont stock was −25% compared to returns of 57%, 43%, and − 3% for the market index S&P 500, S&P Industrials, and S&P Industrial Conglomerates. The 5-year average returns for the DuPont stock was −4.36% while for S&P 500, S&P Industrials, and S&P Industrial Conglomerates, the returns were 11.22%, 8.56%, and 1.07%, respectively.

Table 3 shows the book value and market value of equity of DuPont during the 5-year period 2018–2022. The values are given in millions of dollars.

The average book value of equity as percent of market value of equity was 58.6% during the period 2018–2022.

Table 4 gives the financial highlights of the company during the period 2018–2022. The data source is gurufocus.com. The values are given in millions of dollars.

Table 5 shows the profitability ratios and leverage position of the company during the period 2018–2022.

The average net margin, ROE, and ROA were 23.24%, 7.87%, and 4.55%, respectively, during the period 2018–2022. The average debt-equity ratio was 0.34 during the above period of analysis.

References

1. https://www.dupont.com/about/sustainability.html
2. https://www.investors.dupont.com/investors/dupont-investors/default.aspx
3. Rajesh Kumar, Wealth Creation in the World's Largest Mergers and Acquisitions, Integrated Case Studies, Chapter 3 DowDuPont Merger, Springer, Management for Professionals, page 57–67.
4. Sustainability Report 2022
5. Annual Report 2022

Case 64 M/I Homes Inc

M/I Homes is one of the leading builders of single-family homes in the USA. The company initiated home building activities in the year 1976. The company has sold over 143,400 homes over these years since its establishment. The operations of the company consist of homebuilding and financial services. The home building operations constituted approximately 98% of the consolidated revenues in the year 2021 and 2022, respectively. The financial services segment offers mortgage loans and title services to the customers of the home building operations. M/I Homes design, market, construct, and sell single-family homes and attached townhomes to first time, move up, empty nester and luxury buyers. The company focusses on construction of homes in planned development and mixed-use communities. M/I Homes offer homes for sale in 196 communities within 17 markets which are located in ten states in the USA. The average sales prices of homes delivered by the company in year 2022 was $479,000. The company's financial services operation segment generates revenues basically from origination and sales of mortgages and collection of fees for title insurance and closing services. The company offers mortgage banking services to home buyers through 100% owned subsidiary, M/I Financial, LLC. By December 2022, the company employed 1663 people in home building operations.

Product Lines, Design, and Construction

The company devotes significant resources for the research, design, and development of homes to meet the demand of buyers and evolving market requirements. M/I Homes offer houses whose sales price range between $200,000 and $800,000. These houses are of size which ranges approximately between 1000 to 5500 square feet. The company offers single-family detached homes, first time, millennial, multi-generational, move up, empty nester and luxury homes.

© The Author(s), under exclusive license to Springer Nature Switzerland AG 2024

B. R. Kumar, *Rising Stars*, Management for Professionals,
https://doi.org/10.1007/978-3-031-50032-9_64

Market Scenario

In 2022, the housing construction sector experienced slowdown in home building due to increase in mortgage interest rates and high inflation which impacted the mortgage availability. The market environment was negatively impacted by labor and supply shortages and increasing cost of materials.

Business Strategy

The company focusses on improving profitability by expanding market share using affordable designs, selective investment in land and land development initiatives. M/I Homes focus on effective management of land spend and inventory levels. The company aims at opening new communities and managing overhead spend. The strategic aim is to maintain a strong balance sheet and maintain liquidity levels. The company also emphasizes on customer service, product quality, and design. The company market sells its homes primarily through the M/I Homes brand. The M/I brand is differentiated in terms of high-quality construction located in attractive areas. The company also provides 10-year transferable structural warranty in all of its markets. The Whole Home Building Standards of the company are designed to provide ecofriendly and energy-efficient homes. The design studios and design consultants facilitate homebuyers to select different product and design options. The mortgage financing programs offer competitive fixed rate and adjustable rate loans. The Ready Now Homes program offers homebuyers the opportunity to close on certain new homes in 90 days or less. The company relies on independent RESNET-Certified Raters and the HERS (Home Energy Rating System) Index to measure the performance of its homes, including insulation, ventilation, air tightness, and the heating and cooling system. The company also invests in designing and decorating fully-furnished and distinctive model homes. The company markets its homes using digital and traditional media.

Risk Factors

The home building industry is cyclical and could be adversely affected by changes in general economic, real estate, and other business conditions. The home building industry is fragmented and highly competitive. The company competes with many public and private homebuilders. Increased competition would result in reduction of new contracts and homes delivered with decreases in the average sales prices of homes delivered and/or decreased mortgage origination. The company also competes with community developers and land development companies who also serve as homebuilders or affiliates of homebuilders. Reduction in the availability of mortgage financing or rise in mortgage interest rates or down payment requirements could adversely affect the business operations of the company. The success of the company's business depends on the ability to obtain land for the development of communities at reasonable prices. The land investment processes expose the company to risks such as potential impairment charges which could negatively impact the financial results of the company. The residential construction industry faces labor and material shortages, risks due to work stoppages, labor disputes, shortages in qualified subcontractors, construction personnel, and adequate utility infrastructure and services. These risks for the company would increase costs and delay deliveries. The limited geographic diversification could adversely affect the business of the company if demand for new homes in markets declines. As a home builder, the company is subject to construction defect, product liability, and warranty claims as potential sources of risk. The company is subject to extensive government regulations which could restrict its business operations.

Stock Performance

Table 1 illustrates M/I Homes stock performance in terms of cumulative total return for the recent 5-year period through December 31, 2022. The analysis compares the stock return with that of cumulative total return for market indexes S&P 500 and S&P500 Home building Index. A hypothetical investment of $100 and reinvestment of all dividends is assumed to be made in stock.

The 5-year holding period return for M/I Homes stock was 34% while for the S&P500 and S&P500 Home Building Index, the holding period returns were 57% and 54%, respectively. The average returns for M/I Homes was 15% compared to 11% and 14% for S&P500 and S&P500 Home Building Index during the period 2018–2022.

The next section analyzes the stock returns for M/I Homes in comparison with the stock index returns during the 5-year period April 2018–March 2023. The stock which was trading for $30.48 on April 1st 2018 increased by 1.96 times to trade at $59.93 by March 1st 2023. The cumulative total monthly returns for the stock was 142% for the stock compared to 48% cumulative total monthly returns registered by market index S&P500 during the period April 2018–March 2023. The average yearly return for M/I Homes was 29% compared to 10% returns accounted by market index S&P500. The data source is yahoo finance.

Table 2 gives the holding period return for the M/I Homes stock and market index S&P500 during the period 2018–2022.

Table 1 Cumulative wealth comparison

Year	2017	2018	2019	2020	2021	2022
M/I homes	$100.00	$61.10	$114.39	$128.75	$180.76	$134.24
S&P500	$100	$95.62	$125.72	$148.85	$191.58	$156.88
S&P500 home building index	$100	$67.75	$102.16	$127.18	$191.22	$154.40

Source Annual Report 2022

Table 2 Holding period returns

Year	M/I Homes	SP500	Excess returns
2018	−31%	−5%	−26%
2019	49%	19%	29%
2020	0%	16%	−17%
2021	26%	28%	−2%
2022	−13%	−15%	2%

Table 3 Book and market value of equity

Year	2018	2019	2020	2021	2022
Book value of equity	855.3	1003.48	1258.7	1624.18	2070.73
Market value of equity	578.39	1117.01	1276.17	1772.11	1267.18
BV as percent of MV	147.9%	173.5%	112.7%	127.3%	116.9%

Table 4 Financial highlights

	(In millions of dollars)				
Financial highlights	2018	2019	2020	2021	2022
Total assets	2021.58	2105.59	2643.05	3239.85	3714.92
Short-term investments	21.53	6.08	260.81	236.37	311.54
Total equity	855.30	1003.48	1258.70	1624.18	2070.73
Total revenue	2286.28	2500.29	3046.15	3745.89	4131.39
Total operating expenses	280.61	302.34	357.08	390.62	406.39
Net income	107.66	127.59	239.87	396.87	490.66
Market capitalization	578.39	1117.01	1276.17	1772.11	1267.18
Enterprise value	1377.82	1884.15	1939.71	2549.21	1955.16

The M/I Homes stock had higher returns compared to the market index in the year 2019.

Table 3 shows the comparative book and market value of equity during the period 2018–2022. The values are given in millions of dollars.

The average book value of equity as percent of market value of equity was 122% during the period 2018–2022. Table 4 shows the financial highlights of M/I Homes during the period 2018–2022. The values are given in millions of dollars. The data is sourced from guru focus.com and annual reports.

Table 4 shows the financial highlight of M/I Homes during the period 2018–2022.

During the above period, the total assets and total equity increased by 16.73% and 25% on average basis. The short-term investments were highly fluctuating during the period 2018–2019. The cash investments increased by 14% during the period 2020–2022. On average basis, the total revenues and net income increased by 16% and 49%, respectively. The total operating expenses for the company increased by 10% during the above period. The market capitalization and enterprise value increased by 29% and 12%, respectively.

Table 5 Performance indicators

Ratios	2018	2019	2020	2021	2022
Net margin%	4.71	5.1	7.87	10.59	11.88
ROE%	13.44	13.73	21.21	27.53	26.56
ROA%	5.54	6.18	10.1	13.49	14.11
DER	0.96	0.77	0.73	0.62	0.48

Table 6 Estimation of economic value

Year	2021	2022
Profit before income tax	509	635
Income tax	112	145
Net operating profit after tax (NOPAT)	397	491
Stockholder equity	1624	2071
Long-term debt	1013	1000
Total capital employed	2638	3070
WACC	10.67%	9.60%
Capital charge	281.44	294.74
Economic value	115.41	195.89

Table 5 shows the performance indicators of the firm in terms of profitability ratio and leverage ratio.

The average net margin, ROE, and ROA during the period 2018–2022 were 8.03%, 20.5%, and 9.88%, respectively. The average debt equity ratio during the period was 0.71.

Table 6 illustrates the estimation of economic value for the company in year 2021 and 2022. The values are given in millions of dollars.

The economic value for the company has increased from $115.41 million in year 2021 to $195.89 million in year 2022.

Reference

1. M/I Homes Annual Report 2022

Case 65 Sallie Mae (SLM Corporation)

SLM Corporation known as Sallie Mae is a premier education solutions company which caters to the needs of students in higher education sector. The company provides tools, resources, and information to facilitate students and families make informed decisions and support college completion through its scholarship programs and financing options. The company has been in existence for more than 50 years. The company which operates as Sallie Mae was formed in late 2013. The wholly owned subsidiary Sallie Mae, an industrial bank was established in year 2005. During April 2014, SLM got legally separated through spin off from Navient Corporation which is in the education loan management, servicing, asset recovery and consolidation loan business.

In year 2021, Sallie Mae provided financial support to 397,290 students and families for higher education through 1430 team members. Sallie Mae had authorized $5.4 billion in private student loans during the year 2021. The statistics suggest that less than 2% of the company's loans defaulted in the year 2021. It is estimated that nine out of ten loans are repaid by customers on time.

Business Highlights

Private Education Loans

The primary business of SLM is to originate and service high quality private education loans. These education loans are provided to students and families who are not insured or guaranteed by any state or federal government. SLM also offers range of deposit products which are insured by the Federal Deposit Insurance Corporation. The company originated $6 billion of private education loans in the year 2022. By December 31, 2022, SLM had $19 billion of private education loans as part of its investment portfolio. The primary aim of the private education loans is to bridge the gap between the cost of higher education and the amount funded through family income and savings, scholarships and grants along with federal

© The Author(s), under exclusive license to Springer Nature Switzerland AG 2024

B. R. Kumar, *Rising Stars*, Management for Professionals,
https://doi.org/10.1007/978-3-031-50032-9_65

financial aid. Smart Option Student Loan is the primary private education loan product. Three Smart Option repayment types are available for customers. The first two options of interest only and fixed payment options account for approximately half of the private education loans originated by the company in year 2022. Under these options, monthly payments are required when the student is in school and during the stipulated grace period allowed thereafter. The third repayment option is the traditional deferred private education loan product wherein clients are not required to make payments while the student is in the school and during the allotted grace period. The company also offers both variable and fixed rate loans. SLM offers six loan products for specific graduate programs of study.

Sallie Mae Bank

The Sallie Mae Bank which offers traditional savings products such as high yield savings accounts, money market accounts, and certificates of deposit originates private education loans and manages loan portfolios which also consist of loans insured or guaranteed under the Federal Family Education Loan Program. By December 2022, the bank had total assets of $28.3 billion which include $19 billion of private education loans.

SmartyPig

The SmartyPig™ product is a free, FDIC-insured, online, goal-based savings account with features such as tiered interest rates which enable savings growth for consumers. By December 2022, the bank had $330 million in SmartyPig deposits.

Credit Card

The company has plans to exit the credit card business. By December 2022, the company had $29 million in credit card receivables in loans held for sale.

Strategy

The size of the private education loan market is based on three factors of college enrollment levels, costs of attending college and availability of funds from federal government. SLM focuses basically on students who are enrolled for public and private not-for-profit 4-year degree granting institutions. The federal grant and loan programs are sufficient for the funding needs of students enrolled for 2-year programs. The for-profit schools which do business dealings with SLM basically focus on career training and health care fields. In the year 2021–2022, the private education loan originations amounted to $11 billion.

The company focuses on maximizing the profitability and growth of core private student loan business. The strategy is to expand the client base for private education loans. The marketing strategy of the company is to promote products on campuses through financial aid offices along with online and direct marketing initiatives to students and families. As of December 31, 2022, approximately 3.8% of private education loans repayment was 30 days or more delinquent. The company acquired Nitro College—a Delaware-based education solutions companies which facilitate parents and students plan and pay for college education and manage their financial responsibilities after graduation. The acquisition of Nitro was aimed to enhance strategic growth opportunities for the company and expand its digital marketing capabilities. The acquisition enabled SLM to offer broader education solutions to students.

Sustainability Initiatives

The company made $1.8 million in charitable contributions during the year 2021. The company provided 289 scholarships of value $925,000 to students belonging to minority and underserved communities through its Bridging the Dream Scholarship program in the year 2021. Funds of over $ 3 million have been provisioned for deserving students during the period 2021–2023. Since April 2014, The Sallie Mae Fund has contributed more than $6.3 million in scholarships, grants, and matching gifts to support equity and inclusion in higher education system.

The company helps students and families to make informed decisions by providing accessible tools and resources such as CollegeFit Pro, Free Money Pro, and Graduate School Scholarship Search tool. CollegeFit Pro displays information about different majors, school locations, financial aid packages. Free Money Pro is one-stop-shop scholarship search tool which offers 6 million scholarships worth $30 billion. The Graduate School Scholarship search tool provides details of 1 million graduate school scholarships worth more than $1.25 billion. This search tool also facilitates families to complete the free application for federal student aid. On Campus Pro is an all-in-one resource which facilitates expert guidance for students to explore internship and career opportunities. YourMoney Pro is a free resource which enables students to do proper financial planning to achieve career goals. In 2021, the company has awarded $250,000 to nonprofit organizations for advancement of equity and social justice through educational programs and scholarships to Hispanic and LGBTQ+ students. The company has awarded $50,000 in support of college scholarships to children and spouses of disabled military service members. The vendor management program encourages the use of privately held diverse suppliers which are 51% owned by women, minority, disabled veteran and other diverse category. The Relationship Management team supports campus events organized by Historically Black Colleges and Universities. The Sallie Mae's strategy for loan offerings is based on responsible lending philosophy. In 2021, the company made $193 million in new investments which supported low and moderate income and affordable housing projects. As a part of its environmental initiatives, approximately 5000 pieces of obsolete IT equipment were recycled which was equivalent to 41,000 pounds of materials.

Risk Factors

The company is subject to extensive regulation risks by various federal, state, and local authorities. The company faces concentration risks as its product offerings are primarily concentrated on loan products for higher education and deposit products for online depositors. The company competes with banks and other consumer lending institutions in the private education loan market. Many of these lenders have greater level of diversification in their mix of assets which enable them to be more competitive. The demand for private education loans might decline if the consumers have access to alternative means of financing the costs of education such as pre-paid tuition plans, Section 529 plans, Education IRAs and Government education loan programs such as the DSLP. Consolidation or refinancing of existing private education loans might have a material adverse effect on the financial condition of the firm. Credit risks such as default on loans will adversely affect financial condition of the company. The company also faces interest rate risks as changes in interest rates could adversely affect the operations and financial conditions of the firm. SLM is highly dependent on net interest income. SLM faces asset liability mismatch risks. SLM is also subject to repayment and prepayment risks. The use of derivatives to manage interest rate sensitivity exposes the company to credit and market risk. SLM must effectively manage the liquidity risk inherent in its business. The company fund private education loan originations through asset backed securitizations and deposits. Assets funded through deposits result in refinancing risk since the average term of the deposits is shorter than the expected term of the private education loan assets originated.

Stock Performance

Table 1 compares the 5-year cumulative total returns of SLM Corporation, the S&P Super composite Consumer Finance Sub-Industry Index and the S&P 400 Regional Sub-Industry Index. The analysis assumes an investment of $100 in the stock and

Table 1 Cumulative total wealth generation

Year	2017	2018	2019	2020	2021	2022
SLM corporation	$100	73.5	79.9	112.5	180.6	156.3
S&P Supercomposite consumer finance sub-industry index	$100	83.9	113.2	114.1	155.8	125.5
S&P 400 regional bank sub-industry index	$100	78.6	97.9	89.5	126.8	121.5

Source: Annual Report

Table 2 Book and market value of equity

Year	2018	2019	2020	2021	2022
Book value of equity	2972.66	3311.84	2562.84	2149.71	1726.97
Market value of equity	3620.67	3752	4649.97	5485.96	3995.21
BV as percent of MV	82.1%	88.3%	55.1%	39.2%	43.2%

Table 3 Financial highlights

	(In millions of dollars)				
Financial highlights	2018	2019	2020	2021	2022
Total assets	26638.17	32686.48	30770.42	29221.9	28811.03
Gross loans	22541.04	25025.79	23364.81	21437.09	20942.19
Deposits	19156.26	24476.65	22666.04	20828.12	21448.07
Total equity	2972.66	3311.84	2562.84	2149.71	1726.97
Interest income	1935.35	2331.03	2021.66	1776.84	2031.58
Interest expense	522.29	707.72	541.67	382.02	542.8
Market capitalization	3620.67	3752	4649.97	5485.96	3995.21
Enterprise value	5745.87	3231.39	5634.96	7333.42	4865.27

Table 4 Profitability ratios

Ratios	2018	2019	2020	2021	2022
Return on average assets %	2.01	1.95	2.78	3.87	1.62
Return on average equity%	17.9	18.4	29.98	49.25	24.2
Net interest margin%	6.8	6.76	5.95	5.86	6.54

relevant indexes on December 31, 2017 and also assumes the reinvestment of dividends through December 31, 2022.

The 5-year holding period return for the SLM stock was 56% while for S&P Supercomposite and S&400 Regional Bank Sub-Industry index, the holding period returns were 26% and 22%, respectively. The 5-year average return for the SLM stock was 14% while that for S&P Supercomposite and S&P 400 Regional index, the returns were 7.34% and 6.41%, respectively.

Table 2 gives the book value and market value of equity for SLM stock during the period 2018–2022. The values are given in millions of dollars.

The average book value as percent of market value of equity was 61.6% during the period 2018–2022.

Table 3 shows the financial highlights of SLM stock during the period 2018–2022. The values are given in millions of dollars. The source of data is gurufocus.com

During the 5-year period 2018–2022, the average growth rate of total assets, deposits, and equity were 3%, 4%, and 2%, respectively. The interest income grew by 6% on average basis during the above period. The market capitalization and enterprise value increased by 5% and 20%, respectively, during the above period.

Table 4 gives the performance highlights of SLM during the period 2018–2022.

The average return on assets, return on equity, and net interest margin for SLM during the period 2018–2022 were 2.45%, 30.46%, and 6.38%, respectively.

References

1. SLM Corporate Social Responsibility Report 2022
2. SLM Annual Report 2022

Case 66 MYR Group

MYR Group's oldest subsidiary The L E Myers Co was established in the year 1891. The company has been an industry leader for more than 130 years. Throughout the early 1900s, L E Myers had played an instrumental role in building the national's electrical infrastructure. In the year 1953, L E Myers had built US's first 345 Kv transmission lines for the Ohio Valley Electric Corporation. During the 1990s, L E Myers acquired Sturgeon Electric and Harlan Electric. In 1995, MYR Group Inc. was established as the holding company of L E Myers, Sturgeon Electric and Harlan Electric. MYR Group became one of the largest holding companies of specialty electrical contractors in the USA and Canada. The company went public in year 2008 and began trading on NASDAQ under the symbol MYRG. Through the subsidiaries, the company cater to the needs of electric utility infrastructure, commercial and industrial construction markets. The operations of the company are conducted through wholly owned subsidiaries. Electrical construction services are provided through network of local offices which are established in the USA and Canada. The company provides a wide range of services such as design, engineering, procurement, construction, upgrade along with maintenance and repair services. By December 31, 2022, the company employed 8500 people. The company is among the top five engineering special electrical contractors in the USA for the past 25 years in a row.

Table 1 lists the subsidiaries of MYR Group.

Business Segment

Transmission and Distribution (T&D) Segment

MYRG Group is one of the largest US contractors which services the T&D sector of the electric utility industry. This segment offers a wide range of services related to electric transmission and distribution networks and substation facilities in the USA and Canada. The T&D services offered by the company include the construction and

© The Author(s), under exclusive license to Springer Nature Switzerland AG 2024

B. R. Kumar, *Rising Stars*, Management for Professionals,
https://doi.org/10.1007/978-3-031-50032-9_66

Table 1 Subsidiaries of MYR Group

No	Subsidiaries	No	Subsidiaries
1	L E Myers Co.	6	E S Boulos Company
2	Sturgeon Electric Company Inc	7	High Country Line Construction Inc
3	Harlan Electric Company	8	Huen Electric Inc.
4	MYR Energy Services Inc.	9	CSI Electrical Contractors Inc.
5	Great Southwestern Construction In	10	Western Pacific Enterprises Ltd

Source Annual Report

maintenance of high voltage transmission lines, substations, lower voltage underground, overhead distribution systems, clean energy projects, and limited gas construction services. The T&D segment of the company basically serves the electric utility and power generation firms as a prime contractor through offering services related to traditional design bid build or engineering, procurement and construction (EPC) forms of project delivery. The company provides services to clients through multiyear master service agreements and other variable term service agreements. T&D segment also offers emergency restoration services in response to natural disasters.

Commercial and Industrial (C&I) Segment

The company has been providing electrical contracting services for commercial and industrial construction since the year 1912. The services offered by this segment include design, installation, maintenance, and repair of commercial and industrial wiring. The segment also focusses on the installation of intelligent transportation systems, roadway lighting, and signalization. The C&I contract covers segments such as airports, hospitals, data centers, hotels, clean energy projects, water/wastewater treatment facilities, transportation control, and management systems.

The clients of the company include investor-owned utilities, cooperatives, private developers, government-funded utilities, independent power producers, transmission companies, and industrial facility owners. The company enters into contracts through a competitive bid process. The contracts are basically structured as fixed price agreement, unit price agreement, time and equipment agreement, time and materials contracts, cost plus contracts.

Competition

The T&D segment of the company competes with local independent companies, medium size regional firms, and large national competitors. The barriers to entry into the transmission markets include the cost of equipment and tools for carrying out transmission work, lack of qualified skilled labor and technical skills. Larger transmission projects require specialized heavy-duty equipment as well as strong

Table 2 Acquisitions

Year	Acquisitions
1990	Acquired Sturgeon Electric and Harlan Electric
2000	Great Southwestern Construction (GSWC)
2015	E S Boulos Company, High Country Line Construction
2016	Western Pacific Enterprises
2018	Huen Electric
2019	CSI Electrical Contractors

financial resources. The distribution market faces fewer significant barriers to entry. The C&I segment competes with regional or local firms and with nation firms' subsidiaries. There are fewer barriers to entry in the C&I markets. One of the competitive factors in C&I segment is the strength of the individual relationships which are developed with general contractors for design and construction services for the project. The company bids for bigger and more technically complex projects compared to its competitors.

Table 2 lists the significant acquisitions undertaken by MYR Group during the period 1990–2019.

Sturgeon Electric and Harlan Electric was acquired for geographical expansion. In 2001, MYR Group acquired GSWC to add one of the largest specialty equipment fleets in the USA along with strong financial resources. The acquisition of E S Boulos company for $11.4 million was aimed to enhance transmission and distribution footprint in the northeast region and establish MYR Group's commercial and industrial presence in the region. In 2015, High Country Line Construction was acquired by MYR Group to become strong player on EPC projects throughout the western US region. High Country had expertise in the usage of helicopters to aid construction on environmentally sensitive projects. High Country used innovative construction techniques for complex projects. Western Pacific Enterprises, one of the largest electrical contractors in British Columbia which provided services throughout western Canada was acquired by MYR Group Construction Canada Ltd. The addition of Western Pacific Enterprises to MYR Group strengthened its position in Canada with its expertise in the market segments of Transmission & Distribution and Commercial & Industrial. MYR Group acquired Huen Electric companies in a transaction valued at $47.1 million approximately. The Huen Companies are leading electrical construction firms with offices in Illinois, New Jersey, and New York. The addition of Huen Companies expanded MYR Group's breadth of C&I offerings and geographic reach. In 2019, MYR group acquired CSI Electrical Contractors, Inc. for approximately $79.7 million. CSI Electricals has a strong reputation in the clean energy markets. This acquisition aided MYR Group to expand geographically and strengthened its C&I offerings.

Risk Factors

The operating results may be affected due to industry and market risks. The business is highly cyclical. The success of business may be adversely affected due to timing and volume of work under contract, increased competition, increased cost of performance, cost overruns, supply chain disruptions, delays on projects due to regulatory issues. The industry is highly competitive and fragmented. Negative economic and market conditions, tariffs on materials and recessionary conditions could adversely impact the operations and growth of the firm. The inability of the company to execute or integrate acquisitions could have an adverse impact on the growth strategy and business of the firm. The company also faces project performance issues related to contractual obligation which results in additional costs, delays in revenues or payment of penalties which include liquidated damages. Legislative or regulatory actions related to electricity transmission and clean energy may impact demand for the services of the company.

Sustainability Initiatives

The company gives emphasis on strong board composition comprised of majority of independent members with diverse backgrounds. The company had 80,000 plus total man hours of training. The safety statistics of the company were among the best in the industry. Over the past 5 years, MYR Group companies have won 46 Zero-Injury Awards & Safety Excellence Awards from The National Electrical Contractors Association's (NECA) elite safety program in recognition of its excellence in the field of health & safety. The company uses a formal preventive and correction action system to avoid recurring defects. MYR Group has been involved in the renewable energy market for decades and currently involved in over 50 renewable energy projects. Group subsidiary Harlan Electric supports DTE Energy's MI Greenpower initiative. In 2020, the company launched MYR Group University, an online learning management system. The system has offered 5247 compliance training courses and 782 courses for Microsoft 365 application training. MYR Group and its subsidiaries have made donations worth over a million dollars during the recent years to charities across the world along with investment in pro bono electrical construction work and volunteer hours. MYR Group has also partnered with industry organizations such as OSHA Voluntary Protection Program (VPP), Edison Electric Institute (EEI), Electrical Transmission & Distribution Partnership, etc. to support strategic industry initiatives. The company also focusses on providing supplier diversity training, workshops, technical assistance and education support. The company maintains a zero-tolerance policy toward bribery and corruption.

Market Performance

Table 3 compares the cumulative total shareholder return for MYR Group stock with the cumulative total return on the market indexes S&P500, the Russell 2000 Index and a peer group consisting of 11 publicly traded companies within the industry sector. The period of analysis is from December 31, 2017 to December 31, 2022. The analysis assumes that $100 was invested on December 31, 2017 and dividends if any were reinvested quarterly.

The 5-year holding period return for MYR Group stock was 158% compared to holding period return of 57%, 22%, and 101% for S&P500, Russell 2000, and Peer Group. The 5-year average returns for MYR stock was 29.23%, while for S&P500, Russell 2000, and Peer Group, the 5-year average returns were 11.22%, 5.77%, and 17.81%, respectively.

The following section compares the stock returns with the market index Russell 2000 returns during the recent 5-year period 2018–2022. MYR stock which was trading at $30 on 1st April 2018 increased by approximately four times to trade at $119.90 by March 1st 2023. The cumulative total monthly return for MYRG stock was 171% compared to market index Russell 2000 returns of 26% during the 5-year period April 2018–March 2023. The average 5-year return for the MYRG stock was 35% compared to returns of 5% for the Russell 2000.

Table 4 analyzes the holding period return for the MYRG stock and market index Russell 2000 during the 5-year period 2018–2022. The comparison is based on the assumption of holding period of 1-year period. The data source is yahoo finance.

MYRG stock had superior positive performance compared to the market index Russell 2000 in the year 2020 and 2021.

Table 3 Comparative wealth returns

Year	2017	2018	2019	2020	2021	2022
MYR group Inc.	$100	$78.84	$91.21	$168.21	$309.40	$257.68
S&P 500	$100	$95.62	$125.72	$148.85	$191.58	$156.89
Russell 2000	$100	$88.99	$111.70	$134.00	$153.85	$122.41
Peer group	$100	$76.05	$101.40	$132.33	$190.33	$200.51

Source: Annual Report 2022

Table 4 Holding period returns

Year	MYRG	Russell 2000	Excess returns
2018	−6%	−13%	6%
2019	7%	11%	−4%
2020	109%	22%	87%
2021	99%	8%	91%
2022	−2%	−13%	11%

Table 5 Book and market value of equity

Year	2018	2019	2020	2021	2022
Book value of equity	324.46	364.48	429.29	519.1	560.2
Market value of equity	466.64	542.58	1005.73	1865.04	1525.03
BV as percent of MV	69.5%	78.1%	79.1%	51.6%	30.0%

Table 6 Financial highlights

	(In millions of dollars)				
Financial highlights	2018	2019	2020	2021	2022
Total assets	748.76	1007.87	995.86	1121.09	1398.86
Short-term investments	7.51	12.4	22.67	82.09	51.04
Total equity	324.46	364.48	429.29	519.1	560.2
Total revenue	1531.17	2071.16	2247.39	2498.29	3008.54
Total operating expenses	120.58	160.52	192.12	209.52	231.43
Net income	31.09	37.69	58.76	85.01	83.38
Market cap	466.64	542.58	1005.73	1865.04	1525.03
Enterprise value	553.03	720.57	1035.14	1808.45	1548.54

Table 7 Performance indicators

Ratios	2018	2019	2020	2021	2022
Net margin%	2.03	1.82	2.61	3.4	2.77
ROE%	10.19	10.97	14.81	17.93	15.45
ROA%	4.6	4.29	5.86	8.03	6.62
DER	0.29	0.52	0.12	0.05	0.13

Table 5 compares the book value and market value of equity of MYRG during the period 2018–2022. The values are given in millions of dollars.

The average book value as percent of market value of equity was 40.8% during the period 2018–2022.

Table 6 gives the financial highlights of the company during the period 2018–2022. The values are given in millions of dollars.

During the 5-year period 2018–2022, the total assets, short-term investments, and total equity increased by 17.69%, 93%, and 15% on average basis. The total revenues and net income increased by 19% and 30%, respectively. The total expenses increased by 18% on average basis. The market capitalization and enterprise value increased by 42% and 34%, respectively, during the period 2018–2022. The data source is gurufocus.com.

Table 7 shows the performance measures in terms of profitability position of the firm. The debt equity ratio of the firm is also given for the period 2018–2022.

The average net margin, ROE, and ROA for MYR Group were 2.53%, 13.87%, and 5.88% during the period 2018–2022. The average debt equity ratio for the company was 0.22.

Table 8 Economic value

Year	2021	2022
Profit before income tax	116.31	114.20
Income tax	31.30	30.82
Net operating profit after tax (NOPAT)	85.01	83.38
Stockholder equity	519.10	560.20
Long-term debt	3.46	35.40
Total capital employed	522.56	595.60
WACC	7.51%	9.78%
Capital charge	39.24	58.25
Economic value	45.77	25.13

Table 8 shows the illustration of the estimation of economic value of the company during the period 2018–2022. The values are given in millions of dollars.

References

1. https://myrgroup.com/about/history/
2. https://investor.myrgroup.com/

Case 67 IES Holdings

IES Holdings Inc. was established in year 1997 and headquartered in Houston, Texas. The company designs and installs integrated electrical and technology systems and provides infrastructure products and services to end markets such as data centers, residential housing, and commercial and industrial facilities. By September 2022, the company had 8078 employees.

Operating Segments

Communications

The Communication segment was established in the year 1984. This segment is a major provider for network infrastructure solutions for data centers and missions involving critical environment. The company offers services such as design, installation, and maintenance of network infrastructure for leading Fortune 100 and 500 firms. IES Holding offers services for data centers for co-location and managed hosting customers. The services are enabled for corporate, educational, financial, hospitality and healthcare buildings, e-commerce distribution centers and high-tech manufacturing facilities. IES Holdings also offer services related to design and installation of audio/visual, telephone, fire, wireless access and intrusion alarm systems, and maintenance of data network systems. The company faces competition from large national or regional competitors, small privately owned contractors in the communication segment.

Residential

The Residential segment was established in year 1973. This segment provides electrical installation services for single family houses, multi-family apartment complexes. Residential segment also provides HVAC and plumbing installation

© The Author(s), under exclusive license to Springer Nature Switzerland AG 2024

B. R. Kumar, *Rising Stars*, Management for Professionals,
https://doi.org/10.1007/978-3-031-50032-9_67

services along with cable television installations for residential and light commercial applications. This segment also offers services for installation of residential solar power for new and existing residences. The Residential segment offices are based in 77 locations in the United States. This segment faces competition from small, privately owned contractors.

Infrastructure Solutions

The Infrastructure Solutions segment offers electro-mechanical solutions for industrial operations. The Custom Power Solutions business of the segment includes the manufacture of custom commercial and industrial generator enclosures along with the manufacture of custom-engineered power distribution equipment. The Industrial Services business offers maintenance and repair of AC and DC electric motors and generators; power generation and distribution equipment; industrial lifting magnet manufacturing and repair; maintenance and repair of railroad main and auxiliary generators; main alternators and traction motors. The Infrastructure Solutions segment serves sectors such as steel, railroad, marine, petrochemical, pipeline, pulp and paper, wind energy, mining, and utility industries. This segment faces competition from small, single location service centers to large multinational firms.

Commercial & Industrial

The Commercial and Industrial segment provides electrical and mechanical design, service and construction services to commercial and industrial markets. The construction services are provided for construction projects involving office building, industrial facilities for transmission and distribution projects. The maintenance and emergency services offer services such as critical plant shutdown, trouble shooting, emergency testing, and preventative maintenance. This segment also offers mechanical services such as maintenance agreements, installation or replacement of mechanical equipment for commercial and industrial facilities. This segment offers services for projects related to data centers, chemical plants, refineries, wind farms, solar facilities, municipal infrastructure, and health care facilities. The main competitors are regional or small privately held local firms.

Corporate Strategy

The company gives emphasis on shareholder value creation through increasing market share and geographic and market expansion. The company also aims to acquire businesses which strategically complement its existing business segments. IES Holdings also aim to acquire standalone platform companies based in North America. The focus is on acquiring companies with characteristics such as proven management, low technological or product obsolescence risk, established market position, and strong cash flow characteristics. IES has acquired 15 companies over a period of time. The largest acquisition to date was made by IES when it acquired Technibus for $45 million. IES has made acquisitions in 12 different US states. Electrical equipment and business services were the most targeted sectors for acquisitions made by company which accounted for 40% and 34%, respectively.

On account of technology advancements and changes in data consumption pattern, the Communication industry segment is in need for more computing and storage resources. As the demand in the data center market is strong, the company focusses on providing structured cabling services for applications in data centers, distribution centers, and high-tech manufacturing facilities. The company aims to expand its offerings in this market to broaden its customer base. The long-term strategy of the company is to position itself as a preferred solutions and services provider for large corporations and local firms. The company aims to focus on key elements such as employees' technical expertise, expansion of on-site maintenance, recurring revenue model, and acquisitions for the success of this strategic perspective.

The demand for residential services depends on the demand for single family and multi-family homes. The Texas market has been an important part of the firm's multi-family business. In the Residential segment, the company focusses on different strategies such as concentrated focus on national and regional homebuilders and multi-family developers and a local sales strategy for single and multi-family housing projects. In terms of long-term strategy for residential services, the company aims to become a leading provider of electrical services to the residential market and expand its offerings consisting of plumbing and HVAC services. The company aims to achieve economies of scale in the housing cycle through maintenance of low variable cost structure.

The demand for the services offered by Infrastructure Solutions is driven by growth in data centers, maintenance departments, equipment utilization at heavy industrial facilities. The other driving factors are railroad companies and mass transit systems requirements for capital investments, energy and industrial infrastructure demand for critical power applications, etc. The long-term strategy of Infrastructure Solutions segment is to maintain market leadership position in custom-engineered metal enclosed bus systems and generator enclosures. The company also aims to be the market leader for the preferred solutions provider for outsourced electro-mechanical services, repairs, and manufacturing.

The demand for Commercial & Industrial services is driven by construction and renovation activity levels, economic growth, and availability of financing sources. The electrical and mechanical contracting services industry is generally highly competitive in nature. The bidding strategy in Commercial & Industrial segment is based on industry expertise, project size, location, and past performance.

Risk Factors

The demand for the firm's services is cyclical and vulnerable to economic downturns. Many customers of the company depend on the availability of credit to purchase its services or electrical and mechanical products. Uncertainties in the credit market conditions would adversely affect customers and in turn affect the financial results of the company. The highly competitive nature of the firm's industrial sector would affect the profitability position of the company. The firm generates significant portion of its revenues under fixed price contracts. Bid estimates and changes in commodity and labor costs could have an adverse effect on the firm's profitability. Failure to secure new contracts may adversely affect the cash flows and financial results of the firm. Reductions in backlog on account of cancellation of one or more contracts could significantly reduce the revenue and profits received from contracts included in the backlog. Certain costs may have to be reimbursed in the event of project cancellation. The firm faces risks associated with seasonality, adverse weather conditions, and climate change. The operations of the company are subject to physical hazards. Regulatory requirements may result in significant compliance costs and liabilities. Disruptions in the functioning of IT systems or security breaches of critical data may disrupt the operations of the firm.

Market Performance

Table 1 shows the cumulative 5-year total stock returns for IES Holdings relative to the cumulative total returns for market index Russell 2000 and a customized peer group of four companies consisting of Comfort Systems USA Inc., MYR Group Inc., Sterling Construction Company Inc. and Primoris. The analysis assumes investment of $100 in the stock, Russell 2000 index and in the peer group as on September 30, 2017. The relative performance is tracked till September 30, 2022.

The 5-year holding period return for IES stock was 60% compared to the holding period returns of 19% and 93% for Russell 2000 and the Peer Group. The 5-year average returns for IES Holding Inc. were 15.37% while for Russell 2000 and Peer Group, the average returns were 6% and 18%, respectively, during the above 5-year period.

The following section analyzes the stock returns for IES Holding in comparison with the returns generated by Russell 2000 index during the recent 5-year period. The IES Holding stock which was trading at $16.9 on April 1st 2018 was priced at $

Table 1 Cumulative wealth comparison

Year	2017	2018	2019	2020	2021	2022
IES holding Inc	$100.00	$112.72	$119.02	$183.64	$264.10	$159.65
Russell 2000	$100	$115.24	$105.00	$105.40	$155.66	$119.08
Peer group	$100	$112.56	$96.88	$107.98	$195.85	$193.22

Source: Annual Report 2022

Table 2 Holding period returns

Year	IES holding	Russell 2000	Excess returns
2018	−8%	−13%	5%
2019	53%	11%	42%
2020	84%	22%	62%
2021	11%	8%	3%
2022	−28%	−13%	−15%

Table 3 Book and market value trend

Year	2018	2019	2020	2021	2022
Book value of equity	223.64	249.54	285.12	370.55	390.48
Market value of equity	413.51	435.79	659.62	947.27	561.84
BV as percent of MV	54.1%	60.3%	65.4%	56.2%	41.2%

Table 4 Financial highlights

	(In millions of dollars)				
Financial highlights	2018	2019	2020	2021	2022
Total assets	421.99	445.26	560.53	766.62	934.71
Short-term investments	26.25	18.93	53.58	23.11	24.85
Total equity	223.64	249.54	285.12	370.55	390.48
Total revenue	876.83	1077	1190.86	1536.49	2166.81
Total operating expenses	123.92	140.58	170.91	202.25	262.71
Net income	−14.16	33.21	41.6	66.66	34.76
Market cap	413.51	435.79	659.62	947.27	561.84
Enterprise value	420.06	420.45	639.65	1031.12	703.28

43.50 on March 1st 2023 reflecting an increase of 2.57 times. The cumulative total monthly returns for IES stock was 125% compared to the cumulative total monthly return of 26% for Russell 2000 index during the period April 2018–March 2023. The 5-year average returns for the IES stock was 25% compared to 5% returns for the market index Russell 2000.

Table 2 shows the holding period returns for the stock and market index during the period 2018–2022.

The holding period returns for IES stock was higher compared to the market index Russell 2000 during the period 2019–2021.

Table 3 compares the market and book value of equity of IES stock during the period 2018–2022. The values are given in millions of dollars.

The average book value as percent of market value of equity for the company was 48.7% during the period 2018–2022. Table 4 gives the financial highlights of the company during the period 2018–2022. The values are given in millions of dollars.

The average growth rate of total assets, short-term investments, and total equity were 22.5%, 26%, and 15%, respectively, during the period 2018–2022. The total revenues increased by 26% while the total expenses increased by 21% during the above period on average basis. The market capitalization and enterprise value

Table 5 Performance indicators

Ratios	2018	2019	2020	2021	2022
Net margin%	−1.61	3.08	3.49	4.34	1.6
ROE%	−6.19	14.23	15.71	21.19	9.83
ROA%	−3.34	7.66	8.27	10.05	4.09
DER	0.13		0.11	0.24	0.38

increased by 15% and 20%, respectively, during the period 2018–2022. The source of data is yahoo finance.com.

Table 5 highlights the profitability and leverage position of the company during the period 2018–2022.

The average net margin, ROE, ROA during the period 2018–2022 were 2.18%,10.95%, and 5.35%. The average debt equity ratio was 0.21.

References

1. https://mergr.com/ies-holdings-acquisitions#cma-tab
2. https://iesholdingsinc.gcs-web.com/node/17301/html
3. https://investors.ies-corporate.com/

Case 68 Veritex Holdings, Inc

Veritex is a state banking organization based in Texas. Veritex Holding is the parent holding company of Veritex Community bank. The bank commenced banking operations in the year 2010. The bank offers a wide range of banking services which include commercial and retail lending, checking and savings deposit products to individual and corporate customers. The current primary market for the bank includes Dallas-Fort Worth metroplex and the Houston metropolitan area. Community banking is the reportable segment of the company and generates revenues basically from interest income on loans, customer service and loan fees, gains on sale of government guaranteed loans and mortgage loans, and interest income from securities investment. The customers of the company include small- and medium-sized businesses with annual revenues of less than $30 million. The company has its IPO in the year 2014. Vertex bank is one among the ten largest banks headquartered in Texas. By December 2022, the bank had 763 full-time employees.

Products and Services

Lending Activities

The loan portfolio of the company consists of commercial real estate and general commercial loans, residential real estate loans, construction and land loans, farmland loans, and consumer loans.

Deposits

Deposits are the principal source of interest earning assets for Veritex Holdings. The services offered include safe deposit facilities, commercial and personal banking services. The bank also offers demand, savings, money market, and time deposit accounts.

© The Author(s), under exclusive license to Springer Nature Switzerland AG 2024

B. R. Kumar, *Rising Stars*, Management for Professionals,
https://doi.org/10.1007/978-3-031-50032-9_68

Other Products and Services

The bank offers an interest rate swap program along with a full range of online banking solutions. The bank also offers debit cards, night depository, direct deposit, cashier's checks, and letters of credit. The bank offers a full range of treasury management services which includes balance reporting, inter account transfers, automated clearinghouse origination, and stop payments. The treasury management services of the bank include servicing of commercial deposit and financial institution money market accounts. Cash management deposit products and services offered include lockbox facilities, remote deposit capture, reverse positive pay, account reconciliation services, zero balance accounts, and sweep accounts.

Growth Strategy

Veritex pursues its growth strategy through organic expansion and strategic acquisitions. Since 2010, the company has made seven acquisitions which have led to increase in its market presence in the Dallas-Fort-Worth metroplex and the Houston metropolitan area. The bank aims at organic expansion through the community-focused, relationship-based approach to banking. The bank intends to increase its market share through expanding its customer base and increase of loans and deposits. The bank focuses on organic loan growth and deposit repricing strategy to expand net interest margin.

The team of seasoned bankers facilitate developing banking relationships with current and potential customers. The bank also focuses on improving operation efficiency and profitability. The business development strategy focuses on building market share through personal relationships.

Table 1 lists the acquisitions made by Veritex Holding

Veritex acquired Bank of Las Colinas which provides services that consist of business banking, personal banking, online banking, and mortgage banking. Independent Bank of Texas (IBT), a chartered full-service commercial bank was acquired by Veritex in a deal under which Veritex issued approximately 1.185 million shares of its common stock and paid approximately $4 million in cash for

Table 1 Acquisitions by Veritex holding

Time period	Target Bank	Number of branches acquired
Jan 2019	Green Bank	21
Dec 2017	Liberty Bank	5
August 2017	Sovereign Bancshares	9
July 2015	Independent Bank of Texas	2
October 2011	Bank of Las Colinas	1
March 2011	Fidelity Bank	3
September 2010	Professional Bank	3

Source Annual Report 2022

the outstanding shares of IBT. Veritex added a seasoned SBA lending group and two additional locations through this acquisition. Sovereign Bancshares Inc. was acquired in a deal valued at $162 million. The acquisition of Sovereign Bancshares added one Fort Worth location and two other Tarrant County locations along with entry into Austin and Houston markets for Veritex. Liberty bank was acquired for approximately $64 million in cash and stock deal. Through the acquisition of Liberty bank, Veritex Holdings Inc. added five Tarrant County locations. During the period of acquisition, Liberty Bank was ranked number four among Texas-based banks in the USA and number 11 among bank deposits in Tarrant County. Green Bank was acquired by Veritex Holding in an all-stock deal valued at $ 1 billion. The combined company had approximately $8 billion in assets. This acquisition doubled the size of Veritex bank in terms of employees, assets, and branch locations.

In 2021, Veritex purchased 49% stake in Thrive Mortgage. In the same year, Veritex acquired North Avenue Capital (NAC) LLC thereby catapulting the bank as a leading player in the USDA Business & Industry Loan Program. This acquisition was aimed at diversifying revenue streams for the bank in the form of gain on sale and loan servicing fees. NAC's loan sourcing technology will be used to add value for the bank's products and services. In 2022, Veritex Holding Inc. entered into a definitive agreement to acquire StoneCastle Cash Insured Sweep (interlink), a subsidiary of StoneCastle Partners in a transaction valued at $91 million. The acquisition combined a high growth commercial bank with a tech enabled core deposit gathering platform. interLink on being integrated into Veritex's treasury function would provide flexible and scalable access to approximately $5.7 billion of highly diversified stable core deposits.

The credit risk management strategy of the bank includes centralized credit policies, uniform underwriting criteria by loan type, and ongoing risk monitoring and review processes for different types of credit exposure.

Risk Factors

The business concentration of the bank in Texas may magnify the potential risk consequences of any regional or local economic downturn. Uncertainty in market conditions and economic trends could adversely affect the business, financial condition, and results of operations of the bank. Labor shortages and constraints in supply chain could adversely affect the clients' operations which could impact the operations of the bank. Interest rate shifts have the potential risk to reduce net interest income and would negatively impact the financial performance of the bank. A large portion of the loan portfolio consists of commercial loans which are secured by collaterals like receivables, promissory notes, inventory, equipment, etc. Any deterioration in the value of these collaterals could increase the potential for future losses. The bank's real estate lending activities and its exposure to fluctuations in real estate collateral values are potential risk factors. The small- to medium-sized businesses that the bank lend may have fewer resources to weather adverse business development. The bank is subject to increased regulation on account of being a financial institution with over $10 billion in total consolidated assets. The bank operates in a highly regulated environment and changes in regulation could adversely affect the business, financial condition, and results of operations.

Stock Performance

Table 2 compares the cumulative total shareholder return on the common stock of Veritex Holding to the cumulative total return of the peer group and the Nasdaq Bank Index from the period beginning October 2014 through December 2022. The analysis assumes investment of $100 in the stock in October 2014 in the stock, peer group and Nasdaq Bank Index and the reinvestment of dividends. The select peer group included BancFirst Corporation, Cadence Bancorp LLC., CVB Financial Corp., Eagle Bancorp, Inc., First Financial Bankshares, Inc., Origin Bancorp, Inc., Hilltop Holdings, Inc., Independent Bank Group, Inc., ServisFirst Bancshares, Inc., Simmons First National Corporation, Southside Bancshares, Inc., Pacific Premier Bancorp, Inc., and Independent Bank Corporation.

The 7-year holding period return for Veritex Holding Inc. was 101% while for the peer group and Nasdaq Bank Index, the 7-year holding period return were 84% and 66%, respectively. The average yearly return for Veritex during the 6-year period 2017–2022 was 20.87% while for the peer group and Nasdaq Bank Index, the average yearly returns during the above period were 20.29% and 19.28%, respectively.

The following section compares the stock returns for Veritex Holdings with that of the returns of Nasdaq Bank Index during the 5-year period 2018–2022. The cumulative total monthly return for the Veritex Holding was 45.5% during the 5-year period April 2018–March 2022. The 5 yearly average returns for Veritex Holding was 9% during the period April 2018–March 2022 compared to −1% average returns of Nasdaq Bank Index. The data source is yahoo finance.

Table 3 shows the holding period return for Veritex Holding stock and the Nasdaq Bank Index during the period 2018–2022. The analysis assumes holding period of 1 year.

Veritex Holding stock outperformed the market index Nasdaq Bank with positive gains in the year 2019 and 2021.

Table 4 highlights the book and market value of equity of the company during the period 2018–2022. The values are given in millions of dollars.

Table 2 Comparison of cumulative total returns

Year	2014	2017	2018	2019	2020	2021	2022
Veritex holdings, Inc	$100	$197.79	$153.26	$208.82	$183.94	$285.16	$201.29
Peer group	$100	171.13	138.2	152.67	144.32	208.62	184.08
Nasdaq Bank index	$100	164	134.64	163.23	145.84	203.77	166.36

Table 3 Holding period return

Year	Veritex holding	Nasdaq bank index	Excess returns
2018	−6%	−21%	15%
2019	23%	9%	14%
2020	−24%	−5%	−19%
2021	58%	34%	24%
2022	−18%	−18%	0%

Table 4 Book and market value of equity

Year	2018	2019	2020	2021	2022
Book value of equity	530.64	1190.8	1203.38	1315.08	1449.77
Market value of equity	518.55	1487.49	1266.01	1964.03	1517.16
BV as percent of MV	102.3%	80.1%	95.1%	67.0%	95.6%

Table 5 Financial highlights

	(In millions of dollars)				
Financial highlights	2018	2019	2020	2021	2022
Total assets	3208.55	7954.94	8820.87	9757.25	12154.36
Gross loans	2556.77	5935.15	6807.38	7420.52	9522.27
Deposits	2622.43	5894.35	6512.85	7363.62	9123.23
Total equity	530.64	1190.8	1203.38	1315.08	1449.77
Interest income	145.07	378.79	321.85	316.48	449.41
Interest expense	30.05	93.69	56.05	35.7	84.75
Total non-interest expense	64.04	138.84	146.7	166.89	201.7
Market capitalization	518.55	1487.49	1266.01	1964.03	1517.16
Enterprise value	478.81	2059.38	2075.68	2589.57	2484.86

The average book value as percent of market value of equity was 88% during the period 2018–2022.

Table 5 gives the financial highlights of Veritex Holding during the period 2018–2022. The data source is gurufocus.com.

The average growth rate of total assets, gross loans, and deposits were 48%, 46%, and 43% during the period 2018–2022. The total equity increased by 47% on average basis during the period 2018–2022. The interest income has been highly fluctuating during the above period. The interest expense and the total non-interest expense increased by 39% and 51% during the above period. The market capitalization and enterprise value increased by 51% and 88%, respectively, during the period 2018–2022.

Table 6 shows the performance ratios of Veritex Holdings.

The average ROA, ROE, and net interest margin for Veritex Holding during the period 2018–2022 were 1.33%, 9.59%, and 4.22%, respectively.

Table 6 Performance indicators

Ratios	2018	2019	2020	2021	2022
Performance ratios					
Return on average assets %	1.28	1.63	0.88	1.5	1.34
Return on average equity%	7.72	10.54	6.17	11.08	10.58
Net interest margin%	4.37	5.87	3.62	3.45	3.79

References

1. https://ir.veritexbank.com/financial-information/sec-filings
2. https://ir.veritexbank.com/news-releases/news-release-details/veritex-holdings-inc-completes-acquisition-green-bank-and-now-0

Case 69 The First Bancshares Inc

The First Bancshares Inc., founded in year 1996, is the parent company of The First, A National Banking Association. The First Bancshares operations are based in Mississippi, Louisiana, Alabama, Georgia, and Florida. The company's stock is traded on NASDAQ Global market under the symbol FBMS. As of December 31, 2022, the First had operations in 90 locations which are based in Mississippi, Alabama, Florida, Georgia, and Louisiana. The First is a community-based financial institution which offers a full spectrum of financial services to individuals, businesses, municipal establishments, and nonprofit organizations. The services offered include consumer and commercial loans, deposit accounts, and safe deposit services. In Jan 2022, the First converted from a national banking association to a Mississippi state-chartered bank and changed its name to The First Bank. By December 2022, the First Bank employed 870 employees in five states of the USA.

Products and Services

Deposit Services

The First Bank offers a full range of deposit services which include checking accounts, NOW accounts, savings accounts, and other time deposits which include daily money market accounts and long-term certificates of deposit. All deposit accounts are insured by the Federal Deposit Insurance Corporation. Deposit accounts are solicited from individuals, businesses, associations, organizations, and governmental authorities. The First Bank also offers certain retirement account services such as Individual Retirement Accounts (IRAs) and health savings accounts.

© The Author(s), under exclusive license to Springer Nature Switzerland AG 2024
B. R. Kumar, *Rising Stars*, Management for Professionals,
https://doi.org/10.1007/978-3-031-50032-9_69

Loan Products

The First Bank offers a complete range of commercial and personal loans. Commercial loans include both secured and unsecured loans for working capital, business expansion, purchase of equipment and machinery, etc. The consumer loans include equity lines of credit, loans for automobile financing, home improvements, education and personal investments. The bank also offers real estate construction and acquisition loans. The lending activities are subject to a variety of lending limits which are imposed by federal law.

Mortgage Loan Division

The residential mortgage loan division originates conventional or government agency insured loans to purchase existing residential homes, construct new homes, or refinance existing mortgages.

Private Banking Division

The private banking division of the First Bank offers financial and wealth management services to individuals.

Other Services

The other bank services include online internet banking services, automated teller machines, voice response telephone inquiry services, commercial sweep accounts, cash management services, safe deposit boxes, direct deposit of payroll, social security checks, and automatic drafts for different accounts.

Strategy

The company focuses on strong asset quality metrics and has a well-disciplined underwriting and credit culture. The company focuses on a regional expansion strategy through acquisitions which have enabled the company to expand its footprint in Alabama, Florida, Louisiana, and Georgia. In August 2022, the First Bank completed the acquisition of Beach Bancorp, Inc. (BBI) and merged its wholly owned subsidiary, Beach Bank with the First Bank. The deal was valued at $111.67 million. The holders of BBI common or preferred stock received 0.1711 of a share of company common stock for each share of BBI common or preferred stock. The combined bank has approximately $6.7 billion in total assets, $5.8 billion in total deposits, and $3.6 billion in total loan. During January 2023, the First Bank acquired Heritage Southeast Bancorporation Inc. (HSBI) in a deal valued at $221.5

million. The merger with Heritage Southeast created a unique community banking franchise for the First Bank with market share in the fastest growing economies in the southeastern United States. The combined company had approximately $8 billion in assets, $7 billion in deposits, $5 billion in loans, and over 100 branches across five states in the Southeast. The company faces competition from both federally chartered and state-chartered financial and thrift institutions, credit unions, consumer finance firms, and insurance companies.

Sustainability Initiatives

One of the sustainability aims of the First Bank is to invest and serve underserved markets. The First Bank is one of the largest Certified Community Development Institutions (CDFI) in the USA. This designation is given by US Treasury for financial institutions which carry out 60% of its business activities in distressed markets. Since 2010, the First Bank has awarded over $7.2 million grants for investments in communities to support economic growth and job creation. The First Bank was rated a Superior Bank from Bauer Financial. In 2021, the First Bank's First AID checking account was recertified by the Cities for Financial Empowerment Fund as an account which satisfied the criteria for the updated BankOn National Account Standards. The First Bank is a member owned cooperative of the Federal Home Loan Bank (FHLB) of Dallas which supports housing and economic development of communities which are served by member financial institutions. In 2021, The First Bank awarded more than $1.5 million in Affordable Housing Program (AHP) grants to fund the creation, rehabilitation, or purchase of 172 housing units. The First Bank has used $117,000 in HELP funds to assist 17 first time homebuyers during the year 2021. The First Bank uses FHLB's Special Needs Rehabilitation Assistance Program (SNAP) to provide rehabilitation assistance to very low to moderate income special needs homeowners. The First Bank, partnership with Shred—It is aimed at producing an eco-friendly environment. The First Bank's cybersecurity strategy involves top-down focus on cybersecurity, led by the Board, executive management, and senior leadership.

Risk Factors

Downturn in the economy in geographic markets where the company serves such as states of Mississippi, Louisiana, Alabama, Florida, or Georgia may result in the inability of customers to undertake loan payment obligations in a timely manner. A significant part of the loan portfolio is secured by real estate. The market value of real estate may decline if the economy deteriorates and loan portfolio could become under collateralized and losses incurred upon borrower defaults would increase. The credit loss accruals would negatively impact the earnings of the company. The capital and credit markets are subject to volatility and disruption. Unpredictable market conditions would adversely affect the industry in which the bank operates.

The assets and liabilities of the bank are subject to significant risks which result from changes in interest rates. The bank may be adversely affected by the replacement of the London Interbank Offer Rate with an alternative reference rate. Loan revenues might be adversely affected by the rising interest rates. Changes in the policies of monetary authorities could adversely affect the financial success of the bank. Banks are subject to extensive regulation by various regulatory agencies. Tax laws and regulatory changes could adversely affect the financial condition and results of operations.

Stock Performance

Table 1 compares the cumulative 5-year shareholder return on The First Bank's common stock to that of returns of market indexes Nasdaq Composite-Total Returns index and Nasdaq OMX Banks Index. The analysis assumes an investment of $100 as on December 31, 2017 and reinvestment of dividends.

The 5-year holding period return for First Bancshares was marginal whereas the holding period returns for Nasdaq Composite and Nasdaq Banks Index were 59% and 15%, respectively. The 5-year average returns for the First Bank was 1.53% compared to average returns of 13.68% and 5.47% for Nasdaq Composite and Nasdaq Banks Index.

The following section compares the stock returns of the First Bank with that of returns of Nasdaq Bank Index during the 5-year period 2018–2022. The data source is yahoo finance. The cumulative total monthly return for the First Bank stock was 17.8% compared to 0% cumulative total monthly return for Nasdaq Bank Index during the period April 2018–March 2023. The average yearly return for the First Bank stock during the above period was 4% compared to average yearly return of –1% for the Nasdaq Bank index.

Table 1 Comparison of cumulative returns

Year	2017	2018	2019	2020	2021	2022
First Bancshares, Inc	$100	$88.96	$105.46	$93.24	$118.37	$100.35
NASDAQ composite-Total returns	$100	$97.16	$132.81	$192.47	$235.15	$158.65
NASDAQ OMX banks index	$100	83.83	104.26	96.44	137.82	115.38

Source Annual Report 2022

Table 2 Holding period return

Year	First Bank	Nasdaq Bank Index	Excess returns
2018	−6.49%	−20.95%	14.5%
2019	9.60%	9.38%	0.2%
2020	−10.28%	−4.72%	−5.6%
2021	28.99%	34.09%	−5.1%
2022	−11.26%	−18.18%	6.9%

Table 3 Book and market value of equity

Year	2018	2019	2020	2021	2022
Book value of equity	363.25	543.66	644.82	676.17	646.66
Market value of equity	448.63	667.86	652.03	811.75	769.07
BV as percent of MV	81.0%	81.4%	98.9%	83.3%	84.1%

Table 4 Financial highlights

	(In millions of dollars)				
Financial highlights	2018	2019	2020	2021	2022
Total assets	3003.99	3941.86	5152.76	6077.41	6461.72
Gross loans	2065.26	2611.17	3145.11	2967.23	3778.6
Deposits	2457.46	3076.53	4215.28	5226.78	5494.4
Total equity	363.25	543.66	644.82	676.17	646.66
Interest income	99.98	148.53	179.35	176.75	200.39
Interest expense	15.09	26.72	26.66	19.68	22.58
Total non-interest expense	60.69	79.5	99.98	109.33	120.2
Market capitalization	448.63	667.86	652.03	811.75	769.07
Enterprise value	455.54	797.79	357.03	43.05	908.61

Table 5 Performance indicators

Ratios	2018	2019	2020	2021	2022
Performance ratios					
Return on average assets%	0.88	1.26	1.15	1.14	1
Return on average equity%	7.25	9.65	8.84	9.72	9.51
Net interest margin%	4.08	4.09	4.05	3.54	3.41

Table 2 shows the holding period return for the First Bank stock and Nasdaq Bank index. The holding period is assumed to be 1-year period.

Table 3 shows the book and market value of equity of the First Bank during the period 2018–2022. The values are given in millions of dollars.

The average book value as percent of market value of equity during the period 2018–2022 was 85.7%.

Table 4 gives the financial highlights of the First Bank during the period 2018–2022. The data source is gurufocus.com.

The average growth rate of total assets, gross loans, and deposits were 22%, 17%, and 23%, respectively, during the period 2018–2022. The average growth rate in total equity was 20% during the period 2018–2022. Net interest income increased by 16% whereas interest expense increased by 22%. The total non-interest expense increased by 16%. The market capitalization increased by 16% and the enterprise value increased by 4.86% during the period 2018–2022.

Table 5 highlights the performance indicators for the First Bank.

The average ROA, ROE, and net interest margin for the First Bancshares were 1.09%, 8.99%, and 3.83%, respectively, during the period 2018–2022. The First

Bancshares's Capital Adequacy Tier 1 Ratio % for the year ended Dec 2022 was 15.60% which is higher than 14.10% for the previous year ended in Dec 2021. Capital Adequacy Tier–Leverage Ratio % for the year ended Dec 2022 was 11.10% which is higher than 9.20% for the year ended in Dec 2021. Bancshares Efficiency Overhead Ratio % was 61.42% in December 2022.

References

1. https://www.thefirstbank.com/
2. https://thefirstbancshares.q4ir.com/corporate-profile/default.aspx

Case 70 Brooks Automation (Azenta)

Brooks Automation is a global provider of semiconductor manufacturing and laboratory automation solutions. The company was established in the year 1978. Brooks provides precision vacuum robotics, integrated automation systems, contamination control solutions, and collaborative robots to global semiconductor chip makers and lab automation equipment manufacturers. Brooks Automation has operations in North America, Europe, and Asia. Brooks is the leading global provider of life science sample exploration and management solutions for the life sciences market. Brooks offers a broad portfolio of products and services which represents procurement and sourcing, automated storage platforms, genomic services, range of consumables, informatics, and data software along with sample management solutions. The life sciences division of the company has sales operations in more than 80 countries. This division employs 2900 people globally. In 2021, the company entered into a definitive agreement to sell its semiconductor automation business to Thomas H Lee Partners for approximately $3 billion. The remaining business consisting of Life Science products and Life Science Services were to be rebranded under a single unified brand Azenta Life Sciences during the first half of fiscal year 2022. In this segment the company serves over 8700 customers globally in the pharmaceutical and biotechnology industry.

Segments

Life Sciences Products

The Life Sciences Products business is a major provider of automated ultra-cold storage solutions for biological and chemical compound samples. The storage systems offer reliable automation and sample inventory management at −190 °C temperatures with capacities to store millions of samples. The solutions offered include consumable vials and tubes, polymerase chain reaction (PCR) plates, and instruments which support workflow and informatics. The segment provides

© The Author(s), under exclusive license to Springer Nature Switzerland AG 2024

B. R. Kumar, *Rising Stars*, Management for Professionals,
https://doi.org/10.1007/978-3-031-50032-9_70

customers with complete end-to-end "cold chain of custody" capabilities. The automated ultra-cold storage systems provide standalone systems which can store up to 20 million samples in temperatures which range from ambient temperatures to −80 °C and cryogenic storage with temperatures at −190 ° C. Consumables and Instruments offer a complete range of consumables which include multiple formats of racks, tubes, caps, plates, and foils which are used for storage and handling of samples in ultra-cold storage environments. The products offered assist in genomic sample preparation and services market for sequencing, imaging, plate sealing, liquid handling, and sample processing.

Life Sciences Services

This segment offers solutions for genomic analysis and management and care of biological samples in pharmaceutical, biotech, healthcare, clinical, and academic research areas. The sample management services offered consist of off-site storage services, transport services, laboratory services, and interactive informatics solutions. The genomic services facilitate sequencing and synthesis of genes involving millions of samples every year. These service offerings include Next Generation Sequencing or NGS, Sanger sequencing, gene synthesis, bioinformatics, good laboratory practices (GLP), and regulatory services. The gene synthesis offerings include DNA cloning, gene fragment synthesis, and oligo synthesis. The sample repository solutions offer a full range of services which includes on-site and off-site sample storage, cold chain logistics, bioprocessing solutions, and biospecimen procurement services. Informatics offers sample intelligence software solutions. The informatics suite portfolio offers services to enable laboratory-based workflow scheduling for life science tools and instrument work cells, sample inventory and logistics, environmental and temperature monitoring, clinical trial and consent management, data management, virtualization and visualization of sample collections. Informatics segment offers enhanced on-site and off-site management of biological sample inventories and integration solutions to customers.

In the Life Sciences Product segment, the main competitors are Hamilton company and Liconic AG for automation systems and Thermo Fisher Scientific for consumables and services. In the Life Sciences services segment, the main competitors are Laboratory Corporation of America Holdings, Thermo Fisher Scientific Inc., Integrated DNA Technologies, Novogene Co, Ltd., and BGI Genomics Co Ltd.

Semiconductor Automation Business

In 2021, the company had entered into a definitive agreement to sell its semiconductor automation business to THL. The semiconductor business of Brooks is a leading automation provider in the global semiconductor manufacturing industry. Brooks provides advanced, high precision, high-throughput robots, vacuum automation systems, contamination control systems, and reticle storage solutions to the global semiconductor capital equipment industry. Brooks sells its semiconductor products and services to OEMs and global semiconductor chip manufacturers.

Strategy

The life sciences businesses of Brooks Automation cater to the needs of life sciences trends such as technology, information management, and new sophisticated tools and applications. With the emergence of biologics and personalized medicine, biological samples became the critical assets for drug and therapy pipelines. The market for genomic services is attractive in nature due to the scope of research in biological drug development, personalized medicine, and cell/gene therapy. Major pharmaceutical and biotechnology companies have in-house facilities to do research for sequencing of gene therapy. Many pharmaceutical companies outsource their gene sequencing research to independent laboratories for expert consultative services. In this context, Brooks has clear market opportunity to provide comprehensive sample management and genomic solutions. The company is a value-added laboratory services provider with fast turnaround time. The Brooks Automation platform is gaining significance in the semiconductor industry and has emerged as the leading choice for collaborative robotics within the Life Science lab automation segment.

Acquisitions

In March 2023, Brooks Automation acquired Aim Lab to facilitate its growth strategy to expand solutions within the lab automation segment. Brooks is the market leaders in life sciences collaborative automation sector with leading product solutions such as PreciseFlex™. Aim Lab is a major product design, engineering and manufacturing company with experience in development of innovative robotic instrumentation and modules for the clinical laboratory automation industry.

This acquisition marked the entry of Brooks into the clinical diagnostics market. The acquisition offered Brooks a broader set of capabilities, expanded global presence and opportunity for enhanced collaboration with customers.

Risk Factors

The announcement and pendency of sale of the semiconductor automation business to Thomas H Lee Partners may have adverse impact on the operations and financial prospects of the company. The completion of the sale of the semiconductor automation business to Thomas H Lee depends on obtaining certain regulatory approvals. The revenues and operating margin for the company depend on a variety of factors such as changes in the timing and terms of product orders and service contracts, changes in the demand for the mix of products and services offered, timing and market acceptance of new product and services and costs related to any acquisitions, divestitures, or other strategic transactions. The global nature of the firm's business exposes the company to multiple risks such as longer sales cycles, tariff and international trade barriers, and legal protections for intellectual property and contract rights. As a global company, Brooks is subject to federal, state, local, and foreign regulations which include environmental regulations, regulations related to design, and operation of products and control systems. Changes in tax rates or tax regulation would affect the results of operations of the company. The expiration of patents could lead to increase of competition and decline of revenue for the company. The company may be subjected to claims of infringement of third-party intellectual property rights.

Sustainability Initiatives

In the year 2018, the company developed an integrated environmental, social, and governance program. In 2021, the company recycled 66% of its waste inputs. In 2020, about 14% of the electric usage was based on renewable energy sources. To support women empowerment and leadership, the company initiated Women's EDGE, the grassroots employee resource group (ERG) and has 100 members in six global chapters. As a part of environmental initiatives, the company has installed 600 Kw fuel cell system to improve the energy efficiency of its operations. Brooks Impacting, Communities Initiatives focuses on nationwide initiatives and social issues to support community well-being.

Comparative Stock Performance

Table 1 compares the cumulative total shareholder return for Brooks with that of the Nasdaq Composite index and peer group of companies. The peer group of companies consists of 15 firms which include Advanced Energy Industries, Axcelis Technologies Inc., Bio Rad Laboratories, Bruker Corp among others. The analysis assumes an investment of $100 on September 30, 2016 in the stock, index, and peer group.

The 5-year holding period return for Brooks Automation was 697% while for Nasdaq Composite and Peer group, the holding period return were 100% and 260%,

Table 1 Comparative wealth

Year	2016	2017	2018	2019	2020	2021
Brooks automation	$100	$227.15	$265.67	$284.25	$358.55	$797.18
Nasdaq composite	$100	$120.08	$136.91	$139.19	$159.63	$199.90
Peer group	$100	$162.43	$174	$205	$233.59	$359.77

Source Annual Report 2021

Table 2 Book value and market value of equity

Year	2018	2019	2020	2021	2022
Book value of equity	717.83	1138.95	1213.61	1325.33	3363.39
Market value of equity	2476.7	2677.19	3415.46	7609.43	3215.37
BV as percent of MV	29.0%	42.5%	35.5%	17.4%	104.6%

Table 3 Financial highlights

	(In millions of dollars)				
Financial highlights	2018	2019	2020	2021	2022
Total assets	1095.26	1516	1559.27	1819.51	3716.12
Short-term investments	243.99	335.77	250.7	227.51	1570.04
Total equity	717.83	1138.95	1213.61	1325.33	3363.39
Total revenue	631.56	334.18	388.54	513.7	555.5
Total operating expenses	213.96	180.65	208.07	274.51	279.61
Net income	116.58	437.42	64.85	110.75	2132.86
Market capitalization	2476.7	2677.19	3415.46	7609.43	3215.37
Enterprise value	2428.78	2392.57	3234.08	7476.68	1694.56

Table 4 Performance indicators

Ratios	2018	2019	2020	2021	2022
Net profit margin	18.46	130.89	16.69	21.56	383.95
Return on equity	17.59	47.12	5.51	8.72	90.98
Return on asset	12.52	33.5	4.22	6.56	77.06
Debt equity ratio	0.27	0.05	0.06	0.07	0.02

respectively. The average yearly returns for Brooks Automation was 59.91% while for the Nasdaq Composite and Peer group the returns were 15% and 31%, respectively.

Table 2 shows the book value and market value of equity during the period 2018–2022. The values are given in millions of dollars.

The average book value as percent of market value of equity was 45.8% during the period 2018–2022.

Table 3 shows the financial highlights of the company during the period 2018–2022. The data is sourced from www.gurufocus.com

On average basis, the total assets, short-term investments, and total equity grew by 41%, 148%, and 57%, respectively, during the period 2018–2022. The revenues grew by 19% during the 3-year period 2020–2022. The net income growth rate was highly fluctuating. The net income grew by 1826% in the year 2022 compared to the previous year. The market capitalization and enterprise value increased by 25% and 21%, respectively, on average basis during the period of analysis.

Table 4 highlights the performance indicators of the company.

The average net profit margin, ROE, and ROA during the period 2018–2022 were 114.31%, 33.98%, and 26.77%, respectively. The average debt equity ratio was 0.094.

References

1. https://www.brooks.com/
2. Annual Report 2021

Case 71 SVB Financial Group (SVB)

SVB Financial Group is a diversified financial services company which is also a bank holding and financial holding company. SVB Financial was incorporated in the year 1999. The Group offers diverse set of banking and financial products and services to clients across the United States and other markets. The company offers commercial and private banking products and services through its principal subsidiary Silicon Valley Bank. The California-based Silicon Valley Bank is a chartered bank founded in the year 1983. SVB Financial group also offers asset management, private wealth management, and other investment services. By December 2022, the SVB Financial group had total assets of $211.8 billion and total investment securities of $120.1 billion. The products and services are provided by the bank and its subsidiaries to clients in sectors such as technology and life science, healthcare industries, global private equity, and venture capital. The deposits are obtained from commercial clients within the technology, life science, healthcare, private equity, and venture capital industry sector. By December 31, 2022, the company employed 8553 people.

SVB Financial filed for bankruptcy on March 17, 2023. The group has initiated a separate process to sell various units which include the investment manager SVB Capital and the brokerage firm SVB Securities.

Business Segment

SVB Financial Group has four operating segments: Silicon Valley Bank, SVB Private, SVB Capital, and SVB Securities.

Silicon Valley Bank

Silicon Valley Bank offers solutions to commercial clients through credit, treasury management, foreign exchange, trade finance, and other financial products and

© The Author(s), under exclusive license to Springer Nature Switzerland AG 2024

B. R. Kumar, *Rising Stars*, Management for Professionals,
https://doi.org/10.1007/978-3-031-50032-9_71

services. The credit solutions offered include term loans, growth capital term loan, equipment loans, asset-based loans, revolving lines of credit, warehouse facilities, mezzanine lending, acquisition finance loans, standby and commercial letters of credit, project finance loans, and credit card programs. The global treasury management services consist of deposits, payables/collections, cash management solutions, and mobile banking platforms. The deposit products include business and analysis checking accounts, money market accounts, multi-currency accounts, and in country bank accounts. The global payment services include wire transfer, automated clearing house payments, and fund transfer services. The trade finance products offered by the bank include standby letters of credit, performance guarantees, and commercial letters of credit. The foreign exchange services offer purchase and sale of currencies in the spot market as well as with currency swaps and hedges. The bank offers investment solutions through the repurchase agreement program. The Global Fund banking division offers banking products and services to global private equity and venture capital clients.

The period March 2023 witnessed the biggest banking collapse since the 2008 financial crisis with the bank run on SVB Financial Group. The deposits from the startups and smaller technology companies soared up for the Silicon Valley Bank during the pandemic. SVB bought US treasuries and government backed mortgage securities with the influx of cash. When interest rates started sharply rising and depositors demanded higher returns, the bank was forced to sell some of its bonds at a loss. When the news hit the social media, tech investors panicked triggering a classic bank run. In a government backed deal, First Citizens Bancshares decided to acquire Silicon Valley Bank. The deal for the acquisition involved the purchase of about $72 billion in loans at a discount of $16.5 billion and the transfer of all bank's deposits worth $56 billion.

SVB Private

SVB Private is the private banking and wealth management division of the bank. This segment offers a wide array of financial solutions for private clients. The services offered include mortgages, home equity lines of credit, restricted and private stock loans, capital call lines of credit, vineyard development loans, wealth management, family office, financial planning, tax planning, and trust services. SVB Private also offers deposit account products and services which include checking, money market, certificates of deposits, online banking, and other personalized banking services. SVB also offers private business, commercial real estate, and nonprofit commercial lending and banking which are acquired from Boston Private.

SVB Capital

SVB Capital is the venture capital and credit investment arm of SVB Financial Group which basically deals with funds management. SVB Capital manages over

$9.5 billion of funds on behalf of third party limited partner investors. The SVB Capital family of funds is comprised of pooled investment vehicles such as direct venture funds that invest in companies and funds of funds that invest in other venture capital funds and debt funds.

SVB Securities

SVB Securities is an investment bank and operates as a wholly owned subsidiary of SVB Financial Group. This segment offers investment banking services across all major sub-sectors of healthcare and technology. SVB Securities offers equity research coverage for over 360 healthcare and technology companies. The product and services offerings by SVB Securities include Capital Raising, M&A Advisory, Structured Finance, Equity Research, and Sales and Trading.

Client Industries

SVB provides products and services to serve clients basically in the technology, life science, and healthcare industries. The technology clients represent clients from sectors such as frontier tech, hardware, enterprise and consumer software/internet, fintech and climate technology. The life science or healthcare clients tend to be from industries of biopharma, healthtech, medical devices, healthcare services, diagnostics, and tools. The SVB Start-up Banking practice focuses on serving emerging or early stage clients. The SVB Early Stage practice serves the "mid-stage" or "later- stage" clients who require venture capital for funding. SVB Corporate banking practice serves large corporate clients.

Stock Performance

Table 1 compares the cumulative stockholder return on the common stock of SVB with the cumulative total return of the S&P500 index, Nasdaq Composite and Nasdaq Bank Index during the period from December 31, 2017 through December 31, 2022. An initial investment of $100 and reinvestment of dividends is assumed for the analysis.

Table 1 Comparative stock returns

Year	2017	2018	2019	2020	2021	2022
SVB financial group	$100	$81.24	$107.39	$165.90	$290.13	$98.45
NASDAQ composite	$100	$97.16	$132.81	$192.47	$235.15	$158.65
NASDAQ banks index	$100	75.78	89.41	81.19	114.69	96.14

Source: Annual Report 2022

Table 2 Financial highlights

	(In millions of dollars)				
Financial highlights	2018	2019	2020	2021	2022
Total assets	56927.98	71004.9	115,511	211,308	211,793
Gross loans	28338.28	33164.64	45,181	66,276	74,250
Deposits	49328.9	61757.81	101,982	189,203	173,109
Total equity	5264.84	6621.08	8433	16,609	16,295
Interest income	1969.91	2310	2242	3289	5673
Interest expense	75.92	213	85	110	1188
Total noninterest expense	1150.24	1601	2035	2941	3571

Table 3 Performance indicators

Ratios	2018	2019	2020	2021	2022
Return on average assets %	1.8	1.78	1.3	1.12	0.79
Return on average equity%	20.95	19.63	16.45	14.99	10.37
Net interest margin%	3.79	3.66	2.76	2.2	2.31

The 5-year holding period return for SVB Financial Group was −2% while for Nasdaq Composite and Nasdaq bank index, the holding period returns were 59% and −4%, respectively. The average yearly return during the period 2018–2022 for SVB Financial was 15.35% while for Nasdaq Composite and Nasdaq bank index, the average yearly returns were 13.68% and 1.93%, respectively.

Table 2 shows the financial highlights of the SVB Financial Group during the period 2018–2022. The values are given in millions of dollars. The data source is gurufocus.com

The average increase in total assets, gross loans, and deposits were 43%, 28%, and 42%, respectively, during the period 2018–2022. The total equity increased by 33% during the above period. The average increase in interest income was 282%. The interest expense and noninterest expense increased by 37% and 33%, respectively, during the above period.

Table 3 shows the performance indicators of the SVB Group during the period 2018–2022.

The average ROA, ROE, and net interest margin during the period 2018–2022 were 1.35%,16.47%, and 2.94%, respectively.

References

1. https://ir.svb.com/financials/annual-reports-and-proxies/default.aspx
2. https://www.nytimes.com/2023/03/27/business/silicon-valley-bank-first-citizens.html

Case 72 Alphabet

Alphabet functions as a collection of business with Google being the leading business of the company. Alphabet was created through the restructuring of Google during October 2015 and became the parent company of Google and other Google subsidiaries.

The American multinational technology company specializes in internet-related services and products. Google's products and services include online advertising technologies, search, cloud computing, and software. Google consists of two segments—Google Services and Google Cloud. All non-Google businesses are collectively termed as Other Bets. Google is continuously engaged in innovation and introduction of new products and features. The company has invested more than $100 billion in research and development in the last 5 years. As of December 31, 2022, Alphabet had 190,234 employees. Google Search facilitates people to have trillions of searches on Google every year. YouTube provides entertainment, information, and opportunities about new insights. Google Cloud facilitates customers to solve business challenges and problems. Artificial Intelligence powers Google's core products. AI facilitates Google App to search in new languages. Google products such as Lens and Translate are built using artificial intelligence technologies such as optical character recognition and machine learning. It is estimated that 4 billion photos are encrypted by Google photos daily. YouTube Shorts have over 15 billion each day globally. There are over 1 billion shopping sessions per day across Google. Google has invested over $ 7 billion in data centers and offices across the USA.

Google comprises of two segments—Google Services and Google Cloud.

Google Services

The core products and platforms of Google Services include ads, Android, Chrome, hardware, Gmail, Google Drive, Google Maps, Google Photos, Google Play, Search, and YouTube. The latest generation of hardware products of Google include new

© The Author(s), under exclusive license to Springer Nature Switzerland AG 2024

B. R. Kumar, *Rising Stars*, Management for Professionals,
https://doi.org/10.1007/978-3-031-50032-9_72

Pixel 7, Pixel 7 Pro, and Pixel Watch. Google Services generate revenues through performance and brand advertising which appears on Google Search and other properties, YouTube, and Google Network partners' properties. The advertisement tools facilitate performance advertisers to create simple text-based advertisements. Brand advertising enhances user's awareness and affinity for advertisers' products and services through videos, text, images, and other interactive advertisements. Google generates revenues from Google Play, hardware, and YouTube subscriptions. Revenues are generated from Google Play from the sales of apps and in-app purchases. The Hardware segment generates revenues from the sales of Fitbit wearable devices, Google Nest home products, and Pixel devices. Subscription revenues are received from services such as YouTube Premium and YouTube TV.

Google Cloud

The Google Cloud offerings include Google Cloud Platform and Google Workspace. Google Cloud Platform offers leading technology in cybersecurity, data, analytics, AI, machine learning, and infrastructure. The data cloud facilitates unification of data lakes, data warehouses, data governance, and advanced machine learning into one single platform. Google provides customers with an open, reliable, and scalable infrastructure to run workloads anywhere on the Cloud, at the edge or in their data centers. Google Workspace offers secure communication and collaboration tools which include apps like Gmail, Docs, Drive, Calendar, Meet, etc. Google Cloud Platform revenues are generated from fees derived from infrastructure, platform, and other services. Revenues from Google Workspace is derived from fees for cloud-based communication and collaboration tools for enterprises such as Gmail, Docs, Drive, Calendar, and Meet.

Other Bets

Other Bets segment uses technology to solve issues which affect a wide variety of industries such as transportation and health technology. Other Bets businesses are at various stages of development. Revenues from Other Bets are generated basically from the sale of health technology and internet services.

The company faces formidable competition in different aspect of businesses from general purpose search engines and information services, vertical search engines and e-commerce providers, online advertising platforms and networks, providers of enterprise cloud services and digital video services, etc.

Growth Strategy

The modern-day trend of shift from an offline to online world has contributed to the business growth of Alphabet. Performance advertising and brand advertising constitute the primary source of revenues for Google. Acquisition is an important strategy of growth for Alphabet. Alphabet is one of the largest and most successful acquirers in the technology industry. Google's core search advertising platform and largest businesses like Android and YouTube were resulted from acquisitions. It is estimated that Google had spent over $28 billion acquiring 163 companies since 2001.The purchase of Motorola Mobility for $12.5 billion was the largest acquisition made by Google. In 2011, Motorola Mobility held approximately 14,600 granted patents and 67,000 pending applications worldwide. The acquisition of Motorola enabled Google to supercharge the Android ecosystem which enhanced competition in mobile computing.

Table 1 lists the major acquisitions made by Google.

Sustainability

Google has been a leader on sustainability and climate change over the past two decades since its establishment. In 2007, the company became the major company to be carbon neutral for its operations. In 2017, Google became the first major corporate to match 100% of its annual electricity with renewable energy and maintained that position for the past 5 years. In the year 2020, Google had the largest sustainability or green bond issuance valued at $5.75 billion in corporate history. The net proceeds from the green bond issuance was used to fund environmentally and socially responsible projects in the areas of energy efficiency, clean energy, green building, clean transportation, circular economy and design and affordable housing. The sustainable strategy of Google is based on three strategic pillars of accelerating the transition to carbon free energy, circular economy, technological empowerment, and benefits for society. In 2020, the company launched its third decade of climate action. By 2030, the company aims to achieve net zero emissions in all its operations and value chain which included consumer hardware products. Google became the first major company to run on carbon free energy throughout the year. The company also enabled five gigawatts of new carbon free energy through its investments in key manufacturing regions. Google enables more than 500 cities and local governments to reduce an aggregate of one gigaton (1 billion tons) of carbon emissions annually. The company aims to optimize the reuse of finite resources across operations, products, and supply chains. Google has introduced eco-friendly routing in Google Maps and innovative new features to book flights or purchase appliances which have lower carbon footprints. Google Search shows immense valuable information about climate change from authoritative sources such as United Nations.

Table 1 Major acquisitions by Google

SL	Year	Acquired firm	Deal value	Strategic motives
1	2011	Motorola	$12.5 billion	Acquisition of Patents
2	2014	Nest labs	$3.2 billion	Acquisition for smart thermostats and smoke detectors
3	2007	DoubleClick	$3.1 billion	Expansion in online advertising market
4	2006	YouTube	$1.65 billion	Added the second biggest search engine to Alphabet Portfolio
5	2013	Waze	$966 million	The acquisition of GPS-based navigation application was strategic fit for Google
6	2009	AdMob	$750 million	Facilitated Google's entry into mobile advertising platform
7	2010	ITA Software	$700 million	ITA is a major company in the travel reservations software industry. Aim of this acquisition was to gain infrastructural facilities
8	2007	Postini	$625 million	Google gained the email and web security service
9	2014	Dropcam	$555 million	Acquired video monitoring and security technology to facilitate Nest Lab to increase home automation products
10	2014	Skybox	$500 million	Satellite technology of Skybox was value addition for Google Maps
11	2014	DeepMind Technologies	$650 million	Strategic fit for data mining and artificial intelligence
12	2013	Boston Dynamics	$500 million	The Robots made by the company facilitate delivery of packages for Google
13	2011	Zagat	$150 million	Enhanced the services for Google maps, search and earth

Source: Collated from different sources

Risk Factors

Alphabet generates more than 80% of its total revenues from advertising. The business of Alphabet would be affected in scenarios of reduced spending by advertisers, loss of partners, effect of new and existing technologies which block advertisement online and reduce the ability of company to customize advertisements. The business environment of the company is rapidly evolving and intensely competitive. To compete successfully, the company has to develop innovative, relevant useful products, services, and technologies in a timely manner. The ongoing investment in new businesses, products, services, and technologies is inherently risky and may affect the financial performance of the company. Within Google Services, Alphabet invests heavily in hardware which includes smartphones, home devices, and wearables. In the Google Cloud segment, the company invests significant resources to develop and deploy enterprise ready cloud services such as Google Cloud Platform and Google Workspace. Effective intellectual property rights protection of patents, trademarks, trade secrets, copyrights in different regions of the world is also a significant risk factor. The failure to maintain and enhance the brand image could adversely affect the potential of the company to expand its base of users, advertisers, customers, content providers, and other partners. The company also faces a number of manufacturing and supply chain risks which could adversely affect the business operations of the company. Alphabet relies on contract manufacturers to manufacture or assemble its hardware products, servers, and networking equipment used in technical infrastructure. Supply shortages, raw material availability, logistics capacity, inflation, foreign currency exchange rates, tariffs, trade disputes, geopolitical tensions are risk factors which would have an effect on the operations and financial performance of the company. The failure of the company's information technology and communication system would affect the ability of the company to provide products and services. Alphabet also faces risks related to laws, regulations, and policies.

Stock Performance

In the following analysis, the stock returns of Alphabet are compared with the market index Nasdaq Composite during the recent 5-year period. The Google stock price which was trading at $54.24 on May 1st 2018 increased by 1.93 times to trade at $105.12 by 1st April 2023. The cumulative total monthly stock returns for Alphabet was 84% compared to the returns of 61% for the Nasdaq Composite during the period May 2018–April 2023. The average yearly return for Alphabet stock was 17% compared to market index Nasdaq Composite's return of 12% during the period May 2018–April 2023. The data was sourced from yahoo finance.com.

Table 2 shows the holding period return for Alphabet stock and Nasdaq Composite during the 5-year period 2018–2022. The analysis assumes holding period of 1 year.

Alphabet stock outperformed the market index Nasdaq Composite in the year 2021 and in the rest of the years, the stock performance was inferior compared to the market index Nasdaq Composite.

Table 3 compares the book value and market value of the equity of Alphabet during the period 2018–2022. The values are given in millions of dollars.

Table 2 Holding period return

Year	Alphabet	Nasdaq Composite	Excess returns
2018	−5%	−11%	6%
2019	20%	23%	−3%
2020	22%	41%	−19%
2021	58%	20%	38%
2022	−35%	−26%	−8%

Table 3 Market value and book value of equity

Year	2018	2019	2020	2021	2022
Book value of equity	177,628	201,442	222,544	251,635	256,144
Market value of equity	726827.15	921949.02	1183417.58	1918188.12	1133667.27
BV as percent of MV	24.4%	27.7%	24.1%	21.3%	13.4%

Table 4 Financial highlights

	(In millions of dollars)				
Financial highlights	2018	2019	2020	2021	2022
Total assets	232,792	275,909	319,616	359,268	365,264
Short-term investments	109,140	119,675	136,694	139,649	113,762
Total equity	177,628	201,442	222,544	251,635	256,144
Total revenue	136,819	161,857	182,527	257,637	282,836
Total operating expenses	44,675	54,033	56,571	67,984	81,791
Net income	30,736	34,343	40,269	76,033	59,972
Market cap	726827.15	921949.02	1183417.6	1918188.1	1133667.27
Enterprise value	621699.15	818241.02	1073495.6	1806934.1	1049584.27

Table 5 Performance indicators

Ratios	2018	2019	2020	2021	2022
Net margin%	22.46	21.22	22.06	29.51	21.2
ROE%	18.62	18.12	19	32.07	23.62
ROA%	14.29	13.5	13.52	22.4	16.55
DER	0.02	0.08	0.12	0.11	0.12

The average book value of equity as percent of the market value of equity was 17.3% during the period 2018–2022.

Table 4 shows the financial highlights of Alphabet Inc. during the period 2018–2022. The data source is guru focus.com.

The total assets, short-term investments, and total equity increased by 12%, 2%, and 10% on average basis, respectively, during the period 2018–2022. The total revenues and net income increased by 21% and 24% on average basis during the period 2018–2022. The market capitalization and enterprise value increased by 19% and 22%, respectively, during the period 2018–2022. The total expenses increased by 17% on average basis during the above period.

Table 5 shows the profitability and leverage position of the firm during the period 2018–2022.

The average net margin, ROE, and ROA during the period 2018–2022 were 23.29%, 22.28%, and 16.05%, respectively, during the period 2018–2022. The average debt equity ratio was 0.09 during the period 2018–2022.

Table 6 shows the estimation of economic value of Alphabet Inc. during the period 2018–2022. The values are given in millions of dollars.

Table 6 Estimation of economic value

Year	2021	2022
Profit before income tax	90734.00	71328.00
Income tax	14698.91	11341.15
Net operating profit after tax (NOPAT)	76035.09	59986.85
Stockholder equity	251,635	256,144
Long-term debt	12,844	12,857
Total capital employed	264,479	269,001
WACC	7.37%	10.27%
Capital charge	19492.10	27626.40
Economic value	56542.99	32360.45

References

1. https://abc.xyz/investor/static/pdf/20230203_alphabet_10K.pdf?cache=5ae4398
2. Rajesh Kumar, Wealth Creation-Analysis of Google, Strategic Financial Management Casebook. © 2017 Elsevier Inc, pp 199–208.
3. https://abc.xyz/investor/#esg-updates

Case 73 Malibu Boats

Malibu Boats is the major designer, manufacturer, and marketer of wide range of recreational powerboats consisting of eight Brands—Malibu, Axis, Pursuit, Maverick, Cobia, Pathfinder, Hewes, and Cobalt. The product portfolio of premium brands of Malibu is used for a broad range of recreational boating activities which include water sports, general recreational boating, and fishing. In the performance sport boat category, the Malibu and Axis brands have number one market share position in the USA. The company also has leading market share positions in the fiberglass outboard fishing boat market. The premium brands of the company are used for a range of recreational boating activities which include water sports such as water skiing, wakeboarding, wake surfing, etc. Axis boats are identified with affordable performance sport boat product category. By 2022, the distribution channel consisted of over 400 dealer locations globally. Malibu has seven manufacturing facilities located in five US states and Australia. By July 2022, the company employed 3015 employees worldwide.

Products and Brands

Malibu

Founded in 1982, Malibu offers premium boating experience through its Response series, Wakesetter series, and ultra-premium M series models.

Axis

Axis was launched in the year 2009 to offer an affordable priced high-quality entry-level boat with high performance and the option to upgrade key features such as Surf Gat.

© The Author(s), under exclusive license to Springer Nature Switzerland AG 2024

B. R. Kumar, *Rising Stars*, Management for Professionals,
https://doi.org/10.1007/978-3-031-50032-9_73

Pursuit

Pursuit was launched in the year 1977. The product is a premium brand of saltwater outboard fishing boats which consists of product lines for sports center consoles, dual consoles, and offshore series with options for casual cruising and luxury entertainment.

Saltwater fishing segment consists of Cobia, Pathfinder, and Maverick and Hewes.

Cobia

Cobia model of boats were acquired by Maverick Boat Group in the year 2005. Cobia models consist of center console and dual console vessels for all levels of anglers and boater.

Pathfinder

Pathfinder is the most versatile inshore fishing boat for dedicated anglers to fish with proven technology. The product was launched in the year 1984.

Maverick and Hewes

Maverick and Hewes are designed for shallow inshore flats anglers. These boats are provided with vacuum infused construction and have unique craftsmanship.

Cobalt is the premium luxury sterndrive and outboard manufacturer with five product lines which serve entry level to premium brands with the options to expand some models with patented Surf Gate. Surf Gate is the most innovative feature on all Malibu, Axis, and certain Cobalt models.

Competitive Strengths

The company has a leading market share position in the recreational boating categories. In 2021, the company's sport boat brands such as Malibu and Axis brands held number one market position in performance sport boats. The company had focused on industry leading product design and innovation. The company had vertically integrated a number of key components of its manufacturing process which included manufacturing of its own engines, boat trailers, towers and tower accessories, machined and billet parts, soft grip flooring, and wiring harnesses. One of the competitive strengths of the company is derived from its patented technologies such as Surf Gate, Power Wedge, and Surf Band which drive demand for its products and increase margins across its brands. The brands such as Malibu, Axis, Pursuit,

Maverick Boat Group, and Cobalt brands are widely recognized in the recreational powerboat industry. The company has diverse product offerings. Malibu and Axis are market leaders in the performance sport boat category. Pursuit and Maverick Boat Group compete in the saltwater outboard fishing boat market. Cobalt operates in the sterndrive category.

Strategy of Growth

Malibau boats strategically focus on innovation with dedicated product development and engineering teams located in Tennessee, Kansas, California, and Florida. The company focuses on developing its patented Surf Band technology which allows the rider to control the surf wave, shape, size, and side. Some of the notable innovations offered by the company include Power Wedge III, G5 and power actuated GX Tower, Electronic Dashboard Controls, Flip Down Swim Step, Tower Mister, True Wave. Maverick Boat Group had introduced first of its kind "Hybrid" and "Open" Bay Boat designs in recent years. The company won the Boating Industry Magazine's top award in different categories during the past 5 years. By 2022, the dealer network consisted of over 300 dealer locations in the USA and Canada along with 100 dealer locations in Europe, Asia, Middle East, South America, South Africa, and Australia/New Zealand. The North American dealers purchase boats through floor plan financing programs with third party floor plan financing providers. The company possessed one of the strongest distribution networks in the recreational powerboat industry. The company follows a two-pronged product development strategy. The first strategy focuses on introduction of new boat models to target the underserved segments of the recreational powerboat industry. The second strategy involves development and integration of innovative new or enhanced optional features for its boat offerings. The company aims to strengthen its distribution network by selectively recruiting market leading dealers who sell its competitors' products. The company focuses on expanding its vertical integration capabilities. The company has successfully integrated the production of its own towers and tower accessories, trailers, machine, and billet parts.

The company aims to drive growth in its business through targeted acquisitions. In 2018, the company acquired Swim Step which was part of Cobalt thereby increasing its appeal for its product portfolio. In 2020, the company acquired Maverick Boat Group. The main objective of these acquisitions is to expand its presence in new markets and expand its product lines.

Risk Factors

The profitability of the company may be adversely affected due to the non-execution of its manufacturing strategy in a successful manner. The profitability of the company depends on its ability to spread fixed costs sufficiently over a large number of products sold and shipped. The primary raw materials used in manufacturing of the boats are petroleum-based resins, fiberglass, and vinyl. The shortages or increases in the cost of raw materials, commodities, component parts, and transportation could negatively impact the business operations of the firm. Disruptions in suppliers' operations could disrupt the production schedule. The availability and cost of engines used in the manufacturing of boats are critical. The company solely depends on General Motors for the supply of Malibu and Axis engines. All the outboard motors are purchased from Yamaha. Interruption of informal supply arrangement could have a material adverse effect on the business of the company. The nature of the company's business exposes it to workers' compensation claims and other workplace liabilities. The company's reliance on patents, trademark laws, and contractual provisions to protect its proprietary rights may not be sufficient to protect its intellectual property rights from other companies who sell similar products. The business operations of the company may be negatively impacted by an outrage or breach of information technology and operational technology systems or cybersecurity events. The company also faces market risks related to demand for new recreational powerboats. Weak economic conditions and low consumer confidence could adversely impact the demand for recreational powerboats. Higher energy costs result in increases in operating expenses in its manufacturing facility and in the expense of shipping products to dealers. Changes in laws and policies governing foreign trade could adversely affect the business operations of the firm. As a boat manufacturer, the company has to comply with environmental laws and regulations which could increase the cost of its products and reduce consumer demand.

Stock Performance

The following section analyzes the stock returns for Malibu boats in comparison with the returns for market index Russell 2000 during the recent 5-year period. Malibu stock which was trading at $42.88 on 1st May 2018 increased by 1.30 times approximately to trade at $55.70 by 1st April 2023. The total cumulative monthly return for Malibu stock was 86% during the period May 2018 –April 2023 while the total cumulative monthly return for the Russell 2000 market index was approximately 23%. The average yearly return for the stock was 17% for Malibu stock compared to 5% return for the market index Russell 2000 during the period May 2018–April 2023.The data source is yahoo finance.

Table 1 Holding period return

Year	Malibu	Russell 2000	Excess returns
2018	−19%	−17%	−1%
2019	1%	11%	−10%
2020	43%	22%	20%
2021	−2%	8%	−10%
2022	−19%	−13%	−6%

Table 2 Book and market value trends

Year	2018	2019	2020	2021	2022
Book value of equity	139.87	210.35	261.53	381.15	513.57
Market value of equity	862.09	810.12	1069.96	1528.71	1080.61
BV as percent of MV	16.2%	24.4%	32.3%	35.6%	33.6%

Table 3 Financial highlights

	(In millions of dollars)				
Financial highlights	2018	2019	2020	2021	2022
Total assets	365.77	451.31	477.35	742.78	851.33
Short-term investments	61.62	27.39	33.79	41.48	83.74
Total equity	139.87	210.35	261.53	381.15	513.57
Total revenue	497	684.02	653.16	926.52	1214.88
Total operating expenses	50.28	68.16	63.96	86.71	96.23
Net income	27.6	66.07	61.56	109.84	157.63
Market cap	862.09	810.12	1069.96	1528.71	1080.61
Enterprise value	914.46	902.48	1127.97	1640.26	1129

Table 4 Performance indicators

Ratios	2018	2019	2020	2021	2022
Net margin%	5.56	9.66	9.43	11.86	12.98
ROE%	30.4	39.02	26.84	34.98	35.96
ROA%	9.37	16.17	13.26	18	19.78
DER	0.81	0.56	0.33	0.39	0.24

Table 1 gives the holding period returns for the stock and market index during 2018–2022. The holding period is assumed to be 1 year.

Malibu stock outperformed the market index Russell 2000 in the year 2020.

Table 2 shows the book value and market value of equity of Malibu during the period 2018–2022. The values are given in millions of dollars.

The average book value of equity as percent of market value was 34.6% during 2018–2022 period.

Table 3 gives the financial highlights of the company during the period 2018–2022. The data source is gurufocus.com.

The average growth rate in total assets, total cash investments, and total equity were 24.8%, 23%, and 39%, respectively, during the above period. The total revenues and net income grew by 27% and 64%, respectively. The total expenses increased by 19% during the above period. The market capitalization and enterprise value increased by 10% and 9% on average basis during the above period.

Table 4 gives the profitability and leverage position of the firm during the period 2018–2022.

The average net margin, ROE, and ROA were 9.90%, 33.44%, and 15.32%, respectively, during the period 2018–2022. The average debt equity ratio was 0.24.

Reference

1. https://malibuboatsinc.com/investor-information/annual-reports/default.aspx

Case 74 PayPal Holdings, Inc.

PayPal Holdings, Inc. is a leading technology platform for digital payments for merchants and consumers worldwide. The basic aim of the company is to enable merchants and consumers to manage and make money transactions anywhere in the world in the markets, anytime, on any platform using any device while sending payments or getting paid which includes person to person (P2P) payments. The company offers services which enable customers to use their PayPal or Venmo accounts to purchase and receive payments for goods and services and provide other services such as the ability to transfer and withdraw funds. PayPal enables consumers to exchange funds with merchants using different funding sources such as bank account, PayPal or Venmo account balance, PayPal and Venmo branded credit products which include installment products, credit card, debit card, cryptocurrencies, and products such as gift cards and eligible rewards. PayPal, Venmo, and Xoom products facilitate people to transfer funds to each other. PayPal is at the forefront of digital payment revolution for over 20 years. The PayPal platform facilitates millions of people and businesses across the globe to deal with financial transactions with over 430 million active accounts composed of 392 million active consumer accounts and 34 million active merchant accounts in more than 200 markets. PayPal aims to be a trusted everyday app for consumers and an essential tool to help small- and medium-sized businesses (SMBs). In 2022, PayPal processed 22.3 billion payment transactions and $1.36 trillion in total payment volume across its platform. The company returned over $4.2 billion to stockholders through share repurchases in the year 2022 which represented 80% of its free cash flow. In 2022, PayPal processed 22.3 billion payment transactions and $1.36 trillion in total payment volume across the platforms. The company had provided access to more than $4 billion in capital through its merchant lending services. PayPal had launched PayPal Rewards and Honey extension to consumers to save money on everyday purchases. The company has enabled secure passwordless login to PayPal accounts across platforms and devices with passkeys. PayPal earns revenues primarily by charging fees for payment transactions by customers and other payment related services. Revenues are also generated from customers through fees charged

© The Author(s), under exclusive license to Springer Nature Switzerland AG 2024

B. R. Kumar, *Rising Stars*, Management for Professionals,
https://doi.org/10.1007/978-3-031-50032-9_74

Table 1 Financial and operational metrics

Revenues	$25.37 billion
Active accounts	426 million
Total payment volume	$1.25 trillion
Payment transaction	19.3 billion

Source: Annual Report 2022

for foreign currency conversion, instant transfers from their PayPal or Venmo account to their bank account or debit card. Revenues are also earned through partnerships, interest and fees from merchant and consumer credit products, interest earned on certain assets signifying customer balances, referral fees, subscription fees, and gateway services.

Table 1 gives the key operational and financial metrics of PayPal in the year 2021.

Competitive Strengths

PayPal offers unique end-to-end product experiences through two-sided network payments platform for digital and in-store transactions. The branded and unbranded card processing payment solutions of PayPal offer open ecosystem using a wide variety of different funding options and digital wallet solutions. The company has achieved global scale through organic growth. By December 2022, the company had 435 million active accounts in over 200 markets throughout the world. Over the time period, the company had built and strengthened trusted brands such as PayPal, Braintree, Venmo, Xoom, Hyperwallet, PayPal Honey, and Paidy. PayPal's payments platform offers merchant value proposition by enabling merchants to accept all types of online and offline payments which include PayPal and Venmo digital wallets. PayPal's merchant finance offerings include PayPal Working Capital and PayPal business loan products targeted for small- and medium-sized businesses. PayPal offers consumer value proposition by offering consumers P2P payment solutions through PayPal, Venmo, and Xoom products and services. The company enables both domestic and international P2P transfers across its payment's platform. The business faces competition from wide range of businesses and from all forms of physical and electronic payments. PayPal faces competition from banks and financial institutions which provide traditional payment methods, electronic bank transfers, and payment networks.

Strategy

The company focuses on growing its core business through expanding its global capabilities, customer base and scale by offering solutions to merchants and consumers. PayPal aims to expand its value proposition for merchants and consumers by being technology and platform agnostic. PayPal aims to provide consumers with flexible ways to manage and move money across different markets, merchants, and platforms. The company seeks for growth in both organic and inorganic ways. The focus is on acquisitions and strategic investments in existing and new international markets. The payments platform offered by PayPal utilizes a combination of proprietary and third-party technologies and services to facilitate transactions between merchants and consumers globally across different channels, markets, and networks. Consumers can utilize the payment platform to send payments in nearly 150 currencies, withdraw funds in bank accounts in 56 currencies, and hold balances in their PayPal accounts in 25 currencies.

The company makes strategic investment in companies for innovation in fintech, commerce enablement, digital infrastructure, and crypto/block chain technologies through its corporate venture arm, PayPal venture. In 2021, PayPal ventures have made more than 50 investments which amounted to $850 million. PayPal has developed intuitive user interfaces, customer tools, transaction management databases, and payment network integrations for its platforms. The payment platform, open application programming interfaces, and developer tools enable developers to offer solutions to the global ecosystem of merchants and consumers. The system also maintains the security of the customer information. The technology infrastructure which supports the payments platform simplifies the storage and processing of large amounts of data and facilitates the deployment and operation of large-scale global products and services. The company offers a comprehensive cybersecurity program designed to protect its technology infrastructure and payments platform against cybersecurity threats. The total research and development expense amounted to $11.7 billion in year 2022.

Risk Factors

The company operates in a rapidly evolving regulatory environment which focuses on all aspects of payment industry which include countering terrorist financing, anti-money laundering, privacy, cyber security, and consumer protection. Government regulation significantly impacts key aspects of PayPal's businesses. The activities of non-US entities of PayPal Holding are subject to regulatory supervision by financial regulatory authority in the jurisdictions in which the company operates. PayPal must comply with rules and regulations of the European banking industry specifically with those related to capitalization, fund management, corporate governance, anti-money laundering, disclosure requirements, etc.

Cyberattacks and security vulnerabilities have the potential to severely affect the business and financial operations of the firm. Business interruptions or systems failure could impair the availability of the company's websites, applications, and products or services. Significant and disruptive technological changes could impact the payment technologies. The revenues of the company could decline if the company is unable to keep pace with rapid technological developments and introduce new products and services. PayPal's businesses are subject to extensive regulation and oversight. The failure to comply with complex regulations and changing rules will adversely impact the operations of the company's businesses.

Frequent changes to payment card networks or bank fees, rules could adversely affect the business operations of the firm. The credit products offered by PayPal and reliance on third parties in many aspects of business expose the company to additional risks.

ESG Strategy

The ESG strategy of PayPal focuses on four dimensions of Responsible Business Practices, Social Innovation, Employees & Culture and Environmental Sustainability. PayPal focuses on empowering small businesses to digitize and support an inclusive economy. The company has launched new products and services for its merchants such as Venmo business profiles, Zettle US, Zettle terminal, etc. The company had also enhanced its popular offerings such as QR codes and global pay later solutions. In 2021, the company allocated $535 million for racial equity and social justice initiatives. In 2021, the company made investments in Oyster, Carro, and VNLife. Oyster facilitates startups to hire, pay, and manage employees globally. Carro through its product platform helps merchants to sell inventory on other merchants' sites for expanding their customer base. VNLife offers mobile banking to underbanked populations in Vietnam for economic development. Robust corporate governance practices are critical for the long-term sustainable value creation for the company. 11 out of 12 directors are independent and all the directors stand for annual election. The company has 56% diversity in workforce representation. With respect to social innovation, PayPal has facilitated $3.6 billion in access to capital to small- and medium-sized businesses. Over 21,000 employees accessed over 100 K self-directed courses in order to advance their personal, professional, and business development. The company achieved 100% pay equity in the USA for Black, LatinX, and Asian women compared to white male peers. The company also received 100% global gender and overall US ethnic pay equity. The company introduced Exec Online, a course platform with accreditation from UC Berkeley where over 1600 leaders had participated in classes for developing leadership and team management skills. For employee financial wellbeing, PayPal has provided 800 financial education and coaching sessions which were conducted globally which included tax education course delivered across 21 countries. In 2021, the PayPal-defined estimated net disposable income (eNDI) for hourly and entry-level US employees reached at least 15% in the USA. With respect to environmental sustainability, PayPal aims to reduce absolute operational GHG emissions by year 2025 compared to the base year 2019. The company was able to match 100% of the energy from data center operations with renewable generation in year 2021 based on science-based targets. The company had taken steps to engage 75% of its suppliers by spend to set science-based targets by the year 2025. PayPal had funded the formation of the Digital Finance for Climate Resilience (DF4CR) Task Force. PayPal was a founding supporter of climate focused cohort of Catalyst Fund, a global inclusive tech accelerator which helps startups to build and deliver inclusive digital finance products and services. The company aims to achieve

Table 2 Awards and recognitions

Fortune blue ribbon companies
TIME 100 Most influential companies
Financial times diversity leaders
JUST Capital America's Most JUST companies
2021 CPA Zicklin index—Trend setter
CDP climate Rating A

Table 3 Holding period return

Year	PayPal	Nasdaq Composite	Excess returns
2018	2%	−11%	13%
2019	22%	23%	−1%
2020	106%	41%	65%
2021	−20%	20%	−39%
2022	−59%	−26%	−32%

Table 4 Market and book value of equity

Year	2018	2019	2020	2021	2022
Book value of equity	15,386	16,929	20,063	21,727	20,274
Market value of equity	98721.66	126883.41	274409.8	220261.44	80905.92
BV as percent of MV	15.6%	17.1%	15.8%	7.9%	9.2%

net zero through equitable sourcing practices. In 2021, the company invested in three innovative climate impact projects which led to the retirement of 8000 metric tons of verified carbon credits. In 2021, over 40% of its vendors by spend reported specific activities to reduce their GHG emissions. The company has enabled well over $19 billion in donations to approximately 1.4 million non-profits organizations.

Table 2 lists the awards and recognition received by PayPal.

Stock Performance

The following section analyzes the stock returns for PayPal Holding compared to the market index Nasdaq Composite during the recent 5-year period. PayPal was trading at $82.07 on 1st May 2018. By April 1st 2023, the stock price declined to $76.41. The cumulative total return for the PayPal stock was 31% compared to the cumulative total return of 61% for the Nasdaq Composite Index during the 5-year period May 2018–April 2023.The yearly average return for the PayPal stock was 6% compared to the 12% return for the Nasdaq Composite during the period May 2018–April 2023. Table 3 lists the holding period return for the PayPal stock and market index Nasdaq Composite during the period 2018–2022. The holding period is assumed to be 1-year period.

PayPal stock outperformed the market index in the year 2020.

Table 4 gives the market value and book value of equity of PayPal during the period 2018–2022. The values are given in millions of dollars.

Table 5 Financial highlights

	(In millions of dollars)				
Financial highlights	2018	2019	2020	2021	2022
Total assets	43,332	51,333	70,379	75,803	78,717
Short-term investments	7575	7349	4794	5197	7776
Total equity	15,386	16,929	20,063	21,727	20,274
Total revenue	15,451	17,772	21,454	25,371	27,518
Total operating expenses	6093	6812	8351	9672	9729
Net income	2057	2459	4202	4169	2419
Market cap	98721.66	126883.41	274409.8	220261.44	80905.92
Enterprise value	91610.66	121131.41	270309.8	218919.44	80471.92

Table 6 Performance indicators

Ratios	2018	2019	2020	2021	2022
Net margin%	13.31	13.84	19.59	16.43	8.79
ROE%	13.11	15.24	22.77	19.97	11.52
ROA%	4.89	5.2	6.9	5.7	3.13
DER	0.13	0.29	0.45	0.37	0.51

The average book value as percent of market value of equity was 8.6% during the period 2018–2022. Table 5 shows the financial highlights of PayPal Holding during the period 2018–2022. The values are given in millions of dollars.

The average increase in total assets, short-term investments, and total equity were 16.78%, 5%, and 8%, respectively, during the period 2018–2022. The total revenues and net income increased by 16% and 12%, respectively, during the period 2018–2022. The total expenses increased by 13% on average basis during the above period. The market capitalization and enterprise value increased by 15% and 18%, respectively, during the above period.

Table 6 gives the performance highlights of PayPal in terms of profitability and leverage position during the recent 5-year period.

The average net margin, ROE, and ROA during the period 2018–2022 were 14.39%, 16.52%, and 5.16%, respectively. The average debt equity ratio is 0.35 during the above period.

References

1. https://investor.pypl.com/home/dnefault.aspx
2. https://investor.pypl.com/financials/annual-reports/default.aspx
3. PayPal Global Impact Report 2021.

Case 75 Mid Penn Bancorp, Inc.

Mid Penn Bancorp, Inc. is a financial holding company incorporated in August 1991 and consists of the wholly owned bank and non-bank subsidiaries. In 1991, the Bank became a wholly owned subsidiary of Mid Penn. In 2020, Mid Penn established two additional non-bank subsidiaries of MPB Wealth Management LLC and MPB Risk Services LLC. By December 2022, Mid Penn had total consolidated assets of $4.5 billion, total deposits of $3.8 billion, and total shareholders' equity of $512 million.

Mid Penn Bank was originally established as Millersburg Bank in the year 1868 and became a state-chartered bank in year 1931. In 2015, Mid Penn acquired Phoenix Bancorp Inc. and merged its subsidiary, Miners Bank into Mid Penn. In 2018, Mid Penn acquired the Scottdale Bank and Trust and added five branches in Western Pennsylvania region. In the same year, First Priority was merged into Mid Penn. This merger resulted in the addition of eight offices in Southeastern Pennsylvania region. During November 2021, Mid Penn acquired Riverview Financial Corporation and added 23 community banking offices and three limited purpose offices across Western Pennsylvania. During December 2022, Mid Penn entered into an agreement to merge Brunswick Bancorp into Mid Penn.

By December 2022, the bank had 43 full-service retail banking locations in the Pennsylvania counties. By December 2022, the bank had 580 full-time and 31 part-time employees.

Products and Services

Mid Penn's core business consists of attracting deposits and loans from its network of community banking offices. The bank provides full service commercial banking and trust business. The bank offers wide range of financial services which include mortgage and home equity loans, secured and unsecured commercial and consumer loans, lines of credit, construction financing, farm loans, community development, and different types of time and demand deposits. The bank also offers services such

© The Author(s), under exclusive license to Springer Nature Switzerland AG 2024

B. R. Kumar, *Rising Stars*, Management for Professionals,
https://doi.org/10.1007/978-3-031-50032-9_75

as online banking, telephone banking, cash management services, automated teller services, and safe deposit boxes.

The loan products offered by the bank includes commercial real estate loans, residential real estate loans, commercial and industrial loans, and consumer loans. The bank manages credit risk through portfolio diversification, underwriting policies, and loan monitoring practices. By December 2022, the bank's had highest credit exposure in the commercial real estate sector.

Mid Penn maintains both a held to maturity and an available for sale investment portfolio. These portfolios comprise US Treasury and other government securities, mortgage-backed US government securities, investment grade municipal securities, and corporate bonds. The bank basically uses deposits to finance lending and investment activities.

The bank primarily uses deposits and, to a lesser extent, wholesale borrowings to finance lending and investment activities. The Wholesale borrowing sources of bank include advances from the Federal Home Loan Bank of Pittsburgh, overnight borrowings from Bank's other correspondent banking relationships, and advances from the Federal Reserve's discount window.

Strategy

The bank offers services to commercial businesses and real estate investors, consumers, nonprofit institutions, and municipalities. These services are offered through its 43 full-service retail banking centers along with one loan production, wealth management office, two corporate offices, and one operational facility which are based in Pennsylvania region. The bank's primary market centers are located in diversified manufacturing and service bases across 19 Pennsylvania counties. The bank focusses on developing long-term customer relationships with the focus on maintenance of high-quality service.

The bank competes actively with financial services companies for deposit, loan, trust, and wealth management businesses. The main competitors also consist of commercial banks, credit unions, savings banks, savings and loan associations, insurance companies, securities brokerage firms, finance companies, and mutual funds.

Risk Factors

Mid Penn's earnings and cash flows are largely dependent upon the Bank's net interest income and hence the bank is exposed to interest rate risk. The bank is also exposed to credit risk as approximately 88% of the bank's loan portfolio consisted of commercial real estate, commercial, industrial, and agricultural loans as of December 2022. These loans have higher default risk compared to residential real estate or secured consumer loans. The allowances for loan losses may not be sufficient to cover actual loan losses. The banking subsidiary of Mid Penn faces significant competition from other banks, credit unions, savings institutions, mortgage banking firms in originating both commercial and consumer loans.

The Basel III capital requirements require Mid Penn to maintain higher levels of capital which could result in decline in profitability. The SBA lending program depends on the federal government and the bank faces specific risks with respect to the origination of SBA loans. Mid Penn relies heavily on its information systems. Interruption or breach in security of these systems will adversely affect the operations of the bank. Mid Penn is also exposed to the risks of cyber-attacks as part of its business operations. Mortgage banking income depends on different factors such as mortgage interest rates, conditions of real estate, and refinancing activity. Mid Penn operates in a highly regulated environment and changes in federal, state, and local laws and regulations may have an adverse effect on its business operations. On account of its fiduciary responsibility, Mid Penn is subject to claims and litigation.

Stock Performance

Table 1 shows the wealth generation by means of investment in Mid Penn stock, Nasdaq Bank index, and a peer group during the recent 5-year period. An investment of $100 is assumed to be made in the stock, peer group, and market index by December 31, 2017 and the return generated is examined through the period December 2022. The peer group consists of commercial banks with total assets in the range between $2.3 billion and $9.5 billion.

The 5-year holding period return for the Mid Penn stock was 4% while for Nasdaq Bank Index and Peer Group, the holding period return were 9%, respectively. The average yearly return for Mid Penn stock was 5.05% while for the Nasdaq Bank Index and Peer Group, the average returns were 5% and 4%, respectively, during the period 2018–2022.

In the next section the returns for Mid Penn stock are compared with the market index Nasdaq Bank Index during the recent 5-year period. The data is sourced from yahoo finance. The Mid Penn stock was trading at $35.90 on April 1st 2018. By March 1st 2023, the stock price declined to trade at $23.78. The cumulative total monthly return for the Mid Penn stock was −18.1% during the period April 2018–March 2023.

Table 1 Comparative wealth generated

Year	2017	2018	2019	2020	2021	2022
Mid Penn	$100	$70.57	$91.16	$71.92	$107.54	$104.39
NASDAQ OMX banks index	$100	$82.29	$112.01	$100.46	$138.97	$109.23
Peer group	$100	$89.57	$108.52	$81.65	$114.42	$108.78

Source: Annual Report 2022

Table 2 Holding period returns

Year	Mid Penn Bank	Nasdaq Bank Index	Excess returns
2018	−35.52%	−20.95%	−14.6%
2019	−2.00%	9.38%	−11.4%
2020	2.30%	−4.72%	7.0%
2021	26.91%	34.09%	−7.2%
2022	12.43%	−18.18%	30.6%

Table 3 Book and market value of equity

Year	2018	2019	2020	2021	2022
Book value of equity	223.21	237.87	255.69	490.08	512.1
Market value of equity	194.75	244.25	184.38	506.5	476.11
BV as percent of MV	114.6%	97.4%	138.7%	96.8%	107.6%

Table 4 Financial highlights

	(In millions of dollars)				
Financial highlights	2018	2019	2020	2021	2022
Total assets	2077.98	2231.18	2998.95	4689.43	4497.95
Gross loans	1624	1763	2384	3104	3514
Deposits	1726.03	1912.39	2474.58	4002.02	3778.33
Total equity	223.21	237.87	255.69	490.08	512.1
Interest income	68.65	95.31	107.94	123.32	165.6
Non-interest income	7.4	12.62	17.9	21.53	23.65
Interest expense	12.72	25.16	19.73	14.75	17.77
Total non-interest expense	44.79	59.21	66.08	73.13	96
Market capitalization	194.75	244.25	184.38	506.5	476.11
Enterprise value	283.78	286.37	282.45	486.28	592.06

Table 2 shows the holding period return for the Mid Penn stock and market index Nasdaq Bank Index during the period 2018–2022. The analysis is based on the assumption of holding period of 1 year.

Mid Penn bank had outperformed the bank index in the year 2022.

Table 3 shows the market value and book value of equity during the period 2018–2022 in millions of dollars.

The average book value as percent of market value of equity was 111% during the period 2018–2022.

Table 4 shows the financial highlights of the company during the period 2018–2022.

During the period 2018–2022, the total assets, gross loans, and deposits increased by 24%, 22%, and 24%, respectively. The total equity, market capitalization, and enterprise value increased by 28%, 42%, and 23%, respectively, on average basis. The interest income and non-interest income increased by 25% and 36%, respectively. The interest expense and non-interest expenses increased by 17% and 21%,

Table 5 Performance indicators

Ratios	2018	2019	2020	2021	2022
Performance ratios					
Return on average assets %	0.64	0.82	0.95	0.83	1.22
Return on average equity%	7.75	10.97	14.92	11.68	14.54
Net interest margin%	3.71	3.54	3.63	3.08	3.53
Efficiency ratio%	79.14	72.43	66.51	70.03	58.22
Asset quality ratio					
Non-performing assets to total assets%	0.59	0.54	0.52	0.22	0.21

Table 6 Economic value

Year	2021	2022
Profit before income tax	36.05	67.35
Income tax	6.7	12.5
Net operating profit after tax (NOPAT)	29.3	54.8
Stockholder equity	490.1	512.1
Long-term debt	152.1	58.1
Total capital employed	642.2	570.2
WACC	5%	7.2%
Capital charge	33.2	41.0
Economic value	−3.9	13.8

respectively, during the above period. The data is sourced from guru focus.com and annual reports.

Table 5 highlights the performance and asset quality ratio indicators of the company during the period 2018–2022.

The average ROA, ROE, and Net Interest margin for Mid Penn Bancorp were 0.89%, 11.97%, and 3.50%, respectively, during the period 2018–2022.The average efficiency ratio during the period 2018–2022 was 42%. In 2022, the capital adequacy tier–leverage ratio was 9.57%. Mid Penn Bancorp's Capital Adequacy Tier–Tier 1 Ratio % for the annual that ended in Dec 2022 was 11.18%.

Table 6 illustrates the estimation of economic value of the bank in the year 2021 and 2022. The values are estimated in millions of dollars.

References

1. https://investors.midpennbank.com/corporate-information/corporate-profile/default.aspx
2. https://midpennbank.com/

Case 76 Strategic Education

Strategic Education Inc. is an education services holding company which focuses on providing education for working adults. This education services company provides high quality education through campus-based and online post-secondary education offerings through programs for developing job ready skills. The company operates through its wholly owned subsidiaries Strayer University, Capella University in the USA and Torrens University in Australia. These subsidiaries are accredited post-secondary institutions of higher education. Education Technology Services segment offers industry relevant training, certificate, and degree programs. By December 2022, Strategic Education had employed 3907 employees globally.

Table 1 lists the major events in the history of the company.

By December 2022, the three reportable segments of the company consisted of US Higher Education, Australia/New Zealand and Education Technology Services.

US Higher Education (USHE) Segment

The USHE segment offers certificate and degree programs to working adults through Strayer University and Capella University. The Jack Welch Management Institute MBA is a unit of Strayer University. The USHE offers non-degree web and mobile application development courses through Hackbright Academy and Devmountain. Strayer University which was founded in year 1892 offers undergraduate and graduate degree programs in business, criminal justice, education, health services, information technology, and public administration through physical campuses located mainly in the eastern United States and online. Strayer University is accredited by the Middle States Commission on Higher Education. The curricula of Strayer University are structured to allow students to advance sequentially from one learning level to another by applying credits earned in one program toward attainment of more advanced degree. The target market of working adults and their employers are informed about the programs offered through direct, digital, and social media marketing activities. Strayer University offers career related services

© The Author(s), under exclusive license to Springer Nature Switzerland AG 2024
B. R. Kumar, *Rising Stars*, Management for Professionals,
https://doi.org/10.1007/978-3-031-50032-9_76

Table 1 History

Year	Major events
1892	Strayer's Business College is founded in Baltimore, MD
1904	The second campus became operational and became the cornerstone of the Strayer University
1969	Strayer is licensed to grant Bachelor of Science degree and renamed Strayer College
1991	The parent company of Capella University, Capella Education Company founded
1996	Strayer Education Inc. is established to raise capital for expansion and make Strayer College Public. Strayer introduces online learning program
1997	Capella University graduates its first batch of students
1998	Strayer College granted University Status
1999	The Graduate School of America is renamed to Capella University and student enrollment exceeds 1000 students
2000	Capella becomes member of the Academic Quality Improvement Program (AQIP) of the North Central Association's Higher Learning Commission
2011	Capella Education Company invests in startup Sophia.org, a social teaching and learning platform which integrates education with technology.
2012	Strayer University acquires Jack Welch Management Institute which provide online education program and offers differentiated executive MBA degree and executive certificates
2015	Strayer Education acquires the New York Code and Design Academy, the provider of non-degree web and mobile application development courses.
2016	Capella acquires Hackbright Academy which specializes in software engineering. Dev Mountain was acquired to extend its leadership position in the job ready skills market.
2017	Strayer Education Inc. and Capella Education Company merged to become market leader in education innovation
2018	Strayer Education Inc. is renamed to Strategic Education
2020	Acquired Torrens University and associated assets in Australia and New Zealand. These institutions consisting of Torrens University, Think Education and Media Design School offered diversified curricula to approximately 19,000 students.

Source: https://www.strategiceducation.com/about/history/default.aspx

for its students and alumni. Capella University founded in 1993 is an online accredited higher education institution which offers undergraduate and degree programs in business, technology, health care administration, counselling, psychology, social work, nursing, health sciences to working adults. Capella University focuses on master's and doctoral degree programs. Capella University is accredited by the Higher Learning Commission, the accrediting agency recognized by the Department of Education. The academic offerings of Capella University are offered in a flexible online format and are based on competency-based curricula. The Guided Path credit hour courses of Capella University are offered on a quarterly academic schedule. Capella University offers courses in the FlexPath model wherein students' competencies are directly assessed by faculty when students submit an assessment. FlexPath students set their own deadlines and demonstrate competencies via authentic assessment. Capella University also offers certificate programs whose duration varies from two quarters to approximately 2 years.

Australia/New Zealand Segment

The Australia/New Zealand segment consists of Torrens University, Think Education, and Media Design School. These institutions are collectively called ANZ institutions. Torrens University which was established in the year 2013 is the only investor funded university in Australia which offers undergraduate, post graduate, and specialized degree courses in the field of business, design and creative technology, health, hospitality, and education. The courses are offered both online and at physical campuses. Torrens University is registered with the Tertiary Education Quality and Standards Agency, the regulator for higher education providers and universities in Australia. Think Education is the vocational registered training organization and accredited higher education provider in Australia with campuses in Sydney, Melbourne, Brisbane, and Adelaide. Media Design School is the globally recognized private tertiary institution for creative and technology qualifications in New Zealand. Media Design School offers industry endorsed courses in 3D animation, visual effects, game programming, graphic and motion design, artificial intelligence, and creative advertising.

Education Technology Services Segment

Education Technology Services segment offers employee education benefits programs for employees with industry relevant training. Education Technology Services support employer partners through Workforce Edge, Sophia 12 Learning. Workforce Edge is a platform which offers employers full-service education benefits administration solution. Sophia 12 Learning enables education benefits programs through the use of low-cost online general education level courses recommended by the American Council on Education.

Competition and Strategy

Strategic Education aims to be a leading innovator and provider of career relevant education programs for advancement of students' careers. The strategic priorities of the company revolve around the central pillars of student success improvement, enhancement of student experience, and affordability of programs for students. The company aims to enhance student experience through leveraging technology by using artificial intelligence and automation. The company is actively involved in building relationships with employers to create employee education benefit programs.

The market for post-secondary education is fragmented and competitive in nature. There are no private or public institutions holding a significant market share. Strayer University, Capella University, and Torrens University compete basically with traditional public and private degree granting accredited colleges and universities. The Group also faces competition from nontraditional credit bearing and noncredit bearing educational programs including open online courses offered globally by proprietary, public, and not for profit educational institutions. The key factors which affect the competitive position of the company include the quality of programs and services offered, reputation among the stakeholders, quality of campus facilities and online platforms, the quality and size of alumni base, etc. The company focuses on innovation and actively invests in educational experience to improve student success rates and employability. Initiatives such as FlexPath of Capella which offer competency-based learning infrastructure and direct assessment capabilities; Strayer University's video simulation and content; Torrens University's virtual career expo are examples for improving the skill requirements of employees. The company through its long operating history offers diversified product offering, balanced revenue mix along with financial and operational synergies. The company offers diversified programs in practical areas of adult education. The student support services offered include services such as advising, writing, tutoring, research support, administrative and library services, financial aid counselling and career counselling. The company is also leveraging data and analytics to create personalized experiences for its students. The major focus is on adults pursuing career relevant degree and non-degree programs. The programs offered are flexible and basically comprehensive online program offerings. Both Strayer University and Capella University are well-established brand names in post-secondary adult education sector. Strategic Education considers diversity, equity, and inclusion as core institutional principles.

Risk Factors

Strategic Education Group faces extensive legal and regulatory requirements for higher education institutions. Failure to comply with state and federal requirements may result in significant monetary liabilities and penalties, loss of access to federal student loans and grants for students. Legislation by congress for profit post-secondary education may negatively affect the industry. The Higher Education Act is subject to periodic reauthorization. Congress determines the funding level for each Title IV program on an annual basis. Universities under Strategic Education are dependent on the renewal and maintenance of Title IV programs. In the context on non-compliance, Strayer University and Capella University will not be able to participate in Title IV programs. The loss of state authorization would limit Strayer University's ability to operate in a particular state and could have a material adverse effect on the university business. The failure by the university to comply with Department of Education's credit hour or direct assessment rules could result in sanctions and other liability. The ability of the company to grow its student enrollment depends on a number of macroeconomic factors. The addition of new locations, programs, and services based on demand estimation requires commitment of significant resources.

Stock Performance

Table 2 compares the cumulative stockholder return for the Strategic Education common stock since December 31, 2017 with the Nasdaq Stock market index and a peer group of companies such as 2 U, Adtalem Global Education, Chegg Inc., Graham Holdings, Grand Canyon Education, Laureate Education among others. Currently there are no comparative index for the education industry. The comparison assumes $100 was invested on December 31, 2017 in Strategic Education common stock, Nasdaq Composite and the peer companies. The analysis assumes reinvestment of dividends and the peer group cumulative stockholder return is weighted by market capitalization at the beginning of each year.

The 5-year holding period return for the Strategic Education stock was −1% compared to 59% and 11% return for Nasdaq Composite and Peer Group. The average yearly return for Strategic Education stock was 6.9% compared to 13.7% and 5.07% for Nasdaq Composite and Peer Group.

The following section compares the returns for Strategic Education with that of the market index Nasdaq Composite during the recent 5-year period. The Strategic Education Stock was trading at $109 on 1st May 2018. By April 1st 2023, the stock price declined to $92.9. Strategic stock had cumulative total monthly returns of 17% compared to cumulative total monthly returns of 61% for the Nasdaq stock during the 5-year period May 2018–April 2023. The average yearly return for the stock was 4% compared to the yearly return of 12% for the Nasdaq Composite index during the 5-year period May 2018–April 2023.The data was sourced from yahoo finance.

Table 3 shows the holding period return for the Strategic Education stock and Nasdaq Composite during the 5-year period 2018–2022. The holding period is assumed to be 1 year.

The stock outperformed the market index in the years 2018, 2019, and 2022.

Table 4 gives the financial highlights of Strategic Education during the period 2018–2022.

Table 2 Cumulative stock returns

Year	2017	2018	2019	2020	2021	2022
Strategic Education, Inc	$100.00	$128.00	$182.00	$112.00	$71.00	$99.00
NASDAQ composite	$100	$97.00	$133.00	$192.00	$235.00	$159.00
Peer group	$100	$116.00	$120.00	$176.00	$130.00	$111.00

Source: Annual Report 2022

Table 3 Holding period returns

Year	Strategic Education	Nasdaq Composite	Excess returns
2018	4%	−11%	15%
2019	45%	23%	22%
2020	−41%	41%	−82%
2021	−35%	20%	−54%
2022	31%	−26%	58%

Table 4 Financial highlights

	(In millions of dollars)				
Financial highlights	2018	2019	2020	2021	2022
Total assets	1661.03	1789.41	2295.81	2305.88	2161.75
Short-term investments	41,250	55,021	84,396	96,049	70,026
Total equity	43,549	62,060	93,404	138,245	146,043
Total revenue	232,887	280,522	386,064	469,822	513,983
Total operating expenses	219.73	334.08	359.46	412.84	394.17
Net income	−15.67	81.14	86.27	55.09	46.67
Market cap	2466.15	3490.21	2327.85	1422.41	1911.24
Enterprise value	2119.59	3141.48	2415.57	1478.44	1947.69

Table 5 Performance indicators

Ratios	2018	2019	2020	2021	2022
Net margin%	−2.47	8.14	8.39	4.87	4.38
ROE%	−1.92	5.62	5.37	3.18	2.79
ROA%	−1.58	4.7	4.22	2.39	2.09
DER	0.76	1.02	0.9	0.84	0.96

During the period 2018–2022, the average growth rate of total assets, short-term investments, and total equity were 7.55%, 18%, and 37%, respectively. The total revenues grew by 22% on average basis. The net income showed huge fluctuations during the period 2018–2022. The market capitalization and enterprise value grew by 1% and 5%, respectively, during the above period. The data was sourced from gurufocus.com.

Table 5 shows the performance measures of the company during the period 2018–2022.

The average net margin, ROE, and ROA during the period 2018–2022 were 4.66%, 3.01%, and 2.36%, respectively. The average debt equity ratio during the above period was 0.89.

References

1. https://www.strategiceducation.com/about/history/default.aspx
2. https://www.strategiceducation.com/investor-relations/overview/default.aspx
3. 2022 Annual Report

Case 77 Monolithic Power Systems

Monolithic Power Systems, Inc. is a global fabless company which provides semiconductor-based power electronic solutions. The company was established in the year 1997. The mission of the company is to reduce energy and material consumption. The company offers compact and monolithic solutions for storage and computing, enterprise data, automotive, industrial, communications, and consumer applications. Semiconductors comprise the basic building blocks of electronics systems and equipment. Mixed signal integrated circuits combine digital and analog functions onto a single chip. The company focuses on the analog and mixed signal IC market. The storage and computing market constituted the largest portion of the revenue for the company in the year 2022.

The company has over 3200 employees worldwide in Asia, Europe, and the United States. The company sells its products through third party distributors, value-added resellers, original equipment manufacturers (OEMs), Original Design Manufacturers (ODMs), Electronic Manufacturing Service (EMS) providers, and other end customers. The sales to its largest distributor accounted for 24% of its total revenues in the year 2022. The company has sales offices in China, India, Japan, South Korea, Singapore, Taiwan, United States, and Europe. A typical supply chain lead times for orders are generally 16 to 26 weeks. The research and development team consists of specialists with core competencies in analog and mixed signal design. The R&D initiatives are targeted in the areas of systems architecture, circuit design, and implementation and process technologies.

Product Family

The company's proprietary process technologies enable it to design and deliver smaller, single chip power management ICs. These technologies simplify the design process and have applications within storage and computing, enterprise data, automotive and consumer markets.

© The Author(s), under exclusive license to Springer Nature Switzerland AG 2024

B. R. Kumar, *Rising Stars*, Management for Professionals,
https://doi.org/10.1007/978-3-031-50032-9_77

Direct Current to DC Products

These IC products are used to convert and control voltages within a broad range of electronic systems like portable electronic devices, wireless LAN access points, computers, notebooks, monitors, infotainment applications, and medical equipment. These products are differentiated in the market in terms of degree of integration, high voltage operation, high load current, and high energy efficiency. DC to DC Products consume lower power, incur low cost, and have lower carbon emissions. The DC to DC product family accounted for 95% of total revenues during the recent 3-year period 2020–2022.

Lighting Control Products

Lighting Control ICs are used for backlighting and general illumination products. These products are used to provide light source for LCD panels in computers and notebooks, monitors, car navigation systems, and televisions. The backlighting solutions are basically white light emitting diode lighting sources or cold cathode fluorescent lamps. The lightning control products accounted for 5% of the total revenues for the company during the recent 3-year period 2020–2022.

Strategy

The company continually focuses on improving the energy efficiency of its products through its R&D initiatives. The products of the company are strategically positioned to have lower power loss and significant reductions in circuit board space. The life cycles of the products are usually over 10 years thereby reducing the manufacturing needs and associated carbon emissions related to production of replacement products. The focus of the company is on its core strengths of deep system level knowledge, strong semiconductor design expertise, innovative proprietary semiconductor process, system integration technologies that facilitate Monolithic Power System to offer highly energy-efficient and cost-effective products to customers. The company aims to introduce new innovative products, enter new market segments, and focus growth in regions outside China, Taiwan, and other Asian markets. By December 2022, the company had 1557 patents/applications issued or pending. Monolithic uses a fabless business model involving third parties to manufacture and assemble its ICs. On account of adoption of this model, the company is able to reduce its fixed costs and capital expenditures. The analog and mixed signal semiconductor industry is highly competitive. The primary competitors of the company include Analog Devices, Infineon Technologies, NXP Semiconductors, ON Semiconductor, ROHM Semiconductor, Semtech, and Texas Instruments.

Risk Factors

Monolithic derives major part of its revenues from customers located in Asia through direct sales or indirect sales through distribution arrangements and value-added reseller agreements with parties located in Asia. Hence the company is subject to significant risks due to geographic concentration of business and operations. On account of its dependence on the markets in Asia, the company faces political, cultural, regulatory, economic, foreign currency, and operational risks. Monolithic faces significant risks on account of extensive Chinese government regulations, uncertainties related to China's legal systems, changes in international trade policy with respect to tariffs on export and imports of foreign goods. The operations and performance depend significantly on global economic conditions. Adverse macroeconomic conditions can materially adversely affect logistics or demand for its products. The company also faces inherent risks associated with its manufacturing and testing facilities in China which may result in increased product costs or delay in product shipments. Monolithic is subject to export laws, trade policies, and restrictions such as international tariffs which might adversely affect the business and results of operations. The company also faces political and other risks with respect to conduct of business in Taiwan and Hong Kong due to its tense relationship with China. Fluctuations in the value of US dollar relative to other foreign currencies such as Renminbi may adversely affect the results of company operations. The revenues of the company would decrease if the demand for its products declines in the major end markets served by the company. The ability to increase product sales and revenues is constrained by the manufacturing capacity of its suppliers. The company has supply arrangements with certain suppliers for the production of wafers. In the event of suppliers becoming insolvent or capacity constrained, the company may not be able to fulfill its customer orders. The highly cyclical nature of the semiconductor industry could materially and adversely affect the financial condition and results of operations. Implementation of enhanced ERP or other IT systems could result in significant disruptions to the company's operations. The company is subject to various foreign, federal, state, and local laws and regulations related to environment protection.

ESG Initiatives

Monolithic focuses on powering innovation through clean energy. The products of Monolithic have the highest power density in the industry thereby facilitating customers to meet their energy needs. The products of Monolithic annually save 4.3 TWh of electricity which is equivalent of elimination of 3 million tons of CO2 from the atmosphere. The solutions of the company are integrated into a broad array of electronic devices and products globally which include energy-efficient and green technologies. Monolithic Power System design energy-efficient data center power solutions focus on increasing computing power without increase in energy consumption. The company offers more innovative power architecture approach using a higher voltage solution which is able to significantly reduce power distribution losses. These solutions are designed specifically to provide servers with more power in space constrained environments. The company also provides digital power solutions with more battery life, processing performance, and less power consumption. The intelligent digital power products simplify system designs, results in smaller component footprint and reduces power consumption. The portfolio of LED and WLED drivers and controllers use proprietary technology to improve energy efficiency and reduce wastes. The power saving products are used in numerous smart-home and building applications, such as HVAC systems, electric and gas meters, home remote controls, IP network cameras, as well as gas, smoke, and heat detectors. The solar power solutions offered by Monolithic Power aims to extend solar power system longevity and efficiency. The integrated solutions of the company facilitate energy savings and power density for electric vehicles. Monolithic Power has also initiated steps to partner with the suppliers to develop Scope 3 emission reduction goals.

Stock Return Analysis

Monolithic Power was trading at $131.8 on 1st May 2018. By 1st April 2023, the stock was trading at $461.97 reflecting an increase of 3.5 times in stock price. During the 5-year period May 2018–April 2023, the cumulative total monthly return for the Monolithic Power was 163% compared to the cumulative total monthly return of 62% for the Nasdaq Composite index. During the 5-year period, May 2018–April 2023, the average yearly return for the stock was 33% compared to the average yearly return of 13% for the Nasdaq Composite index. Table 1 shows the holding period return for the stock and market index Nasdaq Composite during the recent 5-year period 2018–2022. The holding period is assumed to be 1 year. The data source was yahoo finance.

The stock had outperformed the market index during the period 2019–2022. In the year 2020, the excess return for the stock was 73% over the market index Nasdaq Composite.

Table 2 compares the book and market value of equity of Monolithic Power during the period 2018–2022. The values are given in millions of dollars.

The average book value of equity as percent of market value of equity was 7.4% during the period 2018–2022.

Table 1 Holding period return

Year	Monolithic power system	Nasdaq Composite	Excess returns
2018	−12%	−11%	−1%
2019	41%	23%	17%
2020	114%	41%	73%
2021	39%	20%	19%
2022	−12%	−26%	14%

Table 2 Book and market value of equity

Year	2018	2019	2020	2021	2022
Book value of equity	640.09	773.49	966.59	1243.99	1668.6
Market value of equity	4941.21	7764.52	16578.13	22819.47	16657.51
BV as percent of MV	13.0%	15.7%	12.4%	7.5%	7.3%

Table 3 Financial highlights

	(In millions of dollars)				
Financial highlights	2018	2019	2020	2021	2022
Total assets	793.43	956.38	1208.49	1585.83	2058.89
Short-term investments	377.28	455.4	595.11	725.08	737.87
Total equity	640.09	773.49	966.59	1243.99	1668.6
Total revenue	582.38	627.92	844.45	1207.8	1794.15
Total operating expenses	207.26	241.3	299.27	416.82	513.77
Net income	105.27	108.84	164.38	242.02	437.67
Market cap	4941.21	7764.52	16578.13	22819.47	16657.51
Enterprise value	4563.93	7311.48	15983.02	22094.39	15919.63

Table 4 Profitability ratios

Ratios	2018	2019	2020	2021	2022
Net margin%	18.08	17.33	19.47	20.04	24.39
ROE%	18.12	15.4	18.89	21.9	30.05
ROA%	14.56	12.44	15.19	17.32	24.02

Table 3 gives the financial highlights of the company during the period 2018–2022. The values are given in millions of dollars. The data source is gurufocus.com and annual reports.

During the time period 2018–2022, the average growth rate of total assets, short-term investments, and total equity were approximately 27%, 19%, and 27%, respectively. The total revenues and net income grew by 33% and 46%, respectively, on average basis. The total expenses increased by 26% on average basis. The market capitalization and enterprise value increased by 45% and 47% on average basis.

Table 4 gives the performance highlights of Monolithic during the period 2018–2022.

The average net margin, ROE, and ROA during the period 2018–2022 were 19.86%, 20.87%, and 16.71%, respectively.

Table 5 shows the estimation of economic value of the company during the years 2021 and 2022. The values are given in millions of dollars.

The economic value for Monolithic Power System increased from $169.51 million in 2021 to $280.01 in year 2022.

Table 5 Economic value

Year	2021	2022
Profit before income tax	272.22	524.94
Income tax	30.18	87.24
Net operating profit after tax (NOPAT)	242.03	437.69
Stockholder equity	1243.99	1668.6
Long-term debt		
Total capital employed	1243.99	1668.6
WACC	5.83%	9.45%
Capital charge	72.52	157.68
Economic value	169.51	280.01

References

1. https://www.monolithicpower.com/
2. https://www.monolithicpower.com/en/about-mps/investor-relations/esg-report.html
3. https://www.monolithicpower.com/about-mps/investor-relations.html

Case 78 Waterstone Financial

Waterstone Financial, Inc. is the holding company of WaterStone Bank SSB and its subsidiaries. WaterStone Bank is a community bank which was established in the year 1921. WaterStone Bank also has an active mortgage banking subsidiary, Waterstone Mortgage Corporation, with 78 offices in 26 states in the United States. The major lending activity of WaterStone Bank involves origination of one to four family, multifamily residential, and commercial real estate loans. WaterStone Bank also offers home equity loans and lines of credit, construction and land loans, commercial business loans, and consumer loans. The sources of funds for WaterStone Bank are primarily retail deposits and home loan bank advances. The deposit offerings consist of certificates of deposits, money market savings accounts, transaction deposit accounts, non-interest-bearing demand accounts, and individual retirement accounts. The investment securities portfolio of Waterstone Financial consists of mortgage-backed securities, collateralized mortgage obligations, government-sponsored enterprise bonds, private label enterprise bonds, and other debt securities. Waterstone Mortgage Corporation originates single-family residential real estate loans for sale into the secondary market.

Waterstone Financial has one wholly owned subsidiary, WaterStone Bank, which in turn has three wholly owned subsidiaries, Wauwatosa Investments Inc., Waterstone Mortgage Corporation, and Main Street Real Estate Holdings LLC. WaterStone Bank's primary market area for deposits also includes communities in which the bank maintains banking office locations. By December 2022, the bank had 742 full-time employees.

© The Author(s), under exclusive license to Springer Nature Switzerland AG 2024

B. R. Kumar, *Rising Stars*, Management for Professionals,
https://doi.org/10.1007/978-3-031-50032-9_78

Lending Activities

One to Four Family Residential Mortgage Loans

In 2022, one to four family residential mortgage loans accounted for 31% of total loans. The one to four family residential mortgage loans have fixed or adjustable rates. The single-family adjustable rate mortgage loans have maximum annual rate adjustments of 200 basis points with a lifetime maximum adjustment of 600 basis points. The adjustable rate mortgage loans are typically amortized over terms of up to 30 years and are indexed to either the 12-month SOFR rate or the 12-month LIBOR. Single-family adjustable rate mortgage loans are originated at community and mortgage banking segment.

Multifamily Real Estate Loans

Multifamily loans accounted for approximately 45% of the total loans by the year 2022. Multifamily real estate loans are offered in amounts up to 80% of the appraised value of the property such that the loans comply with the bank's current loans to one borrower limit. The multifamily real estate loans are offered with interest rates which are fixed for periods of up to 5 years or are variable and either adjusted based on market index. The principal and interest payments are typically based on a 30-year amortization period.

Home Equity Loans and Lines of Credit

Waterstone offers home equity loans and home equity lines of credit which are secured by owner-occupied and non-owner-occupied one to four family residences. The underwriting standards for home equity loans and home equity lines of credit include determination of the applicant's credit history, assessment of applicant's ability to meet existing obligations, payments on the proposed loan, and value of collateral securing the loan. The loan-to-value ratio for home equity loans and lines of credit is limited to 90% when combined with the first security lien if applicable. The interest rates on home equity lines of credit are basically limited to a maximum rate of 18%. The home equity lines of credit have 10-year terms and adjustable rates of interest which are indexed to the prime rate as reported in the Wall Street Journal.

Construction and Land Loans

Waterstone Financial originates construction loans for the acquisition of land and construction of single-family residences, multifamily residences, and commercial real estate buildings. The construction mortgage loans generally provide for the payment of interest only during the construction phase which is typically up to

9 months for family residences. At the end of the construction phase, the construction loan converts to a longer-term mortgage loan upon stabilization. The company requires an appraisal of the property by an independent licensed appraiser. Properties are reviewed and inspected before disbursement of funds during the term of the construction loan. Loan proceeds are disbursed after inspection based on either the percentage of completion method or the actual cost of the completed work. Construction financing has a higher degree of credit risk than longer-term financing on owner-occupied real estate.

Commercial Real Estate Loans

Commercial real estate loans constitute approximately 17% of total loans and consist of loans secured by office and retail buildings, retail properties, and mixed-use properties. Commercial real estate loans are made to corporations, partnerships, and other business entities. The commercial real estate loans are made in amounts of 80% of the appraised value of the property. The commercial real estate borrower's financial information is monitored on an ongoing basis with respect to periodic financial statement updates, payment history reviews, etc.

Commercial Loans

Commercial loans constituted 1.7% of total loans by December 2022. The loans are secured by accounts receivables, inventory, equipment, and real estate. The commercial loans are made to borrowers located in the bank's primary market area. Working capital lines of credit are granted for maintaining inventory and accounts receivables or purchasing equipment. Personal property loans secured by equipment are treated as commercial business loans. The interest rates on equipment loans might be either fixed or variable. Commercial business loans are generally variable rate loans with initial fixed rate periods of up to 5 years. Nonperforming assets consist of nonaccrual loans and other real estate owned which are placed on nonaccrual status when contractually past due 90 days or more as to interest or principal payments.

Mortgage Banking Activity

Waterstone originates from single-family residential mortgage loans for sale in the secondary market through Waterstone Mortgage Corporation. Waterstone sells loans on both servicing released and servicing retained basis. The mortgage bank purchases mortgage-backed securities and collateralized mortgage obligations guaranteed by Fannie Mae, Freddie Mac, and Ginnie Mae. Waterstone also invests in mortgage-backed securities, collateralized mortgage obligations, and private-label mortgage-backed securities.

Investment Activities

WaterStone Bank's investment subsidiary, Wauwatosa Investments, Inc., manages the back-office function for WaterStone Bank's investment portfolio. The government-sponsored enterprise bond portfolio was issued by the Federal National Mortgage Association. The municipal securities consist of obligations which are issued by school districts, counties, municipalities, and agencies and includes general obligation bonds, industrial development revenue bonds, etc.

Sources of Funds

Deposits were the primary source of funds for lending and investment activities. The company relies on advances from the Federal Home Loan Bank of Chicago and borrowings from other commercial banks which are in the form of repurchase agreements collateralized by investment securities. The bank also derives funds from scheduled loan payments, investment maturities, loan repayments, retained earnings, and income on earning assets. The bank also offers deposit instruments which include checking, savings, money market deposit accounts, and fixed-term certificates of deposits.

Risk Factors

Waterstone Financial operates in a highly regulated environment and is subject to enforcement action by banking regulatory agencies such as WDFI, the Federal Deposit Insurance Corporation, and Federal Reserve Board. Hence, the bank is constrained in the manner by which business is conducted. The monetary policies and regulations of the Federal Reserve Board could adversely affect the financial condition and results of operations. The bank is also subject to the Community Reinvestment Act and fair lending laws and failure to comply with the laws could lead to material penalties. The earnings and cash flows are dependent on net interest income and income from mortgage banking operations. Changes in interest rates could have an adverse effect on financial condition and results of operations. Changes in economic conditions could adversely affect the earnings. The bank focusses on origination of commercial businesses, commercial real estate, and multifamily residential real estate loans. These types of loans generally have a higher risk of loss compared to one to four family residential real estate loans. These loans also have greater credit risk than residential real estate loans as repayment is generally dependent on the successful operation of the borrower's business. The allowance for credit losses may be insufficient to absorb lifetime losses in the loan portfolio which may adversely affect the business, financial condition, and results of operations. WaterStone Bank is also subject to environmental liability risk associated with lending activities as a substantial portion of the loan portfolio is secured by real estate. The foreclosure process may adversely impact the recoveries on nonperforming loan. The reliance on certificates of deposits has resulted in higher cost of funds. The risks associated with system failures, interruptions, or breaches of cybersecurity could adversely affect the earnings of the bank. The secondary mortgage market conditions could have a material impact on the financial condition and results of operations.

ESG Initiatives

WaterStone Bank continues to undertake different initiatives as a result of its ESG commitment. WaterStone Bank employees had volunteered over 600 h for community organizations in the year 2022. The bank employees held leadership roles with over 50 community organizations. The WaterStone Bank Foundation awarded more than $650,000 in grants to more than 240 community organizations during the year 2022. WaterStone Bank focusses on a low-carbon business model. The bank has installed energy-efficient lighting and appliances in its premises. The bank adopts technology to reduce carbon footprint such as providing direct and remote deposit capabilities and promote e-statement enrollment to decrease paper and ink use.

Stock Performance

The following section analyzes the cumulative total shareholder return on Waterstone Financial with the cumulative total return of companies listed on the SNL Thrift Nasdaq Index and Russell 2000. The analysis assumes investment of $100 on December 31, 2017, in the Waterstone Financial, Inc. common stock and the two indices along with reinvestment of cash dividends (Table 1).

The 5-year holding period return for Waterstone Financial, Inc. was 40% compared to 6% and 22% return for S&P Composite 1500 Thrifts & Mortgage Finance Index and Russell 2000 Index, respectively. The yearly average 5-year returns for Waterstone Financial were approximately 8% compared to 3.52% and 5.77% for S&P Mortgage Finance Index and Russell 2000 Index, respectively.

In the next section, the Waterstone stock's returns are compared with the returns of the market index Russell 2000 during the 5-year period May 2018 to April 2023. The total monthly cumulative returns for Waterstone stock was −13% compared to

Table 1 Comparative return analysis

Year	2017	2018	2019	2020	2021	2022
Waterstone Financial, Inc.	$100.00	$104.01	$125.22	$134.29	$166.41	$140.19
S&P Composite 1500 Thrifts & Mortgage Finance Index	$100	$81.15	$110.27	$104.12	$128.42	$106.34
Russell 2000 Index	$100	$88.99	$111.70	$134.00	$153.85	$122.41

Source Annual Report 2022

Table 2 Holding period return

Year	Waterstone financials	Russell 2000	Excess returns
2018	−2%	−18%	16%
2019	13%	6%	7%
2020	13%	34%	−21%
2021	13%	2%	10%
2022	−12%	−14%	2%

Table 3 Book and market value of equity

Year	2018	2019	2020	2021	2022
Book value of equity	399.68	393.69	413.12	432.77	370.49
Market value of equity	477.04	516.63	472.16	542.02	382.28
BV as percent of MV	83.8%	82.5%	80.0%	91.7%	68.4%

Table 4 Financial highlights

	(In millions of dollars)				
Financial highlights	2018	2019	2020	2021	2022
Total assets	1915.38	1996.35	2184.59	2215.86	2031.67
Gross loans	1520.76	1608.15	1777.14	1518.52	1641.37
Deposits	1038.5	1067.78	1184.87	1233.39	1199.01
Total equity	399.68	393.69	413.12	432.77	370.49
Interest income	73.7	79.74	78.48	69.88	70.25
Interest expense	19.52	27.54	24.98	14.37	13.29
Total noninterest expense	26.27	26.02	35.68	27.34	28.78
Market capitalization	477.04	516.63	472.16	542.02	382.28
Enterprise value	846.04	925.04	895.24	654.28	732.02

the total monthly cumulative returns of 20% accounted by the market index Russell 2000 during the period June 2018 to May 2023. The average yearly return for the stock was −3% compared to 4% returns of the market index. The data for analysis was sourced from Yahoo Finance.

Table 2 shows the holding period return for the Waterstone stock and market index Russell 2000 during the period 2018–2022. The holding period is assumed to be 1-year period.

The stock outperformed the market index in all years except in year 2020.

Table 3 shows the book value and market value of equity of Waterstone during the period 2018–2022. The values are given in millions of dollars.

The average book value as percent of market value of equity was approximately 80%.

Table 4 gives the financial highlights of Waterstone during the period 2018–2022.

Table 5 Performance ratio

Performance ratios	2018	2019	2020	2021	2022
Return on average assets %	1.65	1.84	3.88	3.22	0.92
Return on average equity%	7.58	9.05	20.12	16.74	4.85
Net interest margin%	3.22	2.98	2.87	3.06	3.23

The data source was annual reports and gurufocus.com. During the above period, the average growth rate in total assets, gross loans, and deposits were 2%, 2%, and 4%, respectively.

Table 5 displays the performance ratios of Waterstone during the 5-year period 2018–2022.

The return on average assets, return on average equity, and net interest margin were 2.30%, 11.67%, and 3.07%, respectively, during the period 2018–2022. Waterstone Financials' Capital Adequacy Tier leverage ratio for the year end 2021 and 2022 were 19.45% and 19.29%, respectively. Waterstone Financial's capital adequacy Tier 1 ratio for year end 2021 and 2022 were, 27.99% and 23.29%, respectively. Waterstone Financial's capital adequacy tier–total capital ratio was 29.01% and 24.36% during 2021 and 2022, respectively.

References

1. https://www.wsbonline.com/
2. Annual Report 2022

Case 79 Willi-Food International Ltd.

Willi-Food International Ltd. (Willi-Food) was incorporated in Israel in year 1994 and is a public company which is traded on the Nasdaq and Tel Aviv Stock Exchange. Willi-Food is one of the fastest-growing companies in the Israeli food and beverage market. The company specializes in high-quality kosher food products. It is one of the largest import companies in Israel. The company focusses on export, import, marketing, and distribution of more than 600 dry, chilled, and frozen food products from 30 categories which are distributed to 5000 points of sale in the retail and professional markets across Israel and Palestinian Authority. In 2018, Willi-Food established a new subsidiary, Euro Dairies. The new subsidiary imports superior-quality dairy products such as specialty cheese, semihard cheese, feta cheese, and yogurts from leading manufacturers in Europe. The company basically imports its products and produces private labels for the leading grocery retailers in Israel and importers throughout the world. These products are then distributed and marketed in the local markets. The products distributed by the company are kosher and are produced under the supervision of different kashrut institutions in Israel and abroad which included "Badatz." In 2022, 99% of the revenues were generated in Israel. The company purchases food products from over 150 suppliers in Israel and other regions which include the Far East, Eastern Europe, South America, United States, Canada, and Southern Europe. The products of the company are marketed and sold to approximately 1500 customers and 3000 selling points in Israel. Most of the products are sold under the brand name "Willi-Food" and certain chilled and frozen products are sold under the brand name "Euro European Dairies." The food market in Israel is very price sensitive and the company faces direct competition from local manufacturers and importers of food products.

The advanced logistics center of the company has a built area of 12,000 square meters for the storage and distribution activity of the company. Willi-Food has 300 employees and subcontractors.

© The Author(s), under exclusive license to Springer Nature Switzerland AG 2024

B. R. Kumar, *Rising Stars*, Management for Professionals,
https://doi.org/10.1007/978-3-031-50032-9_79

Principal Products

The principal products in the import segment consist of canned vegetables and pickles. These include mushrooms, artichoke, beans, asparagus, vine leaves, sour and mixed pickles, vegetables, an assortment of olives, garlic, roasted eggplant, and dried tomatoes. These products are basically imported from China, Greece, Thailand, Turkey, India, and Netherlands. Canned fish include tuna, sardines, anchovies, and salmon. The canned fruit includes pineapple, peaches, apricots, pears, mangoes, cherries, litchis, and fruit cocktail. Edible oils include olive oil, sunflower oil, soybean oil, and rapeseed oil. The dairy and dairy substitute products include hard and semihard cheeses, whipped cream, yogurt, frozen pizza, etc. The products also include dried fruits, nuts, and beans. The other products include instant noodle soup, frozen edamame, soybeans, bagels, breakfast cereals, etc. Dairy and dairy substitute products generated the largest sales volume followed by canned vegetables, cereals, pastas, etc. The products imported and marketed by the company are approved as kosher by the supervisory institutions.

Business Strategy

The company focusses on the promotion of the Willi-Food brand and other brands of the company. The strategy is to increase market penetration through various marketing initiatives and advertising campaigns. The company also aims to expand the current food product lines and diversify into new product lines. The company also focusses on expansion of refrigerated and frozen space through expansion of its refrigerated and frozen logistic center. The company focusses on the development and distribution of additional food products. The company has plans to expand into international food markets of the United States and Europe through acquiring food distribution companies and enhancing collaborations with local distributors and exporting products directly to customers.

Risk Factors

The company depends on a small number of principal clients who have bought products in large quantity though the total number of clients are approximately 1500. The company does not have long-term purchase contracts with the clients. The loss of the clients may adversely affect the business results of the company. The results of the operations may be impacted by monetary risk. The portfolio of marketable securities is subject to various market risks. The company works with a limited number of key suppliers. In the event of suppliers raising prices or terminating the arrangements, the business operations would be affected. The food distribution business in Israel is highly competitive and the company faces competition from existing competitors for imported and locally manufactured food products. The cost of food commodities and other food products is cyclical. Increases or decreases in global product prices may have a material adverse effect on the company's profitability. The results of operations of the company would be adversely affected if the company could not predict the rate of consumption of its products. Consumer preferences change from time to time and failure to respond to these changes could result in reduced demand for these products. The company may be subject to product liability claims for misbranded, adulterated, contaminated, or spoiled food product. The products offered by the company may be subjected to cases of product liability claims and product recalls. The international operations may be adversely affected by risks related to international business.

Stock Performance

The stock price returns of Willi-Food are compared with that of the returns of the market index Nasdaq Composite during the 5-year period June 2018 to May 2023. The Willi stock which was trading at $7.15 on June 1, 2018, increased by 1.87 times to trade at $13.38 by May 1, 2023. The total cumulative monthly returns for the Willi-Food stock were 85% compared to the total cumulative monthly returns of 61% for the market index Nasdaq Composite during the period June 2018 to May 2023. The average yearly return for Willi-Food stock was 17% compared to yearly returns of 12% for the market index during the above period. The data for analysis was collected from Yahoo Finance.

Table 1 displays the holding period return for the stock and market index for the recent 5-year period. The holding period is assumed to be 1 year.

Willi-Food stock outperformed the market index in the year 2019 and 2020.

Table 2 shows the book value and market value of equity of the company during the 5-year period 2018–2022. The values are given in millions of dollars.

The average book value as percent of market value of Willi-Food was approximately 55.4% during the period 2018–2022.

Table 1 Holding period return

Year	Willi-Food	Nasdaq Composite	Excess returns
2018	−2%	−12%	9%
2019	48%	23%	25%
2020	50%	41%	9%
2021	−13%	20%	−33%
2022	−22%	−26%	5%

Table 2 Book and market value of equity

Year	2018	2019	2020	2021	2022
Book value of equity	120.86	134.7	160.58	156.6	153.37
Market value of equity	92.55	157.94	296.89	263.89	182.49
BV as percent of MV	130.6%	145.5%	101.7%	52.7%	58.1%

Table 3 Financial highlights

	(In millions of dollars)				
Financial highlights	2018	2019	2020	2021	2022
Total assets	127.86	147.28	172.69	172.18	166.8
Short-term investments	74.62	72.21	97.74	95.9	73.3
Total equity	120.86	134.7	160.58	156.6	153.37
Total revenue	92.73	108.46	124.49	124.52	136.61
Total operating expenses	16.59	20.99	24.1	24.45	26.93
Net income	6.84	14.12	14.31	12.36	11.39
Market cap	92.55	157.94	296.89	263.89	182.49
Enterprise value	17.94	86.8	199.97	169.14	110.15

Table 4 Performance indicators

Ratios	2018	2019	2020	2021	2022
Net margin%	7.38	13.02	11.5	9.93	8.34
ROE%	5.83	11.05	9.69	7.8	7.35
ROA%	5.53	10.26	8.95	7.17	6.72
DER	0.01	0.01	0.01	0.01	0.01

Table 3 shows the financial highlights of the company during the period 2018–2022. The source of data is from GuruFocus and annual reports.

The total assets and total equity increased by approximately 7% on an average basis during the 2018–2022 period. The short-term investments increased by 2% during the above period. The total revenues and net income increased by 10% and 22%, respectively. The operating expenses increased by 13% on an average basis. The market capitalization and enterprise value increased by 29% and 116%, respectively, on an average basis during the above period.

Table 4 shows the performance ratios and leverage ratio of the company during 2018–2022 period.

The average net margin, ROE, and ROA during the period 2018–2022 were 10.03%, 8.34%, and 7.73%, respectively. The average debt equity ratio for the company was 0.01.

Table 5 illustrates the estimation of economic value of the company in the year 2021 and 2022. The values are given in millions of dollars.

Table 5 Economic value

Year	2021	2022
Profit before income tax	15.85	14.8
Income tax	3.487	3.40252
Net operating profit after tax (NOPAT)	12.36	11.40
Stockholder equity	156.6	153.37
Long-term debt		
Total capital employed	156.6	153.37
WACC	6.02%	6.03%
Capital charge	9.43	9.25
Economic value	2.94	2.15

References

1. https://www.willi-food.com/about/
2. Annual Report 2021

Case 80 KLA

KLA is a global technology leader which provides leading-edge technology and devices using advanced inspection tools, metrology systems, and computational analytics. The company provides advanced process control and process-enabling solutions for manufacturing wafers and reticles, integrated circuits, packaging, printed circuit boards, and flat-panel displays. KLA was established as KLA-Tencor in April 1997 through the merger of KLA Instruments Corporation and Tencor Instruments. In 2019, KLA acquired Orbotech Ltd., a global supplier of yield-enhancing and process-enabling solutions for the manufacture of electronic products.

The company has spent $3.9 billion in research and development during the past 4 years. As of Jan 2023, the company has employed 14,000 people globally. The revenues in the fiscal year 2022 amounted to $10.5 billion. In year 2022, the company invested 15% of its sales back into research and development which exceeded industry standards. The products and services offered by KLA are used by bare wafer, IC, lithography reticle, and disk manufacturers around the world.

Segments

Semiconductor Process Control

In this segment KLA offers a comprehensive portfolio of inspection, metrology, software products, and related services. These products and services facilitate IC, wafer, reticle, and chemical manufacturers to achieve target yields throughout the entire fabrication process.

© The Author(s), under exclusive license to Springer Nature Switzerland AG 2024

B. R. Kumar, *Rising Stars*, Management for Professionals,
https://doi.org/10.1007/978-3-031-50032-9_80

Speciality Semiconductor Process

The products under this segment include advanced vacuum deposition and etching process tools used by manufacturers of microelectromechanical systems, communication, and power semiconductors for automotive and industrial applications.

PCB, Display, and Component Inspection

The products offered include direct imaging, inspection, optical shaping, additive printing, and computer-aided manufacturing and engineering solutions for the PCB market. Display products include inspection and electrical testing systems to identify and classify defects. The inspection and metrology systems are used for quality control and yield improvement in advanced and traditional semiconductor packaging markets.

Strategy for Growth

Technology enables secular demand drivers such as high-performance computing, artificial intelligence, machine learning, and rapid growth in new automotive electronics and 5G communication markets. KLA focusses on these secular trends to achieve market leadership through innovation drivers. These secular trends are instrumental in driving investments and innovation in advanced memory and logic semiconductor devices, complex advanced packaging, and printed circuit board technologies. KLA focusses on investment to drive innovation and create next-generation technologies. The KLA operating model signifying corporate values, strategic thinking, key performance metrics, and operating principles serves as a framework for the execution of long-term strategic objectives. Multiple growth drivers are facilitating the growth of the semiconductor capital equipment industry through the advent of computational power and connectivity for markets such as artificial intelligence and 5G wireless technology. The competitors for the company include firms such as Applied Materials, Inc., ASML Holding N.V., Hitachi High-Technologies Corporation, Onto Innovation, Inc., and Laserte.

Risk Factors

KLA faces commercial, operational, financial, and regulatory risks. The risks related to international operations in terms of tariffs, trade impairments, and longer payment cycles affect the profitability of the company. Intellectual property disputes could affect the company adversely. Trade issues and uncertainty with respect to trade policies such as the ability to obtain import and export licenses and trade sanctions are significant risk factors. KLA is exposed to the risks related to conditions in the financial markets and global economy. The demand for the products is ultimately driven by the global demand for electronic devices by consumers and businesses. KLA is also exposed to different risks related to legal, regulatory, and tax environments. Disruptions or delays on account of third-party service providers could adversely impact the operations of the company. KLA is also exposed to risks related to cybersecurity threats and cyber incidents. The company is also exposed to foreign currency exchange rate fluctuations. The company faces a number of risks specific to ongoing changes in the semiconductor industry. The company is also exposed to risks associated with highly concentrated customer base.

ESG Initiatives

The company develops innovative industry leading equipment and services for the electronic industry. KLA is a part of some of the biggest technological breakthroughs in the electronic industry. The company through collaboration with expert teams powers ecofriendly technologies which are essential for achievement of low-carbon economy. The comprehensive portfolio of software, inspection, and metrology products and other offerings by the company facilitates integrated circuit manufacturers to improve yield and efficiency related to the semiconductor fabrication process. The ESG strategy of KLA focuses on the four pillars of advancing leadership, advancing opportunity, advancing innovation, and advancing stewardship. In the year 2019, KLA conducted its first ESG materiality assessment to identify and prioritize its ESG activities. In the year 2020 and 2021, the company partnered with third-party consultants to build its assessment on ESG reporting based on Global Reporting Initiative standards. In 2021, the company initiated the first enterprise-wide greenhouse gas (GHG) inventory (scope 1, 2, 3). The company offers a comprehensive 2-year Enterprise Leadership Program to help KLA employees to fill future leadership roles. In the year 2021, 211 leaders completed the program. Through the Values in Action training program, 1152 employees were trained. In year 2021, KLA commissioned a multiregional research study to understand the inspirations and barriers which engineers face in their careers. About 27% of KLA Board of Directors are female. The KLA foundation has distributed 115 grants in 12 countries valued at $3.9 million. In 2021, KLA spends $5.5 million as part of total community giving. Under employee giving, the company has distributed matching gifts worth $1.6 million to 151 organizations. In 2021, the KLA Foundation had aligned its programs and activities with six UN Sustainable Development Goals related to community engagement. In 2020, the KLA Foundation established the KLA Social Equity Fund, a 3-year program in partnership with the American Heart Association. KLA Foundation's STEM Inspectors program which was created in partnership with Santa Clara Unified School District has engaged more than 1500 students. The company has plans to globalize its ISO 45001 (Occupational Health and Safety Management Systems) and expand its ISO 14001 (Environmental Management Systems) certifications. As global leader in diversified electronics for the semiconductor manufacturing ecosystem, KLA focusses on sustainable product innovation. In year 2021, KLA introduced four new products for enhancing high yield, reliability, and performance of the chips which power the most advanced automotive electronics. KLA is involved in delivering solutions for SiC and gallium nitride (GaN) power device market for promoting green technologies. KLA introduced the new Voyager® 1035 laser scanning patterned wafer inspector for less waste and high yield. KLA evaluates new and existing suppliers through a rigorous qualification process for a sustainable, responsible supply chain process. Every year, the company assesses key direct suppliers using the RBA Facility Supplier Assessment Questionnaire which provides an overall risk score for evaluation. The company aims to have 100% renewable electricity for its global operations by the year 2030. In 2021, approximately 52% of its electricity was sourced from renewable energy sources. In 2021, KLA conducted its first in-depth climate risk and opportunity assessment which included potential physical and transition risks and opportunities across global enterprise and value chain. In 2022, KLA had created a $1.5 billion, 5-year sustainability-linked revolving facility as a part of its green finance initiatives. In 2021 through KLA's whistleblower and investigation programs, the company conducted around 60 investigations which resulted in 9 terminations and implementation of other remedial actions. KLA's anti-bribery and corruption policies are published in multiple languages in its internal platforms and public websites.

In August 2022, KLA published a new Global Impact Report and had announced new climate targets for achieving 50% reductions in scope 1 and 2 emissions by 2030 and net zero scope 1 and 2 emissions by 2050.

Stock Performance

In the next section, the cumulative 5-year total return of KLA is compared with that of the cumulative total returns of the S&P 500 Index and the Philadelphia Semiconductor Index. The analysis tracks the performance of $100 investment in KLA stock and the indices from June 30, 2017, to June 30, 2022.

Table 1 compares the cumulative returns for the stock and indices.

During the 5-year period, the holding period return for KLA stock was 285% compared to the returns of 71% and 168% for the S&P 500 and PHLX Semiconductor Index, respectively. The average yearly returns for the KLA stock was approximately 34% compared to the returns of 12.5% and 25.79% for the S&P 500 Index and PHLX Semiconductor Index, respectively.

Table 1 Cumulative returns

Year	2017	2018	2019	2020	2021	2022
KLA Corporation	$100.00	114.81	136.14	228.66	$386.46	$384.82
S&P 500	$100.00	$114.37	$126.29	$135.77	$191.15	$170.86
PHLX Semiconductor	$100.00	$129.11	$146.29	$203.84	$346.16	$267.91

Source: Annual Report

Table 2 Holding period return

Year	KLA	Nasdaq Composite	Excess returns
2018	−13%	−12%	−1%
2019	67%	23%	44%
2020	82%	41%	41%
2021	25%	20%	5%
2022	13%	−26%	39%

Table 3 Book and market value of equity

Year	2018	2019	2020	2021	2022
Book value of equity	1387.16	2369.76	2380.74	2801.78	1323.54
Market value of equity	5098.09	5210.05	26136.1	41585.63	43583.46
BV as percent of MV	27.2%	46.5%	45.7%	10.7%	3.2%

Table 4 Financial highlights

	(In millions of dollars)				
Financial highlights	2018	2019	2020	2021	2022
Total assets	4826.66	7972.54	8240.6	8525.03	11916.85
Short-term investments	2465.55	1539.36	1758.66	2070.45	2561.78
Total equity	1387.16	2369.76	2380.74	2801.78	1323.54
Total revenue	2465.55	1539.36	1758.66	2070.45	2561.78
Total operating expenses	899.52	1159.49	1419.04	1376.21	1859.14
Net income	686.74	1040.42	1080.51	1724.98	3142.43
Market cap	5098.09	5210.05	26136.1	41585.63	43583.46
Enterprise value	4547.75	6716.83	27561.04	42456.62	47428.04

The following analysis compares the stock returns of KLA with that of the market index Nasdaq Composite during the recent 5-year period. The KLA stock which was trading at $102.52 on June 1, 2018, increased by 3.77 times to trade at $386.54 by May 1, 2023. The cumulative total monthly return for the KLA stock was 162% compared to the cumulative total monthly return of 61% for the market index Nasdaq Composite during the recent 5-year period June 2018 to May 2023. The yearly average return for the KLA stock was 33% compared to the yearly average return of 12% for the market index Nasdaq Composite. The data source is Yahoo Finance.

Table 2 shows the holding period return for KLA and market index during 2018–2022. The holding period is assumed to be 1 year.

The KLA stock outperformed the market index with positive excess returns in all years except 2018.

Table 3 shows the book value and market value of equity of the company KLA during the period 2018–2022. The values are given in millions of dollars.

The average book value as percent of market value of equity was 7% during the period 2018–2022.

Table 4 shows the financial highlights of KLA during the period 2018–2022.

Table 5 Performance indicators

Ratios	2018	2019	2020	2021	2022
Net margin%	19.87	25.73	20.96	30.04	36.06
ROE%	53.49	55.63	45.78	66.73	152.21
ROA%	14.09	16.26	13.33	20.58	30.75

Table 6 Estimation of economic value

Year	2021	2022
Profit before income tax	1959.18	3300.82
Income tax	11.99%	4.99%
Net operating profit after tax (NOPAT)	1959.06	3300.77
Stockholder equity	2801.78	1323.54
Long-term debt	2840.9	6301.04
Total capital employed	5642.68	7624.58
WACC	8.70%	9.30%
Capital charge	490.91	709.09
Economic value	1468.15	2591.68

The total assets, cash investments, and equity grew by 28%, 5%, and 9%, respectively, during the period 2018–2022 on an average basis. The total revenues and net income increased by 5% and 49%, respectively, on an average basis during the above period. The total expenses increased by 21%. The market capitalization and enterprise value increased by 117% and 106%, respectively, on an average basis during the period 2018–2022.

Table 5 shows the profitability ratios of the company during the period 2018–2022.

The average net margin, ROE, and ROA were 26.53%, 74.76%, and 19%, respectively, during the period 2018–2022.

Table 6 shows the estimation of the economic value of KLA during the year 2021 and 2022. The values are given in millions of dollars.

The economic value of KLA increased from $1468.15 million in 2021 to $2591.68 million in 2022.

References

1. https://www.kla.com/
2. https://ir.kla.com/financial-information/annual-reports
3. https://www.kla-tencor.com/wp-content/uploads/KLA_2021_Global_Impact_Report.pdf

Case 81 Lululemon Athletica

Lululemon Athletica is a designer, distributor, and retailer of technical athletic apparel, footwear, and accessories. The company aims to create transformative products and experiences which offer meaningful connections. The company offers a comprehensive portfolio of products consisting of performance apparel, footwear, and accessories which are marketed under the lululemon brand. The apparel assortment portfolio offers pants, shorts, tops, and jackets which are basically designed for athletic activities such as yoga, training, and sport activities. The company also offers apparels which are designed as fitness-inspired accessories. The design and development team sources technically advanced fabrics with innovative functional features. As a part of its vertical retail strategy, the company incorporates unique performance and fashion needs into its design process. The company offers in-home connected fitness and associated content subscriptions through lululemon Studio.

The women's range accounted for the largest customer group in 2022 which represented 65% of the company's net revenues. North America was the largest market accounting for 84% of net revenues in the year 2022. The business operations are conducted through the two channels of company-operated stores and direct to consumer. Lululemon also operates outlets, serves wholesale accounts, has license and supply arrangements, and sells repurchased products through the "Like New" recommerce program. The company is also involved in selling connected hardware and associated subscriptions through lululemon Studio. By end 2022, the company operated 655 stores in 18 countries across the globe. The retail stores of the company are located on street locations, on lifestyle centers, and in malls. These retail stores are operated by third parties under license and supply arrangements. The direct to consumer channel is effective in building brand awareness in new markets. The company serves its clients through the e-commerce website, www.lululemon.com, regional websites, and mobile apps. The company utilizes outlets to sell moving inventory and inventory from prior seasons at discounted prices. The company sells to premium wholesale locations that offer an alternative distribution channel. The company offers in-home fitness through an interactive workout platform which enables customers to subscribe for live and on-demand classes. The company has

© The Author(s), under exclusive license to Springer Nature Switzerland AG 2024

B. R. Kumar, *Rising Stars*, Management for Professionals,
https://doi.org/10.1007/978-3-031-50032-9_81

employed 34,000 people by year end 2022. Eighty-one new stores were opened in the year 2022. Approximately 91% of the directors are independent and 55% of the directors are female.

Strategy

The renewed focus on the growth strategy is based on the 5-year growth plan – the power of three*2 which leverages the power of three themes of success formula: product innovation, guest experience, and market expansion. Through this strategic focus, the company aims to double its men's business and digital business by the year 2026. The vertical omni operating model focusses on strengthening its guest relationship. The company brought new technical innovations into its merchandise assortment with the launch of Sense Knit, a proprietary fabric technology which offers zoned compression. The company has also made entry into new categories such as play activities with capsule collections for golf, tennis, and hiking. As a part of product innovation, the company launched its inaugural footwear collection made for women. The company's core strength lies in its ability to harness guest relationships through educators and ambassadors. The company launched two-tier membership program which included an Essentials free tier and lululemon Studio premium tier. The company opened 81 net new company-operated stores in the year 2022.

The company focusses on expansion internationally in China, Asia Pacific, and Europe. The expansion strategy in these regions is based on a decentralized model. The company focusses on evolving and integrating its digital and physical channels to provide enhanced omni-channel experience for its clients. The company has license and supply arrangement with partners in the Middle East and Mexico to operate lululemon-branded retail locations in the UAE, Kuwait, Qatar, Oman, Bahrain, Saudi Arabia, and Mexico. Through these arrangements, the company supplies the partners with lululemon products, training, etc. The recommerce program is the sale of repurchased product through the company's "Like New" program. This program facilitates clients to involve in the exchange of gently used lululemon products for credit. After verification and quality check, these products are resold online at likenew.lululemon.com. This program contributes towards the environmental goals of the company. The company has a multifaceted marketing integration strategy to build brand awareness, affinity, and guest loyalty. This strategy leverages owned and paid channels, ambassador network, and brand partners for client engagement. The product design and development team identifies trends based on market intelligence and research. The company has engaged 60 suppliers to provide fabrics for its products.

Competition

The athletic apparel market is highly competitive. The company competes with wholesalers and direct sellers of athletic apparel and footwear such as Nike Inc., Adidas AG, PUMA, Under Armour, Inc., and Columbia Sportswear Company. The retail competitors include the Gap, Inc., Victoria's Secret, and Outfitters Inc.

Risk Factors

The success of the company depends on its ability to maintain the value and reputation of the lululemon brand. Changes in consumer shopping preferences and shifts in distribution channels could materially impact the results of the operations of the company. The diversion of sales from company-operated stores could adversely impact the return on investment and could lead to impairment charges and store closures. The lululemon Studio subsidiary offers complex hardware and software products and services which are affected by design and manufacturing defect. The technical athletic apparel market is highly competitive. Competition may result in pricing pressures, reduced profit margins, or lost market share. The business is subject to significant pressure on costs and pricing attributable to intense competition, constrained sourcing capacity, and related inflationary pressures. The success of the business of the company depends on its ability to identify and originate product trends and expectations to changing consumer demands. The business success depends on the ability of the new company to introduce new products or novel technologies in a timely manner. The future growth of the company depends on its expansion efforts outside of North America. The company is subject to risks associated with leasing retail and distribution space which are subject to long-term and noncancelable leases. The company leases majority of its stores under operating leases and the inability of the company to secure suitable real estate or lease terms could impact its ability to grow. Disruptions of the supply chain system and reliance on international suppliers could have a material adverse effect on the operations and financial results of the company. Lululemon relies on suppliers and manufacturers in the predominantly Asian region for sourcing of raw materials. The failure to comply with trade and other regulations would have an adverse effect on the company's operations. The labeling, distribution, marketing, and sales of products are subject to extensive regulation by federal agencies.

Stock Performance

The following section analyses the cumulative total stock holder return on lululemon stock in comparison with the cumulative total return for the S&P 500 Index and S&P 500 Apparel, Accessories & Luxury Goods Index during the period Jan 2018 to Jan 2023. The analysis assumes the investment of $100 on Jan 28, 2018, in the stock and indices along with the assumption of reinvestment of dividends if any.

Table 1 Cumulative stock wealth

Year	2018	2019	2020	2021	2022	2023
Lululemon Athletica Inc.	$100.00	184.77	302.72	415.63	$399.48	$393.08
S&P 500 Index	$100.00	$94.21	$112.28	$129.29	$154.27	$141.69
S&P 500 Apparel, Accessories & Luxury Goods Index	$100.00	$88.10	$79.56	$76.22	$73.82	$52.03

Source: Annual Report 2023

Table 2 Holding period returns

Year	Lululemon	S&P 500	Excess returns
2018	−3%	−8%	5%
2019	57%	19%	37%
2020	45%	16%	29%
2021	19%	28%	−9%
2022	−4%	−15%	11%

Table 3 Book and market value of equity

Year	2019	2020	2021	2022	2023
Book value of equity	1445.98	1952.22	2558.57	2740.05	3148.80
Market value of equity	19,107.40	31,204.25	42,844.42	42,888.16	39,072.27
BV as percent of MV	7.6%	10.2%	8.2%	6.4%	7.3%

Table 1 shows the cumulative stock wealth created for lululemon and the market indices.

The 5-year holding period return for lululemon stock was 293% compared to holding period returns of 42% and −48% for the market indices S&P 500 and S&P 500 Apparel, Accessories & Luxury Goods Index, respectively. The average yearly return for lululemon was 36% compared to 7.94% and −11.69% for the S&P 500 Index and S&P 500 Apparel, Accessories & Luxury Goods Index, respectively.

In the next section the total returns of the stock are compared with the returns of the market index S&P 500 during the recent 5-year period. The lulu stock which was trading at $124.84 on June 1st, 2018, increased by three times to trade at $376.20 by May 1st, 2023. The total monthly cumulative return for lululemon stock was 146% compared to the total monthly cumulative return of 50% for the market index S&P 500 during the period June 2018 to May 2023. The average yearly return for lululemon was 30% compared to 10% for the S&P 500 market index during the above period. The data source is yahoofinance.com.

Table 2 compares the holding period return for the lululemon stock and S&P 500 for the period 2018–2022. The holding period is assumed to be a 1-year period.

The lululemon stock outperformed the market index S&P 500 in all years expect in the year 2021.

Table 3 gives the book and market value of equity of lulu during the period 2019–2023. The values are given in millions of dollars.

Table 4 Financial highlights

	(In millions of dollars)				
Financial highlights	2019	2020	2021	2022	2023
Total assets	2084.71	3281.35	4185.22	4942.48	5607.04
Short-term investments	881.32	1093.51	1150.52	1259.87	1154.87
Total equity	1445.98	1952.22	2558.57	2740.05	3148.80
Total revenue	3288.32	3979.30	4401.88	6256.62	8110.52
Total operating expenses	1110.45	1334.28	1614.16	2233.82	2766.20
Net income	483.8	645.6	588.91	975.32	854.8
Market cap	19,107.40	31,204.25	42,844.42	42,888.16	39,072.27
Enterprise value	18,226.08	30,850.70	42,492.59	42,509.34	38,987.74

Table 5 Performance indicators

Ratios	2019	2020	2021	2022	2023
Net margin%	14.71	16.22	13.38	15.59	10.54
ROE%	31.8	38	26.11	36.81	29.03
ROA%	23.7	24.06	15.77	21.37	16.21
DER		0.38	0.31	0.32	0.34

The average book value as percent of market value of equity was just 6.9% during the period Jan 2019 to Jan 2023.

Table 4 shows the financial highlights of lululemon during the period 2018–2022. The values are given in millions of dollars. The data source is gurufocus.com.

During the period January 2019 to January 2023, the average growth rate in total assets, short-term investments, and total equity were 29%, 8%, and 22%, respectively. The total revenues and net income increased by 26% and 19% during the above period. The total operating expenses increased by 26% on an average basis. The market capitalization and enterprise value increased by 23% and 25%, respectively, on an average basis.

Table 5 shows the profitability and leverage ratios of lululemon during the recent 5-year period.

The average net margin, ROE, and ROA during the period January 2019 to January 2023 were 14.08%, 32.35%, and 20.22%, respectively. The average debt equity ratio during the above period was 0.33.

Table 6 shows the estimation of economic value of the company in millions of dollars in years 2022 and 2023.

Table 6 Economic value

Year	2022	2023
Profit before income tax	1333.87	1332.57
Income tax	358.54	477.73
Net operating profit after tax (NOPAT)	975.33	854.84
Stockholder equity	2740.05	3148.80
Long-term debt		
Total capital employed	2740.05	3148.8
WACC	9.82%	10.65%
Capital charge	269.07	335.35
Economic value	706.25	519.50

References

1. https://corporate.lululemon.com/about-us
2. Annual report 2023.

Case 82 PerkinElmer, Inc.

PerkinElmer, Inc. is a leading provider of products, services, and solutions for the diagnostics, life sciences, and applied markets. The modern PerkinElmer (Revvity, Inc.) is focused in the business areas of diagnostics, life science research, food, and environmental and industrial testing. The company is headquartered in Massachusetts. The products and services are marketed in more than 190 countries. By Jan 2023, the company has employed approximately 16,700 employees. The stock is listed on the New York Stock Exchange. The company is included in the S&P 500 Index. PerkinElmer is a global leader in analytical testing which offers a comprehensive portfolio of complete solutions consisting of systems, software, consumables, and on-site and online services. This diagnostics and life sciences company addresses critical issues through advanced technologies and differentiated solutions.

Operating Segments

The two operating segments of the company are classified into life sciences and diagnostics.

Life Sciences

This segment offers products and services targeted towards the life sciences market. The life sciences segment consists of automation and liquid handling solutions and analysis and characterization. Automation and liquid handling solutions consists of integrated laboratory automation, liquid handling solution, and OEM solutions. The integrated laboratory automation product of the custom explorer™ G3-integrated workstations offer innovative application-focused laboratory automation solutions for cellular screening, imaging applications, high-throughput screening, and genomics-based applications. PerkinElmer has been providing liquid handling

© The Author(s), under exclusive license to Springer Nature Switzerland AG 2024

B. R. Kumar, *Rising Stars*, Management for Professionals,
https://doi.org/10.1007/978-3-031-50032-9_82

solutions for over 40 years. The company offers a comprehensive lineup of robotic liquid handlers to automate common to complex laboratory workflows. The OEM solutions supply magnetic beads for nucleic acid isolation, components for custom NGS library, and immunoassay technology which includes ChLIA instrumentation.

Analysis and characterization consists of atomic spectroscopy, chromatography, and molecular spectroscopy. PerkinElmer offers atomic spectroscopy technology for the past 60 years. The company offers a comprehensive portfolio which includes reliable flame AA systems, high-performance graphite furnace AA systems, flexible ICP-OES systems, and the ICP-MS system. The diverse portfolio in the chromatography segment includes techniques for liquid chromatography, mass spectrometry, gas chromatography, and Arnel GC engineered instruments. The company offers the most comprehensive suite of sample preparation technology such as autosamplers, headspace GC, thermal desorption, sample handling systems, liquid injection, and solid-phase microextraction options. PerkinElmer also offers a comprehensive portfolio of analytical instruments, software, and consumables in molecular spectroscopy.

Diagnostics

This segment develops diagnostics, tools, and applications related to reproductive health, immunodiagnostics, and applied genomics markets. The company is a major player in the in vitro diagnostics market. The company offers complete solutions consisting of instruments, reagents, automation, services, and software which address the needs of clinical laboratories. PerkinElmer offers a comprehensive range of laboratory solutions to conduct screening through the pregnancy and baby's early neonatal period. Rapid patient testing solutions speed up the time to clinical decision-making. Cord blood banking solutions are offered by PerkinElmer. PerkinElmer Genomics is a global leader in genetic and genomic testing focused on rare diseases, inherited disorders, newborn screening, and hereditary cancer. PerkinElmer also offers solution for SARS-CoV-2 testing. Tulip Diagnostics is one of the leading Indian diagnostic company which is involved in the manufacture and marketing of in vitro diagnostic reagents. Oxford Immunotec is an expert in T cell immunology. EUROIMMUN segment provides assays, instruments, and software for autoimmune, infection, allergy, molecular, and veterinary diagnostics as well as antigen detection.

Table 1 shows the major statistical facts of the company.

Strategy

The company gives importance to develop and deliver innovative products, services, and solutions in high growth markets. The company focusses on investment in research and development and acquisition of innovative technology. The company aims to strengthen its position within key markets by means of expanding its global

Table 1 Highlights of the business ecosystem

Years since established	80
Employees worldwide	6000
Customers served	90,000
Active instruments globally	325,000
Laboratory assets managed	500,000
Global distribution centers	3
Locations worldwide	115
Countries served	168

Source: https://www.perkinelmer.com/uk/company/about-analytical-enterprise-solutions.html#who-we-are

Table 2 Acquisition history

Year	Acquisition details
1992	Acquired Applied Biosystems
2001	Acquired Packard Bioscience which had expertise in robotic laboratory
1997	Acquired PerSeptive Biosystems
2006	Acquired NTD Labs which specializes in prenatal screening
2007	Acquired ViaCell and renamed it ViaCord
2008	Acquired Pediatrix Screening which specializes in screening newborns for various inborn errors of metabolism
2011	Acquired CambridgeSoft and ArtusLabs
2011	Acquired Caliper Life Sciences for US$ 600 million
2016	Acquired Swedish firm Vanadis Diagnostics
2017	Acquired Indian in vitro diagnostic company, Tulip Diagnostics
2017	Acquired EUROIMMUN Medical Laboratory Diagnostics for $1.3 billion
2018	Acquired Australian biotech firm RHS Ltd.; Shanghai Spectrum Instruments, the manufacturer of analytical instruments; and Cisbio Bioassays which specializes in diagnostics and drug discovery solutions
2020	Acquired Horizon Discovery Group for around US$383 million
2021	Acquired Oxford Immunotec Global PLC, Nexcelom Bioscience, Immunodiagnostic Systems Holdings

Source: https://www.biospace.com

product and service offerings. The company also focusses on third-party collaborations and alliances. The company aims for the growth of its core business segments—the discovery and analytical solutions through strategic acquisitions and licensing.

Acquisition History

The modern-day PerkinElmer traces its history to the merger between two S&P 500 companies EG&G Inc. and Perkin-Elmer. Table 2 lists the acquisition history of the company PerkinElmer.

Risk Factors

The major clients of the company include pharmaceutical and biotechnology companies, laboratories, research institutions, public and private health organizations, and government agencies. Downward fluctuations in the customers' market would result in a reduction in demand for the products and services of the company. The company faces risks related to public health crises and pandemics. The global impact of COVID-19 had resulted in an adverse impact on the firm's operations, supply chains, and distribution systems. The company's business is affected by global economic and political conditions as well as the state of the financial markets. The company may lose market share if it does not introduce new products in a timely manner. The company faces stiff aggressive competition from numerous competitors in many areas of its business. Significant disruption in third-party package delivery and import/export services or significant increases in the prices of those services could interfere with the ability to ship products and thus lower profitability. The operations of the company are subject to regulation by different state and federal government agencies in the United States and other countries. The risks related to economic, political, and other risks associated with foreign operations could adversely affect the international sales and profitability of the company.

Stock Performance

The stock price returns of PerkinElmer are compared with that of the returns of the market index Nasdaq Biotechnology Index. The stock which was trading at $62.6 on June 1st, 2018, increased by 1.69 times to trade at $106 by May 1st, 2023. The total cumulative monthly returns for PerkinElmer were 73% for Perkin stock compared to 30% return given by the market index Nasdaq Biotechnology during the 5-year period June 2018 to May 2023. The average yearly return for the PerkinElmer stock was 15% compared to the average yearly return of 6% for the market index Nasdaq Biotechnology during the period June 2018 to May 2023. The data is sourced from Yahoo Finance.

Table 3 shows the holding period return for PerkinElmer and market index Nasdaq Biotechnology during the period 2018–2022. The holding period is assumed to be 1 year.

Table 3 Holding period return

Year	PerkinElmer	Nasdaq Biotech Index	Excess returns
2018	9%	−12%	20%
2019	11%	10%	1%
2020	32%	33%	−1%
2021	47%	−6%	53%
2022	−12%	1%	−13%

Table 4 Book and market value of equity

Year	2020	2021	2022
Book value of equity	74306.41	146495.5	143936.55
Market value of equity	316990.52	486911.54	373469.1
BV as percent of MV	23.4%	30.1%	38.5%

Table 5 Financial highlights

	(In millions of dollars)				
Financial highlights	2018	2019	2020	2021	2022
Total assets	117329.37	123317.32	158346.59	307721.37	275475.65
Short-term investments	3202.68	3618.8	7997.3	12376.51	8858.16
Total equity	50755.59	53068.72	74306.41	146495.5	143936.55
Total revenue	54545.95	54386.07	52976.97	78523.65	64567.28
Total operating expenses	19751.06	18947.77	17164.93	24114.82	24314.07
Net income	4671.7	4291.74	14479.13	19347.92	11096.71

Table 6 Performance indicators

Ratios	2018	2019	2020	2021	2022
Net margin%	8.56	7.89	27.33	24.64	17.19
ROE%	9.35	8.27	22.73	17.53	7.64
ROA%	3.94	3.57	10.28	8.3	3.81
DER	0.73	0.8	0.59	0.72	0.62

PerkinElmer had superior stock market performance compared to the market index in all years except in the year 2020 and 2022.

Table 4 shows the book and market value of equity of PerkinElmer during the 5-year period 2018–2022. The values are given in millions of dollars.

The average book value as percent of market value of PerkinElmer was 34% during the 3-year period 2020–2022.

Table 5 gives the financial highlights of the company during the recent 5-year period 2018–2022.

The average growth rate of total assets, short-term investments, and total equity during the period 2018–2022 were 30%, 40%, and 35%, respectively, during the period 2018–2022. The total revenues and net income grew by 7% and 55%, respectively, during the period 2018–2022. The data is sourced from annual reports and gurufocus.com.

Table 6 shows the profitability ratios and leverage ratio of the company during the period 2018–2022.

The average net margin, ROE, and ROA were 17.12%, 13.10%, and 5.98%, respectively, during the period 2018–2022.The average debt equity ratio was 0.69.

Table 7 illustrates the estimation of economic value for the company during the period 2018–2022.The values are given in millions of dollars.

Table 7 Economic value

Year	2021	2022
Profit before income tax	24,690.28	12,708.21
Income tax	6419.47	2668.72
Net operating profit after tax (NOPAT)	18270.81	10039.49
Stockholder equity	146,495.50	143,936.55
Long-term debt	102,154.33	76,489.57
Total capital employed	248649.8	220426.12
WACC	7.03%	8.00%
Capital charge	17480.08	17634.09
Economic value	790.72	−7594.60

References

1. https://www.perkinelmer.com/uk/analytical-and-enterprise-solutions.html
2. https://www.perkinelmer.com/uk/category/diagnostic-solutions

Case 83 MarketAxess

MarketAxess, the innovative leader in electronic trading was founded in the year 2000. The company is involved in connecting a robust network of market participants through the full trading lifecycle which includes automated trading solutions, intelligent data products and a wide variety of post trade services. MarketAxess Holdings Inc. operates leading electronic trading platforms. The patented trading technology of MarketAxess is used by over 2000 institutional investor and broker dealer firms to trade US high yield bonds, emerging market debt, Eurobonds, municipal bonds, US government bonds and other fixed income securities. The company offers a diverse set of trading protocols which includes request-for-quote, live order books, session-based trading and portfolio trading solutions. MarketAxess offer all-to-all trading ("Open Trading") and automated trading solutions for majority of its products.

MarketAxess offers a number of integrated and actionable data offerings such as Composite+™ and Axess All® to assist clients with real time pricing, trading decisions and transaction cost analysis. MarketAxess offers a range of post trade services such as straight through processing, trade matching, trade publication, regulatory transaction reporting and reference data across fixed income and other products. The company is included in the S&P 500 list.

Approximately 89.3% of the revenues of the company in the year 2022 were accounted from commissions for transactions executed on its platforms. The company derive revenues from information services and post trade services. The company faces competition from Bilateral Trading, Other multi-party electronic trading platforms, EMS and OMS Providers, Securities and Futures Exchanges, Market data and information vendors.

Table 1 lists the average daily volumes of the company.

Table 2 lists the market share of MarketAxess across product areas.

Table 3 list the major milestones of the company.

© The Author(s), under exclusive license to Springer Nature Switzerland AG 2024

B. R. Kumar, *Rising Stars*, Management for Professionals,
https://doi.org/10.1007/978-3-031-50032-9_83

Table 1 Average daily volume statistics

Segment	Value
Total credit	$11.8 billion
US high grade	$5.5 billion
US high yield	$1.7 billion
Emerging markets	$2.8 billion
Eurobonds	$1.5 billion
Municipal bonds	$379 million
US government bond	$21.5 billion

Source: ESG Report 2022

Table 2 Market share across product areas

Segment	Market share
US high yield	17.90%
Emerging markets	29%
Eurobonds	15.40%
Municipal bonds	4.50%
US government bonds	3.50%

Source: ESG Report 2022

Table 3 Major milestones

Timeline	Events
2000	MarketAxess was founded
2001	Acquires Trading Edge and expands trading platform to Europe
2002	Launches Corporate Ticker
2004	Listed on Nasdaq
2010	Acquires Trade West System
2012	Expands into Brazil
2013	Open Trading started; Strategic Trading alliance with Blackrock
2014	European BASI Index launched
2015	Axes All launched; Open Trading extended to European Markets
2016	Launches electronic trading for municipal bonds and leveraged loans
2017	Launches Composite+
2018	Open Trading extended to Asian credit markets
2019	Launches ID Indices, LiveMarkets; Acquires Liquidity Edge; Included in S&P500
2020	Launches Trading for Trees; Dealer dDirect; Acquires Regulatory Reporting Hub
2021	Acquires MuniBrokers; launches Dealer Diversity; Connectivity to China Bond Connect
2022	Launches MKTX US IG 400 Index; Membership of RFQ Hub consortium

Source: Company website

Trading Platforms and Competitive Strength

The electronic trading platforms of the company offers liquidity to the market through the participation of institutional investor and broker dealer clients which basically include all leading broker dealers in global fixed income trading. These brokers provide the principal source of secondary market liquidity for credit and rates products. The Open Trading protocols manage risk, source liquidity and facilitate transactions on behalf of their clients. The total credit trading volume increased from approximately $1.7 trillion in year 2018 to $2.9 trillion in year 2022.Open Trading, the fully electronic, all to all trading functionality is the key differentiator which expand liquidity for trading participants. Open Trading participants have more diverse liquidity options compared to the traditional model of bilateral trading with limited set of dealer counterparties. The Open Trading protocols facilitate institutional investors to realize competitive prices. The platforms also offer global fixed income market participants with trading functionality across Eurobond and emerging markets credit and rates markets thereby connecting clients in over 80 countries to local and global dealers. The MarketAxess emerging markets trading platform offer the most comprehensive offering for local currency bond trading in the regions of Latin America, Central & Eastern Europe, Middle East and Africa and Asia Pacific regions. The platforms provide clients with the ability to trade emerging market local currency debt denominated in 29 local currencies with over 140 broker dealers. The company have developed robust scalable proprietary technology which can accommodate additional volume, products and clients with little modifications and low incremental costs. The company is the only fixed income electronic trading platform which encompasses all to all trading in each of its product areas. In 2022, the clients of the company had executed approximately $939.6 billion in credit trading volume using Open Trading. The company is focused on expansion and diversification in the international business market. By 2022, the institutional investor and broker clients of the company were based in over 80 countries. The company have over 1000 total active international client firms and 5528 total active international traders. MarketAxess offer cross-regional electronic trading services in US fixed income markets for international clients as well as in Eurobonds and emerging debt. The average daily trading volume in the EMEA, Latin America and APAC regions on the MarketAxess platforms had increased from $1.8 billion in year 2018 to $3.7 billion by year 2022.

Fixed Income Products

The proprietary technology facilitates institutional investor and broker dealer clients to trade both credit and rates products on the company's platform. The credit products offered include US high grade bonds, US high yield bonds, emerging market debt (US dollar, Euro, or local currency denominated bonds), eurobonds, municipal bonds etc. The rate products consist of US government bonds, agency bonds issued by federal government department / Freddie Mac or Fannie Mae and other government bonds.

Full Trading Lifecycle Solutions

Disclosed Request for Quote (RFQ)

Through the RFQ protocol, the company enable institutional investor clients to seek competing executable bids or offers from the dealer clients. This protocol facilitates the clients to simultaneously request and receive responses from multiple dealers and execute trades with the dealer of their preference. The disclosed RFQ protocol is available for transactions in all product areas and can be used for multiple dealer inquiries to over 140 dealers. The list trading has the ability to request bids and offers on up to 60 bonds at the same time. The system can also be used for portfolio trading through which market participants can transact bond basket trades of up to 2100 securities in an all one trading protocol.

Open Trading

Open Trading (all to all trading solution) is offered for most of the firm's products and trading protocols. This system allows all participants to interact anonymously in an all to all trading environment encompassing over 1700 potential counterparties. MarketAxess offers several Open Trading protocols such as Open Trading RFQ, Dealer RFQ, Mid-X sessions, Live Markets, Public Axes, Diversity Dealer Initiatives etc.

Open Trading RFQ facilitate participants to display requests for bids and offers anonymously to the entire MarketAxess trading community. Dealer RFQ allows dealers to initiate RFQs to all other dealers or to the entire Open Trading network. Mid-X sessions is a session based mid-point matching tool which enables broker dealers to trade against the midpoint price established by Composite+.Live Market have an order book functionality which creates a single view of two-way actionable prices for most active bonds. Public Axes is an order book style discovery process which gives the participants the ability to view and execute trades upon anonymous or disclosed indications. Diversity Dealer Initiative aims to promote diversity and inclusion in the financial industry by providing clients with the ability to select and support underrepresented broker dealers while benefiting from the enhanced liquidity provided by Open Trading.

Order and Execution Workflow Solutions

The company provide order and execution workflow solutions to meet the specific needs of institutional investor and broker dealer clients.

Data Products

Data offerings support trading activity through diverse trading protocols. The data products consist of Composite+, Axess All, Axess All Prints, Bond Ticker and Relative Liquidity score.

Composite+ is a pricing algorithm which generates near real-time prices for approximately 33,000 corporate and sovereign bonds based on a variety of data inputs. Axess All, the first intra-day trade tape for the European fixed-income market, is sourced from approximately 71,000 bond transactions processed daily by the firm's post-trade services business. Axess All Prints®, is an enhanced, real-time transacted price service for the most actively traded European fixed income instruments. Bond Ticker provides real time TRACE data and analytical tools for market participants to get bond price information. Relative Liquidity Score provides a defined measurement of current liquidity for individual bonds.

Index Solutions

Liquid indices powered by real time data were introduced by the company for passive fixed income investment strategies. The index utilizes Relative Liquidity scores and Composite+ in the construction and evaluation processes.

Post Trade Services

The company also provide trade matching and regulatory reporting services for European investment firms and market and reference data across a range of fixed income products.

Strategy

Open Trading offer meaningful price improvement for its clients and reduces risk in fixed income markets. The company focus on gaining additional market share across its core credit markets. The company aims to utilize its Open Trading functionality and expertise gained from successful market share expansion in US high grade and high yield bonds. With this expertise, the company aims to enhance its product offerings in emerging markets, municipal bonds, US government bonds, European government bonds and Chinese government bonds. This strategic move would broaden the company's product footprint and cater to the evolving needs of clients in diverse investment areas. Each of these markets have unique trading protocols, market structures and settlement solutions. In 2021, MarketAxess acquired MuniBrokers LLC in order to expand its municipal bond trading solution. This strategic acquisition allowed the company to connect its leading trading technology with the extensive liquidity offered by one of the industry's largest electronic inter-dealer marketplaces. The fixed income electronic trading platform offers Open Trading across all product areas. This inclusive approach allows for seamless interaction between broker-dealer clients and institutional investor clients within an extensive all-to-all trading environment, encompassing over 1700 firms. In 2022, the company made significant minority investment in RFQ-hub which is a bilateral multi asset and multi dealer RFQ platform. The company also entered into a strategic collaboration on liquid fixed income indexes, portfolio construction solutions and ESG data with MSCI.

According to Securities Industry and Financial Markets Association data, there were approximately $10.1 trillion in principal amount of fixed income securities outstanding in the US corporate market.

Risk Factors

Global economic, political and market factors could reduce the demand for the firm's services and profitability. The reputation of the firm could be adversely affected if the sustainability practices and ESG disclosures are not up to the mark. The company faces risks related to operations in the electronic fixed income trading markets. Decreases in trading volumes in the fixed income markets would harm the business and profitability of the company. The electronic financial services industry is characterized by rapidly changing and increasingly complex technologies and systems along with increasingly sophisticated client demands. If the company is unable to cope up with these changes, the business operations and financial results may be adversely affected. MarketAxess faces substantial competition which could reduce the market share and affect the financial performance. The company primarily compete with other electronic trading platforms and trading businesses conducted directly between broker dealers and their institutional investor clients. The company is exposed to potential reputational and credibility concerns related to data products and index business. The strategy of leveraging entry of the firm's electronic trading platforms in new markets have risk implications. Any reduction in the use of electronic trading platforms by the firm's broker dealer clients could reduce the volume of trading on the firm's platforms. MarketAxess also rely on a number of third-party suppliers for key products and services. System failures, interruptions, delays in service, catastrophic events could materially harm the business of the company. The failure to comply with privacy, data protection and information security laws, regulations and other obligations could affect the business operations of the firm. MarketAxess business is subject to increasingly extensive governmental and other regulations.

ESG Initiatives

The company's ESG initiatives are aimed at delivering innovation in the global markets of fixed income. The company is adopting the next generation technology across its growing global client base. ESG strategy and initiatives are generally overseen by the Governance Committee. MarketAxess Charitable Foundation is involved in expansion of philanthropic and community partnerships. MarketAxess is ranked as the largest electronic corporate and municipal green bond marketplace for corporate and municipal green bond trading volume. The MarketAxess "Trading for Trees" initiative had completed 4 years by year 2022. This initiative has led to the plantation of 316,000 trees across nine countries in the year 2022. The company launched the Diversity Dealer Initiative in the year 2021 which facilitated minority, women and veteran owned broker dealers to trade with large investment managers. The company twice received Built In's Best Places to Work awards during 2022 and 2023.

In the year 2021, the company conducted its first comprehensive non-financial ESG materiality and prioritization assessment. The three key pillars of the company's Diversity, Equity & Inclusion (DEI) strategy adopted by the Compensation and Talent committee are strengthening of DEI infrastructure, increase of diversity firm wide and congenial environment for employees. MarketAxess offices have had an increased focus on water efficiency and conservation by technology. Two of the three US data centers of the company have a LEED Certification rating level of Silver which stipulate rigorous environmental and energy management systems standards.

Market Performance

The stock was trading at $197.86 on first June 2018. By May first 2023, the stock price increased by 1.43 times to trade at $284.58. The cumulative total monthly return for the MarketAxess stock was 73% compared to the cumulative total monthly return of 61% for the market index Nasdaq Composite during the 5-year period June 2018–May 2023. The average yearly return for the stock was 15% compared to 12% registered by the market index during the above period. The data was sourced from yahoo finance.

Table 4 shows the holding period return for the stock and market index during the recent 5-year period. The analysis assumes holding period of 1 year.

Table 4 Holding period return

Year	MarketAxess	Nasdaq composite	Excess returns
2018	7%	−12%	18%
2019	77%	23%	53%
2020	61%	41%	20%
2021	−24%	20%	−44%
2022	−19%	−26%	7%

Table 5 Book and market value of equity

Year	2018	2019	2020	2021	2022
Book value of equity	607.88	770.09	955.06	1041.31	1081.09
Market value of equity	7953.69	14381.92	21684.3	15594.95	10499.71
BV as percent of MV	7.6%	9.7%	6.6%	4.8%	6.9%

Table 6 Financial highlights

	(in millions of dollars)				
Financial highlights	2018	2019	2020	2021	2022
Total assets	695.54	954.93	1331.43	1530.45	1607.78
Short term investments	246.32	270.12	460.86	506.74	430.75
Total equity	607.88	770.09	955.06	1041.31	1081.09
Total revenue	435.57	511.35	689.13	698.95	718.3
Total operating expenses	113.86	129.39	157.51	190.8	209.32
Net income	172.85	204.9	299.38	257.89	250.22
Market cap	7953.69	14381.92	21684.3	15594.95	10499.71
Enterprise value	7707.37	14,209.78	21,298.77	15,165.44	10,117.64

Table 7 Performance indicators

Ratios	2018	2019	2020	2021	2022
Net margin%	39.68	40.07	43.44	36.9	34.84
ROE%	30.79	29.74	34.71	25.84	23.58
ROA%	27.08	24.83	26.19	18.02	15.95
DER		0.13	0.1	0.09	0.08

The stock outperformed the market index in all years of analysis except during the year 2021.

Table 5 shows the market value and book value of equity trend for the company during the period 2018–2022. The values are given in millions of dollars. The data is sourced from gurufocus.com.

The average book value of equity as percent of market value of equity was 5.9% during the period 2018–2022.

Table 6 gives the financial highlights of the company during the period 2018–2022.

The total assets, short term investments and total equity grew by 24%,19% and 16% on average basis during the 5 year period 2018–2022. The total revenues and net income increased by 14% and 12% respectively during the above period. The total expenses increased by 17% on average basis. The market capitalization and enterprise value increased on an average by 18% during the period 2018–2022.

Table 7 shows the profitability ratios and leverage ratio of MarketAxess during the period 2018–2022.

The average net margin, ROE and ROA during the period 2018–2022 were 38.99%,28.93% and 22.41% respectively. The average debt equity ratio during the above period was 0.10.

Table 8 Estimation of economic value

Year	2021	2022
Profit before income tax	333.92	338.29
Income tax	75.79	87.95
Net operating profit after tax (NOPAT)	258.12	250.33
Stockholder equity	1041.31	1081.09
Long term debt		
Total capital employed	1041.31	1081.09
WACC	5.71%	9.00%
Capital charge	59.46	97.30
Economic value	198.66	153.04

Table 8 illustrates the estimation of economic value for MarketAxess during the year 2021 and 2022. The values are given in millions of dollars.

References

1. https://www.marketaxess.com/
2. MarketAxess ESG Report 2022
3. MarketAxess Annual Report 2022

Case 84 Ameris Bancorp

Ameris Bancorp is a financial holding company whose business is primarily conducted through the wholly owned banking subsidiary Ameris Bank. Ameris Bank offers a full range of banking services to its retail and commercial customers in select markets in Georgia, Alabama, Florida, North Carolina, and South Carolina. The bank operates 164 full-service domestic banking offices. By December 2022, the bank had approximately $25.05 billion in total assets, $20.25 billion in total loans, and $19.46 billion in total deposits. By December 2022, the bank had employed 2847 full-time equivalent employees.

Services

Lending Activities

The bank offers a diversified loan portfolio by offering a broad range of commercial and retail lending services to business entities and individuals. The bank offers agricultural loans, commercial business loans, commercial and residential real estate construction and mortgage loans, consumer loans, revolving lines of credit and letters of credit. By the year 2022, the loan portfolio accounted for 80.8% of the total assets of the bank.

Commercial Real Estate Loans

Commercial real estate loans constitute the largest segment of the loan portfolio of the bank. Commercial and farmland real estate loans are secured by owner-occupied commercial buildings for office, storage, retail, farmland, and warehouse space. These also include non-owner-occupied commercial buildings such as leased retail and office space.

© The Author(s), under exclusive license to Springer Nature Switzerland AG 2024
B. R. Kumar, *Rising Stars*, Management for Professionals,
https://doi.org/10.1007/978-3-031-50032-9_84

Residential Real Estate Mortgage Loans

Ameris originates adjustable and fixed-rate residential mortgage loans. A major part of these loans is sold in the secondary market. The residential real estate mortgage loans which are included in the company's loan portfolio are basically owner occupied and generally amortized over a 20–30-year period.

Agricultural Loans

Agricultural loans are given to finance crop production, purchase of farm-related equipment, operations of dairies, poultry producers, livestock producers, and timber growers. A part of the agricultural loans is guaranteed by the Farm Service Agency Guaranteed Loan Program.

Commercial and Industrial Loans

Commercial and industrial loans consist of loans made basically to manufacturers, wholesalers, and retailers of goods, service companies, municipalities, and other industry sectors. Basically, these loans are made for acquisition, expansion, working capital, and equipment financing and generally secured by accounts receivable, inventory, equipment, personal guarantees, etc. The bank also originates, administers, and services commercial insurance premium finance loans to borrowers in the United States.

Consumer Loans

The consumer loans consist of home improvement, home equity, and motor vehicle loans which are secured by savings accounts and personal credit lines. The terms of these loans typically range from 12 to 240 months based on the nature of collateral and size of the loan.

Investment Activities

The company invests in US Treasury obligations, securities issued by US government-sponsored agencies, mortgage-backed securities, etc. Basically, the company's investments must be investment grade as determined by recognized investment rating service.

Deposits

The company offers a full range of deposit accounts and services to both retail and commercial customers. These deposit accounts have a variety of interest-bearing and non-interest-bearing accounts such as commercial and retail checking accounts, regular interest-bearing savings accounts, money market accounts, individual retirement accounts, and certificates of deposits.

Other Funding Sources

The Federal Home Loan Bank facilitates the company to obtain advances through its credit program. These advances are secured by securities owned by the company. The company maintains credit arrangements with various other financial institutions to purchase federal funds. The company also enters into repurchase agreements which are classified as short-term borrowings.

The company faces competition from commercial banks, thrift institutions, savings banks, insurance firms, consumer finance firms, credit unions, mortgage firms, leasing firms, etc.

Strategy

The bank follows an acquisition-oriented growth strategy to increase its presence and expand the "Ameris" brand in regions of Georgia, Alabama, North Carolina, and South Carolina. The bank also focuses on a prudent operating strategy. The community banking philosophy of the bank gives emphasis on personalized service and deep customer relationships. The bank has adopted a decentralized structure to differentiate itself from large competitors. The bank has maintained its focus on long-term strategy of expansion and diversification of its franchise in terms of revenues, profitability, and asset size. The three fundamental strategic priorities of the bank's business consist of growth of demand deposit, expansion of business banking, and delivery of outstanding customer experience.

In 2019, the bank acquired Fidelity Southern Corporation and added $ 4 billion in deposits. In the year 2021, the bank acquired Balboa Capital Corporation which was a point of sale and direct online provider of lending solutions to small- and mid-sized businesses worldwide.

ESG Initiatives

The bank's sustainability initiatives are based on the principles of diversity, equity, and inclusion (DEI). The Employee Resource Groups (ERGs) focus on the key areas of women in banking; LGBTQIA+; veterans; Black, indigenous, and people of color (BIPOC); multigenerational, caregivers, and mental health. The Leadership

Development Program launched in year 2021 offers opportunity for professional growth. The learning and development team helps teammates establish mentor relationships and prepare teammates to become effective mentors and coaches.

Ameris has programs to support communities. In order to promote access to home ownership, Ameris introduced the Down Payment Grant Program which offers eligible first-time homebuyers amount up to $12,500 for mortgage down payment and closing costs. In 2022, through this initiative, Ameris helped more than 12,063 customers to purchase homes. In 2022, Ameris published its second Corporate Social Responsibility Report (CSR). In order to set carbon footprint reduction targets, Ameris had engaged an energy consultant for the development of conservation strategies for buildings such as energy-efficient light-emitting diode (LED) lighting retrofit for its locations. Ameris had strengthened its partnership with Callanwolde Fine Arts Center in Atlanta to launch an Art Scholars program. For the past 12 years, Ameris has partnered with Feeding America to support Fight Hunger Campaign. Ameris also supports the Georgia HEART Program through donations to around 18 rural hospitals.

Risk Factors

The bank faces significant risks due to changes in interest rates. The ability to generate profits is largely dependent on net interest income. Loan originations and potentially loan revenues could be materially adversely impacted by rising interest rates. A significant decline in interest rates may lead to a notable rise in prepayments within the securities portfolio, resulting in decreased interest earnings generated from those investments. Cyberattacks or other security breaches could have material adverse effect on the business of the bank. Potential decreases in real estate values, which secure the majority of the bank's loan portfolio, may exert pressure on the revenue generated from those loans, potentially necessitating additional provisions to the allowance for loan losses. Greater loan losses would materially adversely affect the earnings of the bank. The performance of bank's business is closely tied to the economic conditions within a specific region of the United States, thereby exhibiting a high correlation to the local economic environment. The bank faces additional risk due to its mortgage banking activities that could negatively impact net income and profitability. The banking industry is heavily regulated and is subject to supervision and comprehensive regulation by various federal and state agencies. The growth and financial performance of the bank may be negatively impacted if the bank is unable to execute its growth plans. The bank faces risks related to its operational, technological, and organizational infrastructure.

Stock Performance Analysis

The cumulative total shareholder return of Ameris is compared with the cumulative return of the Nasdaq Stock Market and index of KBW Nasdaq Bank stocks for the 5-year period starting December 31, 2017, and ending December 31, 2022. The analysis assumes an investment of $100 on December 31, 2017, and reinvestment of dividends and other distributions to shareholders.

Table 1 shows the total wealth generated by Ameris and the market index during the period 2017–2022.

The 5-year holding period return of Ameris Bancorp was 5% compared to 59% holding period returns registered by Nasdaq Composite and 9% return accounted by KBW Nasdaq Bank stocks. The average yearly returns for Ameris Bancorp was 4.45% compared to 13.68% and 5% returns registered by Nasdaq Composite and Nasdaq Bank Stock Index, respectively.

In the following section the returns of Ameris stock is compared with the market index Nasdaq Bank Index during the recent 5-year period June 2018 to May 2023. The total cumulative monthly return for Ameris stock was −11% compared to 0% returns for the KBW Nasdaq Bank Index during the period June 2018 to May 2023. The data is sourced from yahoofinance.com.

Table 2 shows the holding period return for the Ameris stock and KBW Nasdaq Bank Index during the period 2018–2023. The holding period is assumed to be 1-year period.

Table 3 shows the book value and market value of equity of Ameris during the 5-year period 2018–2022. The values are given in millions of dollars.

Table 1 Total wealth generated

Year	2017	2018	2019	2020	2021	2022
Ameris Bank Corp	100	66.31	90.22	82.73	$109.23	$105.04
Nasdaq Composite	$100	$97.16	$132.81	$192.47	$235.15	$158.65
KBW Nasdaq Bank Index	$100	$82.29	$112.01	$100.46	$138.97	$109.23

Table 2 Holding period return

Year	Ameris	Nasdaq Bank Index	Excess returns
2018	−40.64%	−17.42%	−23.2%
2019	12.09%	17.52%	−5.4%
2020	−5.27%	−6.53%	1.3%
2021	27.03%	35.22%	−8.2%
2022	−4.40%	−25.29%	20.9%

Table 3 Book and market value of equity comparison

Year	2018	2019	2020	2021	2022
Book value of equity	1456.35	2469.58	2647.09	2966.45	3197.40
Market value of equity	1504.32	2956.69	2647.44	3458.19	3270.05
BV as percent of MV	96.8%	83.5%	100.0%	85.8%	97.8%

Table 4 Financial highlights

	(In millions of dollars)				
Financial highlights	2018	2019	2020	2021	2022
Total assets	11,443.52	18,242.58	20,438.64	23,858.32	25,053.29
Gross loans	8623.21	14,475.19	15,648.58	17,128.89	20,247.33
Deposits	9649.31	14,027.07	16,957.82	19,665.55	19,462.74
Total equity	1456.35	2469.58	2647.09	2966.45	3197.40
Interest income	413.33	636.39	726.5	703.11	893.89
Noninterest income	114.4	183.21	420.48	335.53	247.56
Interest expense	69.93	131.23	88.75	47.79	92.86
Total noninterest expense	269.13	383.93	571.22	525.9	522.58
Market capitalization	1504.32	2956.69	2647.44	3458.19	3270.05
Enterprise value	1089.99	3885.28	1099.39	279.74	4155.98

Table 5 Performance ratios

Ratios	2018	2019	2020	2021	2022
Return on average assets %	1.3	1.15	1.43	1.79	1.49
Return on average equity%	10.71	8.22	10.24	13.43	11.24
Net interest margin%	4.06	3.92	3.94	3.83	4.06

The average book value of equity as percent of market value of equity was approximately 93% during the period 2018–2022. The data is obtained from gurufocus.com.

Table 4 shows the financial highlights of the bank during the period 2018–2022.

On an average basis, the total assets, gross loans, and deposits grew by 23%, 26%, and 20%, respectively, during the period 2018–2022. The total equity grew by 24% on an average basis during the above period. The average growth rate of interest income and noninterest income were 23% and 36%, respectively, during the above period. The interest expense and total noninterest expense increased by 3% and 21%, respectively. The market capitalization increased by 28% on an average basis during the above period. The data is taken from gurufocus.com.

Table 5 highlights the profitability ratios of the company.

The average return on assets, return of equity, and net interest margin were 1.43%, 10.77%, and 3.96%, respectively, during the period 2018–2022.

Ameris Bancorp's efficiency overhead ratio for the year ended December 2022 was 51.65% which was lower than 54.87% for the previous year 2021. The capital adequacy tier 1 leverage ratio for Ameris Bancorp was 9.36% in 2022 which was higher than 8.63% in the year 2021.

References

1. https://www.amerisbank.com/
2. Ameris Bank Annual Report 2022.

Case 85 Shyft Group

Shyft is a US-based niche market leader in speciality vehicle manufacturing and assembly for the commercial vehicle and recreational vehicle industries. The products offered by the company include walk-in vans, truck bodies, cargo vans, pickup truck upfits which are used in e-commerce/parcel delivery, etc. Products such as upfit equipment which are used in the mobile, retail, and utility trades are offered by the company. The company also offers contract manufacturing and assembly services. Shyft also supplies replacement parts and offers repair, maintenance, field service, and refurbishment services for the vehicles manufactured by the company. The operating activities are conducted through wholly owned operating subsidiary, The Shyft Group, USA. The vehicles, parts, and services of the company are targeted for commercial users, original equipment manufacturers (OEMs), dealers, and government institutions. This innovative organization consists of nine brands in the last mile delivery and other specialty vocations which focus on building chassis and bodies and offers upfit services.

Over the past 5-year period (2018–2022), the revenues of the company witnessed compounded annual growth rate of approximately 16%. The company doubled its cash dividends in the year 2022. In 2022, it allotted $26.8 million capital to shareholders. With respect to research and development, the company has spent $4.4 million, $8.5 million, and $25.3 million during the period 2020–2022.

Segments

The company operates under two reportable segments – fleet vehicles and services (FVS) and speciality vehicles.

© The Author(s), under exclusive license to Springer Nature Switzerland AG 2024

B. R. Kumar, *Rising Stars*, Management for Professionals,
https://doi.org/10.1007/978-3-031-50032-9_85

Fleet Vehicles and Service Segment

The company manufactures commercial vehicles used in the e-commerce/last mile/parcel delivery, beverage and grocery delivery, laundry and line, mobile, retail, and construction industries in diverse locations in the United States such as Bristol, Indiana, Pennsylvania, Charlotte, and Michigan. The commercial vehicles are marketed under the Utilimaster brand name. The company also offers vocation-specific equipment upfit services which are marketed through the Utilimaster Upfit Services brand. By December 2022, the FVS segment employed approximately 2600 employees and 400 contractors. The company offers fleet vehicles in the gross vehicle weight rating class 1 through class 7.

Products

Walk-In Vans

These vans are used across different types of vocations for multiple delivery and mobile service options.

Truck Bodies

The Utilimaster dry van truck bodies are basically the industry benchmark standards for heavy-duty commercial delivery. The truck bodies are installed on chassis from a wide variety of manufacturers which are supplied with finished cab.

Cutaway

Cutaway truck bodies are designed for medium-duty commercial delivery and are installed on chassis from different manufacturers who are supplied with finished cab.

Velocity

Velocity is an ergonomically designed walk-in van lineup built on commercial cargo van chassis across OEMs.

Specialty Upfit

The company installs specialty interior and exterior upfit equipment for walk-in vans and truck bodies for added safety, cargo handling efficiency, and improved vocational functionality.

Parts and Accessories

The company also provides a full line of parts and accessories for walk-in vans and truck bodies. The company markets its commercial vehicle products such as walk-in vans, cutaway vans, and truck bodies under the Aeromater, Velocity, Trade master, and Utilivan product brand names. The company sells its fleet vehicles to leasing companies and national and fleet accounts.

Specialty Vehicle Segment

The speciality vehicle segment consists of Spartan RV Chassis and Builtmore Contract Manufacturing brands, service bodies, and vocation-specific upfit. Upon confirmation of purchase orders, the specialty vehicle products are manufactured according to customer specifications. The chassis and vehicles under this category are sold through original equipment manufacturers. The service bodies and aftermarket parts and accessories are sold to dealers and distributors or directly to consumers. By December 2022, the specialty vehicle segment employed approximately 1000 employees.

Products

Motorhome Chassis

The company specializes in the custom manufacturing of luxury class A motorhome diesel chassis which are tailored to the individual specifications of its motorhome OEM customers. These chassis are produced under the brand name Spartan RV Chassis.

Contract Manufacturing

Under the brand name Builtmore Contract Manufacturing, the company offers final assembly services for Isuzu N-Gas and F-Series chassis which are specifically designed for the North American market.

Service Bodies

The speciality vehicle segment manufactures and assembles truck bodies for different trades and vocations.

Speciality Upfit

The company specializes in designing and installing custom lighting and upfit solutions to cater to the unique requirements of different fleet industries. The services are extended to a wide range of specialty sectors such as law enforcement, transportation department, security companies, funeral services, towing, and utility providers.

Parts and Accessories

The company provides truck accessories under the Magnum brand.

Strategy

In the context of rapidly changing e-commerce market, the company focusses on leveraging opportunities with respect to capitalizing last mile delivery. The solution experts of the company focus on innovation for efficiency improvements and cost savings in the service segment, utility industry, food and beverage delivery sectors, and mobile and retail industry. Innovations developed include safe loading equipment, keyless entry and cargo access systems, backup camera systems, and refrigeration solutions. Innovations developed by the product development team include a new walk-in van format termed the Velocity. The company has implemented the Shyft Production System, lean manufacturing, and continuous improvement for all its four fleet vehicle facilities for maximizing efficiency and reducing costs.

In the speciality vehicle segment, the company has made innovations to motor home and speciality chassis. These innovations include Premier Drive system with custom tuned shocks, independent front suspension, and passive steer tag axle which improve ride and handling efficiency. In order to gain pricing advantages, the company has embarked on establishing long-term supplier agreements and consolidating its supplier wherever beneficial.

The introduction of Blue Arc signifies the commitment of Shyft to create commercial fleets with zero-emission vehicles and double its revenues by the year 2025. The company emphasizes on sustaining high-growth brands which are uniquely focused on last mile delivery and infrastructure.

Shyft Group has adopted strategic well-executed acquisitions for value creation. The infrastructure-focused brands Royal® Truck Body, DuraMag®, and Builtmore Contract Manufacturing™ are actively integrating their distinct capabilities and utilizing their diverse footprints to expand their product offerings into untapped geographic markets. The company has made sustainable investments in electric vehicles.

Sustainability Initiatives

The ESG strategy of the company focuses on advancement in sustainability, diversity, equity, and inclusion. The company believes that innovation is the key to environmental stewardship. The company's newest go-to-market brand, Blue

Arc™ EV Solutions, offers a full ecosystem of end-to-end electric-powered solutions to achieve sustainability and performance goals.

With investments in electric vehicle solutions for commercial fleets and introduction of the Blue Arc go-to market brand in the year 2022, Shyft Group aims to achieve approximately 30% growth in revenues through sustainability-focused initiatives by the year 2025. The fleet vehicle and service segment specializes in the production of commercial vehicles which are used in different industries such as last mile parcel delivery, beverage and grocery delivery, laundry and linen services, and mobile retail as well as trades and construction. With these strong products, the company could capitalize on the trends of e-commerce expansion. The company expects to produce its all electric class 3 delivery walk-in van by mid-year 2023. In 2021, the company has generated revenues of $305 million from products which were designed to increase fuel efficiency and reduce emissions. In 2021, 78% of the waste was recycled. The company has established a 5-year DEI roadmap to foster an inclusive culture and diverse environment. The company requires the suppliers to comply with robust supplier policies which include a formal supplier code of conduct, conflict mineral policy, and a global supplier standard manual.

Risk Factors

Uncertainty in the global macroeconomic and political conditions could adversely affect the business and financial operations of the company. Any negative impact with respect to relationship with major customers could have significant adverse effects on revenues and profits. The markets which the company serve are undergoing rapid transformation with respect to parcel delivery services and electric vehicle technologies. The company faces challenges with respect to maintaining its competitive position in the rapidly changing markets. In the event of cancellation, the backlog and anticipated revenue would decrease as backlog consisting of agreements and purchase orders from customers is subject to modification, cancellation, or rescheduling. The integration of businesses or assets that the company have acquired or may acquire in the future poses challenges that have the potential to disrupt the operations and negatively impact the operations and financial standing of the company. The reconfiguration or relocation of the production operations may have a negative impact on the firm's earnings. Disruptions within the dealer network could adversely impact the business of the company. Potential factors such as rising labor rates, changes in labor practices, supply chain disruptions, implementation of new tariffs, or restrictions could lead to increased costs of raw materials and component parts and might result in the reduction of operating income. The EVs and EV operations of the company heavily rely on intricate third-party and in-house software and hardware components. The development of complex software and technology systems in collaboration with vendors and suppliers is crucial for the achievement of mass production of EVs. However, there are no guarantees that these systems will be successfully developed or integrated.

Stock Price Performance

Table 1 compares the cumulative total stock holder return on Shyft stock with the cumulative total return on the Nasdaq Composite Index and the Dow Jones US Commercial Vehicles & Trucks Index for the period beginning on December 31, 2017, and ending on the last day of the year 2022. The analysis assumes an initial investment of $100 in the stock and market indexes.

The holding period return for Shyft stock was 63% compared to 59% and 88% returns accounted by the market indexes Nasdaq Composite and US Commercial Vehicles & Trucks Index, respectively. The average yearly return for the stock and the market indexes of Nasdaq Composite and US Commercial Vehicles & Truck were 36%, 13.68%, and 14.76%, respectively, during the period 2017–2022.

The following section compares the stock returns of Shyft with that of returns of Nasdaq Composite during the recent 5-year period. The stock which was trading at $15.1 on June 1st, 2018, increased by 1.61 times to trade at $24.42 by May 1st, 2023. The total monthly cumulative return for Shyft was 127% compared to the total monthly cumulative return of 61% for market index Nasdaq Composite during the period June 2018 to May 2023. The average yearly return for the stock was 26% for the stock compared to 12% yearly return for Nasdaq Composite during the period June 2018 to May 2023. The data for analysis is sourced from yahoofinance.com.

Table 2 shows the holding period return for the stock and market index during the 5-year period 2018–2022. The analysis assumes holding period of 1 year.

The stock Shyft outperformed the market index Nasdaq Composite in all years except in the year 2018 and 2022.

Table 3 shows the comparative book and market value of equity of the company in millions of dollars during the period 2018–2022.

The average book value as percent of market value of equity was 23% during the period 2018–2022.

Table 1 Wealth comparison

Year	2017	2018	2019	2020	2021	2022
The Shyft Group, Inc.	$100.00	$46.34	$116.85	$184.42	$320.05	$163.08
Nasdaq Composite Index	$100	$97.16	$132.81	$192.47	$235.15	$158.65
Dow Jones U.S. Commercial Vehicles &Trucks Index	$100	$83.73	$105.66	$136.09	$160.10	$188.00

Source: Annual Report

Table 2 Holding period return

Year	Shyft	Nasdaq Composite	Excess returns
2018	−52%	−12%	−40%
2019	115%	23%	92%
2020	67%	41%	26%
2021	63%	20%	43%
2022	−41%	−26%	−14%

Table 3 Book and market value of equity

Year	2018	2019	2020	2021	2022
Book value of equity	186.08	171.75	200.16	266.86	268.69
Market value of equity	255.37	639	1003.06	1739.99	871.74
BV as percent of MV	72.9%	26.9%	20.0%	15.3%	30.8%

Table 4 Financial highlights

	(In millions of dollars)				
Financial highlights	2018	2019	2020	2021	2022
Total assets	353.78	450.54	359.05	447.87	580.48
Short-term investments	27.44	19.35	21	37.16	11.55
Total equity	186.08	171.75	200.16	266.86	268.69
Total revenue	570.53	756.54	675.97	991.79	1027.16
Total operating expenses	50.63	69.41	97.43	115.21	132.92
Net income	15.01	−12.57	32.82	68.93	36.56
Market cap	255.37	639	1003.06	1739.99	871.74
Enterprise value	252.88	748.55	1056.21	1758.11	991.44

Table 5 Performance indicators

Ratios	2018	2019	2020	2021	2022
Net margin%	2.63	−1.66	4.86	6.95	3.56
ROE%	8.44	−7	17.62	29.51	13.66
ROA%	4.58	−3.12	8.11	17.08	7.11
DER	0.14	0.75	0.37	0.21	0.49

Table 4 gives the financial highlights of the company during the period 2018–2022.

The total assets increased by 15% on an average basis during the period 2018–2022. The total equity and total revenues increased by 11% and 18%, respectively, during the above period. The total expenses increased by 28% on an average basis. The market capitalization and enterprise value increased by 58% and 65%, respectively, during the above period.

Table 5 shows the profitability ratios and debt equity ratio for the company during the period 2018–2022.

The average net margin, ROE, and ROA during the period 2018–2022 were 3.27%, 12.45%, and 6.75%, respectively, during the period 2018–2022. The average debt equity ratio during the above period was 0.39.

Table 6 gives the estimation of the economic value of the company during the year 2021 and 2022.

Table 6 Economic value in millions of dollars

Year	2021	2022
Profit before income tax	84.48	43.93
Income tax	14.51	7.03
Net operating profit after tax (NOPAT)	69.97	36.90
Stockholder equity	266.86	268.69
Long-term debt	0.74	56.27
Total capital employed	267.6	324.96
WACC	9.71%	9.00%
Capital charge	25.98	29.25
Economic value	43.99	7.65

References

1. https://www.myshyft.com/
2. ESG Report 2022

Case 86 Progressive Corporation

The Progressive Corporation is an insurance holding company based in the United States with subsidiaries and affiliates. The insurance subsidiaries of the company offer personal and commercial auto insurance, personal residential and commercial property insurance, and workers' compensation insurance basically for transport sector. The insurance services are also provided to business-related general liability insurance and other specialty property casualty insurance and related services. The noninsurance subsidiaries offer support services for insurance and investment activities. On account of the nature of insurance, legal and regulatory requirements, the insurance and claims organizations are generally managed on a state by state basis. The investment portfolio of the company consisting of fixed maturity securities, short-term investments, and equities are valued at $53.5 billion by December 2022. By December 2022, the company employed 55,100 employees.

Business Segments

Personal Lines

The personal line segment consists of personal auto and special line products. The personal auto insurance represents approximately 94% of the total personal line net premiums written in the year 2022. The special lines products write insurance for personal autos and recreational vehicles. Fifteen private passenger auto insurers including Progressive writes over $2.5 billion of premiums annually which constitute 84% of the market in the United States. Special line products include insurance for motorcycles, TVs, RVs, watercraft, and snowmobiles. The competitors of the company are specialty companies and large multiline insurance carriers. The personal line products are sold through agency and direct channels. The agency business includes business written by the company's network of more than 40,000 independent insurance agencies which are located in the United States. The agency business is involved in writing insurance through strategic alliance partnership with

© The Author(s), under exclusive license to Springer Nature Switzerland AG 2024

B. R. Kumar, *Rising Stars*, Management for Professionals,
https://doi.org/10.1007/978-3-031-50032-9_86

other insurance companies, financial institutions, and national agencies. In 2022, the total net premiums written through agency channel accounted for 47% of the personal line businesses. The direct business consists of business written directly by the company on the Internet through the Progressive mobile app and through phone.

Commercial Lines

The commercial line segment is involved in writing auto liability and physical damage insurance along with business related general liability and property insurance for small businesses and workers' compensation insurance. The commercial line business accounted for approximately 18% of the total net premiums written in the year 2022. The company's commercial auto customers insure approximately two vehicles per policy. In the year 2022, the company wrote approximately 90% of its commercial auto business through the agency channel. The commercial line business operates in the commercial auto business market targets of business auto, for-hire transportation, contractor, for-hire specialty, and tow. The business auto segment consists of autos, vans, and pickup trucks used by small businesses. The hire transportation segment includes tractors, trailers, and straight trucks used by regional general freight and long-haul operators. The contractor segment includes vans, pickup trucks, and dump trucks used by light contractors. For-hire specialty segment consists of dump trucks, log trucks, and garbage trucks. The tow segment includes tow trucks and wreckers used in towing services and gas/service station business. The commercial line business offers its clients UBI options. UBI program such as Smart Haul uses driving data from motor carrier's existing electronic logging device. Snapshot ProView is another UBI program offered to commercial auto customers without their own electronic logging device.

Property

The company also offer business-related general liability and property insurance through business owner's policy insurance. The property segment writes residential property and enters insurance in all states of the United States through independent agency channel and through select agents under the Platinum program. Property business accounted for 5% of the total net premiums written in the year 2022.

Reinsurance

The reinsurance business includes both regulated and nonregulated businesses. The nonregulated arrangements reinsure activities in the property business and commercial line business. The property program consists of contracts which cover multiyear period. The company also maintain an excess of loss reinsurance treaty which covers personal umbrella business. The reinsurance program in the commercial line business aims to manage certain exposures in the commercial auto, TNC, BOP, and worker's compensation products.

Competition and Strategy

The insurance market is highly competitive. The major factors which determine competition in the insurance market are price, agent commission rates, coverages and product features, claims handling, and geographic coverage. The company faces competition from national players as well as from smaller regional insurers in both agency and direct channels. These competitors have broad distribution networks of employed or captive agents. Many competitors invest heavily in advertising initiatives and expand their online or mobile service offerings. In the year 2022, the company acquired Protective Insurance Corporation and subsidiaries to expand its portfolio of offerings to larger fleet and provide worker's compensation for trucking industry. The company focusses on Destination Era strategy for promotion of property business. The agency channel of the company offers customers the opportunity to bundle auto, special lines, and property offerings. The company offer Platinum program to select agents who have the appropriate customers for the bundled offerings. By 2022, the company had over 4000 Platinum agents. In the direct channel segment, the company bundle Progressive auto with property products in different states as well as with home owners and renters' products which are provided by unaffiliated insurance carriers throughout the United States. These bundled packages provide a single destination to consumers to fulfil their auto and property insurance needs. The special line products and umbrella insurance coverage offered by the company can be combined with any of the auto, home, or renters' coverages which are offered under direct or agency channel. Bundled products are an integral part of the firm's consumer offerings and significant part of the strategic agenda. HomeQuote Explorer is the multi-carrier direct to consumers online property offering by the company.

The personal line strategy of the company is focused on becoming a competitively priced provider of wide range of personal auto and special line insurance products. The company gives importance for refining its personal auto segmentation, underwriting models, and pricing strategy. The company aims to improve the auto insurance rates for the customers through usage-based insurance (UBI) program such as Snapshot. The company offer Snapshot through its hardware-based or mobile app-based versions. This mobile app aims to improve user experience while monitoring costs. The data collected via the mobile app offers valuable perspective on mobile device usage, vehicle operations, and accidents. The company also offers independent agents an agency quoting system which facilitates firms to bundle multiple policies.

Risk Factors

Progressive Corporation faces different risks such as insurance risks, operating risks, market risks, liquidity risks, credit, and other financial risks. The success of the financial operations of the company depends on the ability of the company to underwrite and price risks and to charge adequate rates to policy holders. The inherent risk in the process of establishing property and casualty insurance loss reserves is a significant factor for the financial success of the business. The insurance operating results would be materially adversely affected by natural events, epidemics, other widespread health risks, etc. The success of the business depends on the ability to accurately predict reinsurance needs, receive sufficient reinsurance coverage for property and other businesses, and collect reinsurance contracts. The company also faces operating risks in terms of uninterrupted operations of systems, facilities, business functions, and operation of various third-party systems. The business could be materially adversely affected by security breach or other attacks which involve technology systems or systems of one or more vendors. The markets in which the company sell insurance are highly competitive. The company faces competition from large, well-capitalized national and international companies as well as smaller regional insurers. The insurance businesses also operate in highly regulated environment. The existence of patents and other claimed intellectual property rights creates legal challenges for the business practices of the company. The performance of the fixed income and equity investment portfolios of the company is subject to variety of investment risks. The company faces financial and other credit risks as the business is dependent on the performance by third parties due to contractual or service arrangements and government programs.

Sustainability Initiatives

The company aims to foster a learning culture and offer several leadership development programs such as multicultural leadership development program. With respect to diversity, equity, and inclusion, the company is one among the few public companies with a female CEO as well as a female independent board chairperson. The company aims to double the representation of people of color in senior leadership from 10% to 20% by the end of year 2025. The company has nine employee resource groups (ERGs) to help build communities for the employees with common background, life experiences, interests, and professional goals. The company also offer competitive pay through combination of fixed and variable compensation.

Stock Performance

The Progressive stock which was trading at $ 60 on June 1, 2018 increased by 2.16 times to trade at $129.8 by May 1, 2023. The Progressive stock had cumulative total monthly returns of 89% compared to the negative returns registered by market index

Table 1 Holding period returns

Year	Progressive	Nasdaq Financial	Excess returns
2018	12%	−6%	19%
2019	11%	9%	2%
2020	19%	14%	5%
2021	26%	14%	13%
2022	29%	−16%	44%

Table 2 Book and market of equity

Year	2018	2019	2020	2021	2022
Book value of equity	10,821.80	13,673.20	17,038.60	18,231.60	15,891.00
Market value of equity	35,184.46	42,321.37	57,864.58	59,988.66	75,867.38
BV as percent of MV	30.8%	32.3%	29.4%	30.4%	20.9%

Table 3 Financial highlights

	(in millions of dollars)				
Financial highlights	2018	2019	2020	2021	2022
Total assets	46,575.00	54,910.50	64,098.30	71,132.30	75,465.00
Short term investments	69.5	226.2	76.5	187.1	203.5
Total equity	10,821.80	13,673.20	17,038.60	18,231.60	15,891.00
Total revenue	31,954.70	38,997.70	42,638.10	47,676.50	49,586.40
Net income	2615.30	3970.30	5704.60	3350.90	721.5
Market cap	35,184.46	42,321.37	57,864.58	59,988.66	75,867.38
Enterprise value	40,013.76	46,996.17	63,678.08	65,194.26	82,546.08

Nasdaq Financial 100 during the recent 5-year period June 2018–May 2023. The average yearly return for the stock during the period June 2018–May 2023 was 18%.

Table 1 shows the holding period return for the stock and market index during the 5-year period 2018–2022. The holding period is assumed to be 1 year.

Progressive Corporation stock outperformed the market index Nasdaq Financial in all years during the period 2018–2022.

Table 2 shows the book value and market value of equity during the period 2018–2022. The values are given in millions of dollars.

The book value as percent of market value of equity was 25.7% during the period 2018–2022.

Table 3 gives the financial highlights of the company during the period 2018–2022. The values are given in millions of dollars.

The total assets and short-term investments increased by approximately 13% and 78%, respectively, on average basis during the period 2018–2022. The total equity and revenues increased by 11% and 12%, respectively, during the above period. The market capitalization and enterprise value increased by 22% and 20%, respectively, during the period 2018–2022. The data is taken from annual reports and www.gurufocus.com.

Table 4 Performance indicators

Ratios	2018	2019	2020	2021	2022
Net margin%	8.18	10.18	13.38	7.03	1.46
ROE%	26.01	32.42	37.15	19	4.23
ROA%	6.13	7.82	9.59	4.96	0.98
DER	0.41	0.32	0.32	0.27	0.4

Table 5 Estimation of economic value

Year	2021	2022
Profit before income tax	4210.00	922.1
Income tax	847.89	200.56
Net operating profit after tax (NOPAT)	3362.11	721.54
Stockholder equity	18,231.60	15,891.00
Long-term debt	4898.80	6388.30
Total capital employed	23130.4	22279.3
WACC	4.57%	6.00%
Capital charge	1057.06	1336.76
Economic value	2305.05	−615.21

Table 4 shows the profitability ratios and leverage ratio of debt equity ratio during the 5-year period 2018–2022.

The average net margin, ROE, and ROA were 8.05%, 23.76%, and 5.90%, respectively, during the period 2018–2022. The average debt equity ratio during the above period was 0.34.

Table 5 illustrates the estimation of economic value of Progressive Corporation. The values are given in millions of dollars.

Reference

1. Annual Report 2022.

Case 87 SmartFinancial

SmartFinancial was established in the year 1934. The company has over 70,000 members. SmartFinancial is a bank holding company which is registered under the Bank Holding Company Act of 1956. SmartFinancial owns and operates SmartBank. The bank is federally insured by NCUA and is an equal housing lender. The Tennessee-based chartered bank was established in the year 2007. The bank attracts deposits from general public and offers commercial loans, commercial and residential real estate loans, leases, consumer loans, and residential and commercial construction loans. The major source of income for the bank is interest and fees collected on loans and leases, fees collected on deposit accounts, and interest and dividends collected on other investments. The principal expenses of the bank include interest paid on deposits, employee compensation, benefits, office expenses, and other overhead expenses. As of March 2023, SmartBank has 41 full-service bank branches and 1 loan production office. By December 31, 2022, the bank employed 583 full-time and 13 part-time associates.

Banking Services

With respect to general lending activities, SmartFinancial maintains a diversified loan portfolio consisting of a wide range of commercial and retail lending services to business entities. SmartFinancial offers commercial business loans, commercial and residential real estate construction and mortgage loans, agricultural loans, leases, consumer loans, and revolving lines of credit and letters of credit. The company engages in the origination of residential mortgage loans, primarily focusing on one to four family properties. Typically, the company enters into commitments to sell these loans within the secondary market. By December 2022, SmartFinancial's net loan and lease portfolio totaled approximately \$3.2 billion which comprised 70% of the total assets. Commercial real estate loans consist of owner-occupied loans for operating businesses, providing long-term financing for land and buildings, while loans secured by income-producing properties, such as apartment buildings, office

© The Author(s), under exclusive license to Springer Nature Switzerland AG 2024
B. R. Kumar, *Rising Stars*, Management for Professionals,
https://doi.org/10.1007/978-3-031-50032-9_87

and industrial buildings, and retail shopping centers, are repaid through rental income and are sensitive to real estate valuations. Consumer real estate loans consist of real estate loans secured by first liens, second liens, or open-end real estate loans such as home equity lines.

Real estate construction and development loans are repaid through cash flow generated by property operations, sales, or refinancing, with this portfolio segment involving credit extensions to developers or investors where repayment depends on real estate sales or income generated from collateral. The commercial and industrial loan portfolio segment offers commercial and financial loans, leases which are used to finance working capital needs, equipment purchases, or expansion project. The lease portfolio segment offers leases to small- and mid-sized companies for equipment financing leases. The consumer loan portfolio offers direct consumer installment loans, overdrafts, revolving credit loans, and educational loans. With respect to investment activities, SmartFinancial invest in federal, state and municipal obligations, corporate obligations, public housing authority bonds, and securities issued by government-sponsored enterprises.

Deposits

SmartFinancial offers a full range of deposits and service to both retail and commercial customers. These includes commercial and retail checking accounts, regular interest-bearing savings accounts, money market accounts, individual retirement accounts, and certificates of deposit. The bank strategically utilizes brokered deposits to achieve specific objectives, including obtaining desired maturity and dollar amounts without impacting the current customer base's deposit costs and managing interest rate risk through targeted maturities and amounts.

Other Funding Sources

In this category, the Federal Home Loan Bank facilitates firms to obtain advances through its credit program. The company participates in the federal reserve discount window borrowings program. The company also enters into repurchase agreements which are treated as short-term borrowings.

Investment and Insurance Services

The bank has contractual agreement with registered broker dealer Raymond James Financial Services Inc. to offer and sell different securities and other financial products to the public. The brokerage and investment advisory program offered by Raymond James complements the bank's general banking business. Rain Insurance, a subsidiary of the bank, provides insurance products in the property and casualty area, commercial, transportation, and life and health sectors.

Growth Strategy

The company aims to become a high-performing community bank by focusing on organic loan and lease expansion and deposit growth and maintaining disciplined merger and acquisition practices. In 2019, SmartFinancial acquired Progressive Financial Group. Through the merger with Sevier County Bancshares, the company increased its assets by approximately $485 million in the year 2021. In 2021, the company acquired Fountain Leasing LLC which offered construction equipment financing to small- and medium-sized businesses. In 2022, the indirect wholly owned subsidiary of SmartFinancial entered into a purchase agreement to acquire Sunbelt, an independent full-service insurance agency which offers personal, commercial property, and casualty insurance as well as life and health insurance. Sunbelt also has an insurance department which provides insurance services to transport sector.

Risk Factors

The interest rate adjustments by the Federal Reserve Board would have an impact on the net interest income of the bank. The bank depends on information technology, telecommunications systems, and third-party servicers for its operations. Systems failure, interruptions, or breaches of security would have an adverse effect on the operations of the bank. The bank operates in a highly regulated environment and is subject to supervision and regulation by a number of government regulatory agencies. The success of the banking operations depends on the quality of assets, in particular, the loans and leases. The operating and financial results will have adverse effect if the bank has significant loan and lease losses. Changes in accounting standards could materially affect the financial results of the bank. Economic downturn caused by inflation, recession, and unemployment may contribute toward the deterioration of the quality of the loan portfolio and reduce the level of deposits thereby causing adverse effect on the business of the bank. The bank also faces competition from financial institutions and other financial service providers. The organic loan and lease growth may be limited by regulatory constraints. The concentration in loans secured by real estate is subject to risks which might adversely affect the operations and financial conditions of the business. By year end 2022, approximately 77% of the loans and leases had real estate as the primary or secondary component of collateral. The largest loan relationships make up a significant percentage of the total loan portfolio. A downturn in the customers' businesses or industries may lead to higher credit losses and reduced loan balances which could potentially impact the financial performance of the bank.

Table 1 Comparative wealth creation

Year	2017	2018	2019	2020	2021	2022
SmartFinancial	100	84.19	109.23	84.86	$129.28	$131.32
Russell 3000	$100	$94.76	$124.15	$150.08	$188.60	$152.37
S&P Small Bank Cap	$100	$83.44	$104.69	$95.08	$132.36	$116.69

Source: Annual Report 2022

Table 2 Holding period returns

Year	SmartFinancial	Nasdaq Bank Index	Excess Returns
2018	−28.91%	−21.49%	−7.4%
2019	13.76%	5.20%	8.6%
2020	−16.10%	−4.72%	−11.4%
2021	38.18%	34.09%	4.1%
2022	2.57%	−18.18%	20.8%

Stock Price Performance

Table 1 compares the cumulative 5-year shareholder return on SmartFinancial stock assuming an investment of $100 on December 31, 2017 and reinvestment of dividends thereafter to that of returns of the Russell 3000 index and the S&P SmallCap Bank Index. The S&P SmallCap Bank Index contains securities of NYSE and NASDAQ-listed companies with market capitalizations between $250 million and $1 billion. Russell 3000 tracks the performance of 3000 largest US traded stocks.

The holding period return for SmartFinancial was 31% compared to 52% and 17% return registered by market index Russell 3000 and S&P Small Bank Cap. The average returns for SmartFinancial was 9.11% during the above period compared to returns of 10.62% and 5.42% accounted by market index Russell 3000 and S&P Small Bank Cap.

The next section compares the stock returns of SmartFinancial with that of the market index Nasdaq Bank Index during the recent 5-year period June 2018–June 2023. The total cumulative monthly return for the stock was 5.2% while the average yearly return was 1%. The data source is yahoo finance. Table 2 shows the holding period return for SmartFinancial and market index during the recent 5-year period 2018–2022. The analysis assumes holding period of 1 year.

The stock outperformed the market index in the year 2019, 2021, and 2022.

Table 3 shows the book value and market value of equity trends during the period 2018–2022. The values are given in millions of dollars.

The average book value as percent of market value of equity was 104.5%.

Table 4 gives the financial highlights of the bank during the 5-year period 2018–2022. The data is sourced from guru focus and annual reports.

Table 3 Book and market value of equity

Year	2018	2019	2020	2021	2022
Book value of equity	283.01	312.75	357.17	429.43	432.45
Market value of equity	254.57	331.29	274.04	459.73	464.77
BV as percent of MV	111.2%	94.4%	130.3%	93.4%	93.0%

Table 4 Financial highlights

	(In millions of dollars)				
Financial highlights	2018	2019	2020	2021	2022
Total assets	2274.41	2449.12	3304.95	4611.58	4637.50
Gross loans	1777.24	1903.25	2393.96	2644.79	3187.95
Deposits	1921.96	2047.21	2805.22	4021.94	4077.10
Total equity	283.01	312.75	357.17	429.43	432.45
Interest income	92.21	108.46	117.61	125.23	158.83
Non-interest income	4.53	6.72	15.43	23.95	27.72
Interest expense	15.57	24.58	16.75	11.84	21.33
Total non-interest expense	53.12	57.74	72.15	87.69	105.73
Market capitalization	254.57	331.29	274.04	459.73	464.77
Enterprise value	189.16	235.46	−26.52	−418.33	292.77

Table 5 Performance ratios

Ratios	2018	2019	2020	2021	2022
Return on average assets %	0.91	1.12	0.85	0.88	0.93
Return on average equity%	7.41	8.91	7.26	8.85	9.98
Net interest margin%	4.42	4.11	4.24	3.86	3.83

During the above period, the total assets, gross loans, and deposits grew by 21%, 16%, and 22%, respectively, on average basis. The total equity of the bank increased by 11%. The interest and non-interest income increased by 15% and 62%, respectively, during the period 2018–2022. The interest expense declined by 1%. The total non-interest expense increased by 19%. The market capitalization increased by 20% on average basis.

Table 5 shows the performance measures of the bank during the period 2018–2022.

The average ROA, ROE, and net interest margin for the bank were 0.94%, 8.48%, and 4.09%, respectively, during the period 2018–2022.

Table 6 shows the estimation of the economic value of SmartFinancial during the year 2021 and 2022. The values are given in millions of dollars.

Table 6 Economic value

Year	2021	2022
Profit before income tax	44.32	54.91
Income tax	9.5	11.9
Net operating profit after tax (NOPAT)	34.8	43.0
Stockholder equity	429.4	432.5
Long-term debt	129.5	66.6
Total capital employed	559.0	499.1
WACC	6%	9.8%
Capital charge	34.4	49.0
Economic value	0.4	–5.9

Reference

1. Annual Report 2022

Case 88 Superior Group of Companies

Superior Group of Companies (SGC) was established in 1920. The three business segments of Superior are branded products, healthcare apparel, and contact centers. The branded product segment, through its signature marketing brands BAMKO® and HPI®, produces and sells customized merchandising solutions, promotional products, and branded uniform programs. The branded products are manufactured in house or through third parties. These products are targeted toward customers in a range of industries such as retail, hotel, food service, entertainment, technology, and transportation. The sales offices of the segment are located in the United States, Canada, Brazil, the United Kingdom, and Colombia. The segment has support services in China and India. Superior's healthcare apparel segment through its signature marketing brands such as Fashion SealHealthcare® and WonderWink® manufactures and sells a wide range of healthcare apparel such as scrubs, lab coats, protective apparel, and patient gowns. The healthcare segment sells healthcare service apparel to healthcare laundries, dealers, and physical and e-commerce retailers in the United States. SGC's contact centers segment through multiple The Office Gurus® entities provides outsourced nearshore business process outsourcing contact and call center support services to North American customers. The branded product segment offers customized products to support branded marketing programs, branded uniform programs, corporate awards, incentives and recognition programs, event promotions, and specialty packaging and displays.

The healthcare apparel segment offers career and service apparel for personnel of hospitals and healthcare facilities. In addition, the segment offers miscellaneous products for use by linen suppliers and industrial launderers. In 2022, the branded product segment accounted for approximately 67% of net sales, while the healthcare segment and contact centers accounted for 20% and 13% of the net sales. SGC offers outsourced, nearshore business process outsourcing, contact and call center support services to North American customers through its contact centers segment.

The major competitors in the branded product segment include multitude of national and regional companies such as BDA, HALO Branded Solutions, Staples Inc., Cimpress PLC, HHGlobalGroup Limited, and Land's End Inc. The major

© The Author(s), under exclusive license to Springer Nature Switzerland AG 2024

B. R. Kumar, *Rising Stars*, Management for Professionals,
https://doi.org/10.1007/978-3-031-50032-9_88

competitors for the healthcare apparel segment include companies such as Medline Industries, Careismatic Brands, Barco Uniforms Inc., FIGS Inc., Encompass Medical, Standard Textile Co Inc., etc. The competitors in the contact centers segment include TaskUs, Transparent BPO, WebHelp, Focus Services, Ubiquity, CCI, and RDI.

The principal fabrics used by SGC for the manufacture of finished apparel goods are cotton, polyester, spandex, cotton synthetic, and polysynthetic blends. The majority of the fabrics are sourced from China. Majority of the products are manufactured in Bangladesh, China, Haiti, Madagascar, and Vietnam.

By December 31, 2022, Superior Group of Companies had approximately employed 6800 employees worldwide.

Acquisitions

In 2013, the company acquired all of the assets of HPI Direct Inc. which specializes in the design, manufacture, and distribution of uniforms to big domestic retailers, food service chains, transportation, and other services in the United States. In 2016, the company acquired all of the assets of BAMKO Inc. which is a full-service merchandise sourcing and promotional products based in Los Angeles with subsidiaries in Hong Kong, China, Brazil, and England as well as an affiliate in India. In 2017, through BAMKO, SGC acquired all of the assets of Public Identity, a promotional products and branded merchandise agency which offers promotional products and branded merchandise to corporate clients and universities. In the same year, BAMKO acquired the assets of Tangerine Promotions Ltd., a promotional products and branded merchandise agency which is the leading provider of point of purchase (POP) and point of sale (POS) merchandise. In 2018, SGC acquired CID Resources which manufacturers medical uniforms and lab coats and sells its products to specialty uniform retailers, e-commerce, etc. In 2021, BAMKO acquired Gifts by Design Inc. which is a promotional products and branded merchandise agency which develops and supplies corporate awards, incentives, and recognition programs for world's biggest brands. In 2021, SGC acquired assets of Sutter's Mill Specialties which is a vertically integrated manufacturer of high-quality decorated promotional products. Sutter Mill prints on demand and creates customized promotional programs and products. In 2022, the company acquired the assets of Guardian Products of Georgia which is a leading provider of promotional products to automotive dealers in the United States.

Risk Factors

The operational results may be negatively impacted by shortages in sourced goods or raw materials from its suppliers, disruptions in manufacturing processes, and local condition in countries in which business operations are conducted. Safeguarding of trade names, trademarks, and other intellectual property rights is critical for the success of the firm. A significant portion of the firm's sales is reliant on fulfilling customer order on a per order basis. The failure to meet customers' order requirements in a timely manner could result in order cancellations and strained customer relationships which could negatively impact the business operations. Noncompliance with data privacy and security laws and regulations may have a detrimental impact on the operational outcomes and business activities of the company. In the event of interruptions or failures in the company's information technology systems, including cyberattacks, the business operations may experience disruptions, potentially leading to adverse impacts on the financial condition. The company is subject to international, federal, national, regional, state, local, and other laws and regulations which might expose the company to potential liability. The company also face intense competition within its industries. The branded uniforms, healthcare apparel, and promotional products industries are susceptible to pricing pressures, which could necessitate a reduction in the prices which the company charge for its products. This could have an adverse impact on its financial performance. The apparel industry, encompassing branded uniforms and healthcare apparel, is influenced by ever-changing fashion trends. If consumer preferences are misjudged, it could result in a negative perception of the brands and result in subsequent decrease in demand for its products.

Sustainability Initiatives

Superior Group of Companies (SGC) received numerous recognitions in the year 2021. SGC was ranked 10 out of 100 by *Forbes* America's Best Small Companies. SGC was also ranked as 88 of 100 by *Fortune Magazine* 100 Fastest Growing Companies. SGC also received the Best Garment Innovation award from Network Association of Uniform Manufacturers and Distributors (NAUMD). The Code of Business and Ethical Conduct outlines SGC's approach toward conduct of business activities under ethical framework. Additional policies include Anti-Corruption and Anti Bribery Policy, Anti-Discrimination and Anti-Harassment Policy, Insider Trading Policy, and Supplier and Vendor Compliance Manual. The board of directors monitor the company's compliance with code of conduct under the guidance of legal team. Whistle Blower Policy outlines different avenues to report concerns. Data privacy, security training, certification, and compliance are given top priority in the company. Information security and data privacy teams follow industry best practices related to data security. The company focuses on its supply chain by frequently assessing the supplier relationships to identify and mitigate potential risks to the company and its customers. SGC's branded merchandise team focuses on increasing spending with domestic suppliers who engage in sustainability initiatives. Among the selected suppliers, approximately 90 percent have shown a positive response by enhancing their sustainable product offerings and implementing changes to their production practices in order to decrease their carbon footprint. SGC's Supplier and Vendor Compliance Manual defines the audit programs and expectations for suppliers to specify requirements with their employees, supply chain partners, and subcontractors. The manufacturing partners are subject to regular social compliance audits by the company or third-party auditors. SGC has a zero-tolerance policy for sourcing raw materials from suppliers whose products contain conflict minerals. The labor policies require suppliers to provide safe, healthy work environment for their employees and follow labor practices in compliance with applicable laws and regulations. The company invest in a variety of programs to attract and retain employees which include training, diversity, and inclusion along with bonuses. In 2021, the company established the SGC University to focus on learning and development initiatives. SGC is committed to create a diverse, equitable, and inclusive workplace to support its employees. Approximately 80 plus charitable organizations receive cash contributions from SGC and its divisions. In 2021, SGC donated 132,638 units of clothing valued at over $2.6 million to 10 humanitarian and healthcare organizations in the United States. In the context of environmental management initiatives, the company utilizes recycled plastic bottles to produce garments. In 2021, through the bottle recycling program, SGC recycled approximately 14.75 million plastic bottles. In 2021, approximately 7% of uniform sales of the company represented garments manufactured from recycled products. As part of waste reduction initiatives, SGC reuses storage and shipping cartons and recycles 100 percent of unusable corrugated and other paper waste. In 2021, SGC started production of its award-winning products made with WonderWink Renew™, the newest line of recycled fabric which is used for a range of products which include uniforms and hospital scrubs. In line with ESG values related to product quality, SGC ensures that 100 percent of the fabric acquired for apparel manufacturing holds Oeko-Tex certification which serves as a guarantee that products have undergone testing and are confirmed to be free from harmful levels of toxic substances.

Stock Price Performance

The stock returns of Superior Group of Companies are compared with the returns of market index Nasdaq Composite during the 5-year period July 2018–June 2023. The total monthly cumulative return for Superior Group was −11% compared to 69% return registered by market index during the 5-year period July 2018–June 2023. The average yearly return for the stock was −2% compared to 14% registered by market index during the above period.

Table 1 Holding period return

Year	Superior Group of Companies	Nasdaq Composite	Excess returns
2018	−15%	−14%	−1%
2019	−22%	23%	−45%
2020	106%	41%	65%
2021	−2%	20%	−22%
2022	−49%	−26%	−22%

Table 2 Book and market value of equity

Year	2018	2019	2020	2021	2022
Book value of equity	150.92	157.55	191.63	226.99	192.6
Market value of equity	268.32	206.18	357.70	353.84	164.75
BV as percent of MV	56.2%	76.4%	53.6%	64.2%	116.9%

Table 3 Financial highlights

	(In millions of dollars)				
Financial highlights	2018	2019	2020	2021	2022
Total assets	335.09	358.93	393.92	470.25	456.94
Short-term investments	5.36	9.04	5.17	8.94	17.72
Total equity	150.92	157.55	191.63	226.99	192.6
Total revenue	346.35	376.7	526.7	536.99	578.83
Total operating expenses	97.1	109.24	137.47	151.67	178.44
Net income	16.98	12.07	41.03	29.44	−31.97
Market cap	268.32	206.18	357.7	353.84	164.75
Enterprise value	380.48	320.16	442.91	466.85	309.42

Table 4 Performance ratios

Ratios	2018	2019	2020	2021	2022
Net margin%	4.9	3.2	7.79	5.48	−5.52
ROE%	12.31	7.82	23.5	14.07	−15.24
ROA%	6.13	3.48	10.9	6.81	−6.9
DER	0.78	0.78	0.47	0.54	0.84

Table 1 shows the holding period return for the stock and market index Nasdaq Composite during the 5-year period 2018–2022.

The stock outperformed the market index in the year 2022.

Table 2 shows the comparative book value and market value of equity during the period 2018–2022. The values are given in millions of dollars.

The average book value as percent of market value of equity was 90.5% during the period 2018–2022.

Table 3 gives the financial highlights of the company during the period 2018–2022.

The total assets, short-term investments, and total equity increased by 8%, 49%, and 7% on average basis during the period 2018–2022. The total revenues increased by 15%, while operating expenses increased by 17% during the period 2018–2022. The market capitalization and enterprise value declined by 1% on average basis during the above period.

Table 4 shows the performance ratios of Superior during the period 2018–2022.

The average net margin, ROE, and ROA were 3.17%, 8.49%, and 4.08%, respectively, during the period 2018–2022. The average debt equity ratio during the above period was 0.68.

References

1. ESG Report 2021.
2. Annual Report 2022.

Case 89 Meta Financials Group Inc. (Pathward Financial)

Meta Financial Group Inc. is a registered bank holding company which was incorporated in the year 1993. The group includes Pathward Financial and the Bank along with the subsidiaries of Pathward Financial. MetaBank, the wholly owned full-service banking subsidiary of Pathward Financial operates through the segments of consumer, commercial, and corporate services. MetaBank collaborates with partners through the BaaS business line to provide solutions to attract low-cost deposits and generate fee income. The low-cost deposits are primarily invested into loan and lease products offered through the commercial finance business line. The bank also sells loans such as consumer credit product loans, refund advance loans, and government guaranteed loans to third-party buyers. The bank also sells and purchases loan participations as well as mortgage-backed securities. The consumer segment which include the BaaS business line offers prepaid cards and deposit accounts to payment processing and consumer lending. The company offers innovative solutions such as payment, issuing, credit, and tax. The payment solutions process payments for all customers' personal and business needs. Pathward is one of the leading debit and prepaid card issuer in the United States. Tax solutions offer electronic refund advances and refund transfers with some of the largest tax companies in the world.

Pathward Venture Capital, LLC., the wholly owned service corporation subsidiary of the bank, was formed in year 2017 for minority equity investment purposes. First Midwest Financial Capital Trust was established in year 2001, and Crestmark Capital Trust was acquired in the year 2018. These subsidiaries were established for issuing trust-preferred securities.

Table 1 shows the important milestones for the company.

© The Author(s), under exclusive license to Springer Nature Switzerland AG 2024
B. R. Kumar, *Rising Stars*, Management for Professionals,
https://doi.org/10.1007/978-3-031-50032-9_89

Table 1 Milestones

Year	Event
1954	Storm Lake Savings and Loan Association is founded
1993	First Federal Savings Bank of Midwest is established
2004	First Federal launches Meta Payment Systems to provide banking technology and infrastructure to partners
2005	First Federal changes name to MetaBank
2014	MetaBank acquires AFS/IBEX, provider of premium financing to property and casualty industries
2015	MetaBank acquires Refund Advantage, provider of services for tax professionals
2016	MetaBank acquires EPS Financial, a provider of tax-related financial transaction services, and Specialty Consumer Services, a provider of consumer credit services
2018	MetaBank acquires Crestmark, a commercial lender
2022	MetaBank rebrands as Pathward

Source: Pathward website

Lending Activities

The company focuses its lending activities on the origination of commercial finance loans, consumer finance loans, and tax services loans. The company places significant emphasis on the quality of credit and strives to prevent excessive concentrations of loans and leases within a single industry or reliant on a solitary class of collateral.

Commercial Finance

Pathward's commercial finance business line offers different products through its working capital, equipment finance, structured finance, and insurance premium finance lending solutions. The products offered include term lending, asset-based lending, factoring, lease financing, insurance premium finance, and government guaranteed lending. The bank offers a variety of collateralized conventional term loans and notes receivables. These term loans are secured by equipment, recurring revenue streams, or real estate. The bank adheres to standardized loan policies and adheres to authorized credit limits. It employs diligent portfolio management practices, which encompass monitoring past-due accounts, evaluating financial performance, assessing financial covenants, and staying abreast of industry trends. The weighted average life of these loans is approximately 53 months.

Asset-based loans offered by the bank are secured by short-term assets such as accounts receivables and inventory. The asset-based loans are secured by equipment supported by third-party independent appraisals. Loans are typically revolving lines of credit with terms of 1–3 years.

The bank offers factoring lending services, wherein clients provide comprehensive accounts receivable reporting for lending arrangements. The factoring clients are diversified across various industries and geographical locations. Credit risk is mitigated through standardized advance policies, authorized credit limits, receivables verification, portfolio management, lock box agreements, and similar arrangements, with clients typically providing guarantees for purchased accounts receivable.

The bank offers adaptable and innovative lease solutions for client equipment requirements, with leases structured as sales-type or direct financing leases that transfer ownership benefits and risks to the lessee, including provisions for ownership transfer at the lease's end, bargain purchase options, or equipment purchase at fair market value.

The bank offers nationwide short-term collateralized financing, known as insurance premium financing, to assist commercial customers in purchasing insurance for different types of risks, such as commercial property, casualty, and liability. Premiums are advanced to the insurance carrier or intermediary and repaid with interest by the policyholder over the policy term, typically with a 20–25% down payment and the remaining amount financed over an average period of 9–10 months.

The bank extends loans to small businesses and professionals through programs that receive partial guarantees from the SBA or USDA. In some cases, portions of these loans that are guaranteed are sold to the secondary market. The company also offer healthcare receivables loan portfolio which are comprised of loans to individuals for medical services received. Majority of these loans are guaranteed by the hospital which provides the service to the debtor. This loan category includes commercial real estate loans.

Consumer Finance

The company's BaaS business line offers its consumer credit products and Emerald Advance products through its credit solutions. The bank designs its program credit protections with the aim to earn a reasonable risk adjusted return. The loans offered under these programs are generally closed-end installment loans with terms between 12 and 84 months. Through the bank's partner program termed Emerald Advance, the bank serves as the originator of a line of credit where customers draw on a line of credit.

Other Consumer Finance

The other consumer finance segment consists of student lending, tax services, and refund advance loans. The student loan portfolio consists of seasoned floating rate private portfolios serviced by a third-party servicer. The bank's BaaS business line offers tax solutions which includes short-term refund advance loans and short-term electronic return originator advance loans. Refund advance loans are unsecured loans offered to tax payers that are basically determined based on underwriting criteria designed for the product. On account of the nature of refund advance loans, it typically takes no more than three e-file cycles from when the return is accepted by the IRS to collect from the borrower. ERO advance loans are unsecured advances that are typically utilized by tax preparers to purchase tax preparation software. The bank engages in various collateral-based warehouse lines of credit, holding a senior, secured position as the first-out participant. These credit facilities are predominantly backed by consumer receivables, with the bank benefiting from a senior collateral position strengthened by a subordinate party structure.

Originations, Sales, and Servicing of Loans and Leases

The bank sells loans and leases generally without recourse. The company may sell the guaranteed portion of its SBA 7(a) loans and USDA program loans in the secondary market.

Investment Activities

The general policy of the bank is to purchase investment securities which are US government-related securities, agency, and instrumentality securities. The company's mortgage-backed and related securities portfolio consisted of securities issued by US government agencies or instrumentalities, including those of Ginnie Mae, Fannie Mae, Freddie Mac, and Farmer Mac, along with private label institutions.

Funding Activities

The bank's sources of funds are deposits, borrowings, amortization and repayment of loan and lease principal, interest earned on or maturation of investment securities, and funds provided from operations. The borrowings include FHLB advances, overnight federal funds purchased, repurchase agreements, short-term borrowings, and funds available through the FRB discount window. The bank offers a variety of deposits which primarily consists of demand deposit accounts, savings accounts, money market savings accounts, and certificate accounts. The bank also periodically utilizes brokered or other wholesale deposits to target strategic maturities related to its seasonal refund advance lending. Historically, the company has primarily relied on advances from the FHLB, secured by a blanket collateral agreement covering a portion of unencumbered loans and specific investment securities.

Risk Factors

Pathward Financial has established processes and procedures to identify, measure, monitor, report, and analyze different types of risks such as liquidity, credit, market risk, interest rate risk, operational risk, legal and compliance, and reputational risks. The bank is subject to credit risk in connection with lending and leasing activities. The net income is bound to decrease if the bank's actual loan and lease losses exceed its allowance for credit losses. The earnings of financial services firms are significantly affected by general business and political and economic conditions. The bank invests in certain tax advantaged investments which support renewable energy resources. These projects may not generate returns as expected and may have an adverse impact on results of operations. The bank operates in extremely competitive environment. The bank would suffer if there is a decline in the use of prepaid cards or adverse developments with respect to the prepaid financial services industry in general. Security breaches involving the bank or third parties could expose the bank to liability and protracted and costly litigation.

Market Performance

Table 2 compares the cumulative total stock return on Pathward Financial common stock over the last 5 fiscal years with the cumulative total return of the Nasdaq Composite index and Nasdaq ABA Community Bank index. The analysis assumes the investment of $100 in stock and each index on October 1, 2017, and reinvestment of all dividends.

The 5-year holding period return for Pathward Financial was 30% compared to holding period return of 70% and 10% accounted by market index Nasdaq Composite and ABA Community Bank index. The average yearly return for Pathward Financial was 24% compared to average yearly return of 14.13% and 7.62% registered by Nasdaq Composite and Nasdaq ABA during the period 2017–2022.

The following section analyzes the stock returns for the MetaBank stock and market index Nasdaq Bank index during the 5-year period August 2018 to July 2023.The total monthly cumulative return for the stock was 96%, while the average yearly return for stock during the above period was 20%. The data is sourced from Yahoo Finance.

Table 3 shows the excess holding period return during the 5-year period 2018–2022.

Table 2 Comparison of cumulative returns

Year	2017	2018	2019	2020	2021	2022
Pathward Financial	100	106	126.51	75.2	$206.25	$130.12
Nasdaq Composite index	$100	$125.17	$125.82	$177.36	$231.03	$170.37
Nasdaq ABA Community index	$100	$103.35	$95.14	$65.70	$119.36	$109.76

Table 3 Holding period return

Year	Pathward Financial	Nasdaq Bank index	Excess returns
2018	−32.83%	−17.42%	−15.4%
2019	55.03%	17.52%	37.5%
2020	−1.77%	−6.53%	4.8%
2021	54.44%	35.22%	19.2%
2022	−27.60%	−25.29%	−2.3%

Table 4 Book value and market value of equity

Year	2018	2019	2020	2021	2022
Book value of equity	747.73	843.96	847.31	871.88	645.14
Market value of equity	1079.06	1232.89	660.42	1662.04	948.86
BV as percent of MV	69.3%	68.5%	128.3%	52.5%	68.0%

Table 5 Financial highlights

	(In millions of dollars)				
Financial highlights	2018	2019	2020	2021	2022
Total assets	5835.07	6182.89	6092.07	6690.65	6747.41
Gross loans	2960.60	3800.19	3497.72	3397.96	3339.66
Deposits	4430.99	4337.01	4979.20	5514.97	5866.04
Total equity	747.73	843.96	847.31	871.88	645.14
Interest income	158.53	325.73	292.84	285.85	312.2
Non-interest income	144.68	188.24	184.2	229.28	193.96
Interest expense	27.99	61.52	33.8	6.86	4.87
Total non-interest expense	188.36	289.2	280.75	299.24	334.76
Market capitalization	1079.06	1232.89	660.42	1662.04	948.86
Enterprise value	1493.68	1968.23	334.88	1442.01	596.82

Table 6 Performance Indicators

Ratios	2018	2019	2020	2021	2022
Performance ratios					
Return on average assets %	8.76	12.25	12.44	16.53	20.63
Return on average equity%	0.93	1.61	1.71	2.22	2.33
Net interest margin%	3.06	5.2	5.18	5.54	5.87

The MetaBank stock outperformed the market index during the period 2019–2021.

Table 4 shows the book value and market value of equity during the period 2018–2022. The values are given in millions of dollars.

The average book value as percent of market value of equity was 77.3% during the period 2018–2022.

Table 5 shows the financial highlights of Pathward Financial during the 5-year period 2018–2022.

The average growth rate in total assets, gross loan, and deposits were 4%, 4%, and 7%, respectively, during the period 2018–2022.The interest and non-interest income increased by 26% and 9%, respectively, on average basis during the period. The interest expense declined by 2 percent on average basis. The total non-interest expense increased by 17% on average basis. The average increase in market capitalization and enterprise value were 19% and 55%, respectively. The data is sourced from annual reports and gurufocus.com.

Table 7 Economic value

Year	2021	2022
Profit before income tax	156.45	187.32
Income tax	10.7	28.0
Net operating profit after tax (NOPAT)	145.7	159.4
Stockholder equity	871.9	645.1
Long-term debt	92.8	36.0
Total capital employed	964.7	681.2
WACC	6.05%	6.98%
Capital charge	58.4	47.5
Economic value	87.4	111.8

Table 6 shows the financial performance ratios of Pathward Financial during the period 2018–2022.

The average return on assets, return on equity, and net interest margin were 14.12%, 1.76%, and 4.97%, respectively, during the period 2018–2022. Pathward Financial's efficiency overhead ratio was 64.09% in year 2022 compared to 62.05% in the year 2021. The capital adequacy tier 1 ratio for Pathward was 12.39% for the year ended 2022 compared to 12.46% in the year 2021.

Table 7 illustrates the estimation of economic value of Pathward Financial in the year 2021 and 2022. The values are given in millions of dollars.

The economic value increased from $87.4 million in 2021 to $111.8 million in 2022.

Reference

1. Annual Report 2022

Case 90 Meta Platforms

On October 28, 2021, Facebook, Inc. changed its name to Meta. Meta was incorporated in Delaware in July 2004, and completed its initial public offering in May 2012, and its common stock is currently listed on the Nasdaq Global Select Market under the symbol META.

Meta Platform's primary objective is to foster a closer connection between communities and the world. With a focus on bringing the metaverse to life, the company offers a range of innovative products and apps that support this vision. Through cutting-edge technology, Meta Platform facilitates seamless connections, empowering people to discover and engage with diverse communities while also nurturing the growth of businesses. Meta Products connect more than 3 billion people around the world. Beyond conventional 2D screens, Meta Platform is leading the charge toward immersive experiences in the realm of social technology, such as augmented and virtual reality. By embracing these transformative technologies, Meta enables individuals to share their experiences, ideas, photos, and videos in unprecedented and captivating ways. The company's dedication to pushing the boundaries of connectivity and interaction opens up exciting new possibilities for the future of social engagement and virtual exploration. The company employs nearly 72,000 people across 80 cities.

The financial results of Meta are reported in terms of two segments: Family of Apps (FoA) and Reality Labs (RL). The company generates most of its revenues from selling advertising placements on its Family of Apps to marketers. Marketers purchase advertisements which can appear in multiple places such as Facebook, Instagram, Messenger, third-party applications, and websites. Approximately 82% of the total costs and expenses of Meta were accounted by the FoA segment and about 18% by the RL segment. The FoA investments amounted to $71.79 billion in the year 2022. The total RL investments amounted to $15.88 billion in year 2022.

© The Author(s), under exclusive license to Springer Nature Switzerland AG 2024

B. R. Kumar, *Rising Stars*, Management for Professionals,
https://doi.org/10.1007/978-3-031-50032-9_90

Family Products of Apps

Facebook

Facebook serves as a powerful platform, empowering individuals to forge communities and foster global unity. It provides a space where people can freely share life's cherished moments, engage in meaningful discussions about current events, and cultivate and strengthen relationships. Facebook facilitates the discovery of shared interests and enables seamless connections within various communities. Moreover, it acts as a catalyst for economic growth by offering opportunities to create and expand businesses. This multifaceted platform offers a variety of features, such as feed, reels, stories, groups, and more, to facilitate these enriching experiences and interactions.

Instagram

Through various features like Instagram feed, stories, reels, videos, live, shops, and messaging, users and creators alike can establish meaningful connections and express themselves freely through captivating photos, engaging videos, and private messaging. Moreover, Instagram acts as a hub for discovery, enabling users to explore and patronize their favorite businesses while staying connected to the latest trends and innovations. It's a dynamic platform that fosters genuine connections, self-expression, and a seamless blend of social interactions and shopping experiences.

Messenger

Messenger is a versatile messaging app that effortlessly connects people with friends, family, communities, and businesses across platforms and devices, offering text, audio, and video call capabilities.

WhatsApp

WhatsApp is a globally trusted and secure messaging app, widely utilized by individuals and businesses for private communication and transactions.

Reality Labs Products

These products of Meta Platform are aimed at exploring new technologies such as neural interfaces using electromyography which facilitates people control their devices using neuromuscular signals and innovations in artificial intelligence and hardware to build next-generation interfaces.

Meta's current product lineup comprises Meta Quest virtual reality devices and a diverse selection of software and content accessible through the Meta Quest Store, enabling an array of social experiences, such as gaming, fitness, entertainment, etc. Meta has introduced Horizon Worlds, a social platform fostering interactions, gaming, virtual events, and meeting new people, alongside Horizon Workrooms, a VR space designed for seamless team collaboration and communication in a work setting. As a part of Meta's virtual reality efforts, Meta Reality was unveiled on Meta Quest Pro, thereby incorporating mixed reality capabilities that blend virtual immersion with real-world grounding for heightened user experience. As a part of its augmented reality initiatives, Meta has introduced Ray-Ban Stories smart glasses and Meta Spark, a platform which enables creators and businesses to build augmented reality experiences.

Strategy

The businesses of Meta are characterized by rapid innovation, rapid change, and disruptive technologies. The strategy of the company focuses on metaverse, the next evolution in social technology where an embodied Internet provides immersive experiences beyond two-dimensional screens. During 2021, Meta revealed a shift in its business and product strategy, prioritizing efforts to contribute to the realization of the metaverse. This initiative is expected to be a multifaceted, dynamic, and long-term endeavor, encompassing the advancement of new and emerging technologies and persistent investment in infrastructure, privacy, safety, and security endeavors, along with extensive collaboration with other companies, developers, partners, and participants.

The core of Meta's product development philosophy revolves around perpetually innovating to craft and enhance socially designed products. Meta is heavily investing in AI and machine learning to leverage an AI-powered discovery engine for recommending relevant content; enhance advertising tools and ad delivery, targeting, and measurement capabilities; and create new product features using generative AI.

Acquisitions[1]

Facebook has acquired 66 companies. The largest acquisition was WhatsApp messenger acquisition. Other notable acquisition of Facebook includes that of Instagram

[1] Rajesh Kumar, Wealth Creations in the World's Largest Mergers and Acquisitions Integrated Case Studies Chap. 39, Major Acquisitions by Facebook, Pages 321–327. Management for Professional series, Springer Nature

and Oculus Virtual Reality. In 2011, Facebook bought Snaptu, an Israeli startup which enabled people to use smartphone like applications on simpler "feature" phones which formed the majority of mobiles in use globally. During April 2012, Facebook acquired mobile photo-sharing app Instagram for approximately $1 billion in cash and stock. After acquisition, Instagram remained as an independently branded standalone app which was separate from Facebook. At the time of acquisition, Instagram was increasingly positioning itself as a social network with 27 million users on IOS alone rather than a social network. Through the deal Instagram gained massive design and engineering resources. Facebook allowed Instagram to grow organically. By 2014, Instagram had approximately 300 million users who were sharing 70 million photos and videos every day.

In June 2012, Facebook acquired the Israeli startup facial recognition company Face.com in a deal valued at approximately $100 million. Facebook's facial recognition technology was already used to offer auto tag suggestions when users upload photos to Facebook. Face.com also had a mobile photo app called Kli. In 2013, Facebook acquired Parse to mark its entry into the new business segment of paid tools and services for developing mobile apps. In 2014 Facebook acquired Oculus VR, the leader in immersive virtual reality technology for $2 billion. At the time of deal, Oculus had received more than 75,000 orders for development kits for the company's virtual reality headset, the Oculus Rift. Facebook acquired Oculus with the strategic aim to extend Oculus' existing advantage in gaming to new verticals which included communications, media and entertainment, education, and other areas.

WhatsApp was acquired by Facebook in the year 2014. The deal was valued at $19 billion. WhatsApp continued to run its operation completely independent since its acquisition. In other words, Facebook kept WhatsApp as a separate service just as it did with Instagram. WhatsApp services were not based on any monetization model. With approximately 450 million monthly active users, WhatsApp allowed users to send text messages to other users for free without advertisements. The company offers the app for free, but to aid in the cost of the service, users pay $0.99 every year. According to *Forbes* estimates, WhatsApp makes money by charging $1 a year subscription in a couple of countries which have clear carrier billing systems and where credit card penetration is high, thus accounting $20 million in annual revenue at the time of acquisition. After acquisition, Facebook scrapped the annual fee charged by WhatsApp. The acquisition of WhatsApp bolstered Facebook's strong position in the messaging arena. Facebook's standalone messaging app for mobile devices was second only to WhatsApp with respect to its share of the smartphone market. As a part of the deal, Facebook paid WhatsApp $4 billion in cash and $12 billion in stock. By May 2018, approximately 1.5 billion users were sending 65 billion messages via the WhatsApp mobile app and web client per day up from 1 billion users when the company was launched. The acquisition gave Facebook the most popular messaging service in the world. The acquisition of WhatsApp provided major benefits to Facebook in terms of large user base in the direct messaging area, smartphone engagement, and penetration across various geographical regions.

ESG Initiatives

In 2021, Meta announced a joint $925 million commitment alongside Stripe, Shopify, McKinsey, and Alphabet to accelerate the development of carbon removal technologies over the next decade. Meta conducts regular assessments to understand ESG topics which are important to the stakeholders. In 2021, Meta made good progress on net positive water goal objectives. Meta restored 2.3 million cubic meters of water in year 2021. By 2021, the company had contracts for more than 7500 megawatts of renewable energy. The six new data center buildings were awarded LEED Gold certification. The company was 30% more water efficient than LEED baseline and avoided 10.5 million gallons of water annually. It recycled 86% of construction waste, thereby saving 32,000 tons of waste from going to landfill. The company had also launched the $1 million Climate Misinformation Grant in partnership with the International Fact Checking Network. The company also has started working with select group of suppliers to calculate and report their greenhouse gas emissions. The company aims to be water positive by the year 2030. In 2021, Meta reached the milestone of contracting 1 billion gallons of water per year for restoration. In order to address physical climate-related risks, Meta executes assessments using models and potential risk scenario. The company launched Happiness Series Initiative to increase supply chain worker morale and sense of belonging. In 2021, Meta Platform launched its first Culinary Sustainability Program focused on embedding environmental and social responsibility into culinary operations. The company operated more than 60 cafes and 700 micro-kitchens globally to serve employees and visitors healthy, delicious snacks, and meals. As a leader in efficiency and renewable energy, Meta is a platinum member of the US Green Building Council and active member on the LEED Advisory and Technical Committees. The building projects completed in year 2021 recycled over 50,000 tons of construction waste. The company had also piloted the use of recycled ground glass as a substitute for cement in various concrete applications in its data center locations. The company also prioritize the use of recycled materials in new system designs. Meta is targeting a 50% reduction in the carbon impact of workplace operations by year 2030. Meta is one of the largest corporate buyers of renewable energy. The solar and wind projects of Meta spans 18 states in the United States. Meta partnered with DigDeep to fund water systems for Navajo families.

The Trinity River wetland adopted by Meta aims to restore over 200 million gallons of water annually.

Risk Factors

The company is subject to variety of laws and regulations in the United States and abroad. The company faces risks related to product offerings. The size of Meta's user base and user's level of engagement across the products are critical to its success. The financial results will be negatively affected if the company fail to retain existing users or add new users or decrease their level of engagement with its products.

Substantially all of the revenues of Meta are generated from advertising. The loss of marketers or reduction in spending by marketers could seriously harm the business of the company. Meta's advertisement targeting and measurement tools utilize data signals from both external websites and services and its own products; however, changes in regulatory environment, third-party mobile operating systems, and browsers may impact the availability of these signals, potentially affecting the advertising revenue. Meta's user growth, engagement, and monetization on mobile devices are reliant on seamless integration with mobile operating systems, networks, technologies, products, and standards which are beyond the control of the company. The chances of potential lack of success in the metaverse strategy and investments may have adverse implications on Meta's business, reputation, or financial outcomes. The competitors of Meta include companies offering online connection, sharing, discovery, and communication products and services to users, along with firms engaged in advertising sales for businesses targeting consumers, as well as those developing tools for optimizing advertising campaigns. Competition presents an ongoing threat to the success of Meta's business. The company receives a high degree of media coverage around the world. Unfavorable publicity with respect to privacy practices, advertising policies, product decisions, product quality, litigation or regulatory activity, or government surveillance is a risk factor which affects the financial results of the company. Investments in virtual and augmented reality have the effect of reducing operating margin and profitability. Real or perceived inaccuracies in community and other metrics may harm the reputation and negatively affect the business of company. The company face risks related to design, manufacturing, and supply chain management of its consumer hardware products. Meta is exposed to inventory risks with respect to its consumer hardware products due to rapid changes in product cycles and pricing.

Stock Performance

Meta Platform stock which was trading at $175.72 on August 1, 2018, increased by 1.67 times to trade at $294 by July 1, 2023. The total monthly cumulative return for Meta was 95% during the 5-year period August 2018–July 2023 compared to the total monthly cumulative return of 69% for market index Nasdaq Composite. The average yearly return for Meta during the above period was 19% compared to 14% accounted by market index Nasdaq Composite during the period August 2018–July 2023.

Table 1 shows the holding period return for Meta stock and Nasdaq Composite during the 5-year period 2018–2022.

The market index had superior returns in all years except in the year 2021.

Table 2 shows the book and market value of equity trend for the company during the period 2018–2022 in millions of dollars.

The average book value of equity as percent of market value of equity was 26.8% during the period 2018–2022. The market value of equity had peaked in the year 2021 thereafter declining by approximately 66% in value the following year.

Table 1 Holding period return

Year	Meta Platform	Nasdaq Composite	Excess returns
2018	−25%	−5%	−20%
2019	23%	31%	−7%
2020	35%	36%	−1%
2021	30%	21%	10%
2022	−62%	−27%	−35%

Table 2 Book and market value of equity

Year	2018	2019	2020	2021	2022
Book value of equity	84,127.00	101,054.00	128,290.00	124,879.00	125,713.00
Market value of equity	374,130.86	585,373.00	778,232.84	921,935.35	314,568.76
BV as percent of MV	22.5%	17.3%	16.5%	13.5%	40.0%

Table 3 Financial highlights

	(In millions of dollars)				
Financial highlights	2018	2019	2020	2021	2022
Total assets	97,334.00	133,376.00	159,316.00	165,987.00	185,727.00
Short-term investments	10,019.00	19,079.00	17,576.00	16,601.00	14,681.00
Total equity	84,127.00	101,054.00	128,290.00	124,879.00	125,713.00
Total revenue	55,838.00	70,697.00	85,965.00	117,929.00	116,609.00
Total operating expenses	21,570.00	33,941.00	36,602.00	48,527.00	62,416.00
Net income	22,112.00	18,485.00	29,146.00	39,370.00	23,200.00
Market cap	374,130.86	585,373.00	778,232.84	921,935.35	314,568.76
Enterprise value	333,516.86	540,842.00	726,932.84	887,810.35	300,421.76

Table 3 shows the financial highlights of the company in millions of dollars.

During the period 2018–2022, the total assets, short-term investments, and total equity of the company increased by 18%, 16%, and 11% on average basis. The average growth rate of revenues and net income were 26% and 9%, respectively. The total operating expenses increased by 32%. The market capitalization and enterprise value of the company increased by 10% and 13%, respectively, during the above period. The market value declined by approximately 66% in 2022 compared to the previous period.

Table 4 shows the performance measures of the company during the period 2018–2022.

The average net margin, ROE, and ROA for Meta Platform were 30.59%, 24.58%, and 19.53%, respectively, during the period 2018–2022. The average debt equity ratio during the above period was 0.10.

Table 4 Performance indicators

Ratios	2018	2019	2020	2021	2022
Net margin%	39.6	26.15	33.9	33.38	19.9
ROE%	27.91	19.96	25.42	31.1	18.52
ROA%	24.32	16.02	19.92	24.21	13.19
DER	0.01	0.1	0.08	0.11	0.21

Table 5 Estimation of economic value

Year	2021	2022
Profit before income tax	47,284	28,819
Income tax	7915.34	5475.61
Net operating profit after tax (NOPAT)	39368.66	23343.39
Stockholder equity	124,879.00	125,713.00
Long-term debt		9923
Total capital employed	124,879	135,636
WACC	9.64%	10.00%
Capital charge	12038.34	13563.60
Economic value	27330.32	9779.79

Table 5 illustrates the estimation of economic value of Meta during the period 2021 and 2022. The values are given in millions of dollars.

References

1. https://investor.fb.com/home/default.aspx
2. Annual Report 2022
3. Meta Sustainability Report 2021

Case 91 Mercury Systems

The technology company Mercury Systems Inc. is a technology-intensive company related to global aerospace and defense industry. The company is headquartered in Andover, Massachusetts. The end-to-end processing platform of the company offers broad range of aerospace and defense programs. The processing technologies of the platform consist of signal solutions, display, software applications, networking, storage, and secure processing. The innovative solutions provided by the company are software defined, open, and modular to meet high-tech needs of customers. The company is the lead manufacturer of essential components, products, modules, and subsystems. The products of the company are sold to defense prime contractors, the US government, and original equipment manufacturers (OEM) commercial aerospace companies. Mercury Systems' comprehensive range of products and solutions has been successfully implemented in over 300 programs, which cater to the needs of more than 25 diverse defense prime contractors and commercial aviation customers. At the forefront of innovation, Mercury is spearheading the advancement and integration of commercial technology into aerospace and defense solutions. The company's expertise spans from chip-scale to system-scale and encompasses diverse data domains, including radio frequency ("RF") and digital up to decision-making levels. The customers of the company rely on its mission-critical solutions for a wide range of applications, including command, control, communications, computers, intelligence, surveillance, and reconnaissance ("C4ISR"). Additionally, the firm's expertise extends to electronic intelligence, mission computing avionics, electro-optical/infrared ("EO/IR") systems, electronic warfare, weapons and missile defense, hypersonic, and radar technologies. In fiscal 2022, the company made revenues of $988.2 million. By 2022, the company employed a total of 2386 people.

© The Author(s), under exclusive license to Springer Nature Switzerland AG 2024

B. R. Kumar, *Rising Stars*, Management for Professionals,
https://doi.org/10.1007/978-3-031-50032-9_91

Strategy

According to Renaissance Strategic Advisors ("RSA"), as of September 2021, the global aerospace and defense electronics market is estimated to be $130 billion in 2021, growing to $155 billion by 2026.

The market opportunity for the company arises from emerging need for domestically designed, sourced, and manufactured electronics in important aerospace, defense, and intelligence applications. The primary focus is on making advanced commercial technologies readily available and accessible to aerospace and defense sector. Primarily, Mercury Systems aims to enhance command, control, communications, computers, and intelligence (C4I) systems, sensors, and electronic warfare which cater to different commercial markets. The surging demand for tactical intelligence, surveillance, and reconnaissance (ISR) is driving substantial growth in sensor data generation. As a result, there is an even greater need for the company's products' capability to securely store and process data onboard platforms.

In 2021, Mercury adopted a companywide initiative termed IMPACT which laid the foundation for the next phase of the company's value creation mechanism in terms of growth, margin expansion, and free cash flow generation. The IMPACT initiatives focus on the areas of organizational efficiency and scalability, procurement, and supply chain. Mercury aims to excel in the aerospace and defense industry by providing accessible, secure technologies through their Mercury Processing Platform, offering innovative solutions tailored to meet the market's demand for speed and affordability. Their strategy centers on differentiated market positioning and significant R&D investments. The company primarily focus on growing organically through investment in people, processes, systems, and trusted manufacturing assets. The company supplements its organic growth through expansion of capabilities, market access, and penetration through mergers and acquisitions. Since 2014, Mercury has completed 15 acquisitions with investment of approximately $1.4 billion. Mercury develops leading edge technologies which are customized for aerospace and defense applications. The company aims to improve operational capability and scalability by driving transformational and sustainable business improvement and value creation across enterprises. As a premier commercial technology company in aerospace and defense, the strategies revolve around leveraging key strengths through innovation, scaling existing capabilities, and targeted acquisitions of adjacent technologies. The company has successfully initiated strategic programs such as Aegis, Patriot, Lower Tier Air and Missile Defense Sensor ("LTAMDS"), Surface Electronic Warfare Improvement Program ("SEWIP"), Terminal High Altitude Area Defense ("THAAD"), Predator, F-35, Reaper, F-18, F-16 SABR, E2-D Hawkeye, Paveway, Filthy Buzzard, PGK, P-8, Advanced Integrated Defensive Electronic Warfare Suite ("AIDEWS"), Common Display System ("CDS"), Aviation Mission Common Server ("AMCS"), and WIN-T.

Mercury's expanded capabilities, especially in integrated subsystems related to defense threats and increased system complexity, have led to increased outsourcing

Table 1 Major acquisitions

Name of acquired entities	Year of acquisition
Lewis Innovative Technologies, Inc.	2015
Microsemi Carve-Out Business	2016
CES Creative Electronic Systems S.A.	2016
Delta Microwave, LLC	2017
Richland Technologies L.L.C.	2017
Themis Computer	2018
Germane Systems, LC	2018
GECO Avionics, LLC	2019
The Athena Group, Inc.	2019
Syntonic Microwave LLC	2019
American Panel Corporation	2019
Physical Optics Corporation	2020
Pentek Systems, Inc. and Pentek Technologies, LLC	2021
Avalex Technologies, LLC	2021
Atlanta Micro, Inc.	2021

Source: Annual Report 2022

from prime defense contractors and OEM customers. Mercury has expanded into new submarkets within major markets. For instance, the company has moved into electronic warfare, weapon systems, acoustics submarkets, C4I, and mission computing. Through vertical expansion, the company seeks to apply technology on all its aerospace and defense platforms. The company also focuses on investment in next-generation chiplet technology.

Table 1 lists the major acquisition of Mercury undertaken in the last decade

Competitive Strengths

The company is a major subsystem solution provider for the C4ISR and electronic warfare markets. The products and solutions of the company have been deployed on more than 300 different programs and over 25 different defense prime contractors. The company serves high-priority markets for the DoD and foreign militaries such as UAVs, ballistic missile defense, guided missiles and precision munitions, airborne reconnaissance, and electronic warfare system. The company is the leading technology company which serves the aerospace and defense industry. The company has a portfolio of open standards architecture technology building blocks across the entire sensor processing chain. The company also offers secure processing expertise which is built in to its pre-integrated subsystems. The company have invested in advanced domestic design and manufacturing capabilities. Over the years, the company has prioritized investments to build internal capabilities and capacity for defense electronics design and manufacturing in the United States. Mercury Systems has established long relationships with defense prime contractors, US government, and other key organizations in the defense industry over 30 years in defense electronics industry. These customers include Airbus, BAE Systems, Boeing, General Atomics, General Dynamics, L3Harris Technologies, Leonardo, Lockheed Martin Corporation, Northrop Grumman Corporation, and US Navy. By July 2022, the company held 185 patents of different duration issued in the United States.

Solutions and Products

The technology provided by Mercury Systems fits at the crossroads of the high-tech and defense sectors. The key differentiators of the Mercury Systems are in terms of mission-ready, trusted and secure, and software-defined, open and modular. The Mercury Processing Platform is designed to comply standards in terms of computer intensive, signal processing, image processing, and command and control applications.

The products offered by Mercury Systems can be classified into different categories.

Components

Components represent the basic building blocks of an electronic system.

Modules and Subassemblies

Modules and subassemblies combine multiple components to serve range of complex functions which include processing, networking, and graphics display.

Integrated Subsystems

Integrated subsystems consist of components, modules, and/or subassemblies into one system which are enabled with software. The company uses the latest Intel® server-class processing products, Xilinx Field Programmable Gate Arrays ("FPGA"), as well as NVIDIA GPU products in its embedded high-performance processing technologies. Embedded systems security has become a requirement for new and emerging military programs. The company has pioneered the development of defense industry's current and emerging open standards, including standards such as RACEway, RapidIO, VXS, VPX, REDI, and notably OpenVPX.

Risk Factors

Mercury Systems depends heavily on defense electronics programs and faces the risk of potential termination and reductions and delays in government spending. Economic conditions adversely affect the business, results of operations, and financial condition. Price inflation for labor and materials would adversely affect the business of the firm. The loss of one or more of the largest customers, programs, or applications could adversely affect the results of operations. The markets for the company's products are highly competitive and are characterized by rapidly changing technology, frequent product performance improvements, and evolving industry standards. The competition from existing or new firms could cause to experience downward pressure on prices, fewer customer orders, and reduced margins and loss of market share. The potential unavailability of critical components from sole source suppliers might disrupt or delay product deliveries to customers.

Stock Return Analysis

Mercury Systems (MRCY) was trading at $54.50 on August 1, 2018. By July 1, 2023, the stock price declined by 0.67 times to trade at $36.7. The total cumulative monthly return for Mercury stock was −3% during the 5-year period August 2018–July 2023 compared to 69% total cumulative monthly return of market index Nasdaq Composite. The data is taken from yahoo finance.

Table 2 shows the holding period return of Mercury Systems and Nasdaq Composite index during the 5-year period 2018–2022.

The stock underperformed compared to market index Nasdaq Composite in all years except in the year 2022.

Table 3 highlights the book and market value of equity trend during the period 2018–2022. The values are given in millions of dollars.

Table 2 Holding period return

Year	Mercury Systems	Nasdaq Composite	Excess returns
2018	−13%	−5%	−8%
2019	18%	31%	−13%
2020	15%	36%	−21%
2021	−23%	21%	−43%
2022	−21%	−27%	5%

Table 3 Book and market value trends

Year	2018	2019	2020	2021	2022
Book value of equity	771.89	1284.74	1384.78	1484.15	1537.19
Market value of equity	1785.94	3816.31	4302.88	3661.38	3581.88
BV as percent of MV	43.2%	33.7%	32.2%	40.5%	42.9%

Table 4 Financial highlights

	(In millions of dollars)				
Financial highlights	2018	2019	2020	2021	2022
Total assets	1064.48	1416.98	1610.72	1955.14	2304.42
Short-term investments	66.52	257.93	226.84	113.84	65.65
Total equity	771.89	1284.74	1384.78	1484.15	1537.19
Total revenue	493.18	654.74	796.61	924.00	988.20
Total operating expenses	173.18	207.56	261.30	288.99	324.48
Net income	40.88	46.78	85.71	62.04	11.28
Market capitalization	1785.94	3816.31	4302.88	3661.38	3581.88
Enterprise value	1914.41	3558.38	4143.03	3819.05	4037.61

Table 5 Performance measures

Ratios	2018	2019	2020	2021	2022
Net margin%	8.29	7.14	10.76	6.71	1.14
ROE%	5.46	4.55	6.42	4.33	0.75
ROA%	4.35	3.77	5.66	3.48	0.53
DER	0.25		0.05	0.18	0.34

The average book value of equity as percent of market value was 41.7% during the 5-year period 2018–2022.

Table 4 shows the financial highlights of the company during the 5-year period 2018–2022.

The total assets, short-term investments, and total equity increased on an average by 21.5%, 46%, and 21% during the period 2018–2022. The total revenues increased by 19% on average basis, whereas the net income declined by 3% on average basis. The total operating expenses increased by 17% on average basis during the period 2018–2022. The market capitalization and enterprise value increased by 27% and 25%, respectively. The source of data is annual reports and gurufocus.com.

Table 5 gives the profitability and leverage position of the company during the period 2018–2022.

The average net margin, ROE, and ROA for the company were 6.81%, 4.30%, and 3.56%, respectively, during the period 2018–2022. The average debt equity ratio during the period was 0.21.

Reference

1. Annual Report 2022

Case 92 National Bank Holdings Corporation

National Bank Holdings Corporation (NBHC) is a Denver-based bank holding company which provides community banking services. National Bank Holdings through its bank subsidiaries NBH Bank and Bank of Jackson Hole Trust operates a network of over 95 banking centers to serve individual consumers, businesses, and government institutions. NBH Bank operates through brands such as Community Banks of Colorado, Community Banks Mortgage, Bank Midwest, Bank Midwest Mortgage, Hillcrest Bank Mortgage, Bank of Jackson Hole, etc. The banking centers are located primarily in Colorado, greater Kansas City region, Utah, Wyoming, Texas, New Mexico, and Idaho. By December 31, 2022, NBHC held $9.6 billion in assets, 7.2 billion in loans, $7.9 billion in deposits, $1.1 billion in shareholders' equity, and $0.8 billion of trust and wealth management assets under management.

During the period 2010–2022, NBHC completed eight bank acquisitions. In 2022, NBHC completed the acquisition of Community Bancorporation and merged it. The deal was valued at $140.4 million. During 2022, the company completed the acquisition of Bancshares of Jackson Hole, the bank holding company of Wyoming-based Bank of Jackson Hole. The transaction was valued at $213.4 million. As of December 31, 2022, the bank employed 1255 full-time and 67 part-time associates.

Business Strategy

The growth strategy of NBHC focuses on capitalizing on market opportunities. The company aims to generate strong organic growth along with pursuing selective acquisitions of financial institutions and other complementary businesses. NBHC focuses on organic growth through strong banking relationships with small- and medium-sized businesses and consumers. NBHC focuses on client-centered relationship-driven banking strategy. The bank's subsidiaries offer a complete array of loan, deposit, and treasury management products and services with focus on small- and medium-sized businesses with an advisory approach. The business and commercial bankers are supported by treasury management teams in each of the markets

© The Author(s), under exclusive license to Springer Nature Switzerland AG 2024
B. R. Kumar, *Rising Stars*, Management for Professionals,
https://doi.org/10.1007/978-3-031-50032-9_92

which the bank serve. The consumer bankers offer a complete portfolio of loan, deposit, online, and mobile banking solutions. NBHC also aims for expansion of commercial banking, business banking, and specialty businesses. The bank originates high-quality loan portfolio which are diversified across industries and granular in loan size. The bank has preferred lender status with the Small Business Administration and offers a leveraged platform for growth in the business lending segment. The bank focuses on providing small- and medium-sized businesses with alternative digital access to address borrowing, depository, and cash management needs. NBHC is involved in the development of digital solution 2UniFiSM, a national platform for providing banking services to small- and medium-sized businesses, digital payment tools, and financial services information management. NBHC leverages its comprehensive underwriting and risk management processes under one operating platform. The company has maintained a conservative risk culture with adherence to comprehensive and seasoned policies across the organization. The policy of the bank has been to implement self-imposed concentration limits on loan portfolio to ensure granular and diverse loan portfolio and protect against downside risk for any particular industry sector. The strategy of NBHC is to acquire or expand into financial services franchises which exhibit attractive demographic attributes and business growth trends. The major focus for acquisitions is in primary markets of Colorado, the greater Kansas City region, Texas, Utah, Wyoming, New Mexico, and Idaho. The strategic objective of the bank is to serve small- to medium-sized businesses in its markets.

Products and Services

Commercial and Specialty Banking

The commercial bankers focus on small- and medium-sized businesses and commercial real estate investors and developers. This division offers a complete suite of loan, deposit, and treasury management products and services. The bank originates commercial and industrial loans and leases which include working capital loans, equipment loans, lender finance loans, food and agribusiness loans, nonprofit loans, owner-occupied commercial real estate, and other commercial loans and leases. Working capital loans have terms of 1–3 years which are secured by accounts receivable and inventory and personal guarantees of the principal amount. Nonowner-occupied commercial real estate loans ("CRE") consist of loans to finance the purchase of commercial real estate and development loans. A range of Small Business Administration (SBA) loans are offered to support manufacturers, distributors, and service providers targeted to small businesses and entrepreneurs. The bank also offers value-added commercial deposit and treasury management products to clients to optimize their cash management program. The bank focuses on full relationship banking which include banking core operating and ancillary accounts. Commercial clients are provided with money market and short-term repurchase reserve accounts. The bank offers an array of treasury management solutions to clients which include business online and mobile banking, commercial credit card services, wire transfers, automated clearing house services, remote deposit capture services, controlled disbursements, and fraud prevention. Business loans consist of term loans, line of credit and, real estate secured loans whose terms vary by purpose and by type of underlying collateral.

Residential and Personal Banking

Residential real estate loans encompass loans secured by the borrower's primary or secondary residence, along with properties acquired by the borrower for investment purposes. These closed loans are typically amortized over a 10–30-year term. Consumer loans are structured as small personal lines of credit and term loans. The bank offers variety of deposit products to clients such as checking accounts, savings accounts, money market accounts, health savings accounts, fixed maturity time deposit, and individual retirement accounts. The bank offers comprehensive user-friendly mobile and online banking platforms. The bank also offers trust and wealth management services.

Lending Activities

The loan portfolio consists of commercial and industrial loans, commercial real estate loans, residential real estate loans, business loans, and consumer loans.

ESG Initiatives

The bank focuses on equity, diversity, and inclusion principles. Approximately 64% of company's workforce is female, and 54% of the females have managerial roles. Minorities account for 23% of the company's workforce.

Risk Factors

The business and operations are sensitive to general business and economic conditions in the United States. The business of the bank is highly susceptible to credit risk and fluctuations in the value of real estate and other collateral securing such credit. A decline in residential real estate market prices and reduced home sales could negatively impact the value of collateral securing mortgage loans, leading to higher charge-offs in the future, and also affect mortgage loan originations and gains on sale of mortgage loans. The allowances for credit losses and fair value adjustments may prove to be insufficient to absorb losses inherent in loan or other real estate-owned portfolio. The increasing federal, state, and local regulations on loan servicing, collections, or other aspects might raise compliance costs and noncompliance risks. The SBA lending program is dependent on the US federal government, and hence the bank faces specific risks associated with originating SBA loans. Consumer and commercial banking are highly competitive. The company faces significant competition from other financial institutions and service providers. The bank faces risks of system failures and interruptions on account of heavy dependence on the Internet, cloud technologies, and third-party providers. The banking industry is subject to extensive regulation, supervision, and legislation by federal and state regulators and bodies.

Stock Price Performance

Table 1 presents a comparison of NBHC stock price performance with that of indices performance during the recent 5-year period. It assumes $100 invested on December 31, 2017 with dividends invested on a total return basis.

The 5-year holding period return for NBHC was 44% compared to 19% and 22% holding period returns accounted by market indices KBW Regional Banking Index and Russell 2000 Index. The 5-year average returns for NBHC stock index and Russell 2000 Index were 8.7%, 5.48%, and 5.74%, respectively.

Next section analyzes NBHC stock returns during the recent 5-year period in comparison to the returns of Russell 2000 Index. The stock was trading at $37.65 on Sept 1, 2018. By Aug 1, 2023, the stock price declined to $34.90. The total cumulative monthly return for NBHC was 15% during the period Sept 2018–Aug 2023. The market index had returns of approximately 28% during the above period. The average yearly return for the stock during the period was 3% compared to 6% returns registered by the market index Russell 2000.

Table 2 gives the holding period return for the NBHC stock and the market index during the 5-year period 2018–2022.

Table 1 Stock performance

Year	2017	2018	2019	2020	2021	2022
NBHC	100	96.57	112.55	107.53	$147.37	$144.19
KBW Regional Banking Index	$100	$82.51	$102.20	$93.33	$127.53	$118.71
Russell 2000 Index	$100	$88.97	$111.65	$133.90	$153.70	$122.25

Source: Annual Report 2022

Table 2 Holding period return

Year	NBHC	Russell 2000	Excess returns
2018	−18.01%	−20.51%	2.5%
2019	10.20%	11.27%	−1.1%
2020	0.49%	90.88%	−90.4%
2021	32.07%	−7.77%	39.8%
2022	−7.33%	−8.36%	1.0%

Table 3 Book and market value of equity

Year	2018	2019	2020	2021	2022
Book value of equity	695.01	766.92	820.69	840.11	1092.20
Market value of equity	949.84	1098.04	1003.58	1316.39	1582.19
BV as percent of MV	73.2%	69.8%	81.8%	63.8%	69.0%

Table 4 Financial highlights

	(In millions of dollars)				
Financial highlights	2018	2019	2020	2021	2022
Total assets	5676.67	5895.51	6659.95	7214.01	9573.24
Gross loans	4140.43	4532.85	4601.54	4652.53	7243.24
Deposits	4535.62	4737.13	5676.23	6228.17	7872.63
Total equity	695.01	766.92	820.69	840.11	1092.20
Interest income	221.39	240.83	216.85	200.13	283.65
Non-interest income	70.78	86.94	137.07	106.5	63.51
Interest expense	23.95	36.77	25.06	13.82	17.85
Total non-interest expense	57.31	45.83	54.34	53.68	75.49
Market capitalization	949.84	1098.04	1003.58	1316.39	1582.19
Enterprise value	1141.95	1195.52	398.01	510.17	1825.57

The NBHC stock outperformed the market index in the year 2018 and 2021. The data was sourced from Yahoo Finance.

Table 3 compares the book value of equity and market value of equity during the 5-year period. The values are given in millions of dollars.

The average book value as percent of market value of equity was 71.5%.

Table 4 gives the financial highlights of the bank during the 5-year period 2018–2022. The data source is annual reports.

During the period 2018–2022, the average growth rate of total assets, gross loans, deposits, and total equity were 14%, 17%, 15%, and 12%, respectively. The interest and non-interest income increased by 8% and 4% on average basis. The interest expense declined by 8%, whereas the total non-interest expense increased by 9%. The market capitalization and enterprise value increased by 15% and 56% on average basis.

Table 5 highlights the performance ratios of NBHC during the 5-year period 2018–2022.

The average ROA, ROE, and net interest margin for NBHC for the 5-year period 2018–2022 were 1.23%, 10.16%, and 3.71%, respectively. The average efficiency ratio during the above period was 64.62%. In terms of asset quality, the ratio of nonperforming assets to total assets have shown a declining trend. The average nonperforming assets to total assets was 0.41%. By December 2022, the consolidated tier 1 leverage ratio for the bank had been 9.29%, whereas the common equity tier 1 and consolidated tier 1 risk-based capital ratios were 10.54%.

Table 5 Performance ratios

Ratios	2018	2019	2020	2021	2022
Performance ratios					
Return on average assets %	1.17	1.39	1.41	1.35	0.85
Return on average equity%	10.01	10.99	11.16	11.27	7.38
Net interest margin%	4.2	3.91	3.52	3.24	3.69
Efficiency ratio%	70.89	62.63	61.88	64.48	63.22
Asset quality ratio					
Nonperforming assets to total assets%	0.6	0.49	0.47	0.24	0.23

References

1. https://www.investorrelations.nationalbankholdings.com/corporate-information/corporate-profile/default.aspx
2. Annual Report 2023

Case 93 Addus HomeCare

Addus HomeCare is a leading provider of comprehensive home care and support services which focuses on innovative patient services. The company has been in 40 plus years of service. Addus focuses on home care services which include personal care services that assist with activities of daily living along with hospice and home health services. Addus' consumers are persons who are at risk of hospitalization or institutionalization such as the elderly, chronically ill, and disabled. The payor clients of Addus include federal, state, and local governmental agencies, managed care organizations, commercial insurers, and private individuals. Currently Addus offers home care services to approximately 44,000 consumers through 212 locations across 22 states in the United States. In 2021 and 2022, Addus Home served 67,000 and 66,000 discrete consumers. The company provides all three levels of care, personal care, home health, and hospice services in Ohio, Illinois, and New Mexico.

The services and operating model of the company cater to the crucial needs across the healthcare continuum. The operating model offers significant value to managed care organization. The costs involved are less for care provided in home rather than facility-based care which is typically preferred by families of consumers. The company lower the cost of chronic and acute care treatment by delaying or eliminating the need for care in more expensive settings. The company offer services to private pay consumers. The reimbursement for the majority of services provided by Addus comes from federal, state, and local government programs which include Medicare, Medicaid state programs, managed care organizations, other state agencies, and the Veterans Health Administration.

Growth Strategy

The demand for personal care services is witnessing a surge within managed care delivery models, encompassing programs such as Medicaid Long-Term Services and Supports (LTSS) and Medicare Advantage Plans. These managed care

© The Author(s), under exclusive license to Springer Nature Switzerland AG 2024

B. R. Kumar, *Rising Stars*, Management for Professionals,
https://doi.org/10.1007/978-3-031-50032-9_93

initiatives strive to effectively control costs, optimize resource utilization, and enhance service quality by fostering a close collaboration between health insurance plans and healthcare providers. The growth of the company's business depends on its ability to provide high-quality care, maintenance of existing payor relationship, establishment of new payors, increase of referral sources, and retention of caregivers.

The company focuses on providing high-quality care. The caregivers of Addus adhere to individual care plans monitored through supervisory visits. They receive preservice training, evaluations, ongoing in-service education, and in some states, mandatory certified training with state certification maintenance. To drive organic growth, Addus focuses on strengthening sales, marketing, and business intelligence analytics, investing in technology, and optimizing operations for efficiency. Addus expects increased demand due to an aging population and enhanced alignment with referral sources and payors, while selectively expanding with new offices in existing markets when viable opportunities arise. In order to capitalize on the industry's shift toward managed care models to enhance care coordination, Addus strategically collaborates with managed care organizations. By offering a larger, experienced partnership, sophisticated technology, electronic visit records, and outcome-focused services, Addus anticipates being competitive in the evolving narrower provider networks. Addus focuses on integrated care model, expansion into hospice and home health, and alignment with the broader healthcare sector making the company an appealing choice for managed care organizations seeking diversified home-based care solutions. Addus HomeCare also focuses on acquisitions as a part of its growth strategy. In 2022, the company acquired JourneyCare Inc. and Apple Home Healthcare Ltd. In year 2021, the company-acquired Armada Group and Summit Home Health.

Addus Services

The company operates three business segments: personal care, hospice, and home health.

Personal Care

The personal care segment offers nonmedical assistance to elderly, chronically ill, or disabled who are having increased risk of hospitalization or institutionalization. The services offered include assistance related to bathing, grooming, oral care, feeding and dressing, medication reminders, meal planning and preparation, housekeeping, and transportation services. The personal care segment encompasses staffing services for various clients such as assisted living facilities, nursing homes, and hospice facilities. Each payor client independently sets eligibility standards, service type, amount, duration, and scope and establishes reimbursement rates following relevant laws, regulations, or contracts.

Hospice

The hospice segment offers services which include palliative nursing care, social work, spiritual counselling, homemaker services, and bereavement counseling. The patients receiving hospice services have life expectancy of 6 months or less.

Home Health

The home health segment offers primarily medical services to individuals who may need support during illness or after hospitalization including skilled nursing and physical, occupational, and speech therapy.

Payors

The payor clients are principally federal, state, and local governmental agencies and managed care organizations. The commercial insurance payor clients of the company are generally profit companies. The majority of the services offered by the company is rendered through agreements with state and local governmental social and aging service agencies, usually lasting 1–2 years with an option for renewal typically ranging from 1 to 5 years, subject to a 60-day termination notice.

Risk Factors

The challenging economic conditions marked by significant inflationary pressures, elevated interest rates, difficult labor market conditions, and supply network disruptions are risk factors for the company which have financial consequences. The impact of the CARES Act and other stimulus or relief legislation along with the government responses to aid healthcare providers can impact the operations and cash flows of the company. Given the nature of the company's consumers and the physical proximity required in the operations, the company might be more susceptible to the impacts of a public health emergency compared to other businesses. Liquidity problems might arise due to timing differences in reimbursement. The industry segment is subject to extensive government regulation. The company's consumer caseload, units of service, and profitability could be negatively impacted by reductions in reimbursement and other changes to Medicare, Medicaid, and other federal, state, and local medical and social programs. Service providers in the healthcare and long-term care industries face intense competition.

The healthcare and long-term care industries are highly competitive among service providers. The competitors for the company include personal care services providers, hospice providers, home health providers, private caregivers, hospital-based agencies, community-based organizations, and self-directed care programs.

The insurance liability coverage may not be sufficient for the business needs of the company.

Market Performance

Addus stock which was trading at a price of $70.15 on September 1, 2018, increased by 1.33 times to trade at $93.82 by August 1, 2023. The cumulative monthly return for Addus stock was 55% compared to cumulative monthly returns of 29% for the market index Russell 2000 during the 5-year period September 2018–August 2023. The average yearly return for Addus was 11% compared to 6% yearly returns accounted by market index Russell 2000 during the above period. The source of data was Yahoo Finance.

Table 1 shows the holding period return for the Addus stock during the recent 5-year period compared to the holding period return for the market index Russell 2000.

Addus HomeCare had excess returns compared to market index in the year 2019 and 2022.

Table 2 compares the book value of equity and market value of the equity during the period 2018–2022. The values are given in millions of dollars.

The average book value of equity as percent of market value of equity was 39% during the period 2018–2022.

Table 3 gives the financial highlights of Addus HomeCare during the 5-year period 2018–2022.

During the period 2018–2022, the total assets, short-term investments, and total equity increased by 32%, 13%, and 27%, respectively, on average basis. The total revenues and net income increased by 17% and 31%, respectively, on average basis. The total expenses increased by an average of 20% during the period. The market capitalization and enterprise value increased by 20% and 24%, respectively, on

Table 1 Holding period return

Year	Addus HomeCare	Russell 2000	Excess returns
2018	−100%	−9%	−91%
2019	62%	2%	59%
2020	24%	40%	−16%
2021	−17%	−8%	−9%
2022	25%	−6%	30%

Table 2 Excess value

Year	2018	2019	2020	2021	2022
Book value of equity	268.49	475.59	518.68	574.34	633.54
Market value of equity	890.99	1518.28	1853.07	1490.55	1604.57
BV as percent of MV	30.1%	31.3%	28.0%	38.5%	39.5%

Table 3 Financial highlights

Financial highlights	(In millions of dollars) 2018	2019	2020	2021	2022
Total assets	348.09	636.75	892.58	947.59	937.99
Short-term investments	70.41	111.71	145.08	168.90	79.96
Total equity	268.49	475.59	518.68	574.34	633.54
Total revenue	516.65	648.79	764.78	864.50	951.12
Total operating expenses	113.98	144.49	181.73	203.91	231.00
Net income	16.43	25.24	33.13	45.13	46.03
Market capitalization	890.99	1518.28	1853.07	1490.55	1604.57
Enterprise value	837.87	1488.00	1947.66	1585.20	1702.67

Table 4 Performance ratios

Ratios	2018	2019	2020	2021	2022
Net margin%	3.18	3.89	4.33	5.22	4.84
ROE%	7.39	6.78	6.66	8.26	7.62
ROA%	5.3	5.13	4.33	4.9	4.88
DER	0.06	0.17	0.46	0.46	0.28

average basis during the above period. The data was sourced from annual reports and gurufocus.com.

Table 4 shows the performance ratios of the firm during the period 2018–2022.

The average net margin, ROE, and ROA were 4.29%, 7.34%, and 4.91%, respectively, during the period 2018–2022. The average debt equity ratio for the company during the above period was 0.29.

References

1. https://addus.gcs-web.com/investor-overview?c=231191&p=irol-irhome
2. Annual Report 2022

Case 94 LHC Group

LHC Group is a post-acute healthcare service provider. By the year 2022, the company had 920 service providers in 37 states in the United States. LHC provides services in five segments – home health services, hospice services, home- and community-based services, facility-based services, and healthcare innovations. The facility-based services are primarily offered through its long-term acute care hospitals (LTACHs). The home health services offer a broad range of services such as skilled nursing, medically oriented social services, and physical, occupational, and speech therapy. Home health agencies facilitate nurses, home health aides, and therapists to design and implement individualized treatment plan for patients in accordance with a physician-prescribed plan of care. In 2022, LHC operated 527 home health service locations. The hospice segment offers end-of-life care to patients with terminal illnesses through the services of interdisciplinary teams consisting of physicians, nurses, home health aides, counselors, and volunteers. The hospice segment offers wide range of services which include pain and symptom management, emotional and spiritual support, homemaker services, and counseling. By the year end 2022, the company offered 159 hospice locations. The home- and community-based segment offers services related to activities of daily living to elderly, chronically ill, and disabled patients. This segment had operations in 128 locations. The LTACH location offers services primarily to patients with complex medical conditions who have been transitioned out of a hospital intensive care unit. By 2022, the LTACH had 367 licensed beds. The healthcare innovation (HCI) segment, comprised of Imperium Health Management, LLC; Long Term Solutions, Inc.; and Advance Care House Calls, aims to enhance the provision of services in other segments to benefit patients and payors, offering accountable care organization enablement, in-home assessments for the long-term care insurance industry, and primary medical care for patients with chronic and acute illnesses who struggle to visit a doctor's office. In the year 2022, LHC Group Inc. and UnitedHealth Group entered into an agreement and plan of merger with UnitedHealth Group and its subsidiary Lightning Merger Sub Inc. As a result of

© The Author(s), under exclusive license to Springer Nature Switzerland AG 2024

B. R. Kumar, *Rising Stars*, Management for Professionals,
https://doi.org/10.1007/978-3-031-50032-9_94

Table 1 Segment revenues in millions of dollars

Segment/year	2020	2021	2022
Home health	1466.779	1551.542	1531.491
Hospice	243.806	311.218	407.489
Home and community based	194.584	189.561	180.587
Facility based	128.578	132.098	127.916
HCI	32.457	35.203	35.288
Consolidated	2066.204	2219.622	2282.771

Source: Annual Report 2022

the merger plan, LHC Group was delisted from the Nasdaq stock market. The company employs approximately 30,000 employees in 37 states of the United States.

Table 1 gives the net service revenue for LHC for the recent 3-year period.

Strategy

The company aims to become the leading provider of in-home healthcare services in the United States along with providing complementary suite of post-acute healthcare service offerings through its facility-based and HCI segments. In 2019, there were approximately 11,356 Medicare-certified home nursing agencies which operate in the United States. Approximately 18% of these Medicare-certified home health agencies serve rural areas, and 87% of them are privately owned. There were 4840 hospice agencies which participated in the Medicare Program in the year 2018. The goal of the company is to become the preeminent provider of high-quality post-acute care in the markets where the company serves by nurturing long-lasting relationships with local hospitals, physicians, and other healthcare providers.

One of the strategic pursuits adopted by the company is to drive internal growth in existing market. The company has plans to expand the number of healthcare providers who have been referred to the company and broaden its service offerings in each market through education, community engagement, and focus on high-quality care for patients. The company aims to improve margins and net income by expansion into new markets. The company aims for organic growth through utilization of point of care technology, development of de novo locations, and acquisition of existing Medicare- and/or Medicaid-certified agencies in attractive markets. As a part of its growth strategy, LHC partners with hospital and health systems along with acquisition of free-standing agencies. The company also focuses on strategic acquisitions in new and existing markets. By December 31, 2022, the portfolio of LHC comprised of a total of 82 equity joint ventures. Among these, 75 were formed in collaboration with hospital and health systems, encompassing a network of more than 350 hospitals. Additionally, the company had four joint ventures involving physicians and three with other parties. The equity joint ventures are structured as either manager managed or board managed.

Services

Home Health Services

The registered nurses and licensed practical nurses of the company provide different variety of services to homebound patients who suffers from acute or chronic illness. These services include wound care and dressing changes, cardiac rehabilitation, infusion therapy, pain management, pharmaceutical administration, and patient education. The company has also designed proprietary clinical pathways to treat chronic diseases such as diabetes, hypertension, arthritis, Alzheimer's and Parkinson's disease, osteoporosis, and complex wounds. LHC offers skilled nursing, ventilator and tracheotomy services, extended care specialties, and medication administration and management. The company also provide management services to third-party home nursing agencies. LHC's physical, occupational, and speech therapists offer therapy services to patients in their home. Speech and language therapists provide corrective and rehabilitative treatment to patients suffering from physical or cognitive deficits or disorders.

Hospice Services

The Medicare-certified hospice operations of the company facilitate full range of hospice services to terminally ill patients and their families. The company's hospice agencies offer comprehensive services including pain and symptom management, palliative medication, emotional and spiritual support, inpatient and respite care, homemaker services, dietary counseling, and family bereavement counseling, with social worker visits available for up to 13 months following a patient's passing.

Home- and Community-Based Services

The home- and community-based services offer a wide range of services to patients such as grooming, medication reminders, meal preparation, assistance with feeding, light housekeeping, respite care, transportation, and errand services.

Facility-Based Services

LTACHs, the facility-based services segment, specialize in providing high-level care and continuous monitoring for patients with severe medical conditions, including those deemed medically unstable for treatment in non-acute settings, such as those with respiratory failure, neuromuscular disorders, cardiac disorders, nonhealing wounds, and renal disorders.

Healthcare Innovation Services

The HCI segment comprises Imperium Health Management, LLC (an ACO enablement and management company); Long Term Solutions, Inc. (an in-home assessment company for long-term care insurance); and Advanced Care House Calls (offering primary medical care for patients with mobility challenges), with the goal of ultimately benefiting patients and payors through enhanced services.

The home health agencies and hospice agencies which are operated in one segment are separated into multiple geographical regions and further separated into individual operating markets or clusters. The home- and community-based agencies which are operated in one segment are separated into multiple geographic regions. All home health agencies, hospice agencies, and home- and community-based agencies hold licenses and certifications granted by both state and federal authorities. The home health service locations use proprietary clinical resource allocation model and cost management system called service value point system. Patient care is coordinated on-site at the agency level of each home health service, hospice service, and home- and community-based location.

HCI's main business segments primarily offer assessments and associated services to the long-term care insurance sector, along with management services to accountable care organizations (ACOs) that oversee more than 400,000 Medicare beneficiaries.

CSR Initiatives

The agencies and employees of the company contribute locally and nationally to organizations such as United Way, Boys & Girls Clubs, Toys for Tots, and the American Heart Association. In 2022, the company made $2 million in charitable contributions. The company is part of a select group of global brands that support the American Red Cross's Annual Disaster Giving Program as sponsors. The compliance and ethics program of the company encompasses auditing, improved communication channels with the chief compliance officer, ethical standards consistency, and heightened awareness through comprehensive training and education. The company maintains an autonomous third-party "Integrity Line," which promotes employees to report any apprehensions regarding unethical conduct, conflicts of interest, harassment, discrimination, abuse, or workplace safety infractions. The clinicians of the company are provided with the necessary personal protective equipment and supplies to ensure proper patient care aligning with each patient's clinical diagnosis.

Risk Factors

If the planned transaction with a wholly owned subsidiary of UnitedHealth Group does not proceed, it could potentially have adverse effects on the trading price of the company stock and impact the future business and operational outcomes. A significant portion of the company's net service revenue comes from Medicare. Any alterations in Medicare rates or payment methods, or the firm's inability to manage costs, may lead to substantial declines in operations and cash flow. As a healthcare service provider, LHC faces substantial government regulation and alterations in laws, regulations, their interpretation, or enforcement which may necessitate operational changes which might potentially impact financial results and cash flow adversely. The company also undergo both routine and nonroutine governmental reviews, audits, and investigations. The scenarios in which there is loss of certifications for the company's list of long-term acute care hospitals could negatively impact the operational results and cash flows. LHC faces competition from competitors with more substantial resources which may pose challenge for the company to compete effectively as a provider of post-acute healthcare services. LHC's business often experiences reimbursement delays which range from the point of requesting payment for its services to actually receiving reimbursement or payment thereby creating liquidity problems.

Stock Market Performance

Table 2 compares the cumulative 5-year total shareholder return on LHC Group with the cumulative total return of the Nasdaq Composite Index, the S&P Health Care Index, and a customized peer group of three companies consisting of Addus HomeCare Corp, Amedisys Inc., and Encompass Health Corp. The analysis assumes that $100 was invested in the stock, in each index, and in the peer group including reinvestment of dividends on December 31, 2017, through December 31, 2022.

The 5-year holding period return for LHC Group Inc. was 164%. During the same period, the holding period return for market indexes Nasdaq Composite and S&P Health Care and peer group were 59%, 80%, and 73%, respectively. The average yearly return for LHC Group Inc., Nasdaq Composite, S&P Healthcare, and peer group during the period were 27.40%, 13.68%, 12.98%, and 17.46%, respectively.

Table 2 Comparative cumulative returns

Year	2017	2018	2019	2020	2021	2022
LHC Group, Inc.	$100.00	$153.27	$224.91	$348.28	$224.05	$263.98
NASDAQ Composite	$100	$97.16	$132.81	$192.47	$235.15	$158.65
S&P Health Care	$100	$106.47	$128.64	$145.93	$184.07	$180.47
Peer group	$100	$159.91	$205.29	$298.16	$199.42	$173.24

Source: Annual Report 2022

Table 3 Financial highlights

Year	2020	2021	2022
Total assets	2938	2895.621	2896.957
Revenues	2063.204	2219.622	2282.771
Net income	137.933	143.616	60.248

Table 3 shows the financial highlights of the company during the period 2020–2022. The values are given in millions of dollars.

Reference

1. Annual Report 2022.

Case 95 Metropolitan Bank Holding Corp

The Metropolitan Commercial Bank (MCB) is the subsidiary of Metropolitan Bank Holding Corporation. MCB offers a wide range of business, commercial, and retail banking products and services to small and middle market businesses and public entities in the New York metropolitan area. The bank is basically a solution-oriented relationship bank which focuses on middle market companies and real estate entrepreneurs. The bank has merged the advanced technological service and community-oriented approach of a local bank along with a comprehensive range of financial solutions and offerings. The bank also offers corporate cash management and retail banking services. The bank holds a prominent position in BaaS via its Global Payments Group delivering worldwide payment infrastructure and acting as an issuing bank for third-party debit card programs, while also offering financial infrastructure such as cash settlement and custodian deposit services. The company operates in a diverse economic region, characteristic of urban hubs, where services, wholesale/retail trade, finance/insurance/real estate, technology firms, and construction constitute the primary sources of employment. The bank issues prepaid cards for nationwide card programs which are managed by third-party program managers. The bank operates six banking centers strategically located within close proximity to target clients. The company competes with regional and national banks within its markets, along with nationwide nonbank commercial finance firms, for competition spanning lending, fund attraction, and merchant processing services, facing challenges from commercial banks, savings associations, credit unions, consumer finance firms, pension trusts, mutual funds, insurance companies, and mortgage-related entities. By December 31, 2022, the bank had assets, loans, and deposits totaled $6.3 billion, $4.8 billion, and $5.3 billion, respectively. By December 31, 2022, the bank employed 239 full-time employees.

© The Author(s), under exclusive license to Springer Nature Switzerland AG 2024

B. R. Kumar, *Rising Stars*, Management for Professionals,
https://doi.org/10.1007/978-3-031-50032-9_95

Products and Services

Lending Products

The commercial real estate (CRE) products offered by the bank include acquisition loans, refinance loans, loans on owner-occupied properties, and construction loans. The loans are provided with collateral involving different asset classes such as multifamily, mixed use, retail, office, hospitality, healthcare, and warehouse. The C&I products consist primarily of working capital lines of credits. The term loans are offered for the acquisition of equipment and other company assets, trade finance, and letters of credit. Majority of C&I loans carry the personal guarantee of the principals of the borrowing entity.

Commercial Real Estate

The largest component of the bank's real estate loan portfolio is comprised of nonowner-occupied CRE mortgage loans which are secured by office buildings, mixed-use properties, commercial condominium units, retail properties, hotels, and warehouses. Environmental report is generally required for all new CRE loans. The loans are generally written for terms of 3 to 5 years. The interest rates may be fixed or floating and repayment schedules are generally based on a 25–30-year amortization schedule. As of December 31, 2022, approximately 31.5% of the company's real estate loan portfolio consisted of loans made to the healthcare industry which were made basically to the nursing and residential care facilities.

Multifamily Loan

The multifamily loan portfolio includes loans secured by multi-tenanted residential properties, mainly in the New York City area, with underwriting standards akin to nonowner-occupied CRE.

Construction Loans

The company originates construction loans for both significant renovations and new ground-up construction.

Commercial and Industrial Loans (C&I)

C&I credit facilities are made to a wide range of industries which include healthcare with focus on skilled nursing facilities, auto leasing firms, wholesalers, manufacturers, and importers and exporters of wide range of products. The company's lines of credit, usually assessed annually, and term loans with terms of 2–5 years, also reviewed annually, can be established with fixed or floating rates.

Deposit Products and Services

Global Payments Business

The bank administers both local and global digital financial transactions for its fintech clientele and operates as an issuing bank for external debit card initiatives. The bank also handles prepaid and debit card payments for diverse businesses.

Corporate Cash Management Deposit Accounts

The bank also manages corporate cash management deposit accounts. Deposits are the primary source of funds used by banks for use in lending and investment activities. The company accumulates deposits through prepaid third-party debit cards, fintech clients, its cash management platform for various entities including bankruptcy trustees and property management firms, local businesses, individual referrals, other partnerships, and its retail branches. The bank sustains a variety of funding sources which include credit lines from the Federal Home Loan Bank and access to the Federal Reserve Bank (FRB) discount window.

Business Strategy

The bank aims to build a relationship-oriented commercial bank through organic strategy of growing its client relationships and developing new long-term clients. The major focus of the bank is on New York metropolitan area middle market businesses with annual revenues of $200 million or less and New York metropolitan area real estate entrepreneurs with net worth of $50 million or more. The company initiates and manages commercial real estate (CRE) and commercial and industrial (C&I) loans typically ranging from $3 million to $30 million, identifying this as a segment of the market with potential for growth. By prioritizing comprehensive client business support encompassing cash management, lending options, and a dedicated approach, the company enhances its ability to offer a wide array of services catering to both present and future client requirements, showcasing its adaptability and dedication to crafting personalized solutions for individual clients. The company focuses on a diversified funding strategy which enables it to be less reliant on branches. The bank generates significant deposits from its borrowing clients. The company actively issues debit cards for third-party debit card programs and manages digital payment settlements, both domestically and internationally, on behalf of its fintech clients.

Risk Factors

Major portion of the company's loan portfolio includes multifamily real estate loans and commercial loans which have a higher degree of risk than other types of loans. By 2022, approximately 99.5% of total loans consisted of CRE and C&I loans. The performance of the bank's multifamily and mixed-use loans could be adversely impacted by regulation. Inflation has an adverse impact on the business and on its customers. Low-interest environment may adversely affect the net interest income and profitability of the bank. Interest rate shifts might reduce net interest income and negatively impact the financial condition of the bank. Breakdown in the operational systems or infrastructure of the company as well as those of third parties could negatively impact the bank's liquidity and disrupt its operations.

Stock Market Performance

Table 1 compares the cumulative shareholder return for the MCB stock with the cumulative shareholder return for S&P 500 Index and KBW Index during the period 2017–2022. The analysis assumes that $100 was invested in the common stock and each of the indices on December 31, 2017.

The 5-year holding period return for the MCB stock was 39%, while for S&P 500 and KBW Bank Index, the holding period returns were 57% and 19%, respectively. The average yearly return for MCB stock amounted to 30.89%. During the same period, the market indices S&P 500 and KBW Regional Bank Index registered returns of 11% and 5.5%, respectively.

The following section analyzes the stock returns for MCB stock and Nasdaq Bank index during the 5-year period September 2018–August 2023. The stock was trading at $41.11 on September 1, 2018. By August 1, 2023, the stock price reached $42.5 per share. The cumulative monthly return for the MCB stock was 56.7% compared to zero return for Nasdaq Bank index during the 5-year period September 2018–August 2023. The average yearly return for the stock was 12% compared to 1% return accounted by Nasdaq Bank index during the above period. The source of data was Yahoo Finance.

Table 2 shows the holding period return for the stock and Nasdaq Bank index during the 5-year period 2018–2023.

MCB had registered excess return over the market index in the year 2019 and 2021.

Table 1 Comparative cumulative returns

Year	2017	2018	2019	2020	2021	2022
MCB	100	73	115	86	$253.00	$139.00
S&P 500	$100	$96.00	$126.00	$149.00	$191.00	$157.00
KBW Regional Bank Index	$100	$83.00	$102.00	$93.00	$128.00	$119.00

Table 2 Holding period return

Year	MCB	Nasdaq Bank index	Excess returns
2018	−24.98%	−19.04%	−5.9%
2019	37.80%	9.38%	28.4%
2020	−26.21%	−4.72%	−21.5%
2021	168.61%	34.09%	134.5%
2022	−36.46%	−11.80%	−24.7%

Table 3 Book and market value trends

Year	2018	2019	2020	2021	2022
Book value of equity	264.52	299.12	340.79	556.99	575.9
Market value of equity	253.5	400.93	300.87	1163.37	642.44
BV as percent of MV	13.1%	14.8%	16.9%	27.6%	28.5%

Table 4 Profitability indicators

Ratios	2018	2019	2020	2021	2022
Performance ratios					
Return on average assets %	1.3	1.09	1.03	1.06	0.89
Return on average equity%	10.19	10.69	12.33	13.49	10.49
Net interest margin%	4.24	4.05	3.97	3.9	4.39
Efficiency ratio%			58.16	48.32	52.51

Table 5 Financial highlights

	(In millions of dollars)				
Financial highlights	2018	2019	2020	2021	2022
Total assets	2182.64	3357.57	4330.82	7116.36	6267.34
Gross loans	*1867.35*	*2677.92*	*3142.32*	*3739.53*	*4853.50*
Deposits	1660.55	2790.77	3829.61	6435.57	5277.91
Total equity	264.52	299.12	340.79	556.99	575.9
Interest income	83.95	129.78	143.1	173.28	260.74
Non-interest income	*12.16*	*10.63*	*17*	*23.7*	*26.59*
Interest expense	12.72	32.17	18.18	16.28	31.58
Total non-interest expense	17.81	28.71	32.68	37.55	86.82
Market capitalization	253.5	400.93	300.87	1163.37	642.44

Table 3 shows the excess value created by MCB stock in the market. The values are given in millions of dollars.

The average book value of equity as percent of market value of equity during the period 2018–2022 was approximately 20%.

Table 4 shows the performance ratios of the bank.

The average ROA, ROE, and net interest margin for the bank were 1.07%, 11.44%, and 4.11%, respectively. The average efficiency ratio was 53%.

Table 5 gives the financial highlights of the company during the period 2018–2022.

During the period 2018–2022, the total assets, gross loans, and deposits grew by 34%, 27%, and 39% on average basis. The total equity and market capitalization increased by 23% and 69% on average basis during the above period. The interest income and non-interest income grew by 34% and 25%, respectively, on average basis. During the same period, interest expense and non-interest expense increased by 33% and 55%, respectively. The sources of data were annual reports and guru focus.com.

Reference

1. Annual Report 2023, Metropolitan Bank Holding Corporation.

Case 96 Lennar

Lennar was established in the year 1954 as a local Miami homebuilder. Over the years, the company has built over 1 million new homes in the United States of America. Lennar serves different communities in terms of lifestyles and family dynamics. In terms of deliveries, revenues, and net earnings, Lennar is the second largest homebuilder in the United States. Lennar is an originator of residential and commercial mortgage loans, provider of title insurance and closing services, and developer of multifamily rental properties. The company is also the sponsor and manager of funds and joint ventures which focuses on the development and ownership of multifamily rental properties.

The common stock of the company was listed on the New York Stock Exchange in the year 1972. During the 1980s and 1990s, the company expanded its operations into a number of homebuilding markets in California, Florida, and Texas through both organic growth and acquisitions. In 1997, the company acquired Pacific Greystone Corporation. In year 2000, the company acquired US Home Corporation and expanded its operations in States of New Jersey, Maryland, Virginia, Minnesota, and Colorado. During the period 2002–2005, the company acquired different regional homebuilders. During the period 2010–2013, the company expanded its homebuilding operations into Georgia, Oregon, Washington, and Tennessee. In 2017, Lennar acquired WCI Communities, the homebuilder of luxury single and multifamily homes. In 2018, the company acquired CalAtlantic Group Inc., a major homebuilder with presence in 43 metropolitan areas covering 19 states.

In 2022, the company delivered 66,399 homes and had reported $15.72 of EPS. In the same year, the homebuilding operations generated $3.5 billion in cash flows. During the recent 5-year period, Lennar had generated over $12 billion in homebuilding cash flow which enabled the company to retire $5.4 billion of senior notes, repurchase $3.4 billion of common stock, and paid $ 1 billion of dividends. In 2022, the homebuilding operations generated $32 billion in revenues which accounted for 95% of its consolidated revenues. By November 2022, the company employed 12,012 individuals of whom 9357 were involved in the Homebuilding operations.

© The Author(s), under exclusive license to Springer Nature Switzerland AG 2024
B. R. Kumar, *Rising Stars*, Management for Professionals,
https://doi.org/10.1007/978-3-031-50032-9_96

Table 1 Time line

Year	Event
1954	Gene Fisher and Arnold Rosen form F&R Builders in Miami, Florida
1956	Leonard Miller establishes partnership with Arnold Rosen and becomes co-owner of F&R Builders
1971	The company changes its name to Lennar and becomes a public company
1972	Lennar is listed on NYSE
1981	Lennar diversified into mortgage financing business with the formation of Universal American Mortgage Company
1989	Lennar unveils Everything's Included®, presenting homebuyers with an array of luxurious features worth thousands of dollars, all included at no additional expense
2000	Lennar's acquisition of US Home propels the company to double its size
2011	Lennar debuts Next Gen® – The Home Within a Home, specifically crafted to cater to the needs of multigenerational families. Quarterra is unveiled, focusing on the development of upscale rental apartment communities with a touch of luxury
2014	Lennar launches Lennar International establishing itself as a leading US real estate provider in the global market
2017	Lennar's acquires WCI Communities, a developer specializing in lifestyle communities and luxury single- and multifamily homes Nationwide, UAMC changes name to Eagle Home Mortgage and becomes a comprehensive mortgage lender within the Lennar family of companies Lennar pioneers the world's inaugural Wi-Fi CERTIFIED™ Home Designs, which facilitated effortless voice control and home automation integration
2018	Lennar merges with CalAtlantic Homes to create the largest homebuilder in the United States Len^x is introduced to integrate technology solutions across Lennar
2020	The family mortgage company of Lennar, Eagle Home Mortgage LLC, is renamed to Lennar Mortgage LLC for aligning homebuilding and financial services brands CalAtlantic Title is renamed to Lennar Title

Source: https://www.lennar.com/about/history

Table 1 lists the chronological sequence of the company's time line.

Business Segments

Homebuilding Operations

The homebuilding operations of the company include the construction and sale of single-family attached and detached homes along with the purchase, development, and sale of residential land. The company basically sells homes in communities which are targeted to first time, move up, active adult, and luxury homebuyers. In 2022, the average sales price amounted to $480,000.

Residential Mortgage Financing

The company primarily provides conforming conventional, FHA-insured, and VA-guaranteed residential mortgage loan products, along with other home mortgage options, to buyers of its homes through its financial services subsidiary, Lennar Mortgage. In the year 2022, Lennar Mortgage offered loans to 72% of its homebuyers. In the fiscal year 2022, Lennar originated approximately 37,700 residential mortgage loans totaling $14.4 billion.

Title, Insurance, and Closing Services

Lennar is licensed to provide title insurance and closing services for residential and/or commercial transactions in 40 states. During the fiscal year 2021 and 2022, the company closed 67,500 and 68,800 real estate transactions.

Commercial Mortgage Origination

The LMF Commercial subsidiary originates and sells into securitizations first mortgage loans which are secured by income-producing commercial properties. The loans are generally in the range of $5 million to $50 million. LMF Commercial also originates floating rate loans which are secured by commercial real estate properties.

Lennar Others

The company strategically invests in companies which are involved in technology initiatives in order to enhance its homebuilding innovation initiatives.

Multifamily Operations

Lennar is involved in the development of multifamily communities since the year 2011. Since its inception through 2022, the multifamily business has developed 116 multifamily residential communities with approximately 34,900 rental units across 20 states in the United States. The multifamily business offers residents a mix of studio, one-, two-, and three-bedroom homes. It is one of the businesses which is included in the proposed spinoff program of the company.

Single-Family Home Rentals

Lennar formed the Upward America Venture which is engaged in the acquisition of single-family rental properties consisting of townhomes, duplexes, and condominium buildings. Lennar subsidiaries are the manager and the general partner of Upward America. By November 30, 2022, Upward America had purchased 4129 homes in 103 communities across 19 metropolitan statistical areas.

Five Point Holdings, LLC

Lennar owns an indirect 40% interest in Five Point Holdings LLC which is a publicly traded developer of three large master planned mixed-use developments in California.

Strategy

The company has well-laid out strategies in place to strengthen its market leading position in the industry. The company focuses on adjusting pricing to market conditions and maintain reasonable delivery volumes. The company relies on proprietary dynamic pricing model to guide volume-based pricing in order to drive sales at market pricing. The company associate with trade partners to right size its cost structure to current market conditions. The company focuses on managing its operating costs and SG&A expenses and maintain tight inventory control. The articulated strategy of the company is to purchase strong margin and high return land opportunity at today's pricing. The strategic objective of the company is to enhance building process efficiency; lower selling, general, and administrative costs; and reduce customer acquisition expenses through technology and innovative strategies. The focus is on cutting construction costs, shortening cycle times along with the achievement of consistent production flow. The company aims to create a subsidiary called Quarterra Group Inc. to spin off its multifamily and single-family home rental asset management businesses along with certain investment assets. The Next Gen® home is basically innovative homes. The purchasing power alongside technology-driven cost reduction and debt paydowns has led to high gross profit and operating margins. The company differentiates its products by utilizing the Everything's Included® approach, which leverages its purchasing power to incorporate luxury features as standard elements in its homebuilding processes. The company increasingly focuses on advertising homes through digital channels to increase the cost effectiveness of its marketing efforts. The company invests in technology companies to improve the homebuilding processes and reduce customer acquisition costs. The company focuses on land light strategy which involves decreasing owned homesite inventory and expanding control over land though options, agreements, and strategic partnerships rather than direct ownership. The acquisition of land through option contracts allows the company to control portions of properties which are owned by third parties which include strategic land funds. In 2021 and 2022, approximately 59% and 63% of the total homesites were controlled through options and joint ventures. The company uses independent subcontractors for major aspects of home construction. By 2022, the company was actively involved in building and marketing homes in 1208 communities. Lennar provides a diverse range of homes for various types of homebuyers, from first time to luxury and multigenerational, in locations spanning urban infill to suburban golf course communities. The company competes for homebuyers with numerous national, regional, and local homebuilders.

Risk Factors

The company faces market and economic risks. The demand for Lennar's homes hinges on a range of macroeconomic factors, including employment rates, interest rates, stock market trends, consumer sentiment, housing demand, financing accessibility, new home supply, existing inventory prices, and demographic factors. Supply shortages and inflation could adversely affect the profitability of the company.

Residential homebuilding and apartment development are governed by diverse local, state, and federal regulations, encompassing environmental laws related to health and ecological safeguards, which may lead to delays, substantial compliance expenses, and potential restrictions in environmentally sensitive zones. The mortgage and title subsidiaries have to comply with applicable real estate, lending, and insurance laws and regulations. A decrease in new home prices may necessitate the reduction of the recorded value of land holdings and the write-off of option expenses. The homebuilding, mortgage lending, and home rental sectors are highly competitive, and intense competition may have negative implications for the firm's business and financial performance. Rising interest rates may elevate the construction costs of the homes which the company develops. Noncompliance with the terms and conditions of the borrowing agreements may limit the company's ability to secure future loans or trigger the immediate repayment of outstanding debt.

CSR Initiatives

Lennar aims to build healthier and more energy-efficient homes which have less impact on the environment than prior generations of home. In 2022, the company contributed $1000 for each home delivered totaling $66 million to the Lennar Foundation. Approximately 16% of the homes built by Lennar in the year 2021 were ENERGY STAR® certified. At least 90% of homes build by Lennar have one or more ENERGY STAR® appliances installed. At least 80% of the systems in Lennar homes have compliance with respect to high-efficiency furnace and high SEER air conditioning. The company has made 48,100 solar power home deliveries since the year 2013. The company maintains a comprehensive companywide environmental compliance program known as the Lennar Environmental Management

System (LEMS), designed to establish uniform standards and processes aimed at enhancing environmental condition assessments and ensuring compliance with applicable environmental regulations. The company has established strategic relationship with companies to integrate technology solutions across the homebuilding industry. For example, for renewable energy and energy efficiency, the company has partnered with Sunnova – the residential solar and energy storage provider – Dandelion the provider of home geothermal system, and Rheia the compact air distribution system provider. For water conservation, the company has partnership with residential-scale water recycling system-based company Greyter. Potential new homebuyers can access free credit education and gain a deeper understanding of the home financing process through Lennar Mortgage's Home Buyers Solutions Group. Lennar Single Family Rental (LSFR) aims to provide affordable living through the Upward America Venture. The company has initiated a series of awareness and education panels to encourage ideas with respect to inclusion and diversity. The Lennar Foundation aims to improve the lives of the most challenged community members. Lennar Foundation with grants in the range of $10,000 to $25,000 encourages different divisions of the company to host caring and fundraising events for their local partner charities. The sustainability strategy of the company is inspired by the 17 Sustainable Development Goals set forth by the United Nations. The company offers over 10,000 jobs throughout its operations. All of the hardwood is sourced from certified, responsibly managed forests.

Stock Market Performance

Table 2 compares the 5-year cumulative total return of common stock with the Dow Jones US Home Construction Index and the Dow Jones US Total Market Index. The analysis assumes $100 invested on November 30, 2017, in the stock and indexes and reinvestment of all dividends.

The 5-year holding period return for Lennar Corporation was 49% compared to 44% and 56% returns for market indexes Home Construction Index and Total Market Index. The average yearly return for Lennar stock was 12.52% compared to 12.13% and 10.15% accounted by the market indexes.

Lennar stock which was trading at $46.68 on September 1, 2018, increased by 2.55 times to trade at $119.05 by August 1, 2023. The Lennar stock had cumulative monthly returns of 132% compared to cumulative monthly return of 68% accounted by market index Nasdaq Composite during the 5-year period September 2018–

Table 2 Cumulative returns

Year	2017	2018	2019	2020	2021	2022
Lennar Corporation	$100	$70	$98	$126	$175	$149
Dow Jones US Home Construction Index	$100	$71	$104	$127	$178	$144
Dow Jones US Total Market Index	$100	$102	$117	$139	$176	$156

Source: Annual Report 2022

Table 3 Holding period return

Year	Lennar	Nasdaq Composite	Excess returns
2018	−16%	−18%	1%
2019	18%	23%	−6%
2020	15%	41%	−26%
2021	40%	20%	20%
2022	−6%	−26%	21%

Table 4 Book value of equity and market value of equity

Year	2018	2019	2020	2021	2022
Book value of equity	14,682.96	16,033.83	18,099.40	20,996.28	24,240.37
Market value of equity	13,854.69	18,843.02	23,721.35	31,455.54	25,454.01
BV as percent of MV	106.0%	85.1%	76.3%	66.7%	95.2%

Table 5 Financial highlights

	(In millions of dollars)				
Financial highlights	2018	2019	2020	2021	2022
Total assets	28,566.18	29,359.51	29,935.18	33,207.78	37,984.30
Short-term investments	1562.62	1497.93	2916.54	2963.40	4814.20
Total equity	14,682.96	16,033.83	18,099.40	20,996.28	24,240.37
Total revenue	20,571.63	22,259.56	22,488.85	27,130.68	33,671.01
Total operating expenses	343.93	321.19	333.45	398.38	414.50
Net income	1695.83	1849.05	2465.04	4430.11	4614.13
Market cap	13,854.69	18,843.02	23,721.35	31,455.54	25,454.01
Enterprise value	22,510.55	27,003.09	28,330.94	35,050.36	26,978.81

August 2023. The average yearly return for Lennar stock was 27% compared to 14% of market index Nasdaq Composite during the period September 2018–August 2023.

Table 3 shows the holding period return for Lennar stock and market index Nasdaq Composite during the recent 5-year period.

Lennar stock had excess returns in the year 2021 and 2022 compared to the market index Nasdaq Composite.

Table 4 shows the book value of equity and market value of equity during the 5-year period 2018–2022. The values are given in millions of dollars.

The average book value of equity as percent of market value of equity was approximately 81% during the 5-year period 2018–2022.

Table 5 gives the financial highlights of the company during the period 2018–2022.

During the period 2018–2022, the total assets, short-term investments, and total equity increased by 7.5%, 39%, and 13%, respectively. The total revenues and net income increased by 13% and 32%, respectively, on average basis. The total expenses increased by 5% on average basis. The market capitalization and enterprise

Table 6 Performance ratios

Ratios	2018	2019	2020	2021	2022
Net margin%	8.24	8.31	10.96	16.33	13.7
ROE%	15.11	12.11	14.52	22.83	20.55
ROA%	7.17	6.38	8.31	14.03	12.96
DER	0.69	0.6	0.41	0.31	0.26

Table 7 Economic value

Year	2021	2022
Profit before income tax	5819.06	6014.57
Income tax	1362.24	1365.91
Net operating profit after tax (NOPAT)	4456.82	4648.66
Stockholder equity	20,996.28	24,240.37
Long-term debt	6378.36	6199.14
Total capital employed	27374.64	30439.51
WACC	8.67%	8.88%
Capital charge	2373.38	2703.03
Economic value	2083.44	1945.63

value increased by 19% and 6%, respectively, on average basis during the period 2018–2022. The data for analysis was sourced from guru focus and annual reports.

Table 6 shows the performance ratios of the company during the period 2018–2022.

The average net margin, ROE, and ROA for Lennar were 11.5%, 17.02%, and 9.77%, respectively, during the period 2018–2022. The average debt equity ratio was 0.45 during the above period.

Table 7 illustrates the estimation of the economic value of the company during 2021 and 2022. The values are given in millions of dollars.

References

1. https://investors.lennar.com/?
2. Lennar Social Responsibility Report 2022

Case 97 1-800-Flowers

1-800-Flowers.com, Inc. and its affiliated companies offer a wide array of gifts crafted to facilitate customers in conveying their sentiments, forging connections, and commemorating special occasions. The company began operations in the year 1976. The firm started off with the acquisition of a single retail florist and later on expanded to a 14-store chain. The company took advantage of the rapid emergence of toll-free calling. The company acquired the right to use the toll-free telephone number 1-800-FLOWERS and established it as its corporate brand. The star family of brands of the company include 1-800-Flowers.com®, 1-800-Baskets.com®, Cheryl's Cookies®, Harry & David®, PersonalizationMall.com®, Shari's Berries®, FruitBouquets.com®, Moose Munch®, The Popcorn Factory®, Wolferman's Bakery®, Vital Choice®, Stock Yards®, and Simply Chocolate®. The company operates BloomNet®, a global floral and gift industry service provider. It also oversees Napco℠, specializing in floral gifts and seasonal décor; DesignPac Gifts, LLC, a gift basket and tower manufacturer; and Alice's Table®, a nationwide digital livestreaming platform which offers floral, culinary, and lifestyle experiences. By July 2022, the company employed approximately 4700 full-time and part-time employees in the United States.

Growth Strategy

The company aims to be the leading brand on thoughtful gifting which focuses on customers' celebratory needs. The company aims to strengthen its valued customer relationships which offer convenient access, thoughtful gifts, and superior service. The company aims to foster increased human expression and connections in today's evolving landscape. 1-800-Flowers.com is one of the most recognized brands in the floral and gift industry. The superior power of its brand has enabled the company to extend its product offerings from floral category into complementary products such as gourmet popcorn, cookies and related baked and snack food products, premium chocolate and confections, wine gifts, gourmet gift baskets, fruit bouquet

© The Author(s), under exclusive license to Springer Nature Switzerland AG 2024
B. R. Kumar, *Rising Stars*, Management for Professionals,
https://doi.org/10.1007/978-3-031-50032-9_97

arrangements, gift-quality fruit baskets, dipped berries, as well as steaks, chops, and prepared meals. In 2020, through the acquisition of PersonalizationMall.com, the company added an extensive selection of personalized products to its offerings. In 2021, the company acquired Vital Choice Seafood which is the source of wild caught seafood and sustainably farmed shellfish, pastured proteins, and organic foods. In the same year, the company acquired Alice's Table® to extend its product portfolio with lifestyle offerings which included fully digital livestreaming floral, culinary, and other experiences. These acquisitions facilitated the company to extend its line of gift offerings for customers in variety of celebratory occasions. These strategic initiatives will help the company to increase the purchase frequency and average order value for existing customers along with attracting new customers. The firm's consolidated customer database and multibrand website has been designed to dynamically engage its customers. The company aims to enhance its position as a leading one stop destination for every customer's gifting and celebratory needs. The company's vision is to build a "celebratory ecosystem" consisting of collection of premium gifting brands and suite of products and services. As a part of strategy, the company focuses on both organic growth and acquisition of complementary businesses.

Brands

Consumer Floral and Gift Segment

1-800-Flowers.com

It is a direct-to-consumer, multichannel provider of fresh flowers, plants, fruits, gift basket products, balloons, candles, keepsake gifts, jewelry, and plush stuffed animals.

Fruit Bouquets

This brand is a direct-to-consumer, multichannel provider of artistically carved fresh fruit arrangements.

Flowerama

It is the franchisor and operator of retail flower shops, acquired in year 2011.

Florists.com

It is the direct-to-consumer provider of fresh flowers, plants, fruits, and gift baskets.

Personalization Mall

It is the e-commerce provider of personalized gifts and keepsakes which were acquired in year 2020.

Alice's Table

It is the provider of lifestyle offerings, which included fully digital livestreaming floral, culinary, and other experiences.

BloomNet

It is the provider of products and services to the professional florist.

Napco

Napco is the wholesale merchandiser and marketer of floral industry and related products.

Gourmet Foods and Gift Basket Segment

Harry & David

It is the multichannel specialty retailer and producer of premium gift quality fruit, gourmet food products, and other gifts which are marketed under the Harry & David® and Cushman's® brands, which were acquired in September 2014.

Wolferman Bakery

Wolferman Bakery which was acquired in year 2014 is the manufacturer and retailer of indulgent bakery gifts which include super thick English muffins, toppings, and desserts.

Moose Munch

It is the multichannel retailer and manufacturer of small batch gourmet buttery caramel and chocolate-covered popcorn, acquired in September 2014 in conjunction with the purchase of Harry & David.

Stock Yard

It is an e-commerce provider of gourmet steaks, chops, burgers, and other gourmet meat gifts.

Vital Choice

It is an e-commerce provider of wild-caught seafood and sustainably farmed shellfish, pastured proteins, organic foods, and marine-sourced nutritional supplements.

The Popcorn Factory

It is the manufacturer of giftable premium popcorn and specialty treats.

Cheryl's Cookies

It is an e-commerce baker and retailer of premium cookies and related baked gifts, acquired in March 2005.

1-800-Baskets.com

It is an e-commerce retailer of gift baskets and towers.

DesignPac

DesignPac, the designer, assembler, and distributor of wholesale gift baskets, gourmet food towers, and gift sets, was acquired in the year 2008.

Simply Chocolate

It is an e-commerce retailer of artisan chocolates and confections.

Shari's Berries

It is an e-commerce retailer of dipped berries and other specialty treats, acquired in August 2019.

Products and Service Offerings

A wide variety of products such as fresh-cut flowers, floral and fruit arrangements and plants, gifts, dipped berries, popcorn, gourmet foods and gift baskets, cookies, chocolates, candy, wine, and gift-quality fruits are offered by the company. The company's product development and production teams collaborate to create floral arrangements, gourmet foods, gift baskets, and other products tailored to meet customers' celebratory or sentiment-sharing needs.

Flowers and Plants

The company's flagship 1-800-Flowers.com brand offers fresh-cut flowers and floral and fruit arrangements for same-day delivery. The company offers customers a variety of florist-designed products, encompassing traditional floral and gift items, the Fruit Bouquets brand of fruit arrangements, and fresh farm-delivered flowers. The company additionally provides an extensive range of popular plants to enhance both indoor and outdoor settings. Through the acquisition of Alice's Table, Flowers.com offers fully digital livestreaming, floral, culinary, and other experiences.

Personalized Gifts

Through its Personalization Mall brand, the company offers a diverse array of products featuring sublimation, embroidery, digital printing, engraving, and sandblasting techniques to deliver a distinctive and personalized customer experience.

Gourmet Foods and Gift Baskets

Harry & David is a vertically integrated, multichannel specialty retailer and producer of premium gift-quality fruit, food products, land- and sea-based proteins, and gifts under the Harry & David, Wolferman's Bakery, Vital Choice, Cushman's, and Moose Munch brands.

The company utilizes the Stock Yards name under license for the sale of premium meats.

The company produces high-quality cookies and baked gift items under the Cheryl's and Mrs. Beasley's brands, presented in creative gift packaging, offering customers a wide selection of assortments. Additionally, The Popcorn Factory brand specializes in premium popcorn and specialty snack products. The 1-800-Baskets.com brand showcases an array of gourmet gift baskets and associated products crafted by DesignPac, in addition to offerings from third-party sources. Simply Chocolate offers artisan chocolates and confections.

BloomNet

The company's BloomNet business offers its members a range of products and services, encompassing order settlement processing; advertising through member directories; access services via BloomLink®; additional offerings such as web hosting, marketing, designer education, and point of sale systems; and wholesale floral supplies.

Risk Factors

Fluctuations in financial and credit markets, along with shifts in consumer sentiment, may lead to substantial volatility that could negatively impact customers' spending behavior and consequently affect the company's business and operational outcomes. Consumer spending on products sold by the company may vary with general economic conditions.

Elevated shipping expenses and supply chain interruptions could have a detrimental impact on the company's product sales, given that a significant portion of its products are shipped either directly from manufacturers or from the company's fulfillment centers to customers. The reliance on international vendors for the supply of flowers, along with specific components and products, exposes the company to substantial risks related to regulations, global economic conditions, taxation, and political instability and can have adverse effects on the financial stability. The recent growth rates may not be sustainable or indicative of future growth. The company's growth potential may be constrained if it fails to establish and sustain strategic online and social media partnerships that generate substantial traffic. Intense competition within the floral, plant, gift basket, gourmet food, and specialty gift sectors necessitates a proactive response to competitive pressures to prevent potential revenue loss.

Sustainability Initiatives

The company has partnered with No Kid Hungry and has provided 1.5 million meals to children. In 2021, the company donated nearly $6 million of perishable product to local nonprofit food banks across the United States. BloomNet has a robust scholarship and research underwriting program and has donated over $100,000 as scholarships to support the careers of budding florists. The company has donated more than $1 million in product donations from food brands to aid local communities. Employee resource groups (ERGs) support diverse populations across its family of brands. The ERGs of the company include Women and Allies, LGBTQ + and Allies, Latinx and Allies, and African American/Black and Allies. As part of BloomNet Diversity Program, approximately 20 percent of the florists in the network are identified as businesses owned by minorities, veterans, women, members of the LGBTQ+, and disabled. From 2007 onward, the company has directed more than $200,000 in monetary funds and in-kind donations to support the work of GLAAD, the leading LGBTQ+ media advocacy organization.

Stock Market Performance

Flowers.com was trading at $10.45 on October 1, 2018. By September 1, 2023, the stock price declined by 0.67 times to trade at $7.08. The cumulative monthly return for Flowers.com was 32% for the Flowers stock compared to cumulative monthly return of 60% for the market index S&P 500 during the 5-year period October 2018–September 2023. The average yearly return for the Flowers stock during the period October 2018–September 2023 was 6% compared to 12% returns for market index S&P 500.

Table 1 shows the holding period return for the Flowers stock and market index S&P 500 during the period 2018–2022. The analysis assumes holding period of 1 year. The data was sourced from Yahoo Finance.com.

The stock had higher returns compared to market index in the year 2018 and 2020.

Table 2 shows the book value of equity and market value of equity during the period 2019–2023. The values are given in millions of dollars.

Table 1 Holding period returns

Year	Flowers.com	S&P 500	Excess returns
2018	17%	−8%	25%
2019	−9%	19%	−29%
2020	71%	16%	55%
2021	−24%	28%	−52%
2022	−44%	−15%	−29%

Table 2 Comparative value

Year	2019	2020	2021	2022	2023
Book value of equity	342.71	399.77	509.07	509.41	471.84
Market value of equity	1216.21	1286.96	2071.66	613.75	505.25
BV as percent of MV	28.2%	31.1%	24.6%	83.0%	93.4%

Table 3 Financial highlights

	(In millions of dollars)				
Financial highlights	2019	2020	2021	2022	2023
Total assets	606.44	774.44	1076.68	1094.89	1051.43
Short-term investments	172.92	240.51	173.57	31.47	126.81
Total equity	342.71	399.77	509.07	509.41	471.84
Total revenue	1248.62	1489.64	2122.25	2207.89	2017.85
Total operating expenses	481.01	541.83	747.34	779.64	727.95
Net income	34.77	59.00	118.65	29.61	−44.70
Market cap	1216.21	1286.96	2071.66	613.75	505.25
Enterprise value	1140.26	1209.26	2168.96	881.37	707.93

Table 4 Profitability ratios

Ratios	2019	2020	2021	2022	2023
Net margin%	2.78	3.96	5.59	1.34	−2.22
ROE%	10.57	15.89	26.11	5.81	−9.11
ROA%	5.91	8.55	12.82	2.73	−4.17

The average book value as percent of market value of equity was approximately 52% during the period 2019–2023.

Table 3 gives the financial highlights of Flowers.com during the period 2019–2023.

During the period 2019–2023, the total assets, short-term investments, and total equity increased by 16%, 58%, and 9%, respectively. The total revenues increased by 14% while the total expenses increased by 12%. The market capitalization and enterprise value were highly fluctuating during the above period. The data source was annual reports and gurufocus.com.

Table 4 gives the profitability ratios of the company during the period 2019–2023.

The average net margin, ROE, and ROA during the period 2019–2023 were 2.29%, 9.85%, and 5.17%, respectively.

References

1. Annual Report 2022
2. https://www.1800flowers.com/?utm_medium=direct&utm_source=flowerscom

Case 98 FS Bancorp

FS Bancorp was established as the holding company of the First Security Bank. The First Security Bank is a relationship-driven community bank which delivers banking and financial services to local families, local and regional businesses, and industry niches. Initially the bank was chartered as a credit union to serve various select employment groups. The banks have headquartered office, an administrative office, 20 full-service bank branches, and 10 home loan production offices. By December 31, 2022, the company had consolidated total assets of $2.63 billion, total deposits of $2.13 billion, and stockholder's equity of $231.7 million. The bank is a diversified lending institution which focuses on the issuance of loans for commercial real estate, single- to four-family residences, and home equity. Its lending portfolio encompasses consumer loans which include various indirect home improvement loans secured by fixtures as well as marine loans and commercial business loans. Fixture-secured loans represented the largest portion of the company's loan portfolio. The company also focuses on real estate lending products such as one-to four-family and commercial real estate loans which include speculative residential construction and commercial business loans. The company also focuses on residential mortgage loans. The bank aims to leverage its strength in indirect consumer lending.

In 2016, through the purchase of four retail bank branches, the company acquired $186.4 million in deposits and $419,000 in loans. In 2018, the bank completed the acquisition of Anchor Bancorp with acquisition of $357.9 million in deposits and $361.6 million in loans. The Anchor Bancorp acquisition facilitated the expansion of retail footprint by the addition of nine full-service bank branches. The First Security Bank is regulated by the Washington State Department of Financial Institutions and Federal Deposit Insurance Corporation.

© The Author(s), under exclusive license to Springer Nature Switzerland AG 2024

B. R. Kumar, *Rising Stars*, Management for Professionals,
https://doi.org/10.1007/978-3-031-50032-9_98

Lending Activities

The bank primarily focuses on the origination of consumer loans, one- to four-family residential first mortgages, and second mortgage/home equity loan products. In the active indirect consumer lending program, the company focuses on non-mortgage commercial business loans and commercial real estate loans consisting of construction and development loans. Recently the bank has expanded its loan products by offering residential mortgage and commercial construction warehouse lending to diversify revenues. The chief credit officer approves multiple loans to single borrower up to $20 million. Loans in excess of $20 million and up to $35 million require additional approval from management's senior loan committee. The bank's largest lending relationship in the year 2022 totaled $47.9 million and consisted of a mix of acquisition and construction real estate loans, multifamily construction loan, and commercial line of credit.

The company offers a variety of commercial real estate loans. Most of commercial real estate loans are secured by multifamily residences, retail centers, warehouses, and owner-occupied buildings. By end 2022, 25% of the gross loan portfolio was accounted by commercial real estate loans. The commercial real estate loans secured are originated with a fixed or variable interest rate for up to a 15-year maturity and 30-year amortization. The variable rate loans are indexed to the prime rate of interest of 5-, 7-, or 10-year FHLB rate. The loan-to-value ratios on the company's commercial real estate loans typically do not exceed 80% of the appraised value of the property securing the loan. The loans secured by commercial real estate are generally underwritten based on the net operating income of the property and the financial strength of the borrower.

Construction and Development Lending

Construction and Development Activities

The construction lending program of the company focuses on construction of both speculative and presold one- to four-family residences with acquisition of in-city lots for later development of one- to four-family residences and single-family residences. These loans are provided to known builders and developers in the market area. Construction loans are generally made with a maximum loan amount of the lower of 95% of cost or 75% of appraised value at completion. The company also makes land acquisition and development loans to builders or residential lot developers on a limited basis. The company addresses the risks associated with construction development lending by adhering to underwriting policies, disbursement procedures, and monitoring practices.

Home Equity Lending

The home equity lines of credit have adjustable rates tied to the prime rate of interest with a draw term of 10 years plus and a term to maturity of 15 years. Monthly payments are based on 1% of the outstanding balance with a maximum combined loan-to-value ratio of up to 90% including any underlying first mortgage. Fixed second lien mortgage home equity loans are typically amortizing loans with terms of up to 30 years. By December 2022, total second lien mortgage or home equity loans amounted to $55.4 million accounting for 2.5% of the gross loan portfolio.

Residential

The company originates loans secured by first mortgages on one- to four-family residences. These loans are originated through referrals from real estate agents, financial planners, and builders. Retail banking customers are also important referral sources for the company's loan originations. In the year 2022, the company originated $828.8 million of one- to four-family mortgages. The loans were sold to investors such as Fannie Mae, Ginnie Mae, and Freddie Mac. By 2022, one- to four-family residential mortgage loans totaled $469.5 million accounting for 21.2% of the gross loan portfolio. The one- to four-family loans are generally underwritten based on the applicant's ability to repay.

Consumer Lending

Consumer lending is primarily though home improvement contractors and dealers. Consumer lending accounted for approximately 25.6% of the gross loan portfolio in the year 2022. The indirect home improvement loans also referred to as fixture-secured loans constitute the largest portion of the consumer loan portfolio. The indirect home improvement loans were originated through a network of 119 home improvement contractors and dealers located in Washington, Oregon, California, Idaho, Colorado, Arizona, Minnesota, Nevada, Texas, Utah, Massachusetts, and Montana. Five dealers were responsible for 53% of the loan volume. The fixture-secured loans were offered for products such as replacement windows, siding, roofs, HVAC systems, pools, and other home fixture installations. The loans are processed through the loan origination software, and approximately 40% of loan application received an automated decision based on information provided. The company follows internal underwriting guidelines in evaluating loans received through the indirect dealer program including using a Fair, Isaac and Company Incorporated credit score. The company's fixture-secured loans generally range in amounts of $2500–$100,000 and carry terms of 12–20 years with fixed rates of amortizing payments and interests.

Commercial Business Lending

The company originates commercial business loans and lines of credit to local small- and mid-sized businesses and are secured by accounts receivables, inventory, or personal/business property, plant, and equipment. Commercial business loans are offered at fixed rate but are usually adjustable-rate loans indexed to the prime rate of interest plus a margin. The company has commercial construction warehouse lending lines secured by notes on construction loans and are typically guaranteed by principals with experience in construction lending. By 2022, the company had $60 million in approved commercial construction warehouse lending lines to four companies in the range from $10 million to $20 million. The company originates both fixed-rate and adjustable-rate loans. The ability to originate loans is dependent upon customer demand for loans in the market areas.

Risk Factors

The business of the bank may be adversely affected by downturns in different economies. Adverse economic conditions adversely impact business, financial condition, and results of operations. Inflationary pressures and rising prices affect the results of operations and financial conditions. The loan portfolio faces increased risks due to large percentage of consumer loans. As a result, the level of provision for credit losses on loans would reduce profits. The consumer loans are originated indirectly by or through third parties which present greater risk than direct lending products. Commercial real estate lending is subject to various risks which could adversely impact the results of operations and financial condition. The residential construction lending is subject to different risks which would adversely affect the operations and financial conditions. The company makes real estate construction loans to individuals and builders primarily for the construction of residential properties. Residential construction lending is subject to various risks which would adversely impact the financial results of the company. The residential mortgage warehouse lending program is subject to various risks which could adversely impact the results of operations and financial condition. If the allowance for credit losses on loans is not sufficient to cover actual loan losses, the earnings could be reduced. The business may be adversely affected by credit risk associated with residential property. Changes in interest rates may reduce the net interest income and may result in higher defaults in a rising rate. Revenue from mortgage banking operations is sensitive to changes in economic conditions. The securities portfolio may be negatively impacted by fluctuations in market value, tax code changes, and interest rates. If the hedging against interest rate exposure is ineffective, it would result in volatility in operating results. The commercial real estate loan portfolio will be subject to additional regulatory scrutiny. The company faces risks related to cybersecurity, third parties, and technology. Ineffective liquidity management could adversely affect the financial results and conditions.

Market Performance

Table 1 compares the cumulative total shareholder return for the bank with the cumulative total return on market indexes such as Nasdaq, S&P 500, US Nasdaq Bank index and SNL Thrift index. The analysis assumes investment of $100 on December 31, 2017, and reinvestment of all dividends.

The 5-year holding period return for FS Bancorp was 34% compared to 57% for S&P 500 and 17% for SNL Bank index. The 5-year average yearly return for FS Bancorp was 8.96% compared to 11.22% for S&P 500 and 5.42% for SNL Bank index.

The stock was trading at $22.57 on October 1, 2018. The stock price increased by 1.31 times to trade at $29.41 by September 1, 2023. The total cumulative monthly return for FS Bancorp stock was 46% compared to total cumulative monthly return of 5.85% for Nasdaq Bank index during the recent 5-year period Oct 2018–September 2023. The yearly average return for FS Bancorp stock was 9% compared to 1% return for market index Nasdaq Bank index during the period Oct 2018–September 2023. The data source is Yahoo Finance.

Table 2 shows the holding period return for the stock and market index Nasdaq Bank index during the period 2018–2022. The holding period is assumed to be 1-year period.

FS Bancorp had excess return over the market index Nasdaq Bank index in all the years of analysis.

Table 3 displays the book value of equity and market value of equity during the period 2018–2022. The values are given in millions of dollars.

The average book value as percent of market value of equity was 88.5% during the period 2018–2022.

Table 4 gives the financial highlights of the company during the period 2018–2022. The data is sourced from annual reports and gurufocus.com.

Table 1 Comparison of returns

Year	2017	2018	2019	2020	2021	2022
FS Bancorp	100	79.35	119.54	104.7	130.64	133.8
S&P 500	$100	95.62	125.72	148.85	191.58	156.88
SNL Bank index	$100	83.44	104.69	95.08	132.36	116.69
SNL Thrift	$100	87.21	117.82	112.28	143.69	116.8

Source: Annual Report 2022

Table 2 Holding period return

Year	FS Bancorp	Nasdaq Bank index	Excess returns
2018	−5.01%	−11.05%	6.0%
2019	31.39%	9.38%	22.0%
2020	0.15%	−4.72%	4.9%
2021	25.44%	15.26%	10.2%
2022	0.66%	−16.47%	17.1%

Table 3 Book and market value of equity

Year	2018	2019	2020	2021	2022
Book value of equity	180.04	200.24	230.01	247.51	231.70
Market value of equity	192.64	284.44	232.24	274.75	258.70
BV as percent of MV	93.5%	70.4%	99.0%	90.1%	89.6%

Table 4 Financial highlights

	(In millions of dollars)				
Financial highlights	2018	2019	2020	2021	2022
Total assets	1621.64	1713.06	2113.24	2286.39	2632.90
Gross loans	1377.43	1421.59	1740.68	1879.99	2238.95
Deposits	1274.22	1392.41	1674.07	1915.74	2127.74
Total equity	180.04	200.24	230.01	247.51	231.70
Interest income	62.33	89.63	88.84	96.37	118.69
Non-interest income	16.71	19.96	53.29	34.71	15.39
Interest expense	10.23	19.32	14.72	9.73	14.41
Total non-interest expense	44.65	57.39	62.56	75.5	75.57
Market capitalization	192.64	284.44	232.24	274.75	258.70
Enterprise value	284.80	317.73	246.09	334.43	455.01

Table 5 Performance ratios

Ratios	2018	2019	2020	2021	2022
Performance ratios					
Return on average assets %	1.87	1.36	2.05	1.7	1.21
Return on average equity%	16.12	11.95	18.25	15.67	12.37
Net interest margin%	4.42	4.7	4.32	4.3	4.55

The average growth rate of total asset and gross loans was 13% during the period 2018–2022. The total deposits and total equity increased by 14% and 7%, respectively, during the above period. The interest income and non-interest income grew by 19% and 24%, respectively. The interest expense and total non-interest expense increased by 10% and 15% on average basis. The market capitalization and enterprise value increased by 10% and 15%, respectively, during the above period.

Table 5 shows the performance ratios for FS Bancorp during the period 2018–2022.

The average ROA, ROE, and net margin for the bank during the period 2018–2022 were 1.64%, 14.87%, and 4.46%, respectively. The average efficiency ratio in 2022 was 64.70% compared to 61.41% in the year 2021. FS Bancorp's capital adequacy tier-leverage ratio % for the annual that ended in Dec. 2022 was 9.70%, which is lower than 10.80% for the previous year ended in Dec. 2021.

Reference

1. https://investorrelations.fsbwa.com/corporate/default.aspx

Case 99 Arch Capital Group Ltd.

Arch Capital Group Ltd. (ACGL) is a publicly listed company which is a part of the S&P 500 Index. Arch Capital was established in September 2000. Arch Capital offers insurance, reinsurance, and mortgage insurance through its wholly owned subsidiaries. The company is recognized as a leading global financial services company in the world. Standard and Poor's rating was A+ for the company in year 2022. The company has a global presence with 5800 plus employees. Arch's Global Mortgage Group is a global leader in aggregating, managing, and syndicating mortgage credit risk. The company offers a range of property, casualty, and mortgage insurance and reinsurance lines along with the focus on writing specialty lines of insurance and reinsurance. The mortgage operations of Arch Capital included the United States and international mortgage insurance and reinsurance operations as well as participation in government-sponsored enterprise (GSE) credit risk sharing transaction.

The gross total premium in the year 2022 amounted to $17.3 billion. The total net reserves amounted to $14.9 billion. The investment approach of Arch focuses on improving the company's return on equity through thoughtful target allocation and periodic rebalancing. The underwriting income across three underwriting segments amounted to $1.8 billion in the year 2022. In 2022, the net premiums written increased 21% to $5 billion. Underwriting income for the mortgage segment increased 32% to a record $1.3 billion in 2022. In 2022, Arch Capital leveraged the overall strength of the portfolio to deliver $1.3 billion in terms of underwriting income.

The company classifies its businesses into three underwriting segments of insurance, reinsurance and mortgage and two operating segments of corporate and other.

© The Author(s), under exclusive license to Springer Nature Switzerland AG 2024

B. R. Kumar, *Rising Stars*, Management for Professionals,
https://doi.org/10.1007/978-3-031-50032-9_99

Operations

Insurance Operations

The insurance operations of the company are conducted in Bermuda, the United States, the United Kingdom, Europe, Canada, and Australia. The insurance operations in Bermuda are conducted through Arch Insurance, a division of Arch Re Bermuda and Alternative Re Limited. In the United States, the insurance group's subsidiaries include Arch Insurance Company, Arch Specialty Insurance Company, Arch Indemnity Insurance Company, and Arch Property Casualty Insurance Company. The company conducts insurance operations on several platforms in the United Kingdom such as Arch Insurance and Lloyd's syndicates. The insurance business in Canada is operated through Arch Insurance Canada Ltd. The insurance group aims to excel in underwriting intensive lines of business with the focus on talent-intensive business rather than labor-intensive business across all product lines on gross and net basis.

Reinsurance Operations

The reinsurance operations are conducted on a worldwide basis through reinsurance subsidiaries such as Arch Re Bermuda, Arch Re US, Arch Syndicate 2012, Arch Syndicate 1955, and Arch Re Europe.

Mortgage Operations

Mortgage insurance offers protection to the insured lender, investor, or GSE against loss in the event of a borrower's default. The group offers various credit risk sharing products to government agencies and mortgage lenders. The mortgage operations include mortgage insurance and reinsurance business in the United States, Bermuda, the United Kingdom and Australia. In the United States, the mortgage operations are primarily conducted through Arch Mortgage Insurance Company, United Guaranty Residential Insurance Company, and Arch Mortgage Guaranty Company.

Growth Strategy

The insurance group aims to expand its portfolio by identifying profitable underwriting opportunities, including specialty lines, and capitalizing on market trends. Arch Capital centralizes underwriting responsibility by assigning each product line to an underwriting executive who manages all aspects of product development within their respective line. The underwriting philosophy of the insurance group focuses on generation of underwriting profit through prudent risk selection and proper pricing. The company also focuses on providing superior claims

Table 1 Key ratios

Ratios	2021	2022
Loss ratio	67.80%	64.90%
Underwriting expense ratio	26.40%	27.30%
Combined ratio	94.20%	92.20%

Source: Annual Report 2022

management. The company has adopted a multichannel distribution system through collaboration with international, national, and regional brokers along with managing general agencies and program administrators to efficiently serve its diverse customer base.

The company aims to maintain a disciplined approach to select risks and price them in all phases of the insurance cycle. The company focuses on underwriting specialty lines. Capital allocation is based on the most attractive opportunities. The cycle management strategy facilitates underwriting teams to grow business during favorable market conditions. The company also aims to foster strategic partnerships in stable and niche sectors to achieve long-term alignment with partners for accessing niche opportunities, scale businesses, and dependable defensive lines. The insurance group primarily distributes its products through licensed independent retail and wholesale brokers.

The reinsurance group's strategy leverages its financial capacity, experienced management, and operational flexibility to offer a diverse range of products through its operations. The reinsurance group exclusively underwrites profitable business, prioritizing disciplined underwriting over premium expansion. The reinsurance group aims to exploit opportunities on account of shifts in demand or favorable pricing trends. The reinsurance group employs a meticulous, data-driven underwriting approach to determine appropriate premiums for specific risks, aligning them with the anticipated capital at risk. The mortgage group aims to utilize its financial capacity, advanced mortgage insurance technology, operational adaptability, and seasoned management to provide mortgage insurance, reinsurance, and other risk sharing products globally. The mortgage group adheres to a disciplined, data-driven underwriting approach using proprietary and third-party models which include delinquency and home price forecasting to ensure premiums match the insured risk.

In 2014, Arch Capital acquired Somerset's motor insurance managing general agent, distribution capabilities through direct and aggregator channels, affiliated insurer, and fully integrated claims operation. During the year 2016, Arch Capital became the leading provider of mortgage insurance in the United States through the acquisition of United Guaranty Corporation for approximately $3.3 billion. In 2018, the company acquired McNeil and Company Inc. which was market leader in specialized risk management and program administration in the United States. In 2019, Barbican was acquired to strengthen the company's reinsurance operations. In 2021, the company completed the acquisition of Somerset Group.

Table 1 highlights the key ratios for the company.

Risk Factors

The company operates in a competitive environment. The insurance and reinsurance industry exhibit cyclical patterns, with potential periods of excessive underwriting capacity and unfavorable premium rates. Inflation and global recessionary conditions can adversely affect the business, financial health, and operational results within insurance and reinsurance industry. Claims resulting from natural and man-made catastrophic events have the potential to generate significant losses and have a material adverse impact on the financial position of the company. Customers and policyholders may also experience impacts from regulatory, technological, market, or other climate change-related risks in various ways. The availability of reinsurance, retrocessional coverage, and capital market transactions to mitigate its risk exposure might be constrained, and the credit and other risks which are linked to the company's reinsurance agreements could lead to losses which might negatively impact its financial stability. The insurance business could face significant adverse effects in the scenario if the crucial third-party partners fail to adequately manage their risks, engage in fraudulent activities, or breach their obligations toward the company. Potential technology glitches and cyberattacks such as ransomware or state-sponsored incidents could disrupt services and harm businesses. Adverse developments in the financial markets have a material adverse effect on the results of operations and financial position. A decrease in low down payment mortgage originations or shifts in government housing policies could lead to reduced US mortgage insurance, thereby impacting the revenues.

ESG Initiatives

The company's specialized insurance coverages and services promote wealth building through homeownership. The businesses of the company aid decarbonization efforts by facilitating energy transition. Approximately 26% of the company's offices are LEED certified, and 60% of them have a formal recycling program. The company incorporates investee firms' ESG rating into its investment analysis. Arch Capital has made investments of $138 million in green bonds which are issued to fund green projects or other sustainability activities. The company's assets under management (AUM) of value amounting to $772 million are in investments with an ESG focus. Approximately $7.1 billion of AUM of the company are with asset owners who are signatories of the United Nations Principles for Responsible Investment. The company also focuses on expanding its diversity and inclusion initiatives. Approximately 23% of employees participate in employee-led networks. About 600 employees completed course on fostering inclusive leadership. The Arch Group Foundation awarded grants of over $450,000 to nine nonprofit organizations aligned with Arch's priorities related to accessible safe housing, academic and career success, and environmental resilience. Through the matching gift program, the company donated over $2.4 million, and employees donated $2.1 million to organizations.

Stock Performance

Table 2 compares the cumulative total shareholder return for Arch Capital shares for the last 5 years through December 31, 2022, to the cumulative total shareholder return of S&P 500 Composite Stock Index and the S&P 500 Property and Casualty Insurance Index. The analysis assumes an initial investment of $100 in 2017 along with reinvestment of dividends.

The 5-year holding period return for Arch Capital Group Ltd. was 107% compared to 57% and 82% holding period returns of S&P 500 Index and S&P500 Property and Casualty Insurance Index. The average yearly returns for Arch Capital Group, S&P500 Index, and S&P500 Property and Casualty Insurance Index were 19.48%, 11.22%, and 13.26%, respectively, during the period 2017–2022.

The stock was trading at $28.37 on October 1, 2018. On September 8, 2023, the Arch Capital stock was trading at $77.26 representing an increase of 2.73 times compared to the price on October 1. The cumulative total monthly return for Arch Capital during the recent 5-year period October 2018–September 2023 was approximately 121% compared to 58% total cumulative returns of S&P 500 market index. The average yearly return for the Arch stock was 25% compared to 12% yearly returns for market index S&P 500. The data was sourced from Yahoo Finance.

Table 3 shows the holding period return for Arch stock and market index S&P 500 during the period 2018–2022.

Arch Capital stock outperformed the market index S&P 500 in the year 2018, 2019, and 2022, respectively.

Table 4 shows the book and market value of equity of Arch Capital during the recent 5-year period. The values are given in millions of dollars.

The average book value as percent of market value of equity was approximately 79.8% during the period 2018–2022.

Table 5 shows the insurance segment's net premiums written by major line of business.

Table 2 Comparison of returns

Year	2017	2018	2019	2020	2021	2022
Arch Capital Group Ltd.	100	88.31	141.75	119.21	146.91	207.49
S&P 500 Index	$100	95.62	125.72	148.85	191.58	156.88
S&P 500 Property and Casualty Insurance Index	$100	95.31	119.97	128.31	153.05	181.93

Source: Annual Report 2022

Table 3 Holding period return

Year	Arch Capital	S&P 500	Excess returns
2018	−6%	−8%	2%
2019	46%	19%	27%
2020	−18%	16%	−35%
2021	−48%	23%	−71%
2022	36%	−15%	51%

Table 4 Book and market value of equity

Year	2018	2019	2020	2021	2022
Book value of equity	10,437.68	12,315.55	13,987.44	13,555.13	12,920.90
Market value of equity	10,753.60	17,397.00	14,670.43	16,843.17	23,250.32
BV as percent of MV	97.1%	70.8%	95.3%	80.5%	55.6%

Table 5 Net premiums written

Year	2021	2022
Professional lines	1,177,144	1,502,448
Property, energy, marine, and aviation	722,582	878,067
Programs	595,824	611,922
Travel, accident, and health	305,390	484,847
Construction and national accounts	431,952	469,717
Excess and surplus casualty	359,458	460,798
Warranty and lenders solution	146,984	139,247
Others	408,859	473,596
Total	4,148,193	5,020,642

Table 6 Financial highlights

	(In millions of dollars)				
Financial highlights	2018	2019	2020	2021	2022
Total assets	32,218.33	37,885.36	43,282.30	45,100.95	47,990.51
Short-term investments	646.56	726.23	906.45	858.67	855.12
Total equity	10,437.68	12,315.55	13,987.44	13,555.13	12,920.90
Total revenue	5474.33	6781.69	8291.79	8926.15	9657.04
Net income	757.97	1636.32	1405.52	2156.85	1476.93
Market capitalization	10,753.60	17,397.00	14,670.43	16,843.17	23,250.32
Enterprise value	14,074.10	20,624.86	18,442.33	19,548.13	25,961.44

Net premiums written by the insurance segment were 21.0% higher in 2022 than in 2021.

Table 6 gives the financial highlights of the company during the recent 5-year period.

The total assets, short-term investments, and total equity increased by 10.6%, 8%, and 16% on average basis during the period 2018–2022. The total revenues and net income increased by 15% and 31% on average basis during the above period. The market capitalization and enterprise value increased by 25% and 19%, respectively, on average basis. The data source is annual reports and gurufocus.com.

Table 7 shows the profitability ratios of the company during the period 2018–2022.

The average return on assets, return on equity, and net margin were 3.71%, 12.51%, and 18.88%, respectively, during the period 2018–2022.

Table 7 Profitability ratios

Ratios	2018	2019	2020	2021	2022
Return on assets %	2.36	4.67	3.46	4.88	3.17
Return on equity%	8.13	15.63	11.43	16.19	11.17
Net margin%	13.85	24.13	16.95	24.16	15.29

Table 8 Economic value

Year	2021	2022
Profit before income tax	2103.35	1488.89
Income tax	128.51	79.95
Net operating profit after tax (NOPAT)	1974.84	1408.94
Stockholder equity	13555.13	12920.90
Long-term debt	2724	2725.00
Total capital employed	16279.13	15645.90
WACC	6.84%	7.79%
Capital charge	1113.49	1218.82
Economic value	861.34	190.12

Table 8 illustrates the estimation of economic value of the company during the period 2021–2022. The values are given in millions of dollars.

Reference

1. https://ir.archgroup.com/financial-reports/annual-reports/default.aspx

Case 100 First Horizon Corporation

First Horizon Bank had its origin in the year 1864 when First National Bank of Memphis was established by Frank S Davis. First Horizon Corp is a leading regional financial services company headquartered in Memphis, Tennessee. First Horizon operates in 12 states across the southern United States. The bank and its subsidiaries offer commercial, private banking, consumer, small business, wealth and trust management, retail brokerage, capital markets, fixed income, and mortgage services.

First Horizon is a bank holding company under the Bank Holding Company Act and a financial holding company under the Gramm-Leach-Bliley Act. The common stock is listed on the New York Stock Exchange under the symbol "FHN." By December 31, 2022, First Horizon's subsidiaries had over 450 business locations in 24 US states.

As of June 30, 2023, the total assets of the company stood at $85.1 billion; deposits and loans amounted to $65.4 billion and $61.3 billion. The company has 413 banking centers. By December 31, 2022, First Horizon had 7542 associates or 7397 full-time equivalent associates.

Table 1 shows the timeline of establishment of the bank.

Table 2 highlights the principal businesses and brands of the bank.

Business Segments

Regional and Specialty Banking Segments

The loans and deposits offered by the bank are basically in the regional banking and specialty banking segments. Larger portion of the net interest income and non-interest income for the bank is sourced from regional banking and specialty banking segments, respectively. The principal lines of business in the regional banking segment are commercial banking, business banking, consumer banking, private client, and wealth management.

© The Author(s), under exclusive license to Springer Nature Switzerland AG 2024
B. R. Kumar, *Rising Stars*, Management for Professionals,
https://doi.org/10.1007/978-3-031-50032-9_100

Table 1 Timeline

Year	Milestones
1864	First National Bank of Memphis was established
1941	First National built its first suburban branch at 1338 Union
1964	On its 100th anniversary, First National moved into a new 25-story corporate headquarters at 165 Madison
1977	First National changed its name to First Tennessee
2004	First Horizon National Corporation became the parent company
2014	First Tennessee celebrated 150 years of service to the community
2017	Merger with Capital Bank to make First Tennessee the fourth largest regional bank in the southeast
2019	The entire company operated under the unified First Horizon brand name
	First Horizon National Corporation and Lafayette, Louisiana-based IberiaBank Corporation, agreed to merge
2020	The merger with IberiaBank was completed. The combined company became one of the largest financial service companies headquartered in the south and one of the top 25 banks in the United States in deposits
	The parent company dropped "National" from its name, becoming First Horizon Corporation

Source: https://www.firsthorizon.com/First-Horizon-Corporation/About-Us-Rev/History

Table 2 Businesses and brands

Businesses	Principal brands
General banking and financial services	First Horizon and First Horizon Bank
Fixed income/capital markets	FHN Financial
Mortgage lending	First Horizon Bank
Insurance brokerage and management services	First Horizon Advisors
Wealth management and brokerage services	First Horizon Advisors

Source: Annual Report 2022

The principal lines of business in the specialty banking segment are fixed income/capital markets, professional commercial real estate, mortgage warehouse lending, asset-based lending, franchise finance, equipment finance, corporate banking, correspondent banking, and mortgage origination.

Table 3 showcases the list of services offered by First Horizon through its subsidiaries and divisions.

Growth Strategy

The bank focuses on targeted and opportunistic expansion of consumer and commercial banking products and markets. The bank also focuses on expansion of commercial lending through strategic and tactical transaction, talent development, and acquisitions. The focus is also on rigorous expense management with continued investment in revenue-generating initiatives. The bank also focuses on managing

Table 3 Services offered by First Horizon

General banking services for consumers, businesses, financial institutions, and governments
Fixed-income sales and trading; underwriting of bank eligible securities and other fixed-income securities
Eligible for underwriting by financial subsidiaries; loan sales; advisory services; and derivative sales
Mortgage banking services
Brokerage services
Correspondent banking
Transaction processing: nationwide check clearing services and remittance processing
Trust, fiduciary, and agency services
Credit card products
Equipment finance services
Investment and financial advisory services
Mutual fund sales as agent
Retail insurance sales as agent

Source: Annual Report, Page 11

business units and products with strong emphasis on risk-adjusted returns on invested capital. The company has made substantial investment in scalable technology and infrastructure to attract and retain clients. The bank has pruned and adapted its physical banking center network to reflect long-term trends in client usage of banking centers. The company also focuses on the inorganic growth strategy involving mergers and acquisitions. In the year 2020, Horizon Bank completed the merger with IberiaBank corporation. At the time of merger, Iberia had $31.7 billion of total assets and operated over 190 banking centers in 11 states. In the same year, the company purchased 30 branches from Truist Bank. In 2022, the Horizon Bank entered into an agreement to be acquired by Toronto-Dominion Bank. The shareholders approved the transaction in May 2022. The transaction has to be approved by regulators.

The key competitors in many markets for the bank include Wells Fargo Bank, Bank of America, First Citizens Bank and Trust Company, JPMorgan Chase Bank National Association, BankUnited, Hancock Whitney Bank, and Pinnacle Bank.

Risk Factors

The bank faces regulatory risks due to the pending mergers and acquisitions undertaken by the bank. The bank faces competitive risks in primary areas of consumer and commercial deposits, commercial loans, financial planning, wealth management, and fixed-income products and services. The bank also faces strategic and macro-risks with respect to management of liquidity and capital requirements associated with organic growth and cash-funded acquisition. Disruptive shifts in the business landscape propelled by emerging technologies and evolving customer preferences have the potential to negatively affect the banking sector. Operational risk encompasses various factors, such as errors in processes, technology failures, fraud, theft, security breaches, and external events, creating potential challenges for the bank. The bank may be adversely affected by economic and political environment in the United States and other parts of world. The company encounters credit risk as the clients may not fulfill their loan repayment obligations, and the collateral's realizable value may prove inadequate to prevent a charge-off. The company is exposed to risks wherein various other parties across diverse circumstances may default on their commitments to make payments. The company faces regulatory, legislative, and legal risks. The bank is subject to geographic risks of operating in various jurisdiction.

ESG Initiatives

In 2021, Horizon Bank had invested approximately $2 million in preservation and restoration of the environment. The bank has made lending to businesses in LMI communities and businesses with revenues less than $ 1 million in 2021. Approximately 53% of management roles are held by women. There is a 35% diversity among board of directors in terms of race, gender, or ethnicity. In 2021, the bank offered $ 1 billion as home mortgage lending to LMI borrowers in LMI communities. In the same year, over $19 million was distributed by the First Horizon foundations through nonprofit partners. Horizon Bank has provided capital in excess of $750 million to renewable energy project financings during the past 5 years. In 2021, the scope 1 and 2 location-based greenhouse gas (GHG) emissions were reported for the first time. Throughout the pandemic, First Horizon provided essential relief funds to small businesses through the SBA Paycheck Protection Program. By partnering with Operation HOPE, First Horizon provides complimentary credit and financial management workshops that encompass subjects like enhancing credit scores, establishing budgets, enhancing financial well-being, and launching small businesses. Under Operation HOPE program, about 48,254 financial empowerment services were offered to 7466 clients. Through the program, 356 entrepreneurial training program services and 4118 credit and money management group education classes were offered. The bank focuses on maintaining resource efficiency. In 2021, 1400 laptops/PCs were recycled and 1.5 million pounds of paper were recycled.

Stock Market Performance

First Horizon was trading at $16.13 on October 1, 2018. The stock price was $11.83 on September 1, 2023. The total cumulative monthly return for First Horizon stock was 20% for the recent 5-year period October 2018–September 2023 compared to the total cumulative monthly return of 5.85% for the market index Nasdaq Bank index. The average yearly return for First Horizon stock during the 5-year period October 2018–September 2023 was 4% compared to average yearly return of 1% for the Nasdaq Bank index.

Table 4 Holding period returns

Year	First Horizon	Nasdaq Bank index	Excess returns
2018	−18.46%	−11.05%	−7.4%
2019	12.81%	9.38%	3.4%
2020	−20.25%	−4.72%	−15.5%
2021	17.57%	15.26%	2.3%
2022	43.19%	−16.47%	59.7%

Table 5 Book and market value of equity

Year	2018	2019	2020	2021	2022
Book value of equity	4785.38	5076.00	8307.00	8494.00	8547.00
Market value of equity	4192.42	5157.93	7082.20	8713.31	13,158.97
BV as percent of MV	114.1%	98.4%	117.3%	97.5%	65.0%

Table 6 Financial highlights

	(In millions of dollars)				
Financial highlights	2018	2019	2020	2021	2022
Total assets	40,832.26	43,311.00	84,209.00	89,092.00	78,953.00
Gross loans	28,214.68	31,655.00	59,254.00	56,031.00	58,692.00
Deposits	32,682.99	32,430.00	69,982.00	74,895.00	63,489.00
Total equity	4785.38	5076.00	8307.00	8494.00	8547.00
Interest income	1546.00	1624.00	1898.00	2158.00	2683.00
Non-interest income	667	608	903	997	728
Interest expense	326	414	236	164	291
Total non-interest expense	1164.00	1153.00	1614.00	1968.00	1859.00
Market capitalization	4192.42	5157.93	7082.20	8713.31	13,158.97
Enterprise value	3764.13	8741.93	974.20	−4058.69	15,112.97

Table 4 shows the holding period return for the stock and index during the 5-year period 2018–2022. The holding period is assumed to be 1-year period.

First Horizon outperformed the market index Nasdaq Bank index in years 2019, 2021, and 2022, respectively. The source of data was Yahoo Finance.

Table 5 gives the book value and market value of equity of First Horizon during the recent 5-year period. The values are given in millions of dollars.

The average book value of equity as percent of market value of equity during the period 2018–2022 was approximately 98.5%.

Table 6 shows the financial highlights of Horizon Bank during the period 2018–2022. The source of data is annual reports.

The total assets, gross loans, and deposits increased by 24%, 25%, and 27%, respectively, on average basis during the period 2018–2022. The total equity increased by 18% during the above period. The interest income and non-interest income increased by 15% and 6%, respectively, during the above period. The interest expense declined by 16%, whereas the total non-interest expense increased by 14% during the above period on average basis. The market capitalization

Table 7 Performance ratios

Ratios	2018	2019	2020	2021	2022
Performance ratios					
Return on average assets %	1.33	1.05	1.33	1.15	1.07
Return on average equity%	12.42	9.51	13.21	12.32	10.94
Net interest margin%	3.47	3.33	3.14	2.95	3.49
Efficiency ratio%			54.37	68.56	61.24

Table 8 Economic value

Year	2021	2022
Profit before income tax	1284.00	1159.00
Income tax	274.0	247.0
Net operating profit after tax (NOPAT)	1010.0	912.0
Stockholder equity	8494.0	8547.0
Long-term debt	1544.0	1551.0
Total capital employed	10038.0	10098.0
WACC	8.43%	8.43%
Capital charge	846.2	851.3
Economic value	163.8	60.8

increased by 34% on average basis during the above period. The data source was annual reports.

Table 7 shows the performance ratios of the company during the period 2018–2022.

The average ROA, ROE, and net interest margin for the bank during the period 2018–2022 were 1.19%, 11.68%, and 3.28%, respectively. The average efficiency ratio was 61.39%.

By December 31, 2022, the tier 1 capital ratio and total capital ratio were 11.92% and 13.3%.

Table 8 illustrates the estimation of the economic value for the company during the year 2021 and 2022. The values are given in millions of dollars.

References

1. https://ir.firsthorizon.com/investor-home/default.aspx
2. ESG Impact Report 2022

MIX
Papier aus verantwortungsvollen Quellen
Paper from responsible sources
FSC® C105338

If you have any concerns about our products,
you can contact us on
ProductSafety@springernature.com

In case Publisher is established outside the EU,
the EU authorized representative is:
Springer Nature Customer Service Center GmbH
Europaplatz 3, 69115 Heidelberg, Germany

Printed by Libri Plureos GmbH
in Hamburg, Germany